ALSO BY ALLAN BLOOM

Giants and Dwarfs: Essays 1960–1990
The Closing of the American Mind
The Republic of Plato (translator and editor)
Politics and the Arts: Letter to M. d'Alembert on the Theatre
  (translator and editor)
Emile or On Education (translator and editor)
Shakespeare's Politics (with Harry V. Jaffa)

Love and Friendship

Allan Bloom

SIMON & SCHUSTER   New York   London   Toronto   Sydney   Tokyo   Singapore

SIMON & SCHUSTER
Simon & Schuster Building
Rockefeller Center
1230 Avenue of the Americas
New York, New York 10020

Designed by Liney Li
Manufactured in the United States of America

10 9 8 7 6 5 4 3 2 1

Library of Congress Cataloging-in-Publication Data

Bloom, Allan David, 1930–1992
    Love & friendship / Allan Bloom.
        p.   cm.
    Includes bibliographical references and index.
    1. Love in literature. 2. European literature, Modern—History
and criticism. 3. Shakespeare, William, 1564–1616—Criticism and
interpretation.   I. Title. II. Title: Love and friendship.
PN56.L6B56   1993
809'.93354—dc20   93-1380
                                                            CIP

ISBN 0-671-67336-X

ACKNOWLEDGMENTS

Before his death on October 7, 1992, Allan Bloom completed the final revision of this book. Tim Spiekerman, Christopher Nadon, and Christopher Lynch assisted him during the writing and revision. In revising it he had the benefit of comments on a previous draft from Saul Bellow, Werner J. Dannhauser, Charles H. Fairbanks, Hillel G. Fradkin, Pierre Hassner, Steven J. Kautz, Edward O. Laumann, James H. Nichols, Jr., Donna Orwin, and Nathan and Susan Tarcov. Over the previous twelve years he taught with Saul Bellow all the novels and plays discussed in this book and often remarked on how much he learned about them from this experience. A timely grant from the Earhart Foundation made possible preliminary work on Rousseau's *Emile* in the summer of 1985. Generous support from the John M. Olin Foundation for the University of Chicago's John M. Olin Center for Inquiry into the Theory and Practice of Democracy made possible a leave of absence in 1990–1991 during which he wrote the first draft, and supported the author's work in other ways. The staff of the Olin Center, first Judy Chernick and Terese Denov, and later Stephen B. Gregory and Anne Gamboa, patiently and meticulously processed this book with the assistance of Marian Felgenhauer.

The author's executors, Hillel G. Fradkin and Nathan Tarcov, were left with the tasks of responding in his place to the editing of Simon and Schuster's Robert Asahina (whose work on *The Closing of the American Mind* Allan Bloom greatly admired and appreciated) and supervising the completion of the notes by Christopher Lynch and Paul Ulrich. Susan Tarcov assisted them at every stage. Queries were

8   *Acknowledgments*

answered or emendations offered by Peter Ahrensdorf, Alice Behnegar, Nasser Behnegar, Janis Freedman Bellow, Saul Bellow, Adam Breindel, Joseph Cropsey, Werner J. Dannhauser, Charles H. Fairbanks, Borden Flanagan, François Furet, Robert T. Gannett, Victor Gourevitch, Bette Howland, Steven J. Kautz, Christopher J. Kelly, Marilyn Klein, Mark Kremer, Catherine Lynch, Jonathan Marks, Arthur M. Melzer, Christopher Nadon, Peter Nichols, Clifford Orwin, Donna Orwin, Marc F. Plattner, Anne Ruderman, Richard S. Ruderman, David Schaefer, Diana Schaub, Joel Schwartz, Andrew Sloniewsky, Astrida Tantillo, William Thomson, Richard L. Velkley, Kenneth Weinstein, and Michael Z. Wu.

Hillel G. Fradkin
Nathan Tarcov
Chicago, March 1993

To Michael Z. Wu

CONTENTS

Introduction: The Fall of Eros   13

PART ONE/ROUSSEAU AND THE ROMANTIC PROJECT   37

1. Rousseau   39
2. Stendhal, *The Red and the Black*   157
3. Austen, *Pride and Prejudice*   191
4. Flaubert, *Madame Bovary*   209
5. Tolstoy, *Anna Karenina*   231
6. Conclusion   259

PART TWO/SHAKESPEARE AND NATURE   267

Introduction   269
7. *Romeo and Juliet*   273
8. *Antony and Cleopatra*   297
9. *Measure for Measure*   327
10. *Troilus and Cressida*   347
11. *The Winter's Tale*   375
12. Conclusion   393

INTERLUDE ON TWO STRANGE COUPLES:
HAL AND FALSTAFF, MONTAIGNE AND LA BOÉTIE   399

PART THREE/THE LADDER OF LOVE   429

Epilogue   547
Notes   553
Index   565

INTRODUCTION:
The Fall of Eros

This book is an attempt to recover the power, the danger, and the beauty of eros under the tutelage of its proper teachers and knowers, the poetic writers. Against my will I have to use the term "eros," in spite of its alien and somewhat pretentious Greekness as well as its status as a buzzword since Freud and Marcuse. There is an impoverishment today in our language about what used to be understood as life's most interesting experience, and this almost necessarily bespeaks an impoverishment of feeling. This is why we need the words of old writers who took eros so seriously and knew how to speak about it.

The word "love" now applies to almost everything except the overwhelming attraction of one individual for another. And sex is a timid pseudoscientific word that tells us only that individuals have certain bodily needs. There is an appalling matter-of-factness in public speech about sex today. On television schoolchildren tell us about how they will now use condoms in their contacts—I was about to say adventures, but that would be overstating their significance. On talk shows young collegians tell us about how they decide whether they have been raped in their various encounters. There is nothing about this of the now impossible complaint about outraged virtue. Sex is spoken about coolly and without any remains of the old puritanical shame, as an incidental aspect of the important questions of disease and power. The sexual talk of our times is about how to get greater bodily satisfaction (although decreasingly so) or increasingly how to protect ourselves from one another. The old view was that delicacy of language was part of the nature, the sacred nature, of eros, and that to speak about it in any other way would be to misunderstand it. What has disappeared is the risk and the hope of human connectedness embedded in eros. Ours is a language that reduces the longing for an other to the need for individual, private satisfaction and safety.

Isolation, a sense of lack of profound contact with other human beings, seems to be the disease of our time. There are great industries of psychotherapy that address our difficulties in "relationships"—that pallid, pseudoscientific word the very timidity of which makes substantial attachments impossible. This way of describing human connection begins from the tentativeness of our attachments, the alleged fact that we are naturally atoms wanting to belong to clusters without the wherewithal to do so, a situation that would, at best, make contractual relations possible. This abstract term puts citizenship, family, love, and friendship under the same makeshift tent and abstracts from their very different foundations and demands. Yet one has to have a tin ear to describe one's great love as a relationship. Did Romeo and Juliet have a relationship? The term is suitable only for expressions like "they had a relationship." It betokens a chaste egalitarianism leveling different ranks and degrees of attachment. "Relationships" are based on "commitments," as in "I'm not ready to make a commitment." It is a term empty of content, implying that human connectedness can arise only out of a motiveless act of freedom. It reeks of Sartre's *No Exit*—"Hell is— other people."[1] It is this contemporary condition that led me once to describe us as social solitaries. I meant by this not that we have attained the condition of solitary self-sufficiency that Rousseau so vividly characterized and Kant, looking to Rousseau, calls the very model of the sublime, but that we are lonely while living in society, with all the social needs for others yet unable to satisfy them.

Nevertheless the most insistent demand nowadays of people in general, and young people in particular, remains human connection, a connection that transcends the isolation of personal selfishness, and in which the thought of oneself is inextricably bound up with the thought of another. Politically, the demand for human connection is to be found in the quest for community, which is something other than a collection of liberal individualists. There is a lot of serious thought and some action dedicated to this goal (though it is probably impossible given the structure of our society and its basic principles), but there is practically no attempt to build upon eros, the one natural inclination, always present in every society and beyond particular social or political principles, that links us indisputably. There is much lamenting about the collapse of the family, but practically no attempt to revive the romantic rituals that once led to it and underlay it. We witness a strange inversion: on the one hand, the endeavor to turn the social contract into a less calculating and more feeling connection among its members; on the other hand, the endeavor to turn the erotic relation into a contractual one. The characteristic modern way of describing human relations as those between self and other appears to have dug an unbridgeable chasm between the two.

The de-eroticization of the world, a companion of its disenchantment, is a complex phenomenon. It seems to result from a combination of causes—our democratic regime and its tendencies toward leveling and self-protection, a reductionist-materialist science that inevitably interprets eros as sex, and the atmosphere generated by "the death of God" and of the subordinate god, Eros. It is summed up in debased and ridiculous fashion when the young women entering Smith College are told that lookism is included among the currently recognized vices along with racism, sexism, and homophobia. Yet eros begins, sad but true, in preferences founded in the first place on what is seen with the eyes, founded on ideals of bodily beauty. Nobody serious ever suggested that this is where it ends, but if this essential beginning is suppressed, farewell eros. A good education would be devoted to encouraging and refining the love of the beautiful, but a pathologically misguided moralism instead turns such longing into a sin against the high goal of making everyone feel good, of overcoming nature in the name of equality. (As though Americans already had an overdeveloped taste for the beautiful and a capacity to discriminate among its kinds!) Love of the beautiful may be the last and finest sacrifice to radical egalitarianism.

Perhaps a way to begin investigating the fall of eros would be to take a glance at that great work which influenced Americans so profoundly, the Kinsey Report.[2] It rose in the American sky like a comet, giving comfort, consolation, and encouragement, as well as a lot of exciting detail about what everyone else does, to people who guiltily thought they were alone in doing these things. Open and broad public discussion of the diversity of sexual practices in America was unusual in 1948, so the Kinsey Report was satisfying to people who wanted to talk or think about their private sexual lives but did not have the nerve to do so. There was some attempt to make it a scandal, alleging perversity or unhealthy prurience in its authors. But this is America, and the purity and objectivity of science cannot be tainted by the attacks of moral and religious fanatics. The attacks on Kinsey's good faith met a response something like "This man is a scientist!"—meaning that his objectivity put him beyond all such complaint. Kinsey was the truth, and we had to face it, which was not too difficult for most people to do.

Kinsey himself was a big, hearty, crew-cut man, a paragon of American virtues. He allegedly studied sex as he had also studied wasps. A scientist does not have to tell us why he does what he does, what his private motives are; he looks for truth in many areas and adds his research to the store of knowledge. He does not have a moral agenda, and he necessarily abstracts from questions of good and bad, which are the themes of subjective moral prejudice. He just tells you the facts, and you can do whatever you like with or about them.

In fact, Kinsey very obviously did have a political intention, though not one stemming primarily, or even at all, from personal and perverse self-interest. He really was a scientist in a certain decayed Enlightenment tradition that told him that science would ultimately make men happy. He believed that the statistics would speak for themselves and show everyone that there is an astonishing diversity of sexual practices, and that the official versions, which told us that the great majority of people did and should satisfy themselves essentially in monogamous marriages, were untrue. Such a statistical approach would have the effect of saying that the practices being studied are real and the moral judgments about them are mere prejudices, particularly prejudices of religion, still understood at that time to be the great enemy of science. At the time there was a whole system of guilt and extreme social stigma, as well as laws in many places that prescribed prison sentences for solitary masturbation, adultery, homosexuality, and even acts between married couples in the privacy of their own bedrooms that deviated from the purpose of producing children. Kinsey appears to have believed that these constraints caused immeasurable suffering and loss of legitimate pleasure. Kinsey thought both that it would relieve men's guilt if they recognized they were part of a great public and that lawmakers would then be influenced to wipe away archaic laws. Kinsey made the move from the fact of promiscuity to its legitimacy. Everybody does it, "so it does not mean that I am a bad person." He clearly believed that what men actually do is natural and that the constraints are merely the vestiges of a Puritan heritage. It was all very simple and simpleminded.

There may have been a bit of playing the *beau rôle* in Kinsey's talking about what is shocking to most men without any pathos of shock. But, in general, I believe that his motives were good and that he was not deriving some private kick from his researches. Both science and society were meant to benefit from what he did. He surveyed a broad panoply of sexual acts from masturbation to homosexuality and even intercourse with animals (an activity engaged in mostly by farm boys in that period), and found that there were a surprising number of people who had participated at least once in them, and a smaller number, although surprisingly large, who found their specific preference in one or another of them. The gentleness of his approach is striking. There is hardly any reference to sadism and masochism, and he did not formulate questions about incest, intercourse with children, or other similarly shocking behaviors. His bias toward gentle and harmless sex, which ought to be able to name itself, is revealed here. The brutal and dangerous temptations are excluded from study, although they too take place. Another startling aspect of Kinsey for a contemporary reader is his stark elitism—the lower classes do not know how to do it and have no imagination. Only the educated can liberate themselves from mythology and can think through the differences between plain and fancy sex.

Kinsey's approach shows much of what is typical in the modern treatment of what were once erotic phenomena. In the first place, it both reveals and strengthens Americans' reliance on public opinion. Look at Gallup before you leap! This approach thereby gives more support to timidity in an arena classically reserved for the daring. It attempts to render conventional what always had a refreshing element of violation of convention and of reliance on one's inner demons. Kinsey never enters into the psychological effects of various sexual preferences or, most important, the ways in which they promote or detract from truly human union on all levels. He rather caters to the public taste for a respectable way of talking about sex and the need for confirmation of one's tastes. He uses public opinion to influence public opinion about sexual matters.

The Kinsey Report appeared pretty early on in our polling madness, which now appears to be the only element in decision making, transcending all questions of good and bad, prudent and foolish. It was significant both because it was early on and because it touched on the most intimate parts of a man's or woman's life. Kinsey contributed to the reduction of eros to sex, a view from the outside utterly destructive of what one feels on the inside. This perspective, of course, does not remain confined to the laboratory, but becomes everybody's way of looking at it.

When the Kinsey Report came out, I was seventeen years old. At one of those bohemian parties that took place in the environs of the University of Chicago, a rather seductive lady—from my point of view very old, at least thirty—said to me, "You are at the peak of your sexual potentiality." She was referring to Kinsey's discovery that seventeen-year-old males had more orgasms daily than any other age group. I began to wonder what I had to do in order to keep up with the norm. Kinsey's counting contributed to a certain mathematical reductionism. Such an enumerating of the variety of taste may even encourage people to acts that did not originally tempt them, just to keep up with the Joneses. It tells them to go ahead with what they desire because it is the common human practice. But it does not encourage people to think about what they desire and its consequences. The great disservice done by the school that Kinsey represents is to make it unnecessary to think about or discuss the meaning of one's desires on their own level, not shorn of the hopes and fears and infinite ramifications by which they are naturally accompanied. As a corollary to this, Kinsey and his compeers take away the very language that makes a truly scientific self-examination possible. Any good novelist can teach us more that is true about the meaning of our desires than can any of these amateurish scientists.

Kinsey notes that devout Jews and Christians do much less out of wedlock than do the less devout. But he does not reflect on this fact or ask about how much of sexual behavior is a matter of will and education. He probably thinks that such abstinence is archaic, and that he presents the nature of sex stripped of the prejudices that frequently accompany it. Whether or not he was entirely aware of it, he was an advocate of a scientific version of the distinction between convention and nature and firmly planted himself, as his natural science dictated, in nature's camp. He can protest as much as he likes that his work has no normative implications, but the presentation of some kinds of facts necessarily carries a morality with it. If someone tells you that sex is pleasant, that there is a wonderful variety of ways to have it, that there is no rational basis for inhibition, and that practically everybody does it, what implications for action do you suppose follow? It is one thing to be a virgin because God commands it and love and respect depend upon it, and another to say it is just a matter of choice, some do, some don't. Inasmuch as there is a positive drive to have sexual satisfaction, virginity becomes an empty heroic pose. Kinsey really knew all this because, in a very good-hearted way but without much refinement of taste, he wanted to help people out.

The upshot was that sex became behavior, a part of the then new behavioral sciences, which made the distinction between fact and value. Their practitioners thought that, once liberated from values, they could produce a true science of man. When you see in the *New York Times* a picture of two smiling fifteen-year-olds emerging from their high school displaying the condoms that were distributed to them, you fear that "behavior" is the only thing that counts now, and that we are so far away from natural intimacy and all the complex things that surround it that it is hardly worth trying to discuss love and eros anymore with such pupils. Everything is so routine and without mystery.

But the question remains whether it is possible to study man, as opposed to the other animals, without taking account of will, reason, and imagination. These are the distinctively human faculties that allow sex to actualize itself as eros in human beings. Animals have sex and human beings have eros, and no accurate science is possible without making this distinction. Kinsey pays no attention to the fact that animals, although they indulge themselves whenever they can, have a much smaller range of sexual desires, almost exclusively directed toward procreation. The strange variety of human sexual desires points toward an indeterminateness that requires molding for a truly human life. It is comparable to the indeterminateness in human beings requiring politics, which the brute animals have no need of. One cannot ignore man's imaginative and rational contribution to his own formation, which is absent in the other species. As Aristotle says, the political community comes into being for the sake of life, but its end is the good life, a goal that was not evident in the first impulses.[3] Likewise, coupling begins in sexual desire, but has as its end love. The various kinds of love affairs, like the various kinds of political orders, are human beings' often inept attempts to realize inchoate potentialities that are specific to man. Without examining the ends that these associations aimed at, no one can give an adequate account of them.

Still, what Americans wanted was respectable public talk about sex and liberation from old constraints that had become too painful to endure. Yet in America, imprisoned eros turned for liberation not to a romantic literature but to scientific reductionism. This turn expressed an overpowering urge, more important than any desire for real satisfaction, to make various kinds of sexual expression conventional. Everyone must be brought out of whatever closet he was forced to hide in before gratification will be possible; it fits perfectly our system of delayed gratification, which says that fun is for later. Compare this with Stendhal's Julien Sorel (whom I shall discuss later), who had no desire or need to make adultery respectable and was totally dedicated to his private relations with the two women he was deeply engaged with. The turn to science is connected with a longing to simplify and domesticate the raging and chaotic feelings within us. Kinsey, and most of those who teach us about sex, can tell us nothing about the arts of love or seduction, and nothing about the delicate interplay of giving one's body to someone else in such a way as to gain trust and respect. For Kinsey a description of sex is no different from a description of eating habits, and the object of desire is essentially indifferent, except for the platitudinous and abstract rules that stem from a democratic society. Kinsey instead established the grounds for the endless and empty demands for sexual "rights" and for the utterly unerotic movements generated to further those rights. On the whole, scientific sexology has done us much more harm than good, when one balances its contribution to doing away with harsh and unfeeling laws against a loss of the human perspective on eros.

Kinsey shared the stage with the much more interesting Freud, with whom he had in common only the public discussion of sex. As Kinsey made sex matter-of-fact and simple, Freud made it omnipresent and complex. The two together appealed to contemporary taste in these questions, making sex pervasive at the same time as easy to go public with. The enduring appeal of Freud, even to sophisticated people like Jacques Derrida, is the license he appears to give for talking endlessly about sex in relation to all things. He brings an unbeatable combination of sex, science, and the promise of being well-adjusted.

Of course, reading Freud is the most unerotic experience one could imagine. Hardly a page or a line of Freud could arouse erotic excitement in any normal reader. Can one really discuss eros without arousal? Freud does not appear to have been a very sexy man, and he brought a grim and brutal view of man and society to his treatment of sex. It is all unmasking and showing the miserable effects of sex on our souls. In Freud, sex is the most important thing in our lives, but it is certainly not a beautiful one. The sex life of civilized man, as opposed to that of the other animals, is complex and interesting, but not precisely attractive or the kind of thing one would write poetry about. Freud inherits the same kind of distinction between nature and society as does Kinsey, but with a much less smiling view of the kind of satisfactions possible in society. His nature is what Hobbes described, where men are engaged in a war of all against all for survival,[4] and society is a way of palliating that war bought at the cost of all kinds of repressions. Sex in the state of nature is brutish and essentially uninteresting. It becomes interesting in society because of what society does to it. And what society does is to distort it, repress it, and thereby extend it as an intruder into all areas of life. Freud remained throughout his life an unquestioning prisoner of natural science's unerotic view of nature. Eros is a by-product of society, which is necessary, but society is in no way an object of desire and joy.

Ancient views of politics taught that man's nature has an impulse toward society and that society is not necessarily a maiming or division of man but potentially his perfection. Similarly, the ancients believed that eros is a natural longing for the beautiful, which, given the complexity of man and of things, can be damaged and misled but is in itself a perfection of human sociability by way of the passions. Nothing like this is present in Freud. He popularized the Greek word *Eros*, but this was probably only an aspect of Viennese bourgeois pride in German classical *Bildung*, the *Bildung* ridiculed by Nietzsche as mere gilding on the cage of modern mediocrity. Freud failed completely in establishing a real distinction between sex and eros, although his good sense accorded him a protean view of the effects of sex on the soul, effects that are absolutely inexplicable on the basis of his underlying philosophy.*

Still, Freud, unlike Kinsey, enters into real interior experience, talks about what it means to people, and is concerned with the different kinds of sexual gratification in relation to the whole person. He has no difficulty whatsoever with talking about good and bad sexual wishes and expressions, although he hides his moralism and makes it less interesting by speaking instead of healthy and sick. Like the doctor he was, he begins from the sick, and it is difficult to tell whether the healthy is anything other than the absence of the unhealthy. It is certain that society is merely a bleak necessity to which man must adjust, but which is no fulfillment for him. The real satisfactions of eating, sexual intercourse, and sleeping are rooted in low nature, which is not yet human and gone forever. The higher things, the civilized ones, the vocations of citizen, doctor, father, and

---

* Marcuse, the other writer who contributed to making eros an almost unusable word for serious conversation, only went Freud one better by promising polymorphous delight once Freud's moralism was shorn away. History was making it possible to have satisfactions like the first natural ones, not embellished by civilization, and Marcuse thereby achieved the goal, so pervasive among intellectuals of this century, of wedding the two great forces, Marx and Freud.[5]

all the rest, have no natural support, and are secondary expressions. So why should one want them, since they provide only secondary satisfactions and are attained only by terrible wounds to man's nature?

Freud tried to encourage people to look at themselves and to take their inner life seriously. But his psychology causes men and women not to take their real experiences seriously but rather to look beneath them to motives that their psychoanalytic therapists teach them to look on as the real causes. Thus the independence and the charm of what they actually feel, think, and do is drained away. For Freud practically everything has become sexualized, and men learn to see sexual motives behind tastes and activities where they would never have thought to look for them in the past. A statesman or an executive who undergoes psychoanalysis or who gets caught up in psychoanalytic theory cannot take his activities on their own level but only as the complex result of lower or more primitive causes. Such people get into the bad habit of being ironical about what they do in life, for it must always be interpreted in terms of other things for which it is only a cover-up. In an age where men and women are more and more actors and role players, this habit only reinforces their inability to *be* something, totally. Constantly looking at one's motives in this way is demystifying and furthers rationalizing calculation. This is peculiarly deadly to love, where being serious about the reality of the perfection imagined in another is essential to self-forgetting in passionate concern with that other.

Freud is a good example of the impossibility of moving from lower to higher in the study of psychology. His education and his taste compel him to take account of great works by writers and painters in order to produce a psychology worthy of its name. This distinguishes him from Kinsey or typical American practitioners of the behavioral sciences who are not aware that they must discover adequate psychological explanations for the high in man, partly because they do not recognize that there is anything high in man. However, dragged down by the leaden weight of his interpretive framework, when Freud actually goes to work on these sublime products of genius, he falls ridiculously beneath their level, interpreting their works mostly in terms of the materials derived from psychosexual deviations.[6] The surface is dissolved, and the depth and beauty of the work itself are reduced to its boring components. Listen to Mozart and then see what psychoanalytic interpreters do to his work. You have to have become very perverse (in a nonpsychoanalytical sense) to think such interpretations tell us anything about the music itself, which opens out onto a higher real world that cannot conceivably be constructed out of Freud's childish building blocks. He cannot believe that there is such a thing as a natural writer, because his natural man has no such inclination. The writer must have been diverted from his natural satisfactions and sought to satisfy them in a socially respectable way, adding an erotic charm to things that have no real eros. I remember a bright student who summed it up very neatly for me almost thirty years ago. When he told me that a person has to be neurotic to create, I asked him why. "Why else would one create?" was the response. The very imagination of poets, which from their own point of view is a divination of the highest beings, to Freudians must be the same as or akin to the erotic dreams that express and repress the coarse sexual energies. It all goes downward. Freud's views on religious figures are shockingly crude and distort the phenomena for the sake of a theory, whereas the theory could be proved only by those phenomena. This theory is utterly inadequate to explain saints, artists, lawgivers, or even the scientists themselves who propound the theory. But people soon began to see the theory as the reality and to forget what does not fit the theory, just as economists have become persuasive about people's material motives although one has never actually met a person who cared only about maximization of profit. There is no reason to doubt Freud's genuine attachment to and pleasure in our artistic heritage. In his essay on Dostoyevsky, Freud exclaims that, before such greatness, psychoanalysis must lay down its arms.[7] But he cannot resist picking them up again almost immediately and using them to round up the usual suspects, in Dostoyevsky's case, his father. Thus, people who read Hegel are at the outset asking themselves what his sexual motives might have been and cease asking whether his infinitely richer account of the world around us is true. Pretty soon we become abstract in our very souls.

Freud's theory of sublimation is his desperate attempt to preserve the phenomenal richness of psychological life while remaining faithful to his clear and simple scientific reductionist causes. But it does not work. Even from the outset the higher psychological life has to be made much cruder and less ambiguous than it actually is in order to admit of modern scientific treatment. And then Freud is really unable clearly to distinguish unhealthy repression from healthy sublimation, unless it is by the degree of torment undergone and the social acceptability of the adjustment to it. He cannot explain what is sublime about sublimation, and the question that inevitably follows is, "Why sublimate? What is higher or better about sublimation?

Why not try to do what comes naturally?" Sublimation collapses back into its primitive elements, like a great tower that has neither foundation nor purpose. Freud is not distinguished by subtlety or refinement in his study of the higher life, but that is nothing compared to what his legions of followers are now capable of. The literary theory called deconstructionism, which has unaccountably filled up the emptiness of its categories with Freudianism, deconstructs what were once thought to be great writers. This is revealing of the whole tendency of contemporary high cultural life: whether represented by natural science or deconstructionism, it can only deconstruct—it cannot construct or reconstruct. Eros has become only a fancy way of saying sex.

Kinsey and Freud, who seem so different, the one smiley and the other gloomy, the one dealing with behavior, no questions asked, the other concentrating on what he considers to be the deep and dark origins of behavior, actually begin from the same view of nature in which sex is mere sex. These two versions of that view have provided the frame for the way we talk and think about eros. Eros, in its Freudian version, is really all just selfishness and provides no basis for intimate human connection. At best it allows only a compromise that has nothing to do with the demands of love. Such theories make possible the repulsive speech, so open, so dull, so flat, about what used to be thought to be perhaps the most mysterious, exciting, and deepest animating force in man.

Yet simply put, human sex is inseparable from the activity of the imagination. Everybody knows this. The body's secret movements are ignited by some images and turned off by others. Ideas of beauty and merit, as well as longings for eternity, are first expressed in the base coin of bodily movements. A biologist can describe male erection and female readiness and tell us what bodily processes make them possible, but he cannot tell us when and by whom they will be set off. The truth of erotic arousal defies materialism. One sees action at a distance. And it is imaginative activity that converts sex into eros. Eros is the brother of poetry, and the poets write in the grip of erotic passion while instructing men about eros. You can never have sex without imagination, whereas you can be hungry and eat without any contribution of imagination. Hunger is purely a bodily phenomenon and can safely be left to the scientists, and now to the dieticians. But our sexual dieticians are absurd. The best you can do by neglecting or denigrating imagination is to debauch and impoverish imagination.

In a better world, sexual education would be concerned with the development of taste. All the great lovers in literature were also lovers of tales and had their heads full of sublime rivals in their divine quest. The progress of civilization is intimately connected with the elaboration of erotic sensibility and a real examination of the delicate interplay of human attractions. But everything today conspires to suffocate imagination. There have been hardly any great novelists of love for almost a century. Scientific sex claims to tell us about the real thing. Reading classic books has become less and less of a taste among the educated, although cheap romantic novels, the kind that are sometimes stuck into boxes of household detergent, apparently flourish among housewives who haven't heard that Eros is dead. And now the most respectable authorities in the study of books tell us that their messages were always pernicious and sexist. There is practically nothing within our horizon that can come to the aid of ideal longing. Sure, you can be a romantic today if you so choose, but it is a little like being a virgin in a whorehouse. It just doesn't fit with the temper of the times and gets no support in the current atmosphere.

Talking about love has suffered the most. Eros requires speech, and beautiful speech, to communicate to its partner what it feels and wants. Now there is plenty of talk about relationships and how people are intruding on one another, and there is talk akin to discussions on the management of water resources. But the awestruck vision of the thing-in-itself has disappeared. It is almost impossible to get students to talk about the meaning of their erotic choices, except for a few artificial clichés that square them with contemporary right thinking. Out of self-protectiveness, no one wants to risk making arguments, as Plato's characters did, for the dignity of his or her choice and its elevated place within the whole of things. What one cannot talk about, what one does not have words for, hardly exists. Richness of vocabulary is part of richness of experience. Just as there is a disastrous decline in political rhetoric, rhetoric necessary to explain the cause of justice and form a community around it, so there is an even more disastrous decline in the rhetoric of love. Yet to make love humanly, the partners have to talk to each other.

Students, like many other Americans, have a tendency to leave their reflections on eroticism at "You've got a right to do anything in the privacy of your own bedroom." This is a decent liberal opinion adopted to protect people from the prying eye of the law or the disapproval of public opinion. It is indifferent to what is actually being practiced, whether it is vice or virtue. It is self-protective and makes sex boring, a harmless pursuit of taste, like choosing among

Baskin-Robbins' 31 flavors. One wishes that we Americans could develop formulas for tolerance that did not at the same time destroy private discrimination of good and bad, noble and base. Does tolerance necessarily require a relativism that goes to the depths of men's and women's souls, depriving them of their natural right to prefer and to learn about the beautiful? As always is the case with contemporary moralistic formulas, this one nourishes our easygoingness, our unwillingness to judge ourselves. Yet however uncomfortable such an activity is, those who are not willing to undertake it are depriving themselves of the transcendent pleasures of eros. It is difficult for me to understand how people can accept the trivializing formula that their sexual tastes don't do any harm, when they are talking about what is, or what should be, a thing so central to their hearts and so close to the very meaning of life that it could confer the greatest benefit.

But now there is a new illiberal tendency that strangely both contradicts and supports liberal tolerance and easygoingness: the imperial project of reform promoted by radical feminism. It wants to enter the bedroom and much more the psyche in order to alter male sexual taste and behavior. It is not so much acts but the meaning of those acts and the disposition of those who perform them that now count. The new discussion of male sexuality—for it is almost exclusively males who are the subjects of this—produces a distinctly unlovely vision of erotic relations. Male lust, male treatment of women as objects—in general, machismo—are the themes of this new sexual education. It is an education directed not to the sublime or sublimation, but to control. The object is not the relatedness of male and female, but liberation from male oppression, or nature's oppression, in order to provide women with power or choice, the great word of the movement, choice to make oneself whatever one wants to be, free from the patriarchal structures that are said to have kept even what appeared to be the freest women imprisoned. Male and female are no longer to be reciprocal terms, and the male habit of supposedly forcing women into such reciprocity is what must go. Of course, rape was always forbidden, and there was a codicil to the liberal formula that limited the right to do anything in your own bedroom to "consenting adults." But now we are alleged to have a much higher consciousness of what rape and consent mean. What used to be understood as modes of courtship are now seen as modes of male intimidation and playing on the weaknesses and anxieties of women.

The education of male sexual desire in the past was intended to make men into gentlemen, a term reciprocal to lady, a person whose chastity was priceless and needed protection. The new feminist women make no claim to chastity and even ridicule it. It is an affront to raise the question of chastity as a part of the criminality of rape. Whether it be a prostitute or Mother Teresa is unimportant, although not all juries have yet been persuaded of this. Rape is considered bad no longer because it assaults a weak and defenseless person's modesty, which is necessary to her exclusive attachment to the man she loves. Rape is now bad because it deprives women of power. Males are the rapists, the date rapists, the sexual abusers of children, the pornographers, the sexual harassers. Male and female sexual relations have to be adjusted to an abstract program of reforming them. There is no thought of the beauty of eroticism or love in any of this.

Supporting this unerotic treatment of eros is the hot new principle that all human relations, especially sexual ones, follow from the one motivating principle in man, the will to power. Everything is power relationships, crude power, the will to dominate, to have things one's own way. The relationship between government and the governed is one of exploitation. The teacher-student relation is a power relation with the teacher interested only in imposing his views and his person on the student. And above all, the relation between man and woman is a power relationship in which men have exploited and dominated women. The coarseness of this interpretation is beyond belief, making Marx's notion of economic relations seem a masterpiece of subtlety. Of course there is power in the government-governed connection, but can anyone who has experienced politics think that is the whole or even the central story? Can Lincoln and Roosevelt be understood not to have cared for the governed, for the just and the good? And was Socrates merely deluded when he believed that his vocation was that of midwife, evoking only what is already within his students, respectfully trying in the first place to test their potentiality? If one compares Socrates to today's more advanced teachers, one cannot help but be shocked by the latter's insouciant indoctrination and abusive treatment of students, which have come to be seen as all too natural, justified by their suppression of the distinctions between knowledge and power, between teaching and propaganda.

The worst distortion of all is to turn love, a relation that is founded in natural sweetness, mutual caring, and the contemplation of eternity in shared children, into a power struggle. This is another one of those games that intellectuals can play. But why would anyone want to do such violence to real experience? It is the war of all against all again, and the only possible peace is to be found in artificial constructs. This is the last stage in the attempt to found all human relations on contract, the discovery of complementary interests, rather than on natural inclinations. Abstract reason in the service of radically free men and women can discover only contract as the basis of connectedness—the social contract, marriage contract, somehow mostly the business contract as model, with its union of selfish individuals. Legalism takes the place of sentiment. It is now asserted that the relation between men and women is not based on their pointedness toward each other and can properly result only from a haggle that conciliates their separate wills to power. All the rest was a long-standing set of myths made up by the phallocrats. The demands of the imperial phallus are the source of all the problems. Its imperialism is to be deconstructed and Plato's interpretation of it in the *Phaedrus* as the wing that powers the flight from becoming to being is rank ideology not to be taken seriously.

The power and the pervasiveness of this view among the current intellectual elites are hardly to be believed by those who are not *amateurs* of those elites. It authorizes a veritable thought police, whose actions are legitimized by an almost religious guilty conscience about the harm that sex can do. The cure for sexism is a much more complicated affair than the cure for racism, because the sexual organs are naturally connected to human functioning, as skin color is not. This view reinforces the lack of sexiness in the liberal view, but it is in a radical tension with the liberal view's *laisser-aller*. Radical feminists insist that the liberals' consenting adults, especially the women, consent only because they are forced to by sexist education and public opinion. So we must in the first place reeducate the partners so that they no longer think they need each other. This will put off enjoyment for a good long time.

All the things that used to be thought to be natural must now be overcome in the name of abstract equality. As one says these days, "Gender is not a natural phenomenon, but a cultural one." The de-eroticization of the world began in our materialistic science and has culminated practically in this last great movement of radical egalitarianism. The most secret and interesting parts of one's body and soul are being subjected to the intense public light of the third degree.

It is difficult to say how people, particularly young people, react to this attempt, which has swept over the educational system, to dictate the character of erotic feeling and reflection. One can expect that nature will rebel, at least in a few, as it does against all attempts by one tyranny or another to suppress it. When the Chinese government in the 1950s responded to a proliferation of rats who ate inordinate portions of the crop by putting a bounty on them, the peasants started raising rats. This was a hint that nature might be alive and well in China. I suspect it was our historicism, our belief in the primacy of history over nature that caused us to underestimate the natural resistance to the projects of the communists and made us think they might succeed in molding man in the long run according to their wishes. The most important reason for communism's fall was forgotten nature.

Nature is, in a way, always present, and that is a great source of hope, but if one has been taught to interpret it perversely, and if all the institutions and writings around one support that perversity, it requires a great effort of thought and sentiment to recognize it for what it is. The present has a tendency to appear to be permanent and natural. For those who rebel against the orthodoxies of our day and the prescriptions about what they should feel and think, there is a need to recover nature, which is buried under successive layers of ideological ash. Rousseau gives a model for this kind of recovery when he compares his search for natural man in *The Discourse on the Origin and Foundations of Inequality* to scraping the barnacles off the statue of the sea god Glaucus, which has for ages lain on the bottom of the sea.[8] Rousseau had to move from the bourgeois who dominated the scene in his time to the sources out of which he came, and of which he was only a distorted reflection. The selfish and tepid passions of this man who appeared to be man simply were revealed to be what they were by comparison with what man really is, as Rousseau reconstructed him by observation of other times and places.

I suggest that we need a generation or two not of theory but of an attempt to discover the real phenomena of eros. This means a flight out of our own time to those times and places that believed in it more and did not share our peculiar projects for transforming it. I can think of no better way of beginning our journey than by reading classic writers, poets or poet-philosophers, who cared about love. As I have said, speech about love by lovers is essential to the being of love; therefore, turning to the writers is not like turning to the encyclopedia for information but is to share in the experience of love. When I was young, I used to hear Freudians say, condescendingly, that Shakespeare and Dostoyevsky were wonderful and, through their poetic genius, glimpsed what Freud established theoretically by his science. They meant that one really no longer needs Shakespeare or Dostoyevsky because Freud can teach us the comprehensive truth.

I have always thought that this is a pretty silly way of looking at things. Shakespeare knew love, and unless Freud can explain it in all its power and subtlety as Shakespeare presents it, which Freud manifestly does not, his theory is inadequate. I ask for what might in our jargon be called a phenomenology, a detailed and comprehensive description of what it is we are trying to explain as we experience it before we enter into explanation. Such endeavors are surely also needed in politics and religion after two hundred years of abstractions from which they have emerged unrecognizable. But nowhere is this a more urgent task than in matters of eros, the first and best hope of human connectedness in a world where all connectedness has become problematic. The best books not only help us to describe the phenomena, but help us to experience them. They are living expressions of profound experiences, and without such knowledgeable advocates of those experiences we would find it very difficult to gain access to matters that depend so much on educated feeling and for which merely external observation is not sufficient. Books may provide a voice for whatever remains of nature in us.

But, as with eros itself, we find books under attack. We live in a country in which the activity of solitary reading, with its need for leisure and calm, has diminished to the vanishing point. And, worse still, there are theories reigning in the land which tell us that books can have no permanent meanings or intrinsic beauty, that their authors' conscious intentions are deceptions, especially self-deceptions. The texts can be interpreted only by scholars who know their contexts, who know the class, gender, and race of their writers, and who have recently broken the code of writers' unconscious motives. Books as unities speaking to all men have been smashed to smithereens. Most of all, they have to be explained in terms of the will to power of their writers, and of those who supposedly canonized them as the tyrants of our tastes. The same people who tell us that relations of love are really relations of power also tell us that books themselves have nothing to do with the love of truth or beauty, but only with the love of power, if you can call it love. Thus they would close the routes through which we might escape the confines of their view of love. The American tendency to indifference to the study of what is outside our horizon is now given the imprimatur of the highest intellectual authorities. A great wall surrounded by a moat full of snapping crocodiles protects us from the corruptions of eternity.

This book is intended for the use of those who can still be charmed by books and who have an irreducible interest in the depiction of love. Such persons use books for pleasure and instruction. Books about love inform and elevate the fantasy life of their readers and actually become part of their eros while teaching them about it. Their appearance has to be taken for their primary reality, and they tell stories that can be naively apprehended and naively thought about. This does not mean that study of such texts with persons who know them well and have reflected on them for a long time is not useful and even necessary. Moreover, it is hard for someone to read Stendhal, for example, without knowing who Napoleon is. But Stendhal can help us to begin our reacquaintance with him. Such writers can begin the enrichment of lives, feelings, and experiences that have become impoverished. The popular power that Victor Hugo's or Dickens' novels exercised for more than a century required no sophistication, and people have understood them pretty well and with a fair degree of agreement concerning what they were about. This does not preclude greater intelligence or finer taste from seeing more in those novels, but persons possessing them must begin where less sophisticated readers begin.

I know all the current critics' objections to this way of reading, and I can already hear choruses of protest that I do not understand them. This is not the place to respond at length. All I can say here is that since I was a young man and a student in Europe, I have paid serious and sustained attention to the sources of these views: Nietzsche, Heidegger, Lacan, Foucault, Levinas, Lyotard, Deleuze, and others whose names it is now so fashionable to throw around. I am persuaded that all their theories, in the form that they have come to the United States, are nothing but a fad that will pass, one can only hope before they have done too much damage to the study of literature. I see a much greater depth and attractiveness in the books as they present themselves, rather than as they appear through the lenses of these new critics, equipped with their complicated decoders. I cannot help thinking of Groucho Marx at the racetrack being gulled by Chico, who tells him that he can't place his two-dollar bet until he has purchased a breeder's guide, and then a whole series of other guides. By the time Groucho has looked into all of them and been utterly confused, the race is over. With the new critics, it is life that will be over.

Readers will have to decide who tells them more about these books and who allows these books to tell them more about their lives. I believe the writers whom I interpret in this book are much more intelligent than I am and probably know the questions better than I do. I do not share the assumption of our dogmatic critics that we are the first ever to know the sources of all things. Part of my intention in this book is to restore our awareness of the ambiguities and the conflicts in nature as it presents itself to us. True intellectual openness consists in trying to understand the writers as they understood themselves, which is possible if one is not arrogant about one's own understanding of things. One begins by picking up a story and reading it with the same wonder that one had as a child. The combination of innocent experience and cultivated intelligence is what we seek. I am sure that many of my particular statements about the books in the following chapters will raise objections in the minds of my readers, and I hope that this will encourage them to make better interpretations on their own—but without turning away from the writers and their books to seek ill-fitting keys in Freud or Derrida. You may disagree with my explanation of something that Darcy says to Elizabeth in *Pride and Prejudice*, or one of Julien's strategies for the seduction of Mathilde, but the means for correcting me should be your careful observation and your good common sense. I am, of course, mindful of the contemporary prescriptions for what can and cannot be said about the relations between the sexes. I try not to pay too much attention to them and let the writers speak for themselves.

Always before my mind's eye while writing this book was a passage from Xenophon where Socrates in the simplest and most accessible way tells a hostile critic what he does and what counts for him:

> Antiphon, as another man gets pleasure from a good horse, or a dog, or a bird, I get even more pleasure from good friends. And if I have something good, I teach it to them, and I introduce them to others who will be useful to them with respect to virtue. And together with my friends I go through the treasures of the wise men of old which they left behind written in books, and we peruse them. If we see something good, we pick it out and hold it to be a great profit, if we are able to prove useful to one another.

Xenophon comments, "When I heard this I held Socrates to be really happy . . ."[9] Here there is none of the grand, mysterious rhetoric about the Delphic oracle, the *daimonion*, and the divine mission, which are the stuff of Socratic mythology. This, in contrast, we can understand immediately. What is more, such Socratic philosophizing is possible almost everywhere and at all times—"good-natured" persons sitting around reading the books of wise men and seeing together what they can get out of them for the guidance of their lives. "Friend," "good," "profit," and "pleasure" are the powerful words that cluster around the reading of books in Socrates' life. At the origins of philosophy and right up to our day this has been the life-perfecting activity, and the preservation of this naive but ever so mysterious and vulnerable pursuit will, I am certain, prove decisive for access to the reality represented by those wonderful words.

I wrote this book while recovering from a serious illness, and strangely this activity turned that period into one of the most wondrous times of my life. Every day I could consort with Rousseau or Stendhal or Austen and learn such wonderful things about loving and hating, benefaction and doing harm. When I went to bed at night I looked forward to getting up in the morning and resuming this living relationship to the books, and I was lifted above my petty concerns by them. I have attempted to communicate some of that experience here. How much more delight there is in learning about the virtues and the vices from Jane Austen than in emptily trying to teach them to her. Friendship and love may very well consist in sharing such experiences with another. In itself and immediately this transports us out of our dreary times. I hope that by this book I may touch at least a few potential friends who can love literature in spite of the false doctors who try to cure them of it.

I have no desire, and the facts do not permit me, to preach a high-minded and merely edifying version of love. If you still have the heart to proceed with reading this book, you will see that, as there is light here, there is also darkness, much hope and much disappointment, possible adornment of life and real ugliness and terror. I simply try to act as an honest broker for greater persons and writers than I am. As I have said, I present no theory, nor do I have one, although my observations cannot help but call into question other theories. I have constructed no schema to act as a clothesline on which to hang all the books of the tradition, as the estimable and enduring Denis de Rougemont does in his *Love in the Western World*.[10] He wanted to judge it all, as a good Catholic, in terms of the struggle between *Eros* and *agapē* and the futility of the former in the face of the latter. I have no such high aspirations, hoping only to show you what some great writers thought these things are.

A word about the plan of this book. I do not try to give a total historical account of love or a survey of all the opinions that have been held about it. Instead I try to take the most eminent examples of rich descriptions of love to which we can have immediate access. I begin with Rousseau and four novelists—Stendhal, Austen, Flaubert, and Tolstoy—who were strongly influenced by him. Rousseau was both a philosopher and a literary man, with the two sides interrelated. He taught that philosophy had to have both the insight and the form that poetry lends. He was the greatest modern describer and proponent of love, and he initiated a movement of love, Romanticism. This great movement aspired to the establishment of a new basis for human connection amongst the isolation of bourgeois society. Its conception of love attempted to combine the purest longing with the fullest bodily satisfaction. It tried to rescue sex from Christian original sin and to recover the union of body and soul of Platonic eros while guaranteeing the reciprocity missing from the Platonic understanding of love and friendship. It did so through an ideal of love between radically different and hence totally complementary men and women, an ideal constructed out of newly legitimated sexual energy and an imagination emancipated from nature.

The Romantic movement is the precursor to some extent of the later movements that tried to manipulate rather than discover eros, and to dissolve it into its crudest elements shorn of the illusions of the imagination. But Rousseau's project still bows toward nature, eschews reductionism, and possesses an infinite awareness and delicacy, which inspired very great independent artists after him. Rousseau and the Rousseauans play a double role in this book. They are great witnesses to love, but the failure of their movement also was connected with the collapse of love as a theme of literature toward the end of the nineteenth century. Rousseau is closest to whatever reminiscences we have of love. His attempt to save love by fostering belief in an illusion of our own creation was in the long run, I believe, necessarily a failure. But from that failure we can learn about ourselves and also be motivated to look elsewhere. I do not wish to use Rousseau as a straw man for my preferences, but he and the novelists who followed him clearly display a set of common themes that still affect us and are the alternatives against which our sexual thinking rebelled.

The novelists of love whose works I interpret were both fascinated and repelled by Rousseau's charm. They explored all the alternatives he opened up: from a romantic love with a core of friendship between intelligent and virtuous though imperfect partners culminating in marriage, to a radical opposition between romantic love and the legal sanctity of the family. Romantic love became a standpoint from which to judge a bourgeois world in which there were no longer men worthy of love, marriage had become contemptible, and art for art's sake seemed to be all that was left.

After Romanticism, I turn to Shakespeare, who tries not to create love out of illusions but to present its reality. Shakespeare is to me the purest voice of nature, and he does not meddle with nature. His plays provide us with the greatest variety of erotic expression, and with Shakespeare eros is the proper term to use. All kinds of men and women, in all kinds of situations, are given us by Shakespeare to appreciate and understand, not to transform according to our will or our apparent needs. He takes lovers with the utmost seriousness and portrays with sympathy love's promise of unity, its mysterious attraction to beauty, and its hope to overcome even the ugliness of death. Yet he also shows its folly and disappointment. He helps us marvel at love's transcendence of political loyalty and ambition, and still reminds us of its need for legal limitation. Finally, he lets us see that love has a history from pagan antiquity to modernity—and that Christianity is the source not only of the repression decried since the Romantics, but of a deepening of women and a new sensitivity of men.

Lastly, I turn, with the help of Montaigne, that great mediator between Ancients and Moderns, to Plato, the classical philosopher of love, who, while sharing Shakespeare's fidelity to nature, treats of eros's expressions across a wider spectrum than could be suitable for the theater and with a more explicit rational account of their meaning. Plato's works, in addition to their philosophical content, are arguably works of art comparable to the greatest. He presents eros not only as a painful and needy sign of our incompleteness, but as giving and productive. He explores the tensions between love of one's own and love of the good, and between the politically necessary subordination of eros to the family and the liberation suggested by such questionable erotic phenomena as incest, pederasty, and promiscuity. He sees in eros the possibility of both individual happiness and true human community.

Almost half this work is devoted to Rousseau and Plato, enriched by the personages depicted by the other artists treated in the book. This book bears witness to a confrontation between the two greatest philosophical teachings about eros, another chapter in the quarrel between the Ancients and the Moderns.

PART ONE

Rousseau and the Romantic Project

1. Rousseau

I A Swiss told the French that they did not know how to make love. What is even more astonishing, they believed him and took him as their master in the art of love. The Germans became the apprentices of the French, and in turn instructed the English. He, Rousseau that is, introduced them all to the *romantic* taste—ideal and sincere—to take the place of their *gallantry*, which he treated as a school of vanity. This marks the beginning of the frantic sexual search for genuine human contact and reciprocity in the isolation of bourgeois life that endures in one form or another up to our own day. Edmund Burke spotted it at its birth and recognized it as the sexual revolution accompanying the political revolution, the private life suitable to modern public life. Burke thought it was all degrading:

> The passion called love has so general and powerful an influence; it makes so much of the entertainment, and indeed so much of the occupation, of that part of life which decides the character forever, that the mode and the principles on which it engages the sympathy, and strikes the imagination, become of the utmost importance to the morals and manners of every society. Your rulers were well aware of this; and in their system of changing your manners to accommodate them to their politics, they found nothing so convenient as Rousseau. Through him they teach men to love after the fashion of philosophers; that is, they teach to men, to Frenchmen, a love without gallantry; a love without anything of that fine flower

of youthfulness and gentility, which places it, if not among the virtues, among the ornaments of life. Instead of this passion, naturally allied to grace and manners, they infuse into their youth an unfashioned, indelicate, sour, gloomy, ferocious medley of pedantry and lewdness; of metaphysical speculations blended with the coarsest sensuality. Such is the general morality of the passions to be found in their famous philosopher, in his famous work of philosophic gallantry the *Nouvelle Eloise*.[1]

But his disapproval of Rousseau's romantic project was no more successful in preventing the spread of this enthusiastic infection than was his opposition to Rousseau's political project. Oceans of novels and poems—beginning with Rousseau's own *La Nouvelle Héloïse* and the *Paul and Virginia* of his disciple Bernardin de Saint-Pierre, and continuing with almost all the greats of the nineteenth century—flooded France, Germany, England, Russia and educated the tastes of peoples while at the same time watering the seeds of a psychology of sex. Burke failed, but he as clearly as anyone recognized the culprit and his power.

Burke captures the curious character of this sexual revolution when he calls it a medley of lewdness and pedantry. On the one hand there is a fervid and single-minded dedication to the beautiful, to love in its purest, most unqualified sense; and, on the other hand, a scientific concentration on the coarse material facts of sex—sex, not eros or love. The laboratory experiment and the passionate embrace do not go together nor are their devotees alike—the scientific man with his method of disenchantment versus the lover with his art of enchantment. This ill-assorted match between objectivity and commitment is at the core of modern love from the outset, apparently combining contrary charms that at the same time threaten its coherence. Great romantic longing and fullness of bodily satisfaction is the winning formula.

This odd combination, plus the public confession of an irregular and even perverse sexual life by the promoter of idealistic longings, provokes Burke's disgust.[2] And no philosopher told us so much about his sex life and its peculiarities as did Rousseau. As a matter of fact, only Montaigne told us a bit about himself, while Plato provided some tantalizing details about Socrates. Not even Rousseau's philosophic successors followed him in this. We are as starved for information about Kant and Hegel as we are about Bacon and Spinoza. They were either all ashamed or thought that private sexual tastes were irrelevant to their thought. But artists of all kinds followed Rousseau's lead, appealing ever more to sexual interest while revealing themselves in explicit detail as part of their stories. Thomas Mann said that German schoolboys studied the loves of Goethe as Greek boys once studied the loves of Zeus.[3] Rousseau was the philosopher of the artists and the artist of the philosophers. Sex is connected with the love of the beautiful. But it should not be forgotten that the experience of erotic love links Rousseau with Socrates at the very origins of philosophy.

And it is quite a list of experiences Rousseau offers the world for examination: masturbation, exhibitionism, incest, sexually charged acts of punishing and being punished, now called sadomasochism, adultery, visits to prostitutes, experiments with *ménages à trois*, children produced and abandoned, and even homosexual assaults on himself[4]—all taken quite seriously as part of his quest for self-knowledge. Today this may appear tame, as writers continue to compete in the sincerity sweepstakes. But it remains quite respectable, and it comes from the man who invented the game, the man most likely to have thought through why it is a good thing to concentrate on such matters. The strangeness of Rousseau's procedure can be sensed by imagining how we would react to Newton's or Einstein's having left us detailed discussions of their sex lives. It just would not seem suitable and would at best be considered irrelevant to gravitation or relativity, their real studies and their real lives. Such confessions would have appeared to prove that their science by itself was not a fully satisfying way of life and that they could not merely as scientists be taken as exemplary human beings. Rousseau's life too is dedicated to knowing, and, in spite of Burke's strictures, and in spite of our common sense or received opinion, he succeeded in making his sex life a part of his life as a knower. Not only artists but philosophers, theologians, and statesmen accepted him, as he was, as a model of the man devoted to the most comprehensive knowledge.

Freud, more than a century later, took up the endeavor to found a natural science of psychology with sex in the starring role, making it the equivalent in psychological science of atoms in physical science, removing the stain of dirtiness or merely personal indulgence from those who pay attention to it. But Freud, unlike Rousseau, did not entrust us with anything significant about his own sexual tastes or practices. He adopted the pose of a Newton, the pure subject looking disinterestedly at the object, or, to put it conversely, objectivity analyzing the dearest illusions of subjectivity. I do not suggest that Freud was dishonest. He seems to have thought that one could be a scientist of the soul in the manner of the great Enlightenment tradition of the science of bodies. This meant that within us all, or at least in those of us trained in scientific method, there is an anonymous observer capable of seeing things as they are, not distorted by our imagination, or our vanity, or our desire. All it takes is filtering out all those impurities or wiping the mirror clean.

Rousseau, on the contrary, seems to hold that our consciousness is thoroughly constituted by the impurities, chief among them sexual desire, and that knowing the knower is the hardest of all intellectual enterprises. One has to take what is going on in oneself—all of it—seriously in order to attain self-knowledge. Reason is only one of many things working simultaneously in us, and not the most powerful at that. The sexual arousal that occurs when one is supposed to be studying plant morphology contributes to the result as does the thought of the woman who may admire one's scientific brilliance. Love of truth does not appear to be man's primary motive, and, therefore, it is a long way to the truth from what one sees through the filter of the passions. Rousseau moves toward the primacy of the individual and unique human being over against the general and uniform natural law. He has no doubt that there is a human nature, but it is so far away from us—hard to reach and covered over with so much unnatural history—that as individuals we can hardly even attempt to live naturally. Rousseau allows us to witness his attempt to discover nature by living and meditating on his peculiar, acquired sentiments and experiences in order to find nature's tracks within. This cannot help but make most of us think about similar things in ourselves. We begin to take them more seriously, and we too wish to become sincere about ourselves instead of forgetting or lying.

The Rousseau of the *Confessions* is an unusually sensitive modern man with all the distortions that civilization produces in the life of the passions. This is the beginning point from which he proceeds in two directions, back to the sex of brutish man in the state of nature, and forward toward a possible ideal life of love that combines the unity of natural desire with the profundity and self-consciousness of civilized man, all of whose capacities have been developed. Rousseau's life, as opposed to his thought, requires him to compromise owing to the almost instinctual conflicts resulting from his mixed-up education. Erotically he does a bit of this and a bit of that in order to allow his desires to express themselves, always considering what will satisfy him while doing as little damage as possible to himself or others. There are sensual loves and sensitive ones, passionate loves and domestic ones, perfect and ideal loves existing only in fantasy, licit and illicit loves, loves that give him a mother's rather than a mistress's care, almost meaningless sex and almost too meaningful love, loves tending to eternity and self-sufficiency competing, on the one hand, with the unsexual love of justice and the common good and, on the other, with the charms of natural solitude and self-awareness.[5] All of these alternatives are at least in part unsatisfactory, and none satisfies the longing for perfect love with reciprocity and permanence or the longing for lost wholeness that is the very core of the Romanticism he founded. Never does he say, "This is what I do, and that's all there is to it." He knows there are degrading lusts and acts, just as there are exalting and fruitful ones. He always keeps an eye on what sexual desire does to his whole soul and judges it accordingly. As Freud was the unsexy knower of sex, Rousseau was its sexy knower.

The present human condition, represented at its peak by Rousseau, is according to him so far from nature that it is no longer possible to live naturally. Not much of the complexity of the sexual life of civilized man can be attributed to nature—only raw individual desire and the reproduction required by the preservation of the species. The rest is due to acquired sociability and is likely to be chaotic and to set man at war with himself and others. The original sexual desire, which is to have sexual intercourse, has been transformed and become a murky stream in which many other kinds of desires now swim and pervade every aspect of life. Love, the desire to be loved in return, family and its duties and prohibitions, possessiveness and jealousy, shame and guilt, among many other things, are now set in motion by sexual desire. All the agony of the separation of the self from "the other" now follows from the innocent and in itself easily satisfiable arousal of the sexual organ. The very objects that move it are changed as imagination has come to dominate and dictate to the body's need. The achievement of a true personality, some sort of harmonious whole, is a work of art. Nature does not support or guide the artist in his work. Thus each such achievement, as the work of a serious artist, bearing as it does the stamp of his unique self, is bound to be different from every other. Man requires art, but few possess it. As natural men are all the same, civilized ones are all different. And most of them are a mess. Without Rousseau's art, another man with the same sexual tastes and history would be a monster. The lack of a natural standard for judging does not lead simply to relativism. The standard, however, is not a natural but an aesthetic one.

But only in nature or according to nature is man's happiness to be found, for it is there that a perfect equilibrium exists between his desires and his capacity to satisfy them. The movement from nature to society destroys that equilibrium. New kinds of desires or modifications of old ones emerge, and imagination invents satisfactions or dreams of satisfactions that make desire infinite. Nature makes man whole, society divides him. The trouble with man comes from society, not from his nature. He is not suited for social life, and this is not his fault. His desires are, as it were, plugged into the wrong circuits. An older moral philosophy, which goes back to Aristotle, taught that desires are by nature infinite and that man possesses the faculty of will, guided by reason, which can control desires for the sake of the good. The language of this philosophy was that of virtue and vice. Virtue was in this older view understood to be natural and the control exercised by it to be productive of at least one part of happiness. Virtue is happiness according to Socrates' formula. Courage controls man's fear of pain; moderation his love of pleasure. This control of pleasure, a willed harmony in tension, was itself understood by this tradition to be a pleasure. The existence of such virtues and their pleasurable character—except perhaps for the vain pleasure of superiority over others—is flatly denied by Rousseau. In particular, it is the virtue of moderation, which governs the desires connected with food and sex, that concerns him so much. To Rousseau, man is naturally moderate.* Society enflames his desires, and the control exercised over them is not that of virtue but that of fear, of external command, of what we now call repression. The new language is that of health and disease. The wound inflicted by society produces sexual neurosis. Fear and vanity attach sexual desire to imaginary and distorted objects. Healing, rather than appeals to morality, is what is needed in order to attain the bit of happiness possible for social man.

	Sexual desire, the source for him of so much misery as well
II	as of the most sublime moments, played such a role in Rousseau's consciousness and in his observations of the men and

women of his time that he could hardly help imagining an education that would take sex seriously and overcome the essential conflict

---

* This view is somehow maintained in Marx, where it is capitalism that creates artificial and limitless desire. Socialism will restore desire to its original condition. Capitalism, on the contrary, adopts the classical view that desire is infinite, although it shares the modern view about virtue. It rejects attempts to control desire and channels it instead.

between desire and duty. This would be an education for happiness (327, 419).* Sexual intercourse, he asserted baldly, is the greatest pleasure. A happy life must, therefore, have an important place for this pleasure. In their projects for the reform of man and politics, Rousseau's immediate predecessors and contemporaries had concentrated on avoidance of pain, on things men fear. Reduction of suffering was the negative goal of their thought. Economics, the dreary science, was the instrument of their reform. Rousseau went for the other half of the pleasure-pain dichotomy and concentrated on the positive. He was, of course, not such a fool as to think that a civilized life could be dedicated to sexual intercourse, but the civilized extensions of sex can be made the theme of a serious human being. Love, family, children, as well as poetry, can be made a way of life. An eroticizing of the world of concern to us is possible. The novel became the instrument of Rousseau's reform, and he hoped his educational novel, *Emile*, would someday cease to be imaginary, a novel, and turn into the history of man (416).

In *Emile* Rousseau takes the two evidently natural aspects of sex, individual pleasure and reproduction, and links them across a vast spectrum of sentiment and knowledge. For sex, he discovers, has an amazing or even miraculous power in man. Rousseau is some kind of materialist, but he finds in semen a capacity to turn flesh into spirit (232, 252). In comparison with hunger, the focus of his education of the child Emile (152), so much more can be done with sex. A refined palate and the vanity connected with the presentation of rare food and drinks splendidly served can take eating pretty far away from the fruits and nuts gathered from the trees and ground and eaten with dispatch by natural man. But for all the art and ceremony that can surround food in a country like France, it remains food. No one will die to preserve this luxury, and no great poet will celebrate it. Gluttony is not the worst of vices, but it is the most contemptible. It is a sign of small-mindedness. One can fantasize about a great dinner; but if that is the limit of one's fantasy life, it is a puny thing, morally and aesthetically handicapped. But sex, which is in fact no more naturally spiritual than eating, and, as Aristotle says, just another satisfaction of the sense of touch, the meanest of the senses,[6] is able to produce the most splendid flights of the soul as well as terrible tragedies. The energy emanating from the sexual fluids is at the root of world-transforming and adorning fantasies. Ideals of vir-

---

* All parenthetical citations in this chapter are to pages in Jean-Jacques Rousseau's *Emile: or On Education*, translator, Allan Bloom (New York: Basic Books, 1979).

tue and sacrifice for others are part of its legacy, as told in the medieval romances. Natural man is flat-souled, even machinelike in his response to bodily stimuli. It is from the plasticity of sexual desire that his depth emerges. Moreover, unlike the other grand passions that, as Rousseau knows, develop in social man, especially religion and patriotism, this one has a natural base, a natural organ of satisfaction, and perhaps a natural end.

Rousseau believes this erotic component in man is both a force underestimated by his liberal predecessors, hence dynamite in the repressed bourgeois, and an opportunity for the harmonization and moralization of man. Locke, the greatest spokesman for liberalism, wrote an influential educational treatise that does not mention sex, offering instructions in how to rear the child in decent, even gentlemanly social habits, with a view to rational foresight concerning safety and security. He is to be a family man, but what that means is hardly discussed. At the end Locke simply leaves his pupil "to his mistress" (357).[7] Rousseau's pupil, on the other hand, does practically nothing but prepare for that moment. One might say that Locke trusts that nature will take care of the marital relationship if the two partners have otherwise decent characters, while Rousseau denies that there is any natural teleology pointing toward marriage and the family. Nature provides man only with an occasional desire for a casual contact with a woman. That is a long way from caring for and protecting a wife and children for a whole lifetime. Nothing natural makes a man *desire* that. Force and habit can achieve such a goal, but Locke, who intransigently returns to natural freedom as the basis for human relations, cannot found the family on traditional grounds. It would seem, from Rousseau's perspective, that Locke was politically radical while remaining largely conventional with respect to the family. Rousseau held, and put into practice, the belief that once nature has been invoked, all forms of human relationship have to be reconstructed in its light. The primacy in the liberal tradition of "the economic man," rational and industrious, controlling his desires not from virtue but from calculation of future benefit, will result in a neglect of the sexual force in man, with unforeseeable results. It will be there, but it will be treated as if it were not, or as if it were unimportant and easily dealt with. The striking innovation in Locke's book on education is a training in how to produce a perfect stool daily and thus gain mastery over disorderly nature,[8] while in Rousseau's book it is a training in how to have a perfect orgasm (not necessarily daily), thus assisting nature to a new level of satisfaction. As Locke never speaks of sex, Rousseau almost never speaks of the toilet. Two different perspectives, and it is not difficult to predict which is likely to flatter men most.

Modern liberalism, unlike Greek philosophy and Christian theology, has no serious teaching about sex. Freudian psychoanalysis, a semi-Rousseauan enterprise, had to be invented in order to deal with the sexual neuroses of the bourgeois. The most authentic Rousseauan influence, however, is to be found in the great Romantic novels, which were meant not to help people adjust, but to found a life of sublime sexual expression.

An obscene and comic example can help to show how novel Rousseau's treatment of sex is and how much it distinguishes him from his predecessors, not only modern but also ancient. A story told by that great purveyor of gossip about philosophers, Diogenes Laertius, recounts that Diogenes the Cynic was found masturbating in the public square. When reproached for his shameful behavior, he explained, without trying to excuse himself, "I wish I could rub my stomach to satisfy its hunger."[9] This way of dealing with sexual desire is in accordance with the views of Cynicism, the school of philosophy that argued that men should live like dogs, that is, free of the tyranny of opinion and in accordance with nature. Make nothing more of sex and hunger than nature demands at minimum! This is an extreme case, but a similar attitude is present in much ancient philosophy, and Cynicism is a school that derives from Socrates. The last part of Book IV of Lucretius' *On the Nature of Things*, a book important in Rousseau's own intellectual life, conveys something of the same message: Free yourselves from the illusory power of the desires; give nothing to them other than the vital minimum! Then you can go about your business—which in the case of this select few, philosophers, is presumably thinking.

This question of masturbation is also mentioned quite frequently in Rousseau, usually as a bad practice but one to which he himself is addicted. In his own case, however, it is treated not as a compulsion or a compensation for frustration but as an opportunity for idealizing imagination to produce more perfect partners than the real world supplies. This is almost an act of creativity, and Rousseau's use of the word "creation" is one of the first applications to human, as opposed to divine, making.[10] Rousseau does not get rid of desire but increases and heightens it. In sex, at least, as opposed to food, he is not a minimalist, and he shows how far his naturalism is from the ancient variety. In general, he moves away from the austere treatment of the passions and imagination in all previous philosophy, early modern as well as ancient. Aristotle, who says there are two peak pleasures, sex and thinking, urges sexual moderation because one cannot think while engaged in sexual intercourse.[11] But one can fantasize, and Rousseau is not sure thinking is such a wonderful thing. Between feeling and sexual desire there is no such tension as that between thinking and sexual desire. Rousseau helps to render man whole again. A result of this way of uniting man is a preference for sincerity over truth. Romantic novels, music, and painting represent the new status of the passions. In Aristotle tragedy purges the passions, whereas after Rousseau the arts augment them and render them ecstatic.

III   Rousseau understood his romantic project as a response to a grim assessment of modernity, well known from his *Discourse on the Sciences and Arts*. This condition can be summed up as individualism, not that virtue of rugged self-sufficiency so prized in American folklore, but a needy isolation in the midst of society. Rousseau foresaw the collapse of all the structures that tie men together. He originated the still fashionable analysis of human relations in terms of the opposition between self and other, with no bridge connecting them. Common humanity is only an abstraction that has no effects on individuals and produces no felt common good. Each knows others as a scientist knows natural bodies—not from within, but through a peephole in the Cartesian closed box of consciousness. The new philosophy and the new natural science had reduced men to atoms without natural connectedness. Everyone needs everyone else, but no one really cares for anyone. Hobbes said that all are naturally at war with all, and in spite of some disagreement with that formula, Rousseau accepts that civil society is founded on that premise. Civil society and the relations among men in it are only extensions of that war by peaceful means, substituting various kinds of competition and exploitation—mainly economic—for mortal combat. The primary relationship is constituted by contract, that is, between two individuals who remain individuals entering into a contract valid only as long as it contributes to the individual good of each. The links between them are artificial and calculated and, above all, tentative. In this condition, man's defense system is always on alert.

The psychological effects of this unending alert are devastating. A being concerned only with himself has to spend his time worrying about the intentions of others and trying to hide his own from them, threatening, flattering, lying. In his selfishness, he forgets himself. His soul goes wandering out over the world of men and never returns, while he becomes hypocritical, envious, vain, slavish, measuring himself relative to the success or failure of others. This is the condition of alienation, which Sartre defined as "Hell is—other people."[12]

The selfishness of man is not for Rousseau merely a fact of modernity, the result of contemporary immorality or of false philosophy. It is always; it is human nature. What is new is that now everyone knows this fact, and modern politics, instead of trying to forget it, builds on it. This is the deadly truth. In the past, great legislators like Lycurgus and Moses denatured man in order to found communities (40).[13] The device they used was the transformation of individual selfishness into collective selfishness. Men lived within sublimating structures of family and nation, founded by force and fraud, decked out with myth and religion, to such an extent that their concern for family and country was barely distinguishable from their concern for themselves. Selfish deeds were punished by law and selfish thoughts by conscience. Now, full awareness of one's selfishness is not only permitted but encouraged as the foundation for voluntary association. Rousseau thought that this is a disaster, and much of his writing is devoted to describing and characterizing its product, the bourgeois.[14]

However, for all that, Rousseau, unlike Burke, does not suggest a return to the old way or even an attempt to prop up what still remains of it. And this is not only because he did not think it worthwhile to cry over spilt milk. Rather, in spite of its nobility, he thought that the old way was incomplete or imperfect. The very term he uses, "denaturing," points to the reasons. Nature is good. If social life requires its abandonment or its maiming, then it is social life that is questionable. Man, thus distorted, had shown great spiritual force in the ancient city or in the Christian faith. Would he be not only happier but greater if his social life were an expression rather than a denial of nature? The opportunity provided by the modern crisis is a complete, self-conscious rebuilding of man.

This is the project of *Emile*, which Rousseau begins by stressing that the opposition between natural man and social man, between desire and duty, is the core of the human problem, which is not soluble. The modern crisis results, precisely, from the false opinion that the two can be reconciled, an opinion that produces the bourgeois—neither natural man nor citizen, not knowing what he is, suffering from the identity crisis of all identity crises, a nothing. But a few lines later Rousseau tells us that his book is intended to unite the two opposite poles, nature and society, to overcome, as it were, the principle of contradiction (40–41). This became the project of much of nineteenth-century philosophy, most notably in the great syntheses of Kant, Hegel, and Nietzsche. The means chosen by Rousseau to this end is an education and transformation of sexual energy. From the outset this is a promising beginning, because sex is the only human need that naturally requires the participation of other human beings. But it is not as promising as it might appear because it treats those others as means to one's own satisfaction, not as ends in themselves. There is less harm done in treating a potato as a means than a man or a woman. The most likely outcome of using sex as the ground for relationship is reciprocal and tortured exploitation, desperate attempts to get others to give up their self-love without giving up one's own (213–214).

IV Civilized sex, the kind having to do with what men call love, is in Rousseau's psychology a product of imagination and *amour-propre* (a term I shall not translate from the French). Imagination is the great and dangerous potential faculty dormant in the state of nature (213–214).[15] When it is aroused, man's separation from nature begins and becomes ever greater, for it suggests infinite fears and hopes, extending man's sensibility over the entire universe, transforming his needs by ideas of beauty and merit. In the limited area of hunger, Rousseau presents this change by the depiction of two dinners Emile eats, one with farmers, where he is served the simple natural food produced by the labors of those who consume them, and one splendid feast *à la française,* where he is awestruck by the richness of the silver, china, and crystal, the formality of the service, the rareness of the food and the elaborateness of its preparation, the grandeur of the company and the gallant relations between the men and the women. The second meal is heady stuff, but Emile is stopped dead in his tracks by a question put to him by Jean-Jacques: "Through how many hands would you estimate that all you see on this table has passed before getting here?" Emile realizes on reflection that the whole world and thousands of men and women have been forced to contribute to what he eats at noon and what "he is going to deposit in his toilet at night" (190–192). But for a Frenchman all this is a necessity (which he can perhaps overcome by an act of vanity that is even worse than this luxuriousness itself). Such factitious necessities are the inevitable stuff of the life of civilized man. The imaginary or vain pleasures (and pains) cake over the natural ones so that they are no longer recognizable. His love is like this, but ever so much more so. In the state of nature any female suffices for man's desire, and she is always desired for the same old monotonous deed, but imagination makes civilized man choosy about his objects and gives him complicated ideas of what he wants to do with them.

Desire for exclusive possession and reciprocity are born of *amour-propre*, that mysterious keystone of Rousseau's understanding of the soul. The partners in a purely natural sex act could not care less what the other party thinks or feels, or has done before, or will do after. The relationship is hardly more significant than that between a man and his food. These sexual partners may be aware that they belong to the same species, but this does not mean much. Everything is related to the individual I, not to an unfelt thou or we. Rousseau, unlike older moralists, does not blame or struggle against this egotism. That is nature; to complain about man's selfishness would be like complaining about his not having been born with wings.

This exclusive self-concern Rousseau calls *amour de soi* (literally translated, self-love). It involves natural man in providing himself with food, an occasional woman, and a repose in which he enjoys sensing his own existence. He is absolute unto himself. Rousseau praises this selfishness, setting himself against the Christian moralists who take it to be the source of evil and oppose it with the command to "love thy neighbor as thyself." Rousseau suggests that the proper opposition is not between egoism and altruism, or something of the sort, but between good and bad self-love, *amour de soi* and *amour-propre* (92, 213–215, 243).[16] This distinction links Rousseau to Machiavelli and his followers who argued that men, instead of trying futilely to live in terms of imaginary oughts, should come to terms with and live according to what they really are. This is the first step toward an effective morality. And Rousseau's distinction determined the nineteenth and twentieth century way of treating egoism. It is understood no longer as a problem of man's sinful nature but as one of alienation from his true goodness.

To Rousseau, man is the only animal whose self-love can become altered or doubled in response to the recognition of others' existence. He can convert his simple search for exclusive well-being to a concern for being first among men. This means that his absolute being is turned into a relative one, dependent on the opinions and deeds of others. The small change from *amour de soi* to *amour-propre* constitutes *human* psychology. A dog will sometimes fight with another dog over a bone, but it can never be concerned with what the other dog thinks of it. It may be discontented over the loss of the bone, but it cannot be insulted by the other dog, swear vengeance and spend its life trying to punish the other. But this is what civilized man does always, beginning from earliest childhood. The baby who learns that he can command his parents by tears forgets about his real needs and spends his time asserting his will over that of his parents. Food becomes less important than his relations of mastery and slavery. To love himself means others must love and serve him, and finally real need disappears in preoccupations of sacred honor. And this is the beginning of evil in man, which is the desire to harm and punish others (64–69). This transformation of self-love makes men aware of one another's intentions and hence, in this terrible way, the consciousness of the other's consciousness arises. Having relations to others means that existence has become relative to them and life is lived in terms of their opinions. Previously man thought only of himself. Now he thinks of himself through others and wants them to prefer him to themselves.

The movement to *amour-propre* from *amour de soi* came to be called alienation, that is, becoming involved with others and forgetting oneself. The precise mechanism of the misery of social man is to be found here. Vanity and pride are born along with their effects: competitiveness, ambition, anger, envy, jealousy, hypocrisy, deceitfulness, among others. A Rousseauan psychotherapy would treat the distortions of *amour-propre* in civilized man. Rousseau can sometimes sound like a biblical prophet when he denounces *amour-propre*. He does not however look to the virtues to overcome it but suggests various strategies for the recovery of the real self. He is *the* modern of the moderns.

But Rousseau, in spite of appearances, was not simply the enemy of *amour-propre*. It is, in his view, a two-edged sword. Mostly, as with all things human, it cuts in the wrong direction, but properly directed it can be the source of greatness of soul in the quest, for example, for political or literary or scientific glory, or for love. All these begin in the desire to be recognized by others as best.

Sex, of course, is where the expression of *amour-propre* is most inevitable. A man can be reared to be a Robinson Crusoe in society, independent of others in the provision of life's necessities, free of material or spiritual dependence on others. But as soon as a civilized man meets a woman, he has to care about her will, not out of respect for her, but out of respect for himself. Her opinion is more important than the sexual act itself. She must not simply give herself; she must wish to give herself.

Of course, it is most likely, once *amour-propre* is in play, that a man will seek to conquer a woman's will without engaging himself in any way. Seduction, the attempt to get her testimony to his desirability, becomes the art of love. In its most subtle and artistic form ever, according to Rousseau, this art dominated the life of aristocratic France. Men without honor and women without modesty trifled elegantly with love. Neither really committed him- or herself, mocking the substance of love with its forms. The sexual act was adorned by imagination and vanity but was not informed by the morality of true love, in which sex is a testimony of permanent mutual esteem. The logic of this kind of relation was developed by Rousseau's disciple Choderlos de Laclos in *Les Liaisons dangereuses*, in which the whole pleasure of the two protagonists, the Vicomte de Valmont and the Marquise de Merteuil, is in sexual victory, a pleasure much enhanced by breaking the rules of conventional decency and taking advantage of innocence and, especially, virtue.[17] Deception rules and joy reaches its climax in the manipulation of the sexual desires of persons who believe they have moralized and tamed those desires, leaving them, in the end, with no self-respect. In this erotic war of all against all, the inevitable conclusion is that the two masters must, after having mastered the minor players, take each other on, with the results everyone knows. This exploitation and conflict is much more terrible than any connected with business, where relations are purely external and the individuals are explicitly self-interested. It is *almost* impossible, given human self-love, that the promise to care for another as for oneself be anything but deceitful.

But, to repeat, *amour-propre*, although it is already a perversion of his nature, is the only thing in man that unites souls. And education in love, connectedness, and even morality uses as its means sexual desire, imagination, and *amour-propre* judiciously formed into an artistic unity by the educator. This is a radically different kind of education from that proposed by Socrates, who asserts that he merely evokes what is already naturally in man.[18] Rousseau's education forms rather than evokes, and is a project and an act of creativity.

V In the last stages of man's sojourn in the state of nature, before he was subjugated by or subjugated himself to civil society and its laws, when man was still free, Rousseau finds an equivalent to the biblical Fall. Men ceased their wandering and began settling down with companions. In such little communities they began to make comparisons and to have preferences. No longer was just any man or woman good enough. Ideas of merit and beauty, the two components of love, led to exclusive taste for a single partner who possessed them and who, of course, was supposed to reciprocate. But when these wishes are frustrated, jealousy is born, bringing in its wake hatreds and desire for revenge. For the first time blood is spilled with the intention to do harm. But this is not all. These still essentially idle men and women, gathered in herds, devote themselves to singing and dancing, the companions of love. But some are better at them than others. Each wants to be attractive, to be looked at and preferred. Thus a certain kind of half-natural inequality establishes its throne among men, along with the pain and conflict such inequality produces. Happiness now depends on the opinions of others. Singing and dancing best, being most beautiful, most adroit, strongest, or most eloquent are essential to esteem, especially of the opposite sex. Those who possessed these gifts became vain and contemptuous; those who did not were ashamed and envious. Those thus deprived were tempted to feign possessing these goods and hence to become dissemblers and hypocrites, beginning the underground life of capricious torment in their dependence on others for their self-esteem. And all this for sex![19]

In spite of all these unhappy accidental consequences of the first cohabitations, Rousseau pronounces this to have been the happiest time, midway between the brutish sloth at the beginning and the perfervid activity of *amour-propre* we have at the end. Finally money, a merely conventional thing, will come to be the only distinguishing attribute, because it can buy all the others. Rousseau's analysis resembles Marx's, but for him the sex wars preceded the class wars and point to scarcities economics cannot remedy. Rousseau appears to have anticipated those twentieth-century intellectuals who tried to combine Marx and Freud.

| VI | "It is now that man is truly born to life and now that nothing human is foreign to him" (212). This is Rousseau's description of what he calls "the crisis" of puberty. It is a second |

birth, moving man from individual self-preservation to concern with the species. The meaning and the secret of life enter into Emile's bloodstream at this moment, and Rousseau can apply to him the classic formula for the wise man. The key to humanity is sex. Until this time the boy has learned his relations to dead physical being, the realm belonging to natural science. Now he must study man and his relations to his fellows. His understanding of humanity depends on the new condition of his body. Never has puberty been described in more portentous terms. This is the fatal moment, for good or for ill.

Rousseau is partly a naturalist and sees man as part of the animal kingdom. All animals appear to live in order to reproduce. Young animals become what they are at the moment when they can reproduce. There is an evident movement toward a peak. When they reach it, they are all that they are ever going to be. Then, in their fullness, their primary activity is the reproductive act, which they perform with pleasure while propagating their species. Nature would seem to have motivated their most necessary function with the most powerful pleasure, and the orgasm is the peak of their existence, when they are most fulfilled. When they cease to be able to perform the sexual act, they are on the downward slope toward death, useless, alive but no longer what they really are. Puppies are cute, old dogs can be touching, but everybody sees that these are the imperfections on either side of a perfection that defines the species. There is no prize at the Westminster Dog Show for the best puppy or the best old dog. And so it is with all the species. These are not scholastic ravings but the palpable evidence of our senses that the life sciences can perhaps not explain but with which they cannot dispense. We see it also in humans, although, since Rousseau, we have romanticized the innocence of children because he made us doubt whether there is a civilized maturity. Nobody except those who profit from the conventions of patriarchy, like Swift's Struldbruggs, would prefer the last part of life.

Man, though, stands out among all the animals as the only one who needs a sex education. Most other animals require some kind of education or apprenticeship to life, but it ends when they are able to reproduce. With man, the most serious part of education can only begin with the capacity to reproduce. Offspring is all that is required of the other animals, and they, particularly the males, have nothing else to do for that than engender. But human children, especially civilized ones, require extended and complicated care from both of their parents. Biologists say that man's sexual maturity comes earlier in his development than does that of other animals, which would seem to argue for some kind of inexplicable natural intention.[20] To interpret the problem that Rousseau addresses in a way suggested by Kant,[21] man has two puberties, one the physical capacity to make children, the other the moral and intellectual capacity to care for them. At least ten years separate the two puberties. A real culture consists in their coincidence. This means that, unless one's sexual desire is for not only the act but the act with someone one admires and will always admire, one is bound to live in perpetual conflict between desire and duty. Desire naturally must rebel against the limits or laws imposed on it from outside. There is a war in the soul, constant guerrilla attacks, small victories by each side, compromises, spurious peace treaties, a struggle that exhausts the soul while the two combatants lose sight of their original goals. This is the condition of civilized man. A cultured person is one in whom the sexual desire has been transformed in such a way that it longs for the true, the good, and the beautiful as seen in a single permanent partner with the orgasm as the fulfillment and reward of such longing. This is a return to the original state when the performance of natural duty, reproduction, was rewarded with the greatest pleasure.

But now duty, no longer natural, includes producing future parents and citizens as well as human animals. The coincidence between the greatest pleasure and the performance of duty is henceforward most improbable. In civilized man pleasure is weakened and perverted by the bad conscience with which society saddles it, and noble duty is performed only for mercenary motives and halfheartedly. The one light Rousseau sees leading from real civilized man to the ideal of cultured man is the simple fact of love, a thing rare but not impossible, where the sweetest inclinations join the noblest aspirations and even sacrifices. In its usual form it is not enough, but encouraged and enlightened it points the way. The unity of man on a high level, his acquired faculties enhancing him rather than dividing him, would be the result. Society would be the instrument of realizing his sexual desire in the family rather than its oppressor. This is how Kant saw Rousseau's project, expressed, he said, in *La Nouvelle Héloïse* and *Emile*: making man whole again after the tragic split in him between nature and society described in his celebrated early writings. Kant's was probably not an exhaustive interpretation, but it identified what turned out to be the most edifying strand of Rousseau's thought. The story of human community was concentrated in this precise and detailed description of the sexual drive for more than a century, with aftereffects enduring up to our own time.

Education from puberty on is sex education, just as education from birth to puberty is self-preservation education. And sex education does not consist in telling children who are not in a position to understand what mommy and daddy do, how to avoid pregnancies or venereal diseases, or how to recognize, ward off, and denounce vicious adults, particularly their closest relatives. All this is like lobotomizing them in order to avoid possible overaggressiveness, a kind of popular mechanics without thought about the uses of the machine. No child, Rousseau insists, can understand anything whatsoever about sex, because he has none of the experiences that make understanding possible. He must distort such useless information to fit what he can understand. A child can be a great expert on sweets or dogs. He cannot grasp politics, God (Rousseau will say later), or sex (255ff., 380–381). Who knows what crazy notions will come into the head of a kid who is told about such things. Sex education is properly education in the capacity to love and not in how to make love, an art not so difficult to learn as it is made out to be. A sublime utilitarianism that asks in the first place, "What's the use of it?" must precede the teaching of the sexual facts. As in so many other things, concentration on the means prior to consideration of the ends would turn the means into ends. Furthermore, this preparation cannot be a perfunctory statement prior to showing the pictures. The pupil must really understand and, more important, feel what he is looking for. If he does not love his ideal before practicing sex, he will never love it. The separation of sex from love is fatal to love. It must seem impossible to practice the former without experiencing the latter, for sexual energy is necessary to real love. Therefore sex education essentially deals with the development of the imagination.

The miracle of sex, according to Rousseau, is that although it is purely material, it becomes in civilized man utterly dependent on imagination, which is purely immaterial. Imagination most palpably moves the flesh. Most men and women physically reject persons who could quite easily satisfy their physical desire because such persons do not fit their imaginary model of beauty or merit. The body just won't perform. No civilized sex is simply physical. It is always mixed up with some image of what the other party is or what one is oneself in relation to that other party. None of this is natural. Rousseau's project is to form the imagination in such a way that men's preferences will tend toward serious objects, the enjoyment of which might result in happiness and a life in conformity with decent social relations. This means that sex education can be undertaken only by a philosopher, someone who has reflected on man's nature and his place in the order of things. It is not an affair for sexual plumbers.

How to perform this delicate operation of uniting desire and sublime imagination is demonstrated in Books IV and V of Rousseau's *Emile*. Perfect sexual satisfaction is the end of this education, and sexual desire is its means. Illustrative of Rousseau's point is an anecdote John Aubrey, the author of *Brief Lives*, recounted to a friend who had expressed the opinion that "the only time of Learning is from nine to sixteen, afterwards Cupid beginns to Tyrannize." Aubrey responded that "Mr. Hobbes told me, that G. Duke of Buckingham had at Paris when he was about twenty years old, desired Him to reade Geometrie to him: his Grace had great naturall parts and quicknese of witt; Mr. Hobbes read, and his Grace did not apprehend, which Mr. Hobbes wondered at: at last, Mr. Hobbes observed that his Grace was at mastrupation (his hand in his Codpiece). This is a very improper age; for that reason for learning."[22] The young man was experiencing what Socrates' companion Glaucon called erotic necessity, altogether different and more intense than geometric necessity. The simple fact is that all young people, especially boys, as soon as they start feeling these new things in themselves, even more so if they have some idea what they mean, are incessantly preoccupied by them. Anybody who has dealt with them at that age knows their obsession. If you say, "It's a nice day," they see some hidden sexual reference and laugh. I remember a science teacher when I was in high school demonstrating something with a tube out of which a white substance emerged sporadically. The continuous giggling of the class drove him wild until he yelled, "Only perverts could see something funny in this." He was greeted by sustained uncontrollable laughter. All our wit and intellectual energy were otherwise engaged, and the teacher simply made perversion seem interesting while adding the fillip of the forbidden to our glee. At a certain age adolescents start having new interests that conventional studies do not address. Their lives become split between what they are learning in school and what really concerns them. There is an immense literature about the double lives of adolescents.

They have got to learn, say the pedants. Rousseau says the study of mathematics and physics is unerotic, as are the specialties and the arts of self-preservation. That is why Rousseau has made such an effort to give Emile a basic knowledge of nature and the skills of natural science prior to puberty. He must have submitted himself to the iron laws of natural necessity before his imagination comes into play and fills up the world with its tales. Otherwise he will bend nature to his whims as do the savages with their myths. Natural science can be taught in such a way as to appeal to the primary concerns of children—self-preservation and being able to get around on their own. But natural science cannot be taught to appeal to adolescents with their special concerns. What a shame it is, Rousseau laments, to waste that pure source of curiosity and energy, which could be used for humanizing studies, just because adults want them to learn something else. The trick is to find things for an adolescent to learn that attract his new sensibility and at the same time instruct it. Now is the moment when the old saw "The proper study of man is man" becomes true and when consciousness finally begins to be self-consciousness. Otherwise youngsters will have dead studies and untutored experiences. And deceptions of all kinds become the order of the day. The hidden life becomes the real one.

Rousseau was a shrewd observer of human motivations and made neat calculations of how they operate on the various ages of man. A five-year-old will promise to jump off a tower tomorrow if you give him a cake today, because he does not know what tomorrow is and does not know what a promise is. You can come to collect on his promise, and he will refuse without understanding what is bad about it. You can spank him, which gives him a real motive to keep his promises. But this does not mean that he recognizes that breaking promises is bad, only that he knows that being spanked is bad. The cause of the spanking is not in the nature of the deed but in you. The way out is simple: the child will do what he pleases while hiding it from his parents. There is no escaping this, Rousseau argues, so better not exact promises from children. A twelve-year-old knows what tomorrow is and can calculate that it is probably wise to sacrifice today's pleasure to avoid a greater pain tomorrow. Honesty is the best policy, he understands, but the evil of lying is still beyond him. Rousseau accuses Locke of not being able to get beyond this stage in his education, which, as earlier noted, does not include sex. The twenty-five-year-old Emile can promise fidelity to his Sophie, not because of the pleasure he is going to get or the pain he is going to avoid, but because of his respect for her and his respect for himself. His pleasures and pains have become drastically changed by his attachment to the ideal.

The postulate of Rousseau's reasoning about this subject is that man is by nature an idle beast willing to make no more effort than is absolutely necessary to get his food and shelter in order to be able to lie around dreamily. There is no inborn desire for self-improvement. Therefore, it is very difficult to get man to learn anything other than what the most immediate pleasures and pains would urge. Education must consist in finding motivations for what it is good for man to know. Rousseau indicates that up to his day educators had found only three motives, all of which have bad side effects and can even destroy the value of learning. They are fear, gain, and vanity (89–90). These turn out to be motives that dominate bourgeois life in general, prepared for by bourgeois education. Translated into childish terms they are presented in the form of spanking and scolding, gifts and other such payments, and honor and praise. The trouble with all of these is that learning is never for its own sake and that it encourages certain spiritual deformities. Fear produces anxious human beings, concerned with avoiding pain but incapable of experiencing the sweetness of existence. Slavishness and toadying to authority along with learning understood only as a way of avoiding pain or death are the results. Hobbes's man. Base gain reduces learning to its market price, and its possessor understands only the mercenary. The child thinks that his studies have their *raison d'être* in the rewards. Locke's man! The worst of all is vanity. Omnivorous *amour-propre* is set in motion from the earliest age, feeding on the highest things only for the sake of the subject's sense of superiority over others. Vanity is a profound source of inequality among men, and its effects are described harshly in the second part of the *Discourse on the Sciences and Arts*. This is a critique of the Enlightenment, but also a critique of the pride of the theoretical life altogether. Socrates' man? Young Emile is treated harshly only once by his teacher, Jean-Jacques. That is when he learns about magnetism and uses his knowledge to gain the applause of ignorant people. Jean-Jacques arranges to have him humiliated publicly by a greater expert on magnetism and the manipulation of crowds. He does so because vanity is the most powerful distorter of souls (172–175). A child will soon forget the artificial lesson in history or the theorem of geometry you teach him in this way, but the effects of the methods used to teach him last forever and determine his disposition toward life as a war against others for the sake of security, profit, and esteem.

In response to this problem Rousseau finds two alternative motives for learning that do not corrupt his pupil's natural goodness. The first is food and especially sweets. All children are gluttons, particularly when it comes to sweetmeats. This is beyond the brutish desire for any nourishing food, though it does not go very far from nature. A child will make an effort beyond that required to stay alive to get sweets. The charm in the first three parts of *Emile* is Rousseau's subtle use of food as the means of instruction. Emile learns to read because he receives invitations to go and eat custard at some neighbor's place but does not know where and when. He perfects astronomy when he is lost in the woods at lunchtime and tries to orient himself in order to get home and eat. Rousseau rings every change on this theme, and it is the means of almost the entire early education. He argues that the food, if properly distributed, appears to the child to be connected to the thing he is asked to learn and does not cause him to look away from it to the will or the whim of the adult who teaches him. Rousseau gives the example of an Italian boy who learned the whole of Archimedes' geometry from cakes made in the various geometric shapes. Since he was allowed to eat only one a day, it was very much in the little glutton's interest to figure out which one had the greatest volume. The final advantage of this method is that the desire for sweets, unlike fear and vanity, will become unimportant when the child reaches puberty. He will have other kinds of sweets on his mind. No young man in love is at risk of corruption from gluttony. The result of the use of sweets in teaching is the opposite of that of the other methods: the learning remains, while the superadded motive disappears. This procedure, in its use of sugar, imitates the sweetness of being (117, 180–181, 146).

The second motive invented by Rousseau is of course sex, sexual desire, sexual energy, or however one ought to describe the effects of the fluids that enter Emile's body at puberty. The last two thirds of the book are only a detailed account of Emile's sexual development. This is the golden thread, so often missed by interpreters, uniting the diverse matters treated that make the book appear to be an ill-organized and ill-assorted compendium. Rousseau says, concerning food, that he can lead armies of children to the ends of the earth by the mouth (153). He implies that he can do the same with adolescents using the instrument to which the promised satisfaction is addressed. The genius of *Emile* consists in Rousseau's exclusive use of these two simple motives from beginning to end to accomplish the whole complex work of culture.

But there is this difference: the sweets are covertly added by Rousseau to provide a motive for the child that is not naturally in him; the sexual yearning is in the adolescent, and the task is to mislead him about its true object. The child Emile runs for sweets; the adolescent seeks God and other ideals because he does not yet know what he really longs for. The task is to enrich his desires before they are satisfied. It is not to forbid his satisfaction, which would be to repress him and divide him against himself. The goal is to sublimate his desires prior to his capacity to distinguish sex from love, so that when he learns about the distinction it no longer interests him.

We find ourselves here, as it were, at the source of the Nile, the almost unnoticed origin of a great stream that overflowed its banks and produced a tropical proliferation of exotic plants. Although he never used the term, Rousseau is the founder of sublimation in the precise sense of the word. Kant understood Rousseau to be a teacher of the sublime, and from then on the movement from the material to the spiritual, a movement not natural but cultural, was called sublimation. Popularly this is thought to be an invention of Freud, but here we have it in an inspiring rather than a grim form, with a clear and persuasive answer to the critical question "What is sublime?", a question hardly addressed by Freud.

Rousseau's intention is to create longing in the soul of man. Natural man does not long. He has desires that lead to immediate satisfactions. And bourgeois society, in a perverse imitation of nature, provides small goals and small satisfactions for its typical man. Romanticism, Rousseau's child, tried to encourage, within the confines of bourgeois society, a small band, the happy few, men of genius, the artist-lovers with the greatest longing for the greatest goals. Rousseau tries to construct eros. Eros is a word I try not to use in relation to modern writers, for none of them can consistently assert that the longing for the ideal is what sexual desire is really all about. They have to fabricate eros with "the stuff dreams are made on." Merely imaginary or illusory ideal objects made by poets are supposed to solicit the desires of men. Can such insubstantial images really persuade men for long against the force of real bodily desire?

This is the question that makes one doubt the whole Romantic project and makes one wonder whether today's dreary scene of boring and meaningless sex is not its consequence. For Rousseau and his followers were trying to make something out of nothing, to draw men out of the primal slough with a rope that cannot be attached to anything above, other than a hope and an aspiration. Goethe expresses this romantic faith in the formula "The Eternal-Feminine attracts us higher." Nietzsche scoffed at this.[23] Freud and Kinsey are waiting at the end of the garden path.

| **VII** | Rousseau begins his education with the observation that the passions, particularly the sexual passion, are naturally good and that God would never condemn or wish to an- |

nihilate them (212–213). This apparently casual remark goes to the heart of his intention. It is an attack on the notion of original sin and the whole Christian revelation. This was, of course, a hot topic, Rousseau's treatment of which resulted in his exile from Catholic France and Protestant Geneva. The dividedness of man in this most intimate area of his life is caused by the universal acceptance of the Fall as the cause of his misery—his vices and perversions. The essence of Rousseau's project is to heal the guilt poisoning modern men, to lift them up again to complete and unhampered love. To use the jargon favored by Denis de Rougemont, Rousseau works for the final triumph of eros over *agapē*. The very commandments concerning man's sinfulness make him into both a rebel and a slave and ruin his sexual experience. God corrupted man. Rousseau underlines this by his silence about the Bible, God, and religion throughout Emile's childhood. Rousseau even writes, "I hate books," just prior to giving Emile the only book he reads until his teens, *Robinson Crusoe*, about a man who survives alone on an island by his own resource and without any higher authority (184). Rousseau does not point it out, but we can observe that Emile is not baptized or taught the catechism, so as to preserve him from theological contamination with its stimulation of the terrified imagination.

There is nothing particularly novel about the project of unifying man, of suppressing the difference between how he ought to live and how he does live, reducing the tension between body and soul, and doing away with the conflicting demands of the heavenly and the earthly city. From Machiavelli on, this was the goal of the Enlightenment writers. We still see the remains of their work in such institutions as the separation of church and state. But none of them concentrated on the sexual damage done by the Christian teaching. There were a lot of obscene jokes about priests and nuns, and sexual libertinism was used as a sign of rebellion from the divine law, but the discovery and reconstruction of the pre-Christian disposition toward sex or an improvement on it does not seem to have interested any of the Enlightenment thinkers—as opposed to some of the very early moderns like Boccaccio, Chaucer, Montaigne, and Shakespeare—because they thought either that it was unimportant or that it would rectify itself. Nietzsche said, "Christianity gave Eros poison to drink. He did not die, but became vice."[24] Rousseau made the undoing of that mistake central to his writing. He did so for all the reasons that I have already discussed. He moved from concentration on individual rights concerned with property and security to concentration on what is now called the private life. We are aware that when people talk about privacy these days, they mean sex and what is connected with it. Rousseau is the modern philosopher who most loved Plato's *Symposium* and gave the nineteenth century a taste for it. Rousseau originates Blake's notion of "the botched creation" and the attempt to begin over again with a new Adam, which means without the Fall. This theological background, likely to go unnoticed today, is necessary to understand what Rousseau is about. As he was, along with his great predecessors, the enemy of Christianity in politics,[25] so he was also its enemy in the realm of love.

This does not mean that Rousseau is for "letting go." Man is now an artificial being, full of factitious desires and passions, afflicted by the sinful view of sex propagated by Christianity and the materialism of modern philosophy. Breaking through ancestral restraints now would put into practice all the contradictions nourished within men over millennia and debase their human contacts all the more. So far are we from nature that we must begin over again in the new Eden Rousseau depicts in his education. The biblical tradition knew some things about sex that have to be incorporated into a natural education, and they concern its danger and its sacred character. When God made the covenant with Abraham, promising that his offspring would become a great people, countless as the sands of the desert or the stars in the sky, it was in return for the circumcision, meaning that God was to take charge of the organ of generation, which He would then loan to man. This great loan from God was not a thing to be played with. Fathers then still had vast views of the meaning of their acts of generation. They were not to waste their precious seed on the ground or in any other way. The future depended on it. In such a light, talk about the "right" to control one's own body, especially all the parts that have to do with reproduction, sounds pretty silly. The sexual organs in their movements are the visible presence of the sacred. Rousseau wishes to maintain this kind of divine possession without the authority of God and all the nays of the biblical commandments. So extreme is his intention.

As I have said, the beginning point of all this is puberty. And Rousseau's view is that early puberty is a curse. It means that there is that much more time for an immature person to get corrupted and that much less learning before having to cope with the crisis of puberty. The asexual things that have to be learned get mixed up with the sexual ones, which means that unerotic necessity will have less sway over his judgment while imagination will tend to feed on everything without limit. The distance between natural and civil puberty is greater, and it is more difficult for Rousseau to reduce that distance to nothing. His two techniques for filling the gap before explicit sexual knowledge is made available to the young man are (1) delaying puberty and (2) keeping him ignorant of the meaning of his feelings.

To many contemporary readers, Rousseau, after liberating sexual desire from the yoke of sin, seems to impose a similarly severe but merely human yoke. He is charged with vestigial Calvinism (his Genevan religion) or, more loosely, with puritanism. But one must remember that the restraints he imposes derive their authority from nothing other than supreme sexual pleasure. It is precisely to give man freedom from brute desire and to avoid the imposition of necessary social restraints from outside that Rousseau is the proponent of love. Man is naturally attracted to any available object. But when he is really in love, all females lose their attractive power except for the beloved one. There is no adultery or infidelity in the heart of a lover. Love is immeasurably more effective than religious stricture in civilizing sexual desire. This is the very model of Rousseau's promotion of moral ends without morality. Morality would be only a less effective substitute for love. This goes with, not against, the grain. No nays; only yeses (327ff.).

These are the kinds of things that elicit the apparently cranky sides of Rousseau's thought. If one does not see the crucial importance of attaching idealism to sexual desire from the outset, making the two separate things into a seamless unity, all of Rousseau's remarks concerning late puberty, particularly the view that the psychological surroundings have much to do with the age of puberty, as well as his strictures against loose language and masturbation, seem silly.

Rousseau is aware that in primitive societies a thirteen-year-old can be considered a man because the duties and learning of man's estate are very simple, but the complexities of civilized society make it impossible for any young person to put together the demands of immediate raw nature and those of civilization. If one does not attempt what Rousseau attempts, the opposition between desire and morality will divide men. He presents us both a hope and a great doubt. The hydraulics of the soul are such that if you use its energy in one direction, it will not have any available for the other. Even early knowledge of the facts so fixes the imagination that it is impossible to turn it to other objects.

 VIII Rousseau states with exceptional force the whole principle of his education, which leads from brutish nature to high civilization or culture, at this decisive moment:

> Do you wish to put order and regularity in the nascent passions? Extend the period during which they develop in order that they have the time to be arranged as they are born. Then it is not man who orders them; it is nature itself. Your care is only to let it arrange its work. If your pupil were alone, you would have nothing to do. But everything surrounding

him influences his imagination. The torrent of prejudices carries him away. To restrain him, he must be pushed in the
opposite direction. Sentiment must enchain imagination, and
reason silence the opinion of men. The source of all the passions is sensibility; imagination determines their bent. Every
being who has a sense of his relations ought to be affected
when these relations are altered, and he imagines, or believes
he imagines, others more suitable to his nature. It is the errors
of imagination which transform into vices the passions of all
limited beings—even those of angels, if they have any, for
they would have to know the nature of all beings in order to
know what relations best suit their nature.

This is, then, the summary of the whole of human wisdom
in the use of the passions: (1) To have a sense of the true
relations of man, with respect to the species as well as the
individual. (2) To order all the affections of the soul according
to these relations.

But is man the master of ordering his affections according
to this or that relation? Without a doubt, if he is master of
directing his imagination toward this or that object or of giving it this or that habit. Besides, the issue here is less what a
man can do for himself than what we can do for our pupil by
the choice of circumstances in which we put him. To set forth
the proper means for keeping him in the order of nature is to
say enough about how he can depart from it. (219)

This provides an outline for the rest of his education. The young
boy prior to puberty had a sound relationship to things based on
natural experience and a science that explains their regularity. Now
the problem of his relation to men becomes the great question, and
this is ever so much more difficult because men, unlike things, do
not behave with regularity and permanence, but are capricious.
Imagination is the wild card, and Rousseau's intrusive education
depends upon giving the imagination guidance about what things
are and what is desirable in them in such a way that it can correspond to the demands of unity and autonomy. Unlike older views
that imagination, though deceptive, reflects or hints at natural reality, Rousseau teaches that imagination must compensate for what
nature does not provide for human existence. Therefore it is up to
man himself to establish a rank order of goals from his own freedom
or spontaneity. Here Rousseau makes it clear that only a philosopher
can do this. The philosophic teacher exists to get the ball rolling, and

enable man's imagination to become independent. This teacher begins by showing how sentiment can enchain imagination with the first step of his sexual education, which is compassion.

Rousseau tells us that human relations properly begin only when man's sensibility or capacity for feeling extends beyond himself. What he means by sensibility here is that capacity for feeling new sensations, beyond the self-preservative ones, that arise with sexual maturity. Rousseau radicalizes the modern view that man is essentially a being of feeling rather than a rational animal. Hobbes argues that man is a being of feeling or passion, but in the end makes man's connection to others a result of calculating reason. Rousseau insists that unless there is a relationship of feeling among men, the opposition between self and others will make it impossible for them to have a moral connection with one another. The youngster whose imagination is occupied with the pursuit of sexual pleasure will have an entirely different perspective on things from the innocent one who, full of feelings whose meaning he does not know, will investigate his new relatedness to other persons.

Another way of putting the same thing is that Rousseau agrees with modern thought, as over against ancient thought, that reality resides in the unique, individual beings. The universal is abstract. Therefore, humanity is an abstraction unless there is a bridge built by the unique individual to it by feeling. This is the work of compassion, and its emergence is the first stage in overcoming the natural opposition between self and others.

Rousseau had argued in his earliest writings, in particular *The Discourse on the Origin and Foundations of Inequality*, that there is present in both brutes and man a feeling of connection with the sufferings of others of their kind.[26] In *Emile* he develops that view but transforms it by making compassion both more central to the soul and more active in guiding the actions and sentiments of his pupil. It is immediately clear why Rousseau prefers feeling to reason in this context. Natural pity makes us immediately sympathize with the sufferings of others, but reason can assure us that it is the other who suffers and that we are not necessarily in the same boat with him. Excessive rationalism individuates man and strengthens natural selfishness. Therefore liberalism's attempt to use reason as the ground for the social contract goes in the wrong direction. The only connection is in the passionate sense of bodily and spiritual suffering. Human beings can be understood to share a common fate on the basis of their vulnerability. Only feeling finds ground for true common cause.

Compassion in its civilized and active form is the first important work of imagination in man (220–226). A suffering human being observed by a neutral observer is an absolute other. But if one sees oneself in the other, he becomes one's fellow. He becomes a human being by an act of the imagination. So imagination, rather than real sameness of species, is the reality of common humanity or human-kindness. The young child, actually a natural savage, with his exclusive concern for self-preservation, has little in him to identify with others. The young man, trained to self-sufficiency, but with an excess of sensibility due to his new sexual energy, is the one who can extend his feeling beyond himself by acts of the imagination without rivalry. It is at this crucial stage of life, between the selfish atomism of the child and the development of his social relations, that Rousseau inserts the sentiment of compassion, which, properly trained, will temper his relations to his fellows and determine the limits of his selfishness.

In performing this high-stakes operation, Rousseau is extremely hardheaded about what human nature permits. Man's selfishness does not allow him to sacrifice his own interest to that of another. The happy other who has all the things one would like for oneself is an object of resentment and envy. A suffering man is no threat. Rousseau asserts, with characteristic boldness and harshness, that nobody can share the happiness of even his best friend without envy. He won the lottery and got all the money. I congratulate him, but actually I would prefer to have the money myself. His happiness robs me of mine. Aristotle would say that the true friend, although very rare, is possible, that he could rejoice in his friend's good luck, whereas Rousseau insists that this is simply impossible. It is only the friend's neediness which one can succor that brings out the generous, as opposed to the corrosive, sentiments. Rousseau goes so far as to say that a truly self-sufficient man would have no concern for others and that his happiness would be a kind of solitary monstrosity (221). Rousseau does not even consider the ancient view that men have a natural unity in their exercise of reason.

The spiritual development Rousseau attempts to foster goes from the first immediate but imaginary shock we feel at the sight of another's pain to the recognition that it is the other suffering and not us, that we can be of use to the other, and that this would speak well of us while benefiting the other. This may sound like hypocrisy, but it can become part of a person's self-awareness, a gentle habit of the soul, as opposed to a harsh conflict between self-interest and duty.

This development and elaboration of compassion is made possible by the emergence of sexual sensibility and imagination, but it is made necessary because of the emergence at this moment of *amour-propre*. In relation to nature, man is absolute and has no term of comparison or rivalry. But among men, comparison of relative worth or status is inevitable. The happy man is an insult to the unhappy man, and the unhappy man is an affirmation of his worth to the happy man. To be surrounded by the rich, the famous, the titled, brings out the ugly and diminishing passions, whereas the presence of the needy brings out the gentle ones. So as a result of what I have called the hydraulics of the soul, the first social relations that the newly sensitive young man must observe are those of ordinary people whose life is made up of more pain than joy. The experience of pain for others is to be accompanied by a limited self-sufficiency gained from the early training. It is a fine line that must be walked between indifference to others' suffering, stemming from a sense of invulnerability, and envy of their supposed happiness. Since *amour-propre* must necessarily come to be in social man, everything depends on this development as to whether there will be a proud and generous relationship to other men or one of hypocritical good fellowship grounded in murderous competition.

An expansive view of man's being permits him to establish out of his inchoate sexual energy a sensitive attachment to others, to experience the same thing others experience. This permits a broader understanding of self-interest. The compassionate man has pleasures unknown to the one whose life is devoted to the cramped pursuit of self-preservation.

Although the awakening of compassion has important social consequences, Rousseau's primary intention is to respond to the either/or posed by *amour-propre*. The gentle awareness of human suffering is no threat to the pupil's self-esteem, whereas the man who is happier, or is thought to be happier, than the young Emile both usurps the first place that Emile claims and adds insult to injury by having no need of him. Compassion encourages inner independence while envy is the chorus master of all the vices connected with dependence. Compassion is not, Rousseau knows, just in itself, but it is the preparation for understanding and practicing justice. Compassion lends itself to the demand for equality because it gives Emile the experience of the life of the people as opposed to that of the rich or the noble. Emile will not be poor, but his sentiments will prefer the poor to the rich.

At a more advanced stage of this education Emile must face the reality of a society dominated by inequality and the apparent disproportion between position and merit. The natural bent of *amour-propre* would be to covet the places of the socially privileged, and avoiding this is the most difficult part. The child Emile learned that he preferred his own simple, rustic dinner to the splendid one laid out by the rich. This was part of the education of the mouth. The mature equivalent will consist in arousing pity for outstanding men and women. The young Emile was not taught Plutarch's *Lives* because he could not have understood the moral teachings, and its effect would have been alienating, making the youngster into an imitator (243). Now, with the independence and self-satisfaction of his childhood and with compassion as a new armor against rivalry, Emile is brought to Plutarch, but in a strikingly novel way, which reverses the entire tradition. Rousseau extends compassion to the privileged, who are usually the objects of hatred and revenge. Plutarch's heroes, from the point of view of the self-sufficient man, are dependent and tragic, pitiable men and women seeking imaginary goods and suffering the most terrible consequences from that pursuit. Plutarch becomes a compendium of the splendid vices of the ancients rather than of the supreme examples of virtue. Rousseau, unlike the old moral teachers, wants no imitation on the part of his pupil because such imitation brings on all the corrosions of self-hatred. His young man is not the imitation of a classical hero but a *personality* in his own right. Tolstoy, a great reader of Rousseau, depicts this in *War and Peace* with the opposition between Prince Andrei, the noble imitator of the heroic and admirer of Napoleon, and Pierre, clumsily marching to his own drum even when he tries not to. Emile, properly educated, will experience a sympathetic horror in contemplating the emptiness of the goals of those who seek to be first among men, and will be content to be himself.

Without this disposition he would be full of moral indignation and invoke just punishment. The first experience of compassion would institute class war between those who seek equality and those who enjoy inequality. Rousseau attempts to extend compassion to both classes in order to avoid the ugly passions connected with what most people call justice. Rousseau makes a great effort to avoid moral indignation, which is the great sophist in the soul and persuades people that their wounded self-interest can be converted into a high moral calling. Compassion indicates the road to reform while keeping envy at bay.

It must be stressed again that Rousseau is constructing a rank order in the soul, not relying on one that is already there. The Platonic and Aristotelian tripartite division, into reason, spiritedness, and desire, is not the reality of the self. The self is, as Hobbes and others described it, an undifferentiated mass of desires without natural rank order. Rousseau, following nature, reorders the passions to make those connected with self-sufficiency dominate. Politically, he corrects the teachings of self-interest, and he convinced nineteenth-century liberals (e.g. Tocqueville[27]) that democracy is best founded on the fellow-feeling of compassion. But for Emile himself, compassion is only the extension of his sensibility made possible by his unconscious sexual awakening in order to protect him from the deceptions of imagination. He is no less selfish than he was naturally before, but his selfishness now includes a pleasurable feeling connected with his discovery of his human-kindness. This is really not yet moral obligation, and when his self-interest conflicts with the dictates of compassion, he will follow his self-interest. And above all, the activity of the compassionate man is not a way of life for Emile. There is, of course, real human attachment, but it is generalized and does not constitute the bond of sociality and mutual admiration that we seek but have difficulty finding. This Rousseau will find only in love, the erotic love of a couple. Emile does not yet care for another as he cares for himself.

Rousseau is perfectly aware of the danger of the hypocrisy of compassion, the self-indulgence of caring mixed with superiority. He attempts to cure this by reading the fables, ancient and modern, that teach men the folly of vanity (240–249). But most of all he tries to achieve this end by generalizing compassion so that the young Emile does not take an individual whom he knows and likes to be the only object of compassion, but thinks as a legislator what compassion would achieve for a whole community or for mankind at large. Such feelings intimate the idea of justice prior to Emile's having heard the word "justice." From the bawling child who thinks that the world must come to a halt to succor his slightest pain, we arrive at a young man who conceives of the pains of all humanity and puts his own pains in proportion to them. Rousseau calls this sublime and gives us a hint of what he would mean by sublimation. Thus concludes the first stage of the education of erotic sensibility. This is what he meant when he said: "sentiment must enchain imagination" (219).

IX Now Rousseau turns to the second part of that sentence, "and reason silence the opinion of man." This is the most famous part of *Emile*, "The Profession of Faith of the Savoyard Vicar" (260–313). It rivals *The Social Contract* and the *Confessions* as Rousseau's most famous work; it is frequently simply extracted from the book and taught to schoolchildren out of context. It is apparently Rousseau's statement about metaphysics. The "Profession" had undoubted power, as proved by Rousseau's banishment from society and condemnation by Catholics and Protestants alike, and by the inspiration it gave to later theology. Its teaching is all too familiar in the liberal religious positions of the nineteenth and twentieth centuries. It is ecumenical and independent of revelation. But it is clearly not Rousseau's final reflection about metaphysics or the question of God because it is explicitly put into the mouth of another and is less radical than reflections pronounced in Rousseau's own name.[28] It is necessary but difficult to understand the "Profession's" place in the plan of *Emile*, applying as it does to the young Rousseau as opposed to the young Emile. Properly understood, the "Profession" reveals the deepest stratum of Rousseau's thought and seeks to find an entirely new dimension of the soul.* The "Profession of Faith" is nothing less than Rousseau's presentation of the sublime, the underlying experience of greatness that anchors the profound soul. The quest for God is a result of erotic sensibility, and the necessity for this reflection comes from the need to regulate erotic expression. This is the foundation of the notion of sublimation and provides its lofty model for the sublime. It is both interesting in itself and very up-to-date for us. The impulse emanating from it transformed not only religious thinking but also literature, music, and painting. Not least, it motivated the system of Immanuel Kant, who attempted to ground Rousseau's sentiments. Kant took Rousseau's teaching to be the culmination of culture, that is, the harmonious and unified perfection of civilized man.

Ordinarily civilization means only a honing and exacerbation of

---

* This dimension is shrewdly assessed by one of the most intelligent theologians of the twentieth century, Karl Barth, in discussing Rousseau's article on "Genius" in his *Dictionnaire de musique*:

This is not the eighteenth century anymore, it is not the genius of Bach nor the genius of Haydn (quite apart from the fact that a book of instruction in accordance with their way of making music could scarcely have contained an article on "genius" at all), it is not Mozart either, but it is unmistakably Beethoven, Schubert and Mendelssohn, line for line. Music which holds the universe in thrall, which reflects ideas in the form of feeling, which aims at expressing and awakening the passions, which as feeling for life addresses itself in a mysterious way to the feeling for life, music which does not wish to be understood as beautiful, but as enchanting and only in a delirium, music which according to whether it moves one or not, reveals a kind of predestination to blessedness or damnation—all that might very well be found in Schleiermacher's Address on Religion, but not in any book previous to the age of Goethe, nor in any heart or head either. Anyone who read this article in those days was immediately called upon in the field of music to decide whether to receive the new message, that art is prophetic of feeling, as something rich with new promise or as something in the nature of a declaration of war; and whether he should welcome or hate it accordingly.[29]

the intensity of private satisfaction, whereas, according to Kant's interpretation of Rousseau, culture requires the generalization of the private so as to encompass the public. But the teaching on compassion in *Emile* does not complete this work. Tension remained between self-interest and the interest of the whole, along with the inevitable primacy of the former. The Savoyard Vicar's teaching, if successful, would suppress the claims of the private and brutish natural man.

Another way of putting it is that Rousseau has given the sexual destiny of Emile's desires the slip by attaching them to compassion, extending sensibility from the individual to the species. But he has given Emile no way of thinking about the opinions and practices of men in matters sexual that will protect that attachment. There is a need to correct calculating reason by making it sensitive reasoning. But most of all, the Savoyard Vicar provides an object of intense satisfaction far beyond those that result from pitying others.

To begin with, Emile's education has been totally silent about what would have been the most important theme of education in his time, that is, religion. Rousseau's silence was heavy with disapproval of the Christian, both Catholic and Protestant, treatment of children. He implicitly accuses the biblical teaching, with its burden of "nos" and its attribution of original sin to all, of corrupting children, of dividing them and robbing them of the autonomy of their judgment (98–101). It is only when the adolescent senses of civilized man cry out for enlightenment that the quest for God becomes a felt need on the part of pupil and teacher alike. The longing for pure spirituality now seeks its fulfillment. This longing is fraught with the greatest dangers, for the imagination easily turns it into that maddest and most dependent form of ignorance called superstition. Rousseau here relies on the most fundamental meaning of enlightenment: liberating men from superstition. The newly vital imagination must gain its satisfaction only after being subjected to reason. But how can a purely sensual being such as man even have abstract thoughts? Rousseau presents the movement from sensibility or sensuality to abstract thought as a kind of miracle. It would seem that he attributes this movement to the miraculous seminal power that puberty provides.

The mystery of eroticism is encapsulated in these reflections. The mystery is how spirituality can arise in a being who seems so material as Rousseau's man. Rousseau must tread a fine line between superstition and unbelief. Naturally, man is superstitious, Rousseau tells us in a surprising confession (134ff., 256). It is surprising because Rousseau has seemed to tell us elsewhere that natural man has no imagination. That natural man seems to be a kind of model constructed by Rousseau by which to judge man, whereas here he explains that without enlightenment man will inevitably interpret natural physical phenomena as acts of will threatening or protecting him. This is why the early education of Emile is directed to understanding corporeal nature and bending him to unquestioning acceptance of nature's yoke.

The "Profession of Faith" gives a model of the kind of reflection appropriate in matters of religion, a model free of the distortions resulting from man's fear. One might ask, "Why not be an unbeliever?" Rousseau answers that the unbeliever has no standard for judgment beyond the maelstrom of society's opinions. One must not forget that Rousseau is trying to avoid the power of priests while fully aware that the man liberated from the priests, in the absence of any other authority, is most likely to be a slave to public opinion. The boy Emile could count on instinct to preserve his independence. He knows that the simple country dinner tastes better than the elaborate one given by the rich and powerful. But his sexual instinct has become so plastic as to give no guidance. God seems to be the only resource. Social man must begin to think, and he inevitably arrives at a view or an imagination of the first causes of all things. So experience of a higher order confirmed by reason is a necessary part of education at a time when the passions grow great and imagination becomes unbridled. Thus a balance is kept between passion and enlightenment. This restores, on the level of society, the natural equilibrium of the savage.

The Savoyard Vicar presents a new kind of rationalism, which I shall call sensitive rationalism. It is intended to satisfy the demand for reason while avoiding the modern uses of reason as the arm of selfish satisfaction. God, as anchor of independence and object of satisfaction, is the goal of the religious views expressed by the Savoyard Vicar. This is no mere civil or useful religion. It is a powerful temptation and satisfaction for the religious longings in man. No poets would be inspired with religious enthusiasms in reading Hobbes or Locke. But Rousseau did indeed solicit such enthusiasms and reinjected the religiosity that Enlightenment tried to suppress. He states the problem simply:

Let a Turk who finds Christianity so ridiculous at Constantinople go and see how they think of Mohammedanism at Paris! It is especially in matters of religion that opinion triumphs. But we who pretend to shake off the yoke of opinion in everything, we who want to grant nothing to authority, we who want to teach nothing to our Emile which he could not learn by himself in every country, in what religion shall we raise him? To what sect shall we join the man of nature? The answer is quite simple, it seems to me. We shall join him to neither this one nor that one, but we shall put him in a position to choose the one to which the best use of his reason ought to lead him. (260)

The stakes are in all ways very high.

Rousseau seems to present what is called natural religion, that is, a religion accessible to all men through their natural faculties unassisted by the revelations of scripture. This is the kind of theology one finds in Aristotle's metaphysics and the religious reflections of modern philosophy. But in Rousseau's hands natural religion is quickly transformed into the religion of nature. The beauty and order of nature inspire an enthusiasm that we know all too well since Rousseau. This is a far remove from the matter-of-fact accounts of natural religion in earlier thinkers. A new kind of belief becomes the capstone of Enlightenment, replacing distorted and impure beliefs of imperfectly civilized man. The beauty of nature's order acts as a standard and as a satisfaction compared with the disorder of society and the paltriness of its satisfactions. And the hints of the limitless power of the God who lurks behind nature give the pleasurable but frightening experience of the sublime. Gone is the contempt for nature that results from the biblical accounts of a God who is so superior to nature that we can learn nothing about Him from it, who shakes our attachment to our senses and our reason and demands a faith against all odds. Again Kant gives voice to Rousseau's intentions when he says that a man with a feeling for the beauty of nature can hardly be simply corrupt or immoral.[30]

Moreover, as Arthur Melzer has said, Rousseau replaces faith by sincerity in the profession of faith.[31] Faith means belief in another, in the mysterious God who exists objectively. Sincerity puts the onus on the subjective certainty of the self without reference to further authority. The shift in focus is reflected in our parlance when we say we have faith in someone as opposed to saying we are in good faith. The primacy of the latter reflects the dignity and legislative power of the individual. It is a proud affirmation of the dignity of the self rather than the pious annihilation of the self before a higher dignity.

Reciting ancient propitiatory oaths to the angry gods, Rousseau undertakes the dangerous task of speaking about them. Rather than giving a discursive account of his theology and how it suits Emile,

Rousseau tells a story about how a good priest saved him from corruption, the second of three passages in *Emile* about Rousseau's own development (135–137, 260–313, 344–355).[32] These passages outline how he, so deeply affected by the injustices of society, liberated himself and was hence able to educate men so as to be free. He is the philosopher who experiences the distortions of social man and founds an education that produces a man who does not require Rousseau's genius to be free. The young Jean-Jacques is very different from Emile, in fact he may be said to be Emile's contrary. Whereas Emile was raised according to nature, that is, free from the opinions of men, Jean-Jacques was caught in the maelstrom of their prejudices.

The first story about the young Jean-Jacques tells of him as a ten-year-old orphan who is taken into the home of a distant relative, a Protestant pastor with a son of the same age (135–136). Jean-Jacques cannot bear his dependency and helplessly tries to make himself the equal of his spoiled cousin Bernard, whom Jean-Jacques does not regard as his equal. Competition for primacy is the whole business of his life at an age when Emile does not even recognize the existence of others. He tries to show his courage by recovering a Bible from a dark church. It almost ends in a terrible humiliation as the demons of the night nearly defeat him in the church. But he triumphs over the kingdom of darkness because of his even greater fear of the laughter of the august company assembled by his cold step-parents. He is especially sensitive to the presence there of a young woman who has induced premature sexual desire in him. All kinds of fears and shames awake his wounded *amour-propre* and launch him into a furious battle for recognition. In the *Confessions* this young woman is said to have punished him in such a way as to make him seek erotic pleasure in punishment.[33] All the bad actors are paraded in this little story—rivalrousness, religion, and premature sexual desire.

The "Profession of Faith" picks up the story of Jean-Jacques in his adolescence. The Savoyard Vicar's teaching addresses itself to a young man in the grips of angry indignation, full of envy, resentment, lust, and the spirit of vengeance. Wounded *amour-propre* is the center of his soul. The addressee of the "Profession of Faith" tells us as much about it as does its substantive content. Jean-Jacques had to leave his Protestant hometown as a result of an escapade and became a destitute fugitive in an Italian city. The young rascal, so charming in his picaresque adventures, in order to survive converts to the dominant religion of the place, Catholicism. Entering into a home for converts, he becomes the victim of all the corruptions so vividly characterized by Enlightenment antitheological ire against Catholicism. He is a prisoner of hypocrites, an object of perverse sexual harassment, the pawn of unbelieving priests concerned only with comfort or worldly power. His just complaints turn him into the accused. He ends up utterly alone and without resources: he almost came to have "the morals of a tramp and the morality of an atheist" (263). The disorder of society and the triumph of injustice in the world made him concerned only to triumph in the opinions of men. Spite is his dominant passion. He is still sexually innocent but only out of a shameful timidity. As a result of his experience in the almshouse, he is disgusted by sex, but has a libertine's opinions about it, preparing the way for a degraded erotic life. Here we find again united the themes of *amour-propre*, religion, and sex.

The Vicar enters as *deus ex machina* for the salvation of Jean-Jacques' soul, whether it be for this life or the one afterward. His story is also interesting and partially parallels that of Jean-Jacques. He is disgraced in the Church because of his independence and is barred from all advancement. In spite of this, he has a gentle and pious demeanor in punctiliously fulfilling the obligations of Catholic ritual. He is in outward observance a pious Catholic while not hating the dogmas of Protestantism and open to a humane ecumenism. The Vicar suffers from the quarrel among the sects and their conflict with the true religion. For Jean-Jacques, he is another loser like himself, an object of puzzlement but not of emulation.

The Vicar's specific crime was sleeping with unmarried girls (267). Rousseau, of course, presents the celibacy of priests as unnatural, therefore justifying certain kinds of promiscuity on their part. They are left with the choice of maidens who have not yet sworn their marriage vows or married women who have. The Vicar chooses the naturally more innocuous, while the Church, respecting vulgar opinion, preferred that its priests have sexual relations with married parishioners whose offspring can be attributed to the cuckolded husband, thus avoiding scandal. The Catholics prefer to soil the most sacred vows in order to silence the rumors. The theological-sexual problem is recapitulated in the Vicar as well as in the young Jean-Jacques. Rousseau wryly remarks that the Vicar is still "not too well corrected" (265) in his sexual habits.

The Vicar is an enigma for Jean-Jacques because he seems to have Protestant beliefs while rigorously observing Catholic practice. He is a model of how a wise man adapts himself to the practices of the nations while keeping his inner self free. Thus he provides a kind of response to both the religious and the sexual problems with which Jean-Jacques is unable to cope. The Vicar, like Jean-Jacques, stands between the two sects, Protestant and Catholic, and this position illuminates the religious madness. On opposite sides of arbitrary lines drawn on a mere map men have contrary views of salvation and all the most important things of life and are willing to kill those who do not share them. But anyone who tries to cross these spiritual lines must be disloyal to his father, his country, and his religion. Since too much depends on family and national attachment to leave such decisions to every individual, the Vicar states the practical principle that everyone should adhere to his father's religion (311, 381). But this is too conventional a solution to satisfy anyone who thinks. So he takes two individuals who, against their wills, each in his own way, have stepped outside the limits of their fathers' religions and have had to think them through for themselves. This provides a dim reflection of the problem Rousseau faces in starting all over again with the natural man, the new Adam, who will require a new or natural religion. He never addresses this problem directly and the Vicar's "Profession" is a kind of halfway house between the religions of the nations and the religion of nature. The religions turn out to have the same incoherence as do the different ways and laws of the nations. On the one hand, they express the furious passions of the nations, involved with all their injustices and hypocrisies, while, on the other hand, they point toward the highest things men have in common and toward images of justice.

The Vicar has found a standpoint outside the opinions of men that allows him to judge them, and provides him with an independent source of satisfaction. In his education of Jean-Jacques he at first presents himself as a victim just like Jean-Jacques. It does not occur to Jean-Jacques to regard his humble priestly pal as an object of admiration. He possesses none of the goods that Jean-Jacques thinks constitute happiness. Jean-Jacques thinks that the ones who are on top in society are the happy ones and either schemes to be among them or moralistically denounces them. Eventually, however, the curiosity of this unusual boy directs itself toward the priest who lives with equanimity in what would seem to be an unbearable situation. Finally the priest asserts to the incredulous Jean-Jacques that he himself is the happy man (266). Against his inclination Jean-Jacques wonders at the priest's standpoint outside, and the priest offers to explain it to him.

For his "Profession" the Vicar very carefully chooses a gorgeous locale with the background of mountains, rivers, and flowing valleys. Rousseau says that it is "the most beautiful scene that can strike the human eye" (266). This passage reminds us of an earlier moment when Emile, in an equally beautiful setting, discovers the seasonal changes of the sun's position in the sky, and Rousseau warns us not to expect the child to have any awareness whatsoever of that beauty. The ecstasy of the peculiar beauty of the seasons, the beauty of nature and its relations to the sentimental life, are impossible for Emile at this stage of life (168–169, 181). His is a purely material mathematical observation of the astronomical facts. After puberty the ecstatic condition that gives him eyes to see the beautiful and the sublime comes into being. The seminal fluids provide the missing ingredient without which nature is but matter in motion, whether its beauty is in the things themselves or is a product of man's creative or poetic power. Suffice it to say that to address his particular target the Vicar's rhetoric requires erotic sensibility. The enthusiasm for nature is the ground of contempt for the artificiality of social life.

The "Profession" is a modified Cartesian meditation, an attempt to find the minimum certitudes for a thoughtful man to live by. The Vicar underlines more distinctly than does Descartes the moral dimension of his metaphysical undertaking. The contradictions in the social and theological order have so uprooted his habitual principles of moral conduct that he is forced to go back to the roots and begin all over again if he is not to be buffeted solely by the winds of fortune. The first certitude is the thinking subject, but the essence of man is individual feeling rather than universal reason. "I feel, therefore I am" goes alongside "I think, therefore I am." The method is what one might call the logic of the heart rather than the logic of the mind, and sincerity, that judge whose authority is so mysterious, is the arbiter of the proofs of God's existence. Although he is always aware that there are unrefuted objections to his conclusions, the Vicar is sure that his sincerity overbears the reasonings of his critics. He outlines Kant's critical project, the essence of which is to bridle metaphysical imperialism by its command, "Thus far proud reason and no further." Both the Vicar and Kant wish to silence reason's attempts to disprove that God exists. They want a religion that, if not reason itself, at least is not unreasonable.

The first principle the Vicar uncovers is based upon the fact of motion. There must be a first cause of motion and that is the first attribute of God that the doubter encounters. There are two substances—matter and will. Will or power somehow lies behind this world of continuous motion that we experience (270–274). I would not hesitate to identify this dark force with the terrifying sublime that underlies the Romantic artist's awareness.

The second principle of certitude is order, that is, nature. Nature reveals an intelligible order, whatever its status, that cannot help but attract any thoughtful man (275–276). The Vicar means here not primarily the order found in reductionist physics but those obvious phenomena of growth or teleological motion present in the most ordinary experience, especially in the plant and animal kingdoms. These correspond to the energy, especially erotic energy, of the young Rousseau and Emile. Rousseau, as did Goethe after him, concentrates on such phenomena in an attempt to recover a world in which man can live fully. Rousseau spent much time in his later years botanizing.[34] The Vicar thinks that anyone insensitive to this splendid order is only partially human, even if abstract reasoning might seem to support him. The admiration of nature's realm I will call the love of the beautiful, the aesthetic accompaniment of the sublime. This order, unlike the sublime, is totally present and accessible to contemplation and understanding. It is pleasant without an element of the terrifying.

The principles of will and order in nature guarantee a realm of splendid contemplation that not only satisfies reason, like Plato's contemplation of transcendent Ideas, but stimulates energetic imagination. These first two principles, although they are not uncontroversial, belong to the attributes of the God of the philosophers and contain little admixture of hope. The Vicar's next step, toward moral obligation, is much more tenuous and fraught with difficulty. But this is where his enterprise necessarily takes him. He begins by looking at the place of the species, man, within the ordered whole of nature. Man is the best of the animals in both his bodily and his mental powers. No one would choose to be anything other than man if he had his choice among the animals. The first glance that man takes at himself is most satisfying to his collective *amour-propre* (277–278).[35] It is well to note here that the Vicar is much more certain of man's special status within the ordered whole than is Rousseau himself in his accounts of man in the state of nature, where man is less distinguishable from the brutes and where one finds proto-evolutionary suggestions.[36] The Savoyard Vicar either is more certain than is Rousseau himself of the purposeful ordering of nature or takes his bearings not from the state of nature but from the point of view of developed man in civil society. But when one looks from man's exalted station in the order of nature to society, one finds not order but chaos and the worse ruling over the better. Everywhere power, money, and family triumph over virtue, and there is no proportion between merit and desert. So the choice of the moral life appears unsupported.

Nonetheless, the Vicar sees in this bleak perspective not the proof of a world indifferent to morality, where justice is the benefit of the stronger, but the proof of man's most distinctive faculty, his freedom. There must be abuse of freedom in order for men to deserve praise for their proper use of it. There is a clear morality in concern for the common good. The concern for the whole or the exercise of the general will, or as Kant put it, the categorical imperative, is easy to understand but difficult to practice. It is likely that most men will order their lives according to their private good. Yet true self-esteem, the highest of goods, is the reward for crushing private interest in favor of the common good. The good civil society has a legislation like that of the order of the whole as planned by God, but since God leaves the governance of humans to humans, it is of course less likely to be achieved. Otherwise man would live instinctually without choice like the brutes, without the dignity of responsibility. Man is an imperfect God in his little sphere, endowed with an irrepressible certainty of his free capacity to choose or to will and his capacity to order.

The Vicar traces the private versus the public inclinations of man to a dualism in his nature following from the two substances—matter or extension versus mind—that are postulated by his teaching. Man's body is private and vulnerable and leads him to be concerned only with his own preservation or pleasures and pains. His mind or his soul partakes of a community with other men and looks to the general. Virtue or morality consists in the triumph of soul over body. The two substances have different natures or constitutions and they are uneasy partners. The soul is not made to serve the body and the body serves the soul reluctantly and only when whipped.

Although the Vicar insists on this traditional and readily grasped dualism, up to this point there has been no such dualism in *Emile*. Its absence is part of the radicalism of Rousseau's own teaching. Emile has followed only his inclination, and to the extent he has begun to be concerned with others, he has done so only by an expansion of his feelings without any tension akin to that between morality and self-interest. Emile, at least thus far, is seamless, whereas the Vicar praises a divided man whose glory is in the victory of the higher over the lower. We must remember this difference when we come to reflect on Rousseau's own final judgment of the Vicar's sublime teaching.

In order to avoid a completely chaotic freedom for man the Vicar is constrained to prescribe a guiding principle for his freedom. He invokes the conscience, which is one of the most vexed and controversial themes in moral thought (279ff., esp. 289). The Vicar argues that in all of us this regulating principle causes us to take pleasure at the sight of justice or concern with the common good and to feel pain at the sight of injustice or concern only with one's own individual good. This voice or sentiment thus both directs action and rewards and punishes the man to whom it speaks. Just as hunger and other such passions are the voices of the body, so is conscience the voice of the soul, which is itself akin to the animating principle of the cosmos. It is the felt expression of the universal. Conscience is particularly esteemed in the Christian tradition and is therefore peculiarly appropriate to this enlightened ecclesiastic, even though his account of it is closer to a philosophic one than to the Christian.

In contrast to the Vicar, Jean-Jacques almost never speaks of conscience to Emile, although Rousseau insists in his own short statement at the end of the "Profession" that morality cannot be preferable to immorality without the sanctions of conscience (314–315). The only thing in *Emile* up to now that has any kinship to conscience as described by the Vicar is the ultimate generalized pity or compassion that motivates Emile in his relations to all men and is thus somehow legislative. But that generalized pity is not in mortal combat with Emile's own self-interest. It does not constitute a triumph in a divided man but is itself an inclination energized by sensuality. To the extent it conflicted with the more primitive inclinations, it would have to give way. Emile is to be a whole man at one with this earth. The Savoyard Vicar accepts the imperfectness of this life in the light of another, imagined or real. His account of conscience, and hence of a real and noble morality, is an absolutization of compassion, which Rousseau insists is real in man but not absolutely authoritative as the voice of true morality.

The Vicar must take one more step. However much morality depends upon the purity of intentions, no decent man can rest satisfied with simply unrewarded justice or with no relation between morality and happiness. The human longing for happiness may not correspond to the demands of morality and may even have to be subordinated to them, but the simple opposition between happiness and morality would be too tragic to bear and would appear to give witness to a godless universe. Yet, the evidence for the convergence of the two is not strong. Rousseau's own beloved Plutarch is just another witness to the victories of the Caesars over the Catos. The defense of morality, at least in the Vicar's situation, requires the possibility and the postulate of another life where rewards are proportioned to deeds, not so much for the sake of vengeance against the malefactors, but for the sake of vindicating the decent. The peak of the pyramid built by the Vicar is the most philosophically doubtful of his arguments, that is, the immortality of the soul. The good man is moral not for the sake of eternal happiness but for the sake of morality itself, but he must be allowed to hope for eternal happiness when he sacrifices this worldly happiness to morality (284). This is the Vicar's most effective argument for the absoluteness of morality when presenting it to a doubting and tormented youngster.*

The culmination of the Vicar's sentimental meditations is the life that Jean-Jacques sees him leading. Assured of his place in the cosmos and enjoying satisfactions that do not depend upon political regimes or the conditions of society, he does good according to the natural religion while adapting himself to the aberrations of the particular sects (311). His earthly joy comes from his good conscience and his ecstatic contemplation of the intelligible order of nature. These are the natural or the permanent things that do not depend on men.

Yet for all the power and eloquence of the Vicar's "Profession" it surely does not represent Rousseau's own last word about the right way of understanding things or living a good life. The simplest proof of this is that Rousseau, who regarded his own life as exemplary, was very unlike the Savoyard Vicar. Moreover, Emile, the best of the ordinary men, does not become an ecclesiastic but a lover, husband, and father, none of which the Vicar is. In the dramatic context of *Emile*, the Vicar acts as a cure or a palliative to Jean-Jacques' *amour-propre*, incarnating a way of life in which self-knowledge does not depend upon the arbitrary opinions of men. The Vicar's great speech is fraught with difficulties, but his Orpheus-like eloquence silences Jean-Jacques' objections (261, 294). The spell, however, will be broken, as we shall soon see.

The problem is that the fidelity to the voice of conscience adopted by the Vicar leads to a certain otherworldliness. The happiness that a man seeks is not available to him on this earth if he lives morally. This world is drained of much of its charm, and there is a longing for

---

* In order to remind ourselves of the significance of the "Profession," we can see that Kant's great system is meant to ground on the highest level the intention of the Vicar's morality. Kant's entire philosophical undertaking was deeply influenced by his encounter with *Emile*. The Vicar responds to the three great questions of serious men and of the philosophers: what can I know? what ought I to do? and what may I hope? Kant's three postulates—God, freedom, and immortality—are the Vicar's own, and just as the Vicar cannot prove them, so Kant postulates them, and, more rigorously than the Vicar, proves that metaphysics cannot refute them. Likewise, the two things that cause wonderment in Kant, the starry firmament above and the moral law within, are identical to those of the Vicar.[37] It is not sufficiently understood, however, particularly in the Anglo-Saxon world, how much Kant was inspired by Rousseau, and how much more the latter provided Kant's inspiration than did Hume's critique of causality. This is because the profundity and the necessity of Rousseau's battle for human dignity in the world of scientific atomism do not touch very deeply persons more interested in the "theory of knowledge" than in how to live a good life.[38]

death. The Vicar offers compensations in this world, but they are pale compared to those offered in the next.

Another aspect of this problem is the Vicar's attitude toward sex. Rousseau indicates that sexual satisfaction is a natural necessity, without which even profounder distortions of the soul come into being. The Vicar could have satisfied this need if he had been a Protestant, as Rousseau had been, and able to marry. But even Protestantism taints sexual expression with the poison of original sin. The Vicar still continues to have relations with young girls, but his sexual pleasure has to be treated as nothing more significant than the pleasure of scratching when one itches. It is not a fulfillment of his highest aspiration, which is unerotic. His contemplations have no admixture of the Platonic eroticism that somehow unites body and soul and which Rousseau attempts to recover on the new continent of modernity. The Vicar's erotic life is a kind of trash can that does not contribute to his moral vocation, whereas Emile's own education tends to make his erotic life the most important thing. The whole organic structure of Emile's education strains toward a unified eroticism that itself can found moral obligation or make a contract between human beings that engages their hearts and their souls. Emile never speaks or acts as though he knew of the Vicar's point of view. He speaks of God only at the summit of romantic excitement (426). His is the God of lovers rather than the God of the moral man. In some sense the Vicar's "Profession" is meant to make the thoughtful reader measure the difference between conventional morality and the new morality that Rousseau proposes.

But this is not the whole story. The "Profession of Faith" is an exquisitely constructed mechanism that addresses itself to the ordinary practices of mankind. It is too much to expect that most men will have Emile's education and that their lusts will correspond to their duties. Some kind of limit or repression of their bodily desires is likely to be necessary, and Rousseau offers a gentle version of Christianity to accomplish this end. The "Profession" points toward life after death while still leaving joys to be tasted in this world. It is Christian, but it is not exclusively Christian, meaning to say that all men could practice this religion without being humiliated by a conversion to Christianity. The "Profession" provides a basis for an ecumenism without disloyalty to one's own people and religion. It unshackles the "few great cosmopolitan souls"[39] of whom the real priests are jealous. The priests can regard the Vicar's situation as a punishment for his sexual proclivities, which in themselves lead toward nature, but the real reason they have demoted him is that he is free of their preachments. In the second part of the "Profession," where the Vicar treats revealed religion (295–313), he provides a compendium of all the conventional objections to the revealed texts that are the source of the exclusive articles of faith at the root of the dictum "outside the Church, no salvation." These texts force the abandonment of reason, encourage fanaticism, and guarantee that reason will be at war with religion. A book read in this way, whether it is the Bible or Plutarch (which Rousseau delicately uses as his example) (240–244), alienates man from himself and makes it impossible to rely on sincerity. This is what underlies Rousseau's confession "I hate books" (184). The proper way to read books is indicated by the Vicar's reading of the Gospel. The Vicar cannot be sure that Jesus was the son of God, but he (unlike Rousseau, who at the end of his life most enjoys reading Plutarch[40]) has a taste for reading the Gospel because Jesus is the highest example of conduct, whether he is the man-God or simply man at his best (307–308). Rousseau failed in his own personal attempt to walk the thin line between reason and revelation but he succeeded in transforming his successors. As Karl Barth tells us, Rousseau actually changed much of religious doctrine and practice, and we see his effects all around us.[41] The botched creation proclaimed by Blake and the call for a new beginning where nature and man are in harmony are a reflection of Rousseau's articulation of the religious problem. The Vicar boldly tells the young Rousseau to acknowledge God among the philosophers (i.e., the atheists) and to preach tolerance among the fanatics (i.e., the priests) (313). This may all seem boring to us now because it is so familiar, but it was an ingenious and in many ways an admirable project.

The ambiguous character of Rousseau's own teaching about religion is expressed in the long footnote with which Rousseau concludes the Savoyard Vicar digression (312–314). In it he does something unexampled in philosophy: he makes a defense of fanaticism—political, moral, romantic. Although in the body of the text he shares the Enlightenment concern for and hatred of intolerance, with its conviction that one's nonbelieving neighbors are damned, he has also come to the conclusion that the tolerance of the philosophers issues in a selfish indifference. Reason is most frequently a tool of the particular passions and dissolves the humane sentiments in the acid of its criticism. So fanaticism is indeed dangerous and ugly. But it is powerful, self-forgetting, and above the petty creature comforts of the bourgeois. The choice, as Rousseau seems to outline it, is between ignoble reasoning and noble fanaticism—political, moral, romantic. This observation casts a dark shadow over Rousseau's text when one recognizes that he gives at least partial license not only to the extremes of the French revolutionaries who admired him so much, but also to the other even more extreme fanaticisms, apparently for the first time blessed by philosophers or intellectuals, that characterize the two centuries since Rousseau wrote. To meditate on this important question one must ask whether the great fathers of liberalism had not become easygoing in their theological-political-moral teachings, leaving Rousseau with the choice between selfish reason and dedicated extremism.

X   For the young Rousseau, the Vicar's influence can be crudely understood to be a course of study in sexual restraint. The Vicar provides a glimpse of the grandest, the most splendid, the most exalted objects to which man, this vulnerable brute, can attain, and he does so in such a way that most men can at least admire his lofty disinterestedness. Rousseau indicates that this loftiness is to be attained by a ladder constructed out of imagination, *amour-propre*, and sexual energy. In the Vicar's case, sexual energy is converted into his asexual contemplations. The most complete teaching of *Emile* is to be found in Emile's life. Not only is that life powered by sexual energy, but its explicit, conscious fulfillment is found in the sexual life. If the splendor of the Vicar's teaching can be combined with the natural ends of man here on this earth, Rousseau may, as Kant said, be said to have solved the problem of culture.[42] Romantic love and the family are to be the answers to the problem. As conscience is the Vicar's answer to the problem of noncontingent obligation or contract, Rousseau tries to find the answer in the love of a couple rightly understood.

The Vicar's education of Jean-Jacques immediately precedes what one might call the sexual revelation designed for Emile, "The true moment of nature comes at last" (316). He has compressed the seminal fluids and they produce energy as does boiling water in a steam engine. His sentiments have enchained his imagination and reason silenced the opinions of man. Rousseau hopes, by his various tactics, to have maintained Emile's ignorance of the true meaning of his desire up to the late teens. He knows that as soon as a young man really knows it, he will make the fulfillment of his desire his primary goal. Therefore this satisfaction must be promised to him, and no study that does not relate to it will take. The simplest thing is to marry him off immediately, which is probably what nature wants. But since man is now so far from nature, force and fraud are necessary to fulfill nature's intention, inasmuch as the fulfillment of society's moral demands is not part of nature's scheme. The choice usually appears as one between libertinism or asceticism, each obviously unsatisfactory. Rousseau suggests that the joys of libertinism can be combined with the highest moral calling, thus avoiding the tedious shuttle back and forth between indulgence and repression, which is to be found not only in individuals but in the habits of societies. Rousseau, from now until the end of *Emile*, shows how this is to be done.

First, the boy must be told. He has been prepared to listen because his teacher has never bored him with moralisms that he suspects the teacher does not himself believe. Emile is curious and trusting, and his early independence and satisfaction will continue in his passage to adulthood. He does not have the child's usual sense that childhood is an enforced discipline to be cast aside when he grows up. Not for him the former choirboy's or Eagle Scout's fall into debauchery. He is a partner with his teacher and does not feel that his enlightenment is at odds with what his teacher wants to teach. The young Emile divines that what the teacher has to teach him is as important for him as was the Vicar's teaching for Jean-Jacques. And just as the Vicar prepared Jean-Jacques' passions to be attentive to his speech, so must the teacher prepare Emile's passions.

"The pedant and the teacher say pretty much the same things, but the former says them on every occasion, while the latter says them only when he is sure of their effect" (319). An erotic rhetoric must be invented. Plato's *Phaedrus* must be reinvented. The passage on rhetoric is for me one of the most telling in the whole of Rousseau's amazing book. Rousseau teaches us about the subtlety and grandeur of the arts of persuasion, the knowledge of nature and human nature required by a teacher. The most human form of speech, as Aristotle tells us, is that used by men to communicate their knowledge or their understanding of good and bad and of just and unjust.[43] A science of the passions is requisite to this noble persuasion, and has its proper place in the great lost art of rhetoric. After having used his last deception to put Emile off the scent, engaging him in the lusty, sanguinary hunt in the forests where the sport vies with the erotic charms of the nymphs, Rousseau summarizes the modern condition with respect to rhetoric: "I observe that in the modern age men no longer have a hold on one another except by force or by self-interest; the ancients, by contrast, acted much more by persuasion and by the affections of the soul because they did not neglect the language of signs" (321). For the economists, all rhetoric consists of dollar signs, and the tyrants speak endlessly to captive audiences who are too frightened to listen. Persuasion, as it was practiced by the ancients, appealed to grander and nobler motives corresponding to powerful beliefs about the world.

The gods were witnesses to men's oaths, and they saw everything, whereas men can know only appearances:

> Stones, trees, heaps of rocks consecrated by these acts and thus made respectable to barbaric men, were the pages of this book, which was constantly open to all eyes. The well of the oath, the well of the living and seeing, the old oak of Mamre, the mound of the witness, these were the crude but august monuments of the sanctity of contracts. None would have dared to attack these monuments with a sacrilegious hand, and the faith of men was more assured by the guarantee of these mute witnesses than it is today by all the vain rigor of the laws. (321)

All of these references are to the Hebrew Bible, and, as is so often the case with Rousseau, he gives early witness to a theme that began to preoccupy the minds of intelligent Europeans a century later. Rousseau is speaking of the demystification or the disenchantment of the world resulting from a new science that wiped the slate clean and left no place for the tales about the gods and their involvement in human affairs. This demystification is the center of Rousseau's doubts about the parallelism between the progress of civilization and the moral improvement of man, who is now moved like the atoms, which are pushed by other atoms rather than persuaded by noble rhetoric. Nature must be full of gods in order to motivate men, and the persuasive rhetoric has to have this as a corollary in order to strike awe into men.

As he uses the Bible for the gods, he uses Roman practice for the language or signs that persuade and bind political man. Again, the symbols have disappeared. Therefore, the art of speech that appeals to such things has disappeared. A modern orator would make empty discourses about Caesar's wounds; an Antony produces the body and points to them. That is the style of ancient rhetoric. Rousseau appears to believe that the living presence of the gods has been made impossible by Enlightenment reasoning and that political myth and ritual have disappeared because the state is now just a business contract. As always, Rousseau's arguments can cut both ways. He regrets the human cost of Enlightenment. But he also believes that its reasonings are true and that it is good to be liberated from the tyranny of false and fanatic belief. He uses ancient rhetoric in order to show the force of persuasion, but he will propose a new enchantment of the world intended to regain the advantages of such rhetoric but without its obscurantism.

Rousseau wants to fill the world with poetic imaginations, dreams about love. The scene he chooses as background for his sexual revelation is akin to the one the Savoyard Vicar chose for his religious revelation. Rousseau wants to inspire awe by means of the splendor of the setting and, as it were, give tongues to the mountains, the valleys, and the rivers. This is the very model of the Romantic use of nature; the scenery sets the stage for the passions and itself shares them. The mystery of human generation fits into a nature that is itself full of human meanings. Rousseau wishes to reestablish on modern grounds Plato's erotic nature, where everything is striving toward a fulfillment and perfection, as opposed to the randomly moving atoms, which have no such longing. The sublime experience of nature to which we are induced by the "Profession of Faith" remains. With the Vicar, however, the culmination is a rejection of the sexual or a consigning of it to the dross we must bear with in this life. With the sexual revelation, sex becomes the core of the highest experience and will be a part of the divine on this earth.

Rousseau prepares us to hear what he will tell this healthy adolescent about the meaning of sex, which is driving him now without his knowing it. But he stops short and tells us that it is impossible to talk about these things today, especially in the French language, without being obscene instead of sublime. Thus he leaves it to our imagination to invest this most important instruction, which is usually conveyed by rascally servants, corrupt playmates, or scientific quacks. The point is to give Emile the poetry along with the merely material facts. The very idea of Emile's sexual fulfillment must act as a restraint against trivial or debauched sexuality.

> . . . if in speaking of this inconceivable mystery of generation, one joins to the idea of the allure given to this act by the Author of nature the idea of the exclusive attachment which makes it delicious, and the idea of the duties of fidelity and of modesty which surround it and redouble its charm in fulfilling its object; if, in depicting marriage to him not only as the sweetest of associations but as the most inviolable and holiest of all contracts, one tells him forcefully all the reasons which make so sacred a bond respectable to all men, and which bring

hatred and maledictions to whoever dares to stain its purity;
if one presents him with a striking and true picture of the
horrors of debauchery, of its foolish degradation, of the gradual decline by which a first disorder leads to them all and
finally drags to destruction whoever succumbs to it. . . . (324)

Here again one glimpses the central thrust of Romanticism and sees
why adultery became the underlying theme of so many Romantic
novels. Marriage is the true human attachment and is the contract of
human connectedness. It is more profound than, and a prerequisite
of, the essentially selfish social contract. Civil society will be formed
out of couples of lovers, and fathers and mothers, rather than out of
atomistic individuals. It will remain derivative, but its elements will
be more potent than those of more ordinary contract teachings. The
goodness of sex is affirmed while the high stakes it entails are underlined. Man's dangerous responsibility is maintained but without
belief in the badness of the body or original sin. Emile will be moderate because his desires are immoderate. The tutor will depict love's
passion "as the supreme happiness of life, because in fact it is" (327).
This is a most unusual statement for a philosopher, but a Goethe can
take it as his own.

Given these high stakes and the education Emile has had, the
tutor is sure that the young man, awestruck, will come begging for
help in navigating these uncharted seas. He will ask the tutor to take
care of him. And the tutor will use this occasion to get him to make
the first promise of his life. Up to now Emile has lived according to
his inclination, doing what comes naturally, and has never been
asked to bind himself in such a way that duty conflicts with inclination and divides him. Now he will become divided, but on the basis
of his own inner recognition that it is really for his own deepest
satisfaction. This is Emile's first obligation, but the tutor will call in
the chit only at the very end of *Emile*, proving thereby that morality
can be truly self-legislated rather than being a merely external force
put in place by others.

Of course Emile is not aware of the epoch-making importance of
the contract he has just made with Jean-Jacques. When he agrees to
do or to refrain from doing as his tutor commands, he does not
realize that his soul will become double, divided between desire and
duty. The savage lives as Emile has always lived, according to his
desires. The civilized man is split between desire and what is commanded. Emile will be the first man who has true will, commanding
himself. This is a loss of innocence, but it is arguably, if not demon-

strably, a higher stage of human development. Another way of putting it, which refers us back to the little boy in his garden who learns about forbidden fruit, is that unlike God, Rousseau will give commandments that his creation can understand (98–101).

Once this sacred and legal obligation is put in place, the tutor prescribes a course of action to satisfy the now urgent demands of sexual awareness. What he proposes is a modern knight errant's quest for the ideal woman who will satisfy together Emile's physical and moral demands. Prior to seeking her, Emile, alone or with the help of his tutor (the novelist), must create her in his imagination (328ff.). His tutor proposes the name Sophie for this ideal woman. When he encounters the woman who incarnates the ideal, who turns out actually to bear the name Sophie, he will experience the shock of recognition or, to put it Platonically, the reminiscence of what he already knows within himself as his own. Finally Rousseau addresses the real problem: how one cares for another as one cares for oneself rather than as an other, a leap that Emile has not yet made and that most people never make. He provides the erotic equivalent of his solution to the political problem: obedience to the law one gives oneself. One obeys oneself, not an other or others. One's self-esteem depends on one's capacity for such law giving and obedience. In love all this comes into play, now supported by a powerful inclination promising happiness.

This is Rousseau's radical teaching about love. Love is imaginary. It is not the love of the self-subsistent Idea of the beautiful, as in Plato. Nor, given the illusory character of love, does Rousseau follow Lucretius in trying to free man from the illusions of love. He weds the Lucretian view of love as illusion with the Platonic seriousness about love. "And what is true love itself if it is not chimera, lie, and illusion? We love the image we make for ourselves far more than we love the object to which we apply it" (329). The enigma of Rousseau's whole undertaking is how one can believe in what one knows to be a product of one's imagination. He teaches that imagination plays a much more important role in sex than do the physical facts. That is why the preparation of the imagination is a lifetime's work, from childhood on. He goes so far as to say that a man who lived alone on a desert island would die never having felt sexual desire. Only within society and its poetic speech do sexual desire and love bloom. By such means Rousseau attempts to overcome the radical isolation of man posited by modern thought, the fundamental principle of which he accepts.

The presence of the ideal object of desire in Emile's imagination is a substitute for the innocence that kept him from early sexual indulgence. Now he will reject the nasty and debauched possibilities offered to him as unworthy. He will be looking at every woman who presents herself and saying, "Oh, that is not she." Thus Rousseau hopes to prolong Emile's virginity while he is still learning things necessary for the state of adulthood. This method kills two birds with one stone: it instills longing in a being used to immediate satisfactions (and shows that the capacity to long for higher fulfillments is very necessary to the fully developed human being) and enables him to learn about society close up without being corrupted by it. With his ideal, Emile will pay the closest attention to the societies into which he will enter but will have a standpoint from which to despise most of what he finds in them.

Discovering standpoints for sound judgments is the most important part of Rousseau's education. The little boy has his immediate, natural pleasures and pains unaffected by others' opinions. The merely corporeal suffices. All he needs is healthy senses, and that is why the education of the senses is so important in the first two books of *Emile*. Later, when utility supersedes pleasure and pain as the guide of his action, he has the comparison between the dinner of the rich and the noble and that of the country people which gives him perspective on luxury and the division of labor. Next, when he enters the sentimental or moral dimension of life, he has compassion, which makes him pity rather than envy the great. Now the complete and most privileged standpoint will be to judge all that he sees and experiences against the standard of *amour-passion*. By cultivating such standpoints in the soul of his educated ordinary man, Rousseau provides him with the philosopher's touchstone, which liberates him from the tyranny of opinion, or its alienation, and its sinister relativism. He concludes with an astonishing declaration:

> If there were a single man among [the youth of our day] who knew how to be temperate and sober and who knew how in their midst to preserve his heart, his blood, and his morals from the contagion of their example, at the age of thirty he would crush all these insects and become their master with less effort than he had exerted in remaining his own master!
>
> No matter how little birth and fortune had done for Emile, he would be that man if he wanted to be. But he would despise these young men too much to deign to enslave them. (335)

So much power does Rousseau attribute to nurture or education over nature that this ordinary man, properly educated, can be seen as a harbinger of Nietzsche's Superman. Here one also finds the roots of the Marxists' great expectations for socialist man. Rousseau rebels against the decisive effect of nature with its unjust distribution of capability.

Rousseau makes many interesting and sensible suggestions about how to ride the wild steeds of adolescent sexual desire while avoiding the dangers of becoming their accomplice, on the one hand, or their hated and discredited censor, on the other. In this context he condemns masturbation unequivocally (333–334). He says he would prefer that Emile frequent prostitutes rather than use this "dangerous supplement." This is a strong opinion, particularly striking since Rousseau speaks in the *Confessions* about his own use of the "dangerous supplement" in much less categorical terms.[44] The difference is that Emile unlike Rousseau is to be a social or a married man: going to a prostitute implies the need for another, whereas masturbation implies the possibility of solitariness.

The solitary man has roots in the state of nature, which must be overcome by social man. But social man is somewhat less natural for Rousseau than he makes him appear to be; therefore conventions and habits must reinforce the somewhat doubtful teleological attachment of sexual desire. Rousseau tells us that imagination is the core of sexual attachments and that he is the virtuoso of the imagination in this regard. There is a sense in which the naughty Rousseau is more the poet than is the lover because he feeds totally and freely off the imagination and actually provides the imaginary object of love for his pupil. Rousseau the philosopher-novelist attempts to provide the erotic imagination for mankind at large. This is why I say that the modern romantic disposition, initiated by Rousseau, is somehow a construction rather than a natural growth. The "dangerous supplement" is a response to the conflicting inclinations of civilized man and in Rousseau's case helps to soften the conflicts. *Emile* is an attempt simply to overcome them, but one might wonder whether it isn't just covering over them. That there is a sexual teleology is a lot less certain than Rousseau would have us believe in this aspect of his teaching. But he is still an excellent corrective for thinking about a question that is no longer a question for us—the acceptance of all forms of sexual arousal. The powerful and exclusive sexual attachment to another depends upon the habit of thinking that the object of one's affections is the sole and unique satisfaction. Otherwise one is likely to get only watery and legalistic attachments.

XI Emile, equipped with his new standards, goes out into society to learn its ways. More precisely, Rousseau takes him to live for a year in Paris (334–344). This choice suffices to show that Rousseau does not so unequivocally despise Paris as he would have us believe. Rather, civilized and divided man produces twin peaks of accomplishment or fulfillment that are incompatible. For the ancients they were Athens and Sparta, for Rousseau in his own way, Paris and Geneva. Sparta and Geneva represent moral or civic excellence; Athens and Paris represent, if not excellence, at least a rainbow of the intellectual achievements. The purpose of the Paris sojourn is to teach the young man who has lived so much alone to live with his fellows. This is not so much for the sake of morals, for this young man is already essentially moral, although bad social ties might threaten his morality. It is to teach him to live with men as they are while maintaining his distance. Or, to put it another way, this is his education in taste, the experience of elegant pleasures that are not necessary but bespeak noble concerns. This is the arena of the gentleman as he is described by Aristotle—an arena so neglected by the modern thinkers—who likes beautiful but useless things. Such things are the objects of disinterested but passionate attachment, unalloyed by base necessity, a sign of man's freedom. Rousseau is alert to what is lost in modernity. The modern writers simplified the moral teaching of the ancients. The ancients always spoke about the good and the beautiful in their moral writings, while the moderns speak only of the good or useful. Thus the human significance of art is trivialized, reduced to entertainment. Restoring art to its throne as the expression of the soul's most sublime heights is Rousseau's intention.

Thus the incipient lover is best prepared for art. Poetry, painting, and music express the intention of love while heightening it and civilizing it. The young Emile, prior to puberty, is a perfect mirror of nature, the decent but crude product of so much democratic education—pragmatic, learning the method of the sciences as the highest achievement—whereas Rousseau, in the same way Tocqueville does after him, holds that unpoetic or unartistic democratic man lacks something of great importance that was known to aristocratic ages. Modern education concentrates on what Pascal calls *l'esprit de géométrie*,[45] whereas Rousseau proposes to bring together in one person the opposed traits of *l'esprit de géométrie* and *l'esprit de finesse*. Emile must combine the exquisite taste found in aristocracies with the decent, common general morals of healthy democratic man. Of course, Rousseau holds that good morals are the most important thing, but taste contributes much more of what makes everyday life agreeable.

The artist is a teacher of the subtle distinctions among things and corrects the tendency to scientific abstractness, providing a rich and varied natural consciousness. It is in such things that Paris excels. Although Rousseau often appears to denigrate the art world, introduction to it is the capstone of his education of Emile. Even though taste is corrupt in Paris (because the arts are objects of vanity for the rich and the powerful, and the link to healthy morality that gives art its power is broken), one can find there a subtler observation of man as well as an attachment to classic literature that is both healthy and profound. Emile will be protected from that corruption because his love goal prevents him from being caught up in the petty intrigues of the artistic and political worlds that dominate Paris.

Essential to the cultivation of taste is the relation between the two sexes. That is where even Emile is dependent on the opinions of others and therefore has a deep interest in pleasing (338, 341). And this is also where Emile's love of poetry and that of the modern Frenchman diverge. The Frenchman is only playing an artificial game promising eternity in return for enjoyment now to women who bestow their favors easily while presenting the false front of chasteness. But for the real lover, love is a life-and-death matter, and its artistic expression reflects that seriousness. Great art is sublime and sublimating. This relation of love and art parallels what Rousseau said about rhetoric—in modern, demythologized nature, force and interest dictate because there is no longer a beautiful persuasive speech. The French of Rousseau's time used an artificial and thin expression that reflected the character of their gallantry. Lovers had been struck dumb because of a loss of even the memory of great erotic passion with its great risks. Here the dull voice of calculating reason was the same as that used in accounting. Neither the grand passion nor the delicious obscenity of the great poetry was to be found. Without the words for the expression of passion, passion itself disappears. The grunt will not do. Real love requires a language to express itself. This is why Rousseau adores the Platonic dialogues about love, the *Symposium* and the *Phaedrus*, where men serious about love invent marvelous speeches.* Emile will learn gorgeous

---

*As always, it is the ancient Greeks who have the best taste and the greatest power in expressing the natural human emotions. As in so many other cases in *Emile*, Rousseau convincingly shows his own taste and power of discrimination in his interpretation of literary texts, be it Thucydides, Plutarch, La Fontaine, or Tasso (239; 110–111; 112–116, 248; 385, 415). He defends his restoration of ancient literature with a killing response to Fontenelle, the great proponent of the moderns in the "Battle of the Books," who said "that this whole dispute about ancients and moderns comes down to knowing whether the trees

speech without which he could not convey his sentiments to his beloved. This peak of sublimation will be put into practice as soon as Emile meets his Sophie in Book V.

As a conclusion to the sublimating education of Book IV, Rousseau again speaks about himself, not Emile. This is the third passage reflecting on the development of the tutor rather than the pupil (344–355). It is a mirror of the soul of the grown-up or fully developed Jean-Jacques and completes the trilogy that begins with his night games at the Lamberciers and passes through his encounter with the Savoyard Vicar. Now he indulges in a fantasy about what he would do with his life if he were rich, meaning if he had no need to concern himself with the deforming and unpleasant provision of the necessary. The most remarkable aspect of this fantasy is the utter absence of the indignation, the wounded *amour-propre*, at the center of his other tales about himself. He has learned to consult his own inclinations and not to sacrifice the present for hopes and fears about the future. What we get here is an essay that presents a refined epicurism in taste, a substitute for morals. The grown Jean-Jacques is oceans away from the Savoyard Vicar as well as from Emile the ardent lover.

In Rousseau's fantasy everything would be measured in terms of pleasure. As one would expect with Rousseau, the entertainments Jean-Jacques would offer to his friends take place in the country and feed off the unadorned joys of nature itself. Everybody there is somehow an isolate. They have no duties, and each will separate off when it is his inclination to do so. No one is married, it seems; there are no lovers à la Emile. It is their shared pleasure in natural entertainment that binds them together. Rousseau seems to suggest that, for a man like himself, with his doubts and his independence, something like this is the best solution of the tension between nature and civilization. This is a side of Rousseau that does not figure in Kant and leads toward *Reveries of the Solitary Walker*.

This fantasy belongs to a middle-aged man, and the sexual life treated in it is appropriate to that age. Rousseau knows that it is unseemly for a graybeard to pursue the nymphs who might people his forest. This is not because he no longer feels desire but because the desire would not be reciprocated. He would be a ridiculous figure, if he forgot, as most men do, how unseemly the coupling of

---

in the past were bigger than those today," and to whom Rousseau rejoins, "If agriculture had changed, it would not be impertinent to ask this question" (343). Education is the agriculture of the human soul, and Rousseau's education seems to want the improbable synthesis of modern natural science with ancient human wisdom. This importance of taste for human existence is reflected in Kant's *Critique of Judgment*.

youth and age is. There are no moral considerations here, as there are for the Vicar. It is simply not fitting for a man to live off illusions and be a disgusting sight to the object of his desires and to the world at large. He does not renounce sex, but for the sake of his own self-awareness, he will not take it seriously. This is part of good taste and shows how good taste can supplement or substitute for morality. Purchased love is best not taken seriously, particularly not by the purchaser. As the Savoyard Vicar presents otherworldly overcoming of the body's lusts, Rousseau presents himself as the practitioner of a worldly overcoming. Whether this solution is preferable to Emile's passionate, moralizing love is a question. In any event, Rousseau has presented us with the materials for putting together the puzzle of the alienated man's struggle with his own dividedness, as opposed to his pupil's simple sincerity, which has never had to cope with the corruptions of dividedness.

| XII | Once Emile completes his junior year abroad in Paris, his judgment has been formed while he has developed an immunity to the big city's glitter. Now he and his friend leave Paris without regret to look for Sophie in less civilized or more rustic places. This is the climax of Emile's education, which finally determines the course of his whole life.

Emile as a whole is a novel and within this novel there is a second novel, a romantic novel, Book V, where the bourgeois knight-errant finds his lady, courts her, and wins her. Here Rousseau gives an outline of the themes that must be treated by novelists if they wish to interest the heart of modern man. With *Emile* Rousseau founded a whole genre of novels called the *Bildungsroman*, or education novel, the most notable example of which is Goethe's *Wilhelm Meister*. And Rousseau succeeded in imposing his taste on many of the greatest writers of the nineteenth century, who constitute the core of the classic tradition of the novel. There followed a century-long elaboration of the delicate psychology of men and women in love, the most appropriate discourse for modern man.

Rousseau says, "It is not good for man to be alone" (357). So did God. Rousseau tells us critically that Locke just brings his pupil together with his mistress and leaves it at that. Again, so did God. Neither gave man or woman the education necessary to overcome their loneliness in marriage. That is a much greater task.

Here I encounter the greatest difficulty facing anyone who dares to speak of these questions in our age. There is a powerful orthodoxy today that limits the kind of speech possible about the nature of woman and about the nature of man in relation to woman. This orthodoxy has its roots partly in the egalitarian principles of democratic regimes. Such regimes do not admit the existence of decisive differences of nature but rather insist that all human beings are essentially the same and reject any political conclusions drawn from whatever differences there may actually be. This orthodoxy is reinforced in our own time by radical feminism, which is something more potent and more extreme than the teachings of traditional egalitarianism. Poor Jean-Jacques, who suffered during his lifetime at the hands of outraged piety, now suffers something similar at the hands of outraged feminism. He is considered to be one of the great sexists and a source of the oppression of women. Some persons don't want him to be read, even though his radical egalitarianism and his initiation of the movement in favor of participatory democracy make him appealing in other respects. Mostly, as is the case with much of our past, he is simply ignored; but if he is discussed, it goes without saying that it is only to diagnose and dismiss his wrongheadedness.

It is my view that what is held most passionately at a given moment is that which most needs criticism from persons, places, and times at a distance from the current convictions. It is always dangerous to be such a critic or to seek out those who are, and that is why philosophy is perpetually a risky undertaking. There are a number of ways to arrange the relations between men and women, in sex and love, in marriage and in parenthood, ranging from the harem depicted in Montesquieu's *Persian Letters* to the virtual disappearance of the difference between the sexes in Plato's *Republic*. There is no reason to assume that the arrangement we opt for is the only one or the best. These differences seem to be rooted in "cultures" and one must either leave it at cultural relativism and say that these are simply different ways, or attempt with an open mind to determine which culture is best and most enhances the human beings who belong to it. Neither of these stances justifies the atmosphere of indignation and recrimination prevalent today. With resignation I face the fact that I shall lose much of my audience by taking Rousseau seriously and keeping open the possibility that he may understand these things as well as or better than we do. I could mumble that I am only reporting Rousseau's opinions and that I do not wholly share them, which is true, but such an apology is already too much of a concession to the mere power of the present. These are important questions and, as is always the case, we shall have need of deeply thought through alternatives when the prevailing orthodoxy wears thin. I could not, however, in good conscience prescribe such a course to a young professor who does not yet have tenure.

It must be admitted that this little Romantic novel in Book V presents peculiar difficulties. We must understand that his florid rhetoric is meant to provoke the coquettish Parisian ladies who kept the salons where elderly philosophers turned their thought to pleasing them and made themselves ridiculous. And the novel's Romantic taste with its idealization of woman is far from the taste of generations formed by the hard-headed reaction to Rousseau. We have moved from sentimentality to brutality, and it is our peculiar perversion to believe that the brutal is more authentic than the sentimental. Moreover, we are so much further on the road to the equality of women that we fail to recognize how radical Rousseau's proposals were.

The strong reaction to Rousseau today is in large measure on target, for, although he evinces the most sacred respect for women, he argues strongly against the possibility of the total transformation of "gender relations" and deplores the hostility toward, or even the denial of, what he calls the law of nature in sexual relations (358). Yet, Rousseau uses the notions of nature and natural ambiguously (consciously so). Here he is somewhere between nature in the rigorous sense, as depicted in *The Discourse on the Origin and Foundations of Inequality*, and merely edifying public doctrine. Rousseau at this point takes the family to be natural, while in the real state of nature neither men nor women have families. This is confusing, and one must interpret him to mean that in the passage from nature to society, the family, on natural grounds, becomes necessary to minister to the more complicated needs of children in society. This is natural only in the sense that nature constrains man's freedom in such a way as to restrict the satisfactory nonnatural or civilized solution to the problems of producing and educating offspring. Actually, what is presented in Book V is closer to what one ought to call culture than nature, with the difference being that culture is not simply a free creation accomplishing what it wants with unlimitedly plastic man, but a creation precisely limited, if not determined, by nature.

Rousseau's presentation here is a project, something that he makes up, and is therefore not compelling in the same way nature is. But his project bows toward nature and attempts to preserve in civilized fashion the inclinations found in nature. Here he is at odds with modern persons like Simone de Beauvoir and her particular brand of Existentialism that is so appealing to many Americans.

Rousseau was very much aware of the almost inevitable collapse of the differences between the sexes resulting from liberal society and the principle of equality that informs it, so what he says can be practically understood to be a response to what is going on today. In general, the thinkers of the past saw pretty much what we see in erotic matters and, to put it boldly but truly, no serious thinker ever regarded women as slaves. The charge that they did is a piece of demagoguery to which we have become far too used. At least since Aristotle, the truest principle of feminism has been asserted by everyone: the hallmark of barbarism is treating women as slaves.[46] But unlike earlier thinkers Rousseau shares our situation. He was the first critic of liberalism or bourgeois society and was so prescient that he saw from the beginning what others began to see only a century later. Marx owes to Rousseau the things he said in the *Communist Manifesto* and elsewhere about the homogenization of men and women produced by bourgeois society.

The special problem to which Rousseau addresses himself is the atomization and egotism produced by modern bourgeois society. Rousseau is as great an egalitarian as either Hobbes or Locke, if not more so. But if selfish natural man is translated as is into society, the only human relations possible are founded on selfish individualism; and the original egotism, which in nature was self-sufficient, becomes complicated by the need to use other human beings as means to our ends. The decay in human connectedness is a problem of which we are only too aware across the political spectrum, from right to left. Even those who are most eager to transform the relations between men and women also deplore modern isolation and uprootedness, which they regard as the results of bourgeois society's and capitalism's tendency to use human beings as commodities rather than as ends in themselves. All of these lamentations are not, however, accompanied by persuasive remedies, because we also are unwilling to give up the individual independence that is at the root of the problem. Older, more organic communities were based on forcing men and women into a social mold, partly by use of traditions or untrue myths. Now we see through them. Modern democratic man has to have arguments that are rational and compelling to his individual judgment and to which he can give his assent or dissent. Rousseau, just as he passionately wishes to remain faithful to equality, also insists on freedom, and these conditions define the problem he sets out to solve. Therefore one must seek a powerful and nonmercenary motive for relations among human beings that can be affirmed by free and equal persons. Rousseau is able to find only love and family feeling which might be compelling to such persons. There is something natural about family relations, and Rousseau makes a great effort to make them appear totally natural. Nature, in spite of all the critical philosophical objections to the very idea, is still compelling to common sense. "It's only natural" always seems to be a justification that is not merely ancestral or mythical and which is hence persuasive.

People who are in love present a visible disproof of the selfish economic model of man. The kind of attachments possible in the family and that flow from love can be reduced to individuals' selfish calculations only by sophistic arguments. A people made up of families is selfish in an entirely different way from one made up of individuals. It is imperative for Rousseau to discover a molecule out of which to build society rather than the atoms out of which it is today built. The parts of the molecule are already moved by different kinds of motives founded in real attachments and concern for others. Rousseau attempts on modern grounds to reconstitute the family as the prepolitical unit out of which civil society is constructed. He is far too modern to argue, as did the ancients, that one must begin with politics because man is naturally a political animal. The parts precede the whole and the high must be constituted out of, or reduced to, the low. This is the modern difficulty, which Rousseau faces squarely, although one can always wonder whether its solution is possible. Instead Rousseau makes a powerful case for the centrality of the sexual passion and its connectedness with other persons. The differentiation of the sexes opens the possibility for the social differentiation in which human beings are not simply individuals. Rousseau tries to prove the complementarity of man and woman. If man and woman are a pair and unable to be complete without each other, contributing equal but different shares in a common work, then one can speak plausibly of a certain natural sociality; whereas if they are all the same or whatever they want to be, we are back to the war of all against all. Rousseau is aware that mere exhortation or legal arrangement will not succeed in producing genuine commonality if there is not natural inclination to support it. He affronts contemporary convictions with arguments about nature that attribute to it a teleology that is at least doubtful.

He begins by treating human beings, on the analogy of the plant and animal kingdoms, as instruments of reproduction, as though they have one supreme function or work and must be interpreted with respect to it. A certain scientific objectivity would seem to confirm the soundness of this beginning, but it shocks the sacred sense of individual freedom, and it does not jibe with the subjective sense of individuals who frequently need sex and enjoy it, without any thought of the eternity in children, let alone fulfilling the responsibilities connected with them. Rousseau appears to argue that our being or our natures will be unfulfilled unless the natural function becomes the subjective goal of civilized man. He thinks, or wants us to think, that a man as father and a woman as mother are clearly more deeply human than persons with careers in the modern marketplace. But his rhetoric about love and family, profoundly moving to men and women of the nineteenth century, no longer seems so to us today.

He begins his treatment of love by stating certain undeniably natural facts that he admits are not the "law of love" but that underlie love. The bodily performance of the sexual act requires different things from the two sexes. A man must have an erection, and it is up to woman to provide the attractions necessary to produce one if she wishes to engage in sex with him. He must will and be able, whereas she must simply not put up too much resistance. It follows, according to Rousseau, that for the sexual union to succeed, woman must make herself charming or agreeable to man. "The surest art for animating [a man's] strength is to make it necessary by resistance. Then *amour-propre* unites with desire, and the one triumphs in the victory that the other has made him win" (358). Attachment requires not only one's own desire but the uncertainty of whether one is really desired by another. This is the beginning of all the complexity of erotic artifice. One must doubt, the other must feign, all in the name of a successful outcome that both desire. The male doubt about the seriousness of female resistance and the consequent testing of the finality of refusal, which so infuriate some of our contemporaries and are taken to be assaults on women leading to date rape, are an essential part of the game of love according to Rousseau. He of course is unequivocally opposed to any real forcing of a woman to do a man's will. But discerning the difference between a woman's modesty and her actual distaste is the core of an essential delicacy that must be learned. There are risks in this game but the partners must learn to play it if they are to have a real engagement of their souls. Man is the victor in a gentle combat with someone who appears to favor him exclusively. He can be moved by the discreet mixing of his sexual desire and his *amour-propre*, and modesty is the magnet that draws him. Rousseau gives two reasons for this: first, that female modesty is attractive to men, and second, that a woman's stakes in the sexual act are much greater because she alone can become pregnant. The first reason has to do simply with the pleasures of making love, the second with the protection of children (359ff.). One may well doubt whether feminine modesty represents a natural harmony between the requirements of sexual pleasure and those of child raising. The two reasons can be joined, however, by asserting, as does Rousseau, that it is up to the woman to attract the man to herself and by extension to the children because of her interest in getting someone to protect and provide for them. Rousseau thus outlines the key role of woman in providing the link between father and children, which is not provided by instinct. It is a woman's heavy burden to turn the man into a lover and give him a second nature, a love of his children.

A third reason for modesty is that women have more powerful and constant sexual inclinations than do men. They can perform many times what men can do less often. And they do not, like the brutes, have seasons. With an unabashedly teleological formula, Rousseau says that modesty is nature's gift to the human female which guides the freedom she has and the brutes do not. Women would, in a shameless state, exhaust men. Modesty, therefore, perhaps a little too much like a *deus ex machina*, both limits women and makes them more attractive, apparently subservient to men while actually enslaving them. There is no doubt that Rousseau gives to women the highest respect as well as the leading role. What is intolerable to many American women (although not so many French women) is that the female must exercise her talents in that role in relation to male nature. There is no insurance that the male will always enter properly into the system, but it is the most thoughtfully considered account of how to get the unattached male to care.

The naturalist looks to the end or final cause of these two disparate but related beings—the reproduction of the species. The male is ordinarily stronger than the female and is free from the handicaps that limit a woman during pregnancy. Therefore, the proper division of labor for men and women who are no longer solitaries in the state of nature is for the woman to care for her children and for herself while the man seeks sustenance for all and protects the woman. Man's strength and woman's softness combine perfectly to constitute the family. Moreover, Rousseau further deduces a different psychology for male and female, distinct but complementary, along with separate but equal talents contributing to the common good. On the basis of the merely bodily differences between man and woman Rousseau establishes a whole way of life for each. He fits together the pieces of a puzzle that when completed presents the picture of the happy family.

Yet despite a certain commonsense plausibility, one cannot help wondering whether he is not forcing the pieces of the puzzle rather than finding them cut out by nature herself. One must always bear in mind that Rousseau is speaking about ordinary people, not the prodigies of art, science, or politics, who cannot be included in a system of democratic education and who must make do for themselves. The parties to the family way of life must agree about the primacy of the family. Rousseau tries to persuade women of that primacy and leaves women to use their charms and talents to persuade men. He insists that the one who appears the weaker in this pair is really the ruler. The essential mechanism she sets in motion is *amour-propre*. Even the most independent-minded erotic man becomes dependent on the judgment of a woman, and a serious woman, one who is looking not only for an attractive man but for one who will love her and protect her, may be the best possible judge of a man's virtues and thus be regarded even by the most serious man as the supreme tribunal of his worth (360, 390–391).

The woman is the first to give evidence of will. Emile has never had to use one part of his soul to control or repress another part, so he can be understood to be an undivided desiring being, even though his desires are gradually sublimated by his education. The woman must from the very beginning desire, but control and dissimulate her desire. The character of the relations between man and woman is determined by the way in which he understands the meaning of her resistance to him. If he believes that her resistance is meant as a test of his virtue and her ceding to him is possible only if he himself is good, then he will endeavor to be or to appear good. But if he believes that a woman's resistance is mere coquetry, that her no always means yes, and that she merely uses the social forms to make herself attractive, he will enter into the game and become a flatterer. In this way, women can be said to determine the character of men in society. Thus, Rousseau draws a sharp distinction between sexual desire that includes the recognition and love of virtue and sexual desire that is for fun and vanity. He may sound to some like a Protestant divine, but his forceful rhetoric is based on the commonsense reason that the goodness or badness of a life is largely determined by the way in which sexual desire fits into the whole economy of the soul.

The power of *Les Liaisons dangereuses* depends upon the recognition of this gravity of sexual behavior. What makes this book so diabolical is that the Marquise de Merteuil and the Vicomte de Valmont have learned the mechanisms of sexual psychology and are able to fool not only innocents but worse, virtue itself. Thus Laclos presupposes Rousseau, whereas contemporaries, who separate the way a person uses sex from his or her character, miss the point. It is possible, as we frequently do, not to pay attention to the natural necessities connected with sexual differentiation and to go ahead and live for other things. But Rousseau would argue that the richness and profundity of life is thereby lost. Nature resides in the first sentiments and provides the link to the general or the common that is only an artificial contract, potent and useful only when it rests on the natural base. In this context, he attacks his admired Plato, who in the *Republic* treats the sexual organs and the facts of procreation as unimportant accidents and uses women exactly as he does men, as artisans, as warriors, as rulers, and even as philosophers. Rousseau responds,

> . . . [this] cannot fail to engender the most intolerable abuses. I speak of that subversion of the sweetest sentiments of nature, sacrificed to an artificial sentiment which can only be maintained by them—as though there were no need for a natural base on which to form conventional ties; as though the love of one's nearest were not the principle of the love one owes the state; as though it were not by means of the small fatherland which is the family that the heart attaches itself to the large one; as though it were not the good son, the good husband, and the good father who make the good citizen! (363)

In strange ways, although we are far from Plato today, we are Platonists, in minimizing the implication of sexual differences. Rousseau has the merit for us of rigorously following through this sexual logic to its end and with all of its consequences. In so doing he makes women into terrestrial goddesses, the worship of whom makes men virtuous. Even though one recognizes all of the differences, one cannot help being reminded of the cult of the Virgin. Of course, these women are not to be virgins.

The most unpalatable immediate consequence of Rousseau's reasoning is a reaffirmation of the deplorable old double standard on new grounds. A woman's fidelity is more important than a man's because of her risk of pregnancy. It is essential, Rousseau affirms, that the man believe that the child is his own. This belief has a great deal to do with transforming his sexual desire into a permanent attachment. The irrational, fierce love of one's own, founded in *amour-propre*, is the glue that seals the parts together. It is easy enough to criticize male distrust and jealousy, but, Rousseau responds, what substitute can you find? A man must see in his child his own product and the possibility of his immortality by way of it. These are hard motives for us to credit, but one could say that their attenuation robs the soul of vigorous although dangerous forces, giving selfish individualizing reason greater sway. Polite people to-day prefer not to talk about such things, and their sense of justice prompts them to say that they would love children equally, no mat-ter what their origins. Yet one must wonder whether this is a progress in morals or an easygoing rationalization for a growing indifference reflected in the collapse of the family. Attenuating a male's concern for children *as his own* does not result in broader attachments but shallower ones: he abandons his own children more readily. Rousseau gives great weight to these terrible but also pos-sibly sublime passions to which natural man was totally indifferent, as he was to the children who might have resulted from his casual encounters with females.

Whole categories of literature, both tragic and comic, turned on this question of a child's legitimacy, but none of it means much any longer now that the legitimacy of the child is no longer so powerful a concern. For Rousseau, it is decisive. Rousseau of course deplores male infidelity, and thinks it deserves harsh treatment, but never-theless insists on greater rigors for the female. This means that a woman is from the outset attached to opinion in a way and to a degree that do not exist for a man. A woman must not only be virtuous but be thought to be virtuous by her husband and the world. Thus women are naturally more conventional than men. The secret of Sophie's education is to restore her spiritual independence while she is mindful of the opinions of men. To live happily in this condition she will have to find an Emile.

The progress of the arts and sciences has contributed since Rous-seau's time to a partial repeal of the law of nature, particularly by way of medicine. The invention of the Pill has made it possible for women to have sex without fear of pregnancy. The increase in life expectancy means that a smaller portion of life is devoted to the preservation of the species in the rearing of children. And in the last fifty years, infant mortality from disease has practically disappeared in advanced countries. Till only yesterday, one of the saddest aspects of human life was that a quarter to a half of children died before reaching maturity, so that the parents' fond gaze was always mixed with the anticipation of loss, and a large number of children had to be produced to ensure the perpetuation of the family.

As a result women can more easily enter the labor force and compete in the liberating or corrupting capitalist marketplace. Rous-seau would surely have to recognize that there is an important dif-ference in this respect between our times and all other times, and this difference has a profound effect on how women must and can live.

And this calls into question the alleged permanence of the human problems, which was the premise of all political philosophers up until the nineteenth century and the advent of historicism. Rousseau's response to the historicist assertion of the uniqueness of every human situation is in this case simple. There are indeed new freedoms and new possibilities opened up by the advance of medical science promised by Descartes in that famous fund-raising brochure, *The Discourse on Method*. However, we now recognize what Rousseau was the first to insist on more than two centuries ago, that the progress of science and the conquest of nature are not simply unproblematic. Our new freedoms depend on that new science, and Rousseau would tell us that these freedoms now dear to us are bought at a high price, above all the demystification of the world and the uprooting of man from it.

Rousseau gives us guidance by his response to the first great medical advance that saved the lives of children, vaccination. This whole issue was fraught with grave political consequences. The thinkers of the Enlightenment were enthusiastically and unqualifiedly for vaccination; the Catholic church, as well as other churches, was against it. Voltaire acted as a publicist for this English discovery in his *Philosophical Letters*.[47] Yet Rousseau again tries to walk in a middle space that neither side wished to accord him. Of course his heart goes out to the children who die, and in each particular case he undoubtedly would have authorized any means to save them. But he does not have Emile vaccinated—because vaccination presupposes the existence of a scientific community that is possible only in large, luxurious, and corrupt nations, and because the world in which doctors are prominent is the one where living becomes more important than living well (131). In this Rousseau follows Plato in the *Republic*.[48] In opposing vaccination he seems to be joining the Kingdom of Darkness, but he was not a welcome guest there either, for his reasons were not religious ones but natural. Rousseau contents himself with a jibe at the Encyclopedists' easygoing self-satisfaction and resolves the rhetorical problem by asserting that contemporary man in already corrupt societies must be vaccinated, thus giving his support to the rational practice of medicine, but he makes it clear at the same time that the quantity of lives saved may be achieved at the cost of their quality. There is little doubt that he would have been even more doubtful about the desirability of the Pill, which by divorcing sex from procreation and the family that gave it meaning liberates men and women from great and noble responsibilities without providing anything to take their place. And as to women in the labor market, his poetic exhortations to family life, which were so moving to many women in his time and after, give us an indication of how he would react. To all of these things his simple response is, "Sure you can make these changes, but the price will be the collapse of the family, and this proves that the human problems are permanent." Nature does not allow costless progress. The great and accidental changes in man that occur on the way from the state of nature to society put Rousseau on the brink of asserting the unlimited plasticity of man alleged in the generations after Rousseau by historicists, but the iron necessity of nature still remains underneath all the changes as Rousseau saw them. The problems of love are pretty much what they always were.

Thus, in Rousseau's teaching a man is always a man and a woman is always a woman, and the well-integrated personality must refer all of its elements to that basic nature. Ultimately, in Romanticism, the distinction between male and female is much more unambiguous than one finds in earlier literature. In Shakespeare, for example, things are often complicated by role reversals and the presence of a combination of male and female elements in a single person, so that a perfect fit of male and female is more difficult to imagine. As a preliminary and very tentative reproach to Rousseau and the movement to which he gave the first impulse, one might say that he presents in all seriousness what Aristophanes presents half jokingly and in a most qualified way, that is, that love is the quest for one's other half, which once found, restores the lovers to perfect wholeness. There is no war between the sexes here, and each desires the other for the sake of wholeness. This might be a subtle and delicate simplification of human nature in the name of real community.

XIII   After having established the interdependent directedness of male and female and the complex psychology of attack and defense, forwardness and modesty natural to male and female, Rousseau turns to the education of the female (364–393). It is not too surprising that this treatment is both much shorter and much more conventional than that given to Emile. Woman, as Rousseau has already observed, is necessarily more dependent, and this education is intended to provide her with independence in the search for a man on whom she can depend and who will sacrifice his independence to become her willing slave. As in "The Profession of Faith of the Savoyard Vicar," Rousseau begins closer to the social state than to the state of nature where he begins Emile's education. All kinds of traits, like conscience and modesty, are taken to be simply natural rather than modifications of nature.

The general tendency of this simple education is to see to it that a girl's taste for pleasing men be to please virtuous men rather than gallant ones, that her desire include ideals of merit as well as those of physical perfection. This is where the great divide between romance and sex is located. The woman's education is something of a blank slate waiting to be filled in by husband and wife together. Not too surprisingly, Rousseau accepts observations about little girls' natural tastes characteristically made by parents, observations frequently contested by critics who say that they are merely responses to the expectations of parents. Little girls, Rousseau asserts, are interested in being attractive and adorning themselves, whereas little boys want only to be independent. Thus the cultivation of the pleasing arts is a good beginning for a girl as the planting of beans was for a boy, a nonabstract beginning point that engages the child's enthusiasm while teaching useful things. Unlike the education of Emile, Sophie's education will be entrusted to her parents. No new beginning here, although this can in part be explained by the fact that fathers no longer educated their sons and in practice really left them to their mothers, who coddled and protected them overmuch, whereas mothers can appropriately educate their daughters and teach them what it means to be a woman. They are made companions of their mothers. Singing, dancing, sewing, penmanship, and so on are the things young girls practice. Rousseau, it must be remembered, wants to combine a traditional strength of soul directed to chasteness with a full, if exclusive, earthy sexual expression. Therefore he in no way reproves apparently natural coquetry, including dancing and singing, the kinds of things reproved by his Calvinist forbears. It seems that a wife must to the outside world have the austerity of a nun, and inside the home create the sensual atmosphere of the harem. Unlike Emile, Sophie is constrained constantly to change her objects of attention, as she will when she is a mother burdened with household responsibilities and various kinds of care of her children (368–369). Hers will be a life more toilsome and less unified in its activities than her husband's.

This toilsome life in relation to the two poles, children and husband, is understood by Rousseau not as subjugation but rather as assuring the exercise of women's real strength and influence. A respectable and charming woman is the great civilizer. Women, Rousseau says, are as intelligent as men, and their intelligence is more precocious. But the intelligences of men and women differ. Men are more abstract and speculative, looking to general rules. Women are more practical and more interested in the particular cases of their children, their husbands, and even of public opinion, which is so important for them. Given the status of the customs concerning inheritance in Rousseau's time, they must even worry about their children's goodwill if they are to have the wherewithal to live as widows. They are better psychologists, partly because they have to pay a great deal of attention to those on whom they depend. Rousseau gives splendidly amusing accounts of the superiority of female address, for example, the embarrassment of a man seated at dinner between two women with each of whom he is having an affair compared with a woman's capacity to manipulate such a situation so as to persuade each of her lovers that he is the preferred one (384–385). This kind of concern with others' opinions was what was most studiously avoided in Emile's education, but for a woman it is necessary, and Rousseau attempts to compensate for it by preparing her primary attachment to a husband who is independent and will protect her. In return she will make him alert to the delicacies of human relationships to which he will respond for her sake. This is the core of the complementarity of male and female, a division of intellectual labor without which there will be no sound product. Rousseau exploits the dangerous desire of women to please in order to further their education in the useful arts as well as their improvement in morals.

This he makes undangerous by subordinating the delicate art of manipulation at which women can be so adept to their desire to have children who love them and whom they love. This manipulativeness, which would be culpable in a man, has its root in the natural necessity for deception in the game of love. This interweaving of male and female is illustrated in the culminating passage of the section on female education by the performance of a husband and wife at yet another of the dinners Rousseau lays on so frequently in *Emile*. The husband is adept at engaging people in conversation because he knows their general social situations and their interests. The wife senses their individual private feelings and their wishes, bodily and intellectual, and what they most need to be fully comfortable. The most delicious moment for the couple occurs after the guests have left, when they are able to compare notes and get a picture of their guests that neither could arrive at without the other (383–384).

The social relationship of the sexes is an admirable thing. This partnership produces a moral person of which the woman is the eye and the man is the arm, but they have such a dependence on one another that the woman learns from the man what must be seen and the man learns from the woman what must be done. If woman could ascend to general principles as well as man can, and if man had as good a mind for details as woman does, they would always be independent of one another, they would live in eternal discord, and their partnership could not exist. But in the harmony which reigns between them, everything tends to the common end; they do not know who contributes more. Each follows the prompting of the other; each obeys, and both are masters. (377)

This sums up Rousseau's project of constituting a subpolitical social molecule out of the individual atoms as the stuff of society, that is, the relation of lovers who are to be procreators of citizens. This notion was picked up by Tocqueville, who describes the American family as though it were the embodiment of Rousseau's family ideal and then crowns American women as the true cause of the success of the American nation.[49] But Tocqueville, with greater modesty than Rousseau, does not give an account of the sexual relations at the base of all of this.

Nothing could underline so clearly the difference between the male and the female educations, and the different natures to which they are directed, as the different religious teachings imparted to each. Emile learned about the first principles of all things and the causes of the movements of nature. Sophie's religion is based on the idea of generation, the birth and death of children and parents, gradually stretching back to the beginning, the ones at the beginning not generated but generating, and forward to the generators who will no longer generate. Generation is the woman's miracle and inclines her to belief in a God who presides over it. This teaching would not be persuasive to a man but, kept within proper bounds, for a woman it kills many birds with one stone. It prepares a woman for the necessary adaptation to her husband's religion, essential for marriage, because its only content has to do with reverence toward the generative aspect of marriage. And it limits a woman's theological imagination to this world and her own most important duty as mother of children here and now. Rousseau finds a greater tendency to religious fanaticism in women than in men, due not only to women's lesser gifts at theoretical reason, but also to their greater dependence on fortune. They are lovers of ephemeral men and children rather than of unchanging and permanent abstractions, and they have greater need of support and consolation in their toilsome lives. Again Rousseau insists both on the importance of religious faith and on the necessity of keeping that faith within the confines of tolerance. Here he stresses the key role of women both for piety and for its abuses (377–382).

This completes the simple education of women, the chief goal of which is to weave together two apparently contrary springs that, in concert, set the perfect female machinery in motion: the desire to please, which attaches women to the caprices of popular prejudice, and conscience, which makes them fanatic and antisocial. Conscience by itself is harsh and unadorned by the pleasant crown of worldly rewards; attention to opinion is the cause of coquetry and dishonesty under an appearance of virtue. The principles of a woman's conscience, on the basis of which her superior capacity to reason from ends to means is founded, are identical to her primitive instincts about her duties to her husband and children. She can and will artfully use her faculty to please people in general, and particularly men, within the limits of these ends.

Rousseau concludes this discussion with an impassioned quasi-sermon about the universal acclaim at all times and places for a virtuous woman. He almost makes one forget that the power of women to lift up men and society as a whole is founded on a great effort of will and reason by which their natural sexual inclination is abandoned in favor of the love of virtue. It is this effort that makes a good woman admired. A woman must forget the difference between sexual desire and eros for the noble, on the one hand, and that between the passionate love of a man and a woman and the responsibilities for a family, on the other.

> I shall say more, and I maintain that virtue is no less favorable to love than to the other rights of nature, and that the authority of the beloved gains no less from virtue than does the authority of wives and mothers. There is no true love without enthusiasm, and no enthusiasm without an object of perfection, real or chimerical, but always existing in the imagination. What will enflame lovers for whom this perfection no longer exists and who see in what they love only the object of sensual pleasure? No, it is not thus that the soul is warmed and delivered to those sublime transports which constitute the delirium of lovers and the charm of their passion. In love everything is only illusion. I admit it. But what is real are the sentiments for the truly beautiful with which love animates us

and which it makes us love. This beauty is not in the object one loves; it is the work of our errors. So, what of it? Does the lover any the less sacrifice all of his low sentiments to this imaginary model? Does he any the less suffuse his heart with the virtues he attributes to what he holds dear? Does he detach himself any the less from the baseness of the human *I*? Where is the true lover who is not ready to immolate himself for his beloved, and where is the sensual and coarse passion in a man who is willing to die? We make fun of the paladins. That is because they knew love, and we no longer know anything but debauchery. When these romantic maxims began to become ridiculous, the change was less the work of reason than of bad morals. (391)

No more explicit a statement of the necessity of illusion for sublime states of soul could be imagined, nor could we find a better place to ask ourselves, "What is the future of an illusion that one knows to be an illusion?" This is perhaps where the poet who loves and believes in his creation overturns the tribunal of philosophy and reason. From here on out men and women are exhorted to put all their eggs in the basket of romantic love, superseding all the exploded old charms that used to be found in religion and country. Rousseau left us with an either/or pitting poetry against philosophy.

It is well to note that this romantic love is entirely reciprocal love: the lover is also beloved, and the beloved is also lover. The classic distinction between lover and beloved, a distinction which teaches that true love need not be reciprocal, is overcome. Man does not love the lovable that cannot or will not love in return. Romantic love flatters our greatest hopes and pretensions not only to love the beautiful but to be loved by it. Rousseau restores imagination, exiled by Enlightenment, to the throne of an imperium more absolute than it ever had been.

XIV To douse the flames of enthusiasm with which Rousseau sometimes can inspire us, I recall the remark of a witty man who asked, "How did a word that used to mean the manliness of man come to signify the chastity of woman?" Rousseau plays some part in this, and when the chastity of women began to appear ridiculous, virtue became a word without a content. However that may be, Sophie is to be the keystone of morality's arch. Women are more necessarily divided than are men because the tension between their sexual inclination, which Rousseau believes to be stronger and more continuous than that of men, and the responsibilities connected with children, is present in their bodies from the outset. The sublimated male is seeking love; the female is seeking love and the family, and the two, although they can become one, are not necessarily the same. Desire has to be controlled in the woman, and the idea of virtue—meaning a willed self-restraint—is present in her from the outset of life. The study of women, therefore, especially requires reflection on the problem of will. Natural man has no will, or, to put it otherwise, he wills his inclination or what he desires. Emile still remains in this condition, whereas Sophie is suffused with the sense of the risk she is running and in awe of the self-overcoming required of her. She can only hope that her senses will not fool her and that she will find a man whose nature and education will give her the opportunity to teach him how to will. A well-educated man will not have a problem of subordinating his desire for food or drink to his nobler desires. But he may very well have great difficulty in subordinating his sexual desire to his manifest duties. This is especially so inasmuch as Rousseau encourages and rests his teaching on the centrality of sexual desire in the souls of human beings. One must desire in order to will. The merely vital desires have been regulated in Emile by the higher desires. His preference for attractive women over good food is not an act of the will. It is merely the substitution of a more powerful desire for others. The view of modern political philosophy was that only desire controls desire, and that will, which traditionally was the source of virtue, is both ineffective and virtually nonexistent. Rousseau does not want to leave it at that, because it is ignoble and a denial of human freedom. The nobility of man consists in willing, even though the will is not natural. In a sense *Emile* is a study of the construction of the will in a being who does not naturally possess will. Dividedness is necessary to man in spite of Rousseau's explicit effort to avoid it. The crucial difference between Rousseau and the received understanding is that this dividedness is self-imposed and not imposed by the great outsiders— God, nature, or public opinion. Sophie's love of virtue is a successful use of the will. Her awareness that her bodily desires here and now are double, to satisfy her individual senses and to continue the species, gives her immediate sentiments on the basis of which she can guide herself. This is the core of her conscience, whereas Emile has no such immediate principle within him. Conscience in a woman requires no questionable religious support, whereas the Savoyard Vicar had to offer a whole system of argument to which Jean-Jacques found "a multitude of objections" (294), stifled only by the Orpheus-like charm of the Vicar's discourse. The woman whose virtue is the crown of her charms can send "her lovers with a nod to the end of the world, to combat, to glory, to death, to anything she pleases" (393). Her virtue can create virtue in men.

At last Rousseau introduces us to Sophie, the object of the hero's quest. She is presented to us in a passage the paragraphs of which begin with "Sophie is . . ." or "Sophie is not . . ." (393–399), thus outlining her salient qualities, which are, like good taste, according to Rousseau, only a compilation of very ordinary qualities, approved by common sense, but which are very rarely combined.

> Sophie is well born;* she has a good nature; she has a very sensitive heart, and this extreme sensitivity sometimes makes her imagination so active that it is difficult to moderate. Her mind is less exact than penetrating; her disposition is easy but nevertheless uneven; her face is ordinary but agreeable; her expression gives promise of a soul and does not lie. One can approach her with indifference but not leave her without emotion. Some have good qualities that are lacking to her; others have a greater measure of those good qualities she does possess; but none has a better combination of qualities for making a favorable character. She knows how to take advantage even of her defects, and if she were more perfect, she would be much less pleasing. (393)

"Sophie is not beautiful," but she is far from ugly. A Helen of Troy is both dangerous and in the long run boring. Yet good looks are essential to the erotic, which still is the foundation of the tower Rousseau is building. Rousseau, for all his tenderness, accepts nature's faulty distribution of its gifts and reminds us that love is the domain of the young and attractive no matter how much we may wish it to be otherwise. "Sophie loves adornment," but the adornment is only an enhancement of the naked body underneath it, rather than a cosmetic dissimulation of it. The sagging structure of a middle-aged woman is for Rousseau rendered ridiculous by all the machinery invented by women in order to trick their gallants. "So-

---

*This is not entirely a social prejudice, inasmuch as it implies that the parents who raised her are both decent and educated.

phie has natural talents," but her dancing and her music and all the other cultivations of these natural talents are not carried to a point of perfection; that would cause her to forget their use as contributions to the grace of life. "What Sophie knows best and has been most carefully made to learn are the labors of her own sex," which make her able to supervise a household and its servants, like the wives described in the writings of the ancient Greeks and Romans. Cooking, sewing, household accounts, etc., will enable her to govern her household and, more important, the man who will be its putative master. She tends to be somewhat obsessed with cleanliness, a vice not usually shared by men, but she does not carry it to the point where the body is preferred to the soul. It is rather a bodily reflection of the purity of her soul. "Sophie *was* a glutton." This possible vice was avoided by her mother's pointing out that bonbons would ruin her teeth and hence her attractiveness. Women share the penchant of little boys for sweets, but they do not naturally outgrow it. This characteristic would seem to be connected with female sensuality.

"Sophie has a mind that is agreeable without being brilliant, and solid without being profound." She will use her intellectual energies not to become a theoretical babbler, but to understand real life and the persons who populate it. This must not be parodied so that she is thought to be a cipher. One has only to read Julie's letters in *La Nouvelle Héloïse* to see the range of educated sensibility and psychological tact that Rousseau sees as the perfection of female intellect and which is far beyond anything one can expect from either a woman or a man today. "Sophie's sensitivity is too great for her to preserve a perfect stability of disposition. . . ." This is part of her attractiveness, and keeps a lover on his toes when it does not become a dominant trait and is counterpoised by a return to gentleness and good sense. Such sensibility appears to be a compensation for a woman's forbearance and sufferance in relation to the injustices of men and society. Men are permitted anger and rebellion, but women represent a gentler persuasion and contribute to reform not by their action but by their example. This is a not inconsiderable power, although it is likely to be despised by the revolutionary temper.

"Sophie is religious, but her religion is reasonable and simple, with little dogma and less in the way of devout practices. . . ." This is self-explanatory, but it is the result of the careful cultivation of her natural aptitude for religion, which, uneducated, would tend to swerve between fanaticism and atheism—either to protect her virtue or to justify its abandonment. "Sophie loves virtue." This is her passion because she has the feelings and the vision to recognize all the power and satisfaction that it can win for her. She desperately wants bodily satisfaction and loving and being loved, but she knows that this will depend on the man "who is going to make solitude sweet for her." "Sophie is knowledgeable about the duties and rights of her sex." She is a sensitive and sure observer of men's qualities. Woman, as judge of man, exercises the greatest influence on his behavior. The belief that a woman's praise or blame is the solidest ground of male self-esteem is one of the most important springs of human connectedness.

"Sophie has little experience of the practices of society," but she has a great sense of the propriety connected with the fundamental relationships. She is respectful of her elders and severe with her contemporaries until she is married. She knows the importance of the ancestral and merely conventional in any society, but she knows that it is from her contemporaries that she will have to choose a husband while keeping all the rest at bay. There is a potential opposition between the generations, the parental authority trying to control the natural desires of the younger generation. Julie comes to grief over this opposition, but Sophie's enlightened parents introduce a reform that allows a uniting of these two poles. Such is the woman not completely appealing to modern tastes, who is made to be the complement of Emile, and whose vindication depends utterly on the success of the relationship she is able to form. Her father can, without being pedantic, address a speech to her about the new significance of marriage he has learned from Jean-Jacques.

This speech introduces the absolutely essential reform that makes marriage the fundamental and sacred contract and, more important, restores to woman her natural freedom on the level of society: she has the right freely to choose whether she shall marry and whom she shall marry (399–401). At least in the West this now appears to be simply a thing to be taken for granted. Parents still worry about their children's choice of spouses, but this worry is frustrated and unable to determine choices. As we all know, marriages arranged by parents remain the common practice in many places in the world. As a matter of fact, the most obvious sign of "westernization" of these "cultures" is the rebellion against parental control and the demand for this right of women to choose. This reform really was an innovation. As is the case in modern political philosophy altogether, Rousseau founds the duties of men and women in an original and fundamental freedom or right. Right precedes duty. But the choice, once made, is determining for the whole of life, and the contract constituted by the agreement between the two spouses is permanent. No divorce! This might sound to contemporary ears like a historical limit on Rousseau's imagination or simply an incapacity to carry the logic of freedom to its conclusion. However, it is just this binding choice that constitutes the morality of marriage and morality itself. The proof of one's freedom consists in a choice by which one will stick and about which one can say, "The result is not as I would have wished, but it is my evident duty to accept the consequences of my choice." If one were to change when things are not going well, it would be desire, the desire of the brutes, that determines action and not freedom or will. If freedom is the essence of man, as the moderns believe, only the capacity to set down laws for oneself that one obeys can demonstrate the possibility and existence of such freedom. The marriage vow contains two elements: freedom and binding, self-imposed commitment. This is the whole reason for Rousseau's total concentration on sexual education in this big book. The sublimation of coarse natural impulse toward the lovable beautiful prepares the ground for the desire of a permanent and unique attachment. Turning that desire into a fixed will to maintain such an attachment is what enables man to convert desire into moral freedom. Rousseau thought this to be the condition of self-respect for modern man, who is no longer a believer or a patriot. When such will disappeared, nothing was left but the empty word "commitment." Just as the older forms of marriage prove the potency of authority, the newer forms really return man to his brutish, externally determined condition. Rousseau, unlike any previous or later thinker, focuses on marriage as the one place where this moralized freedom has its place. The social contract is always tentative and limited to the self-interested advantage of the individuals contracting. Only marriage in its very premise promises eternity and the engagement of all the best of oneself for a whole lifetime. This is the one institution that is founded in human freedom and is accessible to every human being. Beyond it there is nothing; it is the moral microcosm. All the gravity of a responsible life is present in this choice.

Of course one hopes that one's marriage will bring happiness, but in the world of morality, as opposed to that of nature, happiness must give way to morality. Hope, as Kant pointed out, is permitted, but unqualified pursuit of happiness ends in a pragmatism that undermines the self-respect generated by free choice. Human choice ennobles, but imposes a sometimes tragic dualism between happiness and morality, unknown to natural man for whom happiness or satisfaction is the only polar star. Rousseau made marriage bear a very heavy burden. The whole seriousness of life is concentrated in the thrilling but awesome choice of a husband or wife. It is around this choice that the action of the Romantic novel revolves. As a result of Rousseau's analysis, for more than a century the fascination of the plots had to do with fidelity and adultery. When the untamability of the sexual passion and the loss of belief in the dignity of sublimation overcame Rousseau's influence, love was no longer the theme of the novel, and it is difficult to discern what has replaced it.

According to Rousseau, choices of marriage partners are traditionally made up of three elements, the social station of the partners, their wealth, and their inclination or attraction to each other. In most societies, the two former have primacy over the last. Therefore, parents claim the right to determine who will inherit their titles and their wealth. The mere sensual desires of the partners are, at best, a secondary consideration. Rousseau plaintively asserts that the persons are forgotten. Rousseau, rigorously consistent with his project of founding everything on the free choice of individuals and, particularly, on their sentiments, reconstitutes the family in the direction of democracy, where the free election of the partners founds the social contract. But in this case, the women's vote is more important than the man's because the duties it imposes on her are more onerous. The tension between the parents' wishes or commands and the wish of the young people is the most palpable expression of the tension between nature and convention. Nature is most important, but there must always be conventions, and some compromise must be made with them in order to live in society. Therefore, Sophie must choose for herself but must also consult with her parents. The mixture of wisdom and consent is *the* political problem from Plato on up to our own day, and it is represented here in the formation of the family. For Rousseau, consent clearly has primacy, but the sensuality of the young people has been refined by education so that the distance between brute desire and the law is reduced. Sophie's parents will both help her to think about the wisdom of the conventions and help to control her sensitive nature in order that it not be tricked by a clever seducer. Parents still play a role but, in the democratic family, the father's ancestral tyranny is replaced by a free relationship of trust produced by a mixture of utility and gratitude that replaces the rigidity of the law and the expectation of inheritance. The dark thickets surrounding the tension between nature and convention became another central theme of Romantic literature, where ill-sorted lovers tragically struggled to fulfill their natural inclinations for each other against the hostility of the ancestral.

It must be remembered that an older tradition represented by Aristotle would have cast marriage in a very different light. The procreation and education of citizens is, according to Aristotle, what marriage is about. In this austere interpretation, eros tends to disappear as a significant element. Even with perfect awareness of how prejudiced and stupid parents can be, Aristotle thinks that in practice they are better judges of a couple's suitability for this business of running a household. He attempts to correct the possible ignorance of the parents by the guidance of a wise legislator. But Rousseau's advocacy of the rights of love has been so successful that Western men and women can hardly imagine any serious argument for Aristotle's position. Aristotle affirms that man is a political animal and that the family is naturally subordinated to the community.[50] Rousseau affirms that man is naturally a solitary being and that, if he is to become political, it will only be by the mediation of the smaller community, the family, to which the only partially natural connection is sublimated sexual desire. So fundamental are the issues underlying this dispute about the rights of free consent in marriage.

Sophie is lucky because her parents made a conventional marriage, the bases of which were destroyed by fortune. Her mother's family possessed title and her father's money, and somehow events separated her from her title and him from his money. But underneath they found that their love, which alone in marriage is permanent and not dependent on the vagaries of fortune, was real and sufficient unto itself. Thus they in their way can join wholeheartedly in Rousseau's project of a new beginning, helping Sophie to marry appropriately without the conflicts and compromises usually required. It is interesting to note that even within the confines of the conventions according to which Sophie's mother and father were betrothed, the couple was ill-assorted. It would have been better and more according to nature, Rousseau asserts, if the man were titled and the woman brought money, because family titles are at least signs of old virtue and represent certain respectable duties and responsibilities and are therefore more appropriate to the ruler of the constitutional monarchy that is the family.

In his speech to Sophie her father states with admirable baldness the relations between desire and will, the emergence of which is the theme of this last book of *Emile*.

> It is up to the spouses to match themselves. Mutual inclination ought to be their first bond. Their eyes and their hearts ought to be their first guides. Their first duty once they are united is to love each other; and since loving or not loving is not within our control, this duty necessarily involves another,

which is to begin by loving each other before being united. This is the right of nature, which nothing can abrogate. Those who have hindered it by so many civil laws have paid more attention to the appearance of order than to the happiness of marriage and the morals of citizens. (400)

The impulsions of nature, which are not the product of law, must be the foundation on which law is built. One can legislate morality, if it is based on nature, and all the great projects for reforming the relations between men and women will work only if they found themselves in nature. The conversion of changeable desire into unchangeable duty is the work of the will assisted by reason.

Sophie is left to choose for herself. Although questions of wealth and station are not entirely indifferent for human beings living in society, Rousseau, speaking through Sophie's father, gives voice to the permanent human aspiration to be determined in important things not by conventions, by the here and now, but by the essential things such as real merit and beauty. This is to be the decision that will decide everything for Sophie, and she is given every opportunity to choose well, not consulting in her own choice anything but her taste. This freedom can be safely accorded by her parents because her taste has been so well educated. In a remarkable digression, Rousseau offers us "the worst case" of a girl with an ardent temperament whom he claims really existed, whom he also calls Sophie though that was not her real name, and who was granted such freedom by her parents. They were astonished to find that after she looked around, no one was to her taste, and she began to languish. When interrogated, she candidly admitted that she was in love with Télémaque, the hero of Fénelon's epic of the same name (404). Given this book by an eminent Christian author with roots in classical sources, she has fallen in love with its hero. No contemporary man can match the literary depiction of Ulysses' virtuous and handsome son. This supposedly real Sophie was by nature and by education made to love, but that love is not self-sufficient; it requires a worthy object. Without such a love she actually perishes from unfulfilled longing.

This is, in one commonsense perspective, foolish. This Sophie is a victim of an overheated imagination. But she dies for an ideal rather than live with solutions that compromise the most important things. Rousseau tells and perhaps makes up this little story in order to teach us something about women and about imagination. Imagination, as Rousseau has always pointed out, constitutes the quasi-totality of the sexual life of human beings. "There is nothing beautiful except that which is not" (447).[51] But to dismiss this Sophie's death as a result of folly, saying that her love is only imaginary, does not suffice, for almost the whole being of civilized man exists in the imagination, so that the distinction is not properly between real and imaginary but between the sublime imaginary and the degrading imaginary. The so-called realistic use of sex is nothing but degraded or, to speak anachronistically, neurotic imagination. This Sophie's imagination makes the beloved her own, a product of the ideal world created by herself rather than an arbitrary impingement from the outside. This is the mechanism by which Emile will discover his Sophie. The supposedly real Sophie Rousseau speaks of here is in love with a fiction and is living proof of the power of literature. All of the foregoing can apply to men as well as to women, but Rousseau indicates that women are more susceptible to this sublime perversion. This is because they bear such a heavy burden, turning their own and their husbands' desires toward the family as well as to the satisfactions of love. The female seems to be inclined to a sort of semireligious fanaticism and to be able to be caught up in the imaginations to be found in books more easily than does the male. One can see here part of the reason for Rousseau's own strategy in often addressing himself especially to females and using the novel as his vehicle.

It is easy for us to think of another book with another hero with whom Christian women can fall in love and renounce the coarse pleasures of this world. And Rousseau here attempts to explain this phenomenon. The story is meant to cut both ways. It illustrates a kind of folly that forgets the material substrate of the divine satisfaction. The bodily need that is the source and the end of the beautiful fantasy must be part of a healthy human life. Nothing could be further from the notion of original sin. This girl, whom Rousseau calls the real Sophie, is foolish, but she is a noble fool with an exalted soul, a character no realism can rival. The Sophie of our story, the one who marries Emile and possesses an ordinary soul like his, also judges him by the standard of Télémaque, although, characteristically, she has also read, in addition to Fénelon's book, one about keeping the family's accounts. But either because Emile is better than the suitors the supposedly real Sophie encountered, or because Emile's Sophie has a less lively imagination and a healthier sensuality, she judges him to meet the standard. She links the needs of body and imagination as the supposedly real Sophie could not.

After having completed this portrait of the Sophie who awaits Emile, Rousseau makes a few sensible remarks directed toward men about the choice of a wife (406–410). Although a wife should be chosen on natural grounds, any real choice will take place in a conventional social framework. Rousseau advises that equality of station and fortune is desirable so that neither spouse can, as it were, pull rank and cloud the natural suitability. And if there is an inequality, it should be the male who has the advantage. This is because he represents the will of the family as a unit. The woman is to influence the man's decisions. She is not to return to her natural individuality. But the real distinction is not between social classes but between those who think and those who do not. This distinction may be a result of education and reflect economic advantage, but in the actual choice of a husband or a wife one is confronted by those who are able to think and those who are not able to do so, no matter how each got that way. This does not mean that the simple are not as moral as or even more moral than the sophisticated. But the great moral choices do not make up the substance of everyday life as conversation does. In order for there to be the day-to-day community between human beings they must be able to talk to each other usefully and pleasantly. This does not mean that they will think or say the same things. All to the contrary, Rousseau has indicated that man and woman will bring different offerings to the feast, but they must be able to understand each other and take an interest in so doing. The community of understanding and of speech is the most enduring of the bonds between a man and a woman. Thus Rousseau cannot be understood as wanting to enslave women by ignorance. Above all Sophie is educated to be educable by her better-educated husband. Though Rousseau is at the source of our indifference to conventional criteria in the choice of a wife, he adds an important criterion, education, which we now tend to neglect at least in theory if not practice, because in the wake of egalitarianism and relativism, education is not thought to be a real difference.

He concludes with a remark about beauty as a determinant of choice. He says that one's wife should not be too beautiful (a theme in a charming Gérard Depardieu film). Beauty is perhaps the primary attraction for civilized man, and it is not to be counted for nothing, but Rousseau puts it in its place. Once a beauty is possessed, it becomes routine and not a very special advantage. But it can be a source of distorting vanities for both parties. (Remember Gyges' story in Herodotus.[52]) And it draws in its wake almost inevitable jealousies of all those who are as attracted as the husband was before her beauty became routine. Ugliness is, of course, too repulsive and never becomes routine. Therefore, by this strange route, Rousseau reaffirms the ancient principle of moderation.

Now begins the courtship (410–441). It is part love dance like that of those birds who show off their plumage to their intendeds, part a series of love tests like those to which knights-errant were subjected by their beloveds. Courtship is out of fashion today. Actually, it was superseded a couple of generations ago by dating, which has now been superseded by I know not what. The whole purpose of courtship is obviously to acquaint a couple with each other before they make such a momentous and life-determining decision as marriage. Now the overwhelming majority of the educated live together for an extended period before marrying, and neither of the partners is likely to be anything resembling a virgin even when they enter into this premarital stage. Their behavior is sensibly explained by the consideration that they ought to know each other well before they make up their minds to have children. But, Rousseau would respond, the sexual act should be the culmination of and the reward for marital commitment. The separation of the sex from the commitment takes the pressure off and surely separates the sexual act from the "relationship." This degrades the status of the act itself as surely as do teachings about original sin, and as effectively as did the real Sophie, who chose death rather than compromise.

Rousseau says that the time of courtship is the happiest time because the anticipation is better than any fulfillment and that the expectation nurtured during this period extends itself throughout the life of the marriage. It is not so much reality but the creation of an illusion necessary to love that is cultivated during this period. It is true that the lovers will not know just how good they will be together in bed, but Rousseau's view is that a properly primed couple will do just fine on that score. He insists that the first sexual experience is determining for the whole of life, that the furtive and frequently degrading first attempt at lovemaking lowers the sights and takes away much of the idealism that connects the erotic ecstasy to the earthly reward of merit and beauty. Courtship helps to constitute the first attachment and gives free play to the tantalizingly ambiguous relations between individuals as well as to their diverse male and female sexual instincts. The life of two individuals devoted to each other can never be simply without ambiguities that continually require attention, respect, and acts of understanding. There can be no taking for granted. By this measure, our current behavior, although it appears to be sensible, could also be explained as timidity and the fear of running erotic risk. The imagination, as experienced in sexual fantasy, no longer informs the views of lovers, and thus their day-to-day cohabitation becomes routine. The ease of divorce and the fact that today there is no social price to be paid for promiscuity further weaken the erotic tension that is the mainspring of romantic marriage. If love and so much else of what is social are, as most people believe today, really sexual sublimation, then one must really sublimate. If healthy, nonneurotic sex is for social man so delicate and vulnerable a plant, it must be cultivated with the greatest care. The merely bodily has to be inextricably entwined with the higher human aspirations, and this is what Rousseau thinks is very badly done in our times, in which the Christian debasement of eroticism is replaced by the bourgeois debasement of eroticism.

Emile and his faithful Jean-Jacques, like a knight-errant with his squire (or as Sophie, whose head is full of her book, sees it, like Télémaque with his Mentor), arrive in the house of her parents (413). It is worth noting that Emile knows of Télémaque only by way of the *Odyssey*, a purely classical source in which the Christian knights and their romances do not have a place. Sophie recognizes Emile by way of his likeness to Télémaque, while Emile recognizes Sophie by way of his own ideal at which he arrived with the help of Jean-Jacques. This particular woman, at least, requires literary help in love not needed by Emile, who has his tutor-poet. His book is *Robinson Crusoe*, the much harsher story of the solitary, self-sufficient man. When toward the end of *Emile* the couple must separate for a time, Sophie gives Emile her fundamental book, *Télémaque*. In return, Emile gives her his *Spectator*, a much more social book, while remaining silent about Crusoe.

The meeting between the two lovers, so amply prepared for each other, appears completely accidental in a way that makes chance seem to be a goddess (Fortuna) in the eyes of those laboring under love's illusions. Who could think otherwise, when those fated to love each other meet in such distant and isolated places, where they would never have looked intentionally? But all of this has been presumably arranged by the fine hand of Jean-Jacques in cahoots with the parents. In later Romantic novels such meetings do actually take place by chance, but the less trusting philosopher puts on the vestments of Fortuna. He illustrates the philosopher's secondary pleasure, as dream merchant and spectator. These facts are cautionary and make one less hopeful about the perfect success of relations between human beings.

First there must be a mutual recognition and what Stendhal calls, elaborating on Rousseau, crystallization, which is a mixture of desire and doubt where *amour-propre* begins to play a role and engages each in the opinion and judgment of the other while taking away all interest in any others. Sophie sees her Télémaque arriving and is moved by his tenderness toward her parents when they detail the story of their sufferings. Emile hardly notices the girl who could not possibly be the one he has been seeking so assiduously and futilely. But mention of the name Sophie, the very name suggested by Jean-Jacques as appropriate to the ideal woman, galvanizes the young philo-sopher. They look at each other and Sophie blushes and turns away. In a sense everything has already been accomplished with that blush, which appears so much against the will of the modest girl and is so avidly sought by the eyes of the young man.

> If I enter here into the perhaps too naive and too simple history of their innocent love, people will regard these details as a frivolous game, but they will be wrong. They do not sufficiently consider the influence which a man's first liaison with a woman ought to have on the course of both their lives. They do not see that a first impression as lively as that of love, or the inclination which takes its place, has distant effects whose links are not perceived in the progress of the years but do not cease to act until death. We are given treatises on education consisting of useless, pedantic, bloated verbiage about the chimerical duties of children, and we are not told a word about the most important and most difficult part of the whole of education—the crisis that serves as a passage from childhood to man's estate. If I have been able to make these essays useful in some respect, it is especially by having expanded at great length on this essential part, omitted by all others, and by not letting myself be rebuffed in this enterprise by false delicacies or frightened by difficulties of language. If I have said what must be done, I have said what I ought to have said. It makes very little difference to me if I have written a romance. A fair romance it is indeed, the romance of human nature. If it is to be found only in this writing, is that my fault? This ought to be the history of my species. You who deprave it, it is you who make a romance of my book. (415–416)

Emile might seem to be nothing but a Romantic novel but it *ought* to be man's history. Rousseau wrote man's factual history in *The Discourse on the Origin and Foundations of Inequality* with its somber message about the dividedness of man that is its result. Here he tells us that his project is the overcoming of the dividedness, and we understand Kant's enthusiasm for the "illustrious Jean-Jacques Rousseau" who taught us about the possibility of reconciling natural sexual desire with civilized marriage. This overcoming of the opposition between nature and society is the true meaning of culture.[53]

At the outset of *Emile* Rousseau tells us, "Forced to combat nature or the social institutions, one must choose between making a man or a citizen, for one cannot make both at the same time" (39). This opposition and need to choose is the problem revealed in *The Discourse on the Origin and Foundations of Inequality*. Yet the project of *Emile* is stated two pages later in what appears to be a contradiction of this judgment:

> But what will a man raised uniquely for himself become for others? If perchance the double object we set for ourselves could be joined in a single one by removing the contradictions of man, a great obstacle to his happiness would be removed. In order to judge of this, he would have to be seen wholly formed: his inclinations would have to have been observed, his progress seen, his development followed. In a word, the natural man would have to be known. I believe that one will have made a few steps in these researches when one has read this writing. (41)

To repeat, Rousseau's invention of sex education is the bridge over the otherwise uncrossable chasm between natural and social man, between caring for oneself and caring for others.

The courtship is divided into a series of stages in which the ever-eager Emile passes between the ecstasy of apparent acceptance by Sophie and the agony of apparent rejection by this girl, who in acting capriciously makes Emile reveal himself as he is by nature and education, and completes that education. One has to remember that Emile has never before cared about anybody's opinion of him. He feels sorry for those who suffer but is in no way involved with them; he wants nothing from them. He feels gratitude toward his tutor for what he has done for him, but he didn't ask for it and felt no need of him. The teacher, as it were, has disguised himself as a part of nature. Remember that the problem is to educate a human being who can care as much for another as he cares for himself, or to use Kant's formula, can treat others as ends in themselves. Every man understands his own self to be the end, which is equivalent to Hobbes's war of all against all; but starting from this war, one can incorporate the selves of others into one's own self, thus making peace. Parenthetically, it should be mentioned that almost all modern thinkers have started with Hobbes's state of nature, but our perennial problems in understanding human association make it doubtful whether many have succeeded in emerging from it. It is almost forgotten that there once was another route that avoided the land of Hobbes and did not need to sink into the morass of isolatedness. If there is any merit to this book that I am writing, it will be to reopen the quarrel between these two standpoints with respect to what Rousseau and Plato agree to be crucial, love or eros.

At their first meeting Emile and Sophie suspect that each is what the other has been looking for. They do not even speak to each other on the first day. Emile knows what he wants and arranges for his readmission to the household by a ruse, borrowing some clothes that he will have to return. And as soon as he leaves with his tutor he wants to look for lodgings as near as possible. But he is immediately taught a lesson about the difference between how one must behave with males and with females. To pursue a young woman is already to compromise her. If on further acquaintance the young man were to decide that the young woman is not right for him, she would be damaged goods. It might be thought that a more intimate relationship was established, an opinion that would feed the rumormongers. Woman depends on the good opinion of others more than does man. People will talk, and she can become an object of their pity or scandalous rumors. The rejected party is always the object of a certain pity, and the status of beloved does not sit well with an object of pity. Therefore keeping up appearances and even deception are part of the delicacy required of a serious lover. This is lesson number one, which applies, obviously, only where there is a presumption of modesty and chastity on the part of the woman. Emile recognizes that he must think about her, not only about himself, and therefore about the opinion of others. He learns the lesson easily because he is already deeply involved and sees that a directness and openness that would suit him do not conform to what suits her (413–418).

After repeated visits Emile comes to believe not only that he has been accepted as a suitor but that he can directly ask for her hand. She tells him to ask her father, and he is told by him that it is up to Sophie. He is mystified and believes he is rejected. This is his first disappointment and doubt, and it makes Sophie all the more precious in his eyes. The hindrance heightens his awareness of his need and the pain it will cause him if it is not to be satisfied. His loyal friend, who has set himself up as the go-between, informs him that Sophie is worried about his money. Emile is rich, we learn for the first time. It turns out that the natural man in society needs a great deal of conventional currency in order to maintain his position. This whole education and the life he is going to lead with it require money. The aristocratic parents who have ceded their rights to their son's tutor have the duty of providing the tutor with the sums that will make that education possible. Sophie is worried because a moneyed man might think that his contribution to a marriage consists in that and she would have no means to rival him. She has learned all about the various effects of money on character. So Emile immediately wants to throw all his money away, with the archetypical indifference to money of all Romantic heroes. But this would be worse, not only or especially because later he will need it, but because his sacrifice could become an even more powerful proof of his superiority to his wife, who need make no such sacrifice. What to do? Simply, the courtship must go on, and he must prove to Sophie that class and wealth do not obscure his humanity (419–424). This is the purpose of the rest of the courtship. He has won the right to be a suitor but is now in the position of having asked for marriage. In other words, he has become dependent on Sophie while she is not dependent on him.

This is the happiest time of life, when all their youthful joy and expectation produce scenes worthy of the novelist's pen. The very doubt about the outcome that permeates all their pleasant activities together spices the joy, and, again, the absence of the consummation so avidly wished for makes the imagination all the livelier. We see Emile instructing Sophie in singing and dancing, thus depriving the prurient teachers of these things of their vocation. He openly wants the woman he teaches, whereas the apparently neutral professor of these arts must be a deceiver. He conveys all he knows to her without pedantry, and he is no longer interested in any of his store of learning that she cannot share freely with him. The teaching activity is fully erotic, and his favorite pedagogic position is on his knees. What this does to scientific objectivity is worth considering. Together they walk through nature, which belongs to them and to which they lend their feelings. They have none of the cramped existence of modern individuals, and they do not need the expansion of self practiced by kings and nobles with their vain display of themselves in purchased domains.

At such moments they are inclined to turn their vision upward toward the Author of nature, and this is the only explicit reference to Emile's own practice of religion. It is part and parcel of his love affair and is in fact its culmination. The Savoyard Vicar's worship is possible only on the basis of his overcoming of sexual desire, whereas Emile's worship is the consequence of it. The two young lovers, obviously in an excruciating state of sensual excitement, know that they must still sacrifice their fulfillment for a while, and they therefore use God as the reward of their new and freely chosen virtue. This is one of the varieties of religious experience, the one most appropriate to lovers, the one that moralizes nature (426).

Sophie is the master and her commands are law. But law and desire do not coincide, so Emile is constantly trying to evade the law. He kisses her clothing or her hand, a favor she grants but which he turns into a right. Then she tries to prove that it is only her grace by refusing what he thinks is a right. They quarrel, but they also reconcile. Their value to each other and their pleasure are thus enhanced. The game of love is the most enticing game of all.

One of the important steps of the "internalization" of morality in Emile becomes clear at this point. On some days she orders him not to see her. She is testing her authority and his will. On such days he hangs around the neighborhood practicing the art of benefaction among less fortunate folk. It would be easy for him to see her from a distance on the sly. "But Emile's conduct is never devious; he does not know how to be evasive and does not want to be. He has that amiable delicacy which flatters and feeds *amour-propre* with the good witness of oneself. He rigorously sticks to his banishment and never approaches near enough to get from chance what he wants to owe only to Sophie" (436). There is a conflict between his desire and his self-respect, but this first conflict is made pleasurable—by the exercise of his newly discovered will in the name of love. This pleasurable self-restraint will make him independent of Sophie, who is only the fulfillment of what his ideal dictates to him. His is a personal aesthetic, a disinterested love of the beautiful and a sublimation of coarse lust. It is the denial of the Gyges' ring story as told by Glaucon in Plato's *Republic*, which supposedly teaches that there is no interest in morality when one is not seen by gods or men. Even when Emile's goddess Sophie does not see him, she can rely on her lover. Rousseau solves by love of women the problem Plato solved by love of wisdom, philo-Sophie in the place of philosophy.

During this part of the courtship Rousseau stops to reflect on jealousy (429–431), for when one is in love this dark passion is almost inevitably lurking in the wings. Rousseau wishes to avoid the ugly possessiveness and crimes that follow in its wake. Insisting on an exclusive right to the love of another is a tyrannical attempt to control what can never be controlled, natural inclination. Most often it is a form of *amour-propre*, directed not toward the beloved but toward those who aspire to the favor of the beloved. Jealousy is a sign not of true love of the beloved but of competition for primacy among males. All of this is commonplace in the modern criticism of the passion of jealousy. But jealousy contains a nobility and a caring that are usually absent in the critiques of it, which are used to excuse less loving as well as less concern for chastity. The self-sufficiency of the wise man or of the merely selfish one is inimical to love. Rousseau preserves in Emile a jealousy of self-doubt, with no concern for the aspiration of other suitors but only for his own worth. He fears that the highest tribunal of his worth, Sophie, will issue a negative verdict on him. Rousseau laments the loss of his pupil's precious independence in the same way he laments the loss of the innocence of the state of nature in more political writings. But here, as there, and even in a higher degree, he offers a compensation that surpasses the original state. The mutual and reciprocal love of the partners in marriage may not be as dependable as the selfishness of an individual, but it offers greater satisfactions, and freely chosen morality is a more wonderful thing than the mere impulsion of nature. In *The Social Contract* Rousseau says that man was born free but is everywhere in chains.[54] Here the chains are self-consciously and willingly forged, and they are covered with beautiful flowers.

The courtship is completed in two decisive episodes that show what Emile really is. First, Emile, filling out the time when he is not permitted to worship at the feet of his goddess and adorn her, works as a carpenter, the trade he learned in Book III. There he became self-sufficient in society where there is a division of labor. This trade is always necessary and does not depend on the opinions of others. It is presented here with a somewhat different twist, as a way of overcoming the prejudice of gentle folk who despise the necessary things and the practitioners of the crafts that procure them. Sophie and her mother come to watch Emile at work in the master's shop. The rich young nobleman acts as though he were the equal of the other workers and gets a pittance for his labor. What is more, he is not an amateur but appears to be one of the most competent workers. Sophie's mother, playing a role that has obviously been assigned to her by Jean-Jacques, seems to think that Emile is not very serious about this, that it is an aristocrat's condescending pose. In order to test him she invites him to come home with them, the thing he most desires to do. Here there is a clear conflict between desire and duty. But Emile regrets and is apologetic. Without hesitation he pleads his promise to the master who needs his work. Sophie even balks at the suggestion that the master be compensated for the loss that his departure would entail. You don't buy yourself out of commitments. This is the way money bursts the social bonds of equality. Thus Emile shows that he can bow as easily before his freely given commitments as he has always bowed to natural necessity. This is the way that the realm of freedom is established and becomes akin to that of law-governed nature. Sophie's mother seems to take offense at Emile's capriciousness, his lack of *politesse*, which gives Sophie the occasion to defend Emile and to affirm publicly that this lack is a part of Emile that makes him more lovable. Certainly a girl looking for a faithful husband would be reassured by such behavior (437–438).

Sophie demands among many other things that her suitor be punctual, neither early nor late. In the second decisive episode, she expects him one day and he does not show up, nor does he send word. It is not until early the next morning that she gets word that Emile and Jean-Jacques are all right and will be coming along soon. Her anxiety for their safety turns into a cold rage at the insult she has suffered at their hands. The crisis, after running its course of reproaches and explanations, is resolved when Jean-Jacques explains that they found a man with a broken leg in the forest, gave him first aid, and took him to his home, where his pregnant wife, shocked by her husband's accident, immediately went into labor and required their assistance. This is the way they spent the night and what made them unable to come or to give word. Emile concludes this account by adding: "Sophie, you are the arbiter of my fate. You know it well. You can make me die of pain. But do not hope to make me forget the rights of humanity. They are more sacred to me than yours. I will never give them up for you." To which Sophie responds, "Emile, take this hand. It is yours. Be my husband and master when you wish. I will try to merit this honor" (441).

Emile has won his fair maiden. Dedication to human rights has taken the place of the slaying of dragons or wicked knights as the deed that makes him irresistible to his beloved. To prefer the rights of humanity to her is to care more for what she herself cares for and is worth more than any preference for her, stemming from a taste that must necessarily be passing. If he had shirked his responsibility to the injured man and had run to Sophie, this would have been for his own satisfaction. He prefers Sophie to anyone but in a refined way that proves that he respects her rather than uses her. In this episode he displays his peak sentiments, his active compassion, which has become in him the dignity of man, expressed as the specifically human possibility of respecting all men and treating them as ends in themselves. His becoming Sophie's slave has been the way to his freedom as a social man. He is the slave of a woman who loves him because he is a man of principle, obeying his inner lights. He began as a being of mere sentiment or feeling. In his attachment to Sophie he became conscious of himself in the opinions of another. He now becomes self-conscious in obedience to the law he has given himself, which Sophie loves and hence validates. This kind of soul construction is an embryonic expression of Hegel's teaching about the development of man, from sentiment to consciousness to self-consciousness. Rousseau accomplishes this construction with a motor powered by sexual desire. The unity of the couple is made possible by the eroticization of man's capacity for universal, rational moral judgment, a capacity made practically effective by sublimated erotic energy.

XVI Jean-Jacques plays an apparently perverse joke on Emile. He enters Emile's room with a letter in his hand and says, "What would you do if you were informed that Sophie is dead" (442)? Emile angrily responds that he would never again see the man who informed him of it. Like the angry, irrational Cleopatra, he blames the messenger. This is, of course, human, all too human, attributing blame and the intention to harm to whatever is connected with depriving us of what we want. We see that Emile's resignation, his capacity to accept reality as it is, has been undermined by his love. His happiness now depends on fortune, which he must both worship and propitiate. If he did not love he would not behave in this way. This reminds us of the letter Brutus receives from Rome telling of his wife's death, to which he responds, like a true Stoic, that he is unmoved by it because he knew of its possibility. This stoic endurance is impressive to those who are witnesses, but Shakespeare has already let us see that Brutus is an imperfect Stoic and is really very moved. His imperfection and his attempts to hide it touch us because they seem to be human and make Brutus more like us.[55] But we find ourselves before the choice of being rational and apparently not caring, or caring and being irrational. In the latter case our happiness would depend only on fortune. As Rousseau later points out to Emile, even if Sophie were alive but had been unfaithful, his need for her would then make him indifferent to virtue and willing simply to abandon himself to whatever might ensure the possession of his fickle beloved. In spite of everything he is alienated from himself, and his happiness depends on her opinions and caprices.

The engraving that Rousseau commissioned for Book V represents Circe turning Ulysses' incontinent companions into pigs (356, 439). She accorded her favors to Ulysses, who was not tempted by her charms and remained a man. This illustrates the moral condition that Rousseau wants to encourage in Emile. The man who is constant and true to himself in good and bad fortune is the only one who fulfills the requirements of humanity. Emile, who unlike most men is not frightened of death, has only one vulnerable spot, his passion for Sophie. Jean-Jacques compares himself to Thetis, who dips Achilles in the Styx but fails to make him totally invulnerable because the heel she is holding remains out of the water, although it is clearly not Emile's heel that Jean-Jacques has failed to protect. The problem is summed up in Emile's inability to accept Sophie's death. Nature may have taught him to accept his own death with resignation, as do the brutes, thus avoiding Hobbes's insistence that men live in order to avoid death. But the lover who lives for the beloved cannot accept the beloved's death with resignation.

This is the moment of moral virtue when natural inclination no longer suffices for leading a good life (the natural man had no such attachments). Rousseau wants to combine the steadfastness of the natural man with the attachments of the civilized man, or the reasonable man with the passionate man. His analysis of the natural man living in society results in the recognition that such a man must be divided between desire and duty. This is, of course, admitted by everyone, but it has a special pathos for Rousseau, who has traced the source of man's misery to that dividedness and has promised an overcoming of it. He softens our disappointment by propounding a new way of understanding duty, one that comes from within, is noble, and satisfies the new longing to think well of oneself, rather than one that comes from outside, reflecting the merely accidental relation between nature and society. He invents a morality that is something more than a mere calculation of long-range interest and constructs in his pupil a will that is something more than a desire.

Emile must leave Sophie in order to experience what can happen if she were to leave or be taken from him. Jean-Jacques calls in his chit. The sole promise or contract that Emile has made, the long forgotten agreement that he will obey Jean-Jacques if Jean-Jacques is willing to help him through the dangers involved in his search for a wife, must now be honored (326). There have been moments during

his courtship when Emile was divided and sensed the tension between his desire for immediate satisfaction and his ideal of what
Sophie and he are. But that ideal did not involve an absolute obligation, and it remained on the level of sentiment or taste. Essentially,
Emile from the day of his birth up until this moment has done exactly
what he wanted to, whereas morality, at least as understood by
Rousseau, requires doing precisely what one does not want to do.
First Jean-Jacques shocks Emile with the suggestion that Sophie is
dead, and then orders him to leave her for a long time. This entire
scene is a dramatic recapitulation of the deepest sources of our
tradition. It is an explicit imitation of the *Iliad*, where Agamemnon
takes away Achilles' girl (Rousseau has just compared Emile to Achilles) and precipitates the great wrath that is the theme of the *Iliad* and
does so much harm to everyone. Plato, in the *Republic*, counter to the
popular taste, defends the ruler Agamemnon and accuses Achilles of
selfish self-righteousness.[56] Anger is one of the most important
themes of *Emile* and here Rousseau sides completely with Plato's
unorthodox treatment of anger, the tragic passion *par excellence*. Anger is a self-indulgence bespeaking an incapacity to accept what happens to our hostages to fortune—friends, beloveds, and family—a
wanting to make permanent what is changing, a passionate attempt
to give protection to what is our own. In the accents of indignation
it insists on justice where there is no justice. It is a much greater
threat than the mere selfishness of the desires because it clothes itself
in the appearance of morality (87). Emile begins with an Achillean
response, angry at the report of Sophie's death and angrier at the
suggestion that he must leave her. Jean-Jacques is the enemy who
wants to make him do something that he does not want to do. Emile
pleads the immorality of leaving her but the objective observer finds
his plea suspect because Emile's claim of morality is identical with his
most powerful desire, to possess Sophie here and now.

Emile's relation to Jean-Jacques also parallels that of Adam to
God in the Bible, the other fundamental source of our moral understanding. In both the *Iliad* and the Bible, the justice or the reasonableness of the ruler's commands, and hence the obligation of
the subject to obey, is the problem or the question. The modern
liberal tradition attempted to solve this problem by beginning with
the desires or the wishes of the subjects, but in order to do this had
to establish a lax or mercenary morality. Rousseau tried to establish
a high or noble morality but one that is easily understood and rationally accepted by those who obey it. Emile overcomes his anger

when Jean-Jacques reminds him of his obligation, of the promise of obedience he has made. He might have questioned the validity of his contract and the goodwill of his master. Instead he becomes docile and obeys.

We must analyze the psychology that makes this result possible in a being who is naturally motivated only by pleasure and pain. Rousseau, in his explanation to Emile, begins with the strangest imperative imaginable, "You must be happy" (442). This "thou shalt" is quite different from the Ten Commandments' "thou shalt nots." This commandment is identical with the desire of every human being and would seem to be self-enforcing. It is akin to Hobbes's imperative, "Thou shalt preserve thyself," but Rousseau, as opposed to the liberal teachers who spoke not of happiness but of the pursuit of whatever one conceives of as happiness, teaches that happiness has a known content. In this case it is clear that Emile must both love an ephemeral mortal and at the same time recognize that she can be lost. Only if he can combine mortality with the longing for immortality can he be happy. And this requires something more than nature provides us with. At this point Rousseau introduces his fateful distinction between the good man and the virtuous man. The good man is, essentially, the natural savage who lives according to his impulses. As long as he does not need other people, he will have no intention of harming them. His existence is sweet and effortless. Its social version was depicted by Rousseau at the end of Book IV, where he described how he himself would live if he had money. The virtuous man is involved with others and must, if he is not to be a hypocrite, make binding commitments with them, the fulfillment of which is more than a mere matter of taste. So for Emile, who is to be a husband and a father, there is no choice between goodness and morality (444). He must be moral. Rousseau presents an entirely new understanding of morality to Emile. Virtue, he tells him, is not the perfection of desire, but rather the overcoming of desire. Virtue *is* strength, the strength, to put it paradoxically, to want to do what one does not want to do. Where do we get the strength to look at the persons and things we love most and at the same time to be aware of and unmoved by their vulnerability? The incapacity to face the mortality of those we love is partially explained by the weakness of modern man, attributed by Rousseau to the conflict between nature and society. Because of this conflict men do not know what they want and waste their energy in all directions. Rousseau has already told us that Emile, the vigor and unity of whose desires have been carefully preserved, could crush his contemporaries like insects. He has the primitive strength of soul that pursues its goals without conflict. How does he turn this strength against the desires from which it stems?

Emile's moral doubling of himself is made possible by his romantic ideal, which provides him with a counterpoise to his desires. If, after the fashion of the natural man, Emile had merely slaked his sexual lusts by a casual encounter with Sophie, he would have no conflict and no need of virtue. But his sublimation of that desire, which we have witnessed in reading Rousseau's book, requires an image of what he is and what she is, as well as the ground on which they can meet and become one. This idea, fueled by the natural desires and refined by sublimation, permits Emile to command himself rather than to receive his commands from outside. His ideal, the product of imagination and *amour-propre*, gives him an attachment to morality that allows him to get a distance on and conquer his immediate interests. The formation of the ideal, which has been the work of Emile's postpuberty existence, is the origin of will in a soul for which will is not natural. Desire refined is able to project a polar star and at the same time to give man the strength to follow it. To use Nietzschean language, the strong soul becomes both the taut bow which can reach the ideal, and the arrow which has lofted that ideal. This is the highest reach of freedom and the culmination of sublimation.

The ideal of reciprocal love, in which the beautiful soul emerges out of the attraction to beautiful bodies, acts as a self-generated substitute for the laws of nature for civilized and potentially free man, for whose guidance nature provides no law. Out of *amour-propre*, mediated by the desire for the love of a worthy partner, emerges the desire for self-respect. This *constructed* soul and the attachment to another reveal themselves to be extremely fragile, sublime but more dependent on the tutor's manipulations than on nature. The most surprising aspect of Rousseau's teaching is that although the lover recognizes the necessarily ephemeral and vulnerable character of what he loves, he does not turn his love toward the permanent or eternal things, as does the religious man or the philosopher. It is a mystery how a man or a woman can give him- or herself totally to a mortal beloved and at the same time be fully conscious that there is no eternity here and that the beloved is certain to be lost. This attachment to a single human being flatters our desires because very few of us can love God or the Ideas as we love another human being. But it demands of us an ungrounded attachment to the ideal, which is somehow understood as both identical to the one beloved and at the same time transcending him or her. Rousseau tells Emile that "You have enjoyed more from hope than you will ever enjoy in reality. Imagination adorns what one desires but abandons it when it is in one's possession. Except for the single Being existing by itself, there is nothing beautiful except that which is not" (447). Imagination, the medium of romantic poetry, provides the lover's substitute for the real, eternal, and transcendent world of the earlier thinkers. Rousseau asks Emile to live without illusion while under the spell of illusory charms. Such is human love between two persons who believe they want to cleave to each other exclusively.

For Rousseau love is the love between man and woman and must be reciprocal. It must be between man and woman because its source, however distant, is in the crude natural teleology of the body, and Romantic literature has no suitable place for anything other than the attachment of man and woman. There are no Davids and Jonathans properly in it. It must be reciprocal if these two, this couple, are to be faithful to each other. In Rousseau, as I have already mentioned, there is no hint of another aspect of love, prized by the ancients, in which one loves the lovable without expectation that the lovable will or can reciprocate. Love was understood by them to be an uneasy composite of two elements, the longing for the beautiful and the longing to possess one's beloved for oneself. The latter can be the basis of a marriage; the former cannot be. Rousseau has tried to stretch sexual frenzy up the ladder from its bodily source to the moral heights, but he has to admit finally to Emile that over the long run, frenzy cannot endure and principle must fill in for the waning passion. Habit and easy commerce with a woman for whom Emile once had an uncontrollable passion, the love of children, and obedience to the law he has given himself will have to take the place of the raging fire that Jean-Jacques has stoked in Emile and that originally accomplished everything without supplement.

The character of this romantic stoicism Rousseau proposes can be seen in a little, incomplete story, *Emile and Sophie*,[57] which he left among his unpublished papers. It would, of course, be wrong to take this text as authoritative, for who knows what Rousseau intended with it. It may very well be just a game or fantasy he played with one afternoon. However, in it Emile remains true to the education he has been given, especially in this last important scene of *Emile* where he discovers the will and learns that what begins as his master's will becomes his own will. Emile in this story discovers that Sophie has been unfaithful. This is a devastating blow, but he remains faithful to the ideal of what Sophie should be and gains his strength from that. In his head the ideal is separable from the person who incarnated it. He could have forgiven her and had her back, but he rejects this alternative. But he does so not because he is angry with her and revenging himself, as one would expect, but out of delicacy for Sophie. She would always think that he was remembering what she had done to him and that he remained with her out of condescension rather than admiration. He might indeed relearn to respect her, but she could never respect herself as he respects himself. Emile lives faithful to the idea of Sophie, and does not make himself dependent on the fickle real Sophie. Fortune even makes him a galley slave, but he is not broken and, like Epictetus, considers himself free and happy in his slavery because his satisfaction depends only on himself. As I just said, this is all very mysterious, and one can understand why Kant, who begins from Rousseau's analysis, ends up by saying that happiness is not the goal of the moral man. Rousseau makes morality, at least for Emile, emerge out of love, and he makes us hope that the happiness depending on the senses and the possession of the beloved will coincide with morality.

| XVII | So Emile must leave Sophie, but with the assurance that he will return and claim her. This separation is not only for the sake of teaching Emile a salutary freedom that can be exercised in his bondage to Sophie, just as the Emile in *Emile and Sophie* remains faithful to Sophie when they are no longer together. The time of separation is also to be used for travel, in order to learn about politics (450–471). Politics is central because connected with it is the law, which deserves respect and can punish those who disobey it. The independent man is cosmopolitan and can leave the places where laws impede his happiness or make unjust demands upon him. But a married man must find a permanent abode. His attachment to family makes him dependent on politics but also wary of it. And in this passage on travel Rousseau reveals what might be called a conservative side. He presents a résumé of *The Social Contract*, that fiery book which provoked and guided revolutions, and apparently delegitimized all regimes except the one described in it. But Rousseau uses it here to teach Emile not to expect perfect justice in any real nation where he is likely to live, not to cast himself against the rocks of injustice inherent in every regime, and to contain his idealism if he doesn't want to be destroyed. Emile learns that even unjust laws contain elements of justice or aspirations to justice and that he can respect them for this. His passion and idealism will be turned

toward his family, and he will look for a place to live that allows him enough independence to provide happiness for it. Rousseau never argues that there is a right to privacy, but he gives a serious reason for it, the need to leave space for the practice of virtue in regimes that are not dedicated to it. Thus Emile's attachment to his country, to an unsatisfactory political order will be prudential, the consequence of his love of Sophie and his children. Emile will be willing to obey most laws of which he does not approve, because they are necessary to some kind of civic order. He will do so out of his own righteousness and not that of the laws. *Emile* stands halfway between the moral citizen of *The Social Contract* and the solitary of the *Reveries of the Solitary Walker*.

After his two-year voyage, at the age of twenty-four, still a virgin, Emile returns, eager to take possession of his bride. Now they are joined in sacred—sacralized by Rousseau's teaching—matrimony. But Emile and Sophie are still not entirely free of Jean-Jacques, the meddling supplement to nature. After the wedding he persuades Sophie that she should not always give in to Emile's bodily demands on her. Sophie does not particularly like this counsel, and Emile likes it even less. But these refusals give Sophie tools with which to maintain Emile's passion long enough for his inevitable cooling to be the diminishing of his desires *tout court* rather than the diminishing of his desires for her (475–477). Again mere nature does not suffice for married love.

Now the couple is joined, and there is a new beginning for human beings as they emerge from Jean-Jacques' Garden of Eden, cleansed of the stain of original sin. A great philosopher, legislator, and teacher is necessary to unify nature and civilization, but once that has been accomplished, we can hope that equal and ordinary human beings will be able to keep the wheel rolling. This is the ideal suggestion of *Emile*, and at the very end we learn that Sophie is with child. But who is that we see coming over the horizon? None other than Jean-Jacques. They will never be quite rid of him, for they still need his assistance in rearing their children.

LA NOUVELLE HÉLOÏSE

I   We cannot leave Rousseau and move on to the great Romantic novels without at least a few words about *Julie, or La Nouvelle Héloïse*, a book that almost no one reads anymore except when they have to. Although it appears now to be a bore and a pain, it was one of the most popular books ever written and took the whole of Europe by storm. One must never forget, although it is hardly credible today, that practically everything Rousseau wrote had an overwhelming popularity and incalculably far-ranging effects. Not only his ideas, but also the literary forms he invented, were triumphant, and none more so than his novel. There were, of course, important and popular novels prior to Rousseau—Cervantes' *Don Quixote*, Defoe's *Robinson Crusoe*, and especially Richardson's *Clarissa*. But Rousseau transformed the character of the novel and gave it the first place in the rank order of literary forms, particularly displacing the dramatic theater. Rousseau made a powerful critique of both the content of modern drama and the institution of the theater.[58] The great Greek playwrights produced believable and edifying personages. They celebrated demigods and heroes who were the founders of their cities and connected with their religions. He argued that dramatic heroes are no longer believable or interesting to modern men and women, who are equal and essentially private. Nor did Rousseau regard it as simply desirable that such heroes be believable, inasmuch as he wished to encourage a humanity and a virtue accessible to all persons. The traditional literary figures of tragedy take us out of ourselves and alienate us from a heroic model that we cannot attain. In addition, theaters are purveyors of corruption in modern times. They are places for display of wealth and all the vanities that flourish along with it. The celebrated actors and actresses are almost always persons of loose morals, and their celebrity provides bad examples.

The novel, on the other hand, is available without any of this apparatus and is perfectly suited for showing characters who are neither above nor beneath us. The failed dramatist turned himself into the most successful of novelists. His choice of the novel was founded on a comprehensive reflection about the nature of the modern audience and the themes appropriate to it as well as about what would please it. Novels are easily accessible, capable of being read whenever the reader has a bit of freedom, without the formal constraints of verse, and in a sense formless, that is, able to mix philosophic, moral, and political reflection with sentimental interest. It suits the life and the taste of the bourgeois, for, as we have seen, Rousseau believed that the religious and political passions had cooled and that the appeal to love and the intimate interiors of individuals and families was all that remained.

The novel, at least as written by Rousseau, needs no charming evil characters, no real tragedy, but only more or less decent men and women who struggle with the human condition as it is experienced by most people. The drama is essentially aristocratic, the novel essentially democratic. There is little doubt that Rousseau's analysis was correct, at least insofar as it concerns the success of his enterprise. The novel displaced the drama and the epic poem in the affections of modern consumers of fiction. The triumphant bourgeoisie produced a new kind of reader, less educated, less versed in classical literature, and desirous of all kinds of instruction about how to live up to his new eminence in society. Not only did the novelist become an instructor in the human passions and tastes, but he even descended into the most minute details of how proper people should dress and eat and furnish their homes. Such things were of much more immediacy to the new readers than what they might find in Plutarch or the Bible, not to speak of the tragedies of Rousseau's antagonist, Voltaire.[59]

| II | Rousseau always insisted that art must please, whereas sermons do not have to. It is for this reason that sermons are rarely effective. Even if you wish to improve people, you have to begin by flattering their dominant passion. *La Nouvelle Héloïse*, which consists of letters to and from members of a small band of friends and lovers, contains a whole host of Rousseauan sermons that are palatable because they are sweetened by the dominant love theme of the book. One can find in *La Nouvelle Héloïse* the résumés of all of Rousseau's great teachings—the state of nature and the progress toward civilization from *The Discourse on the Origin and Foundations of Inequality*, the principles of politics from *The Social Contract*, the sound education from *Emile*, and so on. Rousseau introduced the didactic rage into literature. Of course Homer and Shakespeare were teachers of their audiences, but modern novelists have been teachers in a manner and to a degree far greater than anything that preceded them. For a long time novelists provided opinions about all kinds of things for their untutored readers, who did not have the time or the learning to judge for themselves and who lived in a world where traditions were being destroyed without anything taking their place. Even today, if one scratches the most cynical novelist, one finds an edifier beneath the surface. William Burroughs, who likes to present himself as a nihilistic enemy of the good, the true, and the beautiful, says that people ought to know about the things he tells them. The

didacticism of the novel constitutes a large part of its charm as well as of its rebarbative character. *La Nouvelle Héloïse* presents all of these traits with a vengeance. One can understand Burke's revulsion at the lack of aristocratic delicacy in Rousseau when one finds a letter from Julie to her lover, Saint-Preux, counseling him to go to a prostitute rather than to masturbate if he absolutely must have satisfaction. There are nauseatingly sentimental letters about the simple goodness of the people, but this entire collection of letters contains models of civilized discourse about the problems of life while telling a fascinating story of how men and women can care for one another within the contradictions of civilized life.

Unfortunately, much of what is innovative in Rousseau's novel has become so banal for us that we can hardly see how well he does it. The letters are suffused with a sexual passion of which the personages are often unaware. The entire book is fueled by frustrated sex that the principals strive valiantly to forget. Their discussions of politics, poetry, landscape, and even God go back to the great erotic mother-source. They give a noble interpretation to life but are brought down by a reality that contradicts the illusions about love and duty. Rousseau can appear to be a lachrymose sentimentalist as he peeps through the pages of the novel, but there is a fine irony at the lack of self-knowledge of his characters.

The action of the novel takes place in Switzerland, one of the last outposts of virtue within corrupt modernity. The scene is domestic and rustic, far from the cities and politics as it is actually practiced. The personages of the novel construct a healthy and tasteful life for themselves, pretty much independent from the rest of the world. They furnish the gorgeous scenery around Lake Leman with the fantasies to which their passions give birth, stormy or calm, dark or sunny, wintry or summery, despairing or content. In this setting their beings are expansive to the furthest horizon. Here Rousseau sets the story that replaces the great medieval romance of Abelard and Héloïse, which ended so badly because of the conflict between religion and the passions of the two lovers. In reading *La Nouvelle Héloïse* one must always remember the problem of original sin and Rousseau's special perspective on it.

The new Héloïse is Julie d'Etange, an intelligent and lovely Swiss bourgeois. Her teacher, Saint-Preux, falls in love with her and seduces her. She truly reciprocates his love, and this love endures, in spite of her wishes to the contrary, until her death. She is eighteen when the story begins, he twenty-three, and she dies in her early thirties. The teacher, who is supposed to be dedicated to his learning and to conveying a part of it to his pupil, is actually motivated by an erotic passion for his attractive charge. The dangerous motives of teachers, about which Rousseau warns his readers so often, are in play here. This romantic young man is an enemy of duty and despises the laws of hospitality in corrupting the daughter of the family that has welcomed and paid him. He is high-minded, which means he deceives himself in the beginning about why he enjoys his teaching, and in the end about the sublime character of his erotic passion, which he is unable to overcome. Thus he is at war, and puts his Julie at war, with the rules of society and especially with the respect and obedience she owes to her father. Rousseau paints this passion and the crimes that follow from it most sympathetically because he knows that he himself would almost certainly behave the same in similar circumstances. Rousseau is always hardheaded about the real motives of people. Teachers, like everyone else, have to have sufficient motives for undertaking their austere functions. And these motives come down pretty much to money or sex. Money is the safer of the two, but not necessarily the one that best energizes the teacher's soul. One cannot help but be reminded of the greatest of all teachers, Socrates, who claims that the only art he possesses is the erotic art. Saint-Preux, at least, has a sufficient motive for his concern, in contrast to Jean-Jacques in his relation to Emile, where the motive remains mysterious. The great legislators of nations have as their motive eternal glory; but this is not psychologically or morally unproblematic, nor is it more in conformity with the nature of things than is the passion of the lover.

Saint-Preux is the archetype of the Romantic hero with his stormy passions and his wild alternations between despair and exultation, at war with society, but not wickedly or cynically like Valmont in *Les Liaisons dangereuses*. He interprets himself, his beloved, and the passion that unites them, nobly. That passion is once and for all, and the few sexual experiences he has with Julie at the beginning of their romance are all that he has for his whole life. The Romantic hero is no Don Juan. Readers cannot help but hope for the lifelong fulfillment of the love between these two charming youngsters. Moreover, these readers are, to say the least, unsympathetic to the prejudiced father, who apparently ruins the affair and the lives of both. One can see why Rousseau begins by saying that any young girl who reads his novel will be corrupted, meaning that respect for the father and the law will give way to the charms of the untrammeled love between two free persons indifferent to the claims of society on them. But Rousseau goes on to say that once she has begun the novel she must continue and finish it, because it offers a corrective to her already corrupt motives. The novel replicates the movement from natural innocence through corruption to virtue, which is the best hope of the historical process.

Julie is horrified by her situation, which has deprived her of her modesty and, especially, of her sincerity, particularly with her parents. But she hopes to right it all by persuading her father, an old soldier who is away doing his duty, to give her to Saint-Preux. This would mean that natural and conventional rights would almost coincide, but only almost, for what society insists should be the last act has come first. A certain myth or self-deception will be necessary for the partners, if only because they will not want their own children to imitate them. But none of this is to be, because her father opposes the marriage violently, even though Julie has recruited her mother and her friend Claire to her conspiracy (for, however benign, it is a conspiracy and a deception). His reasons, which Rousseau's own teaching in the *Emile* opposes and attempts to reform, seem to us to be both stupid and vicious. The young man is not of their social class and he is poor. He possesses none of the kinds of things that attract narrow-minded fathers. Her father is indignant that the tutor who was welcomed into his home should court his daughter and seems to be shocked that such a person thinks he has the right to feel bodily attraction toward his treasure; moreover, her father has promised her to M. de Wolmar, a soldier friend who saved his life. Thus, Julie's father is a résumé of all the worst elements of what today would be called patriarchy: being concerned with property and station rather than love, and arrogating the right to mate one's daughter like a chattel slave. These are all remnants of the old order and should be replaced by the democratic family, where questions of the suitability of partners are matters of prudence, not command, where the inclination of the partners for each other has the highest place in the decision, and the woman has the right to accept or refuse her suitors. And if one reads *La Nouvelle Héloïse* from this angle, one can see it as another literary appeal for reforms of the kind one finds in Ibsen or Zola, reforms now established and hence no longer of compelling interest. As such, *La Nouvelle Héloïse* would be as dead as *Hedda Gabler*. A modern reader would say that if the lovers had been able to ignore or suppress this father, they would have lived happily ever after.

But it is not so simple as that for Rousseau. There is something problematic about the sensual love of Julie and Saint-Preux, and her father doesn't turn out to be such a bad sort after all. This is indicated when, immediately after the letter in which Saint-Preux writes Julie most openly about the sexual pleasures they have enjoyed together (as well as about the hour after the act, which is, according to both him and Rousseau, better than the act itself), there is a letter warning Julie that the story of her love is becoming known. An English lord, Edouard Bomston, who is also interested in Julie and is rebuffed by her, makes a drunken remark alluding to her preference for Saint-Preux, at which the latter takes offense. A duel is requested and about to be arranged. Calumny would make it impossible to keep the cause of the duel secret, and Julie's reputation would be ruined.[60] Adroit damage control by Sophie's friend Claire prevents the duel, and, of course, this leads to letters of many pages detailing Rousseau's views about the practice of dueling and about honor in general. We remember that reputation is important for a woman as it is not for a man. In this men are closer to nature. Thus, the impulsive love of the couple necessarily comes into conflict with social correctness. Saint-Preux, when he recognizes the threat to Julie's good reputation, is willing to renounce his intention to duel, but the burden of maintaining appearances is primarily Julie's. The woman bears within her the conflict between nature and society and the necessity of conciliating the two, required for the happiness of evolved human beings. Saint-Preux's passion is not coarsely sensual. It is stuffed with ideal imagination and respect for virtue, but it is essentially indifferent to opinion and convention. These he neglects and despises and he is willing to confront every obstacle and live alone somewhere with his beloved. This is the Romantic posture that defines itself over against the bourgeois who sacrifices nature to petty concern for reputation. But Julie, although she gives way to her passions, is a bridge between nature and convention. Saint-Preux has no parents of whom one hears, but Julie can be happy only when there is no scandal around her, and more important, when she has the approval of her parents. She is more than just ashamed of her illicit love; she knows that nature and civilization, opposed in principle, must be united if a woman is to live in society and raise children who are to live in it. She knows that society's concern for good morals is not just hypocrisy. The tragedy, if tragedy is the proper word, stems from her failure to unite the two in spite of heroic efforts and sacrifices. The woman is the centerpiece of society and this is why the novel is named *Julie, or La Nouvelle Héloïse*. She is by far the most important person in it. Women have the difficult role and when they play it badly Rousseau is contemptuous; when they play it well, nothing exceeds Rousseau's admiration.

The story of the duel leads inevitably, according to the conventions of Romanticism established by Rousseau in this novel, to Lord Edouard's becoming Saint-Preux's best friend. There are no evil persons in this book, only more or less enlightened or virtuous ones. The charm or the temptation of vice is absent, and Rousseau regards this as the superiority of the novel over tragedy. One might say that for him the interesting struggle is between natural goodness and the need, born of history, for virtue, as discussed by Jean-Jacques in his sermon to Emile. Different capacities, intellectual, moral, and bodily, and different approaches to resolving the problem of man's dividedness, tell the tale. Lord Edouard, as soon as he recognizes the gravity of the situation, apologizes and tries actively to make amends. He is a moody Englishman who thinks himself a philosopher, but his reason is a handmaid of his humors. This sage is involved with two women at the same time, a titled adulteress and a reformed prostitute, and finally decides to marry the prostitute, who instead becomes a nun. Throughout this book he is asking for advice and even wants to introduce the prostitute to Julie, which leads again inevitably to endless discussion about the duties of natural humanity versus social correctness.

Parenthetically, the attachment between Edouard and Saint-Preux raises the whole question of friendship in Rousseau and Romanticism altogether. The primary attachments and the central roles in the novel are always assigned to the lovers, who are driven, however ideally, by sexual desire. There is no way that friendship could be considered, as it is by Aristotle, to be the highest relationship, transcending ties of blood or bodily attraction. Rousseau said in *Emile* that as soon as puberty and sexual awareness arise, the need for friendship is born. One must have a friend with whom to discuss one's mistress. This hardly seems to do justice to the phenomenon of friendship, but the rule is strictly followed in *La Nouvelle Héloïse*. Both Julie and Saint-Preux have a friend whose love life is either puny or botched and who devotes his or her best energy to helping and healing the two wounded lovers. Friendship, then, appears as a secondary offshoot of the original sexual passion. Rousseau's materialism offers no other ground for friendship. For Aristotle, the exchange of speeches, *logoi*, is the ground of friendship and, at the same time, grows out of man's *natural* spirituality, which is reason. But for Rousseau all meaningful speeches refer back to ultimately bodily sentiments or feelings. Friendship must, therefore, be derivative, however noble it may be. Romanticism has room only for the couple made up of man and woman, which is constructed out of the material elements of their respective natures. This is the source of the enduring modern problem of explaining friendship, and perhaps even of practicing it.

Lord Edouard, in his remorse, tries to make amends by approaching Julie's father to recommend his newfound friend as a husband for Julie, and offers to use a part of his fortune to make Saint-Preux the richest man in the Vaud. His proposition is indignantly rejected by Julie's father, who swears that the insolent upstart will never have the hand of his daughter, who is the last remnant of a noble and distinguished family. Moreover, he falls back on his promise to give his daughter's hand to his friend. Thus begins the fatal separation between Julie and Saint-Preux, which makes it impossible for them ever again to fulfill their desires, although those desires remain intact throughout their lives. Julie eventually marries someone else, but it appears that Saint-Preux has only this single sexual notch in his belt to sustain him throughout his life. Everything afterward is played out on the scaffolding of sexual frustration and is excruciating for a contemporary reader. The singularity and permanence of the love object, even when all hope of satisfaction is lost, is a hallmark of the Romantic hero. Even the apparently cynical Stendhal asserts that this provides an intensity and depth of experience totally unknown to the Don Juan.[61] This is Rousseau's legacy to gallant Europe. A Werther-like obsession is the privileged experience of love. It is accompanied by ecstatic alternations between hope and despair. It ends in the contemplation of suicide, which in *La Nouvelle Héloïse* leads to more lengthy discussions, this time about the legitimacy of suicide. This is the overheated world of romantic attachment that so affected everyone's expectations until only yesterday.

Not only does the comically good-hearted Edouard intrude for the purpose of trying to arrange the marriage that would have satisfied nature and convention, but this philosopher who does not know himself also offers the romantic solution of an elopement. With the protection of their noble host, Julie and Saint-Preux would give up everything and feast themselves on each other for a whole life in the English countryside. This would fulfill the romantic aspirations of Saint-Preux, who has no attachments, no family, and whose real name we don't even know. But Julie rejects this alternative, although not without difficulty. Her loyalty to her parents poses an insuperable barrier. This is not merely conventionalism, but a part of her woman's soul, which is incomprehensible to Saint-Preux. The first stage of the separation of these two lovers is understood to be only temporary, until her father can be persuaded. Then, when he appears to be intransigent, the separation is understood to be much longer and even, perhaps, to be without end. But they console themselves by their endless love. They will always be lovers, which in their eyes, if not Rousseau's, is second best to being together, but still a kind of fulfillment in itself. Julie tells Saint-Preux that although she must accept her father's refusal to let her marry him, she will herself refuse anyone else. The final stage comes when she renounces her love of Saint-Preux and insists that he must do likewise.

This last results from the peripeties in her relations with her mother and her father. When Saint-Preux leaves, Julie is pregnant. Not only is she his natural bride, which sets her outside the law, but she is going to be the mother of his natural child, which also puts their child outside the law. Therefore her romantic passion has consequences for another which that other will not have taken responsibility for or had the freedom to choose or reject. She obviously cannot tell her father, who would not complacently accept his daughter's loss of what was once called honor. And more important, she is concerned with hurting him, and she feels that she ought not to tell Saint-Preux, who, aware of her condition, might commit imprudences not only for Julie but for himself. The presence within her of this new being heightens every aspect of the conflict she faces. Only her friend Claire is her confidante. There is almost no way that these conflicts generated by her love can avoid destroying her if her pregnancy becomes visible. She will lose her father, her reputation, and almost certainly her lover. But a terrible scene between her and her father saves her from these consequences while leaving her with her awareness of her criminal situation. In the quarrel that ensues after Lord Edouard's proxy proposal, her father, wrongly deeming himself to be insulted by Julie, strikes her. She falls, and has a miscarriage. This is an immediate solution but one that leaves a terrible trace in her soul. After this she lives at home as an alien, behaving like an obedient daughter while deceiving her father by keeping up the correspondence with Saint-Preux, full of inner rebellion in this world of unjust authority.

She is in contradiction with the world but does not feel herself guilty because she is persuaded of the natural right belonging to true lovers. Guilt intervenes and delegitimizes love when her mother discovers the letters, the very letters that Rousseau has reproduced for us. Her mother, who has a weak constitution and is not well, is distraught by the discovery and torn between her husband and her daughter. Apparently as a consequence of this discovery, she dies, and Julie believes herself to be responsible. This is not original sin, but it is sin, taking away all the good conscience of love. Love now appears to be only an illusion or, rather, a diabolical delusion that tempts its victims to disobedience. Julie's disobedience is not like Eve's, which we know to be sinful revolt against God, but is a necessary outcome of the conflict between nature and convention, goodness and morality.

With the death of her mother, Julie's father learns of the letters and all that has happened between them. He wants to duel Saint-Preux and insists that he relieve Julie of her promise not to marry anyone else. Saint-Preux, contemptuous of him but in love with Julie, renounces his right for her sake. Her guilt and her duty make it impossible for them to maintain their relations. And, finally, she agrees to marry her father's friend. This strong but compassionate girl is able to resist her father's anger but not his tears.

Saint-Preux, although his loss is very great and a happy life is denied him because of his passion, does not have to bear the fateful consequences of that love. He is frustrated but never has to suffer the doubts, the guilt, or the loss of his parents. He is free to love as he pleases. Julie is not. To Rousseau, this is what makes women more interesting than men and the keystones of the social order. He is touched by Julie, pities her, but is not overly hopeful that any reform would entirely solve her problems.

She is momentarily helped by a religious experience. She goes to the altar to marry M. de Wolmar with death in her heart. She loves Saint-Preux and has all the encouragement of nature's superior authority. She is not a hypocrite and wonders how she can swear vows to a man who not only is not loved by her but has a rival in her affections. But once in the church, in the face of its mysteries and impressive ritual, she undergoes a reformation. She suddenly comes to believe that virtue is superior to all inclination and that love of order is superior to love of a man. At that moment she hopes and expects that the overcoming of the opposition between love and duty by the love of duty can make her happy. She declares that her love of Saint-Preux is dead, although their friendship, their respect for each other's virtues, can overcome the newly demonized pleasures of the flesh. Julie is now Mme. de Wolmar in deed as well as name. She is therefore no longer an appropriate object of attraction for any other man. Religion, she believes, teaches the Romantic credo: the marriage contract is the most sacred of all commands and the foundation of decent society. Poor Saint-Preux sets out on the disappointed Romantic's tour of the world, learning the ways of men and nations, but without any expectation of finding any happiness among them.

Julie's account of her religious experience clearly is, to use modern lingo, a rationalization. Rousseau beautifully depicts it as such. Julie is ripped apart by conflict and seeks some kind of peace. She feels guilty about her mother's death and her disobedience to her father. Awareness of the tension between sexual desire and virtue is now added to her old sense of the tension between natural love and public opinion. A harsh rationalist critic would say that her succumbing to the religious charms and the promise of happiness in another life is just an illusory easy way out. The difference between Rousseau and the somewhat sophisticated contemporary who has some acquaintance with Freud is that the latter tends to see the underlying sexual frustration or repression as the reality and to translate the experiences of religion, art, politics, and morals back into the original natural language of sexual satisfaction. "I am obsessed by X, and if I had a healthy sex life, I could rid myself of this obsession and the conflicts that paralyze me." Rousseau, on the other hand, does not give his personages these cheap explanations, and they take the world of their imaginations with utmost seriousness. They are unaware of their unconscious motives, although Rousseau himself smiles with noble irony at their lack of self-knowledge. However, the fundamental conflicts and the grandeur of souls in confronting them are what give meaning and seriousness to life. I believe most contemporaries would think that Julie should have accepted Lord Edouard's solution or some equivalent of it. Rousseau teaches that her rejection of it is her glory. Somehow, in the time between Rousseau and today the sexual teaching has reduced the composite psychological experiences to their crude elements, depriving the moral world and the novel, which describes it, of their compelling interest. Rousseau is still able to present a beautiful and noble world, with all its original contours, to consciousness. He treats the unconscious as though it were a quarry from which the imagination mines the stones for the creation of beautiful statues, whereas we tend to dissolve the imagination's products back into their primal matter once we have discovered the code for doing so. Rousseau cannot be absolved of responsibility for this development because he assigned so central a role to imagination unsupported by reality. He, of course, did so because he was persuaded that in fact imagination has no such foundation in reality for its creations, and he wanted to give human freedom a wholly new and more expansive meaning. He did succeed in doing this for the Romantic movement with its extraordinary flowering in literature, painting, and music. Our views are very much shaped by Rousseau's hopes and their later disappointment.

Rousseau's presentation, as I have frequently noted, is full of what one might qualify as tiresome sermonizing or misplaced philosophic prattle, but as one gains familiarity with this book it becomes evident that Rousseau has not sacrificed literature to edification. These discourses, although substantial in themselves, are always subtly knitted with the personalities of the individuals who write them and reveal their characters. There is most often an element of self-deception that hides behind the appearance of reason, and this delicately heightens our perceptions of the personages and what sort of discourse is appropriate to them. These letters help us to understand the subtle interplay between speech and deed and the specifically human necessity to have speeches to explain one's deeds, a necessity neglected in our times when speeches are understood to be only rationalizations.

The first three books of *La Nouvelle Héloïse* are devoted to the first love between teacher and pupil and the failure of their hopes. The last three books take place six years later, when we are introduced into the home of Mme. de Wolmar and are able to see for ourselves and judge the quality and success of her domestic life. This later half of *La Nouvelle Héloïse* is presided over by the interesting figure of M. de Wolmar. He is a reasonable man of irreproachable virtue, above the snares and temptations of the passions. He is about twenty-five years older than Julie and knows that he cannot hope to be the object of her intense erotic sentiments. He sets up a tasteful and civilized household full of refined pleasures in a society consisting of his wife, their children (for Julie is now a devoted mother), select and worthy friends, servants, and neighbors, including peasants or farmers. Wolmar claims that his only love is the love of order, which he arranges where nature does not suffice, that is, in the realm of human freedom and passion. He is godlike, performing the same function in the household as does the Savoyard Vicar's God in the universe. He apparently has no illusions and is a mere spectator of life's peripeties. His strong character is the foundation on which everything and everyone in the household rests.

These three books of *La Nouvelle Héloïse* give a representation of a healthy and satisfying life within bourgeois society and can even be used as an instruction manual for the bourgeois aspiring to happiness. But this representation is mixed with the complex motives and relationships of the three principals who constitute this system and make it work. I say three principals because, as one would expect, Saint-Preux is back from his travels and is incorporated into the Wolmars' life, thus constituting one of those *ménages à trois* that fascinate Rousseau and with which he was himself involved more than once.

This arrangement is due to Wolmar, who seems to find the life of a couple in need of a supplement. He undertakes to convert the love between Saint-Preux and Julie (for whom it is putatively dead) into friendship. He may very well suspect that Julie too is not entirely his in spite of her protestations and convictions to the contrary. Wolmar trusts, or at least appears to trust, Saint-Preux's virtue and therefore his respect for the marriage ties. There is now a continual chorus by all the parties to this arrangement that such ties are profounder and more satisfying than the erotic ones. The introduction of Saint-Preux has profound consequences for everyone. Julie has informed Wolmar, when she hears of Saint-Preux's return, of the full extent of her relationship with him, but Wolmar is not surprised, either because of his rationalist's imperturbability or because his clear eye had already penetrated the secret long before. He does not react with jealousy and does not feel threatened. He does justify his marrying through the constraint of paternal authority a reluctant woman who is much younger than he is and in love with another man by arguing that this love was flawed and could not produce the happiness it promised. But both Julie and he need something of the remains of that relationship to flesh out their own. Wolmar is fully aware of the ambiguity of motives but takes risks because he can put order into the passions. The question is whether love, with its bodily erotic component, can be converted into friendship, which has no such component, or whether Wolmar believes that the conviction without the reality of such a conversion is sufficient.

Wolmar's project is, after testing Saint-Preux's virtue, to make him the teacher of his children, as he was once the teacher of his wife and her confidante, Claire. Rousseau gives an example of what he means by a friend when he speaks of the impossibility of a father's passing on his duty to educate his children to another, unless the other is a friend.[62] And where to find one? Wolmar makes a friend and provides him with sufficient reasons for caring for another man's children. Wolmar explains his own reasons for not fulfilling his responsibility as a father. He is old and will not likely be able to complete the job. And he hints that there is another reason which would cause his wife to prefer that somebody else other than himself be charged with the education of their children. This he leaves shrouded in mystery for the time being. It will be revealed in its proper place.

So there they are, living this domestic life, dealing with the everyday problems, content with one another, and full of admiration for the orderly existence that Wolmar has imposed on them. Saint-Preux is confronted with a moment of temptation when he and Julie go boating on Lake Leman, that magnificent stage setting with its variety of visages corresponding to every sentiment of those who are near it. A storm occurs, Saint-Preux and Julie are in danger, he saves her, and they are forced into close bodily contact. All the old passions emerge in him in this dangerous proximity. He tells the story, so we cannot know exactly what she felt, but he indicates that she was not exactly indifferent. He describes the experience as being for him akin to the one that Julie had at her wedding. He emerges from it with declamations about the superiority of virtuous friendship to their earlier love alliance. One should remember that Saint-Preux remains in his celibate condition and therefore recognize what all of this must be costing him.

Julie, perhaps mindful of the danger that was so explicitly presented by their trip, attempts, in the spirit of arranging everybody else's life that seems to dominate here and in *Emile*, to arrange a marriage between Saint-Preux and her friend Claire, whose husband has conveniently died. Claire and Saint-Preux make a good-faith effort to love each other or at least to put themselves in a marrying frame of mind but fail for various reasons appropriate to the personality of each.

And then suddenly we find a letter from Julie, who confesses that in spite of very good reasons for being happy, she is not. Happiness, she asserts, must be found as a reward in the other world. Her effort to make virtue and happiness coincide has failed. She protests her deep attachment to Wolmar, her admiration for his character and the world he has created around himself, her love of her children, who correspond to the wishes of the most exacting parent, and her admiration for and satisfaction in her friends. There is just one missing element, but one that robs her of happiness. She remains at this point as mysterious about this as does Wolmar about his mystery. And they turn out to be the same.

The occasion when the mystery must be clarified soon arises. Wolmar is an atheist. The ever more pious Julie cannot endure her husband's failure to recognize the true foundation of all the good things they enjoy. This is not for all the selfish reasons that pious wives frequently use in browbeating unbelieving husbands. It is because she fears that this man she believes she loves will not be saved. She is full of Rousseau's gentle theology that it would be contrary to God's goodness to punish unbelievers who are nevertheless moral men, but she is obviously not quite sure.

Essential to the plot of *La Nouvelle Héloïse* are the different understandings of God belonging to the three central personages. Saint-Preux is a believer whose articles of faith are very near to pantheism. God exists in all the beautiful things he loves and underwrites the satisfactions he expects to get from them. His is a this-worldly faith. Wolmar is thoroughly a rationalist, an example of the Enlightenment view that an unbeliever can be a fully moral man and therefore ought to be more graciously received by a reasonable God than an immoral believer. Whether faith is more important than morality and whether a man can be moral without faith were then the subject of endless dispute. Rousseau surely presents Wolmar as a moral man whose rationality has surmounted the concerns of his individual self in favor of a universal legislation for all men. His satisfaction comes from placing himself within this order. He is practically all-knowing about his subjects, to whom he teaches sincerity much more successfully than did the biblical God who was jealous and punished those who transgressed his commandments. He plays the God in the little world while denying the God of the great world. Wolmar is an atheist because he has experienced the contradictions between religions as well as the fanatical self-righteousness of each. He has studied science and simply finds the Creation too difficult to accept. He is not an atheist in order to give license to his own sins. He has nothing against believers; he simply cannot himself believe. And he cannot simply hide his atheism from his wife as did urbane nonbelievers in hypocritical societies. Sincerity is too much the guiding principle of his order to permit that. Reason suffices and he governs by it alone. Julie's religion seems to be a result of the conflicting responsibilities of lover, wife, and mother, which are in her case, and Rousseau indicates pretty much always, at odds with one another and impose responsibilities at tension with one another on her. The ecstasies of a lover's embraces are very different from those of a mother, and each kind vies for primacy. And unless there is a perfect and enduring harmony between sexual attraction and the duty to the one to whom one is married, there will also be a set of conflicts here too. Julie is sustained by a combination of self-denial, lack of self-awareness, and hopes that acts of renunciation of happiness will bring happiness. Thus the structure of her life is extremely fragile and requires supports that neither Saint-Preux's nor Wolmar's requires. A woman's God is different from a man's. Saint-Preux can understand his frustration as a result of Julie's rigor and his devotion to her command. Wolmar tells himself that he is satisfied by the successful exercise of his reason. But Julie is unhappy without any such resource.

Just prior to the denouement of the novel Saint-Preux accuses Julie of becoming a religious fanatic and criticizes her for subordinating the happiness of this life to imaginations of the next one. The personal reasons for Saint-Preux's criticism, which obviously has a certain basis in fact, are complex. Hope springs eternal and he has grounds for wishing to keep her in this world. She responds with passion and some incoherence. Her tone is pleading, begging for permission to have her consolation in religion. She lets Saint-Preux know that she is fully aware that there is a danger of putting this-worldly sensuality into otherworldly imaginations. But her very awareness, she insists, keeps her from making such a mistake. She is a living exhibit of the relation between imagination, sensuality, and the sublimity of God.

One sees that the poor girl is near the end of her tether, and it is no surprise that immediately after this letter she becomes sick and dies as a consequence of a plunge into the lake to save her drowning son's life. It is not exactly a suicide, but this denouement corresponds to her world-weariness.

In her last letter, written in the agonies of her fatal illness, she admits to Saint-Preux that he has won and she has always loved him, no matter how hard she tried to overcome it or to deny it to herself. The real cause of her dissatisfaction is not Wolmar's atheism but her illicit love for Saint-Preux. Such is the sophistry of a decent woman's heart! Julie's death makes the life of her little community sad and forever full of regret for her loss. Saint-Preux's permanent separation from his beloved gives his life a tragic dimension. And Wolmar recognizes that his reason did not account for his love of Julie. Only an imperfect God loves and cares for others. The emptiness of his claims of the self-sufficiency of reason are exposed to him and leave him without resource. The nobility of Julie's life and death, with all the complex and unavowed motives that made it possible, remains as an example and a consolation. Julie is the goddess of *La Nouvelle Héloïse* and of Romanticism in general.

2. Stendhal, *The Red and the Black*

> **I** In an attempt to understand that moment in our past when Romanticism formed the taste of the reading public and prepared the way for our current taste, I shall discuss four classic novels, Stendhal's *The Red and the Black*, Austen's *Pride and Prejudice*, Flaubert's *Madame Bovary*, and Tolstoy's *Anna Karenina*. All of these books are post-Rousseauan, that is, they breathe the air of a world newly articulated by Rousseau. Their authors all read Rousseau and were both attracted and repelled by him in varying degrees—from Austen, who most easily resisted his spell, to Tolstoy, who was an almost unqualified enthusiast. Their relationships to Rousseau are not as well known as they should be because his once fatal charms have faded and his traces are less recognizable. But for more than a century readers of novels were in the grip of his passionate vision of the way men and women could be together. The only figure today comparable in power to Rousseau, as is recognized more readily now, is Nietzsche, and even he hardly rivals Rousseau.

I do not mean to deny the individuality of the great artists who wrote these novels, nor do I want to appear to violate the aesthetic integrity of the books by reducing the writers' vision to a formula of intellectual history originating in Rousseau. However, even though Stendhal and Austen have almost contrary intellectual, moral, and artistic tastes, they share certain views about what counts that were not shared by earlier or later writers. To both Stendhal and Austen, the intimate contact between one man and one woman seems sufficient to attract readers and hold their attention without much more being added.

Some critics may reproach my undertaking because it insists on the decisive influence of a philosopher on the work of artists. The old New Critics were the first to take this tack, overreacting with the laudable intention of rescuing the texts themselves from doctrinaire intellectual historians. They have been seconded by the newest new critics who have a prejudice against reason and insist that artists cannot be understood to be decisively influenced by the reasoning of philosophers. These reproaches are usually made against those who bring in thinkers whose influence has been exhausted and therefore now belong to the domain of scholarly eunuchs. But it is essential to underline that Rousseau was more potent for thoughtful and sensitive men and women in the nineteenth century than either Marx or Freud is for us. And the fact that these reproaches are themselves doctrinaire can be seen from the way almost all such critics naturally refer to Marx and Freud when treating contemporary writers. This does not mean that all contemporary writers are the same, or that one properly understands or appreciates them by saying that they are Marxists or Freudians. It only means that today artists swim in an ocean discovered by Marx or Freud, and that everybody after Marx or Freud is moved in one direction or another by their tides. It is very rare that a serious person can avoid confronting the thought most important in his times and even rarer that someone can fully overcome those influences. We would not criticize someone for thinking that a poet who lived after the foundation of Christianity was influenced by it, or that his understanding of what counts for man might be different from that of a Greek or Roman poet. Why not, then, attribute something of that power to a philosopher? Somehow in our perspective religion is aesthetically potent and respectable, but not philosophy. Rousseau, however, understood himself to be a rival of Jesus and his writings to be a rival of the Bible, and his claim was accepted by many. Rousseau's new world is one where the attachment of men and women became more central than it ever was before or after, and these writers elaborated that attachment with unrivaled genius, just as the Christian writers carefully examined conscience as it never had been examined before or after. Just as there is a wonderful variety of forms of Christian faith, each interesting in itself but also not to be understood without recognizing the common inspiration of Christianity, there is a similar variety of Rousseauans. This does not detract from any of them, and each must be addressed on his or her own ground and with perfect openness to what he or she says. The phenomenon man appears to reveal itself by way of the interpretations of it. The artists, who of course can themselves be such interpreters, usually begin from the deepest interpretations that are available and seem plausible to them.

As against the most current literary hobbyhorses, I conclude that writers have intentions and knew what they were doing, because they thought so themselves. I cannot arrogate to myself the position superior to my writers that is assumed by so many contemporary critics. This seems to be a misapprehension of the critic's place in the rank order of being, and it also takes away so much of the fun of reading. There is no reason why an artist cannot use his or her genius to present a view of the best way of life and the best human beings. There is nothing anti-artistic about such an endeavor, and the artists' creation of expressions or representatives of that way of life surpasses the persuasive power of almost all the philosophers.

II Stendhal, on the face of it, would seem to be an artist very far from the spirit of the artist who gave us *La Nouvelle Héloïse*. Stendhal is a shameless immoralist, a public atheist, and his heroes are conscienceless adulterers or seducers who live with their beloveds without concern for marriage. And his style is so very different. Stendhal is rapid, dry, and ironic, with an apparent contempt for sentimentality. There are none of the effusions of a Saint-Preux in his works and none of the edification. The action of his books gallops. And there is a distaste for equality, which is Rousseau's fundamental principle. Stendhal's books are written for the happy few and evoke rare exaltations of rare persons. Finally, he expresses regret about the influence that Rousseau had over him. Of course this regret is also an admission of that influence. Stendhal also says that his *On Love* is written for the kind of reader who can understand *Emile*.[1] This cynic was, I believe, one of the better students in Rousseau's school and reveals his teaching more clearly than do more unabashedly Romantic writers such as Hugo or Scott.

Stendhal's cynicism is a consequence of his agreement with Rousseau that the bourgeois has conquered the world and is the most contemptible of beings. Stendhal does not look to revolution to correct this situation, but his art deals with the way in which finer tempers can live within it. This whole novelistic world is, in one way or another, incessantly about the opposition between the artist and bourgeois society. Stendhal's utter contempt for public opinion, a contempt that he repeatedly directs against the United States as the true home of public opinion, could be interpreted as the expression of an aristocratic preference. He does not hesitate to prefer corrupt old heroes to fresh and vigorous democratic America because in America everybody is the slave of shopkeepers' opinions—and there is no opera in America.[2] But actually he is arguing for an Emilean self-legislation, accessible to even the poorest of men, rather than for the haughtiness of the old regime.

Julien Sorel, the hero of *The Red and the Black*, is a nobody whose passions alone separate him from the petty world of the bourgeoisie. He is the son of a coarse peasant who has shrewdly parlayed a sawmill into a small fortune. The beautiful, sensitive Julien is treated like an unwanted changeling by his father and his brutish brothers. Julien hates them all and lives in a private world of imaginations of success, corroded by envy of the rich. His vaulting ambition distinguishes him from everyone else we encounter in the novel. He represents a heroic aspiration no longer to be found in his contemporaries. This is an irreducible fact, a difference of nature, and it is what makes him interesting to Stendhal. In the midst of the society supposedly founded on the natural equality of man there are special kinds of genius deprived of proper vehicles for self-expression. Julien's passion, his anger, and his imprudence are what make him attractive when others only calculate and use everything, including nobility and religion, for the sake of comfort and petty distinction. Julien is incapable of adjusting to this life. His story is his education in what really counts, and he dies young but superior in all the sentiments of the heart. This is clearly a Rousseauan theme, the superior young man whose pride is wounded by everything he encounters but who refuses to be broken by the system. The problem of modern man, as Rousseau tells us, is the emergence of a type of human being whose only concern is property, to be used in the first place for self-preservation, in the second for comfort, and finally for the satisfaction of vanity. There was once an aristocracy that had higher motives, but it exists now only as a reminiscence. And though religion once elevated the soul, it has now been overcome by a Jesuitism that is an imitation of the bourgeoisie. Society as a whole gives witness only to the unjust power of money. There is no relation whatsoever between position and desert. Nothing could be further from the American view that liberal society largely gives witness to the success of equal opportunity. In Stendhal's world no one can make a claim of justice, and all parties are either trying to hold on to advantages acquired or trying to wrest them from those who possess them. Everything is competition and intrigue. There may be ideas of justice, but they do not reflect the actual condition of society. Therefore society's laws and morality have no claim on our loyalty, and the one who manipulates them most skillfully to his advantage solicits admiration. This is pretty much the condition felt so strongly by the youth Jean-Jacques when he encounters the Savoyard Vicar.

A reader of Rousseau's *Confessions*, Julien imitates Rousseau's wounded pride that rebels against the system, but through insisting on being recognized by it he makes himself a part of it. When Julien is hired as a tutor in the house of the rich mayor of Verrières, he makes the same demand, without understanding precisely why, that Rousseau made in similar circumstances,[3] that he not be required to wear a uniform like a lackey and that he dine with the masters and not with the servants (I.5).* As with so many young people in this new nineteenth century, Julien is a reader who gets his instruction about what life is like and how to behave from books. He reads, of course, only a tiny number of books, the real classics for everyday use that take the place of the lost authority of the Bible. As for so many of the most interesting French of his century, Julien's Bibles are Rousseau's works and Napoleon's *Mémorial de Sainte-Hélène*. Stendhal underlines his point by making Julien know the real Bible, especially the Gospels, letter-perfect, by heart, in Latin. This means that he does not take a word of it seriously but uses it as a tool for his hypocrisy to advance himself in a society that is hopelessly and incurably hypocritical. Julien is by instinct an unbeliever, and his real scriptures keep him ever mindful of Rousseau's analysis of modern society and the grandeur of Napoleon's ambition, which conquered that society.

Napoleon is much more Julien's hero than is Rousseau, and Stendhal reflects the sad awareness that dominated Continental literature throughout the nineteenth century and affected not only literary expressions of the human situation but also those of philosophy and sociology. Max Weber, when he spoke of the charismatic leader, really meant Napoleon and lamented his disappearance. This was the Continent's mood. The last of the heroes has disappeared forever, and we must make do in this dull world without him. This post-Napoleonic pathos plays an enormous role in Romanticism and still affects the categories by which we interpret society. Napoleon's

---

* All parenthetical citations in this chapter are to part and chapter of Stendhal's *The Red and the Black*.

vast ambition and his splendid and unabashed pursuit of glory made the world young again and gave the opportunity for the Julien Sorels to play a role on the world stage worthy of them, a role earned by military courage rather than the moneymaker's ruses. Stendhal's most beautiful description of this new youth of the world is to be found in the opening pages of *The Charterhouse of Parma* when the French conquer Milan. The hero of that book, Fabrice del Dongo, is the illegitimate offspring of this conquest; his character and loves are Napoleonic and yet teach how one must live in a post-Napoleonic time. One might say Napoleon is more important for Stendhal than is Rousseau, but the disappearance of Napoleon means only that the victory of the bourgeoisie predicted by Rousseau has come to pass. Stendhal is like those novelists who expressed the mood of the decline of the West, which appeared to be a consequence of the First World War. Nietzsche, however, had already announced that decline forty years before, and the First World War only confirmed his announcement. The disappointments following the French Revolution and Napoleon's Empire served only to confirm Rousseau's articulation of the forces that would move modern society. Thinkers like Rousseau and Nietzsche are prescient, and it takes a half century for events and lesser men to catch up with them. They saw much more and predicted much better than did, for example, Marx; and Tocqueville's remarkable clarity about the future was drawn from his reading of Rousseau.

But, however much the shadow of Napoleon affects the scenery of this drama, Stendhal, like Rousseau, does not so much regret lost heroes as use his loss to discover the highest vocation of man, love. The hard Stendhal represents more unequivocally than any of the other writers we are going to treat, and perhaps more than any other writer, confidence in the redemptive power of love. This is what is paradoxical about Stendhal: he really believes in the possibility of love. He has no sympathy for the charms of the profligate Don Juan, who lacks, according to him, the intense experience of the passionate, exclusive love on which one stakes one's life.[4] But this idealistic view of love seems to clash with Stendhal's unvarnished realism about the deeds and the motives of men. Actually, this love is the standpoint, replacing the aristocratic and religious standpoints that used to serve this function, from which he is able to judge this world so severely. The spirit of Rousseau is, willy-nilly, in Stendhal's blood.

Thus Stendhal, in spite of his apparent lack of didacticism and his concentration on the sentiments of his characters' hearts without any rhetoric or philosophizing about the cosmic scene within which they are experienced, actually does show us all the fundamental alternatives that face a serious man as he saw them. With a few deft strokes he paints the alternatives, Rousseau and liberal society, the Bible and the religious life, the peasant, the bourgeois, the aristocrat, Napoleon and the classical hero. Each of the individuals in his book has an education, a defective education, that is a pale reflection of the great choices and their most persuasive modern advocates. Using his urbane understatement as a cover, Stendhal articulates the whole world of concern to modern man. His hero's private passions and actions are significant because they partake of the interesting conflicts among the fundamental alternatives. Stendhal's unique gifts as a writer permit him to depict all of this with a perfection vouchsafed no other novelist. He proceeds at a breakneck speed, bubbling like champagne in his Rossiniesque superficiality, which is superficial only in the sense that it bathes the surface of things in the sun of the south. His story is always on the move, getting from here to there with amazing rapidity. Within a couple of pages one is already at the heart of the story and already involved with its characters.

The story of *The Red and the Black* is a simple one and was picked out of the newspapers by Stendhal and reproduced without much alteration. A young man of modest origins becomes the tutor in the home of a provincial bourgeois whose wife he seduces. He is forced to leave and ends up in Paris as the secretary of a noble whose daughter he seduces. He is denounced by his first love just when he is on the brink of great worldly advancement, goes to a church where she is praying, and shoots her. He is condemned to death and loses his head, while both of his loves plead for his life. This is the whole story of the newspapers and the novel, nothing more. There are no dissertations and none of the extraneous excitements provided by events to which we are accustomed in so many novels like Dickens' and Zola's. All the excitement, and how very exciting this story is, consists in the intimate psychology of the important characters, particularly Julien. The dangers of Julien when he is in Madame de Rênal's bedroom and his leaping out of her window are dealt with in a few compact lines and are interesting not for their melodrama but for Julien's reactions and reflections about them. Stendhal's marvelous insouciance is described with the greatest skill by Hippolyte Taine in his essay on Stendhal.[5]

The story of the tutor who debauches a woman in the home where he is employed is familiar to us from *La Nouvelle Héloïse*. Julien is different only in that he does it twice and might well have continued to do so if his career had not been cut short. In both homes he expected to further his ambition to make a great career for himself in society, but in spite of himself he makes his career as a lover, not cynically but because this is all that has real emotional force for him. He is not a great sensualist, and his two seductions were not planned. His involvement with the two exceptional women he encounters is all to his credit. No man save him in this novel has any passionate attachment to women. Love is not a vocation for the masses. The only notable successes of this young man, so avid of success and full of fantasies about it, are in the domain of love, which did not figure in any of his Napoleonic projects. And it is our old friend *amour-propre*, not love of the beautiful, that pushes him into his seductions. In both cases, he imposes a duty on himself to sleep with these women because he thinks they think they are superior to him, and, moreover, he is wounded by the humiliating servitude to persons who are merely rich or wellborn. His loves begin as acts of vengeance. His experience is not unlike that of the child Jean-Jacques, whose concern that he was despised by the Lambercier family, with whom he lived as an orphan, led to his braving the terrors of the kingdom of darkness.[6] Inequality is the source of vice, and the motor of vice is *amour-propre*, which seeks revenge, to do harm to those who are superordinated in the management of society and who make others slaves of their opinions. This is surely a vice from the points of view of both Rousseau and Stendhal, but it also constitutes the core of the charm of the two young heroes, for theirs is, apparently due only to nature's dispensation, the version of *amour-propre* that leads to pride rather than vanity.[7] The bourgeois husband of Julien's first love, M. de Rênal, when insulted, plots vengeance, but is always prevented from achieving it by considerations of advantage and of risk involved, whereas Jean-Jacques and Julien act foolishly and impetuously without calculation to restore their self-respect in their own eyes. Just as Jean-Jacques passed through the graveyard while thinking he was, by his daring, making himself worthy of Plutarch's Roman heroes, Julien is constantly trying to measure his deeds against his Napoleonic vision of himself. He conducts his seductions as Napoleon conducted the operations of the Grande Armée. The self-mockery of Rousseau is paralleled by Stendhal's mockery of Julien, although they both think well of their heroes. They are both extremely alienated, buffeted by their sense that they come off badly in comparison with other men, and both use literary models to distinguish themselves from the herds of sheeplike men who surround them. Nothing starts from the heart, but they both have great hearts. They are both great reasoners about schemes for their advancement, but these schemes are comically unrealistic, and they always end up following an unexpected, even unconscious, prompting of their hearts. The task of both Rousseau and Stendhal in their sentimental education of their heroes is to make them discover the truth and beauty of love and thus cure them of their alienation. Their *amour-propre* is the engine of self-awareness that passes through a long moment of self-deception while providing their souls with the wings to take them upward toward the sublime. Stendhal's operative word is "sincerity," and he watches his little hypocrite Julien destroy the most delicious experiences because he does not yet have the courage to be sincere. Sincerity (as opposed to hypocrisy), which prior to Rousseau was a virtue testifying to quality of religious faith, becomes with him the religion of the godless subjective self. Its rituals are dedicated to inducing it to reveal itself, and its devotees seek not to be faithful to the true God with all their hearts and their minds but to be true to themselves.

This Rousseauan psychology is present in aspects of Julien's character that are rather surprising given his single-minded ambition, self-absorption, and harsh view of people's motives. He is capable of tears for the suffering poor. He is indignant, à la Rousseau, at M. Valenod's dishonest administration of the funds destined for the indigent and his mistreatment of them (I.7). Julien has the compassion of natural goodness that is lacking in the others, and Stendhal apparently is so soft as to justify Julien's extreme egotism and ambitiousness by emphasizing the unnaturalness of the society against which he struggles, a society in which hopes for justice are forlorn. Stendhal's dislike of moral pieties, which suits his themes, his tastes, and his talents, breaks down a bit in the passages that reveal Julien's compassion, along with those that show Julien's pious respect for revolutionaries and their causes. All this seems to smack of the Rousseauan sentimentalism with which Stendhal wishes to break. This intention is gainsaid by his indignation at the injustices of the new bourgeois society as well as its philistinism. Julien is interesting because he cannot play that game and thus reveals it for what it is.

Similarly, Julien's admiration of persons of single-minded dedication and high moral standards who are persecuted precisely because of their virtue is unqualified. In spite of his unbelief, he respects those who do really believe and live according to the precepts of Christianity. The two examples are priests, the Curé Chélan and the Abbé Pirard, both of whom are assigned roles akin to that of the Savoyard Vicar. Julien's incredulity seems to have to do less with a critique of faith than with a doubt about its vitality in modernity. He anticipates Nietzsche's "God is Dead," which means that the trouble with God is not his nonexistence but his incapacity to act and motivate men in our times. Chélan and Pirard are throwbacks, and therefore not unqualified objects of imitation, but they are impressive in that they believe in *something* that affects their lives, whereas everybody else is motivated by money, and their relation to higher things is but an ineffective veneer or self-justification. For Stendhal or Julien, believing in something is more important than truth. Stendhal seems to say that a clear-sighted person who has lived the experiences of our time can believe only in passionate love. Julien, who wants to be Napoleon and who chooses the life of a priest because, in this hypocritical age, the Church is a support for the existing social order and the path to power and riches for parvenus, actually ends up being only a bedroom warrior. All of his spirituality is exhausted in his wars with the ladies, and his daring and ready wit are almost exclusively demonstrated in his descents from bedroom windows with the risks of angry husbands or parents discovering, disgracing, or killing him. These sexual escapades are compelling realities whereas all the rest is insubstantial acting, dissipated by the love game as are the morning clouds by the sun.

Even the Rousseauan opposition between city and country is preserved in Stendhal. It is striking in a writer who manifests little of the Romantic taste for nature, and who hardly pauses to describe natural settings, that Julien's moments of greatest inner freedom and exultation come when he sees the mountains and looks down over the valleys from them (I.10). This partakes of the peculiarly Rousseauan sublimation of the highest spirituality into landscapes. In Shakespeare, nature is translated into the human element and gets its dignity as it gives cosmic meaning to the aspirations and deeds of human beings. In Rousseau it is the contrary. Man is translated into nature. The human perspective is lost in empathy with the mountains, the seas, the heavens, storms, calms, etc. The experience of nature in this sense is with the capacity to experience compassion. Nature is strongly contrasted with the artificiality of a society whose chains are anything but natural. Only the love experience is truly compelling for Stendhal, but its special character comes to light in the context of a specific view of the relation between nature and society. And, although the men in the provinces can hardly be said to be more natural than those in Paris, the contrast between Mme. de Rênal and Mathilde de La Mole is founded on the perfect naturalness of the former and the perfect artificiality of the latter. Stendhal even echoes Rousseau's attack on the corrupting effect of novels. In Paris the literary modes determine how men and women make love. Mme. de Rênal's innocence of any literary influence makes her love true and sincere because she discovers it for herself and in herself, whereas Mathilde not only reads novels but wants to be a character in one (I.7, I.13, II.11). How Rousseau and Stendhal can square this view of the effect of novels with their own vocations as novelists is a vexed question. Taken from the highest point of view, their case is not entirely dissimilar from that of Plato, who attacks writing in writing. Here one can only say that all three are conscious of a problem and respond to it by being writers of a different kind from the others.

This provides the key to the special brand of immoralism to which Stendhal is addicted. We are so used to something akin to what Stendhal presents to us that we forget how shocking it is, and, more important, how different it is from the tastes of earlier writers. Shakespeare and the Greek dramatists, for example, do not celebrate the immoral deeds of their heroes and usually end by supporting the conventional moral order, perhaps in an unconventional way. For the last two centuries our sympathies have been attached to the destroyers of the moral order, so much so that, without any awareness of what this really means, we use the word "subversive" as a synonym for art. Every bubbleheaded movie star or rock star thinks it is sufficiently impressive to describe his or her art as "subversive." Stendhal is not so foolish as to take any such description as sufficient, but he has contributed to the success of this point of view, and its deep source is in Rousseau's distinction between the moral man and the good man. Although Rousseau makes much more of morality than does Stendhal, he describes himself as a good man and not a moral man, and thereby seems to give a certain preference to goodness. In the wake of this distinction one finds a gradual degradation of morality into bourgeois morality, meaning merely the hypocritical and repressive rules of the game of a competitive and exploitative society. A sign of this change is to be found in the "Prologue in Heaven," which introduces Goethe's *Faust*, where Faust is referred to by God as a good man.[8] He is certainly not a moral man. In so much of the literature that provides our immediate education the major characters break the moral rules, and there are no counterbalancing moral characters who indicate by their example the superiority of the moral way. It is not that earlier writers did not see that there are problems with conventional morality, but they believed that conventional morality was an imperfect reflection of true morality, and they were inclined, not merely out of concern for edifying the public, to look in the direction of a perfected morality and moral heroes for their elaboration of the most interesting human types. After Rousseau that direction appeared to be a dead end, and frankly immoral types began to epitomize the most interesting ways of life. Julien is a liar, a thief, a cheat, a seducer, an ingrate, but this does not prevent Stendhal from preferring him to everyone else in his book. All of this prefigures Nietzsche's *Beyond Good and Evil*, and Stendhal was a novelist very much to Nietzsche's taste.[9] Goodness seems to consist in a combination of natural sentiments like compassion combined with energy of soul, and above all, sincerity. A large part of sincerity is the frank admission of the natural selfishness that conventional morality does not overcome but lies about. Machiavelli's quick-witted and daring characters provide a text for this taste, and Machiavelli's laughter becomes part of the seriousness of this new perspective on morality and human interestingness. All of modern moral and political science gets an artistic expression in these new heroes. Balzac's criminal hero Vautrin, with his strength and explosive energy, which contrast with the weakness of the social forces of justice, is another such character. What is new in the Romantic idiom is the linkage of these low motives with the highest idealism and poetry. It is Machiavellianism with a powerful erotic charge.

The corollary of this taste is an utter contempt for the classic virtue, moderation. Daring, ready wit, and even a quixotic love of justice, which are elements of the other virtues in the classical canon, remain respectable and attractive, but moderation comes to light as merely repulsive. Moderation is the most important ingredient of Socratic irony, and if irony remains at all, it is a far cry from that delicious style one discovers in Xenophon's Socrates. Moderation appears now to be equivalent to the bourgeois' careful concern for his self-preservation and avoidance of any life-threatening risks. It was always believed that men have to be willing to risk their lives for what they care about, but it never before went to the extreme that risking one's life is in itself the proof of seriousness. But that is what Mathilde de La Mole, and many fictional and non-fictional personages after her, set as the single test for lovers and other high types. Nietzsche expresses and parodies this tendency when he says a good war hallows any cause.[10] Julien does worry about getting killed, but mostly out of *amour-propre*: he doesn't want his inferiors and rivals to get the better of him. This risks becoming merely a reaction to the contemptible bourgeois version of prudence, allied as it always is with moderation. Thus reason is inevitably sacrificed to his taste, for reason, as we have already noted, is now understood to be calculating, reductionist, and destructive rather than creative of beautiful ideals. Romanticism restores imagination to the throne usurped by reason with the support of the Enlightenment's troops. Julien's reasonings are always ridiculous while his instincts are exciting and admirable. All this is a gloss on Machiavelli's dictum:

> I judge this indeed, that it is better to be impetuous than cautious, because fortune is a woman; and it is necessary, if one wants to hold her down, to beat her and strike her down. And one sees that she lets herself be won more by the impetuous than by those who proceed coldly. And so always, like a woman, she is the friend of the young, because they are less cautious, more ferocious, and command her with more audacity.[11]

One might add that this passage seems to be a complete and exhaustive interpretation of the part of *The Red and the Black* that concerns Julien's affair with Mathilde.

The preference for youth, beauty, and daring simply dominates *The Red and the Black*, which is the purest profession of Stendhal's faith, but it should be noted that in its rival, *The Charterhouse of Parma*, there is a certain qualification of this faith. In it there are two poles of interest, the romantic hero, Fabrice del Dongo, and the charming, cynical, Machiavellian political man, Mosca. He is a bit ridiculous because he is no longer young and was never beautiful and is in love with the beautiful, but past her prime, Duchess of Sanseverina, who is really in love with her nephew Fabrice, who loves someone else. In spite of this, Mosca charms by his intellect and real knowledge of life. There is a certain parallelism here to Homer's two books. In the perspective of the Trojan War, the angry young Achilles is unquestionably the most attractive figure, but in peace the wily Odysseus and his observation of the various ways of men capture our attention. I doubt that Stendhal fully worked this problem out, but Julien seems to represent the fantasy life of Stendhal, what this unprepossessing writer would like to have been like, while Mosca represents the wisdom and the insight of Julien's creator. Stendhal may have cherished a preference for his creation but he cannot suppress the creator's significance, and that creator does not quite fit into the system.

<table>
<tr><td>III</td></tr>
</table>

Stendhal leads Julien through the life of the nineteenth century that he so despises. He is elevated from his home, where he is surrounded by cruel peasants who hate this sensitive changeling, to the home of M. de Rênal, who, in the ridiculous parody of the *ancien régime* that was the restoration of Charles X, tries, out of vanity, to capture a semi-aristocratic status based on his family origins.

The regime is on its last legs. The novel is written in the light of the liberal, that is, the commercial or capitalist revolution of 1830 that brought Louis Philippe to power or, rather, to the shadow of power. The active political opponents of M. de Rênal and his newfangled reactionary party are the Liberals, who want to reform the social order in such a way as to favor their own rise to wealth. Persons like M. de Rênal try to win the distinction of those who lived and acted when throne and altar were still intact. There is a respectable aristocratic past in France, in contrast to America, and this solicits the imagination or, if you please, the snobbism of M. de Rênal and, in one way or another, everyone else on the scene. Once they have their money, they want to play at being aristocrats. They fill their future with imaginations of new and cheapened titles, distinguished ceremonial positions, and medals and sashes. He and his class live in terror of a renewal of the Revolution, expecting that their own servants will cut their throats and pillage their houses. They rely on the police and the Church to suppress the dangerous *canaille*, which threatens them with socialism.

M. de Rênal can dedicate himself to embellishing himself and his properties because he already has made his money—out of manufacture. He is, of course, distinguished from the true aristocrat because he takes these bagatelles with infinite seriousness whereas the latter, while requiring these things, as Aristotle tells us, despises them.[12] M. de Rênal is an infinitely vulgar man who thinks about the price he has paid for everything, although he is distinguished from the liberal upstart Valenod, who will tell all comers what those prices were. The Valenods, however, are more attuned to the spirit of the times and are about to win the next round, with the help of the Jesuits. Reactionary imitators like M. de Rênal affect to represent traditional culture and wish to have tutors who know Latin to educate their children. They have no interest whatsoever in the content of Latin literature but care only about the good reputation attached to the dead language. From the moment Julien arrives on the scene he is in a continuous battle of vanities with M. de Rênal, and Julien almost always gets the better of him. No real aristocrat would put himself in a position where a youngster whom he wishes to treat as a servant continually humiliates him. The key to Julien's success in the house is M. de Rênal's fear that Julien will be hired away by M. Valenod and thus his own distinction will be lost.

After showing us M. de Rênal and his entourage of typical provincial characters with their constant intrigues, Stendhal gives us a picture of the religious establishment through Julien's stay at the seminary. Religion is still the great educator and is understood by Stendhal to be the highest expression of a culture. Its debility is the best symptom of what Stendhal thinks is wrong with nineteenth-century culture. This interlude is very much like Rousseau's account in the *Confessions* of his incarceration in a religious institution in Turin,[13] except that Stendhal does not play upon a putative superiority of contemporary Protestantism, which he would regard as merely the dull ideology of liberalism. For him Catholicism had much more poetry and provided a better stage for the various interesting varieties of the psychology of faith and the lack thereof. Stendhal wishes to present a true history of the practice of his own time while measuring it against its highest claims for itself. He is hard on religion as almost no one is today because he has, perhaps in spite of himself, such high expectations from it.

The scene in the seminary is of interest because it presents a world with the highest moral and spiritual pretensions, whose most striking element is the unrelieved materialism of its actual life. The heavy and graceless children of peasants are there to escape the poverty of their lives and are preoccupied with the food they get in the present and, for the future, exhaust their imaginations about the comfortable functions they will fulfill when they are priests. Mere convention and opinion dominate their every thought and deed while the professors spin the blackest plots for the sake of power and influence. The seminary contains a discrete mixture of mediocrity and moral ugliness seasoned with unbelievable stupidity. The most typical priest is concerned with caring for and manipulating the dead symbols of a once potent religious impulse, the shell of which is the great churches still rising impressively above the cities, reminiscences of an omnipresence of religion hardly credible to us who have no such monuments. The body is immortal while the soul was killed by the Enlightenment and the Revolution. The fallen inheritors of this legacy calculate their survival on the basis of usefulness to the political classes while those political classes count on religion to serve as an opiate of the masses.

Stendhal's analysis differs from Marx's only in that he expects strictly nothing from the masses. Julien is the very model of the superior man who is hated and distrusted because he does not share the motives and aspirations of those around him. He does, as I have mentioned, deeply admire the severe Abbé Pirard, who is a real believer and adheres to the strict principles of Jansenism. He is the only person in the book who has moral weight as compared with Julien. But like the old hermit in *Zarathustra*, he just hasn't heard that God is dead. Like so many nineteenth-century atheists, Stendhal is an admirer of Pascal and Port-Royal. There is an undigested element of religious extremism in them, feeding on the cult of sincerity and contempt for bourgeois materialism, rebellious against the spirit of Voltaire and the Encyclopedists, the atheists of the eighteenth century. The intense element of the soul had been forgotten and was ready to boil over. This reflects Rousseau's preference for extremism—in politics, morals, love, and religion—as over against the easy-goingness of his contemporaries. Fanatics at least believe in and care about something. Similarly, the Curé Chélan, the only decent man in Verrières, is thought to be a Jansenist. The Jesuits who are in control represent a flexible semirationalism, an ends-justifies-the-means morality, and an admixture of calculation about political possibilities with their faith. Julien's appearance in this novel in the habit of a novice represents his attempt to adapt to and master the circumstances of his time. His hypocrisy is justified by the character of that time, but his true self is present underneath that habit.

This religious interlude between the two halves of the novel—provinces versus Paris, parvenus versus aristocrats, Mme. de Rênal versus Mathilde de La Mole—is an essential part of Stendhal's sketch of the history of his time. It concludes, appropriately, with Julien's encounter with the bishop of Besançon, a true remnant of the *ancien régime*, the cultivated ecclesiastic without excess of principle, a man of perfect taste and true tolerance. He sees right through Julien while being complicit with the vicar and his cohorts who persecute Julien, all in the spirit of worldly wisdom. The bishop is the incarnation of the *disinvoltura* that delights Stendhal. He concludes his relations with Julien by giving him a magnificent edition of the pagan Tacitus, who provides an alternative account of the same period in history presented in the New Testament.

At last having arrived in Paris, we actually find the true aristocrats who have the most exquisite manners, some taste, a pride that is second nature, because at least there was a past where they had a great place, and a breadth of views unknown in the provinces. Julien is honestly seduced by the charms of the old Marquis de La Mole, who treats him with infinite politeness, which is, on deeper reflection, an insult because it is founded on the Marquis' unassailable conviction of Julien's social inferiority. The Marquis is not a man to feel threatened by this clever and talented youngster. He only wants to make use of him; and, when he finally takes Julien's measure, he is amused by him, providing him with a blue suit that he is to wear when they are just friends, in addition to the black suit he wears when he is the Marquis' secretary. This little world with its palaces and its titles is a work of refinement developed over centuries, and the actors on its stage continue to believe that they play a central role in Europe, and hence in universal history. (Stendhal admires this world and was an enthusiastic participant in the opera, which was the preferred entertainment in it.) This aristocracy is the representative of tradition and partakes of its strengths and weaknesses. It presents a heady atmosphere to this boy from the country who perfects his manners and manages to become a man *à la mode*. He is even able to test his skills as a factotum in the political conspiracies. This is an excellent education, but it is all too easily learned, and once he is the master of the Parisian ways, he still remains without anything significant to do. The prospects of a bishopric or even, finally, a dukedom fail to satisfy his quest for something important to do. Although from the point of view of the social hierarchy, he remains a man of the lower class, he has all the natural gifts that would allow him entry into the highest aristocracy. But when he gets a clear look at the world of Paris, he recognizes that it is tainted by the furious vanity of fashion and the quasi-impossibility of sincerity. This is a diminished scene, not one to satisfy an ambition like Julien's. The Marquis and his friends have become a part of the money world, as has everyone else, and their powerlessness as aristocrats has culminated, except for a few halfhearted political conspiracies, in the boring routine of a high society that has no true vocation and lacks all firmness of soul. Napoleon, always Julien's hero, represented a vital new beginning in which individual greatness and great politics seemed for an illusory moment to be possible in modernity. In the end the depiction of Paris here is nothing but a rerun of Rousseau's, though presented in Stendhal's elegant idiom. Julien's stay in Paris is like Emile's. Each completes his education there, protected against its corruptions by the presence of a high ideal that makes him more of an observer than a participant. Julien, however, unlike Emile, has the misfortune of meeting a woman in Paris who appears worthy of his attention.

IV And now we must turn to the two women who together constitute the whole of Julien's sexual experience as well as the real excitement of this novel. Each is truly extraordinary, standing far above the world in which she is placed. Like every single good person in *The Red and the Black*, they are both irresistibly attracted to this beautiful and singular, but absolutely selfish, young man. They join the Curé Chélan, Abbé Pirard, Marquis de La Mole, and Prince Korasof in this strange, supramoral fascination. Each woman represents one of the two kinds of love Stendhal distinguishes in the novel, Mme. de Rênal, heart-love, and Mathilde, head-love. Mme. de Rênal is true love, without tincture of *amour-propre* and the role playing that accompanies it, whereas Mathilde is a potent actress, taking as her role the reenactment of the most vigorous moments of French history. Julien, of course, brings his overdose of *amour-propre* to both affairs, but with Mme. de Rênal there is the possibility of immediate sentimental union, whereas with Mathilde the entire mechanism is the fevered imagination and the alternation of mastery and slavery. To contemporary readers, Mme. de Rênal is the stereotype of the submissive woman, passively accepting the role assigned to her by a male-dominated society, whereas the proud and rebellious Mathilde seems to represent the possibility of liberation. In fact, neither Mme. de Rênal nor Mathilde is a promising candidate for liberation because their whole being and the meaning of their lives are involved with the existence of a man such as Julien. Mme. de Rênal's superiority consists precisely in the unalloyed naturalness of this vocation in her. Our difference in perspective on these characters is the single most revealing sign of the distance between us and Stendhal, although he is in so many ways a modern just like us. He knew that the relations between the sexes had become boring.

Stendhal uses as the epigraph for one chapter a quote from Barnave: "So this is the beautiful miracle of your civilization! You have made an ordinary business out of love" (II.31). What he admires is either a thing of the past or a theme of novels for the happy few, but he uses all of his art to convince us that the only interesting life is the one dominated by *amour-passion*, that of men and women living for each other, supported by shame, modesty, and idealization of the sexual act. Nothing of the interesting relationships Stendhal depicts would be possible for women for whom the sexual act is not a matter of life and death and sacred honor. These relationships, constructed like the most complicated movements of great old watches, have as their mainspring the conviction that the gift of the body comes from grace of the whole soul, and these special connections are given to

Julien alone against all counsels of prudence and in an act of over-coming the will. Each gives herself to Julien with a fair degree of ease in the circumstances and rather shamelessly, but in the conviction that the overpowering love they experience is itself the standard for good and evil. Their passions are natural, especially in the case of Mme. de Rênal, but so in another sense are the conventions that forbid them to have or indulge such passions. They live in societies where what they do is condemned, and necessarily so. For these women, their giving themselves necessarily entails civil death, a banishment from society, unlike the hypocritical affairs of ordinary adulteresses. Each of these women is heroic in her utter abandon, which is a kind of social suicide for the sake of the imperious demand of her attraction. Neither Mme. de Rênal nor Mathilde could hope to hide her involvement with Julien for very long, whereas Julien could easily hide his involvement, and for a man the consequences are much more benign in any event. The loosening of bourgeois morals in the generations after Stendhal did not so much make life easier for lovers as destroy the conditions of love. This is what is anticipated in the quote from Barnave. Love is really the business of "the happy few."

In Stendhal, a man who surely knew all the physical charms of sex, there is almost no description of them. Stendhal's descriptions of the act itself do not go beyond remarks like "when Julien left Mme. de Rênal's room, it could have been said, in novelistic style, that he had nothing more to desire," or "she had nothing more to refuse him" (I.15). Stendhal's reticence is not in any sense prudishness, although an earlier literature that was coarser could speak more openly, perhaps because it believed less in love. In Shakespeare, both modes are present, but certainly most of his loves (Cleopatra's is the great exception) seem to support Stendhal's way. This reticence is due partly to Stendhal's agreement with Rousseau that the illusions of love and the interesting psychological effects of the illusions are far more important than the act of love itself. But it also has to do with the fact that the physical details of the act, reproduced in pictures or words, are not what the sexual act really is for those who participate in it, for their imaginations are engaged with their specific relationship, and mere spectators cannot see this. Everything is in the sentiments leading up to the bodily act and following upon it, the attractions and repulsions connected with this fulfillment, and the spiritual exaltations and excesses surrounding what is in the world of nature the most banal and ordinary satisfaction. This is what is wrong with pornography. It distorts and impoverishes sensuality. Stendhal wants his readers to imagine, after he has seduced them into becoming lovers of his personages, what they do together, so that they themselves can be accomplices in the romantic illusion. Stendhal believed that his descriptions would be much more sexually exciting to his readers of choice than any explicit depiction could ever be. The reader has to contribute, if he is to be a participant in the novelistic description. Far from being hampered by the various kinds of imagination, the sexual act is nurtured by them.

None of this is meant to gainsay the fact that much of what Stendhal hints about Julien's sexual experiences indicates that he, like so many other men and women, rarely really enjoys sex because he is thinking about other things while doing it, or is, not to put too fine a point on it, worried about how he looks to his beloved or to a watching world. But this is all part of the story of love, and Julien ends up by being cured.

Moreover, the wild and misguided *amour-propre* that Julien brings to his relationships with women is not simply a vice. Without it there would be no relationship. One has to worry about what the other party thinks, and that is difficult, if not impossible, to know. *Amour-propre* is, to repeat, the instrument of human sociality because it is the part of us concerned with others' wills. The imperious need to subjugate another's will leads to many perversions, because every ounce of one's self-esteem depends on success in the venture. And, as all the searing complaints of jealous men and women tell us, there seems to be no way to predict or control the esteem that is necessary for our self-esteem. Will can overcome our desires, but it cannot make us sexually attractive. The seduction of another's desire can easily become an end in itself, therefore culminating in contempt or at least loss of interest in the one who is conquered, and in simple self-hatred when one fails. Further, the demands of *amour-propre* in love relationships escalate, so that one wants the other not only to respond but to respond to what one really is, truly and sincerely. The game is ever more subtle and the truth of the relationship is difficult to determine. And there is so much pain in all of this that *amour-propre* must constantly prepare safety nets so that desperate doubt does not send us into an abyss. Self-protective interpretations distort the truth of the affair. Finally, one begins to wonder how there can ever be a reciprocity of affection, mutual and sincere admiration, without each of the parties misinterpreting and using the other. But these are the facts, perhaps sad facts, about the difficulty of human relationships. How much simpler isolation or frank acceptance that one is just using others would be. Love is the no-man's-land, studded with mines, between these alternatives. The true meaning of the civilized sexual act is that one has successfully navigated this mine-field.

But the fact of this book is that Mme. de Rênal is naturally and wholly in love with Julien, without reflection and without second thoughts. Her inclination is everything a man could ask for. Julien's problem is double: he has to persuade himself both that Mme. de Rênal's attachment is really like this and that he reciprocates and can get his satisfaction in the calm acceptance of a love that excludes so many others and so many objects of ambition.

Mme. de Rênal is an innocent even though she is a product of and lives within a very corrupt society. She is so indifferent to the charms which attract the other provincials that she is proof against their influence. It is as though she were sleepwalking, and only her accidental meeting with Julien awakens her and brings to the surface the depths of passion hidden beneath what appears to be a perfect calm. Her imagination is not inflamed, and she alone is able to have immediate enjoyment without fantasies that surely embellish affairs but that also mean that one is enjoying the fantasy and not the reality. She is, of course, not a natural savage, which means she has her share of *amour-propre* and imagination, but hers is the kind that Rousseau prescribes for Sophie and Emile, so that her worry about the opinions of others concerns only Julien's opinion, and her imagination embellishes her own situation rather than imitating other persons'. Julien is always calling the whole world to witness everything he does, particularly the inner witness he has constructed for himself. If Mme. de Rênal had read novels, she would have been way out ahead about what really happens in her relation with Julien and would have been deprived of the deliciousness of the experiences, which she would have interpreted prior to having them. She is a natural, but she is also something of an aristocrat, with a great inheritance in prospect. Her education—for Stendhal education is of the essence for knowing what a person is—was the typical convent education that did not in any way attach the young girls' sensuality to a true religious experience but taught a conventional and routine piety. It left her untouched, and its failings were compounded by the fact that she was treated with the greatest respect by the nuns because she was an heiress. She did not experience contempt for those around her, but her aristocratic superiority was expressed by her indifference to them.

Mme. de Rênal is the archetypical Romantic heroine in her inno-cence, her unpretentious high-mindedness, and her unalloyed fem-ininity. A woman in one of my classes once exclaimed, "She's nothing but a cow!" And it could look this way to persons for whom the sentimental life is a drag or too much of a burden, but Mme. de Rênal is capable of the tenderest and most passionate relationship. One wonders how long a couple could go on like this, but that is not such a problem. Stendhal thinks this experience is worth it, no matter how brief. Julien has only a few days to enjoy the perfectly unselfconscious love of Mme. de Rênal, and Fabrice del Dongo's Clélia dies after only three years of a furtive affair. Unlike Rousseau, Stendhal does not think of marriage and family but concentrates only on the love affair of two partners, which is, in spite of its claims, of short duration. The intense episode is preferred to the calm of the philosopher or the security looked for by the bourgeois.

Mme. de Rênal is the typical Romantic heroine also in that she is a married woman whose marriage is loveless but who is very capable of love. When she encounters a man she can love, she is caught in the conflict between duty and love. This is an endlessly interesting situation for people who take both marriage and love seriously and it provided the theme for the literature to which the bourgeoisie was addicted well into the twentieth century. Mme. de Rênal and her kind cannot be blamed because they had no idea of what love is when they married and took marriage to be a social institution into which one enters for good and prudent reasons. The assumption is that love, passionate, physical love, is a very good and important thing. If this does not justify adultery it at least makes us sympathetic to the sinner.

She is, like Julie, above all a mother. Her deeply felt obligations to her children split her between them and Julien. Julien enters her life by way of her children and almost as a substitute father to them. When she gets to know him she wishes he were the father of her children. This not only gives her heart the excuse for occupying itself with him but allows it to formulate the sophistry that her love of him is part of her love of them. In spite of her having been married for a dozen years, Mme. de Rênal is to all intents and purposes a virgin. The experience of sex with her husband has left her utterly unmoved. It is part of the social convention of marriage, even though it has resulted in the very natural product of her sons. This merely serves to underline the difference between love and motherhood, which is for Mme. de Rênal the major contradiction produced by civilization. She never succeeds in resolving this contradiction, although her behavior with respect to both elements of it is tragically noble. Her husband simply has no substantial existence for her. She doesn't hate him, and her adultery serves only to bring to light the fact that he was never anything real for her. He is as crude in his relation to women as he is to everything and everyone else. He is used to her and counts on her, but he has taken her for granted and is incapable of understanding or sympathizing with the movements of her soul. In a recapitulation of the human relations of the bourgeoisie in general, she is for him the other who remains intransigently the other, whereas love is the story of the other becoming one's own or one's self. His sufferings are only comic and are themselves a justification for her adultery. He thinks about having a duel, which Julien would have agreed to in an instant, but after thinking it through decides that it would be imprudent. The appearance of prudence covers over the fact of cowardice. He cannot send her away because that would compromise the inheritance from her rich aunt. He is really very unhappy, but the ways of his unhappiness are contemptible and ridiculous. Stendhal stacks the deck in favor of Mme. de Rênal's adultery. He underlines the fact that she is an adulteress by making us always think of her as Mme. de Rênal, while Mathilde is always Mathilde, and Julien always Julien. We learn that her Christian or intimate name is Louise only when Stendhal lets us enter the mind of M. de Rênal, who reflects that he is very used to Louise (I.21). She is always clad in the respectability of marriage, even and especially when she is committing adultery.

As Mme. de Rênal comes to admire Julien more and more she knows only delight and pleasure. Her little bit of *amour-propre* expresses itself when she finds out that her servant Elisa loves Julien and she fears that Julien may reciprocate. This *amour-propre* deceives her into thinking she is performing a disinterested deed when she offers to aid Elisa in her hopes for Julien. Thus *amour-propre* assists in making her aware that she loves and in adding value to Julien's love. She suddenly asks herself, "Is it possible that I am in love . . . ?" (I.8). Then one night while tossing in her sleep she is struck by the frightful word "adultery," prior to the actual event (I.11). As Taine points out, the mere word, a kind of abstraction, terrifies her and changes the whole meaning of what is going on in her heart.[14] It never stops what is going on there. It doesn't even poison her affections. When she is with Julien she is purely and wholly in love with him, but this word fractures the unity of her being, while it also deepens the love and its significance. The detailed depiction of this psychology is where Stendhal excels, and it is what interests him most. If one does not have or has lost the taste for such examination, Stendhal's book becomes a hollow shell, at best a tame story of adventure. For a real psychologist, which is what Nietzsche thinks Stendhal is in the highest degree, his novels are endlessly fascinating because they observe these phenomena with precision and without interpretive abstraction. The loss of this taste accounts, at least in part, for critics' need to look to all kinds of external things in order to keep in business. They want to teach Stendhal their boring science because they are deaf to the fascination of all he has to teach us.

Mme. de Rênal goes through the motions of resisting Julien at his first approaches, but this is mere habitual behavior, appropriate to her position as the proper wife of the mayor of Verrières, and her resistance rapidly melts. One never doubts that she will give in or that she will be faithful to her choice. Her token resistance, somewhat reinforced by doubts about Julien's seriousness, disappears rapidly because she is so sure of her instincts. This woman, who appears so passive and gentle, evinces the daring and the firmness of a general when she is involved in her affair and needs to protect Julien, her children, and herself. There is no weakness, and she behaves perfectly. She has no more bad conscience about deceiving her husband in these circumstances than does a general about deceiving an enemy. Her reaction to the anonymous letters that denounce her is quick-witted and subtle. All of this is a surprise to us and to her.

The affair's vulnerability comes from Mme. de Rênal's attachment to her children, that other pole of her nature. When the eldest of her sons gets sick she is overcome with guilt and terror, fearing that this is punishment, divine punishment, for her adultery. The tension between her love and her children is expressed in her religious terrors. This tension is the most essential characteristic of female psychology in Stendhal's world. The love of her children is very real but also relatively feeble compared with the total passion she has for Julien. She experiences no need to reinforce her sentiments toward her husband, but her concern for her children does require this religious supplement. This is exactly the same mechanism that was at work with Julie when she covered over her love of Saint-Preux with worry about her husband's atheism. In the actual presence of Julien she is completely his and confident in what she does, although she does not forget her children. In another twist on the status of children with respect to the erotic life, Julien at the very end wants Mme. de Rênal to be the real mother of his child, with whom Mathilde is pregnant. The child who naturally belongs to the individual who bears it apparently should really belong to the one with whom one is in love. This is what nature should want, if the law of love is believed to be primary. Goethe plays on this theme with great delicacy in

Elective Affinities when husband and wife, who are each in love with someone else, make love, or make-believe love, with their true loves in mind. The child who results from the act resembles the true loves who were imagined during it.[15]

Mme. de Rênal's religion is most powerful when she must do without Julien. She is no longer able to return to her pre-Julien routine, so only a life of dedication to religious duty and consolation can maintain her without Julien. Although she has faith in her faith during these periods, the mere presence of Julien suffices to dispel all that. During the time when Julien is in the seminary and cannot communicate with her, she devotes herself to religious practice. But an impromptu visit by Julien late in the night encounters only *pro forma* resistance, although that resistance is almost too much for the eager Julien. He always deprives the poor woman of her self-deceptions that make it more or less possible for her to exist without him. But one is not sure whether this cruelty is so awful, because she is at her best when she is loving Julien.

Julien makes love to this prodigy in ridiculous ways appropriate to his proud nature. He meets her and says, as it were, to himself, "This means war." He conducts his seduction as Napoleon conducted his battles, and he issues bulletins to himself. He begins his attachment to her out of revenge against her husband's superior position and gradually moves closer to her out of revenge for what he takes to be her belief that she is superior to him. M. de Rênal does wish to humiliate Julien because he thinks such behavior is aristocratic. (The real aristocrats humiliate Julien without meaning to do so, although Julien always sees slights as intended.) Julien imagines putting himself in the position of being rebuffed and then actually being rebuffed. He plots real revenge in response to this humiliation that exists only in his imagination. Self-respect is his only motive, and he has absolutely no interest in the love of Mme. de Rênal. Because he has such a need to keep his defensive forces on the alert, he cannot permit himself any trust in the enemy. He misinterprets almost every signal she gives him. He makes holding her hand a duty. Hours of anxiety and fear precede his grasping the forbidden hand, and his only interest is whether he will have the courage to do so. He owes it to his Roman character to do this. Again, when the moment has come, his great interest is whether he will be able to fulfill his project by taking the ladder and climbing up to the room. His intrepidity, which is the half-false variety founded on his *amour-propre*, is in stark contrast with hers, which is set in motion without doubt or hesitation simply because of the supreme value for her of their being together. All of this is high comedy as presented by Stendhal. Julien has moments, when he calms down a bit as a result of his habitual intercourse with her, when he is actually present in the love affair without making it into a war. But these moments are short-lived, and he is always ready to go off to new adventures that will further his Napoleonic ambition. When he returns for the one night after leaving the seminary on his way to Paris, his adventure is fueled by the desire to reassert himself over the powers of religion. It takes him a couple of hours to break down her resistance. Stendhal points out that if she had acceded to his requests a little earlier, he would have enjoyed the lovemaking. But it took too long and again the whole business became an issue of the vanity of winning instead of the pleasure of being together.

Julien's silliness does not lead simply to a negative evaluation of him. He does have an element of Don Quixote in him, but the comedy is that of the talented upstart in a world where there are no longer roles for his talent. Stendhal laughs through his tears and suggests that Julien would have put it all in place if he had lived longer and healed his wounded *amour-propre*. Yet that *amour-propre* is the source of what is best about him. Stendhal appears unable to depict a fully ripe man. Successful maturity is doubtful for him, and he may in this reflect a problem with the Romantic mood altogether. As the Marquis de La Mole, no mean observer of men, says, Julien responded to his condition not by seeking petty advantage but by asserting himself against contempt, real or imagined. Thus, while being the slave of these others who might despise him, he insists on himself, on his own dignity, on what is within him and what he owes himself. At the very end he regards his peculiar merit, the quality that saves him from being a nothing, to be the law of *duty* that he has imposed on himself. This is his characteristic form of *amour-propre* and an illustration of Rousseau's ideas of soul construction. Ultimately, Rousseau hoped that this formation of the idea of duty would become independent of the slights of others in which it began, and Stendhal's admiration for Julien's character echoes this hope. The man who bases his action precisely on rejection of petty desires and petty fears is the antibourgeois.

The comic side of Julien is represented by his encounter with a bully in a bar in Besançon, who challenges Julien by looking at him. It does not come to a fight or a duel, but Julien senses himself to have been humiliated, a condition that endures for more than a year. This bully is a low type who should not engage the vanity of a gentleman and with whom a gentleman would refuse to fight. Julien runs into him again in the street in Paris, challenges him to a duel, and takes his card. When he goes for the ritual visit with his second, he finds that the name and address on the card are those of a fatuous young diplomat whose servant the bully turns out to be. So Julien has to have a parody of a duel with the master. The servant is dismissed by his master and is beaten by Julien, who is then wounded in the duel and becomes the friend and companion of the man who wounds him. The whole business of dueling is a now absurd remnant of the *ancien régime*.[16] There is not enough vitality in the idea of honor to justify it, although the decent Marquis de Croisenois dies in a duel in defense of Mathilde's lost honor. Once Julien is able to put his Besançon antagonist in his proper place, he never thinks about him again. But this haughty will to assert his natural place against the insults of the conventional world remains the central aspect of his soul. We are a step away from the triumph of the will. His capacity to experience love can emerge only when he is definitively cured of this feverish *amour-propre*, but it is the condition for his tasting true love, which itself is free of this struggle.

By contrast, without that true love, the relation between Julien and his Parisian love, Mathilde de La Mole, consists entirely of *amour-propre*. If Stendhal didn't carry this episode off with such wit, it would be the stuff of Hollywood melodrama, the provincial who arrives on the great stage and immediately has a love affair with the greatest and apparently most unattainable of stars, in this case, the richest, the noblest, and most beautiful of Parisian women. Their epic struggle is framed by the fact that she is condescending to him and he appears to be social climbing. Neither can accept the indignity of this disproportion in their social positions. Mathilde, of course, unlike Julien, has everything and need not aspire to anything in the real world around her. She is bored, and it is this boredom that expresses the ultimate situation of man in the nineteenth century. Julien is too busy climbing the ladder to be bored, but Mathilde, who is born on its highest rung, is able to survey the scene and recognize that, once there, nothing is worth doing. Boredom had become a theme of French literature in the seventeenth century with Pascal's account of it as the special experience of the man without God. Nothing is left to do in a world whose beautiful surface has been dissolved by the rational criticism of the Cartesian *cogito*. The life of such a man alternates between furious, self-forgetting activity and boredom, which homogenizes everything on the outside and makes nothing appear to be worthy of concern. This is the strand in French thought that counters the Enlightenment and its optimistic this-worldly concerns. Pascal is the genius invoked by nineteenth-century French literature in its antipoetic Enlightenment science and politics. But what is striking about Stendhal and many other Romantics is that they adopt Pascal's analysis without the radical religious faith that made it possible. For Pascal it is the absence of God for those who are hungry for Him that is the source of their boredom. Only the presence of that hunger makes it clear that the ordinary food of the soul does not nourish. But Stendhal denies that there is or ever was a God. A nothingness becomes the standard for the judgment of the world. Longing, not the object of longing, is his standard for such judgment. The emptiness at the top haunts this literature. Stendhal tries to fill this emptiness with love or poetic creation.

The impoverishment of Mathilde's world comes to light by way of her imagination of a world where there were real men and real lovers, willing to die for their causes and their beloveds. Her criticism is simply the old refrain: what's wrong with the bourgeoisie, above all, is the absence of anything to die for or the willingness to die. Willingness to die is the touchstone for her and is her great mystery. Her boredom seeks drama, which would permit self-forgetting. The historical epoch to which she attaches herself, her novel, is the age of Henri III, which was indeed the peak of French vigor, the moment of the religious wars where faith was still compelling enough to fight about. This was also close to the moment of the Fronde, when proud, independent aristocrats still could rebel against the creeping absolutism of the monarchy. Aristocrats were aristocrats then and kings were kings, which neither are now. One of her ancestors was the lover of a queen and was put to death because of his participation in a conspiracy. This was a stage worth acting on; and, although Mathilde's imagination injects too much of the romantic element into the great theological and political issues of that day, that element was certainly present in France more than in other countries. The proud and willful girl makes a cult of this family tradition, and each year she celebrates the anniversary of her ancestor's execution and forces the family to play along, using the antique names for her various relatives. The nineteenth century as presented here through Mathilde's eyes is the careful, self-protective moment of the bourgeoisie, prior to the spurious corrective of bohemianism and the even later attempt of the bourgeoisie itself to be bohemian. Stendhal would, I believe, say that the fundamental motives are revealed in this earliest stage and that what came later was elaborate deception and self-deception.

There is no moment when Mathilde simply sees someone and

loves or hates him. Everybody must pass through her internal casting bureau in order to see whether he fits a role in the play she produces. This casting is the framework in which her relationship with Julien evolves. At first he is a matter of no more interest than any servant to her, and he thinks that she is really unattractive in her haughtiness. Then she notices his firm heroic stance when she hears him talking about politics. Her first reflection is that this is not a man born on his knees. The two previously had a certain union of taste, both filching volumes of Voltaire from the Marquis' library, the notorious Voltaire, forbidden in Julien's seminary and Mathilde's convent as well as by the public opinion of the Bourbon restoration. Unlike Mme. de Rênal, both Julien and Mathilde are readers, and readers who read essential books. Her first attraction to Julien occurs in the context of his relationship to the Count d'Altamira, who is the leader of a conspiracy to overthrow the monarchy of Naples and is under sentence of death. That makes Altamira interesting too. Julien certainly is attracted by him, and his discussion with Altamira makes him forget the mannequins who inhabit the Marquis' salon. But Altamira's attractiveness for Mathilde is ruined by the fact that he is a Liberal, which means that his standard is *utility*, the last thing Mathilde wants. She would want a revolution against utility, in which one sacrificed one's life for the *beau geste* alone.

Perhaps it should be added that the Count d'Altamira is apparently not very good-looking, whereas Julien is exceptionally beautiful. Mathilde would not see it in this way. Julien's good looks would have to be an expression of his proud rebellious soul for her, but that soul would probably be uninteresting to her if it did not come in such a body. Of course Mathilde has to think about how she could square an affair with Julien with her grand sense of her position. She engages in a great deal of sophistry with herself about natural aristocracy and the possibility of raising Julien in the social order. All of this fantasizing is an essential part of the passion that is developing. Its gestation is furthered by Julien's apparent indifference to her, which makes him a special challenge. How dare this *roturier* be indifferent to such a great lady? Julien, on his side, thinks he has no interest in her, but he is really preoccupied with the improbability of such a great lady's being interested in him or, if she were, the probability of her merely playing with him. His sensitive vanity furthers the romance because he appears to manifest a noble indifference, something worth the effort to combat. Thus, mutual misunderstanding is the stuff on which imagination and *amour-propre* feed. When the involvement reaches its culmination, the immediate response of this girl is, "How could I have done such a thing with such a low person?" The release of sexual tension puts Julien, not precisely back into perspective, but into another false perspective. Then she hates and wounds him to the extent of her appreciable gifts at doing so. This leads to a scene in the Marquis' library where Julien pulls an antique knife from its scabbard and threatens to kill her. She is ravished by this sign of affection. There follows another great night together, this time with the drama continuing after the act. Julien, disappearing, as is his wont, through the window and down the ladder, receives a huge lock of his mistress's hair, which is thrown after him. This permits Mathilde to use her art of doing up her hair in such a way as to hide what she has done from her family while providing an exciting secret understanding between Julien and herself. Piquancy is added by a certain desire to be discovered and to flaunt the conventions openly. These are the kinds of things that fuel the mad passions essential to her.

The fact is that the entire affair between these two strange persons is an erotic version of the dialectic of master and slave. When she is up, he is down, and vice versa. It is a struggle for mastery over another's desires, and as in all such conquests, the interest is only in the acquisition, not in the enjoyment of what has been acquired. Each seeks the validation of his or her worth by another who is a worthy judge. The problem is that as soon as this other has capitulated, he or she is no longer a worthy judge. The capitulation proves weakness, and the struggle comes up empty. The only things that keep this affair going are the counterattacks of the apparently defeated enemy and the need to come back to the charge in order to make the conquest final. In this war no prisoners are taken and the psychological cruelties are barbaric. Julien goes through the most extreme sufferings, where he accepts her negative judgments as definitive and true evaluations of his small worth. He lives entirely in the capricious movements of her soul. This is exquisite torture and as extreme an alienation as can be imagined. Life is drained of all content except obsessive reflection about what has happened and how he can restore himself. This too is a variety of love. No one can doubt the connectedness here, but there is no moment of true reciprocity or enjoyment of each other for what each really is.

Finally, Julien explicitly recognizes that he must *subjugate* Mathilde. He restores himself in one of Stendhal's great comic inventions, paralleled only by Fabrice del Dongo's sermons as archbishop of Parma in which he makes love to Clélia. A wild Russian suggests that he court the prudish and ridiculously snobbish wife of a field marshal in order to make Mathilde jealous and provides a packet of ready-made love letters written by a Russian friend in an attempted seduction of an English lady. Julien sends these letters off daily, sometimes forgetting to change London to Paris in them or to perform any of the other alterations necessary to make the letters appropriate. He does not bother reading the responses. He coolly tortures Mathilde, who is reengaged by his indifference and the appearance of an apparent rival on the stage. Mathilde loses all dignity, sidling up to Julien in the salon to hear what he is saying to the field marshal's wife. By a great act of will and the aid of the ready-made battle plan of the Russian, he for the moment brings her back to heel. This is when he begins using the word "subjugation" and asks for guarantees. The final guarantee that Mathilde offers is her pregnancy, which means that she has sacrificed everything to him.

This affair might well today be characterized as sadomasochistic. And this language would not be completely groundless if one stripped it of its perverse and pseudoscientific overtones. The Marquis de Sade, who wrote not long before this time, seemed to think that the most intense pleasure was the pain one could cause another, and used the sexual excitement he hoped to generate as an excuse for sermonizing about alienated social relations. There seems to be a certain advantage contained in relations of pain in a world where it is doubtful whether pleasures can be social or shared. This doubt seems justified in the gentler sexual activities, but there is no doubt in the mind of someone who causes pain that his screaming victim is relating to him. It is also true that the passive partner is gratified by the real interest expressed by the active one in his torture. Sadomasochism is a peculiarly modern form of lovemaking. The elaborate and absurd rituals that often accompany sadomasochistic relations as they are practiced today indicate that this is where we now find the free play of imagination in erotic encounters and almost the only place where ritual is still alive. Although I would not deny the possibility that there were such experiences among men and women in earlier ages, I doubt they were very central. I am inclined to think that sadomasochism achieves its new power only at a time when the possibility of love based on nature has become doubtful. It is an eroticization of the will and the peculiar pleasures of its exercise in imposing order on a chaotic world. Merely labeling sadism and masochism as a perversion does not deal with the existential situation underlying them. Nature, homogenized, no longer authorizes relations of sub- and superordination, nor does free consent or convention. Rank order is constituted merely by the will and the force the will can generate. The stronger will wills the weaker will's willing to be formed and put into an order. This is the struggle between form and matter when form no longer naturally informs matter. Stendhal is not a follower of Sade, but he does depict powerfully, attractively, and amusingly a love whose content is entirely provided by *amour-propre*, the desire for primacy. He offers an alternative in the love of Mme. de Rênal, but if there is no Mme. de Rênal, one has to make do with Mathilde. Just as she longs for the willingness to die without much consideration of that for which one dies, she admires the pure will of the one who is able to dominate her. The absence of men who care enough to enter into this struggle is an abiding theme of much Romantic literature. The distinction between seduction and force, both based upon man's superior strength, begins to disappear, and leads to Nietzsche's dictum, "Are you going to women? Don't forget the whip."[17] In sum, when the will to power has become our metaphysics, love becomes a derivative expression of power.

When Julien is winning his war with Mathilde, after getting the habit of the ups and downs of the relationship and before he has a chance to become bored and contemptuous in his turn, he develops a certain real affection for this spirited girl and her passion to play a role in the human comedy. But there is little time for such self-aware affection, and it is not, in any event, substantial enough to sustain itself. Almost immediately, she is lifting him to the heights, arranging a brilliant military and diplomatic career, and presenting him with what he assumes will be a son to be an heir to his achievements. He is on the verge of a dukedom, his natural father being declared not to be his father while he becomes the son of an old duke, a status fitting his nature. This is the peak of what the nineteenth century can offer to ambition, but for him it is also the peak of alienation; he lives the actualization of dreams that arose out of envy.

Just at the moment of fulfillment, as he approaches the sun in his winged chariot, he is shot down by his old provincial love. The denouement of this novel is induced by Mme. de Rênal's piety. Julien has disappeared in the vortex of Parisian life, and she has returned to her remorseful observance. He has the gall to suggest that she be a reference for him to the Marquis de La Mole, who is deciding whether to accept Julien as a son-in-law for his daughter. Under the direction of her scheming confessor, who is trying to make a reputation for himself, Mme. de Rênal writes a letter, not utterly counterfactual, accusing Julien of moving into households and using the women in them to further his ambition. Julien, in a rage, goes and shoots her in church. But by his attempted murder he purges himself of his *amour-propre* and the indignation that defends it. The only person whom this hero actually shoots in the novel is a praying woman. She of course repents her religious excess and returns to her true religion, Julien. Everything about the piety of this woman is said by her confessor: she is in love with Julien and calls it remorse. This is all a very curious and interesting commentary on competition between religion and eroticism for the spiritual energy of the human soul. Which of the two is more real and more satisfying is obvious. Finally, Julien recognizes that what he regarded as only an episode or a stepping-stone was and is the thing in itself. The very being together, the total absorption in each other, is now accompanied by the awareness that this is sufficient happiness because he has had the experiences that prove its worth. Poor Mathilde is reduced to her true proportions. False love is destroyed by true love. With her, no such being together is possible. Without any ill will or any involvement of vanity, he is convinced that she will go on to others and another life, whereas with Mme. de Rênal and him this is all there is. Their senses of their own existence depend on each other without any contradiction between them. One might say, as Julien sometimes does in prison, that he has ruined his life by his incapacity to recognize this. But Stendhal appears to suggest that the few days of perfect harmony between Julien and Mme. de Rênal are enough to judge their lives happy. Similarly, the death of Julien at twenty-three might seem to be tragic, cutting off a life before it has begun, but again, Stendhal suggests that Julien has had the most important experiences and that no sequel could live up to the richness of what he has done with his life and its conclusion. Intensity is ever so much more important than duration, and no adult bourgeois life is anything but duration. Julien imitates Socrates, Boethius, and many others who proved that happiness can be completed in a prison. They demonstrated the power and the consolation of philosophy. Julien demonstrates the power and consolation of love. This is Stendhal's legacy.

In prison Julien goes through many hesitations, doubts, and reversals of sentiment and opinion. He continues to worry about what men will think of him. His speech in the court is a mixture of bravado and pathetic complaint about the injustice to the poor in conventional political orders. Terror of death assaults him, and he wonders whether the law of firmness he has prescribed to himself will suffice to overcome this animal instinct and permit him to go proudly to his execution. But amid all of this confusion, the presence of Mme. de Rênal conquers, and he dies with the same gay abandon with which he lived when he was at his best. His love gives him a little touch of eternity when there is no other eternity for him. Mathilde, like the queen of Navarre, gets his head after bribing the craven priests who are in charge of death and its public interpretation. She buries him in a grotto with suitable pageantry and establishes a shrine for a cult dedicated to this great lover. Three days after Julien's execution, Mme. de Rênal, who is not jealous of Mathilde and needs no aping of sacred ceremony for the public expression of her love, for whom the only witness is Julien, simply dies with the thought of Julien and in the presence of her children, the only two things that had any reality for her and which express the problem of a human life for a good woman. The end of the two lovers is sad but also somehow sweet and heartening. The utter despair we find in *Madame Bovary* is not to be found here.

Julien and Mme. de Rênal did find each other in spite of the thickets of propriety and convention. This is Stendhal's response to any suspicions that human existence is futile.

3. Austen, *Pride and Prejudice*

I Jane Austen's world seems to be as far away from Stendhal's as is possible. Here one breathes a totally different air. The language is that of reason rather than of sentiment, virtue rather than sincerity, and moderation rather than daring. Accommodation to the social order is inevitably preferred to the Continental's criminality. All attachments are directed to marriage and fidelity to the marriage contract. Neither the adulteress nor the seduced maiden is justified, although they may be the objects of sympathy—a very qualified sympathy. Everyone is held to standards of duty and morality, and individual responsibility is the incessant theme of her novels. And in her world, duty and morality are not the subject of complicated or sophisticated interpretation. They are the results of principles that every tolerably well raised ten-year-old knows—obedience to the law, honesty, respect for one's parents, loyalty to friends, and gratitude to benefactors. The admirable qualities in Jane Austen's world sound like a list of contraries to the list one finds in Stendhal. Jane Austen is the steadfast defender of *bon sens* against self-expression and commitment. These characteristics are present so consistently and insistently that Jane Austen can appear to some to be a defender of conventional morality against the rights of individuality and to others as a partisan of Aristotelian rationalism against the dominant principles of modernity.

Any personage in her novels who presents the charms of the Romantic hero or heroine or who feels, does, or expresses extreme things is cast in a negative light. The acceptable emotional range in

Jane Austen is very limited, to say the least, compared with French or Russian novelists. There are bad people but none of the monsters that one finds in Stendhal, Balzac, or Dostoyevsky. Wickham in *Pride and Prejudice* is thoroughly disagreeable and contemptible, but more weak than evil, certainly no highway robber or murderer. And the other bad persons suffer from vices like envy, jealousy, snobbism, and too great a concern with money. All of them are normal parts of respectable country life.

Nothing much really happens in Austen's novels. The action is confined to the quest for mates and the more or less successful outcomes of such quests. There are no politics, no conspiracies, no high crimes, no wars. In *Pride and Prejudice* soldiers play a certain role, but that there is a great war on with Napoleon, or that these men might be called upon to fight and die, is at best hinted at. The only reference to the grand politics of the day, the memory of which is for Julien Sorel the great scene against which he measures his own deeds and ambitions, is that the "peace" caused the disbanding of the military units in the Bennets' neighborhood (III.19).* The soldiers and their uniforms are introduced only for their sexual attractiveness, to show the frivolousness of some girls, in particular Lydia Bennet. The good men, Bingley and Darcy, seem to have in no way participated in the great political and ideological events of the day. Austen's horizon is so narrow and cramped that one might accuse her of being simply feminine, unable to recognize or appreciate politics, war, and the movement of great ideas. The alternatives presented are impoverished compared with those presented by Stendhal. Religion is present in the person of the ridiculous Mr. Collins, but it is only part of the scenery, neither a great enemy nor a great hope.

What we have is a class of country gentry who do absolutely nothing. Mr. Gardiner has a business, and he is in that regard an outstanding exception. Everyone else has an income of one kind or another that permits him or her to live more or less comfortably without working. The Bennets are not wealthy, but they have a house that would appear to be a palace to contemporary homeowners, and they have three servants. The time of this class is spent in passing time, visiting one another (a six-week visit is considered insultingly short by Lady Catherine de Bourgh), letter writing, playing cards, unenlightening conversation, gossip, and, above all, endless matchmaking. Austen seems calmly to accept what would

---

* All parenthetical citations in this chapter are to volume and chapter of Jane Austen's *Pride and Prejudice*.

appear to Stendhal to be an unheroic bourgeois life, the hatred of which animates his literary career. The great heroic models are simply absent from the consciousness of her personages and are not regretted. This is the life that for Stendhal justifies rebellion and despair. In short, Jane Austen's world, when one comes to *Pride and Prejudice* fresh from *The Red and the Black*, is boring. But when one actually reads Austen, the intensity and excitement are as great as or greater than what one discovers in other writers. It is a kind of miracle, but the fate of Jane and Elizabeth Bennet in their relations to Bingley and Darcy engages us. Stripped of all external drama, the history of the heart as presented by Austen is endlessly fascinating.

The excitement of these stories is accompanied by the laughter Jane Austen provokes in her readers. It is the laughter produced by irony. One thing all critics agree upon is that Jane Austen's prevailing tone is ironical. In a gentle way, she ridicules practically everything, not only the pretensions of inferior persons like Mr. Collins or the Bingley sisters with their concerns for money and place, but also the self-deceptions of her protagonists, and even the hopes and expectations attendant upon the marriages that seem to be their fulfillment. And it is this irony that perhaps most links her to the classical tradition. Real irony has a lot to do with the virtue missing in modern thought, moderation. It is the tone of superiority politely exposing inferiority without wounding it, leaving things in their place while nevertheless understanding them. It is a certain art of deception, the mode of radical thought that accepts conventional life while itself remaining free. Irony flourishes on the disproportion between the way things are and the way they should be while accepting the necessity of this disproportion. It is a classical style because the ancients did not expect that reality could become rational. Stupidity they thought to be inexpungible. Moderation, rather than being the expression of a timid or easygoing soul, was for them the expression of one who has overcome hope and therefore indignation. The reserve that one finds in Jane Austen, which Leo Strauss has compared to that of Xenophon,[1] is a result not of simple-mindedness or naïveté but of an awareness of nuance and a contempt for vulgar sophistication. It obscures superiority in an egalitarian world rather than trumpeting superiority and complaining about its lack of recognition. It is the means of maintaining proportion in an essentially unchanging and unchangeable world. In short, irony seems to presuppose the distinction between theory and practice, and is far away from *praxis*, that recent invention which is neither one nor the other. Socrates is the ironical figure *par excellence* and always appears to lack sincerity or good faith, the new virtues of a later age. The aggravating conventionality of Jane Austen's mind reflects her aggravating acceptance of the conventional life and goals of the world she portrays. She does not rebel against the idle, propertied class that she depicts, nor does she try to liberate women from their humiliating dependence on men. But she does make us laugh at these things, indicating that there is much joy and strength to be gained simply from knowing. This perspective is largely absent in the Romantics. This woman who writes exclusively of the relation between male and female, and who, as a writer, is nothing but a matchmaker, was herself a spinster, and none the worse for it. Stendhal seems to envy the young and beautiful Julien; Austen does not seem to envy the successes of her heroines. Austen represents and justifies reason and leisure in human affairs when they are in short supply and without much honor in literature and life. She is like Socrates, who appears hopelessly conventional and moralistic to Thrasymachus, with whom he ironizes, while he actually knows everything Thrasymachus knows, and much more, and goes well beyond Thrasymachus' strong critique of justice. But he is angry neither at the fact of injustice nor at Thrasymachus. A decent respect for the perhaps illusory convictions of men who are at least partly decent is his mode, a mode that protects him as well as these men and gets more to the heart of things. Rather than railing at stupidity and boasting, comedy does best to treat them with the greatest apparent respect, as does Socrates in both Plato's and Xenophon's account of him. This is also Jane Austen's mode.

Irony is a branch of humor that has declined continuously since the end of the eighteenth century, and the very word has become almost meaningless—think of an expression like "a tragic irony" or "an ironic twist." I have used the term "irony" in relation to Stendhal when he laughs at his major actors. But this was perhaps too loose a usage. Stendhal loves to shock; Jane Austen avoids it. Stendhal sees only what is wrong with conventions; Austen tries to see what is sound in them. Stendhal really only ridicules rather than ironizes. His rebelliousness and indignation are too great to permit contemplative distance, which is a precondition of irony. Irony disappears when revolutionary politics triumph. The possibilities of truly fundamental change and the writer's conviction that he might contribute to it tend toward humorlessness. Moreover, the writer is inclined to regard himself as part of his age and its movements, denying the speculative distance that earlier writers believed they had attained.

In all these respects Austen seems a part of an older world and far away from the one founded by Rousseau and his followers. But it would be misleading to leave it at that. The centrality and even sacredness of marriage for all of her novels indicates a certain connection with Rousseau's reform of the novel. Much more, the importance of the assent of the sentiments and of love itself, neither of which is simply rational, makes Jane Austen's sobriety appear to be a supplement to, rather than a replacement for, the Romantic quest. There is very much that is sensible and reasonable in Rousseau's view of marriage in *Emile*, and Stendhal's was not the only way for the novelist to go once he or she had fallen under Rousseau's influence. Certainly Jane Austen mutes the effusiveness of lovers, although it is there, for example, when Darcy can finally let himself go. Sympathy for an adulteress, which is the theme of the other three novels we are treating, is simply beyond her reach. But the principle she would and does invoke for rejecting such sympathy is one that Rousseau would surely endorse: a woman should freely choose her husband, but when she has chosen, she must stick by her choice. This woman's freedom to choose is Rousseauan, and it was not a right universally recognized at the time. Moreover, for Austen that choice had to be made on the basis of real love, which she admits is a result of inclination, not reason.

A truly classical view of marriage can be found in Xenophon's *Oeconomicus* where everything is decided reasonably by the husband without concern for love.[2] The only considerations are those of utility relating to the common work or task of the married couple in running the household and raising the children. Austen brings passionate love to marriage where the classical moralists never encouraged it. It was not that they simply rejected or despised love in marriage, but that it got in the way of being reasonable. They appear to have said: be reasonable first and love might follow later. Certainly the virtues of the partners would concern those who determine the match, but they would not insist that those virtues be lovable. Nothing could be further from the spirit of Jane Austen than the arranged marriage, whereas for Aristotle it would probably be the preferred mode of matching a couple. In Jane Austen the parents are distinctly unwise, and this is another sign of the Romantic element in her. Her heroines' ways of asserting their wills against their parents are very different from the characteristically Romantic rebellion, but the assertion of the will is nonetheless essential. Parents are not privy to the sentiments that constitute love in their children. Austen's heroes must think through their attractions and tend not to have the experience of *le coup de foudre*, but this thinking through is an attempt to ascertain the genuineness and seriousness of the sentiments rather than to discover whether having such sentiments is reasonable. Jane Austen would never insist on the illusoriness of love, and she always underpins love with solid supports like property and proof of fixed character.

Nevertheless, like Rousseau she believes that sexual love—and there are plenty of indications that Jane Austen knows a great deal about sexual attraction—ought to be directed toward the virtue of the partner, and courtship is an attempt by each to discover those virtues in the other. The greatest betrayal of the seriousness of the relationship would be to decide about marriage on the basis of mere sexual attraction. The adjustment of the sexual passion to the love of virtue is for Jane Austen the central question, as it is for Rousseau, and the wholly unclassical expectation of these novels is that one's beloved will be one's best friend or that marriage is itself the essential friendship. By contrast, the unerotic and uninstitutionalized character of friendship is fully expressed in Aristotle's *Ethics* and Montaigne's "Of Friendship." Jane Austen presents a reasonable picture of what may be an unreasonable hope, that is, the harmonious union of sexual desire with love, marriage, and friendship.

II The very title, *Pride and Prejudice*, indicates that the involvement of the two lovers, Fitzwilliam Darcy and Elizabeth Bennet, is powered by the psychology of *amour-propre*. The misunderstandings between the two have to do with a struggle for recognition and preeminence. Each becomes interesting to the other because he or she is not a pushover. Contempt and resentment, or opinions about the other's opinions, determine the attachment while impeding it. Elizabeth's problem with Darcy, that he is condescending to her because of the prejudice of his superior wealth, is exactly the same one that Sophie has with Emile at the outset of their romance, and the happy resolution of their affairs can come to pass only when Elizabeth and Sophie are persuaded that their opinion about their suitors' prejudice of wealth is only their own prejudice. Pride is evidently understood to be a vice, particularly by those who think they are victims of Darcy's or anyone else's alleged high self-esteem, but that self-esteem is essential to both Darcy's and Elizabeth's strong characters as well as to their capacity to get along with each other. Each claims to despise other people's opinions; but actually they are both extremely sensitive to the opinions of those they might get romantically involved with or whom they consider to be worthy judges of themselves. There is a delicate balance between the need for self-esteem and the need for the esteem of others, and neither can be sacrificed to the other. This unavowed and perhaps unconscious concern for the good witness of the person one admires is an important mechanism in the most profound sociality, the love between men and women. Elizabeth's extremely amusing father lacks sufficient concern for the opinions of others, and this is a real weakness in him. Rousseau makes a distinction between pride and vanity, but only on the basis of the relative greatness of the objects envisioned by the two dispositions. Elizabeth's pedantic sister Mary says that vanity concerns the opinions of others whereas pride concerns one's opinion of oneself (I.5). This makes sense, but it is not true. The proud persons in this novel, Darcy and Elizabeth, worry very much about what the other thinks. What distinguishes them from Mr. Collins, who is a weathervane, is that everything he is is constituted by his adaptation to the opinions of his conventional superiors, whereas Darcy and Elizabeth pride themselves on their independence of such opinions. Elizabeth's passionate rejection of Darcy's first proposal is a remarkable self-assertion, a refusal of one of the most eligible bachelors in the whole of England by a girl of no position and no means. This is extremely impressive, but it surely depends on her opinion of what his opinion of her is. She cannot tolerate the belief she attributes to him that he is marrying beneath himself. In this scene she is a little like Julien Sorel, strong but self-deluded as to her independence and indifference. She lacks too much self-knowledge to be proud in her sense. The action of the novel helps her to attain self-knowledge. Together the couple and each of its members will be proud.

Darcy, for his part, plays the role of a Romantic hero in the grip of a destructive passion he cannot control. He hides from himself his dependence on Elizabeth by trying to despise her while making a desperate suit to her. "I shouldn't be doing this, and your situation makes you unworthy of me, but you will be gratified to know that I cannot do without you." This is in sum what Darcy says to her, and it certainly provides grounds for rejecting him. But a person wiser than Elizabeth was at that moment would have recognized how purely defensive it was. Elizabeth's vulnerability makes her respond in such a way as to correct the disproportion between their situations by insisting that what she brings naturally is of ever so much more worth than what he brings conventionally. All of this is misunderstanding, which the reader quickly realizes will be set right. The clarification of the misunderstandings will be an education for both and make it possible for them to be together harmoniously forever.

The importance of Elizabeth's *amour-propre* for her romantic attachment is highlighted by her relationships with the two other men who make some kind of claim on her attention. The first is Mr. Collins, who is persuaded that Elizabeth will be delighted to marry him because he thinks himself charming, because he is on the way to a great and lucrative career in the Church, because he is patronized by Lady Catherine de Bourgh, a superior being who also happens to be Darcy's aunt, and because he will inherit the Bennet house when Mr. Bennet dies and expects that Elizabeth will want to keep it in the family. She rejects his suit with ridicule and contempt. She is not angry that someone to whom she is not attracted has the nerve to sue for her hand, but is disgusted by his vanity and lack of real feeling. Within a couple of days this great lover finds someone else. Elizabeth is completely indifferent to Collins and whatever opinion he might have of her, and is therefore an accurate judge of his character and motives. She is a bit like her detached father, who carries on a continuous correspondence with Mr. Collins because the latter's stupidity delights him. The second suitor is Mr. Wickham, who is charming, graceful, and attractive. Elizabeth to some degree seems to fall under the spell of his erotic appeal. He is very good-looking, dances well, and is gallant with ladies. She appreciates his apparent preference for her among all the eligible girls of the neighborhood. She also too easily believes his calumnies about Darcy. She has no reason to resist Wickham's opinions as she does Darcy's, and she is only too glad to have ammunition in her assault on Darcy, who has insulted her. She unabashedly flirts with Wickham, for her a harmless diversion. There is no risk involved, for Elizabeth is beyond the temptation of physical attraction when there is no spiritual force accompanying it. Her relationship with Wickham is at best an amusing pastime, and she feels no pain or resentment when he lightly turns his attention elsewhere. In both of these cases, her instinct and her reasoning are perfect. She is perhaps too ready to believe Wickham's falsehoods, but this is a result of a combination of inexperience of vice and anger at Darcy.

In the gripping drama of Darcy's first proposal and her furious rejection of it, she gives a mixture of good and bad reasons to justify her rejection. She has discovered that Darcy has played a critical role in preventing his friend Bingley from marrying her beloved and truly wonderful elder sister, Jane. He has done so on two grounds, her horrible family and Jane's apparent indifference to Bingley. The connection with the Bennets is evidently unsuitable in Darcy's eyes, although he himself seeks such a connection. But he does so, as he believes, out of an almost tragic necessity. And he can interpret Jane's motives as stemming out of the desire only for a comfortable situation. Both reasons actually have a certain basis in fact. Elizabeth has herself criticized Jane for not expressing her attraction to Bingley more openly. Jane's reticence is due to good taste and modesty, but the misinterpretation is an excusable one. Moreover, Elizabeth's family is, with the exception of Jane and Elizabeth, indeed rather repulsive. We have had ample opportunity to see this with our own eyes, and their behavior at Bingley's ball was mortifying to Elizabeth herself. Their mother is mindless, social-climbing, tasteless, and without any self-control. The three younger sisters are each in her own way equally unappealing. They appear to be a tight band of marriageable predators. Even Mr. Bennet, who is so bright and witty, from the point of view of severe virtue can be understood to be irresponsible and even frivolous. Elizabeth has experienced that most excruciating of pains for a decent person, being ashamed of one's family, being ashamed of one's shame, and the disagreeable uncertainty whether the criticism is in fact justified or is merely an acceptance of the conventional opinions of others. This ambiguity is in Darcy himself. It is not clear whether his strictures stem from the merely social unacceptability of the Bennets, or a real insight into their inferiority. His relative, Catherine de Bourgh, is at least as vulgar as any of the Bennets, and compounds her vulgarity with abuse of her high station. And however different the cases, Darcy's sister agrees to an elopement with Wickham, as does Lydia. A part of Darcy's education in this novel is his coming to clarity about this issue. But Elizabeth responds with the angry defense of her own relations in a way characteristic of proud persons. Aristotle says that a gentleman is ironic to inferiors and insolent to superiors.[3] In this respect, Elizabeth is very much a gentleman.

The second objection to Darcy is his mistreatment of Wickham, whom he is alleged to have cheated out of his rightful inheritance as determined by Darcy's father in his love for his godson. Here the charge is not only pride or prejudice but strictly immoral conduct. Darcy appears to be not only a man contemptuous of others because he is born to high position but also simply a bad man, a breaker of faith and a moral hypocrite.

There is no doubt that Elizabeth believes what she says to Darcy and is truly indignant at his behavior, but her indignation masks the fact that these are only excuses for her dislike of Darcy. Collins' manners are at least as bad, but the passions of her soul do not combine in a passionate attack on him. With him she is objective and detached, or, at most, irritated. But with Darcy she is enraged because of his hold over her, the fact that his opinion really does count. She must make him think that it does not and that she is really independent of him. She has to get to him. If he thinks she is independent, maybe she will be able to believe that she is independent. She is the wrathful Achilles insulting her general Agamemnon. The real objection to Darcy is his taking her for granted and the hopeless inferiority that a marriage with him would entail. All the power is in his hands, and his only attachment to her appears to be an uncontrollable attraction without the support of either the conventional standards or a reverence for her virtue. Throughout a marriage that began in this way, he would have the advantage in every disagreement, for she would merely be a siren who entrapped him counter to all the good reasons for permanent moral attachment. Her accusations help her to avoid admitting the less than noble reasons for her resentment. Her education in the novel is learning to accept her dependence. Marriage between these two savages requires the acceptance by each of slavery to the other, while each thinks that he or she ought to be the master. Elizabeth would never marry a man whom she considered her inferior, while she hates a man who considers himself her superior. Equality of the partners would seem to be the answer, and it is. But the establishment of equality between two strong-willed individuals is not such an easy thing and probably requires each to think the other is superior. The fact is that Elizabeth would very much like to marry Mr. Darcy, and she must only persuade herself that she is taming her own will rather than being tamed by Darcy and that Darcy requires her for substantial and enduring reasons. The correctives to pride and prejudice, and progress in self-knowledge, result from the combative engagement of these two doubting warriors.

Darcy, in turn, responds immediately to the real humiliation that Elizabeth has succeeded in dealing him. He feels for the first time in his life that he must explain himself, not to the world at large but to this Elizabeth whose judgment has become authoritative for him. This reveals Darcy's real defect. It is not that he is not a virtuous man, but that his is a savage virtue, that is, an austere and harsh discipline that needs no explanation to others. Austen's virtuous characters, particularly males, are not the most agreeable or sociable of beings. The seductive Wickham and the easygoing Bingley are too sociable, and this means they are to be taken less seriously. Real virtue, as opposed to the accommodating social virtue of modern man, is at a certain tension with agreeableness. It involves taking virtue very seriously and the recognition that virtuous behavior and character are rare. A distasteful negative judgment, however well hidden, of most men and women is implicit in the virtuous person's conduct. That prickly and unsociable side of virtue is something that writers like Hobbes or Molière, eager above all to further peaceful relations among men, tried to suppress. Rousseau says that the misanthrope, whose truthfulness wins him so many enemies, is a virtuous man and that in ridiculing him Molière is really ridiculing virtue. Rousseau deplores the mean, utilitarian social virtue so effectively promoted by writers like Molière and Voltaire.[4] For the ancient writers on the other hand, virtue has two foci, one community harmony, the other individual perfection, which are not always in total harmony with each other. Balancing these two is difficult and requires rare taste and judgment, too unreliable a prescription for the modern theorists. They simply denied that pride is a virtue.

Given Austen's classical preferences, Darcy's difficult and somewhat unsociable comportment cannot be interpreted simply as a negative. But he carries it to extremes, and the need to explain himself to another forces him to explain himself to himself. This is the immediate effect Elizabeth has on him, and it is probably the deepest long-range effect it will have on him in their marriage. He is softened by the very fact of writing his explanatory letter. Its effect on Elizabeth is to make her think, forcing her to enter into the ambiguities of her feelings. The letter really settles the issue, and their marriage is the inevitable result of their each coming to understand the significance of the act of writing the letter as well as its content. She has to investigate the truth of his claims to virtue, and he has to recognize fully the meaning of his need to gain her good opinion even though he despises the quest for the good opinion of others. Virtue, he learns, is not so self-sufficient as he thought and requires the confirmation of valid judges. This reciprocal recognition is the heart of romance as Rousseau taught it.

Of course there are no wise governors for either Elizabeth or Darcy to guide them to the happy conclusion of their stormy courtship. There is no one to whom either can turn for advice or guidance. For various reasons, everyone else is beneath the comprehension of this true love. In this sense, Austen's novel is Romantic, depending on fateful chance to bring the ship safely into port. If Darcy had not come home a day early, he and Elizabeth would not have had the opportunity for a new beginning; and if Darcy were not present when the news of Lydia's elopement with Wickham arrived, he would not have been able to perform the signal services that recommended him so strongly to Elizabeth and finally proved his good character to her. The happy ending is both necessary and incredible. So, in spite of all of her understatement, Austen is something of a romantic who believes that blind love has good eyes.

Throughout all of Austen's works the heroines are somehow self-generated. She discounts the authority and respectability of the parents, who are distinctly inferior beings, particularly from the point of view of wisdom or prudence. This is a sign of the unconventional or radical side of Austen's point of view. Her heroines fit into the conventional order, but that does not entirely disguise the unconventional grounds of the relationships. They are triumphs of nature over convention. She celebrates the victory of her heroines' wills. This is not to say that virtue is simply strength of will. There is an objective and permanent content to virtue, one that involves certain simple things like honesty, loyalty, and good sense. But to practice these virtues and make a life around them requires unusual strength, inasmuch as the real world is so hopelessly not so much corrupt as stupid and conventional.

Elizabeth's father is an excellent case in point because her relation to him is so subtle and they have so many things in common. They are both extremely witty and, in general, shrewd observers of others' follies. Mr. Bennet, disappointed in marriage and unable to have any sensible communication whatsoever with his coarse and silly wife, simply goes into an inner exile, spending all of his time in his library reading, and ironizing when members of his family force themselves on his attention. He is quite relaxed because he feels himself unable to improve his wife and children or to moderate their conduct. He ridicules them and everyone else incessantly and thus enjoys himself. This level of detachment is, at least in some ways, impressive. It participates in at least the appearance of self-sufficiency while providing a mirror in which one sees the absurdities of low seriousness. He can be said to be cruel to his wife and younger daughters, but they deserve it and also are so used to it that it hardly affects them. Mr. Bennet is a wonderful corrective to the reforming spirit, with its humorlessness, in families and nations. He is not inhuman and appreciates his two elder daughters, who are so decent and fine. He might be criticized for leaving the other three girls under their mother's influence, but he probably assessed his power relative to hers and thought it impossible to counterbalance her. But, however charming Mr. Bennet's detachment, its godlike distance from the things that agitate most people is callous and perverse. Mr. Bennet is a charming dropout. He helps us to see people as they are, but he is not so helpful in understanding the virtuous. Darcy, too darkly serious about morality but therefore a serious man, judges Mr. Bennet harshly as frivolous and neglectful of the fundamental duties of a father, a husband, and the head of a household. Perhaps the most damning thing is the way he hurts both Jane and Elizabeth, especially when he ridicules Darcy without recognizing that Elizabeth is sensitive on this score. This proves that his habitual way of life has made him insensitive even where he does not wish to insult or make fun. Darcy's overseriousness can and will be corrected in his relationship with Elizabeth, but it is clearly closer to the gravity required for decent social life.

Elizabeth has her father's quick wit and lively awareness of the ridiculous, but she cares about people and the serious problems of life, and she can be hurt and be angry. She seeks happiness, as does any healthy human being. In Jane Austen's world, she is a much more perfect specimen than her father—although, to repeat, Mr. Bennet represents the wit that permeates Jane Austen's own writing and is rarely to be found in her personages. His two elder daughters escape the debasement of the social climbing, the shameless search for husbands, and the concern for money that dominate in the rest of the family, but this appears to be a result of their natures rather than parental nurture. Although Austen criticizes the lack of proper education in the Bennet family, Jane and Elizabeth, like so many of Austen's good characters, are self-made. This underlines her belief that nature is far more important than convention, even though she treats the framework of convention with great respect.

Marriage is the most significant of the conventions, but the successful marriage is really the triumph of nature over convention or the use of convention to support nature. The core of the good marriage is the friendship of two people who are attracted to each other and whose virtues are such as both to be admirable and to ensure the fidelity of the partners against temptation and in difficult times. The rules of the marriage relationship, especially with respect to property, can both corrupt and support the natural attraction depending upon the character of the individuals involved. Everybody gets the kind of marriage he or she deserves. The punishment of bad or foolish persons follows immediately from the character of their choice of mates and situations. There is a ladder that goes from Lydia and Wickham at the bottom to Elizabeth and Darcy at the top, passing by way of Mr. and Mrs. Bennet (Mr. Bennet seems to have chosen Mrs. Bennet too much on the basis of good looks, which soon pass), Charlotte and Mr. Collins (Mr. Collins chooses on the basis of what will be most convenient and what will appeal to Lady de Bourgh), and Jane and Bingley. The stakes are human happiness, and people are more or less happy on the basis of their choice of a partner. Very few people have powerful erotic attractions and even fewer are faithful partisans of their attractions. In addition, even fewer persons love virtue. And fewest are those who have a discerning judgment about the character of others and what is fitting. The many have marriages, and hence human relationships, that exist only by law and public opinion. The few have substantial attachments that consist in continuous delight in the company of the other. Charlotte's marriage to Mr. Collins is tolerable only because she is able to arrange her husband's study in such a way that he is not tempted to come out and bother her, whereas Elizabeth wants to be with Darcy as much as she can.

This moral world, viewed superficially, is one of perfect order and justice. The good are rewarded and the bad punished. The high expectations of the central personages are apparently fulfilled. This general niceness could be cloying, not necessarily because we may have vicious tastes but because it does not seem to reflect the nature of things. However, the irony in Austen's books makes us aware that she is explicit only about the nice things, while things are not as harmonious as the surface presents them. The nice Jane Bennet could not be the heroine of one of Jane Austen's novels precisely because she is too nice. She, in a way that is infuriating to Elizabeth, refuses to recognize the nasty motivations of others and always gives them a favorable gloss. She does not recognize that Bingley's sisters' politeness is hypocritical, and that they wish to promote a marriage between Bingley and Darcy's sister in the ultimate hope that one of them will get Darcy. Austen punishes this genial vice in Jane by providing her with a husband who is a bit too weak and accommodating, not the kind of man who provokes ecstasies of admiration. The sharper and shrewder Elizabeth is aware of ambiguous motives and can see them even in herself. When she sees Darcy's magnificent estate, she feels what a wonderful thing it would be to be the mistress of all that (III.1). Austen does not insist on this point, but we have to wonder whether Elizabeth's love would have been as strong or Darcy's so successful without the support of wealth and prominence. In this way, Austen is much harsher than is Stendhal, who shows true love manifesting itself against all such extraneous supports to love. The relationship between Elizabeth and Darcy does seem to be real and powerful, but Austen's pointing to this economic substrate gives us some pause. Her surface is that Xenophontic gentlemanly one, where one mentions only the nice things while hinting at the ones that are not so nice.[5] Modern taste is much more extreme, either reducing things to the lowest common denominator or insisting on a furious idealism. Austen evidently believes she is giving a more honest account of the complexity of human affairs, in which there is a mixture of high and low. Perhaps her position as a novelist outside of the marriage game that is her subject matter permits her relative clarity and freedom from self-deception.

Another example of Austen's pointing toward the ambiguities is Darcy's strenuous and successful efforts to put the best face on Lydia's elopement with Wickham. He says and believes that he tries to mitigate the unfortunate situation because he is responsible for Wickham's presence in their society and therefore, in all his moral rigor, for the elopement. This is duty, but he has no need to explain his conduct to others. One might however ask whether he acts so nobly not only out of a pure love of justice but also from a desire to impress Elizabeth. This incident is what conquers all her doubts about him and persuades her that she must have him. He did indeed make efforts to keep his role in the affair secret, but it did finally come out. Moreover, proving to himself that he deserved Elizabeth might well have been sufficient for him. These relations among men and women are a structure of stresses and balances that requires a sophisticated architecture to remain standing.

Elizabeth somehow recognizes this and she echoes Rousseau's views about the complementarity required to found a solid relationship between a man and a woman. Classical friendship is taught by Aristotle to be essentially a relationship between persons who are alike.[6] The friend is a kind of true mirror in which one can see oneself. By contrast, the friendship of a couple is founded on the imperfections or incompletenesses of each of the partners requiring complements or correctives from the others. Elizabeth wants Darcy to teach her all the things that a man's broader experience of the world, as well as his greater study of the arts and sciences, have brought him, while she can instruct him in tact and civilize his virtue (III.8). The aspiration to independence or self-sufficiency would destroy this unity. They must be "made for each other." Male and female are much more rigidly distinct and unambiguously directed to each other than are the partners in either classical marriages or friendships. For Aristotle, marriage has the common ground of the material interests of the household, a common ground that hardly engages or exhausts the full capacities of the soul, whereas friendship at its peak consists in the common pursuit of the truth. From Aristotle's point of view, Austen's loves would be a halfway house, a mixture of elements that he separates in order to perfect.

But it is friendship that Austen celebrates. Friendship at its peak is for her between male and female whereas for Aristotle it was primarily between male and male. For him, what the female would bring would water down philosophy, the animating principle of friendship. Austen concentrates on the courtships or the discovery of the partners, tests their suitability for each other, adjusts their circumstances in the way Rousseau tells us is desirable (particularly in relation to property and social status, as well as such questions as good looks), and marries them off, presumably to live happily ever after. It is remarkable how little she concentrates on children. There is no discussion of any desire of the partners to have children and to dedicate themselves to rearing them. It is as though Elizabeth and Darcy were to spend the rest of their lives alone together in endless conversation, sharing their intelligence and wit with each other. This is their low-key response to the emptiness of the lives of all the other persons and represents the best of all possible worlds once one has lived out the superficial excitements that preoccupy most people.

Throughout, Austen's heroines are uncompromising about the necessity of woman's chastity and modesty if a serious attachment is to be possible. The apparently shameless Stendhal and the reserved Austen both insist that real connection requires the total cooperation of sexual desire. There is no possibility in their view of a woman's "dealing with her sexuality" in casual or multiple ways and still having the energy of soul left for sublime love. This impossibility is not presented by either moralistically but simply as fact. Elizabeth cannot contain her contempt for those women who give themselves for merely prudential reasons or out of lust, not because she has to resist such temptations, but because sexual desire is of interest to her only insofar as it contains her highest aspirations. It is a woman's responsibility to decide and choose well. She is praised and rewarded for choosing well, blamed and punished for choosing badly. This is the practical arena for her responsibility and the action of her real freedom. Conventional morality may make use of woman's subjection for the sake of stability, but her capacity to deal successfully with the challenge of relationship to men naturally depends on her reserve or self-control. It is precisely the disproportion between male and female that makes this necessary, and in her sober but charming way, Austen affirms the dialectic of *amour-propre* powered by sexual desire that Rousseau insisted was the way to establish profound human connection.

The curiosity of this permanent conversation of friends is that the two partners must be good-looking and that their bodies must be aroused by and attracted to each other. This requirement is unimaginable when one thinks of the intense intellectual sharing between two persons of the same sex, as friendship was traditionally characterized. What does the sexual attraction do to the conversation or the conversation to the sexual attraction? This romantic friendship could be understood as a kind of idealism in which the whole self is engaged without the separating out of the elements that friendship used to require; or, it could be understood as a hardheadedness that, not trusting in the self-sufficiency of the spiritual, gives it an anchor in the body and its passions. In Aristotle, there is a part of man directed to sex and the family, another directed to citizenship, and a third directed to friendship and knowing. They are each distinct and each requires its satisfaction and entails certain duties. The task of the serious person is to give these three elements of a serious life a rank order and subordinate the less important to the more important. For Aristotle, the friendship of shared discourse is the highest thing to which everything else must be subordinated while receiving its due. In Romantic love, friend, lover, father or mother of one's children, and fellow citizen are all the same, and no act of subordination is required. This is a charming and tempting solution, but does it work, and does it give each of the elements its proper due? One cannot help remembering Aristotle's remark that the orgasm and thinking are mutually exclusive.[7] There is no reason why a human being cannot do both, each in its proper time. But if you have a single partner, do you choose him or her primarily for the former or the latter, or on the basis of some compromise? If someone were to say that instead we have to have two partners, one for each of these two great activities, then we are still confronted with the question of which of the two is primary. Those who do not want to face this question are sticking their heads in the ground and will be unable to "know their priorities." This choice depends upon an elaborated view of what is most important. The questions I have just raised may seem inappropriate in a discussion of the austere Jane Austen, but they are necessary precisely because she, unlike the other Romantics, seems to celebrate classical friendship as the core of romantic love.

4. Flaubert, *Madame Bovary*

I | *Madame Bovary* is the simplest of tales, about a small-town adulteress. One has to restore, in thought alone, of course, something of the significance of adultery in order to see why so much of the nineteenth-century novel was devoted to it. Once in a class I said, with a rhetorical flourish, that all nineteenth-century novels were about adultery. A student objected that she knew some which were not. My co-teacher, Saul Bellow, interjected, "Well, of course, you can have a circus without elephants." And that's about it. But out of this material Flaubert made perhaps the most powerful representation of the agony of modern man and especially of the modern artist. This book is a kind of death knell for the great hopes aroused by the Romantic movement. In sum, it represents the longing of a woman who cannot find a man worthy of forming with her that couple which is the bare minimum of the Romantic opposition to bourgeois society. Love had, it appears, no foundation in nature, and eroticism had sunk back into the material system of comfort and safety. The men Emma Bovary meets, and Flaubert means them to be representative, are amorous only as a supplement to their bourgeois concerns. As there are no men to love worthy of Emma, there are no subjects worthy of the epic poet's pen. Emma and Flaubert are full of longing for ideals that cannot be and are really, from the standpoint of reason, foolish. Hence a pervasive sense of groundlessness in the book. The aspiration of author and heroine is impossible to fulfill, and the world they look at in terms of it is dreary past endurance. They share defeat. Flaubert has the advantage over Emma of consciousness of their shared situation, but there is no authentic satisfaction in that, for such consciousness has a reward neither in heaven nor on earth. Flaubert's colossal poetic instrument, his genius of language, was destined to the excruciating labor, a self-crucifixion, of depicting a scene and personages that nauseated him. Aesthetic asceticism was his calling, and his book is as much the tale of a lost artist as of a lost woman.

Madame Bovary is dominated by two related moods—boredom and eroticism. Emma is the focus of both, and they set her apart from all the other characters, who are in one way or another contented or self-satisfied. Everything that Emma does or says is somehow related to an idea of great, self-forgetting love. Her dress, the walks she takes, the decoration of her house, how she serves or eats food, all are suffused with erotic significance. Nothing is neutral, and her despair of finding such a love is reflected in a withdrawal of interest in what surrounds her. She has no access to the world of the bourgeois life, and its inhabitants have no idea what is going on with her. They are all unerotic, although a couple of them manifest a bit of sexual desire. Emma's sexual desire depends on an admixture of the ideal. She is aroused only if her imagination presents her noble objects—in the silly forms recognized by this untutored girl. Romantic heroes and heroines—especially heroines—are indifferent to any sexual experience not touched by the sublime. After Emma's wedding night with the cloddish Charles, who has been previously married and has also had experience with loose women while away from home in medical school, he looks like yesterday's virgin, whereas she gives no sign of anything at all. The mere act is as nothing to her. In this she is like Mme. de Rênal. Later, when she is in a nervous depression and suffering from fainting spells, Emma's maid tells her of a woman she knew who had similar symptoms. They stopped when she got married. "But with me," Emma says, "it didn't come on till I was married" (122).*

This world, the one in which Emma lives, is thus drained of all charm or significance by the almost contentless longing that possesses her. _Ennui_ is what she suffers, brooding over the meaninglessness of life, interrupted only by spasms of self-forgetting and pointless activity. Pascal, as I have already said, describes this con-

---

* All parenthetical citations in this chapter are to pages in Gustave Flaubert's _Madame Bovary_, translated by Allan Russell (New York: Penguin, 1978). Occasionally the translation is modified.

dition most powerfully, but its cause for him is the absence of God and of the love of Him as the only end in itself, whereas for Emma it is the absence of a man. This difference between Pascal and Flaubert reveals a sort of Romantic theology, in which Flaubert has ceased to believe. One can't get to the cosmos adorned by the god Eros from here.

II

Emma's education was incoherent, not suitable for the life she was intended to lead. Such considerations can hardly be talked about today when everybody can aspire to everything, and educators do not even know that wholeness is the real goal. The images cast helter-skelter on the wall of our cave by "the performing arts" present high and low, serious and frivolous without distinction or concern for harmonizing contrary charms. Above all, there are no permanent inspiring models or enduring books. Everything flows and there is nothing to hold on to. Happily none of this education provides young people with higher aspirations that might cause them to despise the world they are going to live in. All this diversity has proved to be a teacher of conformism rather than a source of imagining a good life. But Emma, in her first marital despair, "wondered exactly what was meant in life by the words 'bliss,' 'passion,' 'ecstasy,' which had looked so beautiful in books" (47). For it was books that first injected this poison in her soul. Early on she read *Paul and Virginia*, that most influential and popular novel by Rousseau's devoted disciple, Bernardin de Saint-Pierre, with its rustic setting, away from alienating civilization, and its pure and naive love interest. With this preparation, she was sent to a convent school in Rouen. And here Flaubert with a few precise strokes of his brush gives us a picture, as seen through the eyes of girlish innocence, of the education of the tastes France could still offer. This education is, of course, in the first place, Christian. France *was* a Christian country, and the convent was the prime educator of young girls in the Christian virtues—especially chastity and piety. Many writers prior to the Revolution, particularly Montesquieu[1] and Rousseau, criticized that education as being contrary to the principles that govern modern society, hence leaving the girls unprepared for real life. In the resulting tension between morality and society's conventions, morality was almost certain to give way, leaving them with no guidance. The easy corruptibility of convent girls was a great novelistic theme, best known to us from Choderlos de Laclos' *Les Liaisons Dangereuses* in the person of Cécile Volanges.

The question of Christian education became ever more pressing in France after the Revolution because it had become a liberal nation whose relation to Christianity was now vexed. It might even be said that there was a direct conflict between otherworldly and this-worldly views of happiness. Emma, at first blush, finds the convent thrilling with its high vocations and its function as the repository of intense passions and great deeds. Her attraction, however, is not to the daily round of pious duty but to the rich depiction of heroic men and women that is always present in a French convent with its Gothic buildings and its stunning stained glass. This is what it is all about for her, and the mere routine of the nuns finally puts her at odds with them. For them the age of miracles is definitely long past, whereas it is precisely miracles Emma longs for. The nuns would have been out of place in the era of early Christianity, when faith made the everyday world disappear. Their religion is now nothing but habit. This decrepitude of Christianity is one of the central parts of the drama. Emma, as always, sees it only with her imagination, as what it was at its origins. Moreover, Christianity here is French Christianity, that is, mingled with France's political history. Therefore, the medieval knights and their ladies legitimately enter the religious scene, as well as the life of the later French court, with its splendors, sinnings, and repentings. Everything that attracts her, that has any transcendent appeal in the convent, is food for her nascent sensuality, even confession.

And, of course, there is the inevitable old servant, a Rousseauan commonplace, who tells the girls all about life outside and brings them novels about love, including Walter Scott. This material fuses with the strictly religious objects in the school, and for Emma, without awareness of the opposition between Christianity and Romanticism, it all becomes a religious Romanticism. The high or the inspiring in France is present in either Christianity or Romanticism, both now clichés, and together they constitute poor Emma's aesthetic life.

With such a preparation she marries Charles, who puts his elbows on the table of life and enjoys himself complacently. He has not the slightest notion of what is going on in her head or what she might expect of a man. It is not that she has specific demands or complaints. Her reaction is, "Is this all there is to it? I must be missing something." She is first seduced not by a person but by an event. The Marquis d'Andervilliers, who owns a château in the neighborhood, invites Charles and Emma to a ball. He is a member of the decaying aristocracy, trying to keep a footing in the new dispensation of equality by running for a seat in the National Assembly. Privilege now has to flatter the people in order to maintain itself. But, of course, Emma sees only the characters and the settings of aristocracy from her novels. There are courtly, gallant men and gracious, seductive women. Their bearing is elegant, and their politeness exquisite. In a framework of luxury, *billets doux* are exchanged. Actually the men who seem so extraordinary to her are but the useless remnants of a vanished world, without function in life, pursuing, and securing, banal gratifications. Here she begins to compare Charles with other men, and her dissatisfaction turns into contempt. The peak of her visit to the château is what she sees at dinner:

> At the top end of the table, alone among all these women, sat one aged man, crouched over his plate, with his serviette tied round his neck like a bib, dribbling gravy as he ate. His eyes were bloodshot, and he wore a little pigtail wound round with black ribbon. This was the Marquis' father-in-law, the old Duc de Laverdière, once favourite of the Comte d'Artois, in the days of the Marquis de Conflans' hunting-parties at La Vaudreuil; he was said to have been the lover of Marie Antoinette, between Messieurs de Coigny and de Lauzun. He had filled his life with riot and debauch, with duels, wagers and abductions; had squandered his wealth and been the terror of his family. He pointed to the dishes, mumbling, and a footman stationed behind him named them aloud in his ear. Emma's eyes kept turning in spite of themselves towards that old man with the drooping lips, as though to some august curiosity. He had lived at Court, had lain in the Queen's bed!
> (61–62)

Here Flaubert shows the difference between what Emma sees and what everyone else sees. Others see only a repulsive old man; Emma sees the remnant of the *ancien régime* and its grandeur. In a sense the others are right. This is in fact a senile old man. Emma is silly and inflates the world with her uncontrolled imagination. But Flaubert prefers her delusion to other people's reality. Moreover, the *ancien régime* really did exist, and from full awareness of that fact comes awareness of the deepest fact of Emma's time: the heroes have departed, perhaps forever. Hers are not just childish fantasies, but insights into the way things once were. She is taking a self-destructive course, but her empty longing is more profound than is others' acceptance of the way things are, as though they had always been that way.

III

It is Monsieur Homais who introduces Charles and Emma to the town of Yonville l'Abbaye (where they have moved in the hope of alleviating her depression). He is Emma's great antagonist. He is a most unusual antagonist in that they have almost no involvement at all. They are present together, but neither is concerned with the other. They have no ill feelings toward each other and do no harm to each other. Their closest connection occurs when Emma steals from him the arsenic with which to kill herself. Homais is Emma's enemy in that he epitomizes the man of today, the archetypical product of liberal Enlightenment, the man who is nothing for her and for whom she has no charms. He is self-satisfaction itself, hence unerotic. Flaubert hates him, and this novel's astounding venomousness relates to him: he is *the* bourgeois.

Homais' first words, in advising the innkeeper to buy a new pool table, are "You've got to keep up with the times!" (87). His is an unfaltering faith in progress, progress in science working toward the alleviation of suffering. He is a pharmacist, the link between science and the healing of man's body. The achievement of Enlightenment is, of course, dispelling the shadows of the Dark Ages, the heyday of the Roman Catholic church. Therefore he is suitably anticlerical, ever alert to the threat to science posed by the Church. He is, it almost goes without saying, also a journalist, engaged in the dissemination of the results of science to the people, relieving them of the prejudices taught by the priests. Most of all, his dominant passion is vanity, the quest for small distinctions an aristocrat would despise, distinctions acquired without risk of life.

Flaubert at the outset brings his creation out of the workshop and puts him through his paces. At the sight of the priest, M. Bournisien, Homais bubbles over with scorn. The priest incarnates all that is old and bad about France; he is the vicar of the kingdom of darkness, the permanent temptation of the ignorant masses. The two, Homais and Bournisien, represent the only alternatives available to nineteenth-century Frenchmen, Enlightenment or Catholic reaction. Homais blurts out all the Enlightenment clichés about the priest. When Bournisien turns down a drink offered by the innkeeper, Homais accuses him of hypocrisy, for everyone knows that priests are secret drinkers. In response to the innkeeper's remarks about the priest's physical vigor, Homais warns about the dangers to young virgins from healthy priests. At this the innkeeper rises to the priest's defense and accuses Homais of having no religion. This calumny provides Homais with the occasion to make a full profession of his articles of faith, the faith of a rational man:

> "I have got a religion—my own religion," the pharmacist answered, "In fact I've got more than the lot of them, with all their mumbo-jumbo—I worship God! I believe in the Supreme Being; a Creator, no matter who he be, who has placed us here below to do our duty as citizens and fathers. But I don't need to go and kiss a lot of silver-plate in a church, and support a pack of humbugs who live better than we do ourselves! You can praise God just as well in the woods and the fields, or by gazing up into the vault of heaven, like the ancients. My God is the God of Socrates, of Franklin, Voltaire and Béranger! I am for the Savoyard Vicar's Profession of Faith and the immortal principles of '89! And I cannot worship an old fogey of a God who walks round his garden with a stick in his hand, lodges his friends in the bellies of whales, dies with a cry on his lips and comes to life again three days later: all of which is intrinsically absurd and utterly opposed, moreover, to all physical laws: which incidentally indicates that the priests have always wallowed in a shameful ignorance wherein they strive to engulf the peoples of the world along with them."
>
> The pharmacist paused and glanced round him for his audience, having for a moment imagined himself to be in possession of the floor at a council meeting. (90)

The stupidity of this is unbearable, but it is also hilarious. The fine ear for stupidities is Flaubert's peculiar genius, and he spent his life listening to and reproducing the words of what he believed to be the stupidest age in human history. In this case, it is not a question of the truth of the doctrines expressed. They are a collection of the teachings of several great Enlightenment figures concerning a humane religion. Flaubert's is an aesthetic judgment. The disproportion between the sentiments expressed and the man who expresses them is revolting and such boasting is comic. This is the typical man produced by those teachings put into action, and that is refutation

enough. Flaubert's artistic conscience forced him to the contemplation of this form of modern ugliness: the men who now rule the
world. One can see why, soon after, the gentle love of truth was
replaced by the much harsher notion, intellectual honesty, for the
truth is no longer lovable. But for Flaubert, unlike so many later
writers, the ugly is still recognized to be such in the light of the
beautiful.

One of Flaubert's techniques for illustrating the idle opinions of
his various human types is to orchestrate conversations in which
there is a counterpoint between treble and bass, in which they do not
communicate at all but nevertheless make together a harmony that is
a musical joke. When Charles and Emma arrive in Yonville, they
meet M. Homais and his young boarder, Léon Dupuis, and dine
together. Charles, the doctor, and Homais, the pharmacist, naturally
gravitate to each other, while the handsome Léon and the beautiful
Emma are moved toward each other by spiritual magnetism. While
Homais tells Charles about the attacks of fevers, biliousness, and
enteritis common to the country, as well as the good money to be
made out of them, Emma and Léon find they have a common taste
in travel. The professionals discuss temperatures and the presence of
nitrogen and hydrogen in the air, while the Romantics move from
walks to their passion for the sea and, even better, for the mountains, and from there inevitably to the inspirational power of music,
and finally to reading and the feelings Art should awaken. At this
point the two groups meet as Homais, a lover of culture, offers
Emma the use of his personal library, stocked with the best authors.
Dull materialism and vapid spirituality have played their tunes, the
one with no uplift, the other with no foundation. Homais and Bovary
have established a business relationship; Léon and Emma an erotic
one. Ultimately one player, Léon, will join the other two with their
calculating rationality, his higher concerns being but the amusement
of late adolescence preparatory to tension-relieving sexual experience. That will leave the only true high-stakes player, Emma, alone
at the gambling table.

With Léon she is having her first love affair and courtship, although she is already married and pregnant. This pretty boy, who is
also immersed in the popular Romantic idiom, is the first oasis of
common interest she has encountered. They go through the stages of
love connection—attraction, admiration, doubt of reciprocity, ecstasy
and despair, exclusive concern with each other—as though they were
both unattached youngsters. This section of the book has quite
enough material for the scenario of a typical love novel of the time,

but here it is merely a part of the bleak picture of idle hope smashed against the reality of human isolation.

At the beginning of this insipid affair, Emma is protected from its consequences by hopes that her pregnancy will conclude with a little boy whom she can raise to be the kind of man she would want for herself and through whom she can get her fulfillment at one remove. Men are not the victims of our hypocritical system and can be free. At the end of her labor, the first words she hears are "It's a girl" (101).

The naming of this poor child, who will end up working in a cotton mill, occasions a lively discussion. The naming of children always teaches a lot about the parents, for the child is their link with the future. The deliberation about the child's name indicates the parents' view about the relation between past and future, what kind of a person the parents would like the child to be. It is an occasion for the deepest conflicts within ourselves about identity, about what really counts—religion, politics, art, or tradition. It is also the occasion for the most absurd expressions of conformism and fashion. M. Homais' contribution is the most interesting:

> Monsieur Homais, for his part, was attracted to all names which reminded you of a great man, a glorious deed or a noble conception; he had christened his four children accordingly. There was Napoléon, for glory, and Franklin for liberty. Irma was perhaps a concession to romanticism, but Athalie paid homage to the most immortal masterpiece of the French theatre. For Homais' philosophical convictions did not inhibit his artistic appreciation; the thinker never stifled the man of feeling. He could discriminate. He knew where to draw the line between imagination and fanaticism. (102)

This is *the* statement about what the Marxists call "bourgeois culture," and, going a step further, approaches Nietzsche's Last Man. The best of the past belongs to Homais; equality has put him on the level of the geniuses, and he can appropriate their product to himself. The great historical process, with all of its struggles and great visions, has as its end M. Homais, who is able to put it all in order, take what is valid from each of the actors without their madness. He cannot himself contribute to that process nor can he imitate any of the heroes, as Alexander and Caesar imitated Achilles, or the saints imitated the Jesus of the Gospels. Neither heroes nor saints have the power to alter the fundamental motives of his contemptible self. If

Nietzsche is right in saying that modern man has lost the capacity for contempt,[2] Flaubert is certainly not a modern in this respect.

After her hope is disappointed that her child would make possible a meaningful life within the legal constraints of marriage, Emma becomes obsessed with Léon, as he is with her. There is aching desire on both sides, romantic timidity, and a sense of the impossibility of a happy ending. Moreover, Emma, on the brink of declaring her passion to Léon, becomes aware of the gravity of what this entails—adultery, breaking the marriage vow. Everything has happened unawares, as in a dream. She recoils and dedicates herself to her husband and her domestic duties, playing the ideal wife, appearing so to others, intimidatingly so to Léon. But she is only playing; this moral world has no cosmic force. She experiences a classic conflict between duty and inclination, but, due to no fault of hers, duty has lost its substance and force. It cannot bite back.

In search of some moral force, she wanders to the church, drawn by her childhood sentiments and memories, to see whether there she can find consolation and guidance. This is the moment of the Abbé Bournisien, the shepherd of souls in Yonville. What Emma discovers is the complete debilitation of Catholicism. Bournisien has stubble growing on his face and grease stains on his cassock. He is keeping track of disorderly boys and constantly interrupts Emma. Here there is none of the calm required of devotion. He is thrilled that the bishop condescended to laugh at his dim joke. And when Emma makes halting steps toward revealing the state of her soul, he is uncomprehending of anything that does not relate to material deprivation. He has no inkling that he has before him a woman teetering on the brink of damnation and is no more responsive to her temptations than Homais is to her longing. There is no correlate to her suffering left in the world. The Church, lacking any firm anchor in heaven, has adapted itself to the principles of M. Homais' world. She hurries away with the little boy repeating the catechism, "What is a Christian?" (127), ringing in her ears. This alternative has failed for her. It has failed for Flaubert the artist too.

After Léon departs to study in Paris, the coarse Rodolphe with the gentlemanly allures finds Emma ripe for the picking and completes the seduction of the body after that of the soul has been accomplished by Léon. He has a habit of romance, cannot give anything, and can no longer distinguish one woman from another. Rodolphe is a nineteenth-century equivalent of the *Playboy* man, for whom the pursuit of sexual enjoyment is central, although the nineteenth-century version is infinitely more cultivated and not canned for a mass market. Flaubert gives his opinion of Rodolphe in commenting on his attire. Rodolphe has the stylish Parisian man's contempt for the sartorial inelegance of the provincials, which is supposed to indicate their pedestrian characters:

> He started making fun of the Yonville ladies and the way they were turned out. He apologized for being so carelessly dressed himself. His clothes were an incongruous mixture of the workaday and the elegant, such as is taken by the vulgar to denote an eccentric way of life, an emotional disturbance, or a subservience to aesthetics, combined always with a certain contempt for convention, by which they are either fascinated or exasperated. Frilly at the cuffs, his cambric shirt fluttered out in front between the lapel of his grey drill waistcoat wherever the breeze took it. His broad-striped trousers terminated at the ankle above a pair of nankeen boots vamped with patent leather. These were so highly polished that you could see the grass in them; and in them he went trampling over the horse-dung, with one hand in his jacket pocket, his straw hat tilted to the side of his head. (150–151)

He is typical of nineteenth-century sophistication, decked out with the external style and the speeches now commonly provided by Romantic literature. *Madame Bovary* is unlike either *The Red and the Black* or *Pride and Prejudice* in that there is no engagement of the couples, joined and set in motion like gears, by *amour-propre*. Here there is no human connection, and this is a large part of the story. There are debased rituals of connectedness and illusions of love explicitly constructed for the sake of getting sexual satisfaction. Sublimation is not an inner transformation, but only a tool for overcoming the residual and merely conventional affects of modesty in women. No relationships, but only a hermetically sealed isolation of which Emma is unaware.

Rodolphe provides the occasion for Flaubert's *chef d'oeuvre* in the art of counterpoint. The county fair is to be held in Yonville this year, and Flaubert uses this fair to bring all the representative personages together to act out the incoherent cosmic affair of the nineteenth century. M. Homais is thrilled because he can plug into a larger scene. When the blunt proprietress of the café questions the propriety of his playing a role in an event dedicated to agriculture, hence to real farmers, he speechifies about his chemist's art, which in this scientific age is the true agriculture. But he is there less as pharmacist than as the local correspondent for a Rouen liberal newspaper. The easy, superficial, and mercenary press has become the substitute for real human communication. The article he produces about the fair is a vehicle for his anticlerical prejudices, and he ridicules, after his fashion, the invisibility of the Church on this progressive occasion.

This is the moment of the Liberal or bourgeois Orleanist king, Louis-Philippe, who succeeded Stendhal's Bourbon Restoration kings after the Revolution of 1830. The two official speakers represent the typical rhetoric of the time, a rhetoric designed to keep the potentially rebellious people in harness to the hopes of liberal or capitalist increase of wealth. One speaks of progress, science, and economics. The other presents Rousseau's radical doubts, now incorporated in bureaucratic routine and language. He presents an official history of the progress of civilization, while adumbrating Rousseau's doubts about the relation between scientific progress and happiness. Of course, in his version it all turns out just fine, but he has touched upon and domesticated the themes of radicalism, which were merely rejected and suppressed in the salon of the Marquis de La Mole fifteen years earlier. Flaubert has an almost intolerably sensitive ear for the language of his time and all that it expresses about the contemporary soul. Against this background Rodolphe and Emma carry on their higher conversation.

Emma and Rodolphe go up to the Council Chamber of the Town Hall overlooking the tribune where the festivities are taking place. As we hear the public inanities of the occasion, we are made partners in the private romantic foolishness of Rodolphe, who is cynically manipulating Emma's shy-mindedness toward his goal. As the speaker praises the useful arts that enrich individuals and states, "fruit of respect for law and fulfilment of duty," Rodolphe comments:

> "Duty again!" said Rodolphe. "Always on about duty. I'm sick to death of the word. What a lot of flannel-waistcoated old fogies they are, pious old women with beads and bedsocks, for ever twittering in our ears about 'Duty, duty!' To feel nobly and to love what is beautiful—that's our duty. Not to accept all the conventions of society and the humiliations society imposes on us."
>
> "Still . . . all the same . . ." Madame Bovary demurred.
>
> "No! Why inveigh against the passions? Are they not the one beautiful thing there is on earth; the source of all heroism and enthusiasm, poetry, music, art, everything?"

"All the same," said Emma, "we must take some notice of what the world thinks, and conform to its morality."

"But you see, there are two moralities," he replied. "One is the petty, conventional morality of men, clamorous, ever-changing, that flounders about on the ground, of the earth earthy, like that mob of nincompoops down there. The other, the eternal morality, is all about and above us, like the countryside that surrounds us and the blue heavens that give us light." (157)

Here for the first time the antibourgeois is as ridiculous and contemptible as the bourgeois. That which appeared to be the solution has become part of the problem. Nietzsche said, more than a hundred years ago, that the comedy of the bourgeoisie had been exhausted and become boring (thus providing us with a commentary on our intellectual life, where everyone acts as though critics' banalities were as rare and fresh as they were on the first day). In this observation he was preceded by Flaubert, who made the crisis of the bourgeois all the more acute in announcing the crisis of Romanticism, which was supposed to be its palliative.

Flaubert rings all the changes on this opposition between what is on the ground and what is up in the air, an only apparent opposition between two aspects of bourgeois life. Rodolphe's effusions are accompanied by the mooing of the cows and the bleating of the sheep. He provides the words to this cantata:

"Doesn't this conspiracy of society revolt you? Is there a single feeling it does not condemn? The noblest instincts, the purest sympathies, are reviled and persecuted, and if ever two poor souls do meet, then everything is organized to prevent their union. They'll attempt it all the same, they'll flap their wings and call to one another. And no matter what happens, sooner or later, in six months or ten years, they'll meet again and love—because Fate ordains it, because they were born for one another." (159)

The climax is reached when the prizes for pigs, manure, and an old woman's slavish lifetime service on a farm are distributed to the accompaniment of a discourse on man's progress out of the state of nature. As the speaker raises the doubt about whether this progress was really advantageous for man, Rodolphe harmonizes with magnetism, affinities, and fate. Throughout, Rodolphe has been putting his moves on Emma and has now gained possession of her hand.

Soon after the fair, Rodolphe succeeds in his seduction, using the pretext of teaching Emma how to ride, with the enthusiastic permission of that perfect cuckold, Charles. But it does not take long for Emma to recognize that the affair has easily slipped into routine for Rodolphe. She decides to make one last effort to rehabilitate Charles and establish him as a worthy object of her attentions. She encourages him to operate on the clubfoot of Hippolyte, the errand boy at the inn. Charles, with the cooperation of Homais, brings the latest surgical techniques developed by modern science to ease man's estate. Of course they make a dreadful botch of it, and the offending leg has to be amputated, a leg to which the poor fellow had become adapted. Later, at Emma's funeral, the pitiless Flaubert lets us hear the clump of the peg leg resounding on the floor of the church. Charles is a hapless, useless fellow. His response to the terrible humiliation of his failure is to say to Emma, "Kiss me" (198). She recoils from him and her experiment with him back into the arms of Rodolphe. She gets him to agree to let her run away with him, accompanied by her repulsive little girl, in order to live together on love alone, traveling from one romantic spot to another. This is a lot more than Rodolphe bargained for from this casual amusement with which he was passing his time in the country. Emma is already all packed to go when the fatal letter from Rodolphe comes, and she hears his carriage hurrying out of the town bearing him alone to other parts. The shock almost kills her. Flaubert expresses his opinion of this affair, giving the lie to those who think he regards Emma as being as foolish as everyone else in the book:

> [Rodolphe] had listened to so many speeches of this kind that they no longer made any impression on him. Emma was like any other mistress; and the charm of novelty, gradually slipping away like a garment, laid bare the eternal monotony of passion, whose forms and phrases are for ever the same. Any difference of feeling underlying a similarity in the words escaped the notice of that man of much experience. Because wanton or mercenary lips had murmured like phrases in his ear, he had but scant belief in the sincerity of these. High-flown language concealing tepid affection must be discounted, thought he: as though the full heart may not sometimes overflow in the emptiest metaphors, since no one can ever give the exact measure of his needs, his thoughts or his sorrows, and

human speech is like a cracked kettle on which we strum out tunes to make a bear dance, when we would move the stars to pity. (203)

When Emma recovers, Charles takes her to the opera in Rouen. They are playing *Lucia di Lammermoor*, Donizetti's classic setting of Walter Scott's Romantic novel. The singer is Lagardy:

He had a splendid pallor of the sort that lends a marmoreal majesty to the ardent races of the South. His vigorous frame was tightly clad in a brown-coloured jerkin. A small carved dagger swung at his left thigh. He rolled his eyes languorously and showed his white teeth. It was said that a Polish princess had fallen in love with him hearing him sing one night on the beach at Biarritz, where he had been a boat-mender. She had thrown everything to the winds for him. He had left her for other women; and his fame as a lover served but to enhance his reputation as an artist. This canny player was always careful to slip into the advertisements some lyric phrase about the fascination of his person and the sensitivity of his soul. A fine voice, imperturbable self-possession, more personality than intelligence and more power than poetry, went to complete the armoury of this admirable mountebank-type, with its ingredients of the hairdresser and the toreador. (234–235)

He was a kind of virtuoso, in the style of Paganini, who ministered by his art and his apparent sexual allure to the romantic need of the nineteenth-century bourgeois. Ever the sucker, Emma returns to the psychological charge even though she has hardly recovered from her last disappointment. The intense and tragic lovemaking on the stage thrills her. For a moment the spectator's sympathy satisfies her longing. But, during the intermission, she meets Léon, returned from Paris, and is caught up again in a real affair. Now it is overtly physical and the element of idealism gradually disappears. She is the sexual aggressor, and Léon is scandalized by her genius of sexual corruption. She gradually becomes what used to be known as a fallen woman, satisfying needs of the body with a man she does not respect. The degradation is, of course, founded on the disproportion between what she hoped for and expected from love and the desperate physical expression of it. With Léon, again, nobody's at home, but she is knocking ever more aggressively. This is wild self-forgetting with a passive, flat-souled young man who finally gives her up because his mother disapproves and they are talking at the office. He marries, appropriately, a woman named Léocadie Leboeuf.

Emma's life becomes a web of lies and luxurious expense that she cannot afford. On her return to her home from a tryst with Léon in Rouen, she finds that all her furniture and effects will be seized within twenty-four hours if she does not pay her debts. She has finally become the victim of the shady M. Lheureux, a dream merchant, the nineteenth-century prefiguration of the Visa card, who, purveying to her need for the costumes and trinkets appropriate to her romances, has ensnared her. The web of lies she wove to deceive Charles into mortgaging his property and income is about to come to light. Lheureux is the means of making Emma's passions crash back to earth. In order to save Charles's property and her own reputation, she is reduced to begging from Léon, who says he'll get back to her; from M. Guillaumin, the notary, who offers her money for sex; from Rodolphe, who says he has none. At the end of her tether, she rushes into M. Homais' shop, goes to the storeroom and stuffs arsenic into her mouth.

The scenes around Emma's death are the climax of the novel, and the priest's administration of extreme unction is the peak of Flaubert's art—economy of expression, perfection of language; the subject, erotic blasphemy of Christian ritual and sentiment:

> Slowly she turned her face, and when her eyes lighted on the violet stole she seemed to be seized with a sudden joy. Doubtless she was finding again in the midst of a wondrous appeasement the lost ecstasy of her first flights of mysticism, and beginning to see visions of eternal blessedness.
>
> The priest rose to take the crucifix. Reaching forward like one in thirst, she glued her lips to the body of the Man-God and laid upon it with all her failing strength the most mighty kiss of love she had ever given. The priest recited the *Misereatur* and the *Indulgentiam;* then he dipped his right thumb into the oil and began the unctions: first on the eyes, that had so coveted all earthly splendours; then on the nostrils, that had loved warm breezes and amorous perfumes; then on the mouth, that had opened for falsehood, had groaned with pride and cried out in lust; then on the hands, that had revelled in delicious contacts; lastly on the soles of the feet, that once had run so swiftly to the assuaging of her desires, and now would walk no more. (335)

But this is not Emma's happy ending, for she hears a song through the window:

> "When the sun shines warm above,
> It turns a maiden's thoughts to love."

Emma sat up like a corpse galvanized, her hair dishevelled, her eyes fixed, gaping.

> "All across the furrows brown
> See Nanette go bending down,
> Gathering up with careful hand
> The golden harvest from the land." (337)

The singer is a blind beggar of horrid visage with running sores in place of eyes, whom she used to encounter on her way home from Rouen after her meetings with Léon. He has come to the notice of M. Homais, and that great chemist has undertaken to cure his condition, without brilliant success. Homais' promise to make the ugly beautiful turns out to be instead a cover-up.

> "The blind man!" she cried.
> And Emma started laughing, a ghastly, frantic, desperate laugh, fancying she could see the hideous face of the beggar rising up like a nightmare amid the eternal darkness.

> "The wind it blew so hard one day,
> Her little petticoat flew away!"

A convulsion flung her down upon the mattress. They moved nearer. She was no more. (337)

Her last image is not that of sensuously beautiful salvation, but of ugliness and terror. For her there is no heaven, only a plunge into the abyss.

The watch over the corpse is undertaken by the team of Homais and Bournisien. Homais is terrified of death, the one thing that cannot fit into his rational system. But the fear his thought cannot admit forces him to put on a brave front. For Bournisien it is routine, and he doesn't give it a second thought. The two engage in their endless and tedious theological debate. They really belong together. Homais sits on one side, sprinkling the floor with chlorine; Bournisien sits on the other side sprinkling the air with holy water. They eat, doze off from heaviness of the flesh, wake up and resume their conversation. Finally, Homais says to Bournisien, "We'll get along fine before we've finished" (345). Ain't it the truth. All the while the dead Emma lies between, free at last from their debate and hence triumphant, like Romanticism between the fundamental alternatives. Her suicide is the analogue of the artist's meticulous, dispassionate recording of their terrible story.

Afterward Homais wins out and reigns supreme in Yonville. By a successful campaign in the newspapers he has the blind beggar put away, so that the evidence of his failure to conquer the abyss is protected from public sight. He has learned from the artists that being a bourgeois is shameful, so he starts buying statues, and he performs the ultimate bohemian deed: he takes to smoking. He represents the gradual folding of the world of the artists into the bourgeois dough. The last words of *Madame Bovary* concern M. Homais: "He has just been awarded the Legion of Honor" (361).

IV   As artists became more powerful, and genius was recognized to have superior rights, the states' censors became weaker and weaker. Censorship was no longer what it used to be. It no longer had the good conscience of religion and monarchy behind it. This was another triumph of liberalism, a movement that in the nineteenth century tended to be despised by the artists who profited so much from it. The free market of ideas sounded a bit too commercial to their sensitive ears. The artists are partisans of culture, which demands a unity favorable to censorship, whereas corrupt civilization believes it can afford the artists' subversion. The artists want to be taken seriously, which means they need enemies, especially the officers of the established order. When they are tolerated or simply liberated, they are not taken so seriously. They become just another part of bourgeois society. Censorship has been on the run for these past two centuries, the artists winning victory after victory. The higher ranks of society are against it, and the censors appear to represent religious darkness and the prejudices of the vulgar. Even when the artists are convicted they are supported by the public opinion that counts and are eventually vindicated. Flaubert was the victim of a public accusation against *Madame Bovary*, and there was a trial in which he was acquitted. We all applaud this decision. It is hard for us to read the record of this trial with any sympathy for Flaubert's antagonist. Our reaction is one of these easy, morally superior reflexes that are very close to being self-congratulation. We are on the right side of history, and without having to make much effort to be so. The artists are the enemies of bourgeois society, and yet bourgeois society must embrace its enemies. This is a not unproblematic demand and probably requires some rethinking.

Of course, Flaubert was a man much superior to the prosecutor and immediately engages our sympathies because he is so great a writer and also because here he represents the freedom of speech so dear to liberals. But an open-minded reading of the court record proves that the prosecutor had a few intelligent points and that Flaubert's defense was not quite candid. He was willing to let his novel stand on its own and did not care to make himself a martyr to a cause. He did not argue for absolute freedom of speech, because that was not yet a universally accepted principle. He simply denied that his book was intended to undermine public morals and religion. Public morals, in this case, meant the sanctity of marriage. Any serious reader of *Madame Bovary* cannot help seeing that both marriage and religion are treated with contempt. It is true that sensible persons would not want to imitate Emma and suffer her defeat. But nobody would be inspired by this novel to adhere to the conventional order, which is shown to be so weak, empty, and hypocritical. In order to say that this book poses no threat to that order, he would have to say that literature has no real effect.

The prosecutor argued that there is no counterpoising figure in the novel whose example would show that Emma's choice is wrong, such figures as one would easily find in Jane Austen or Tolstoy. This accusation is surely correct, and it points to that modern weakness of moral principle which we have already mentioned. No public morality has anything of the force of either love or art, which are now both understood to be supramoral. It is a pallid and undangerous sociability of herd men and women. The husbands, politicians, and priests are all contemptible. The choice between them and romantic indulgence is no choice of Hercules. Vice becomes attractive as the opposite to this kind of virtue and as the choice of freedom over conformity. Morality has no teeth as hell disappears. There is no positive social example that solicits the aspirations of the best hearts. This is undoubtedly a real moral crisis for society, although a censor's criticism cannot restore the vitality of morality or provide the artist with an edifying subject matter that is also truly artistic. As it appeared to many of the great Continental writers, the choices were pessimism, nihilism, or "beyond good and evil." Perhaps these writers were too self-indulgent and even irresponsible in their hatred of the bourgeois. Jane Austen may very well prove that it is possible to be both artistically honest and socially responsible.

But to Flaubert, a sincere writer if there ever was one, it did not appear this way. The disproportion between what human nature demands and what any present social reality provides could only provoke nausea in him. He conveyed that nausea to his audience, and in this sense his writing, if not his defense, constitutes a confession of guilt in response to the prosecutor's charges. Flaubert knew this to be a problem. His romantic longing emerges out of a consciousness of the superiority of the myth-driven past over scientific modernity. He tried to write a true romantic novel in which his art would be fully absorbed in trying to depict heroes and heroines, rather than in demonstrations of the superiority of his artistic instrument to any subject that it might try to represent. *Salammbô* really did depict persons of heroic proportions living in the ancient world. But Flaubert could not be a Walter Scott, because Scott's knights and ladies were made of cardboard; they are not the product of a real experience of the present and of the reality on which the artist must feed. Shakespeare could still believe that he and other men of his time were potentially on the level of the Roman heroes, that his audience could lift itself up to them and that his poetry might be an inspiration to the founding of a political and moral order surpassing that of Rome. He himself could be Caesar and more. After the French Revolution and Napoleon, historicism taught that we have little in common with the men and women of the past. Their motives and their deeds as well as the greatness of their souls no longer appeared credible. Earlier artists who roamed in times and places other than their own were now taken to have been naive. But there is, it seems, no way to go from the soul of the bourgeois to that of the great men of antiquity. Mostly literary attempts to return to the past proved to be bloated frauds, and certainly modern audiences, now incapable of authentically appreciating the great literature of the past, would be even less capable of being moved by a modern epic. Rousseau's replacement of Plutarch by *Julie* was decisive. As Flaubert saw it, modern life presents transcendent genius no proper object to express. *Salammbô* was an artistic failure. *Madame Bovary* was, by any standard, a success, certainly a plausible candidate in any contest for the greatest of all novels.

However, it is not entirely true to say that there is no character superior to Emma in the novel. There is a momentary appearance of the great Dr. Larivière, who is called in at the last moment when

Emma's agony from the poison is unstoppable. He is the summit of the medical ladder of which Charles is the lowest rung, a spiritualization of the modern concentration on the body that drags everything down. Charles is the incompetent duffer who learned a few formulas in medical school and applies them unthinkingly to the locals who are sick. He is used by the great pharmacist Homais to impress the mob and feed his vanity on the clichés of Enlightenment. Above these two is Dr. Canivet from Rouen, a vulgar fellow, but one who has some real competence in dealing with the body's coarse needs. These three are bound together in their understanding of the goals of medicine and their place in society. They constitute a pecking order of vanities, with Charles at the bottom, despised by Homais, and Homais despised by Canivet. Larivière, in his profound understanding of this "muddy vestiture of decay," transcends the ordinary limits of concern for it:

> He belonged to that great line of surgeons that sprang from Bichat, that now-vanished generation of philosopher-healers who cherished their art with a fanatical love and practiced it with zeal and sagacity. When Dr. Larivière was angry, the whole hospital quaked. His pupils revered him to the point of trying to imitate him in everything as soon as they set up in practice themselves; consequently, every town for miles around had its replica of his long merino greatcoat and his loose black jacket, the cuffs of which hung down unbuttoned over his firm hands—beautiful hands, always ungloved, as though to be the readier to plunge to the relief of suffering. Disdaining all academic honours, titles and decorations, hospitable and generous, like a father to the poor, practicing virtue without believing in it, he might almost have passed for a saint had not his mental acuity caused him to be feared as a demon. Sharper than a lancet, his eyes looked straight into your soul, piercing through all pretence and reticence to dissect the lie beneath. So he went his way, in all the easy majesty that comes of the consciousness of great talent, wealth and forty years of hard work and irreproachable living. (331–332)

Larivière does not fit into the plot of *Madame Bovary*, but he is not to be ignored as a human possibility. *Practicing virtue without believing in it* is the decisive statement. It would not be exhaustive but it would be revealing to say that there is something of Flaubert as artist expressed in this character. Art for its own sake is all that is left.

5. Tolstoy, *Anna Karenina*

Encountering an old love after thirty-five years of separation produces curious sensations and reflections. Tolstoy's two great novels, *War and Peace* and *Anna Karenina*, were the introduction to high literary taste and Continental thought for a large segment of American college students when I was young. This was one of the last moments of immediate and natural literary influence in the daily life of the more or less educated. The graciousness of life, the incisive presentation of conflicting passions, and the direct presentation of great ideas seemed to be the royal road to an education and the cultivation of civilized sensibilities. The problems of modernity, particularly justice in the organization of the social and the economic order, were addressed directly in Tolstoy and in that other great Russian source, Dostoyevsky, and Russia itself appeared to be the place where the drama of justice would have its denouement. Psychological depth expressing itself in sentimental and unrestrained relations, strange compulsions, triumphs, and especially humiliations appeared to illustrate our Freud, whose victory was still fresh and inspiring. Tolstoy's and Dostoyevsky's characters, more than those of any other writers, were the literary agents of our self-recognition. Reading Tolstoy was one of the dearest experiences of my generation.

Rediscovering Tolstoy brought me a rush of memory of the enthusiasms of youth and the hopes these books engendered for entry into a deeper level of life and really interesting relationships. But the colder objectivity resulting from distance and perhaps also from age and experience changed my responses to what clearly remain transcendent masterpieces of the art of the novel. Tolstoy's antipolitical politics with its critique of rational reform and rejection of liberal democracy, his concentration on national culture in opposition to Enlightenment cosmopolitanism, loom larger for me now. My concern with the individual psychology of his characters had blinded me to the fact that Tolstoy had put his art in the service of a vast political or cultural project. That project now appears more allied to the fanaticisms of this ugly century than to the politics and art that saved at least some of us. Moreover, there is an alien impression, one hardly if at all noticed when I was young, of a gracious, semi-aristocratic civility that is now so far away from anything we can experience or hope to experience in our daily lives. The relationships of love and friendship have a delicacy and an involvement with higher concerns that almost seem inauthentic. Rather than a model for our own lives, the social scene seems to be reminiscent of a lost world where people had the leisure to attempt to make works of art of their lives.

Still, Tolstoy's stories and characters seduce us and lead us toward his perspective on what is noble and base in man. One immediately rediscovers the old charms of Tolstoy's inimitable characterizations, putting us inside their heads, breaking out of the limits of his own consciousness, and giving an independent life to even the most unsympathetic characters. Nobody is just a puppet of Tolstoy's special perspective. He knows exactly what a young girl feels before a great ball or how jealousy arises in a man who denies that he is capable of it. But there is also a great disappointment. Broader learning has made me now able to see a paradox: the variety and liveliness of the characters in the novel are contained within a rigid and doctrinaire framework, one that points to an articulation of human problems that is not Tolstoy's own. Tolstoy turns out to be as faithful and undeviating a follower of Rousseau as any man or artist ever was. In itself there is nothing wrong with this, except that when one knows Rousseau, Tolstoy becomes largely predictable and, coming very late in the Rousseauan day, his vision seems too unproblematic. One can love his characters, or at least some of them, but it is now difficult to think that Tolstoy might be our guide for life. If one knows Rousseau's insistence on the alienating effects of what for him is an abusive reading of Plutarch, Prince Andrei's attachment to Napoleonic heroism and its alienating effect on him in *War and Peace* become a rather heavy-handed textbook illustration of Rousseau rather than an illuminating insight. And the contrast between Prince

Andrei and the sincere Pierre Bezuhov, who, although he tries to find heroic models to imitate, actually can only march to his inner drummer, now appears to be a mechanical device for representing the distinction between the splendid vice of *amour-propre* in overcivilized man and the recovery of nature within. The natural goodness of Bezuhov and Levin is really rather tiresome. Reading Tolstoy now is an exercise in the appreciation of Romanticism and an awareness of its limits in itself and for us. He certainly is a wonderful example of what I have been insisting on, the now implausible assertion that Rousseau could inform the minds and hearts of great men to an unprecedented degree.

It is all there, beginning with the opposition between nature and society and the critique of Enlightenment. The great city, Petersburg, with aristocracy and government bureaucracy, is the contrary of the country with its peasants and its farming, and Moscow plays a provincial middle with naturalness and sincerity. Artificial politeness and competition divide the city folk while compassion produces fellow feeling in simple souls. Rational atheism and the fanaticism of the Old Church are contrasted to a humane religion founded in nature and the sentiments. And above all, the concentration on marriage and the family and the treatment of the various kinds of erotic connections come out of the Rousseau textbook. The gentleness or, if you please, the cloying sentimentality of Tolstoy has this source. Landscape and breast-feeding and all the rest of Rousseau's peculiarities or paradoxes are to be found here. The various types with their alternative lives have the names of characters. Hopeless romantic passion with adultery is Anna Karenina; she is Tolstoy's Julie. The gentleman seducer of high society is named Vronsky. Kitty is the Sophie who successfully becomes only wife and mother. The bourgeois bureaucrat of superficial reform is Karenin. And the sincere man looking for love and trying to find a sincere and honest life is Levin, who plays the role of Tolstoy imitating Rousseau himself.

Russia itself, in a mystic and suprapolitical way, is an actor in the drama, representing a natural growth or a culture, contrasted with France, representing the artificial rationalistic state.

This is a reflection of the split in Russia produced by Peter the Great, who tried to modernize Russia in imitation of France and Enlightenment thought, that aspect of Enlightenment thought, to be sure, that was compatible with enlightened despotism like the rule of Frederick the Great, who attracted the attention and cooperation of many Encyclopedists in the eighteenth century. The emulation of French politics, science, and artistic taste, which became so prevalent among the Russian aristocracy, is treated by Tolstoy as a merely superficial aping of France, particularly Paris, one which suppresses or destroys the national instincts and character. The first page of *War and Peace* is almost entirely in the French language, as spoken by the gossipy natives of Petersburg. Throughout both novels, the broken-back instinct of the Russian aristocrats is pointed out by their movement between French and Russian in expressing their feelings. Petersburg is just a second-rate Paris where even the love affairs are more or less satisfactory to the extent that they can be conceived to be Parisian. The conflict between city and country is reproduced in the conflict between France and Russia.

Tolstoy combines Rousseauan naturalism and nineteenth-century historicism in attempting to show that the Russian people or nation protects and encourages the fundamental human sentiments. Rousseau himself had criticized Peter the Great for introducing French ways into Russia without recognizing that they were not appropriate to it.[1] He said that in trying to civilize Russia in this way Peter had ensured that Russia would remain barbaric, but now with a jumbled and incoherent set of tastes and passions. The source of this criticism is the chapter "On the Legislator" in *The Social Contract*,[2] where Rousseau argues that a founder or lawgiver's function is to make a people with a distinctive way of life, an organic unity, rather than to establish institutions to contain a population of atomic individuals. The opposition between institutions and ways of life as the primary goal of legislation contrasts Locke and the Enlightenment with Rousseau and those who followed him and finds its expression in the continuing debate about individual versus community and civilization versus culture. This debate can easily lead in the direction followed by extreme nationalists, in particular by pan-Slavists in Russia, which culminates in the view that a nation produces a new and separate species, that a person is more of a Russian or a German than a human being. Tolstoy wanted nothing of such fanaticism and tried instead to highlight the Russian way as closest to the human way, rather than separating the two. Such a line was proposed by Rousseau himself, who argued that a properly constructed people would have its own specific character while coming closest to nature within the constraints and perversions of civilization. He regarded the application of universal principles of politics everywhere as a mistake of rationalism, both insensitive to human needs and destined to fail.

This Rousseauan observation does not lead his followers to conservatism but, on the one hand, to a cloudier or vaguer program for revolution and, on the other, to a strange mixture of universal demands of justice and a respect for the traditions of a particular nation. This is illustrated by the French Revolution itself, which began in attempts to liberalize French politics along the lines suggested by the Glorious Revolution of 1688 in England and ended with the much more rigorous and complicated demands of the Jacobins and Robespierre. Liberals, with their rational reforms, always appear in Tolstoy as superficial, ineffective, and vain. Their optimistic zeal comes from lack of rootedness. They may argue well, but they never understand the nature of the people. Whereas Marx speaks of the idiocy of rural life and wishes for the conquest of nature together with the enlightenment of the people, Tolstoy worships the country and wishes the peasants to remain essentially as they are, although he wholeheartedly supports the emancipation of the serfs. Enlightenment would turn the peasants into educated city dwellers, whereas Rousseau and Tolstoy want to make the city dwellers into country people and, at the least, friends of the peasants.

This split in modern egalitarian politics goes back to Rousseau's argument that progress does not lead to happiness, an argument wholeheartedly embraced by Tolstoy. Tolstoy is surely some kind of radical, and Marxists tried to assimilate him. The kibbutz movement in Israel, which had Russian origins, was made up of persons who frequently thought they were Marxists and Tolstoyans, but who established small agricultural communities and a kind of primitive socialism that Marx would have despised and called romantic or utopian. In fine, Tolstoy in both *War and Peace* and *Anna Karenina* sets the private lives he examines in a political world in which the significance of political activity is reduced. In a Rousseauan spirit he goes a step further than Rousseau went, inventing or borrowing a notion of a plantlike existence of national minds that can be disturbed by meddlers but not usefully changed. By dedicating oneself to leading a rich and private life, one makes all the contribution one can to the betterment of mankind. Scientific, instrumental, and manipulative reasoning are the enemies and must be eliminated in such a way as to let sentiment be the guide. With this kind of preparation, the romantic activities of individuals take on a profound and central significance.

Anna Karenina is the tale of two parallel lives belonging to individuals who have the greatest expectations from love, parallel lives that meet and crave each other for only a moment. These two separate stories, Anna's and Levin's, are dealt with simultaneously throughout the book and reflect light on each other: Anna living the tragic life, which seems to be the accompaniment of *amour-propre*, and Levin finding the partner appropriate for having children and, at the end, discovering the need for something beyond that is not self-destructive. Tolstoy thus provides a nuanced picture of the real problems of serious persons who seek to love and be loved while experiencing the tensions or contradictions in any particular solution for civilized human needs. His is the poetic vision of a man who has meditated on Emile, Julie, and the Rousseau of the *Confessions* and the *Reveries of the Solitary Walker*. His message is ultimately one of loneliness, with the critical distinction being between endurable and unendurable loneliness. Levin and Anna are surrounded by more or less inferior types whose lives shy away from facing the ultimate questions. Tolstoy, like Rousseau, never found an ultimate question he did not want to confront.

II   The novel begins with the charming sensualist Oblonsky, who keeps busy trying to forget eternity and is representative of the folly of depending on this attractive but deceptive too too solid flesh. Tolstoy does not precisely concentrate on the opposition between body and soul, but fleshiness in a man is often a symptom of too much expectation from the pleasures of the senses and a superficial disposition toward life. The number of times Tolstoy mentions the thickness or fatness of a man's calf is remarkable, and by that he wishes to indicate the character of the individual involved. The spectrum of this type runs from Kuragin in *War and Peace* all the way up to the highly respectable Vronsky in *Anna Karenina*. These people feel good in their skins and are unable to face the fundamental contradictions of human life. We see Kuragin's fine fat leg cut off at the battle of Borodino. Even Napoleon, the diabolic imperial expression of Enlightenment and its pretensions to transform the human condition rather than face it, has a twitchy calf that is somehow meant to reveal his true nature. The best characters have strong bodies, but they are never sleek.

Oblonsky's situation introduces us to the physical and spiritual problem the novel treats. He has been sleeping with the French governess, and his wife has found out about it. She is a decent woman who is almost exclusively defined by motherhood. She lives in the boring details of taking care of her children and worrying about their health and their good character. Many pregnancies have robbed her of her youthful bloom. She is simply not sexually attractive any longer. This used to happen to women when birth control was hardly used and was not very effective and infant mortality made it necessary to produce many babies in order to maintain the population level. She represents the reproductive aspect of eroticism on which Tolstoy concentrates so brutally. There may have been, at the beginning, a romantic attraction, but that is just nature's way of drawing men into the business of replenishing the species. Now both Oblonsky and his wife, Dolly, feel cheated, he that she is no longer attractive, she that he is no longer attracted. She cannot understand why he would not get a big charge out of playing with the kids. Her shock at Anna's admission that something has been done to her by a doctor to prevent further pregnancies proves her to be a perfectly convinced adherent of what she thinks nature's intention is for the use of her body. She would never say that she has a right to control over her body because nature has such a right over her and is a much higher authority. For a moment she admires Anna's adulterous relationship and the freedom it brings, but this is only comic. She satisfies her little *amour-propre* by imagining that she will have many lovers and make her husband jealous of her as she is jealous of him. Dolly's situation is founded on virtue. Barren women and confirmed bachelors are always outside of the real meaning of life. Rationalists like Koznishev, Levin's half brother, do not love. Tolstoy is very brutal with barren women such as Sonya in *War and Peace* and Varenka in *Anna Karenina* who do not marry. They are perfectly decent but are not equipped for happiness. The only thing wrong with Dolly is that she does not have a faithful husband and this makes her somewhat pitiful, although she is ennobled by her dedication to the family.

But, for all that, Tolstoy does not try to hide under a cloud of moral exhortation the fact that sex with her is not very appealing and that this counts for something, whatever weight one may give it. Oblonsky is one of the very sweetest characters in all of Tolstoy, acting as the sympathetic go-between for Anna (his sister) and her husband, and for Kitty (his sister-in-law) and Levin. He brings life and goodwill wherever he goes. Tolstoy does not blame or punish him; he just presents him as somehow slight and beneath the issues. Not being taken very seriously is his punishment for his superficial eroticism. His easy women and his wonderful dinners are distasteful to the serious Levin. In one way, his sexual activities are simply natural, but in another sense they are a result of the terrifying observation that his wife's loss of her looks is the announcement of mortality itself, a fact that he would like to forget. He cannot face eternity, which somehow both Anna and Levin face constantly. A serious life must come to terms with death, a task at which Anna fails and Levin succeeds. They are both, however, always at grips with it. Romantic love is always allied with death. Only Jane Austen's reserve makes her silent on this question. Love is a life-and-death question. I once had a well-known Freudian teacher to whom I posed the question: "What is the moral conclusion that an intelligent reader can draw from Freud?" He responded, "Don't put all your eggs in one basket." Romanticism says precisely the opposite. Timidity, self-protectiveness, causes love (singular) to deteriorate into relationships (plural). Oblonsky's good humor and real enjoyment save him from the tedious and repulsive serious talk about relationships—which are not in themselves serious—with which we are plagued today.

The connection between the attractions of beautiful bodies and the concern for the well-being of other human beings and of societies is the issue. Tolstoy is extremely impressive in bringing out the full range of this old Rousseauan problem without suppressing the richness of the phenomena, ranging from sensual indulgence to religious mysticism. But one finds less satisfactory the solutions he seems to propose. Anna Karenina is clearly a figure from a moral fable about the dangers of the temptations of the senses and the wickedness of adultery, however deserving of pity she may be. The deaths of Julie, Mme. de Rênal, and Emma Bovary do not testify to their sinfulness as does Anna's. Each in her own way testifies rather to her own superiority and to the unresolvable conflicts contained in her situation. Anna clearly makes a bad choice and she suffers the consequences. At her adultery the cosmos rebels just as surely as it rebels against Macbeth's regicide.

Still, Anna is a marvelous creation. It is difficult from the outset not to love her. Without much descriptive material Tolstoy manages to persuade us of her surpassing beauty. This is why no movie of *Anna Karenina* can be anything but disappointing. Any actress is far beneath what our imagination has prepared us for. Her graciousness, elegance, and sweetness win everyone. She is a good wife and above all a passionately dedicated mother. But she too is a virginal married woman, like Mme. de Rênal or Mme. Bovary. She was married young to a man who had no vocation as a lover, an important man in the bureaucracy, involved in what Tolstoy depicts as the foolish and ineffective business of trying to govern and reform Russia rationally. Anna seems to be skating on the thin ice of bourgeois marriage, persuaded that it is solid and the real thing. The turbulent waters beneath are apparently unknown to her. She thinks of herself as an unassailably faithful wife, whereas she has merely never been tested. She is a perfect subject for testing the promise held out by erotic passion as an end in itself. Her innocence gives her the opportunity to live through the experience without the artificiality or the self-protectiveness of her circle of Petersburg adulteresses. She will go all the way.

Frenzied possession is what Stendhal and, in a modified way, Plato praise, whereas it is condemned by moralists or is at best given a pass to the extent it contributes to the family's reproductive function. Rousseau tried to bring the two together—a passionate love affair and the foundation of a family—without either being subservient to the other. Tolstoy appears ultimately to join the moralists against the convinced romantics, but he does so ambiguously, regretfully, and, perhaps, didactically. Anna is attracted and seduced by a high-grade version of the fleshy man, Count Vronsky, and this first experience of bodily love engages all the spirituality of her rich soul. Is this ephemeral body a deceiver? He begins frivolously, enjoying the idea of yet another beautiful woman who will give him pleasure and the conquest of whom will incite envy and admiration in society. The power of what Anna represents is attested to by the fact that she raises him to the level of tragic devotion to her. He is not a slight man, not one of those substitutes for men encountered by Emma Bovary. He is a gentleman and a soldier, a good son, and a loyal friend. His life prior to meeting Anna was lived comfortably within the confines of the aristocratic conventions of Russia. He is rich and very noble, connected with the court. His bad behavior is that of the typical conventional gentleman: he pays gambling debts before he pays tailor's bills and has erotic experiences that do not rock the boat of his position or his career. Without having had any such intention at the outset, he follows Anna into perdition, breaking with his friends and his mother, resigning his military commission, leaving the society in which he felt so comfortable, for he has discovered that he is unable to live without her. Their lives are deprived of all the ordinary conventional social supports and supplements, and they live off love, off being together. It does not work. There is not enough substance there to nourish them. And there is Anna's guilt.

That guilt concerns her child Seryozha. Anna, like Julie and Mme. de Rênal, is caught up in the contradiction between love and children whose fathers they do not love. In this romantic genre, and well beyond it, women's love of their children is the distinctive element of their nature. They are like men in their capacity for sexual attraction, but unlike them in the fundamental tension they experience between their natural attractions and the other kind of love connected with children. Men have it naturally easy, because they can produce children without caring for them. As Rousseau pointed out from the beginning, a man can be caught up in the web of family relations, but he lacks the immediate natural passions that make women the source of the family. The very existence of Seryozha makes Anna's attempts to live happily with Vronsky an exercise in self-forgetting. Her daughter, the fruit of her liaison with Vronsky, cannot engage her instincts in the same way as the son she left behind. Although her husband was a matter of indifference, their child gives their relationship an authority she is not able to escape. It is difficult to determine whether her guilt is due to her depriving her son of a mother's love, or the likely loss of her son's love, or something more mysterious. The marriage between Anna and Karenin is strictly conventional, and she has all the best excuses for not loving him—he was tricked into marrying her without really loving her, he was by nature one of those barren men, and she was forced into it by her aunt. But somehow or other it is not merely convention that makes her contract to him more binding than any such contract would seem today. Karenin is really Seryozha's father, and although the institution of marriage is made by men and their laws, the obedience to some such law, if the family is to exist, is somehow necessary and even sacred. Anna's quest for happiness with Vronsky is at war with fundamental duty. It is perhaps wrong even to assert that Anna was seeking happiness in her adultery. It seems to have been a fatal and irresistible attraction that she knew from the start would destroy her. However that may be, Anna represents the problem of woman, and Tolstoy uses her to reveal to the world the decisive conflict between erotic love and the love of children that is her core. This is as close to tragedy, the conflict between two noble alternatives, as one gets in the modern poetic dispensation.

It would have been possible for Tolstoy to treat this whole issue in the spirit of a reformer attempting to free women from the oppression of male hegemony. I once heard one of my university colleagues arguing that if Anna had lived in the state of Wisconsin today, a liberal judge would have given her a no-fault divorce and custody of her child. Thus, the book would appear to be only a mirror of worn-out and unjust legal systems. Anna could have had her affair and her child without tension or guilt. But Tolstoy would never consider such a solution, and not only because he is an old fogey. He accepts the Rousseauan view that the seriousness of life is in love and marriage, and modern divorce, the easy availability of replacement parts for the social machine, lacks gravity. As men and women of an older world experienced holy terrors if they profaned a sacred altar, modern men and women should, for Tolstoy, find the true locus for this experience of the sacred in the bonds, spiritual and physical, of marriage. Karenin is a repulsive and weak person, and it is unfair that it is up to him, with his variety of low motives, to decide whether Anna is to have a divorce and her child. But the brute stupidity of the system reveals its necessity. One way or another, in nature's confused and imperfect law, the child must be the product of a couple, and as the child is sacred, so must be the couple that produced it. Tolstoy knows full well that there is a variety of ways of getting along within society while indulging one's whims. Anna's sometime friend Betsy Tverskoy has easy adulterous relations and remains respectable as long as she is hypocritical. But Tolstoy uses all his art to show that she and her kind are slight persons, not to be taken seriously by serious people. Betsy is a great fan of Anna's adultery until Anna takes it so seriously as to cause a scandal. Then she shuns Anna. The society of loose women condemns Anna, and narrow-minded, self-justifying prudes insult her publicly. Tolstoy depicts all of this in such a way as to give us sympathy for Anna, who lives out her sentiments with sincerity. But this does not mean she can get away with it, or that she ought to get away with it. For all that her sad story is the result of the quirks of Karenin's character and the dishonesty of a corrupt society, there is an inevitability to her end. The moral forces of the cosmos work to punish Anna in a way that one would never find in Stendhal. Tolstoy depicts a terrible responsibility that inheres in women and makes them interesting. The abstract fairness that became the dominant theme in the generations after Tolstoy would appear to him to be a means of reducing love and morality to trivial utilitarianism.

All of this points to the problem of the status of love and the beautiful in human relations. Is the beautiful object that one loves only an illusion, or is it something off which and for which one can live? Tolstoy, in part, treats love of the beautiful as nature's momentary ruse in order to ensnare men and women in responsible reproduction. At other times, he presents it as a good in itself, which is what it claims to be. Here we touch upon this ambiguity in the Romantic understanding of love altogether. Rousseau wants to persuade us that love of the beautiful is an illusion, but also that it is somehow beyond illusion. When one attains the goal of erotic union with the beautiful person, can one say that one has lived a fulfilled life? Or does beauty turn out to be an empty promise? In the Romantic understanding there is nothing behind the appearance of the beautiful, and therefore all kinds of disappointments ensue for its votaries. The status of the erotically beautiful is at all times a troubled one when human beings are allowed to take it seriously. But for Plato, there seems to be some kind of being behind the appearance. Whereas Saint-Preux's education of Julie is more a means to the seduction of Julie than an end in itself, Socrates' education of his beautiful youngsters is meant to culminate in a union of souls that is real. With the story of Anna, Tolstoy tries to show that the consuming flame results only in ashes and that one should, however regretfully, eschew its charms. But he fails to explain why those capable of experiencing such love are ennobled by it.

Sexual attraction and the effort to fulfill it are natural. But in almost all civilized societies that satisfaction is severely restricted by conventions and institutions, and even the attraction itself is made somewhat culpable. It is hard for us to imagine today how difficult it was in the past for a man to find a sexual partner, since the married and the unmarried were both forbidden to him by the moral, civil, and religious law. The only alternative was to be found with loose and mercenary women, the commerce with whom destroyed the greater part of the charms of love and brought a risk of mortal disease. A romantic man would want only a beautiful woman who is capable of faithfully reciprocating his passion. The fact that married women were forbidden to him did not mean that they were simply unavailable or that all kinds of evasions were not practiced, but to participate in this game, he had to abandon decency. Unmarried women or maidens were also forbidden, because they were being prepared for marriage, both for their own sakes and their families'. It is not impossible that a young woman who sleeps around prior to marriage will become faithful once married, but the odds are not very good. Rousseau indicates that in case of imperious necessity, like that of a priest, a decent man would choose an unmarried girl rather than a married woman because of the sacredness of the marriage vows. In fact, clever men choose married women because married women are more experienced, are more easily available, and can conceal the responsibility for the children who might accidentally be produced. Prior to or outside marriage, satisfaction was very difficult to obtain and what was obtained was freighted with guilt and degradation. The sexual world was a labyrinth constructed out of natural desire and the conventions then deemed requisite for the maintenance of society. One could get lost in it very easily, and, at best, a man required many wiles and arts of seduction. Of course, much went on, but practically everything was problematic and could end in disgrace, prison, or death. In a mere thirty years, the frustration that was present in one way or another in almost all times and places has become almost unimaginable to us, and we require great effort of both imagination and intellect in order to take seriously problems that we do not face or face in very attenuated form. Today maidens are available, married women are available, and bastards are legitimate. Of course, the availability of abortion makes it easy to avoid illegitimacy, even though the statistics on illegitimacy would seem to prove the contrary. But the rise in illegitimacy is due to the loosening of family ties, which has made it easier to have illegitimate children, easier for those who bear them and for the children themselves. It all seems so sensible. A simplistic interpretation would view this as the victory of nature (sexual desire) over convention (the arbitrary and oppressive laws of society). But both Rousseau and Tolstoy would see something of nature, or if not nature, the divine, in the connection between husband and wife that makes it possible for them to be father and mother. Or, as one sees from this very formulation, a mother is always known to be a mother, but a father must agree to accept the child as his own. Therefore, it is the limitation of the sexual desire that makes it possible for there to be fathers, with all their mysterious powers, rights, and duties. When the chasteness of women and the limitation on men disappear, what disappears with them is fathers. And this one can see in today's proliferation of single-parent households. The expression is too neutral, for they are almost exclusively mother-headed households.

The oversimplification of sexual liberation movements is most obvious here. Julie, Mathilde, and Anna all became pregnant by their natural lovers, and the problem of illegitimacy shines forth. The children who are the products of nature and real love lack something that can be provided only by law and its constraints. If the natural child were sufficient, then nature itself would be sufficient. In Anna's case, the child by the man she did not love was somehow more her child because of her legal and religious connection with that man.

However that may be, Anna's situation highlights the vast gap that separates passionate love and the existence of the family, even though the two seem to be linked by our erotic natures. The family may not be natural, but it is surely not simply conventional, like most of the laws that govern relations among human beings. And it is very difficult to imagine laws that would not frustrate our sexual desires.

A woman's freedom in choosing her mate is as close as serious earlier thinkers came to sexual liberation, and that is still very far away and presupposes unusually virtuous women capable of intelligent and enduring choices, as Jane Austen so beautifully shows us. The free expression of erotic love could still overturn the best resolution. Emile and Sophie might combine passionate love and the family, that highest aspiration of this modern movement, but the novelists, including Rousseau himself, show us the usually unhappy result. Thus, the very great constriction of the alternatives available to passionate men and women in their sexual longings, and their consequent frustration, are part and parcel of the arrangement in which family is central.

In the past, a woman who visibly stepped outside the conventions literally lost her social existence. The maiden who was compromised became almost unmarriageable, and compromised could be taken to mean simple rejection by one who had begun to court her, as Jean-Jacques warned Emile and as in fact happened in the case of Kitty and Vronsky. A girl in this situation was likely to become an old maid living on sufferance with her relatives and expected to serve them. The discovered adulteress, while not precisely wearing a scarlet letter, could not be received in society and lost all of her friends. At best, she could live in a *demimonde*, if there was one available, along with kept women and actresses, the scandalous world of bohemia, which had some artistic allure. There was no respectable ground on which to stand, and this was what Anna faced. Without Vronsky, who protected and supported her, she would have been almost utterly abandoned. This blatantly unfair situation, which weighed so unequally on women, provided a strong incentive to right-thinking people for reforming the entire moral system that underlay it. Such reformers are to be found in *Anna Karenina*, but they are finally dismissed by Tolstoy.

Anna's *amour-propre* is in Tolstoy the primary psychological motive for her involvement with others, and is of the gentle variety, akin to that of Mme. de Rênal. It relates almost totally to the opinions of Vronsky. Unlike Vronsky, who at the outset thought about the affair in terms of the opinions of his whole society, she thought about it only in terms of his affection, on the one hand, and how an attachment to him would affect her opinion of herself on the other. Unlike Mme. de Rênal, she had previously had some self-consciousness, designed to hide her unconscious dissatisfaction. Hers was an alienated self-consciousness because she lived in terms of her opinions about the way she ought to be rather than discover-

ing and expressing her real sentiments. She acted out being a good
wife and mother while being a good wife and mother. Her satisfaction was in her image of herself rather than in that self. It was a kind
of role playing, where the pleasure of life is not so much in being
something as in the appearance to oneself of being that thing which
one actually is. Vronsky's success with her is due to his being able to
touch her real erotic feelings, which would have had to be expressed
in order for her understanding of her self to be in conformity with
her self. At the same time, because she has built a whole world on
that understanding of herself, her affair with Vronsky destroys her
world without providing her with a new self-understanding that
would make her able to bear the truth of her desires. She can think
of herself only as adulteress and bad mother, an almost intolerable
self-consciousness. Therefore so much of her life with Vronsky is
devoted to a kind of charade of self-forgetting and playacting an
imaginary marriage to him. Prior to her relations with Vronsky, she
was living an ought that had very little to do with her is, and during
her relationship with Vronsky she is living an is that she is unable to
make conformable with any ought. When Vronsky is following her
around, as it were courting her, she thinks she doesn't like it and
persuades herself that she wants to be rid of him. But when, one
evening, he does not show up at the salon that they both frequent,
she realizes that she misses him. Her apparent distaste for his attentions was only the ruse of her soul permitting her to use the energy
Vronsky had touched in her as a defense against him. The poor
woman has no arms to defend against this enemy who has breached
the Maginot line on which she counted. In the long run, that is, the
full year during which Vronsky pursues her, it is inevitable that she
surrender.

After that, everything in her life is the desperate struggle of a
trapped animal who is not destined to escape. The sincere Anna
cannot live the hypocrisy of the garden variety of adulteress. Actually, her husband is of the kind who looks for excuses for not recognizing his cuckold's status and all the consequences that come
from it. But Anna has to tell him, to stick his nose in the fact of her
infidelity. When, after the birth of her daughter, she resolves to
return to her husband and to renounce Vronsky, she makes every
effort to resume her old act. But the presence of her husband nau-
seates her and is physically unbearable. Karenin is in fact a nause-
ating human being, and Vronsky's real conversion to the cult of love
is proved to Anna by his attempted suicide. They must be together,
but only for their misery. They are poisoned by what they feed on.

Unlike the case of the couple in *The Red and the Black*, there is almost
no moment when the sweet charm of the natural loving couple is
depicted by Tolstoy.

The agent of Anna's destruction is that most insidious of effects
of *amour-propre*, jealousy. "What," she asks herself, "attaches this
man to me?" Is it the sexual attraction to her beautiful body? But she
is getting older and will lose that. Moreover, sexual attraction is
promiscuous and unpredictable. Is it the joy of conquest? But that
loses its charm for a man almost immediately after he succeeds, and
he must look to test himself against more stubborn enemies. How
can he fail to despise a fallen woman? Maybe he is already playing
her false when he goes away for a time. Or maybe he is sticking by
out of duty, which is not what love wants. How can she know what
he is really thinking, or the inmost movements of his soul? In this
affair there are none of the routines or conventions that artificially
protect attachment. They are thrown back on nature itself, and it is
doubtful whether nature provides forces sufficient for the permanent
and passionate connection of two human beings. Tolstoy represents
jealousy in his characters as Rousseau theorized about it. No other
work of literature, apart from *Othello*, presents so vividly this terrible
passion as does *Anna Karenina*. Dolly, Karenin, Anna herself, as well
as Levin, are victims of jealousy, each in his or her own way. It is one
of the extreme effects of *amour-propre*, the *amour-propre* informed by
eroticism. The comparative and relative existence of a person, which
begins when *amour de soi* is converted into *amour-propre* and which
causes the concern with the opinions of others, is, as we have seen,
converted by the sexual desire to the exclusive concern with the
opinion of the person to whom one is attracted. Smallness or greatness of soul determines the ways in which the torment of doubt
about the other's desire or opinion expresses itself. Rousseau, in
discussing the form Emile's jealousy might take, says that there are
two essential directions possible. The first is to be angry with the
beloved and to blame him or her for the injustice of not loving in
return. The second is to blame oneself for not being worthy of the
beloved. This is the form of jealousy from which both Emile and
Levin suffer. Levin does not hate Kitty or blame her; and although he
feels unable to compete with Vronsky he does not attempt to destroy
him or small-mindedly to denigrate his qualities. His own unworthiness, and hence his not having a right to happiness, is his sole
preoccupation. It is an ugly, melancholy experience that drains life of
any joy. No experience seems to be pleasant without the accompa-

niment of the consciousness of the other. She is the only competent judge.

Anna, on the other hand, experiences a rage against Vronsky, whose every fugitive thought she imagines. Vronsky becomes her enemy. Practically, she needs his protection and his money, which renders the situation a bit ambiguous. But essentially, she cannot live without his enslavement to her, and she has no means to guarantee that. She develops a kind of ideology of possible reasons for his being untrue to her and imagines possible partners in his infidelity, from prostitutes to great ladies. Her mind becomes a grotesque mirror image of what she imagines might be his mind. It is full of obscene reflections of the movements of body and soul. She then becomes a tyrant, without just grounds, wishing to control those movements of body and soul that, if left free, would be promiscuous. She is bereft of any support other than the love of her lover, which is so uncertain a thing. Neither man nor God can help her. Her frenzy is rendered all the more acute by the alternate moods, which at one time tell her she is crazy, and, at another, persuade her that her tormented consciousness sees only the truth. She is torn between wanting Vronsky freely to love her and the awareness that freedom may not necessarily further her need to have him exclusively attracted to her. Tolstoy does not depict Anna's jealousy as mean-spirited, but as the necessary, or even divine, punishment for the dependence constituted by her worldly love.

In fact, Vronsky is sometimes bored with Anna, and the idyllic life they try to live together in Italy or in the country affords Vronsky no fulfilling activity. And her jealousy makes everyday life unpleasant and makes her somewhat contemptible as well. It seems to be in human nature to despise and shy away from neediness and to respect and pursue fullness. Love demands the unity of souls, but the hope for that unity may very well be a snare and a delusion. Love leaves human beings without resource when they are rejected or deceived by the objects of their love. Prudence would suggest "not putting all one's eggs in one basket," but following this counsel would make love impossible and force men and women to revert to merely contractual relations, the permanent opposition between self and other and the state of war that ensues from it. Psychologists today might well call Anna paranoid, implying that her condition is simply an illness. The issue is whether that is not a merely bourgeois judgment, emanating from persons who get along just fine with self-protective half relationships. Nietzsche suggests that distrusting one's neighbor will be considered an illness by the last man, who will go voluntarily to the madhouse (read, into therapy) in order to cure himself.[3] But if human contact is so delicate and so unsure a thing, then distrust is almost surely its partner. Healthy freedom from this "paranoia" is predicated on a useful coarsening of human relations. Love includes the concern for the opinion of another, and that opinion is in so many ways a fugitive thing.

The truly mean-spirited jealousy is experienced by Karenin, who is upset not so much by Anna's infidelity as by his own ridiculousness in the eyes of his society. As the possession of such a woman as Anna makes him an object of envy for others, so the loss of her makes him ridiculous in their eyes. However unjust it may be, the unfortunate lover is almost always an object of contempt, and it is that contempt that concerns Karenin. His love of Anna is not an involvement with her. He was never really in love with her. He has used love as a tool in his desire for primacy over the public at large, whereas love means an exclusive involvement with the one beloved. Moreover, Karenin's jealousy is further degraded by the fact that he is a bourgeois, which means that he is too frightened of death to fight a duel with Vronsky. Duels are indeed folly, but the risk of life adds a touch of nobility to the supposed attachment of love. But, just as in the case of M. de Rênal, we know that his musings on the honorable course of action will never end in the decision to fight. Such a fight would, of course, show even more clearly that he is worried about the opinions of others, but killing Vronsky would certainly make the cuckold look less ridiculous. Instead, Karenin hopes that Anna will die in childbirth and get him off the hook. Then he hopes Anna will repent, bear the burden of public opprobrium, and give the public appearance of returning to duty. He ends up in a mystical Christianity, the low motivation of which Tolstoy despises. Karenin is a poor fish who gets caught up in the great passions of others and whose petty life, which previously seemed so grand, is thereby revealed for what it is. Conventional marriage avoids facing the real dangerousness of love, which should be practiced only by the few who are capable of it.

Anna's suicide is based upon an emotional survey of her situation. There is no place where a sensitive and richly developed soul like hers can get a sure footing. Her unbearable husband, the son who is lost to her, and the social world where she starred and that banished her, have disappeared as a means to fill out some kind of life, however unsatisfying and artificial. Most of all, Vronsky, this decent man who has become a sincere lover when touched by the grace of this remarkable woman, provides nothing really substantial. Their passionate embraces last only for a moment and are tinged by guilt. Their attempts to fill out a life in Italy, with culture, and in Russia, with agriculture, are failures, attempts to live an imagination of a serious life rather than the discovery of what is naturally suitable. Anna actually does what Emma Bovary dreams about, traveling in romantic Italy with her lover, living off love. But Tolstoy teaches that the love of the flesh may ennoble but cannot satisfy. The illusion of love that is so much a part of this Romantic moment in our past is emphasized by him.

It is hard to say what Anna could have done. She might have rejected Vronsky and stayed with her husband as a good wife should. But Tolstoy tells us enough about Karenin to make it clear that no happiness was to be found in that direction and that duty fulfilled would be merely a conventional sacrifice without reward from the gods. The care of her child would have provided her with serious activities for a few years, but only a few, and whatever children may think about it, the life dedicated to them is not a whole life. And the overwhelming attraction to Vronsky leads toward a void. If she had had the luck as an inexperienced young girl to find and choose a Vronsky, she might have lived happily ever after. But that would have been only an accident and would not have revealed the truly composite nature of what is falsely supposed to be a unity—love, marriage, and children. Anna's suicide is the inevitable result of being a woman like Anna, whose ephemeral but real beauty and charm have no status in the eternal order of things. Only a coarse soul could have walked away from the consequences following from real love, a coarse soul not vulnerable to the dependency of love. Tolstoy, more earnest than Stendhal, does not let us lightheartedly celebrate those wonderful moments of perfect union, because there is no perfect union and those moments are always tainted and never self-sufficient. As a good Romantic, Tolstoy points us on a road to happiness and then shows us it is a dead end.

III Tolstoy is, unlike our other three novelists, an expansive writer who tries in his two great novels to present in didactic order his views of the whole world and the forces moving within it. The actions in the novels tend to be more obviously illustrative of his general views than is the case with the others, and he insists on telling us the true story even if it breaks up the speed and intensity of the plot. He is, without doubt, a real novelist, a maker of flesh-and-blood imaginary persons who live within us and act as constant reference points for those of us who have digested his books. But he is also the kind of intellectual who wants to sit around in a coffee klatsch and talk big ideas just like the New York intellectuals who took him and Dostoyevsky as their models. There are endless discussions of various political and philosophic doctrines that preoccupied educated people in his time: materialism, atheism, Enlightenment, political reform, agricultural versus industrial societies, the emancipation of serfs and women, death and nihilism. By contrast, Jane Austen hardly alludes to such things. You have to figure them out for yourself. Stendhal would never reproduce the callow subphilosophy of his time, asking directly, "Is life meaningful or meaningless?" Stendhal's gentlemen might allude to such things, but only in passing, with a touch of irony, and he always subordinates such allusions to the rapid action of his plot. As Stendhal's writing resembles that of his musical genius, Rossini, Tolstoy's resembles that of his, Tchaikovsky. In this, Tolstoy is somewhat more like Rousseau himself, who uses so much of *La Nouvelle Héloïse* as a vehicle for repeating the teachings elaborated in his discursive philosophical works. But Tolstoy is a better novelist and a much worse philosopher than Rousseau. He can sometimes, or even often, bore us with the exposition of his vision of the sentimental unity of Russia threatened by Enlightenment rationalism and the spirit of the French Revolution, or his dilations on the joys of family life. He sermonizes. One need only compare his Napoleon, as presented in *War and Peace*, with Stendhal's. His attempt to demystify Napoleon seems merely edifying, in that his destructive criticism parodies Napoleon. It is a rather mechanical reproduction of Rousseau's criticism of the way Plutarch is used to make men admire the heroic. His creation of the unheroic hero, Kutuzov, the simple, humane representative of his time and his people who conquers Napoleon, is an attempt to replace Plutarch in ways indicated by Rousseau.[4]

No personality in the novels is more illustrative of this tendency than is Constantine Levin, the clumsy but sensitive man who resembles both Russia and Tolstoy himself. Anna is a figure who would not be uncomfortable in French society or a French novel, but Levin is quintessentially what we think of as Russian, and his salient characteristic is high seriousness. His story is told parallel to Anna's, and as she goes down, he comes up, and, in his bumbling way, finds happiness. Tolstoy, fully attracted by Anna, nevertheless tries to demystify her and her romantic world with Levin's awkward sincerity. The alternation between the two worlds, that of Anna and that of Levin, who live in exactly the same milieu, sharing common friends and even relatives, is illustrative of the contrast between bad and good choices in life. Levin's consciousness is riddled with all the incoherent temptations present in his overcivilized and semibarbaric Russia, epitomized by the struggle between Frenchified Russia and the old Russia. He moves in society a little like a Slavic Rousseau, trying to take it seriously but in it rather than of it. When he goes to dinner with Oblonsky, a dinner whose bill of fare is enough to set the mouth of a corrupt person to watering, Levin is both indifferent and contemptuous. The French *grisette* who accompanies the dinner and with whom Oblonsky flirts is revolting to Levin in her erotic looseness. He likes the simple fare produced off his land and cooked by his peasant servant, and he is attracted by modest girls who promise faithful love. He cannot even for a moment enter into the charms of Oblonsky's corruption. He is faithful to his instincts or sentiments, and that is what distinguishes him. They are instincts rooted in the soil of a Russia that is being plowed under by modernity. Even the concerns of the provincial society of Moscow are too much for him, and he is never attractive or at his best when he is in it. He is taken as a good, bluff fellow, but not much fun, a little like Emile is in Paris. He never has time for the gallantry of the salons because he is humorlessly looking for a wife, and he ruins the conversations that are intended to delight the ladies by his humorlessness in seeking the truth, which, according to Tolstoy, pretty much excludes the ladies. He wants a meaningful life, and all he knows is that these people don't even want one, let alone know what it is. His mood tends to be depressive because he sees no way out of the maze of contradictions present in Russian life, but he has fits and starts of enthusiasm when he thinks he has found a way. At the outset we find him having withdrawn from participation in the organizations set up to further local government, because they only make things worse by grafting a superficial reforming spirit onto the old ways, corrupting both. He moves among several alternative schemes for revitalizing agriculture and motivating the peasants. Sometimes he tries to use modern market techniques and at others he tries to reduce himself to the level of the peasants and get deeper satisfaction from their authenticity and naturalness.

We encounter Levin first when he is in Moscow with the intention of asking Kitty to be his wife. He is deeply unsure of himself and thinks that her answer will make the difference between happiness and unhappiness. Kitty refuses him because her head is turned by the apparent courtship of Vronsky, who has much greater romantic allure than Levin and who is strongly favored by her mother because he is a much more splendid match. Tolstoy, unlike Jane Austen, would never show the conventionally perfect marriage to be the good one. Great wealth and high social station must always be empty. Kitty is like Natasha in *War and Peace,* who, for a moment, is susceptible to the attractions of another one of these this-worldly, fat-calved men, Kuragin. These beautiful, enchanting women have in their youth an episode with the merely sensual, which is a part of their makeup but one that must be channeled to a manifest destiny of motherhood.

We can look at Kitty as the anti-Anna woman. With women like her, Tolstoy is at his triumphantly harshest, meaning to say, he propagandizes for her while demystifying her charms. He is marvelous with his descriptions of such maidens at the ball, full of graceful sensuality, loving to be looked at while looking over potential husbands. Their promise of love is irresistible, but they end up, as does Natasha, rather slovenly and with children's urine stains on their blouses. All their allures are part of nature's ruse to turn them into mothers. Tolstoy takes all the romantic charm of love and puts it into Anna, whose end is inevitably tragic. He takes the natural reproductive vocation of women and puts it all into Kitty and delights in disappointing those with high erotic expectations. It is all as nature wants it throughout the whole animal kingdom. With humans and their illusion of freedom, there is need of deception in order to entice them into doing their duty. In good Rousseauan fashion, Tolstoy believes that the family has become a necessity due to the progress of civilization and therefore man must be caught in the web of family involvement. Kitty is an almost exact replication of Sophie. She complements Levin's theoretical reason with her practical reason, constantly reminding him of the little details of their daily life, and makes up for his lack of psychological sensitivity to others. His marriage, the pleasures of which have been seasoned by her first refusal, turns out to be something other than he expected. Rather than bathing in romantic ecstasy and sharing every thought, he finds her to be exactly that complement that he lacked, very much absorbed in their daily affairs, especially after they have a child. She is totally unable to share in his continuous metaphysical speculations. It isn't even worth the effort to try to make her. When his brother is dying, he does not want to take her along to see the agonies of this totally Russian and proto-Dostoyevskian figure who lives with a prostitute and has that extreme range of undignified passions so identified with Russians. Levin believes that Kitty is too delicate to endure the scene, whereas, exactly like Sophie with the injured peasant, she takes over, oblivious to the filth and ugliness.[5] Moreover, she manifests that calm acceptance of the fact of death which Rousseau attributes to natural man and Tolstoy to peasants. Such persons do not need to learn how to die. They know how to die by instinct. In all these ways, she is nature herself, and Tolstoy uses much art to make us accept this in spite of our romantic inclinations.

Levin, on the contrary, is, in spite of his good instincts, alienated from this primordial knowledge by his intellectualism and has to find his way back to it. He becomes almost deranged by the spectacle of his brother's death. The latter is an unbeliever. This is a parallel to Wolmar, but Levin's Julie is not at all disturbed by Levin's spiritual travail, because she knows him to be a good man; and with Rousseauan instinct, as opposed to her churchly upbringing, she knows that God will not punish a good man with eternal damnation because he had wrong opinions that did not affect his action. He is the one who suffers from his atheism. The terribleness of death, which stills all eroticism, makes him obsessed with the questions about why he is alive and the meaninglessness of his existence. He is tempted to suicide. This separates him from his wife, who has no such doubts and whose soul is like a clear stream to the depths of which one can see without obstruction. The Romantic attempt at establishing perfect harmony between two human beings is thus declared a failure, because this man's needs are the concerns of a solitary. Even at the end, when he reconciles himself to reality, his deepest reflections are his own, not to be shared with his wife.

Levin's depression is not primarily due to the vulnerability and impermanence of the union of the two lovers, although that is part of it. Mostly it is due to the meaninglessness of the instant that is life against the background of an indifferent eternity. Levin's unbelief has two sources, both in the modern philosophy that was infecting Russia. The first has to do with religious criticism, the destruction of the authority of sacred texts along with the concentration on the contrary demands of the various sects. He, again like the young Rousseau, is unable to decide which should be authoritative and is appalled by the harshness of the sects with one another. None of the orthodoxies, with their hypocrisy and real indifference to simple moral conduct, can compel Levin. Second, modern natural science presented a reductionist, materialist account of nature with no place for man, his relations with his kind, or providence. There is, according to Levin, no morality possible with such a view of the world. Man is only a belly, concerned with self-preservation, and there are no grounds for caring for others. Levin is astounded by the intellectuals who propound these theories and are still able to live. He thinks they are not serious because they seem to live on, performing their duties, which now appear to be without foundation. This is the pre-Nietzschean meaning of nihilism that preoccupied so many Russians at the end of the nineteenth century: modern natural science is nihilism.

Levin's condition is not atheism as it was classically presented. He has not found an alternative way of life to the religious life. He longs to believe but cannot. His condition could be described as religiosity, as opposed to both religion and atheism. One can say that this is the modern meaning of tragedy, the impossibility of rationally believing in the moral life and the impossibility of living life without morality. It is the condition of the sincere and intellectually honest man. Prior to his marriage and his brother's death, Levin was relatively easygoing about this problem, but these two events set off the chain reaction that leads to his despair. The problem becomes urgent, and up to the last chapter of the novel, it seems that Anna and Levin are, by different routes, coming to the same end—suicide. Tolstoy's books always force the earnest reader to contemplate the meaning of life. His articulation of the problem of life is that reason, essentially groundless itself, destroys the ground of faith, which is the only solution. He never takes seriously for a moment the possibility of a self-sufficient life of reason, an alternative to the life of faith. Philosophy for him is that vice that emerges out of the pride of reason. Every one of the rationalists in his novels—and they come in all shapes and sizes—enters the scene with neon lights flashing "superficial." I look back with wonder on my own youth in which so many dogmatically atheist intellectual teachers loved Tolstoy, but never really took his way of posing the problem seriously, although they could provide no plausible account of the life of reason. Classical love of wisdom disappears completely as the fate of reason is made to appear to be identical to that of scientific materialism, while the study of life takes refuge instead in various abodes such as history, the nation, and sentiment. What distinguishes Tolstoy from Dostoyevsky, who sees the problem in pretty much the same way, is that Tolstoy can still believe in a gentle solution, as represented in such figures as Levin, Pierre Bezuhov, and Ivan Ilyich, whereas Dostoyevsky finds only a terrible abyss and fanatic resoluteness. This is one of the great dividing lines between Romanticism and the nihilism, in the modern sense, that followed it. In Dostoyevsky, Romanticism is dead.

The solution of Tolstoy, hold on to your seats, is the teaching of "The Profession of Faith of the Savoyard Vicar," which Levin recapitulates in every detail. It is a tribute to the perseverance of the Vicar's teaching that more than a century later, Tolstoy could take it for his own profession of faith, although for those for whom Rousseau is too sentimental, Tolstoy's revelation may be a bit disappointing. Levin's success in decent moralism after Anna's suicide is just a bit too edifying. It is similar to the way in which the harsh and almost clinical analysis of the emptiness and senselessness of Ivan Ilyich's life and death is succeeded by the revelation of a Rousseauan compassionate link among human beings in the last paragraph of the story. Rousseau as *deus ex machina*. Levin can return to a simple and pure love of his children while Dostoyevsky's heroes have nightmares about molesting children. For Dostoyevsky, there is no safety net. Levin was in the same condition as the Savoyard Vicar when he, through his semi-Cartesian meditation, found in sentiment a ground on which to stand.

Levin's transforming experience comes when he is working in the fields, in nature, performing the most natural of the arts, farming, when a peasant to whom he talks points out that some people are hard and avaricious and others are good and care for their fellow man. The peasant who is said to be good is named Platon, a name given by Tolstoy to a naturally wise man in *War and Peace* as well, reflecting a kind of primitive Platonic teaching persevering in the Slavic world and asserting the natural intuition of the good. Suddenly, Levin's soul is set ablaze by the insight that will reconcile him with life. He knows the difference between good and bad, although he could not reason to his knowledge. There are two principles in him, his belly, which makes him concerned only with his own preservation, and conscience, which makes him concerned with others. He has always done the good but has not believed in it. In his very nature, the voice of conscience has provided a guide for action very different from the counsels of the belly. Ultimately, Levin echoes Kant's formulation of Rousseau's teaching when he says that he wonders at the starry sky above and the moral law within, neither of which has any status within modern rationalism. His revelation silences the pride of reason, which is man's greatest sin. This permits Levin to affirm life. There is a will and an order in the cosmos and only foolish obstinacy can reduce them to nothingness. This is a revelation, but not one like the others, which depend on the authority of oral traditions or written texts. These latter are kinds of fanaticism, which one hears with one's ears rather than sees with one's eyes, and they separate men rather than bring them together. Tolstoy's faith is a natural religion, accessible to all men at all times and all places. The particular religions are good to the extent they promote the moral conduct proper for everyone. His wife, Kitty, is Russian Orthodox, but she behaves in a way suitable to everyone. All that is intolerant and exclusive in these religions Levin will reject, but for the rest, he will not trouble himself with their truth, which is beyond the reach of his intellect. His is a vague God whose power one sees in nature around us and whose laws are written in the heart with compassion and conscience. There is nothing more in this religion than what is demanded for the support of human morality. The identity of Levin's religion with that of the Vicar leaps to the eye in every sentence. Tolstoy does not, however, enter into any of Rousseau's complex reflections on the relation between God and eros.

Levin supplements Rousseau a bit with a kind of historical theory. The attempts of rational men to govern people are always a failure. This has been demonstrated in Levin's own life with his various dabblings in politics and the reform of agriculture. The destiny of peoples is the sum total of the millions of private deeds performed by individuals who are members of them without concern for the totality. There is a kind of spiritualized Russian hidden hand, and he who attempts to substitute his own rationalized hand for it only causes trouble. The intellectuals are the problem. This theory of Tolstoy's authorizes a turning away from ruling or from politics, the oldest prescription of philosophy from Plato and Aristotle on. Tolstoy's, however, is not a turning away for the sake of philosophy. The individual must devote himself to the little polity to which he is instinctively connected and the members of which he can truly love, the family. Things go well when men's restless energy and intellect accept this sweet limitation, which ensures enduring satisfaction. The sexual connection to the family traces out the high road between selfish intellect and the selfish senses.

Levin's wife and his peasants knew all of this, while he had to engage in mortal combat to arrive at where they always were. This is a bit of a problem, because what are thought to be men's higher powers are primarily used to lead them astray and, when properly clarified, are used to bring them back to the level of the peasants. It would seem that he would do better without these powers. But it is also hard to believe that Tolstoy did not think that a man who possesses these higher powers and makes good use of them is not himself higher. He evidently could not write an entire novel devoted to presenting the consciousness of a peasant or even of Levin's Kitty. As an artist and a thinker, he chose the more complex phenomenon, and this artistic vocation put him in discord with his praise of simplicity. Therefore his art becomes very problematic for him, just as the vocation of the writer was problematic for Rousseau, and it is difficult to understand how Tolstoy resolves this paradox. Is there something better about a man who has gone through all the doubts and deceptions in order to return to original simplicity? Is his a deeper or better soul? It would appear to be difficult for Tolstoy to assert this. Yet this novelist's art is indissolubly connected with the soul of the complicated and the corrupt. The problem is reflected in the renowned first sentence of *Anna Karenina*: "Happy families are all alike; every unhappy family is unhappy in its own way."[6] The complex, the diverse, and the corrupt are the novelist's subjects, whereas the simple and the good are the themes of morality. This would be no problem for Stendhal, who takes morality to be a bourgeois sham, but it certainly is one for Tolstoy. A kind of solution would be to say the moral intention of the artist is to lead the lost sheep back to the fold. He depicts the unhappy family, which is artistically interesting, in order to make the happy families more attractive, which art apparently cannot do by depicting them. The artist would be a protector of morality and innocence. This would mean that art is good where men are corrupt, but bad and tempting where men are good. Rousseau suggested something like this himself, although he went beyond it.[7] It is difficult to avoid believing that the artist is a higher kind of human being, that he is not just a doctor who would no longer be needed if men were healthy. But such a conclusion would go counter to Tolstoy's belief in natural goodness and equality. One must leave it at Levin's family satisfaction recounted by Tolstoy, which is necessarily boring to the palates of those who have been educated by the virtuosos of colorful moral diversity, such as Tolstoy himself.

Tolstoy, more than any novelist, teaches that the family is sacred and the theme of true moral interest. While agreeing with Rousseau that the bodily sexual desire is the ultimate ground of a significant and moral life, he tries to make us forget the tragic tension between the bodily phenomenon of romantic love of the beautiful, and marriage and the family. His great merit, albeit unwilling, consists in the fact that most of us are really more interested in Anna than in Levin and that we cannot forget her in spite of the last section of the novel, which is intended to be a shroud with which to cover her.

6. Conclusion

The Romantic movement was exhausted by the end of the nineteenth century, but the impulses it lent to philosophy and art in Europe and America became part of our common bloodstream. The Romantic hope died, but the Romantic point of view remained until only recently. The prevailing mood was disappointment, engendered by Romanticism's great expectations of salvaging nobility, art, and love from the mediocrity of bourgeois society and the reductions of materialism and natural science. Heaven had disappeared, but hell remained. The ecstatic states of soul connected with the artist's creativity turned out to be groundless. The search for the beautiful ended in the triumph of the ugly. The Romantic began to look like the posturing of the weak soul rather than the overflowing of the rich one. Novels, the privileged form of Romantic communication, in the twentieth century ceased to celebrate love, although they continued to deal with human intimacy and sexual relations. One need only think of Molly Bloom in *Ulysses*, or Odette and Albertine, or Charlus, in *Remembrance of Things Past*. Flaubert's heroine was characterized by belief in love against all odds and all evidence. Robinson, the hero of Céline's *Journey to the End of Night*, is characterized by his resolute decision not to say, "I love you," and his willingness to die in defense of this refusal. Ferdinand, the narrator, is beside himself with admiration when the insistent young woman says to Robinson, "Don't you get a hard-on like everybody else?"[1] and Robinson persists in refusing to admit that that biological fact has anything to do with love or commitment to another. Robinson is the only man Ferdinand has met who believes in something and is therefore above Ferdinand's own nihilism.[2] The extension from the organ and its various manifestations to love and the beautiful is a product of rank hypocrisy. In short, sublimation, Rousseau's great project, is a failure. Human dignity or authenticity depends on intellectual honesty, that great new virtue which consists in the capacity to face the ugly truth, the unlovable truth.

If there is anything to the distinction between sincerity and authenticity, it has to do with the difference between *the* fundamental human experience as described by Rousseau as opposed to that described by Nietzsche. Underlying the contradictions, the injustices, and the hypocrisies of society, there is for Rousseau the sweet sentiment of existence, like that discovered by Levin. Sincerity is the recovery of the self from the maze of alienated opinions and the affirmation of that primary experience which is the core of happiness. Authenticity is the frank recognition of the groundlessness of the sweet and consoling sentiments in the face of a fundamental terror. Rousseau's sincere man appears in this light as the most inauthentic man, one who hangs desperately on to consoling and edifying falsehoods. As Romanticism was a competition for experiencing the most exalted and sublime states, its successor school was a kind of auction in which the victor is the one who has the most terrible things to say about the human condition.[3] Truth began to appear to be whatever was ugliest and most opposed to gentle hopes of love. Rousseau's soft school was replaced by a hard school. A savage reductionism, unlike the cool reductionism of natural science, which proceeded in its work without being very conscious of its consequences, became the order of the day. An angry "I told you so" announced the dashing of Romantic foolishness. The reality is that all the beautiful talk exists only for the sake of seducing others and oneself. This is a far cry from *Les Liaisons dangereuses*, which horrifies us because of its implicit standard of decent conduct against which we measure the deeds of its principals. Such individuals now become the standard of authenticity. Evermore the movement is away from the transcendent unity of the loving couple toward Sartre's assertion that "Hell is—other people."[4] The detailed analysis of this assertion became a great preoccupation of the novelist's art. This is the shipwreck of the attempt to provide a basis for human contact— the discovery that we are really alone. The responses to the situation are either despair or extremisms beyond the imagination of all previous ages. The greatest deniers seem to modern taste to have it all over the greatest affirmers. He who has the most terrible message possesses the most truth.

The simple story that lies behind Romanticism and its successors alike is Thomas Hobbes's account of the state of nature. Chapter 13 of *Leviathan* is a cold and ugly depiction of man's fundamental condition meant to replace that handed down to us in the Garden of Eden and in Plato's *Republic*. This powerful characterization of the life of man as "solitary, poor, nasty, brutish, and short" became the basis of all the modern pieties and was largely accepted by thinkers and governments that succeeded Hobbes. Men are naturally in a murderous condition in relation to all other men, both because of the scarcity that puts them into competition for the means of self-preservation and because of the vaingloriousness, i.e., *amour-propre*, that insists that others evaluate us as we evaluate ourselves. Only by overcoming nature can peace be established, peace that will allow each of these radically individualized individuals to preserve himself. In this harsh light, God's gentle Edenic provisions for man, or nature's community as developed in the *Republic*, disappears like a consoling but illusory shadow. Every man is a means to the ends of every other man, and the peaceful state is only the continuation of war by other means. Human relationship is nothing more than a contract that permits each to pursue his own good. There is no common good. This is obviously a wholly unerotic vision of man. Out of this came all the commonplaces that almost everybody accepts—rights to life, liberty, and the pursuit of property or happiness, limited government founded on the consent of the governed, the natural freedom and equality of men.

Since Hobbes, almost everyone has felt that there is a lot missing in his account of man and has sought to modify him with teachings that further human connectedness. But they all begin by accepting the fundamental truth of Hobbes's teaching, and one can wonder whether the corrections to Hobbes are not too little and too late. Hobbes teaches us that men are "the other" to one another. The history of later moral and political philosophy is an attempt to explain how an other becomes a fellow citizen, a friend, or a lover. All the common talk about "the other" is a testimony to Hobbes's power, although those who speak thus are not aware that this otherness is a substitute for human kindness, a substitute not fundamentally altered by such verbal dodges as "the significant other." Characteristic of such dodges is Martin Buber's construction, which moves from "I" to "thou" and ends up with "we." The issue is whether he has been able to generate enough power to constitute a real "we" or whether this is sentimentalism that will be undermined by deeds. Hobbes has the great virtue of not being sentimental, and he overpowers all those who embrace him and think that he can be brought over into their camp.

The first great philosopher to endeavor to overcome liberal individualism was Rousseau, and I have attempted to outline his effort to create a human eroticism in a nature understood to be without eros, where atoms crash into one another without being naturally attracted. Rousseau, even though his project was conceived as a corrective to Hobbes, also begins from the state of nature, where man is a solitary without any inner attraction to others. Those great thinkers who followed Rousseau, such as Hegel with the dialectic of master and slave, and Nietzsche with the will to power, no longer refer to the state of nature, but they have adopted Hobbes's scheme, which sees war as primary in the relations of men. Nietzsche revels in the opposition of selves and their essential enmity, but all those prior to him try to derive peace from war. Marx is a particularly telling example. He adopts a Hobbesian unsentimental posture when he says that history is the history of class warfare; and then he shows how all the most wonderful things will emerge from that history. We can all see now how well that hope worked out. In other words, all the attempts to get higher or connected man out of reduced, atomic man have failed. Rousseau's complex and deliberate project has concerned us most because it attempts to create love as a replacement for natural fear or hate. It is all too artificial and complex and collapses of its own weight. Make no mistake about it, the specific forms of eroticism that we know have been constructed by modern philosophy in an effort to correct its original defects. They appear, however, to be unable to overcome the force of the clearheaded and fully self-conscious thought of its founders.

The artists who bought into Rousseau's love project because it offered a high function for their genius were the true psychologists of the nineteenth century. They carefully and minutely observed all the manifestations of love and presented a richly detailed picture of it that both taught the public about the sublime and produced enchantment. When Nietzsche said that only in France are there psychologists today,[5] he meant writers like Stendhal, not some professor working in a laboratory. The only comparable psychological subtlety in modernity was manifested by Christians in the examination of their consciences. The Romantics could argue that their standpoint for the observation of the soul was privileged because eroticism is the deeper phenomenon of which the religious impulse is only one of the effects. In antiquity, the greatest psychologist was Socrates, who examined souls from the perspective of the love of truth. All three of these kinds of psychology begin from the premise that the soul reveals itself most fully in its highest aspirations or longings and that the defects and torments of the soul reveal themselves for what they are against the background of that highest aspiration. The observation of the soul is the most difficult kind of observation because it is performed on the very instrument of knowledge itself. In order to begin those researches, it would seem to need the knowledge of itself that it seeks. The anonymous observer of modern science cannot remain anonymous if one wishes to know the knower, and such knowledge requires a different kind of observation than that employed to discover the laws of motion. This kind of knowledge requires plunging into deep and muddy waters teeming with all kinds of monsters. The phenomena of the unknown soul must be catalogued with the utmost detail and refinement. They do not admit of reduction. Causes must be found that are adequate to explaining them. It is so easy to take a part of the whole or to use some theory that plausibly explains but really deforms the psychological experiences. It is the rich depiction of the soul's typical movements that is needed along with a sense of wonder at the force of this protean beast.

For all of this, the novelist or the poet can make a claim for being very well placed. He is, above all, a skilled observer of human beings without any necessary prior commitment to a theory. Everything, of course, depends upon how good his eyes are, but serious artists are likely to be choice human beings. They take seriously what they see and are, in a profound sense, phenomenologists. If love is indeed the highest expression of the soul, the recognized link between love and the poetic muse further fortifies their claim. And so does the fact that love is primarily love of the beautiful, for although it is perhaps difficult to remember it today, art more than any other human endeavor was dedicated to the beautiful. The artist depicting the soul of lovers is also experiencing the genius of the artist himself. He must observe what goes on in his soul as he creates the souls of the lovers. This is all behind Nietzsche's remark about Stendhal's psychological gifts, his capacity to judge the faith of priests and the depth of attachment of women. Finally, Rousseau's emancipation of imagination from reason in art as well as love was equivalent to issuing a hunting license to artists.

Decisive in the sexual history of modern man was the preemption of novelists by scientists in the study of psychology, most notably by Freud. This was the triumph of the thesis that modern natural science is the only form of knowledge, a denial of the view that the methods for studying the instrument of knowing must be different from those appropriate to knowing nature. The special claim of the artists is disallowed, and the artists themselves must be explained by something beneath, if not deeper than, themselves. The artist is no longer qualitatively distinguished from the nonartist and is to be explained by special modifications of the same things that move all men. The artist argued in vain that he was indeed motivated by eros but that his eros was a special form of that passion which could not be broken down into parts or explained as a mere secondary expression due to one kind of frustration or another. As Alexandre Kojève put it, an artist has sex in order to write about it, whereas Freud thought that the writer writes in order to get sex. Although Freud talks about love, he does not help us to distinguish it from sexual desire or habitual connection, and the beautiful has no objective existence for him. The goal of psychoanalytic healing smacks of compromise, in this case compromise between the desires belonging to us by nature and the demands of society imposed on us from outside, between self and other without the mediation between self and other that Rousseau's psychology of love was intended to provide.

Gone is the elaborate edifice, constructed by Rousseau and Kant, unifying the two poles, nature and society, that divided man, and finding in culture the third way, intended to be manifestly higher than either. All the ecstatic experiences built by the Romantics shattered and fell to earth. The high began to appear to be merely moralism, whereas the low looked like what really counts and what had been covered over by Romanticism.

The contemporary legacy of Romanticism in the United States is pretty thin stuff. It comes down pretty much to the centrality of sex, but sex without ideals. The American sex-drenched atmosphere is not like that of the twentieth-century European novelists, whose concentration on failed sexual relations is a thing of despair and torment against the background of Romantic enthusiasm. We hardly got the hopes of sublime love. Rather, what came through was the sexual substrate that supplements the other materialism, that of greed. America's philosophy and literature spoke little of the erotic. This was a country very much founded on the family as an unquestioned unit, a nation of households. Neither the sexual charms that were at the origin of the family nor the temptations that split it apart were allowed to get much play. When sex began to get its due, it was not accompanied by a launching pad pointed toward the sublime. We got indiscriminate liberation, or therapy to cure our hang-ups, or, and this is now the primary one, psychological engineering to complete the project of equality, which had stopped short at the door of the family. Of the great project to establish real connection between human beings by way of sexual love, only a velleity toward oneness with others remains, submerged in vague and groundless talk about community, while actually we all remain selves and others.

PART TWO

Shakespeare and Nature

INTRODUCTION

Arnaldo Momigliano, the great historian of classical antiquity, once said to me that if Shakespeare had only become dominant before the beginning of the nineteenth century, we would have been spared Rousseau. I never asked him precisely what he meant, but I have always construed the remark to mean that to compensate for the human void left by Enlightenment and its natural science, Shakespeare would have been a much healthier influence than Rousseau and the Romanticism he engendered. The Romantics had much to do with raising Shakespeare to the undisputed throne he now occupies, but their mediation tainted Shakespeare, and they were already themselves solidly established. Momigliano's remark appears right to me, for Shakespeare seems to be the mirror of nature and to present human beings just as they are. His poetry gives us the eyes to see what is there. The difference between Shakespeare and the Romantics is measured by the utter absence of didacticism in him. There is no intention in him to reconstruct the soul in order to make a place for human meaning, or to establish ideals in an ideal-less world, or to save the family and its relations from the corrosive of bourgeois rationalism. In short, Shakespeare has no project for the betterment or salvation of mankind. This does not mean that, in general, he did not believe that the truth would benefit men, but he did not think that the artist is defined as the man of responsibility. His plays remind us of the classical goal of contemplation rather than the modern aspiration to transform. Shakespeare did not consider himself the legislator of mankind. He faithfully records man's problems and does not evidently propose to solve them. It is not accurate to describe him as a genius or a creator. He is too much immersed in the wonders of nature to focus on himself as the most important being in it. He does not try to create as did the Romantics; he tries to record nature.

Shakespeare's naturalness is what induces me to meditate on his plays in this discussion of human connectedness. I hope through doing so to articulate something of a premodern view of man's relations with his fellows, to provide serious, and perhaps more satisfactory, alternatives to our characteristic ways of looking at things. For example, Shakespeare's depiction of love does not require an elaborate psychology to explain the miracle of deep involvement, because he does not need to derive community from the premise of radical isolation and selfishness. He does not begin, as does Rousseau, from a Cartesian radical doubt and then try to put the machine back together again. He begins from the evidence that we are involved, presupposing that self and other are not in extreme opposition. Although natural science may teach us many useful things, Shakespeare does not presuppose that it is simply the privileged way of knowing or that it can dissolve the most powerful everyday experiences that men and women have. He preserves the phenomena, and analyzes the difficulties without an *a priori* framework that determines them. Human beings are connected and also disconnected, and the primacy of one over the other is not dictated by plausible postulates. Shakespeare's plays are full of the most beautiful conjunctions and the most brutal disjunctions, and it is an urgent necessity to find out how he saw all of this, because he is wise and because he does not share our common assumptions.

Shakespeare's naturalness is attested to by the strange fact that he is the only classical author who remains popular. The critical termites are massed and eating away at the foundations, trying to topple him. Whether they will succeed will be a test of his robustness. They want to teach us that he is the bastion of all the pernicious prejudices rather than our friend and liberator. But it is still true today that all over the world the titles of Shakespeare's plays have a meaning that speaks to common consciousness. *Hamlet, Lear, Othello* all call forth images in the minds of all classes of men across national boundaries. Perhaps the understanding of, or even acquaintance with, Shakespeare's plays is rather thin, but no one reacts with boredom or the sense that he stands only for bookish edification. This is why the theater is so lively in England and they keep producing such wonderful actors there. Racine and Molière in France, Lessing and

Goethe in Germany, and Dante and Petrarch in Italy have no vitality in the eyes of ordinary young persons. They are dead, merely culture. No normal young person would prefer spending time with one of these great writers to going to a concert of the latest rock group. Shakespeare is practically our only link with the classic and the past. The future of education has much to do with whether we will be able to cling to him or not.

7. Romeo and Juliet

I | *Romeo and Juliet* is always greeted by the young with immediate sympathy, somehow expressing the essence of love, what it ought to be, a permanent possibility, a fulfillment of every renascent hope and a thing to be admired. However far away this love affair may be from any real experience young men and women have today, however alien to the prevalent atmosphere of either careful and contractual relations or careless promiscuity, its two star-crossed lovers engage the admiration of most people without any need for instruction. Love at first sight, tapping the most generous sentiments and focusing the whole of two persons' energies on each other, bringing out the best in each, suppressing the petty and ugly passions, seems to be good manifestly and always possible. Here is a natural imperative. Students find Romantic novels artificial, full of prejudices, and infinitely distant from the way they approach sexual relations, but *Romeo and Juliet*, in a strange way, avoids all this. What Romantic novel could be used to legitimize the life of street gangs as *Romeo and Juliet* was in *West Side Story*? It transcends the quibbles about male and female roles while leaving behind the psychological complexities of attachment characteristic of Romantic novels. Shakespeare's women have a range and diversity that make us forget the constrained and constructed women of the Romantics. The total distinction between men and women and their roles is not present in Shakespeare, and women are capable of assuming male disguise in order to perform the male deeds that men are frequently unable to perform for themselves. Shakespeare is never a sucker for theory, and this communicates itself to his audiences.

Love is very much Shakespeare's theme, and in reflecting on love in Shakespeare one must begin with *Romeo and Juliet*, for it appears to be the purest description of the phenomenon love and depiction of its fate in the world. Shakespeare is a middle ground between the ancient poets whose tragedies hardly spoke of love and the Romantic poets whose sad tales concerned only love. Serious writers in antiquity, with the strange exception of Plato, did not present men and women in love as the most serious of beings facing the most serious of problems. The reasons for this should be investigated further, but we may say that it has something to do with the primacy of virtue and reason over the passions in the classical view, whereas the Romantics made love their theme precisely because of their preference for the passions over virtue and reason. Christian Europe, of course, has an ambivalent and ambiguous history so far as love goes, but certainly the official position depreciates erotic love in favor of Christian love or *agapē*. This is a question that interests Shakespeare greatly.

Two of his tragedies are about couples in love, as their very titles indicate, *Romeo and Juliet* and *Antony and Cleopatra*, while *Troilus and Cressida*, if not a tragedy, approaches that status. They are the only plays that have two names in their titles, indicating that shared tragic fates belong above all to lovers. There are no authentic love affairs in the history plays, where politics, seemingly unerotic, is the primary theme. The comedies, of course, are shot through with sexual themes. And this is perfectly classical, treating man's eroticism as one of the things that make him ridiculous, the angle from which the disproportion between his aspirations and his reality is most evident. The ancients may have relegated love to comedy for reasons of edification, not wanting very ordinary human beings to be encouraged in passions that are most often empty, or for more philosophic reasons, holding that man's dependency on his body and his being duped by illusions are what love is all about. Shakespeare's tragedies are less tragic than those of Aeschylus and Sophocles, and his comedies less comic than those of Aristophanes. The ancients were either all tragedy or all comedy; Socrates at the end of his great discussion about love in the *Symposium* argues against the tragedian Agathon and the comedian Aristophanes and reproaches them for not being able to mix the genres. Shakespeare relaxes the twin tensions that end in either tears or laughter, taking tragedy a bit less seriously and comedy a bit more seriously than did the ancients. And, just as in

Plato, love makes its way onto the scene between high political gravity and low sexual levity. Love appears to be a link between the high and low in man, and Shakespeare devotes much of his talent to looking into this. Love is surely not the whole meaning of life for Shakespeare, but it just as surely flatters some of man's dearest aspirations. What could be more wonderful than uniting one's most intense pleasure with the highest activity and the most noble and beautiful deeds and words? Such is the promise of love.

| II | Romeo and Juliet are the perfect pair of lovers. They are beautiful, they are young, they are noble, and they are rich. People get angry about lookism, ageism, elitism, and so on, |

but, when it comes to Romeo and Juliet, I find that outrage is disarmed, and most everybody becomes a partisan of these youngsters. With envy silenced, even the most sparingly endowed of us gets satisfaction from this love, thus proving that you do not have to make the world ugly in order to compensate us for our defects. Man naturally craves a perfection that he cannot attain. But at least part of that perfection consists in our capacity to conceive it. The greatest writers satisfy this craving, at least for the moment, and thus make us momentarily perfect. Misguided resentment can attempt to destroy the models of perfection in order to balm the wounds of the disadvantaged, but in so doing it deprives all of us of our most natural pleasure. When reading the beautiful words in their love scenes, only the most perverse person would throw the book aside because it hurts too much to think that one will never have anything quite so good. Rather, the natural inclination seems to be, for a moment, to identify and to enhance one's lesser sentiments by the grander ones Shakespeare lays out for us. "This is what I felt but did not have the words to say" is what the healthy reader thinks. Leveling literature and literary theory would deprive us of what is perhaps the dearest longing of our natures, one which Shakespeare satisfies so fully for us.

The crushing of these two winning beings seems the least inevitable ending among Shakespeare's tragedies, the product of mere chance. In other plays, our first rebellion against the fall of a great person is followed by a sad and wise recognition that this end is in the nature of things, residing in the character of the person. Macbeth's ambition leads him ineluctably to crime and death, but Romeo kills himself only because he believes that Juliet is dead. How does that difference between appearance and reality follow necessarily from the lover's nature? This is the mystery of the play. It can appear to be melodrama rather than tragedy. *Romeo and Juliet*, no matter how many times read or seen, always induces a reaction that if this or that little thing had been changed, they would have lived happily ever after. There seems to be no reason why this great tragedy could not have been replaced by the lesser tragedy of their settling down together, watching their beauties disappear slowly with age while they became bored with each other.

In speculating about the tragedy's denouement, one is forced to the conclusion that it has something to do with the problem of family. The names of the Capulet and Montague families are almost as well known as those of Romeo and Juliet. The authority, or even tyranny, of parents induces the classic conflict between inclination and duty, and the love affair between Romeo and Juliet flies in the face of what are at least conventionally understood to be duties. The problem of squaring nature with convention is a suitable theme for drama. The family, which has its roots in erotic necessities, is profoundly anti-erotic. It surrounds young people with all kinds of noes, and, in the grand tradition of the family, it uses sexual alliances for the sake of property, status, and political arrangements.

Romeo and Juliet never have any doubt about the superiority of their love to any commandment that might prohibit it, and Shakespeare presents them in such a way that the audience will have no doubts either about that superiority. This pair represents the natural rights of love. Romeo's side of it is hardly illustrated in the play, but he is fully aware that his love is not a thing his parents would have approved of. And the innocent child, Juliet, proves to be a natural at deception, unhesitatingly lying and misleading her parents. Shakespeare does not argue for the dignity of the family; everyone is meant to side unqualifiedly with the lovers. "All the world loves a lover." The parents are coarse, selfish, and unfeeling. The mother can speak only incoherent platitudes in recommending to Juliet the husband who has been chosen for her. But with his sympathies wholly on the side of love, Shakespeare perhaps wishes to teach us that it, like all idealisms, must come to terms with familial, religious, and political demands. Romeo and Juliet never think of just running away together and living off love, perhaps because everywhere there are conventions.

Love in Shakespeare knows no bounds of propriety, whether laid down by family or country. It has a natural cosmopolitanism. The immediate love of the beautiful is beyond the limits of loyalty, limits that are generally easily accepted where the erotic love of the beautiful does not come into conflict with them. Even in the critical moment when Juliet learns that her cousin, Tybalt, representing her family, has been killed by her husband, she has only a moment of hesitation before returning even more furiously to her faith while becoming indifferent to her cousin's death. This would appear to all of us to be fanaticism if it were not for love, the fanaticism we all adore. Treachery of every other kind seems merely despicable, and it is a great tribute to love that it can provide a passport, recognized by so many, for travel beyond the boundaries. But the loyalists have their day too.

In *Romeo and Juliet*, there is a political problem typical of Renaissance Italy, which is also the seat of modern love in Shakespeare's writings. Machiavelli, a writer whom I am persuaded Shakespeare knew very well, speaks of the family quarrels that racked the independent cities of Italy, quarrels exploited by tyrants and potential tyrants and often connected with political and religious factions. This problem is representative of the more generic question of faction, of which all modern political thinkers, including Shakespeare, were keenly aware. According to the ancient political philosophers, the cities could be founded only when they had enough power to suppress the unlimited powers of the fathers. The blood tie, which forms the clan, must be suppressed, often violently. In Italy, the code of the clan reasserted itself as a result of the feebleness of the political rulers. The too gentle or merciful character of the princes is what Machiavelli blames and Shakespeare depicts. The Prince himself recognizes that he has been too weak, but never acts strongly until it is too late, if one can consider even the end of the play as a real reassertion of his power. He says, in a thought that accords perfectly with Machiavelli's teaching,[1] that "Mercy but murders, pardoning those that kill" (III.i.199).* But he appears not to have been able to act upon this thought. The difficulty is less any lack of brute force than a spiritual weakness, an infection apparently stemming from the attraction of mercifulness. This does not mean that in a less corrupt political order, Romeo and Juliet would not have had to overcome parental resistance, but their problem would not have been rendered tragic by civil war. Friar Laurence tries to use this pair of rare and beautiful love birds as the means of restoring civil peace. But

---

* All parenthetical citations in this chapter are to Shakespeare's *Romeo and Juliet*, ed. Brian Gibbons, Arden Edition (1980; rpt. London: Routledge, 1988).

only their destruction permits the peace of death to descend over the two families, whose only heirs disappear. This tells us much about the relationship of love and politics.

Romeo is the prototype of the Romantic lover and poet in his perpetual longing and his concern for things that the rest of men are too sunk in the mud of daily life to care about; in his moodiness and despair about the fragility of the golden links that bind him to his beloved; in his simultaneous melancholy and enthusiasm. But he is not a Romantic hero because Shakespeare does not permit him to dominate the stage, and although he is sympathetically portrayed, in the whole of Shakespeare's works and even in this play there are many other types that can rival and surpass Romeo. He has a ridiculous side that is properly ridiculed, and that is lacking in a Saint-Preux or a Werther. He is passion without reflection or calculation, and although such passion is rare and attractive, Shakespeare makes it appear to be a thing of youth without making youth appear to be the best age. Romeo is absolutely unqualified in his feelings and in his expressions of them. He is determined and intractable. Neither his enemies nor his friends can have any effect on his behavior, which means that he is an unusually ineffective manager of the conspiracy that would be necessary to bring his plans to a successful conclusion. He thinks that love is sufficient unto itself, self-justifying, and that it has to make no compromises with men or gods. He is a bit of a bore and a pest for his friends and associates because his attention is elsewhere, preoccupied with his hopelessness or his hopefulness, living in a different and higher world than they do. He exists only for the delicious moments of perfect understanding between Juliet and himself. Whatever justification Shakespeare provides for Romeo is in three scenes: their first encounter, the avowal of love in the garden, and the end of the one night they spend together. This last, by the way, may be Romeo's only completed experience of sexual love, as it is certainly Juliet's.

Critics have disputed whether it is a strength or a weakness in Romeo's character that is depicted in the opening scenes of the play, where he is totally and desperately in love with Rosaline (also linked to the Capulet family, which seems to have the only good girls in town) and then he changes his eternal love in an instant. This makes one wonder, if he had lived and Juliet had not, whether he would not have found others. He is certainly in love with love and believes, as lovers must, that the object of his love is unique in the world and that no other could be loved in her place. It is not enough to say that Juliet, unlike Rosaline, is ready to reciprocate. This would mean that

Romeo's love would be willing to compromise on the principle of availability. Certainly love, as Romeo understands it, must be reciprocal, unlike the love directed to a god or a goddess. Yet love for him is a religion, "the devout religion of mine eye" (I.ii.90). And if the eyes were to see another more beautiful, they would be "transparent heretics" (I.ii.93). He rejects Benvolio's reasonable suggestion that he make comparisons and then choose, on the grounds that this would be contrary to his religious faith. "I'll go along, no such sight to be shown, / But to rejoice in splendour of mine own" (I.ii.102–103). He understands love as a product of opposites, like the world itself: "O anything of nothing first create" (I.i.175). His imagery includes pagan and Christian elements.

Does Romeo's initial love for Rosaline portray a man with a natural talent for love just going through his apprenticeship before entering on his vocation? Or does it mean that the whole apparatus of love depends on shifting opinions and mere imagination? Certainly, and this is explicit both in the comments of others and in Romeo's own self-awareness, imagination is his faculty. The vexed question of the desirability and reliability of imagination is raised by this character. In his happy moments, he can beautify the world with the images Shakespeare lends him, but when his lover's imagination fails, he imagines only death, oblivious to or contemptuous of whatever charms reality might offer.

Love is a very strange thing, this powerful desire to be together with another that gets in the way of life's serious activities, such as providing for one's preservation or governing men and nations. It creates an almost unbearable dualism in life unless, by giving oneself to it completely and forgetting the rest, one unifies life. This kind of unity in pleasure and high aspiration is one of man's most flattering hopes. Love is a substitute for the comparatively burdensome and dull practice of the virtues, because it at least seems to substitute for those virtues. A lover is courageous, generous, and beyond the quibbles of mere justice. He is proof against the petty and corrosive desires and passions. He is, of course, not characterized by the less attractive virtues, moderation and wisdom. Romeo is surely bold and willing to risk his life; there is plenty of evidence for that in the play. When he is in his right mind, he is intelligent and clever, as one sees when he is the only one able to keep up with Mercutio. He has friends, like Benvolio and Mercutio, who are clearly decent men. Romeo has no marked virtues, in any strict sense of the word, but he has generous dispositions, and love can turn them into persuasive simulacra of virtue. He might have been a warrior, except that the love of the beautiful predominates over any ambition he might have had. His easy victory over Tybalt shows what kind of a fighter he must have been, but his joys are not those of honor or vengeance or even conquest, except of his beautiful beloved. His virtues and vices are all summed up in the fact of his suicide at the only apparent death of Juliet. He is a perfect youth. We can recognize this only too well when he tells Friar Laurence that nobody as old as that worthy priest could understand his situation. He is all enthusiasm, imagination, and faith, without any appreciation of the sobriety of age.

Juliet's qualities are without the ambiguities present in Romeo. Beauty as the promise of virtue is fulfilled. She has experienced no love before Romeo and was already resisting promising her parents to love the lover they would foist upon her. There is no hesitation from the first moment she exchanges a word with Romeo. Romeo is her life. She is perfectly feminine, but Shakespeare puts her beyond the ordinary demands of modesty. She knows she should say no, but does not. Her assurance of her affections and her belief in what his form promises about his substance are such that she must show herself naked and unprotected to him. She tells him that she could make a show of modesty and reserve, but that she will only remind him that if he is merely a seducer, he will have used her ill. Here her femininity marvelously reminds of the necessity of modesty while dispensing with it. The intensity of her faith takes its place. This is ever so much higher than the games of love practiced by the French. For Juliet, there is neither low nor high in erotic matters, and we are relieved as much by the absence of the high as by that of the low. No love could be more perfect than her innocent eroticism. This child can make the act of love seem to be above all taint of sin. She waits impatiently for her first night with a man, full of bodily longing, faced squarely as such, but understood in such a way as to make that longing and its satisfaction a pure expression of all that seems best. Night will be the day of her love: "Hood my unmann'd blood, bating in my cheeks, / With thy black mantle, till strange love grow bold, / Think true love acted simple modesty" (III.ii.14–16). Never has bodily love had such noble and untarnished expression. Perhaps she represents what Rousseau prescribed in his attempt to reunify man after original sin split him, but it is only Shakespeare who can fill that prescription.

Yet this marvelous creature is treated with astounding brutality by the plot. Her sufferings much surpass those of Romeo. Her isolation in love is much more extreme than his. He is surrounded by friends. His family does not play a role and probably would not have been so fiercely opposed to accepting her among the Montagues, whereas the Capulets would not have gained a son but lost a daughter. Friar Laurence is much more the confidant of Romeo than of Juliet. Juliet has only the support of her nurse, not quite a valid interlocutor, who abandons her at the most terrible time. She has to confront Romeo's killing her beloved cousin and the fury of her parents. And above all, she is the one who has to appear to die and to wake up in the horrors of the grave. She has a moment of doubt when she learns of Tybalt's death and a moment of hesitation before she drinks the potion, but her recovery is so swift and so firm that those moments only serve to heighten her resoluteness.

The relationship between Romeo and Juliet is as powerful and unconditional as human relationships ever are, but when one reflects on it, the substance of their connection remains mysterious. Perhaps this is the mystery of love altogether, but our familiarity with the idea does not reduce its mysteriousness. Love has the advantage over other types of attachment, particularly those connected with family and country, that it does not appear to depend merely on accidents like blood (as is particularly underlined in this play), and that it requires none of the constraints of convention, duty, or law. It is free in every sense. All that one does in it one does with pleasure and enthusiasm. It is one's own, without constraint, although we are not the masters of our falling in or out of love. It is comparable on all these counts only to friendship of the higher kind described by Aristotle. Friendship, however, is a much calmer thing and can give a better account of itself inasmuch as one chooses a friend for his proved virtue. Friendship is a consequence of deliberate choice, whereas love is a kind of possession that requires so much faith, accompanied by a spectacular apprehension of the beautiful. A friend is good, while a beloved is beautiful. The beautiful has it all over the good in attractiveness. The appeal of the good is rational, that of the beautiful is passionate. Friendship is human, while love is divine.

In my own enthusiasm for Shakespeare I can only say that there is no better depiction of all of these qualities of love than in *Romeo and Juliet*. And there is also no better depiction of the strange mating of love and death. This play literally culminates in the tomb. From the outset, Romeo is filled with forebodings of death, and as Juliet bids farewell to him after their night together, she says, "Methinks I see thee, now thou art so low, / As one dead in the bottom of a tomb" (III.v.55–56). She divines here the denouement, which is probably the most horrible scene of death in all of Shakespeare, a writer who does not spare his audiences the sight of death. Juliet, in her terror as she drinks the potion, imagines not only the fearsome sight of death she will encounter, but also all of the human baggage of guilt and dread that accompanies it. The illusion of eternal life and beauty, the delicious, fleshy bodies that embrace and will never decay, is the opposite of the skeletons in the tomb. Shakespeare's joining of the two in this play is what is most shocking about it, the contrast between the hopes of love and the reality of death. Perhaps he is teaching us that the eros for the beautiful is the hopeless attempt to overcome the ugliness of the grave, an attempt of the unwise to adorn a very questionable world.

These two young persons, so admirably equipped for love but so innocent of the world, are sent out into it. We can begin to respond to the question of the inevitability of the tragic ending that seems so undeserved, by saying they are bound to collide with the city. The city with its laws has its own special ways of coping with death or avoiding it (particularly in preserving, by way of the family, the eternity of generations rather than of individuals). The lovers are not the Greek gods of whom we are so beautifully reminded by Greek statues, who are always young and beautiful. The charm of Romeo and Juliet is in their consideration only of the present, which they understand to be there always. But just as powerfully, we know that they are not merely unwise but haters of wisdom:

> FRIAR: I'll give thee armour to keep off that word,
> Adversity's sweet milk, philosophy,
> To comfort thee though thou art banished.

> ROMEO: Yet "banished"? Hang up philosophy.
> Unless philosophy can make a Juliet,
> Displant a town, reverse a Prince's doom,
> It helps not, it prevails not. Talk no more.

> FRIAR: O, then I see that mad men have no ears.

> ROMEO: How should they when that wise men have no eyes?

> FRIAR: Let me dispute with thee of thy estate.

> ROMEO: Thou canst not speak of that thou dost not feel.
> (III.iii.54–64)

If philosophy, as Shakespeare knew that Socrates had said, is learning how to die, then Romeo is not avid of that science. Youngsters are not supposed to be, but this is why youngsters must be supervised. Thus wisdom's superiority, which none of the other characters illustrate, is restored by the message of the play as a whole. Shakespeare flatters our hopes and then smashes them. The sober teachings of moderation are given their due by the results of the charming immoderation Shakespeare appears to celebrate in the early parts of the play. The terrible consequences of their love could have been avoided at many points if either lover had been moderate or reflective, but this would have been like cutting the wings of birds and still expecting them to fly.

III The problem of the play is that there is, with the possible exception of Mercutio, no figure of sufficient weight to counter the charm of love. In the opposition between Romeo and Friar Laurence, it is Romeo who always carries the day, both in the outcome of the plot and in moving the audience. If moderation is merely consolation when one's immoderate schemes fail, it is hardly choiceworthy. In the struggle between age and youth on the stage the preference almost always goes to youth, and wisdom inevitably is an attribute of age while love is one of the two or three primary attributes of hotheaded youth. One does not go to the theater to be taught compromises, however inevitable, between realism and idealism. Unless there are possible splendid representations of wise moderation, in the theater there is a simply tragic choice between the noble or beautiful and life. The choice of life is the coward's part and is never attractive to audiences. So it is represented even by Homer, when the shade of Achilles tells us that now, when he is in a position to survey the alternatives, he would prefer to be a serf on earth than to be the king of all the shades in Hades.[2] If he had acted on that conviction during his life, there would have been no *Iliad*.

To show that these are Shakespeare's own reflections and not merely my own, a glance at *The Tempest* is required. Critics, notably Coleridge, have remarked that Ferdinand and Miranda in *The Tempest* are very much like Romeo and Juliet. The suddenness and intensity of their love, as well as their innocence and good character, are alike. They are also from families at war, the king of Naples, Ferdinand's father, having been part of the plot to unseat the duke of Milan, Miranda's father. Their love has exactly the same potential for tragedy as does that of Romeo and Juliet. But that potential is prevented from being realized by the presence, *per impossibile*, of a genuinely wise man, the sort that would never be present in any real situation. Prospero, who has arranged this affair and brought the young people together, vigilantly supervises their relationship and fulfills a serious political project with their marriage. With Prospero, Shakespeare undertakes *the* most difficult problem for a dramatist, the presentation of a wise man, without making him into a buffoon, a knave, and most and worst of all, a bore. Art's near incapacity to make wisdom attractive was a problem addressed by both Plato and Rousseau.[3] The Platonic dialogues are one kind of partial resolution of this problem. Shakespeare proceeds by presenting him as a magician, a figure always appealing to popular audiences. The Savoyard Vicar may say, "I am happy," but even the mature Rousseau does not seem to believe it, and certainly Rousseau presents himself with an entirely different allure. But Prospero, whose very name means happiness, can, once one has removed a bit of glitter from kings and lovers, stake a claim to being a truly dramatic and appealing wise man. In a sense, *Romeo and Juliet*, as well as several other plays, can be seen to pose problems or conflicts that cannot be resolved in practice but with which a Prospero could in principle deal. Total preoccupation with the agony of the tragic heroes makes us think that there is an absolute impossibility of uniting nobility and happiness. But Prospero, by his person and by the deeds he performs, projects a half light onto the tragic scene that reminds us that life as such may not be tragic.

Miranda, as indicated by her very name, arouses that most specifically human reaction, wonder, which Aristotle tells us leads to either myth or philosophy.[4] Between Ferdinand and Miranda themselves it is all myth, that is, imagination and love. But the philosopher Prospero manages the myth for the sake of a reasonable outcome. "Oh, brave new world." This is what Miranda experiences, but Prospero is fully aware of what villains and clowns really populate this world. He makes Ferdinand pass love tests and actively tames his rebelliousness with punishments. He can prevent their consummation prior to marriage. He imposes an iron law of necessity on them that will protect them from the imprudence which on their own they would almost certainly commit. He delights in their beauty and their mutual attraction, things that he is too old to have any longer. But regret is not what he feels. He sees that they are fond and foolish. His satisfaction comes from his contemplation of them and their fulfilling of his plan. His daughter, from having been the isolated offspring of a failed duke of Milan, will be the queen of

Naples, and her union with Ferdinand will make him into a generous and just king. They will love, and the fruits of their love will be useful to mankind.

The Tempest is a play about motives and motivations. Its lowest characters, Stephano, Trinculo, and Caliban, are creatures of bodily pleasure who can be rendered tolerable in the civil order only by bodily pinches and cramps. The layer above them is inhabited by Italian princes, Antonio, Sebastian, and Alonso, who practice ugly deeds for the sake of acquiring and maintaining rule. They are the princes described by Machiavelli, and for them Prospero prescribes imaginary terrors that produce bad conscience. But they are more human than the inhabitants of the psychological basement, because they, capable of doing more harm, are motivated by a certain spirituality, albeit a dark spirituality. The top floor of the social and political world is occupied by the two lovers, who are also motivated by imagination, but of the beautiful, thus dismissing the base, the petty, and the merely powerful from their vision. They are not wise, but the noble view of things will substitute, if imperfectly, for wisdom, which never truly rules in real states. Prospero with this couple solves the problem of his own succession, and he has channeled the illusions of love to the public benefit. He himself is beyond this house, which he has built and put in order, and above which he floats. Here we have *Romeo and Juliet* without tragedy, a Romeo and Juliet to whom we prefer Prospero. This is perhaps Shakespeare's greatest *tour de force*. Tragedy is prevented by Prospero. We must never forget that the potential of tragedy is here, but we must also never forget that there is something beyond tragedy. Prospero says that he will "retire me to my Milan, where / Every third thought shall be my grave."[5] This is about the right proportion and is the calm statement of a man who knows how to die, very different from the frantic oscillation between love and the tomb.

IV The last two persons in *Romeo and Juliet* who are important to our investigation are Mercutio and Friar Laurence. As soon as one mentions Mercutio's name, one thinks of the problem of obscenity in Shakespeare. A large proportion of Mercutio's lines are devoted to exquisite and witty dirty remarks and allusions. Shakespeare forces us to exercise our imagination in trying to figure out what Mercutio alludes to, and we are already stained by that activity. The commentators remain largely silent about these passages, I suppose because they regard them as comic relief and not part of the serious business of the tragedy, as if comic relief did not require as much explanation as any other aspect of a drama. Why does Shakespeare require comic relief when Sophocles does not? One can answer that he is trying to amuse the audience. But that would imply that so great an artist panders to the public at the expense of the integrity of his work. Maybe. But it should not be assumed that this is so, particularly since it can easily be an excuse for our laziness. Interpreters such as Eric Partridge can be of help, but he is far from being complete, and he postures so much in his role as a freethinker and sexually healthy man in England at mid-century that he himself becomes ridiculous and of doubtful reliability.[6]

Our first observation must simply be that the only character of a human weight perhaps equal to that of the principals has what we would call a foul mouth, which implies a foul mind to go with it. He is a real friend to Romeo, whom he dominates by powerful intelligence. He is also a spirited man, always ready for a fight. His obscenity is largely used in the service of his moonstruck friend, whom he tries to liberate from his attachment to Rosaline by means of ridicule. Of course, like everyone else in the play except for Friar Laurence and Juliet's nurse, he is unaware of Romeo's involvement with Juliet. Therefore his ignorance causes this healer of lovesickness to misdiagnose the case. But his intention is clearly good, although his ignorance contributes to the disaster. He might be said to be responsible for the tragedy by his confronting and provoking the enraged Tybalt, but he does so in order to protect Romeo. It is Romeo's attempt at peacemaking, his lover's vain hope to produce goodwill among men, that results in Mercutio's death. Thus Romeo must fight and kill Tybalt with the consequence that he is banished from Verona. Moreover, he believes the Capulet family will now be absolutely intractable. With Mercutio's death, Romeo loses a close friend who would have been an advisor and a protector. After Mercutio disappears from the scene, all good humor, wit, and obscenity disappear with him. From then on, Romeo is isolated and the atmosphere becomes very grim.

The elements in Mercutio's character are well mixed. He, like Tybalt, is extremely spirited, as Aristotle says friends must be,[7] but he is not eaten up by Tybalt's doglike rage. While not sharing Romeo's uncontrolled imagination and overgreat tenderness, he has a splendid poetic imagination, as is manifest in the Queen Mab speech, a real beauty about fantasy and vanity. And this noble poetic figure is one of the most obscene of Shakespeare's characters. It has been said that the Greeks didn't like to talk about eating or sex because both were signs of man's unfreedom. Something of this view of sex is brought to *Romeo and Juliet* by Mercutio, who is forgotten by everybody, including the audience, during the last three acts when he is no longer present. But to grasp the meaning of the play, we must remember him and the question mark he puts after the seductive sentiments of the lovers. His importance is underlined by the fact that his role in the play is entirely invented, independent of the sources Shakespeare used for it. Such invented characters are of decisive importance in carrying Shakespeare's message, as are Falstaff in the history plays and Enobarbus in *Antony and Cleopatra*. This play is about love, and love is related to obscenity by their common source in eroticism. But love and obscenity are at tension with each other, if not mutually exclusive. Juliet is never obscene, and Romeo is so only in his brilliant exchanges with Mercutio, which prove that when he is himself he is Mercutio's equal in wit and hence his worthy friend. Love and anger have in common that one does not joke about their objects, and if one does, the passions are either doused or are transformed into something else. Both love and anger require belief, and laughter liberates from belief. Only Romeo and Juliet love in the play, and all the others, with the exception of Friar Laurence, are in one way or another obscene.

V One tends to forget just how obscene the first two acts of *Romeo and Juliet* are. Romeo and Juliet are surrounded by persons who talk most explicitly and unromantically about sex. The very first scene gives us a picture of lower-class male manners and morals. The servants of the Montague house chatter about their quarrel with the Capulets and the impending battle:

SAMPSON: I will show myself a tyrant: when I have fought with the men, I will be civil with the maids, I will cut off their heads.

GREGORY: The heads of the maids?

SAMPSON: Ay, the heads of the maids, or their maidenheads; take it in what sense thou wilt.

GREGORY: They must take it in sense that feel it.

SAMPSON: Me they shall feel while I am able to stand, and 'tis known I am a pretty piece of flesh.

GREGORY: 'Tis well thou art not fish; if thou hadst, thou hadst been Poor John. Draw thy tool—here comes of the house of Montagues.

SAMPSON: My naked weapon is out . . . (I.i.20–32)

These false tough guys mix the size and force of their organs into their battle talk. Similarly, in Act I, scene iii, the Nurse, who is permitted to participate in the formal announcement to Juliet that Paris has been chosen to be her groom, cannot help repeating several times over, in the presence of the innocent Juliet, her husband's stupid joke about how Juliet when she was a baby fell on her face but how she will, at an age of improved wit, fall on her back. This seems to her so hilarious and such an appropriate description of the human condition. She completes a perfect pair with Lady Capulet, who stiffly and hypocritically describes the appropriateness and beauty of the match proposed for Juliet. The lower class constitutes a background of the barnyard, a mixture of boasting and explicitness with sly allusions to the mentionable unmentionable. Their behavior seems to be perfectly acceptable in these good families. Perhaps this is because no aristocrat would think of imitating or being influenced by a servant any more than Mme. Duchâtelet was embarrassed to appear naked before her menservants.[8] Clearly, in Shakespeare's world it was not thought that the plant of high eroticism was so frail as to be unable to resist debunking by the brutish couplings of those without any refinement of soul. Love is not simply a construct or a diversion of energy from low to high. Romeo and Juliet are peculiarly invulnerable to this kind of influence, perhaps to their detriment. But Mercutio, who shares the earthy sexual awareness of the inferior persons, translates it to the highest level. He is aware of how our most intense feelings indicate our comic dependence on "pretty pieces of flesh."

Obscenity changes love's transcendence into a fascination with the bodily needs and effects of eroticism. Somehow the disproportion between what we think love should be and what we actually are is laughable. So much of comedy turns on the unmasking of boasting, beginning from the pompous ass who slips on a banana peel and comes back to the level, or beneath it, of ordinary humanity, all the way to the highest claims of love of justice and love of God. We laugh because we are released from pieties in which we cannot entirely believe. This release may be a satisfaction because it allows our natures to go about their business without constantly measuring themselves against our pieties. But our need to laugh, the spirit of comedy, is as mysterious as our need to cry, the spirit of tragedy. Shakespeare never lets us give ourselves completely to either one of these two temptations.

If we follow Leo Strauss's division of Aristophanes' comedy into four kinds, blasphemy, slander, parody, and obscenity, then we must say that in Shakespeare, obscenity predominates. Blasphemy undermines belief in the gods, slander attacks the rulers of the city, parody mocks the tragic poets, and obscenity goes to the root of the family.[9] Obscenity is the gentlest of the four, and is not an utterly useless thing if man needs to take some critical stance toward the myths of the family and the erotic desires that lead us to the family. Surely obscenity is low, but it is not always the lowest or least interesting of Shakespeare's characters who are obscene, as is shown by the example of Falstaff.

Rousseau says that the French are so indescribably filthy-minded that their language is necessarily pure, a sentiment echoed by Goethe.[10] Rousseau says that an unashamed directness is not shameless and that men and women in simpler societies were the masters of such speech, and his Romantic followers made some attempt to enrich the language of eros while recovering its spirit. This, as so much else that stems from Rousseau, had the character of a project, and it sat uneasily with the highness of love and women he promoted. But it does not do simply to say that men were more able to talk about the facts of life in Shakespeare's England than they were in the nineteenth century and everywhere in the West until only yesterday. Shakespeare was able to choose what he wanted from his own times and mold it to his purposes.

Shakespeare's obscenity is peculiarly worthy of our study, because it can help us recognize our incapacity to talk well about certain matters that are very important for our lives. Today dirty talk is routine and meaningless, and, at the same time, the structures of the sacred in love and the family have been dismantled in such a way as to render the point of Shakespeare's humor almost meaningless. The use of the word "fuck" at all times and in all contexts today is not primarily a sign of liberation or willingness to face facts. It certainly does indicate a recent change in the way of looking at things that has complex causes, but the upshot is a radical impoverishment of speech and, correspondingly, of thought and desire. Our use of explicitly sexual language permits two debasements: meaningless and costless sex and also an "objectification" of sex and its manipulation by science, natural or social, for unerotic purposes. Our own "post-Romantic" mode of speech about these matters is inextricably bound up with the attempt to produce a science of sex, which requires an embarrassingly inadequate technical terminology to make it easier for doctors to speak the unspeakable. This both replaces love talk and leads to a simplification and cleaning up of obscenity. The opposite vivid languages of love and obscenity meet now in a pallid middle ground in which the character of each is lost.* Obscene and scientific speech become practically identical, and neither of them has much to do with description of the real world.** The success of a modern theoretical point of view removes imagination from the realm of eros. It is another chapter in the history of modern timidity: love is made undangerous, and those who do the deed think that they are intellectually honest or authentic.

The problem is not that we have too much obscenity. What we lack is an imaginative obscenity. There are no words available for the richness of possible erotic experience—I do not say for our actual erotic experience, which, I suspect, is as flat as the language we use about it. It is amazing, in contrast, how many words and expressions in Shakespeare call to mind that part of our nature which is so dear to us. Not only can he teach us how to talk beautifully and amusingly about sex but he can also help us study the phenomenon much more

---

* So much of our language in all domains has undergone this change that there is no real original popular speech that is not full of "role models," "values," "charisma," and many other words that have no relation to real experience and from which we can learn nothing about it. Nor is there any refined speech that is supposed to give experiences their full due by detailed and subtle description. It has been replaced by an abstract jargon.

** The cult of the simultaneous orgasm, which was a very important issue a few years back, is a good example of all this. Masters and Johnson, in their clinical white smocks, treated masses of couples who wished to achieve this feat. You can imagine what Mercutio, on the one hand, and Romeo, on the other, would have to say about this. Their comedy and tragedy come much closer to reality. Masters and Johnson and all of their ilk are reminiscent of Arthur Murray's Dance School with its slogan, "If you can walk, you can dance." They think they are up to the level of Nijinsky's art.

seriously because it has not been sterilized in advance for us or put through the strainers of various ideologies. His obscenity is never reductionist. It does not dismiss the imaginative overlay of the facts. Rather, it expresses admiration for and wonder at all the strange things that happen to us in the grip of sexual passion.

Obscenity and love find expressions in Shakespeare that reveal them as two aspects of one of the most interesting of all experiences. Mercutio's "the bawdy hand of the dial is now upon the prick of noon" (II.iv.111–112) is a simile of Homeric richness that, in one of its senses, ridicules male boasting while lending itself to it. Mercutio's pricks prove him to be a shrewd and minute observer. Benvolio warns Mercutio that he will make Romeo angry with his irreverent descriptions of Rosaline's parts and what can be done to them (II.i.22). Certainly obscenity is at war with love's moral dimension, that is, the faith in fidelity, reciprocity, and the permanence of attachment. It also attacks the illusion that there can be no other object than the one that has been chosen. But it does not lead to the view that there is no natural erotic attachment. It just renders the whole experience of erotic attraction more ambiguous, and allows one to think about it. Shakespeare's speech about sex is divided between obscenity and love talk, but neither is unerotic like our casual obscenity and sexual science. In these matters, Shakespeare is fully erotic, but points to an ambiguity in eroticism. The moving innocence of Juliet and Miranda is full of a sensuality without shame. Juliet desires Romeo with her body, as Miranda desires Ferdinand. Shakespeare's obscene speakers never represent the disgustingness of the body or its desires. Rather, they glory in the wonderfulness of the senses. There is no indication in Shakespeare that eroticism is sinful, although there is plenty of indication that it reflects an incoherence and dividedness in human nature itself.

VII In *Romeo and Juliet* practically everybody, with the possible exception of Tybalt, is nice, and there are no villains. Good intentions are to be found everywhere, and one cannot help remembering Saul Bellow's firm, "The Good Intentions Paving Company." Old Capulet reveals himself to be a rather decent figure, almost ready for reconciliation with the Montagues because with old age he has even forgotten the reasons for their quarrel. He forbids Tybalt to pick a fight with Romeo in his home and even repeats the local rumors about Romeo's good character (I.v.63–80). Though he plays the tyrant with his daughter, egged on by the grief surrounding Tybalt's death and by his assurance that he knows what is best for his daughter, his behavior is thickheaded but not vicious. The name Benvolio says it all. There is also an all too gentle prince who recognizes that his gentleness is a vice. Romeo, the man of love and a peacemaker, intervenes, professing his love to Tybalt, in the only really warlike scene where harm is done, and becomes responsible for Tybalt's death. The part of life where real hatred is expressed and war reigns is distorted by the well-intentioned profession of love.

And among all of these good intentions, Friar Laurence's are the best. He is usually treated as a charming and prudent man, the wise priest. He is, indeed, in all ordinary senses a nice man who maintains excellent relations with his flock. He is obviously respected by everyone, and his relationship with Romeo is especially sweet. He may be the nicest character in the play. We meet Friar Laurence musing about nature, of which he is a certain kind of occult knower. His musings in the first place argue for a harmoniousness and order in nature. All of nature is understood in its relation to man, its products being beneficial or harmful according to the way they are used. By analogy, he asserts that the conflicting principles in nature are grace and rude will. This is, appropriately to him, a Christian understanding: God is responsible for good and man is responsible for evil. But he does not, as would seem inevitable, leave it at that or, at most, attempt to tame the rude will. He, with his pharmaceutical science, actively plays God. He can mix the natural simples and serve human intentions. He is not merely a priest to whom the various persons confess but also a kind of magician. Underlying his understanding and his activity is the essence of the very gentleness that dominates the play. Everything can be harmonized (II.iii.1–26).

At the end of the friar's speech about nature Romeo enters, and their conversation proves that Romeo has taken the good friar as his confidant. The friar, as a good priest should be, is critical of Romeo's romantic enthusiasms, but he is an accomplice as well as a confessor. One cannot take his strictures too seriously, and one might call him indulgent. A slightly more sinister element in him emerges when he agrees to marry the couple, not because he is won over to their love and for its sake, but because he sees in it the means of reconciling the two warring families. He has a political ambition, which is to do what the prince of Verona himself should have done to restore peace in the city. What he does amounts to a conspiracy in which he uses the two lovers. He cannot act directly because he is timid and without earthly power. The conspiracy, as Friar Laurence elaborates it in the contingencies of the drama, becomes ever more complex and covert. For the sake of enabling Juliet, whom he has secretly married to Romeo, to escape from the marriage her parents plan and go with Romeo to Mantua, he gives her the potion that will make her appear dead. He is a sharp contrast with the skull-and-bones apothecary, who for the sake of money defies the law by selling Romeo real poison. Friar Laurence does finally use love to make peace, but it is a peace of earthly death. As in the case of the compassionate prince, Friar Laurence seems to be a representative of what Machiavelli criticizes in Christian Italy. Earthly peace, according to Machiavelli, can be brought about only by harshness and war, not by compassion and love, and he strongly criticizes the priests for their condemnation of worldly ambition and for their spiritual weakness. They have just enough influence over the minds of men to create chaos but not enough power over their bodies to bring order.

Prior to our discussion of the denouement of the play, we should look for a moment at the two samples given to us of Friar Laurence's priestly rhetoric. When Romeo first threatens suicide on learning that he is banished, Friar Laurence suggests, without success, philosophy. That fails, so he lists the advantages and possibilities of Romeo's situation—banishment is better than death, which was required by the law but mitigated by the merciful Duke, and so on and so on. Romeo tells him that a man like him, referring to his celibacy, cannot possibly understand what Romeo faces. This whole speech is obvious and uninspired, but maybe the kind of thing any of us would say under similar circumstances. The old Nurse, who has wandered in during this scene, expresses delight at what he says, avowing that she could have "stay'd here all the night / To hear good counsel. O, what learning is." She is the priest's typical audience, this ignorant peasant woman, and she likes the sounds he makes. But he persuades Romeo only because he arranges for the first night of lovemaking. Spurred on by anticipation of great delights, Romeo for a moment forgets suicide (III.iii.54–174).

The second speech is close to comedy when Friar Laurence offers a standard set of consolations to the bereaved Capulets. They think Juliet is dead, but Friar Laurence and we know she is alive and have expectations that there will be a happy ending. He tells them that heaven has always been the destination, away from this unhappy earth. The message here is precisely opposite to the one destined for Romeo, when he tells him that life is much better than death. In addition to this decisive ambivalence, the emptiness and the manipulativeness of the friar's rhetoric are underlined by this little sermon pulled out of his file of commonplaces (IV.v.65–95).

Whether or not Friar Laurence should have married Romeo and Juliet in the first place, making use of his transfamilial and transpolitical power over the sacraments, he becomes truly blameworthy, for his elaborate machinations after Tybalt's death have made the marriage much more difficult to avow than it was before. There were two things Friar Laurence might have done if he wished to act boldly and directly. One was simply to encourage Juliet to run away to Mantua, or wherever else, with the banished Romeo. He would have accomplished the same end as he had intended to accomplish with the potion without having to rely on so many accidents governed by the great goddess Fortuna. His other possibility was to go to the families and tell them what he had done and that, like it or not, Romeo and Juliet were husband and wife. This might have been very unpleasant for him, and Juliet recognizes this when she has her terrors about drinking the potion:

> What if it be a poison which the Friar
> Subtly hath minister'd to have me dead,
> Lest in this marriage he should be dishonour'd,
> Because he married me before to Romeo?
> I fear it is. And yet methinks it should not,
> For he hath still been tried a holy man. (IV.iii.24–29)

It is really a potion and not a poison, but Juliet does point to the friar's ticklish situation. This potion is in the end equivalent to a poison for Juliet, and the priest has devised the scheme because he is too timid to be open.

One has to ask what is supposed to be gained from the whole apparent death, other than that the parents and the others concerned would be seeking a corpse rather than the living girl. The disappearance of Juliet's body would have raised all kinds of questions, as would the disappearance of her living unity of body and soul. What has happened is that a young woman has come to her confessor with a personal marital problem, and he devises, with the help of occult knowledge of nature, a miracle. This miracle is, to put it bluntly, a resurrection. Perhaps the friar believes that such a miracle would be so impressive to everyone that they would accept Juliet's infidelity to family and her choice of an enemy lover. He counts on the credulity of everyone. This is easier to do in the post-Mercutio world. Shakespeare does not permit this miracle to appear to the world at large, but it is interesting to speculate about what the opinion of that world would have been if the priest had succeeded.

The miracle fails because Romeo was not privy to the arrangement. He hears that his beloved is dead and never learns that the death is only apparent because Friar John was quarantined in Verona and never got to Mantua. Friar Laurence had not told him how essential the letter was, although it is not clear that he would have been able by dint of greater effort to have gotten it to Romeo. He clearly made no extraordinary efforts to see that the letter reached its destination. A combination of fortune and lack of foresight, perhaps due to Friar Laurence's timidity in not wanting to communicate the contents of the letter or its urgency to Friar John, results in the tragedy. Romeo rushes back, kills the well-meaning Paris, sees what he believes to be the beautiful corpse of his beloved, and kills himself on the spot. If he were less hotheaded or believed less in the appearances, the dreadful result would have been avoided, but he would not then have been the lover he was, and besides, the appearances were, of course, very persuasive.

Friar Laurence might have averted the tragedy if he had gone very quickly to the tomb. He did not, however, imagine that Romeo had heard about the death. He thinks only of being there when Juliet awakens at the end of the forty-two hours—the same time that elapsed between the Crucifixion of Jesus and his Resurrection—he has so precisely specified. He finds the awful scene, Juliet awakens, he tells her what has happened, but he hears the coming of the watch and wants to avoid capture. He tells Juliet that he will consign her to a nunnery, which seems to be the signal of the abandonment of all the earthly hope that Friar Laurence had promised. Then he commits the inexcusable crime of running away and leaving her there, when it is perfectly clear what she will do if left to her own devices. It was his simple duty to prevent Juliet from committing suicide, even though poetic necessity might dictate her death. This is the final statement about the combination of power and weakness that defines this character. His plain confession seems candid, but he apparently thinks that his good intentions exculpate him. And he takes his being scared of the arrival of the watch to be a sufficient reason for leaving Juliet. The friar is a rich study in ecclesiastical politics, and the traditional interpretation of him as a kindly old wise man will not suffice. He maintains a strange and self-contradictory view of the relation between love and death, an either/or that fails to persuade one that his "every third thought" has been the grave.

| VIII | These two lovers want to live on love alone and are at least temporarily well qualified to do so. "What's in a name?" is a very good question when the names are Mon- |

tague and Capulet and they live in Italy. Maybe Shakespeare intends to show us the perpetual ignorance of the conditions of happiness in lovers who cannot adjust their natures to the conventions. But there is sufficient evidence in this play that there is also something specific to this modern Italy with its imperial past, its weak but brutal inde- pendent cities, and its Church, reproduced in Shakespeare pretty much as Machiavelli described it, that affects the permanent aspects of human nature revealed in it. The sharp contrast between the gorgeous bodies and the skeletons in the tomb casts a peculiarly harsh light on hopes and realities, and the role of Friar Laurence only heightens this impression. Prospero knows this modern Italy and has suffered the consequences of its conspiratorial politics. If Ferdi- nand and Miranda had met in this Italy instead of on Prospero's island, they would have been just another Romeo and Juliet. Pros- pero can handle it all. But he is never present in a real Italy. Mercutio with his irreverence and his obscenity, his awareness that Queen Mab flatters the typical passions of lovers and priests, was a useful antidote as long as he lasted. After he departs, the alliance between love and the priest was formally fixed. At this point, we must leave this picture of the charm of love and its vulnerability and turn to consideration of a love that took place in the ancient Italian world.

8. *Antony and Cleopatra*

I Shakespeare was the first philosopher of history. He self-consciously tried to understand the minds of men and women of the most diverse times and places, always with the view to how the permanent problems of human nature are addressed and what are the serious competing visions of the good life. The conflicts of the characters in his plays are always colored by the typical circumstances of their particular place. In commercial Venice, mercenary tolerance permits us to see outsiders in their relation to insiders better than anywhere else. In England, the struggle for legitimate kingship affects the hopes and the actions of many of his most important characters. The student who went to school in Wittenberg brings some of its theological teachings with him in his failed attempt to right the rotten state of Denmark. Shakespeare's utopia elaborated in *The Tempest*, his last play, takes place literally "no place," on an island, that is, on the stage, beyond the specific limits of real regimes. It is always helpful in interpreting Shakespeare to have a map and a chronology at hand. I suspect if anyone were to complete the task of grasping the vast plan of this most comprehensive of artists he would do so only on the basis of seeing his plays in light of time and place. Shakespeare, like a good historian and unlike historicists, needs this knowledge, not to make himself a toady of what is offered to him in the here and now, but precisely to liberate himself from it; he needs to discover the possibilities manifest in other times and places in order to live in the here and now without sacrificing his human potential. This is history as the way to discover the permanent, not to suppress it.

The most important historical distinction for Shakespeare is between ancients and moderns. He shares the Renaissance passion for the rebirth of antiquity and its understanding of Greek and Roman philosophy, politics, and art. What do they say to us moderns, and can we again get inspiration from them? These were questions of burning intensity at the moment when the forgotten beauties of antiquity began to overwhelm the most interesting minds in Italy. It took time for this renaissance to come to England, and Shakespeare was in a position to survey it, think it over, and apply it to his own country as well as to his understanding of man in general. The most important difference between antiquity and modernity is, of course, Christianity. The ancient virtues became in Christianity "splendid vices." The two contrary moralities produced an extreme tension in the spirits of the most interesting men and women of this time and a perhaps productive conflict in the goals of nations. We too can enter into this most interesting of worlds, if we do not assume that these were just passing ideologies of a particular historical moment, but instead see that these are profound and always relevant alternatives that still affect us in various disguising syntheses. The Bible versus Aristotle's *Ethics*, or Plato's *Republic* and Plutarch's heroes versus the prophets and the saints, is a choice that can be as alive to us as it was to Shakespeare. It may be true that Shakespeare presents his Greek and Roman heroes in modern dress on the stage, but they come equipped with ancient souls, which Shakespeare grasped in his profound readings of Plutarch and Homer as well as others. He understood them by imitating them, and in imitating them he allows us to understand them. In them we see the strengths and weaknesses of what is for us the most interesting and decisively different past.

In *Antony and Cleopatra*, a story immediately drawn from Plutarch's *Life of Antony*, Shakespeare gives us a very different kind of love from the one we find in *Romeo and Juliet*. In the latter, we have, relatively speaking, a small-town love affair of a pair of callow youngsters. In *Antony and Cleopatra* we have two world historical figures, mature and far from experiencing their first loves, acting on a stage that was for the time the whole world. It is well for us to remember that prior to the England that was in Shakespeare's time still just aborning, Rome was the most extraordinary political achievement known to man—four hundred years of republican government, and many hundreds of years afterward of imperial rule, the last reminiscences of which disappeared only a few years ago, when the kaisers and the tsars, that is, the Caesars, were pushed off their thrones. The military virtues of the Romans, unequaled by any other people, enabled them to conquer the known world, and they found the formula to make the conquests stick.

At the moment this play takes place, the republic has been destroyed, as Shakespeare depicted in *Julius Caesar*, and the great political issue is who will be the sole ruler of this empire (an empire that is simply identical to what we mean when we say the West), a struggle that is resolved in the action of the play. The issue of principle, republic versus monarchy, has been finally resolved in *Julius Caesar*. There is no dispute about the best form of government, just the question of which man has the resolve and prudence to become the sole ruler of the earth, the most complete and enticing possible prospect of political ambition, beyond that available to any other historical personages, many of whom may have dreamed it, but none of whom ever came within reach of it. It is important to note that the battle of Actium, Octavius' final victory over Antony, takes place just thirty-one years prior to the birth of Jesus and the new kind of empire connected with him that gradually took over the ground where the old kind of empire was encamped. There are two couples in the play, the enemy couple, Octavius (later Augustus) and Antony, and the loving couple, Cleopatra and Antony. Antony's presence as the common element of the two pairs indicates the high-risk and high-stakes game acted out in this play. Never before or after was love actually put in the balance to be weighed against ecumenical imperium. "Let Rome in Tiber melt" (I.i.33),* says Antony at the beginning of the play. This is no idle statement. Rome could be his, and he, for a moment at least, believes that there is no contest, that love is beyond compare more choiceworthy. From the moment the curtain rises the audience must be thrilled by the grandeur of this gesture and all that it entails. The whole world, really the whole world, for a woman. Many men have idly uttered such phrases in their love talk, but no one other than Antony really could prove that he meant it. This play pushes the political and the erotic imaginations to their absolute extremes.

Shakespeare's Antony, as opposed to Plutarch's, cannot help but draw us, at least momentarily, toward a desire to have such a love. Plutarch is not indignant, but rather more contemptuous, while

---

* All parenthetical citations in this chapter are to Shakespeare's *Antony and Cleopatra*, ed. M. R. Ridley, Arden Edition (1954; rpt. London: Routledge, 1988).

Shakespeare seduces us. Antony is drinking poison, but oh how good it tastes! *Antony and Cleopatra* contains some of the lushest language in all of Shakespeare. It is less obscene than *Romeo and Juliet*, although it is suffused much more with eroticism. Mercutio's obscenity would not be alien to the classical world, but it is much more ferocious than what one finds in *Antony and Cleopatra* and is perhaps necessitated by the too sweet and secure quality of Romeo's love. Mercutio and Enobarbus are both debunkers, but Enobarbus unabashedly tells us just how really beautiful Cleopatra is (Antony: "Would I had never seen her!" Enobarbus: "O, sir, you had then left unseen a wonderful piece of work, which not to have been blest withal, would have discredited your travel" [I.ii.150–153]), whereas Mercutio does not tell us of any such unique beauty worthy of extreme aspiration. *Antony and Cleopatra* reeks of the Oriental perfumes of the exotic extremes of Rome's empire. This is clearly a Rome that, having swallowed a world of much richer cultural diversity than it could digest, has become, in the technical sense, decadent, with no view of the future and having lost the impulse that made it soar to such heights. This is no longer the Rome we see in *Coriolanus*, where bravery and continence are everything. It is a garden that presents the most lavish display of exotic flowers in full bloom, but where the soil has become thin. There will be no restorative winter followed by a productive spring. This is a play that reminds us of the human beauty of antiquity and makes us regret the loss of it.

To reflect, once again, upon Momigliano's remark, this antiquity has the living presence of the great god Eros without the artificial imitation of it Rousseau and his Romantic followers tried to reinsert into the unerotic bourgeois world. There was within Christianity a terrible accusation leveled against this dethroned god, but even those like Machiavelli, who tried to restore the unity to man, to close the gap between the ought and the is, were pretty much willing to sacrifice the god rather than to reestablish the sacrifices made to him in antiquity. Machiavelli wrote a marvelous and obscene comedy, *The Mandragola*, which also involves a potion, the plot of which deals with a conspiracy to deceive an impotent old husband and is orchestrated by one who represents the political virtues of captains Machiavelli praises. But this very comedy indicates how unerotic Machiavelli's political vision is, for the erotic theme is meant merely to illustrate a purely political teaching concerning the impotence of Italian politics, the weakness and corruption of priests, and the opportunities existing for potential rulers who know how to make use of fraud. Obscenity here has nothing to do with the erotic life and merely illustrates political life. When one moves from Machiavelli to his greatest students, Bacon, Spinoza, Descartes, Hobbes, and Locke, one sees that they have drawn the consequences of Machiavelli's teaching. Neither great reputation nor comfortable self-preservation has much to do with eros, and these are the motives that Machiavelli primarily recognizes in man. Shakespeare, as I contend and internal evidence strongly supports, understood Machiavelli very well and profited from that great man's teaching, but as *The Tempest* shows, his wisest ruler used the eros for the beautiful as a fundamental motive for his successors. *Antony and Cleopatra* provides evidence for what caused him not to permit the simplification of man for the sake of political purposes. He obviously wants to promote political efficacy and the love of glory, but, as in so many other things, he is dedicated to the preservation of the phenomenon man. He looks all over in the best places in order to be able to describe that phenomenon. Antony and his destructive passion for Cleopatra are an important part of that phenomenon. Shakespeare reproduces both an austere concern for politics and a sympathy with eros that only Plato adumbrates in the enigmatic relation between the *Republic* and the *Symposium*, one apparently giving everything to politics and the other apparently giving everything to love.

The backbones of the human soul are understood by Plato to be spiritedness, the passion of the warrior, and eros, the passion of the lover. Antony partakes largely of both passions, two horses as they are depicted in the *Phaedrus*,[1] but they do not seem to work too well in harness. Love is no less ambiguous here than in a Christian context, but it is so in different ways. Mere sensuality, if it were not allowed to get out of hand, would be more benign than love because the issue is not between chastity and sinning but between politics and love. Antony's is the story of the supreme conflict between the two and, with him, the departure of both from the scene of the world for a very long time, perhaps up to Shakespeare's own time. This does not mean that there were no warriors or lovers after Antony, although in Rome itself there was left only bureaucratic regulation rather than ruling, and sexual decadence rather than love. It does mean, however, that in the new dispensation which overtook the world, both warrior and lover became much more problematic, and one rarely saw them in their pure forms any longer, let alone brought together in the soul of a single man. Shakespeare shows us the end of antiquity in the person of Antony, and he paints a picture, warts and all, that nevertheless is intended to fill us with sympathy, admiration, and perhaps even nostalgia, if this is a sentiment in which Shakespeare indulges himself.

II We see the famous couple first through the eyes of Antony's soldier friends. These men are all admirers of Antony, which is one of the main reasons we are disposed in his favor. Strong and frank men admire and love him. They know him best, and you can judge a man by his friends. Their opinion is most certainly that Antony is being destroyed by his affair. His case is treated not as though he is a sinner, but as though a great warrior is losing his martial spirit and has "become the bellows and the fan / To cool a gipsy's lust" (I.i.9–10). This is simply a soldier's judgment of another soldier, not unlike Hector's view of Paris, who leaves the battlefield to return to Helen's bed.[2] This comparison of Antony to Paris is made by Plutarch himself.[3] The difference is, of course, that Antony was, and to some extent still is, unlike Paris, a great warrior. These soldiers, as Enobarbus tells Antony, do not particularly care one way or another about his sexual escapades, but disapprove only when they get in the way of important business. To put it in Aristotelian terms, Antony suffers from immoderation, which is largely to be judged not in itself but in its effect on his capacity to act well. The category is vice, not sin, and it is a vice that can be linked with great generosity of spirit. Love—and Antony is the only man in the play who loves, and Enobarbus the only one who sympathizes with Antony in his passion—seems to be not only sensually satisfying but a sign of genial human traits in those who are its victims. Octavius, *the* opponent, is painted as utterly unerotic. Antony's response to his critics is winning:

> Let Rome in Tiber melt, and the wide arch
> Of the rang'd empire fall! Here is my space,
> Kingdoms are clay: our dungy earth alike
> Feeds beast as man; the nobleness of life
> Is to do thus: when such a mutual pair,
> And such a twain can do't, in which I bind,
> On pain of punishment, the world to weet
> We stand up peerless. (I.i.33–40)

He invokes a higher perspective in the light of which even Rome appears slight. This is not only the perspective of love; it is also not utterly unlike that of Paul, who looked at Rome in the light of the new faith. This distance on Rome's political achievements—the apparent emptiness of the goal sought with so much patience and so much blood for four hundred years, once it was attained—is something that Antony the lover and the Christians share, and Shakespeare plays on this common ground between the two, although the reasons for the contempt are so very different. This tragedy is redolent with allusions to the secular revolution taking place at the moment when antiquity has reached its peak and modernity is aborning. Soothsayers make predictions of strange new futures, and Charmian hopes to "have a child at fifty, to whom Herod of Jewry may do homage" (I.ii.27–28). The eunuch, one of the stranger products of that East where Cleopatra lives, confesses that he can do only honorable things but has fierce thoughts, and Octavius himself asserts that the day of the olive branch is at hand and that there will be universal peace. Antony is the precursor of the new order as one of love; Octavius is the precursor of it as one of peace. At the climax, soldiers hear trumpets underground and say that they signal the departure of Antony's god, Hercules (IV.iii.15–16). New gods, in no way affectionate toward Antony, will take Hercules' place. Antony's East is where the new religion will come from after he fails, a part of the world full of miraculous possibilities.

Meanwhile, Antony and all his friends are having a wonderful time in Egypt. They drink, they feast, and they make love. It is for them heaven on earth. The picture of the regal Antony and Cleopatra roaming the streets together at night, spying on the pleasures of the common folk, is most enticing. But Antony is clearly a divided man who is uncomfortable in his neglect of his imperial responsibilities. He is not like those later emperors, monstrous men who could devote themselves to monstrous pleasures without too much risk. Antony is not a monster, and he is not yet sole ruler. There is much mopping up to do. He is always on the defensive and has little of the gaiety one finds in Cleopatra or in either of their own entourages. His friend Enobarbus gets a great kick out of Antony's revels, and reproaches him only when he lets a woman get in the way of serious work. Antony seems aware throughout that his involvement with Cleopatra is fatal, but always, as he says, "I' the east my pleasure lies" (II.iii.39). This sense of evasion of responsibility makes him weak in the face of Octavius. He freely admits his guilt and agrees to change his conduct. He is like an apologetic boy facing a reproving parent. He seems to forget the strength of his position, which Shakespeare insists on. He is the only real fighter and general of the triumvirs, he has loyal troops, and in spite of mistake after mistake, like allowing the younger Pompey to be destroyed, he would still have been able to beat Octavius. But his energy is sapped by his love, as is his self-confidence. Almost everything in Antony's defeat is attributed by Shakespeare to his love for Cleopatra.

Antony is, in both his virtues and his vices, an outsized character. His voracity for all the richest experiences of glory and love is enormous. He was ruthless on his road to power and remains capable of great cruelty. He is avid of his honor but careless of many of the details of ordinary decency. He is typical of the late republic in his political criminality and his personal licentiousness. He behaves like an Olympian god, beyond the limits of the moral virtues. There is hardly a hero more impure for whom Shakespeare gives us any sympathy. Shakespeare depicts him as an extraordinary example of the classical morality of unswerving loyalty to friends and implacable hatred of enemies. Shakespeare's dislike of moralism makes him capable of taking this antique type so seriously.

Antony and Cleopatra are enchanted with each other and unabashedly want to have sexual intercourse with each other as much as possible. The act itself and the way they do it are supposed to be memorials of their sovereign superiority. I believe there is no similar example of a love without marriage sympathetically depicted in Shakespeare's plays. It is a love utterly without modesty. Antony, it must be remembered, is a married man whose wife, Fulvia, is quite a force of nature, constantly starting up civil wars on her own. Antony wants her dead but cannot help admiring her and, at least for a moment, regretting her when she dies. Cleopatra torments him endlessly about Fulvia, and when she hears that Fulvia is dead, responds with the stunning line, "Can Fulvia die?" (I.iii.58). She fiercely demands the whole of Antony, but what the Roman Fulvia represents in Antony's life can never die. The love of Antony and Cleopatra is the perfect example of a love for its own sake, at least on Antony's part, because it can never be good for Antony as anything other than itself, and the possibility of marriage or children is never considered. It is literally lawless but undeniably admirable.

The affair is riven with all the doubts and fears that love between two persons unsupported by convention can have. Both of them have had many loves before. The fact that Antony is married to another is a great subject for Cleopatra's complaints. Cleopatra is not ashamed to advertise that she has made love to two great predecessors of Antony in the power struggles, the elder Pompey and Julius Caesar, and has even borne children to both. Her motives are ambiguous because the queen of Egypt has an interest in flattering the ruler of her Roman conquerors. Antony's deeds prove that in spite of his bad track record for fidelity, only Cleopatra involves him now. Eros has rendered him to her completely. He might, from pure self-interest or his sense of responsibility, want to break with her, but he is unable to do so, however great his motives. Still, though one can always retain some doubts about Cleopatra, the overwhelming impression is that she too is in the grip of uncontrollable passion. There is none of the simple assurance and candor of a Juliet in her. Innocence is too far behind her for her to trust in the preservation of attractions. She torments Antony endlessly and artfully in order to keep him on edge. It is not quite the game of *amour-propre*, but she makes him always worry about the significance of her moods. If he is gay she will be sad, and if he is sad she will be gay (I.iii.1–12). This is not the confident and giving love so much admired in modernity. It is utterly selfish, and perhaps reveals more accurately the true nature of love as desperate need of one for the other. The tyrannical character of the total demands made by each are proof of the terrible bonds that tie them to each other. To my mind, Cleopatra's complaint to the dying Antony, "Hast thou no care of me?" (IV.xv.60), is a more powerful statement of love than are selfless expressions of sorrow or regret. Each is directed to the other by ineluctable need. Their admiration for each other means that they must possess each other no matter what the consequences. It is a hunger and a possessiveness more powerful than any other. Few men or women are capable of such selfish self-forgetting.

Cleopatra gives ample testimony to Antony's qualities by her dispositions when he is not there and her plotting to increase her ascendency over him. She is a consummate actress in manipulating him and constantly and guiltlessly exploits his attachments to his wife and to Rome in order to make him prove that they are nothing to him and sacrifice them in her all-consuming fire. There is no prudent balancing of considerations possible with her. She asks for everything and makes it clear that it is a stark choice between her and everything else. He must break with Fulvia in order to prove his thralldom to her, and yet when he wishes to break with Fulvia, that proves he is a man of no faith. Cleopatra's servant cautions her that she is overdoing it, but she responds, probably correctly, that she knows how to catch and hold on to her prey. There is such a mixture of artfulness and artlessness in Cleopatra that it is difficult to choose between the interpretation that she is madly in love with Antony and the alternative interpretation that she simply enjoys her empire over this emperor. I believe that the evidence inclines toward the first of these two, but the doubt is important for Antony and for us. In general, he seems to be sure of her and, at the moments when he thinks of his duties, wishes to liberate himself in the way an opium smoker might wish to free himself from his habit. She is an Oriental goddess who ensnares her votaries. She is active only in converting those votaries, especially those who are rulers of Rome, to her cult. They are attracted by her beauty and the pleasures it promises. The relationship is akin to that between human and god, but this cult is a cult of beauty. In this sense, she is like the old gods.

Her widely alternating moods have a genuineness that astounds. She is what would today be called a real or strong personality. Only a dry or utterly unerotic man, like Octavius, would fail to have at least a fugitive attraction to her, if only to crush it for the sake of more urgent considerations. Perhaps the only time she is unappealing is when she insists on participating in the Battle of Actium and then runs away, and even then . . . Earlier when she has most vexed Antony, who must leave for Rome, she comes to herself, recognizes the necessity, and says, "Courteous lord, one word: / Sir, you and I must part, but that's not it: / Sir, you and I have lov'd, but there's not it; / That you know well, something it is I would,— / O, my oblivion is a very Antony, / And I am all forgotten" (I.iii.86–91). For men and women in love, every parting is a little tragedy reminding them of death, of the final inconceivable separation of those whose bodies and souls are entwined in such a way as to produce the illusion that they are inseparable. When she is alone, she glories in his memory and can think only of his virtues, virtues exceeding those of Pompey and Caesar, whom she loved in her "salad days, / When I was green in judgment, cold in blood" (I.v.73–74). Her beating of the messenger, who brings the news of Antony's marriage to Octavia, a classic example of the misplaced blame that stems from anger, suits her regal superiority to reason and further illustrates her resemblance to the old gods. In spite of the messenger's reminder that "I that do bring the news made not the match," and Charmian's saying that the man is innocent, Cleopatra asserts that "Some innocents 'scape not the thunderbolt" (II.v.67, 77). According to Hobbes, the old gods were admired not for their justice but for their power, and Cleopatra's behavior confirms this observation.[4]

She frequently uses an unadorned erotic language that seems to need no veil of mystery to be enticing. "O happy horse to bear the weight of Antony!" (I.v.21). "Ram thou thy fruitful tidings in mine ears, / That long time have been barren" (II.v.24–25). And, in a complaint that hints at what it is that makes Antony different from Cleopatra and makes her impotent to overcome the difference, "I would I had thy inches, thou shouldst know / There were a heart in Egypt" (I.iii.40-41). Heart and organ would necessarily for her express the same thing. Her sexual allusions are not like those of the serving people in *Romeo and Juliet*, filthy thoughts that have no relation to reality, nor are they like Mercutio's demystifying jabs. They are the full expression of her mode of being at its highest. She is eroticism itself. What an interest in and taste for women Shakespeare had, giving us Juliet and Miranda at one end of the spectrum and Cleopatra at the other, with an astonishing variety in between! The Romantic imagination looks very thin when compared with this.

Unlike *Romeo and Juliet*, where the beauty of the principals is attested to only by them, *Antony and Cleopatra* has the blunt truthteller Enobarbus, who is the very model of *bon sens*, tell Agrippa and us, in some of the most gorgeous poetry written in any language, of how Cleopatra "purs'd up his heart upon the river of Cydnus" (II.ii.186–187). This is an eyewitness account intended to buttress or give authority to the rumor of Cleopatra's being "a most triumphant lady" (II.ii.184). Enobarbus immortalizes the first meeting of Antony and Cleopatra when she arrives on the famous barge. Shakespeare proleptically follows Lessing's rules about the limitation of poetry in representing bodily beauty. Lessing teaches that painting cannot adequately imitate Homer's description of Helen's beauty as seen through the eyes of men who are old and have suffered because of her but who are nevertheless aroused by her. Lessing asserts that a painting which imitates this famous scene in the *Iliad* could show only superannuated lechers looking at a veiled woman. The great ancient artists illustrated this scene by making a statue of the most beautiful naked woman their art was capable of. This was the visual equivalent of the poetry. The sculptor cannot reproduce the actions but must present the essence of what the poet is saying, the impression of surpassing beauty. Similarly, the poet cannot stop his narrative, which is essentially in movement, to give off a list of the various parts of Helen's body, which can in no sense rival the immediate perception of the whole form. This would require a cold act of addition on the part of the reader, which is alien to the immediacy of the experience of actually seeing a surpassingly beautiful woman. The poet must put the experience that he wishes to convey into actions, effects on others, and so on, if, in this case, he wants to rival the sculptor.[5] Enobarbus describes the arrival of the barge and the stunning effect of its movement:

> the oars were silver,
> Which to the tune of flutes kept stroke, and made
> The water which they beat to follow faster,
> As amorous of their strokes. (II.ii.194–197)

And then we impatiently await description of Cleopatra herself, but are both delighted and frustrated by:

> For her own person,
> It beggar'd all description: she did lie
> In her pavilion—cloth of gold, of tissue—
> O'er-picturing that Venus where we see
> The fancy outwork nature. (II.ii.197–201)

Shakespeare refuses the temptation to do what his art cannot do well and instead reminds us of a picture, here asking us to think of any picture of a beautiful woman or goddess that we may have seen.

This last quotation contains one of Shakespeare's most interesting reflections on the relation of art to nature, the kind of reflection too many modern critics do not permit him because they think he was not as sophisticated as they are in the understanding of what art is. It is accompanied by a similar reflection put in Cleopatra's mouth:

> But if there be, or ever were one such,
> It's past the size of dreaming: nature wants stuff
> To vie strange forms with fancy, yet to imagine
> An Antony were nature's piece, 'gainst fancy,
> Condemning shadows quite. (V.ii.96–100)

This is Cleopatra's testimony in favor of Antony to balance Enobarbus' testimony in favor of her. In both cases, nature begins by being considered as low stuff upon which the artistic imagination improves. The artist presents us with a perfection that we ordinary people never encounter in life, although it follows a path indicated by our desires, fed with experiences of nature. Our longing for perfection would appear to depend on artists for its satisfaction. But there is a peripety: these human beings, Antony and Cleopatra, who are not gods, outdo anything art could hope to do. We are prepared, and our desires are sharpened by the artist's superiority to nature in its crude form, to see nature as perfection, which art then imitates. The artist is with respect to nature both humble and sublime. I wonder if this view is that much less satisfying than that of nineteenth and twentieth century artists who are so proud of their superiority to nature and the power of their art. These reflections on nature are most suitable to a tragedy that seems to be meant to remind us of nature.

Nature is still the theme as Enobarbus continues:

> and Antony,
> Enthron'd i' the market-place, did sit alone,
> Whistling to the air; which, but for vacancy,
> Had gone to gaze on Cleopatra too,
> And made a gap in nature. (II.ii.214–218)

Nature itself goes to accompany Cleopatra, and the passage concludes with words of almost unbearable longing:

> MAECENAS: Now Antony must leave her utterly.
>
> ENOBARBUS: Never; he will not:
> Age cannot wither her, nor custom stale
> Her infinite variety: other women cloy
> The appetites they feed, but she makes hungry,
> Where most she satisfies. For vilest things
> Become themselves in her, that the holy priests
> Bless her, when she is riggish. (II.ii.233–240)

I do not say that Shakespeare means Cleopatra to represent nature itself, but there is something here of the ancient appreciation of nature as the almost ineffable standard by which all that time and custom can do is measured. There is nothing in this view of nature to remind us of the abstract, teleological nature that pedants speak of, a nature enveloped in a cobweb of moralistic abstractions that strangle it. It is the wondrous foundation that provides us with those fundamental experiences that are truly ends in themselves and which are almost always forgotten in the lives of toiling mortals. Even the priests themselves must abandon their moralisms to conform to her infinite variety. It is this awareness of nature that I believe accounts for the extraordinary beauty of this play, which stands out among so many other beautiful plays. This tragedy bemoans the perhaps irreparable loss of such a nature, nature expressing itself not as the mountains, the seas, and the forests, but as the microcosm, man. Antony is—as Shakespeare, over against Plutarch, underlines—the man *par excellence* who is open to such an experience. It destroys him, and his capacity to appreciate it is accompanied by important moral vices in him. But Octavius, whose world it is about to become, is utterly blind to this vista. This makes him a perfect administrator. If one wants a model, better expressed than Weber ever could, of what is wrong with bureaucracy, this is it. The erotic passions in Antony are the source of his capacity to apprehend a human satisfaction manifestly greater than that of being the world's sole ruler.

III   And here we must return to the harsh but exhilarating facts of politics, which this play so starkly contrasts with those of love. In order to emphasize the radicalness of Antony's choice, Shakespeare heightens Antony's responsibility for everything that goes wrong. On the evidence of the play, Antony was a sure winner if he applied himself to the political situation. His position is so strong that even after mistake after mistake, he was in a position to recoup himself. But his judgment and his resolve are so compromised by his love affair that we see only the ashes of a man who once had superb military and political gifts.

When we see him together with Octavius upon his return to Rome, he has that peculiar flaccidness we have already mentioned, apparently stemming from the sense that he has behaved dishonorably. The soothsayer speaks of Octavius' preeminence over Antony. He always beats him, even at games of chance (II.iii.10–30). Antony does not wish to confront Octavius directly, although one might judge that the sooner-or-later should be faced sooner. It is perfectly clear that we find ourselves here in a situation beyond law or simple morality. These two powerful Romans stand in a gap between regimes; the old republican laws and structures have been laid waste and the world is waiting for one of these two men to establish the empire and its new kind of legitimacy. In the absence of law, only prudence governs the situation. This is one of those extreme moments that, according to Machiavelli, teach us the true nature of politics, which does not reveal itself in the times when traditional legitimacy covers over such extremes. Treaties are made and broken here according to their momentary utility. Neither Octavius nor Antony ever gainsays that the triumvirate cannot last and that one of them will inevitably win. Three is the number of peace, two is the number of strife. It will end with the two and then the one. If the three partners were of equal power, then the overwhelming ambition of one could be checked by the self-defense of the other two. But Lepidus is the third, and he is not a real third. Lepidus is only a name without power, treated with contempt by his partners, and easily crushed when Octavius makes his move. The difference between Octavius and Antony is that the former is perfectly unified and dedicated in his pursuit of the goal, while the latter dreams that politics will take care of itself while he devotes himself to his pleasures. His dealings with Octavius are interruptions, whereas Octavius' dealings with him are the continuation of a single-minded and long-range plan. The special character of the situation is that the qualities of manliness, which were so important to Rome in its rise, are no longer necessary. Everyone, including Octavius, gives testimony to Antony's preeminence as a soldier. Julius Caesar's strengths are divided between the two rivals—Antony has the soldier's prowess and Octavius has the prudence.

If Antony found that this moment was not the time to make war on Octavius, at least he should never have strengthened the stronger. This is Machiavelli's cardinal rule, and the one most likely to be broken by the weak-willed. Above all, the younger Pompey, who was a real threat to Octavius, should not have been destroyed. Octavius needed Antony in his struggle against Pompey, whereas Pompey was not yet a threat to Antony's eastern hegemony. Politics is normally a continuous struggle with one danger succeeding another, requiring perpetual vigilance. The Roman Empire was approaching an end of politics as all enemies were destroyed. Strangely, Antony wants politics to be over right away so that he can enjoy the fruits of centuries of struggle, whereas Octavius waits in order to establish his secure hold on the empire without any such gratification as Antony enjoys, unless one can count being treated as a god as such a gratification. Both live with the prospect of a wholly new situation in which politics disappears. Antony is simply not up to living with the threat posed by Pompey, even though it is probably a political necessity.

Antony agrees readily to the destruction of Pompey, wanting

only to discharge a debt of honor and then to proceed dishonorably. He then agrees to marry Octavius' sister in order to insure the uninsurable permanence of their relationship. Octavius uses his sister with perfect cynicism and shows off the unerotic political usages of marriage, while Antony hastily agrees to the union in order to put off till tomorrow what he should be facing today. Enobarbus, as in all things, sees clearly from the outset that rather than binding the two together, this marriage will separate Octavius and Antony more radically than ever. Antony will abandon Octavia, and Octavius will be able to use this pretext for his war on Antony.

IV   In one of the truly perfect scenes in which this play abounds, we see Pompey rejecting the empire of the world on moral grounds when it is offered to him by Menas. The triumvirs have foolishly put themselves at the mercy of Pompey by accepting the invitation to be entertained on one of his ships. This is really an illustration of what Machiavelli means by fortune, that is, putting oneself in the hands of another when one ought to keep one's own hands on that other. But perhaps it wasn't all that foolish because they could count on Pompey's morality. He is the only conventionally pious man in this play, obedient to and fearful of the gods. He is also the only one who justifies his own action in terms of republican legitimacy, calling to mind Cassius and Brutus, who fought against one-man rule. None of this has much relevance in the situation Pompey actually faces, and he himself is confused as to whether he is merely vindicating his father, or restoring the republic, or going for one-man rule himself. When Menas tempts him, proposing that they weigh anchor and slaughter the triumvirs, Pompey responds,

> Ah, this thou shouldst have done,
> And not have spoke on't! In me 'tis villainy,
> In thee, 't had been good service. Thou must know,
> 'Tis not my profit that does lead mine honour;
> Mine honour, it. Repent that e'er thy tongue
> Hath so betray'd thine act. Being done unknown,
> I should have found it afterwards well done,
> But must condemn it now. Desist, and drink. (II.vii.72–79)

This calls to mind a similar passage where Henry IV needs and wishes Richard II dead but cannot bear the responsibility of ordering it himself.[6] This is the extreme situation in which the conflict between politics and morality becomes acute, and the whole quest for justice, which should be the goal for both political and moral men, becomes questionable. This conflict can disenchant idealists and open up the field where Antonys play, indifferent to the quest for justice. I think it is clear that Shakespeare believes that Pompey makes a mistake. Though he wishes to profit from unbidden dishonorable deeds of others, Pompey holds that honor has an absolute status, a position justified only if there are gods who reward and punish. There may be a certain nobility in his stance, but if nobility has to be separated from intelligence, and depend on the spontaneous service of the ignoble, it is a pretty lame thing. Antony's heroic nobility is treated much more sympathetically by Shakespeare than is Pompey's moralistic nobility. History hardly remembers the strangled Pompey, and there is not the slightest indication that the gods took on his case. His fame in the world would have been splendid if he had performed the daring deed, and he could have worried about his reputation for justice when he was the sole ruler. He was in the jungle or the state of nature, kill or be killed. He was a pretty good lion but a complete failure as a fox. Fraud was beneath him, and he became its victim. Certainly the nobility and choiceworthiness of the political vocation become doubtful in this perspective. Shakespeare learned very much from Machiavelli's teachings about politics, but unlike Machiavelli, when the splendor of politics is suppressed he could not take politics fully seriously. This may have been the point at which he parted company with Machiavelli and became sympathetic with Antony's eroticism, which links Antony to the poet. When being a Roman was no longer an honorable qualification, the nobility of being the ruling god of the world vanished.

Just after this capital scene, which illuminates the nature of politics, there is another one that is a footnote to this one (III.i). Ventidius, Antony's subordinate, has subdued the Parthians, that previously unsubdued people on the borders of the empire who were a real and immediate threat to Antony's part of it. When Silius suggests to Ventidius that he pursue his advantage over the Parthians, Ventidius responds that it is not a good idea for a subordinate to outshine his master. The master would likely be jealous of the light that puts the master in the shadows. It is dangerous for the subordinate, who then is willing to sacrifice his master's true good for the sake of his own preservation. Envy and jealousy are ugly passions that appear in politics and undermine common goods and loyalty. Moreover, this scene raises the question about the glory attaching to great captains, for it is frequently borrowed from the deeds of subordinates. This may very well tempt the subordinates to overthrow the captains or to serve them ill. Such things were controlled and channeled when there was a functioning republic. But in the naked individualism of anarchy, they make us doubt the possibility of genuine attachments in politics.

V   The peak political moment in *Antony and Cleopatra* is, of course, the Battle of Actium (III.vii.7–10), where Octavius definitively becomes Caesar, his adoptive father's name, which supersedes "king" as the title of monarchs. His victory is utterly Antony's fault. Cleopatra wants to go to war; Enobarbus opposes it as vigorously as he can; and Antony takes it for granted that his female partner should go to war with him. Enobarbus, and everyone else, wants to fight on land, where Antony's superiority lies. Cleopatra wants to fight at sea, and again Antony, without question, simply follows her. The sea seems to be the element of fortune, and the land that of virtue, military virtue. It was on Pompey's ship that the three pillars of the world lent themselves for a moment to fortune. Now Antony risks himself on the sea and loses everything. He belonged to that tradition of Spartan and Roman land fighters who went to war on foot and who the ancient thinkers believed were the most reliable foundations of stable republics. In Athens, the move from land forces to sea forces during the Persian wars introduced the tumultuous democracy. In Shakespeare's time, following Machiavelli, there was an attempt to reintroduce an art of warfare that could rival the ancients. The lack of the ground soldiers who faced the enemy hand to hand was symbolic of the weakness of soul in modern man since the decline of Rome, with its bodily and spiritual arms. Antony had an "absolute" superiority on land, but this captain put a female captain over him. Yet he could have won, had not Cleopatra panicked and run away with her ships. And here is the core of it all. Plutarch quotes someone who said that the soul of a lover lives in the body of another, and in the same context he compares Antony's conduct to that of the recalcitrant black horse in the soul described by Socrates in the *Phaedrus*.[7] No doubt Antony is in love. From the point of view of sound reason, Antony is wholly to blame. When Cleopatra asks Enobarbus whether she or Antony is at fault for the defeat and the death of both now in prospect, Enobarbus answers, "Antony only, that would make his will / Lord of his reason" (III.xiii.3–4).

Enobarbus is a marvelous fiction of Shakespeare. He is made out of whole cloth, the only character who bulks much larger in Shakespeare's play than he does in Plutarch's *Life of Antony*, where he is mentioned in passing, without any characterization. Shakespeare makes him epitomize the friends of Antony, to whom one could speak so directly, thus proving Antony's capacity for friendship, for leaping over the barriers of inequality that make friendship so rare a thing for political rulers. Octavius appears to have advisors, perhaps flatterers, but no friends. Julius Caesar tried, but obviously failed, to keep his old republican equals, like Brutus, on a footing of equality when he topped them all. But Antony, as he could love, also could be a friend, and perhaps this is another aspect of his unworthiness to be king. Enobarbus represents that classical view of reason as the governor of the passions rather than their handmaiden. The contemporary parody of reason as mere calculation is a consequence of this later view of reason. The ancient view meant that the passions, none of them evil in themselves, are to be ruled and used for the sake of the good and the noble. This implied a reflection on the good and the noble that is something other than mere calculation.

At the risk of superficial schematization, I would say that the classical view was succeeded by a Christian one which believed that the passions are both irresistibly powerful and hopelessly corrupt and that reason is too weak and too deceptive an instrument to master them. They can be held in check only by fear, sense of sin, conscience, and guilt. The early moderns accepted the primacy of the passions but tried to cleanse them of guilt and gave reason, in a new function as scout or spy of the passions, an honorable place in the scheme of things. But reason, the prudent ruler of the divinatory but disorderly passions as the object of meditation, was never restored. The crisis of ruling in the soul and its incapacity to function without consent of the passions is paralleled by a similar crisis in politics. Shakespeare, here represented by Enobarbus, never, even when he is making love appear most enticing, ever takes the side of passion against reason, as would a Romantic. The reasonable people in the Romantic novels we have discussed, with the exception of Jane Austen's, are only contemptible bourgeois. With Shakespeare, the old dignity of reason as a perfection of man is present, and the momentary passions of a Julien Sorel and Mme. de Rênal would never be considered by him to be a self-sufficient fulfillment. We would need much reflection on the ancient view of reason in order to make its claims plausible, but those claims peep out in Shakespeare's plays, which deal with the extreme passions of acting men and women. Enobarbus admires Antony. He treats his debauches as the proper amusements of a warrior and can share at the deepest level, as we have just seen, his erotic attractions. But he is contemptuous of the unreason of Antony, and becomes its severest critic when Antony's love destroys his empire and his friends:

> I see men's judgments are
> A parcel of their fortunes, and things outward
> Do draw the inward quality after them,
> . . .
> Caesar, thou hast subdued
> His judgment too.
>
> A diminution in our captain's brain
> Restores his heart; when valour preys on reason,
> It eats the sword it fights with: I will seek
> Some way to leave him. (III.xiii.31–33, 36–37, 198–201)

The conflict between loyalty and reason becomes the source of Enobarbus' personal tragedy, but he is the voice of reason in this play. The difficulty is connected with Shakespeare's obvious sympathy with Antony's erotic passion.

In order to think well about this we should have to understand Plato's *Phaedrus*, where Socrates takes a firm stand on behalf of eros and its immoderation against the moderate, and at least apparently rational, calculations of a nonlover or a lover who wishes to appear to be a nonlover in quest of sexual gratification without madness. The praise of madness can be understood only to the extent that reason itself must be informed by an apprehension of the beautiful or the good in order to be truly what it is. In his most explicit passages about philosophy, Socrates treats it as an erotic activity, nay, *the* erotic activity. Such an understanding of reason and philosophy is entirely absent from all modern thought. That famous black horse is a recalcitrant but essential part of the upward motion of the soul's chariot. Something like this seems to be at the root of the reasonable Shakespeare's sympathy with Antony's erotic mania and his nostalgic backward look at an experience that had disappeared from the world. Antony is ruler, as were many great Romans, and lover, as were few or none. He could not harness the two, and both went down together with him.

| |
| VI |

Enobarbus chronicles Antony's fall in the name of reason, but he does something else very important in addition. In a play where the actors reflect on their historic roles and their places in posterity, Enobarbus acts as Antony's witness. In this he is entirely unlike those witnesses who were just about to appear on the eastern edge of Antony's empire. He gives testimony to the hero Antony was, a testimony that makes Antony survive the disaster of his cause. After the defeat at Actium, Antony's deterioration poses an insoluble problem for Enobarbus. Enobarbus' asides are continuous hints to us about Shakespeare's intentions:

> Mine honesty, and I, begin to square.
> The loyalty well held to fools does make
> Our faith mere folly: yet he that can endure
> To follow with allegiance a fall'n lord,
> Does conquer him that did his master conquer,
> And earns a place i' the story. (III.xiii.41–46)

Telling a story, a sort of alternative Gospel, about the old lost world is of imperative importance for Enobarbus. The suicide of a Cato in the name of the republic, an intransigent refusal to accept the wave of the future, was easy compared with what Enobarbus faced. For Cato, the principle was unquestionable, whereas Enobarbus had to memorialize the example of a kind of man, not as such connected to a principle, decaying before his eyes. He proves unequal to the task, but in doing so, succeeds at it. He defects to Caesar. And Caesar is not just the man Caesar. He is a whole new world containing new kinds of aspiration or perfection. Enobarbus quickly recognizes that this is not a world in which he can comfortably live, that there is no place for him in it. With one of those extraordinary gestures of antique generosity, Antony sends after him to Caesar's camp all of the treasure Enobarbus has left behind, together with some of his own and gentle adieus. Enobarbus is finished. The old world is no longer viable; the new one is unbearable. And he goes to find some ditch to die in. "I am alone the villain of the earth . . ." (IV.vi.30–39). Enobarbus makes Antony the cynosure of posterity's eyes.

> **VII** The transformation of Octavius into Caesar Augustus, who ruled for so long and became a god more securely than did Julius Caesar, the first Roman man to become a god, is chronicled in *Antony and Cleopatra*. The status of god is attained when companions and followers turn into worshipers, when authority is unchallenged. This is godship seen from the point of view of the votaries. From the point of view of the one who becomes a god it is unrivaled and unquestioned authority and the power to live as one pleases. No man can challenge such a god. He represents a conclusion of the dialectic of master and slave with the establishment of a universal master. All fear him, and all esteem him. There is no longer a Coriolanus looking for an Aufidius to challenge him. There are no Aufidiuses left. Octavius is an unprepossessing candidate for the godhead. Without having had to perform Julius Caesar's deeds, he picks up his legacy. In *Julius Caesar*, one sees how Caesar found his worshipers. They were the Roman plebs for whom he provided bread and circuses and who had no greatness of soul with which to challenge him. He was their benefactor, and the great-souled aristocrats were annihilated. There remained millions of slaves and one master, whose protection was sought by all. Octavius simply had, in an efficient and single-minded way, to confirm the result that Caesar's genius had prepared. Manliness, the very meaning of the Latin word "virtue," was, at the beginning of this play, on the point of vanishing. The Roman Empire became peopled by a race of, as Gibbon said, pygmies.[8] In this vast space, another new God was soon to establish His authority, taking the place of the many old gods, the departure of one of which we see in this play, the manliest of them all (IV.iii.15–16). The new religion was to be eagerly embraced by the new breed of Romans. Cleopatra, while preparing her escape from Caesar's realm, for a moment acts the part of one of his worshipers. She calls him the sole ruler of the world, confesses her sexual sins, and recognizes his right to all of her property. His will is the only law. He describes the vista he overlooks when he says, "The time of universal peace is near: / Prove this a prosperous day, the three-nook'd world / Shall bear the olive freely" (IV.vi.5–7).

Octavius is the spirit of history. Throughout the play, Octavius is characterized as lacking any charm whatsoever. He is calculating, self-righteous, hypocritical, merely manipulative in his expressed indignation at the treatment of his beloved sister, unbelievable in the tribute he pays to his fallen opponents, whom he praises only for the sake of building himself up, unerotic, and a party pooper. He is by no means an evil man in Shakespeare's gallery of villains. He is merely the victor who proves the kind of mediocrity men are willing to worship when it succeeds. There is no possible earthly escape from his new modes and orders. However, in Enobarbus, Antony, Cleopatra, and Shakespeare, he ran into nonhistoricists who did not throw in their lots with the providential march of history. He is very eager to prove to the world that he acted justly. From the outset, his concern, in addition to defeating Antony, is to put him in the wrong and show that in spite of Caesar's forbearance, Antony, and anyone else who opposes him, is in the wrong. He takes people to his tent to show them what he has written to and about the other principals and his struggles with them (V.i.71–77). So much depends upon telling his story and giving the color of justice to his victorious enterprise. Enobarbus, Antony, and Cleopatra each want to tell the story of their side without any hope of its victory, intransigently insisting on the superiority of the failed cause.

The rest of the play is devoted to the heroes' response to Octavius' ascendancy. Act IV is devoted to Antony's exile and suicide, Act V to Cleopatra's agony and suicide. Suicide is a great theme in *Julius Caesar* and *Antony and Cleopatra*. One must remember that suicide is a sin in Christianity, and that in Shakespeare's time this was still taken very seriously. The Christian interdiction of suicide could be understood as an attempt to make it impossible to escape God's justice. But there is not a trace of disapproval of these deeds in Shakespeare's presentation of them, and, upon reflection, one can only come to the conclusion that Antony and Cleopatra did the right thing. Suicide was very much a Roman deed, not in the modern style of "the right to death" for people whose bodies no longer work. Nor is it quite like the antibourgeois display of willingness to die, a kind of negative demonstration that one has the wherewithal to be dedicated to a cause even if one doesn't have a cause. These Romans die for country, for liberty, and for honor, not for showing that they could die. Shakespeare's characters all lived in a world, as Churchill described it, where "All had to be endured, and hence—strangely enough—all might be inflicted."[9] There are, of course, cowards in Shakespeare, but most are men who are willing and expect to fight and know that death is always a possibility in a fight. None of them quite likes to die, but they have a certain resignation in the face of the risk of death. Only in the bourgeois world does the risk of death take on an almost erotic attractiveness and become a kind of game to prove that one is not a bourgeois, the typical inhabitant of a world where the right to life is the premise of human action. There is no such right in Shakespeare. Suicide is the proof not of willingness to die but rather of a man's love of freedom, the unwillingness to bend the knee to a tyrant. The suicides in this play are committed not in the name of republican liberty, but in the name of personal freedom from the Caesarean machine. Cleopatra says, "and then, what's brave, what's noble, / Let's do it after the high Roman fashion, / And make death proud to take us" (IV.xv.86–88).

No doubt, this kind of suicide is problematic, especially as it shows concern for the opinions of others. Even in their suicides Antony and Cleopatra are engaged in a struggle with Octavius, who wants to use them as part of his victory. At the very least, they elude him by not permitting him to dispose of their fates as he wishes. Cleopatra will not be marched through Rome in a triumph, the symbol for the mob of the ridiculousness of opposing Caesar. This indicates that the intention of these suicides is not only to frustrate Caesar, but to affect the opinion of the mob.* The contempt for the opinions of the many is part of Greek and Roman aristocratic taste, but classical aristocrats do worry about the opinions of their equals. They may even have to worry about their appearance among the mob, since only through mobs will one's memory be preserved for the special few in after times, as Cato became a model for those who wanted to found republics again, millennia after he committed suicide. Something like this surely preoccupies Cleopatra, if not Antony.

This concern for the honors accorded by others, honors that the proud man thinks he deserves whether others actually accord them or not, is a kind of Achilles' heel in the political man's makeup. Officially, at least, Socrates would be absolutely indifferent to what people think of him because he enjoys pleasures that in no way depend upon honor and because his pleasures are incomprehensible to all those who cannot partake of them. Antony shows some awareness of a possibility of such a life that is both fulfilling and outside of the system of honor

---

* What historicists call History is for Shakespeare only a meaningless succession of mob opinions. When one understands such opinions in this way, concern for them is less justified. No one would want to miss out on the revelation and progress of the Truth. Such a view of things unbends the will to resist in the name of personal conviction.

when he asks Caesar for permission to live as a private man in Athens, that gentle middle ground between Rome and Alexandria. Caesar, of course, will not permit this. Antony's great love is itself a strange mixture of the private independence of two individuals who live for each other and the public life of the ruler. He partakes of a kind of simulacrum of the Socratic experience but without its self-sufficiency, at least on this earth. And it is not to be forgotten that Socrates himself committed a kind of suicide with the intention of gaining a good reputation for himself or for philosophy.

Still, Antony and Cleopatra are splendid suicides. The agonies of these two heroes, which take up an unusually large part of the play, the crucial action having taken place in the middle of Act III, are not at all typical of Shakespeare's plays. There is suffering, sorrow, and regret here, but the abiding impression is more that of an apotheosis. This is not the end of a Macbeth or an Othello, who see that they have done terrible wrongs and have destroyed the meanings of their lives. Both Antony and Cleopatra are glad that they did what they did, and the humiliation of their defeat is counterbalanced by the assertion of the rightness of their love.

Antony has two moments of anger at Cleopatra, although he has many moments of self-deprecation about the conduct that brought him to Caesar's feet and betrayed his very loyal followers. His angers are both occasioned by the defection of Cleopatra's ships and the consequences of those defections. It would not be correct to say that he is jealous of Cleopatra, but he opines that she has played him false with Caesar, turning his love into a foolish infatuation, unworthy of the supreme sacrifices made for the sake of it. After Actium, he finds Cleopatra apparently compacting with Caesar's ambassador. She has a record of coming to terms with rival Romans who get to the top. Her capricious behavior, "her infinite variety," makes her difficult to decipher. The defections that end the second battle persuade Antony that she has "pack'd cards with Caesar" (IV.xiv.19). But in both instances Antony is easily assuaged. Immediately after Actium, Cleopatra's tears, so much ridiculed by Enobarbus, draw forth the response:

> Fall not a tear, I say, one of them rates
> All that is won and lost: give me a kiss,
> Even this repays me. (III.xi.69–71)

Antony's requests for kisses are not to be compared to Charles Bovary's, although both are made at moments of defeat.

The reversal of his fortunes unhinges Antony, and he becomes extremely erratic. His worst moment is when he challenges Caesar to a single fight, rebelling against the unfairness of a poor fighter's winning out over a good one. Caesar answers simply, "let the old ruffian know, / I have many other ways to die" (IV.i.4–5). He also induces his followers to cry for him, of which he is immediately ashamed. But underneath it all there is this continuous stream of erotic feeling for Cleopatra. Even his great speech comparing himself to the illusions projected by the clouds, insubstantial things that quickly dissipate, ends in their mutual expectation of embraces in heaven. At the very end, he says,

> I am dying, Egypt, dying; only
> I here importune death awhile, until
> Of many thousand kisses, the poor last
> I lay upon thy lips. (IV.xv.18–21)

Antony is easily persuaded by Cleopatra's mere speech that she did not betray him at Actium. He has really tragic suffering just after the second battle and the desolation induced by his belief in Cleopatra's dishonesty. He cries out that he is suffering, as did his ancestor hero and god, Hercules, in the shirt of Nessus. His contemplated suicide is at this moment simply the end of everything. But he is mollified when he hears that Cleopatra has preceded him. He then thinks only of joining her. The fact that this is just one of her tricks and that she is still very much alive may cast some light on the genuineness of love, but certainly Antony, even provoked to the limit, always gently returns to his dedication to this woman. And he is vindicated by her extraordinary behavior in the scenes after he dies. They are joined to each other forever. It is one of those marvelous historical accidents that Antony had a servant named Eros, and throughout Act IV his calls for the help of his servant, Eros, Eros, stud his speeches. "Eros!—I come, my queen!—Eros!" (IV.xiv.50) is typical of these passages. Antony wants Eros to kill him, but Eros commits suicide himself, thus depriving Antony of a death administered by Eros. He must do it himself, and he half botches the job, which allows him to spend a delicious last moment with his beloved. The richness of the allusions contained in this, the death of Eros, needs no commentary.

Antony's struggles and his farewell to this world concern fortune and Caesar. In a sort of Stoic reflection on fortune, he recognizes that human autonomy requires independence from the turns of its wheel. Caesar's happiness depends not upon Caesar but on fortune, and

Caesar can tomorrow become a slave. This is Brutus-like, and a certain aping of wisdom. Anyone devoted to politics depends on fortune. Antony's attachment to eros surely reduces that dependency, but this is all part of the incoherence that brings him down. He reiterates the importance of suicide—"a Roman, by a Roman / Valiantly vanquish'd" (IV.xv.57–58)—as part of his independence of Caesar. This is a noble stance, but it rings somewhat hollow. However, Antony, a much less moral man than Brutus, is actually more independent of the political wheel of fortune than is Brutus, and this is undoubtedly due to his love. Brutus dies for an utterly lost cause, whereas Antony has at least for a moment participated in beauties that never change, and in the end dies because of and for them.

Actually, Caesar does not care about bringing Antony back to Rome to decorate his triumph. He simply wants him dead. "We could not stall together, / In the whole world" (V.i.39–40). But Antony does believe that his story will be different from Caesar's. Caesar's world depends on capturing everything that would oppose it. Actually, Antony's story, as something independent of Caesar's and choiceworthy for its own sake, depends on Shakespeare.

Shakespeare makes Cleopatra into Antony's historian as she struggles to come to terms with her loss:

> It were for me
> To throw my sceptre at the injurious gods,
> To tell them that this world did equal theirs,
> Till they had stol'n our jewel. (IV.xv.75–78)

They have had heaven on earth, but the jealous gods have deprived her of her earthly god. But by the end of Act V, she has "immortal longings," and goes to meet her husband in heaven. She is upset that Iras precedes her, for fear that she take the kiss from Antony that was destined for her. The mortality of love between two human lovers is not acceptable to her. She and Antony join in the divine union after death that is required by their love. They both long for immortality, as eros always prompts man to do according to Socrates, but they are able to seek for it only in mortal individuals. From their experience with each other, they divine the divine, but do not grasp it. They are right in thinking that it is eros in man that leads toward the divine and that, unlike many other visions of the divine, it must begin in the divine form of man. Cleopatra's descriptions of Antony, from the moment of his death to her own, are overpowering. His last words to her were intended to justify her love of him. She never needed to justify herself to him because she was the lovable in itself. Her praise of Antony is only heightened by the fact that it is interspersed with flattery of the new god of the earth, Caesar. One is thus forced to compare him with Antony, the god of her soul. Their movement to heaven does not quite persuade us, but we cannot help wishing them well. This is another kind of divinity produced in decadent Rome.

And, finally, again the question of who is to enjoy that famous triumph. All of Antony and Cleopatra's worshipers have converted to Caesar, who says that the converts alone would be enough with which to defeat Antony. With the exception of the regretful Enobarbus, these conversions are painted as low things, the generality of mankind's worship of vulgar success. Cleopatra's passion not to be incorporated in that success, not to be one of those defeated without dignity by the new order of things, is overwhelming:

CLEOPATRA: Now, Iras, what think'st thou?
Thou, an Egyptian puppet shall be shown
In Rome as well as I: mechanic slaves
With greasy aprons, rules, and hammers shall
Uplift us to the view. In their thick breaths,
Rank of gross diet, shall we be enclouded,
And forc'd to drink their vapour.

IRAS: The gods forbid!

CLEOPATRA: Nay, 'tis most certain, Iras: saucy lictors
Will catch at us like strumpets, and scald rhymers
Ballad us out o' tune. The quick comedians
Extemporally will stage us, and present
Our Alexandrian revels: Antony
Shall be brought drunken forth, and I shall see
Some squeaking Cleopatra boy my greatness
I' the posture of a whore. (V.ii.206–220)

Caesar is indeed robbed and disappointed when Cleopatra escapes him. He puts the best face on it when he says, "and their story is / No less in pity than his glory which / Brought them to be lamented" (V.ii.359–361). They are now objects of pity, brought to that condition by Caesar, whose glory, Caesar insists, is enhanced by his having done so. But what Cleopatra most feared does not come. In this play, she is "boyed" (the most improbable role for any of the boys who played women in Shakespeare's plays), but not as a whore. It is only in Caesar's tradition that a Cleopatra would be indistinguishable from a whore. Shakespeare picks up the cause of Antony and Cleopatra, and by his poetry perhaps leads us to the truest meaning of eros. Generation after generation they are renascent on a stage on this earth, and thus Shakespeare pricks our heart with longing, not for a lost world, but for something that is always accessible to man as man. This is really a triumph.

9. *Measure for Measure*

I

Measure for Measure is another play that is dominated by a priest's plot, but, unlike the plot in *Romeo and Juliet*, this equally contrived solution to a problem works. The happy result makes us laugh. The solution to sexual problems is comic both because it is so improbable and because coping reasonably with these desires somehow makes them look ridiculous. Perhaps the plot works because the priest is not really a priest but a genuine political ruler who uses the cloak of religion to hide himself and his designs. Political wisdom seems to require some such religious coloring in order to make itself acceptable to the unwise subjects. Certainly this false friar escapes the law's narrow concentration on men's deeds by using the Church's capacity to get inside men's thoughts.

The explicit intention of Duke Vincentio's ruse is to restore the force of law, which has for either fourteen or nineteen years been allowed to fall into desuetude. The laws in question are perhaps the most decisive of laws, those concerning sexual conduct. They appear to be the most necessary and the harshest, those that go most against nature's grain. Precisely why the Duke has neglected to enforce the laws is difficult to understand. Either he was, like Prospero, too involved with his own thought to pay attention to the unpleasant business of governing, as Escalus suggests, or, as a bachelor, he himself profited from the laxness in the city. There is a hint of this latter interpretation when Friar Thomas takes the Duke's petition for haven to be a request to carry on an affair in his monastic abode

(I.iii.1–6).* This immediate supposition on Friar Thomas' part would seem to be based on prior experience. And as we shall see, the Duke is too honest a man to be simply a hypocrite in condemning practices in which he participates. The Duke knows the legislator is beyond the law, but the law requires his conviction and support. There may be need for terror in order to put law in the seat usurped by lust, but the Duke respects nature and will not lend himself to the dishonesty required simply to deny it. The mercy that tempers the harshness of the newly reapplied law stems from the reflection that "there but for the grace of God go I," that is, both you and I have the same desires and perhaps the same experiences as those who are condemned. The law that condemns erotic activity is made by erotic men. This leads to the heart of the play's ambiguity.

Vienna is the seat of the Holy Roman Empire, and the Church, in both its purity and its corruption, is highly visible there. The Duke effects a kind of Reformation in Vienna, and the astounding fact of the play is that throughout it untamed sexual desire is accepted as a fact of life. Those who do not admit it are as much reformed as those who do.

Vienna is a sexual mess. Bawdy houses are the accepted way to get sexual satisfaction. People talk of them as they do about food markets, and take it for granted that they can be no more easily suppressed than are the food markets, which are necessary. If the proprietors and clients of the bawdy houses, or, in general, all the loose individuals, are something less than admirable, they are either merely comic, which means harmless, or pleasant persons of good company. They are not like criminals who knew they were breaking the law and got caught; they are really surprised that there can be such laws and that they are to blame.

Nobody, but nobody, is married in this town. There is no family, and marriage is not understood to be necessary for procreation. Natural children are hardly thought to be bastards, and the Christian's insistence that a child not born in holy wedlock is a counterfeit has no weight in Vienna. Escalus, a remnant of the old regime, asks Pompey whether Mistress Overdone had more than one husband. He responds, "Nine, sir; Overdone by the last" (II.i.198–199). People once had fathers and mothers, but they are gone. The extreme expression of what is sexually wrong in Vienna is that there is a great

---

* All parenthetical citations in this chapter are to Shakespeare's *Measure for Measure*, ed. J. W. Lever, Arden Edition (1954; rpt. London: Routledge, 1988).

deal of venereal disease, the result of promiscuity.* The Duke apparently finds this situation intolerable. His response, as we shall see, is not "get thee to a nunnery," in either sense. He wishes to reestablish the institution of marriage, which is a mode of sexual expression, although one constrained by law. He apparently is ready to do so because he is now at the point where he is himself willing to marry. It should not be forgotten that his plot culminates in his own marriage, which would have been impossible if the reform had not taken place. What appears to be an extremely severe reform turns out to be actually a gentle one, with license given even to the houses of ill fame for the sowing of wild, that is, unlawful, oats, on the condition that they be less open and be ashamed before respectable institutions. But getting a lot of people married is the central intention of this political deed. The naturalness of marriage is questioned by the action of the play while its political necessity is affirmed.

II The Duke's withdrawal from Vienna is an assumption of a godlike behavior. He is an absent god for whom a human deputy acts. This deputy is watched by another branch of the god's presence in absence, the Church and its priests. The Duke, disguised as a friar, spies out what the law would never see or take into account. This actually reveals a weakness in the written law itself and in its executors. The priest acts deceptively, dishonestly, and abuses the Church's doctrines in order to attain his ends. His behavior is innocuous in *Measure for Measure* because the priest is actually the ruler. The supplement to the law provided by the Duke's prudence, his exceptions of persons, and his privately gained knowledge of the inner life of souls would be requisite for full justice. However, its political institutionalization by means of the Church would be as fraught with difficulties as is the appointment of a deputy. Shakespeare, following Machiavelli as well as the whole classic tradition, is disapproving of the rule of priests. In this case, however,

---

* One cannot help being reminded of Montesquieu's wry hints that the Mosaic Law is so severe, even in its dietary injunctions (Montesquieu asserts that pork is noxious for those with venereal disease), because those inhabitants of the Fertile Crescent to whom it applied were racked by venereal disease, which threatened life at its very source.[1]

the real ruler in the guise of priest is able to make Angelo, his deputy, assume that his position is invulnerable because nobody other than Isabella knows what he has done, whereas the false priest knows it all. Here the Duke's disguise permits him to be omniscient, as is a god, and to manipulate and to mitigate the omnipotence of the political ruler. In extreme cases, such as the basic reform the Duke is effecting, what Machiavelli calls unusual modes are necessary and just.

The Duke's withdrawal and the appointment of an efficient and severe deputy to do the nasty business is a tactic Machiavelli applauds. He gives as an example for imitation Cesare Borgia's appointment of Remirro de Orco as his deputy when he wanted to reduce the Romagna to peace and obedience. When de Orco had successfully completed the tasks given him by Cesare, the latter,

> because he knew that past rigors had generated some hatred for Remirro, to purge the spirits of that people and to gain them entirely to himself, . . . wished to show that if any cruelty had been committed, this had not come from him but from the harsh nature of his minister. And having seized this opportunity, he had him placed one morning in the piazza at Cesena in two pieces, with a piece of wood and a bloody knife beside him. The ferocity of this spectacle left the people at once satisfied and stupefied.[2]

Shakespeare, in his sweeter way, actually imitates Machiavelli's example with his play. The punishment of Angelo is rendered more moral than was Remirro's, because Angelo is actually disloyal to his master, whereas Remirro was not. One gradually becomes aware that the Duke's purpose is as much to humiliate Angelo as to punish fornicators. As a matter of fact, the person who most suffers punishment and humiliation in the play is Angelo, a strange way to go about restoring sexual morals. Rather than being cut in half, Angelo suffers an equally fearsome fate—he must marry. The populace is impressed by both the Duke's harshness and his mercifulness. The Duke, on the one hand, acts like the Moral Majority in the sanctifying of the family. On the other, he acts like the ACLU in impugning the motives of the Moral Majority. He obviously thinks that neither is quite the right thing. The Duke tells Claudio, "Be absolute for death" (III.i.5), whereas the play is absolute for life. Aside from the hapless Claudio, the only person other than Angelo to suffer greatly in the play, in which such severe punishment threatens and in which executioners are so visible, is Isabella. And Isabella is also the only other person with high moral pretensions. Much of *Measure for Measure*'s message is conveyed when Pompey the pimp is appointed deputy executioner. This play illustrates the humanizing of the law by making sure that it is not made by beings who have never felt the human movements of soul and body. A godlike law applied to humans rather than angels results in a perversity that is worse than lechery.

The Duke surely knows what Angelo is prior to appointing him and suggests to the more humane Escalus, more humane in that he remembers in his old age the desires he had when he was young, that he wants to see what Angelo will do. He also knew prior to the action of the play that Angelo had abandoned Mariana in spite of his pledges to her. Angelo is much worse than Claudio, who merely put off marriage until the dowry came through but remained faithful, if that is the word, to Juliet, whereas at the loss of the dowry, Angelo jilted Mariana. Still, he appears honestly tormented when he becomes attracted to Isabella. A sophistry of the heart could have allowed him to forget his bad behavior to Mariana, and there seems to have been no sexual relationship with her. There money seems to have been the theme. Whether the Duke could have counted on Isabella's attracting the attention of Angelo or not, the Duke did expect some such abuse of power. It would seem likely that her brother, Claudio, the first and only real sufferer from the reawakened law, was pointed out to Angelo by the Duke. It is not necessary to assume that Angelo is a Tartuffe, self-consciously using his reputation for piety to gain access to women.

What we see in the great scene with the lecherous Lucio, urging Isabella to heights of rhetoric, is the welling up in Angelo of an erotic attraction to the notion of corrupting virtue (II.ii.26–187). This is a perversity beyond any that might be attributed to the low persons in the play who have frank sexual attractions to good-looking persons or merely have a need for sexual release. There is a refinement in Angelo that sets his senses in motion in the presence of innocence and virginity. It is eroticism heightened and refined by its being forbidden. He confesses to himself that this is infinitely more attractive than natural sexual appeals. Angelo's imperious need for Isabella is inconceivable without the attraction of its being a sin.

The two encounters between Angelo and Isabella are the highlights of this play. He moves, in his own self-understanding, from god to sinner. Before our eyes we see the genesis of guilt. He wills and he does not will. Before, he thought that will and deed were identical in him. He elevates sexual desire into the realm of the forbidden, forbidden by his own standards and his position, and then hates himself for his sexual desire. He becomes disgusted by sexual desire in others, because he attributes to them the same criminality he finds in himself. This makes him into a criminal: he forces Isabella to have sexual intercourse with him and murders Claudio to cover up the rape. At least he thinks he commits these terrible deeds and is foiled only by the Duke's manipulation of appearances. He begins as the cold instrument of the law and metamorphoses into the only malevolent person in the play. This means he delights in doing harm while struggling with his conscience. Sinning and repenting become a way of life for him. Presenting himself as the enforcer of law on fallen man, he actually reenacts the harshness of God at the first Fall.

Shakespeare has very little sympathy for this kind of moralistic sexuality. He has a particular need to humiliate men who make claims like Angelo's. Henry V, in his typically cold fashion, uses the severe Chief Justice to punish the inhabitants of the Boar's Head Inn, especially Falstaff, with whom he has spent his youth and for whom Shakespeare has a great deal of sympathy.[3] He does so for the sake of public morals, as opposed to private satisfaction, now that he is king. He does so also to satisfy the puritanical passions that are rife among the people and which Shakespeare rightly saw would threaten civil peace. These were not the simple moral demands that frighten liberals so, but real puritanical passions of the sort that are today making parts of the Islamic world ungovernable. Something like this is what the Duke is after, though he accomplishes it much more nicely than does Hal. Not only does he wish to channel the sexual affections more or less into family attachments, but he also wants to fend off the threat of extreme reactions by Puritans, whose souls have been prepared for extremism by their religion. The sense of sin grafted on to sexual desire, not a thing to be found in Mistress Overdone's house, accounts for the distortions of Angelo's soul, and Shakespeare's dislike of Puritans is subjected here to profound and fundamental analysis. Nietzsche's reflection I quoted before might be useful also here: "Christianity gave Eros poison to drink. He did not die, but became vice."[4] Most of the others in the play are indulgent or dirty-minded but not perverse. It is imagination, not the body, which causes Angelo to be attracted to the conquest of purity.

III For nothing in the world would Isabella sacrifice her maidenhead, and Angelo would do anything in the world to have it. So she and Angelo are, in a sense, well matched in that they both set an overwhelmingly high price on virginity. Isabella is an attractive, spirited, intelligent girl with a gift for self-righteous rhetoric. She is entering a religious order but has not yet taken her vows. The rigorous "restraints" on the behavior of the sisters are not enough for Isabella, who professes a wish for stricter ones. Her setting among the sisters provides the other pole in the stark opposition that characterizes Vienna —bawdy houses versus holy houses. The center is represented only by the weak Claudio, who floats about between looseness and the sanctity of marriage. The center does not exist in any substantial way, and the Duke's project is clearly intended to make the naturalness and goodness of sex acceptable to one kind of extremist, and to submit its wildness to the yoke of the law in the other kind of extremist. The Puritans are the hardest to persuade because they lead from moral superiority, a great self-satisfaction.

Isabella is pretty easygoing about the habits in Vienna, most probably because she feels superior to them. Her response when she hears that her brother has made a child without the benefit of law with her good friend Juliet is that they should get married. This is perfectly sensible and fits the wishes of the two parties, but it hardly fits with her view of the sacredness of virginity and the base character of those men who would wish to rob her of it. She has chosen chastity, an utter giving up of erotic satisfaction, at least with human beings, although she occasionally seems a bit confused and says that virginity must be kept only to protect the genuineness of any offspring she might have. The premise of this entire play is that there is no way to avoid sexual attraction. Angelo and Isabella, in their own ways, prove to be affected by it. The Duke, when disguised as a priest, tells the Provost that there is no danger in having an unsupervised encounter with Isabella because he is a priest. But he manifestly is attracted to Isabella. The loose must be frightened into curbing their sexual expression; the tight must be made to experience the power of sexual attraction.

As a result of her encounters with Angelo, Isabella begins to see something of the weakness of the grounds on which she stands and becomes a fanatic. She has learned of her rhetorical power under the instruction of the loose Lucio, this worthless fellow, who is more severely punished than any of the other bawdy characters in the play, but less for his sexual practices than for his insults to the Duke. She begins in her first interview with Angelo by meekly and a little too easily accepting her brother's punishment. Then at the end of the first interview, when she has begun to be enchanted with the sound of her own voice (a thing to be denied her according to the rules of the order she is entering against converse with men), she promises Angelo that if he shows mercy, she'll put in a good word with God on his behalf. The speech of Isabella that immediately precedes Angelo's first signs of attraction is intended to remind him that he too is a man and must once have had such feelings as her brother's. This is an appeal to mercy, not as divine grace but as recognition of common human frailty. But in her second interview, where Angelo, now a sexual highwayman, in effect demands, "Your virginity or your brother's life," she engages in a dialogue in which Angelo makes a few real points. She is forced to admit that she sets different standards for her brother and herself and that Angelo simply applies laws, the principles of which she accepts. More important, she is forced to agree that her refusing to have sexual intercourse with Angelo is akin to Angelo's refusal to pardon a similar act by her brother. Angelo tells her that she will be pardoned by God for the intention of her act. The outrageousness of the situation, in which the enforcer of the law is now breaking it, helps to conceal the weakness of Isabella's position. Part of the Duke's intention, as I have indicated, is to make the law, without loss of majesty, more clearly a product of human beings with human frailties and thus less tyrannical. He reduces the gap, the necessary gap, between the ought and the is. Isabella, overheated, starts using erotic language to describe her attachment to her virginity, for which she is willing to die. She says she would "strip myself to death as to a bed / That longing have been sick for, ere I'd yield / My body up to shame" (II.iv.102–104). Virginity has metaphysical status for her now. "Then, Isabel live chaste, and brother, die" (II.iv.183).

This disposition might appear to be noble, but it is understandable that her brother is not totally of Isabella's persuasion. This is perhaps because, although he seems a decent enough fellow, his sexual history makes it clear that he has always had some practical doubts about the sinfulness of sex, including its sinfulness prior to marriage. He and his fiancée, Juliet, are meant to represent the typical subjects of the law's new rigor. They consummated their marriage before it took place because the dowry was held up. Why not enjoy oneself now, since life is so short and the intentions are good? But when he is arrested, he easily accepts the justness of the law and asserts that he suffers as a result of his own licentiousness. Some-how, the principle of marriage was instilled in him, and it is easy for him to acknowledge that he should have waited. This law does not deny sexual satisfaction or make his deed irreparably sinful. Partly, he accepts it passively because he hopes that his acknowledgment of the rightness of the law will save his life. But partly he and his Juliet (who sweetly tells the Duke, when, in the guise of a friar, he is haunting the prison and moralizing with its inmates, that she now honestly regrets what she has done) represent the practice of the great majority of mankind who neither particularly enjoy frequent-ing prostitutes nor have an overwhelming desire to enter monastic orders. The problem in Vienna is partly structural: there is a high view that rejects sex and, perhaps consequently, a low view that simply accepts it in whatever form it is available. These ordinary people are likely, without too much anger or rebelliousness, to re-strain themselves and get married. Such persons are not sufficiently erotic really to run risks, nor do they have the obsessive motives of an Angelo.

IV	Claudio is that poor fish who is the first to suffer from the fresh vigor of a law. He tells the cop, "Why me? I was just following traffic." It is not exactly what you would call a

noble stance, but it touches all those who may have once in a while broken a law that was in disuse, like buying condoms in Connecticut or committing sodomy in one's own home in Georgia (although in old Vienna, there were no lawyers trying to get the laws applied in order to get them discredited). He is scared out of his wits when Angelo, his sister, and the Duke all condemn him to death, in spite of the sympathies of the other characters who think the punishment too severe. The Duke presents one of those moralistic speeches that impress solemn people, but which, in Shakespeare, are meant to be only empty speeches for the consolation of persons in bad situations. We have seen this with Friar Laurence in *Romeo and Juliet* and now we see Friar Lodowick, aka the Duke, doing something similar in *Measure for Measure*. His speech instructs Claudio about how terrible life is and how preferable to it death is (III.i.5–41). This speech, unlike some of the other speeches of the false friar, is not Christian but Stoic. There is no talk of the afterlife or of the immortal soul. Rather, the Duke's sermon concentrates on man's nothingness and his origins in dust. Lessing, with his characteristic good taste, confesses that he never much liked Stoicism because it treats men as though they were gladiators. He denies that the calm expression on the faces of Laocoön and his son as they are being strangled by the snakes has anything to do with the denial of pain. He points out the wonderful passage in Homer where, prior to the great battle between the Achaeans and the Trojans, there was absolute calm in the Trojan camp, for "great Priam would not let the Trojans cry."[5] The Greek camp was full of wailing, which Lessing interprets as proving that the Trojans were barbarians and the Achaeans Greeks, that is, peaks of civilization. In practice, this means that Greeks could accept their tears, and yet be men and fight. Barbarians had to repress nature. I believe that almost all of Shakespeare's Stoical utterances are meant to ridicule the dehumanizing Stoic morality.[6] The contrasts are so overdrawn in the Duke's sermon that it is impossible to understand how anybody ever got any pleasure in life whatsoever. If you are young, you are too poor to have any enjoyment, and if you have money, you are too old to have any enjoyment, and so forth. The Duke denies what Aristotle readily admits, that mere life is pleasant and that is why men hold on to it. The peak of this kind of moralism is to tell you that you do not enjoy what you enjoy. It is literally unbelievable, although for a moment a man punch-drunk from the blows of fortune may say he believes it, as does Claudio: "I humbly thank you. / To sue to live, I find I seek to die, / And seeking death, find life" (III.i.41–43).

This engaging boy is scared witless. This scene prepares for Isabella's arrival in the prison and discussion with her brother about their situations, a discussion spied on by the Duke (III.i.48–149). This is Isabella's worst moment. She tells her brother how horribly she is put upon and expects him to accept, at the cost of his life, the price she puts on her virginity. *He* could not live with *her* shame on his conscience. The death of a brother is as nothing compared with the sacrifice she would have to make. She picks up the Duke's theme in telling him what a little, little thing death is. Death rather than dishonor is her theme song, but humanly, all too humanly, Claudio, and the majority of mankind, wonder whether this is so simply the case. When she makes explicit the terrible, impossible thing she is asked to do in order to save her brother's life, Claudio's resolve to die imperturbably begins to be shaken. This is a chilling scene, but, in its way, one of Shakespeare's most comic inventions. When Claudio realizes that she has no intention whatsoever of saving him by the means Angelo provides, he says with a kind of resignation, "Thou shall not do't." Isabella responds gaily that if it were only her life at stake, as it is only Claudio's life, she would throw it away as easily as she would a pin. To which Claudio responds, one can imagine in what tone, "Thanks, dear Isabella." Then Claudio begins himself to engage in the kind of scholastic casuistry that took place between Angelo and Isabella. He says that Angelo must not regard it as such a big sin, because he is a devout man who would not want to risk being punished in perpetuity for "the momentary trick." "It is no sin; / Or of the deadly seven it is the least." Isabella, in astonishment, asks, "Which is the least?" (III.i.109–111). And then Claudio, in a fully human and moving speech, tells Isabella what he really feels about his execution:

> Ay, but to die, and go we know not where;
> To lie in cold obstruction, and to rot;
> This sensible warm motion to become
> A kneaded clod; and the delighted spirit
> To bath in fiery floods, or to reside
> In thrilling region of thick-ribbed ice;
> To be imprison'd in the viewless winds
> And blown with restless violence round about
> The pendent world: or to be worse than worst
> Of those that lawless and incertain thought
> Imagine howling,—'tis too horrible.
> The weariest and most loathed worldly life
> That age, ache, penury and imprisonment
> Can lay on nature, is a paradise
> To what we fear of death. (III.i.117–131)

Here the issue is not simply the end, no longer existing, as it is in the Duke's speech, but what imagination tells us about the things that happen after death. On the one hand, there is the rotting of one's lovely warm body and, on the other, the experiences of the soul that are told to us by poets, beginning with Homer's guided tour of Hades. Claudio speaks, as does Achilles, of being willing to accept any condition in the world in preference to being king over all of Hades. And he begs, "Sweet sister, let me live" (III.i.132). Nature, gentle nature, gives a dispensation for sacrificing one's maidenhead, as well as one's life, for a friend or a relative.

None of this is the reaction of the philosopher. Lucretius' whole philosophic effort is to persuade the persuadable, a small number, not to be terrified of an afterlife. This liberates men from the fear of afterlife, which can ruin the pleasures of this life, but it takes nothing away from the natural fear of nothingness. Philosophers and ordinary men both fear death, but they do so for different reasons. The philosophers are more inclined to accept it because they have thought it and its necessity through. This only underlines the perfectly decent ordinariness of Claudio. But neither wise man nor ordinary man would very easily accept death when salvation is so easily in their grasp. Only those who accept the framework in which virginity is more highly cherished than anything else could do so. Isabella's rejoinder to Claudio's touching appeal is "O, you beast!" (III.i.135). Her indignation becomes prurient as she equates preserving life at the expense of a sister's shame with incest. She imagines the act and invests it with everything her religious vocation connects with it. Claudio obviously doesn't think of it in this way but quite rationally sees his sister's single contact with Angelo as a means to a very important end. Isabella goes on to impugn her mother's virtue because such a man as Claudio could never have been the son of her father. She works herself up to a pitch where she herself condemns her brother to death all over again.

V   The Duke, seeing all of this, is evidently attracted to this girl, more by her potentiality than by her actuality. He is going to subject her to a number of trials and tortures that will have the effect of taming her spiritedness and bringing her back into the circle of mortality. He immediately makes her privy to the part of his conspiracy directed against Angelo. He has been cultivating Mariana for a long time, and he proposes that she take Isabella's place at the tryst with Angelo. The Duke, who talks only of force, always acts by fraud, and he lies to and deceives almost everyone over and over again. He asks Isabella to participate in arranging an act of carnal knowledge. She does so willingly, partly because she seems concerned primarily with *her* chastity and *her* honor. The friar provides a cover of propriety by saying that a prenuptial agreement is the same as a marriage. It is questionable whether this is so, inasmuch as Claudio is being punished with death for having had sexual relations—or is it perhaps a baby?—after a similar agreement prior to marriage.

What can Isabella think will be the result of Mariana's having sexual intercourse with Angelo? When Isabella first hears of Mariana's plight, with her typical generosity with the lives of others, she says that Mariana would be better off dead. It is very hard to figure out how this covert act would turn into marriage. Isabella does not demand many details inasmuch as she sees a way of saving her brother and not dishonoring herself. The Duke leaves it to Isabella to tell Mariana about the plan, a scene we do not see on stage but on which we are invited to reflect. One must wonder what the faithful Mariana felt about all of this. She is the only person in the play who manifests an undying attachment to anyone, to the man who is the least deserving of love in the entire play. Does she accept this encounter with resignation or delight at the possibility of finally enjoying the fruits of her love? There is no evidence that Angelo had ever experienced a sexual attraction to Mariana, or to anyone, before he met Isabella. Now Mariana has to accept a sexual act with her beloved that is possible only because he imagines he is doing it with someone else. This is at the very least humiliating and argues for an ambiguity in her future sexual relations with the man she hopes will be her husband. Will he ever be aroused by her, or will he always have to imagine Isabella in order to perform the act? His sexual pleasure is, at the least, greatly enhanced by the thought that it is Isabella he is enjoying. Isabella herself must be aware that Angelo will think he has had her and, in a way, will think so for the rest of his life, even though he is to learn that it is untrue. There is a whole dissertation here on the relation between imagination and reality in the commerce between the sexes. The Duke is a refined torturer in such matters. Angelo has had the experience of Isabella and will probably spend the rest of his life comparing Mariana with Isabella. And before his eyes he will see the woman he truly lusted after enjoyed by the Duke. Perhaps the lesson is that these things are all the same in the dark, but Angelo will never believe that. This would be the philosophy of Mistress Overdone's house. The Duke is diabolical.

Isabella, after having acted so efficiently in arranging an act of sexual intercourse, is almost immediately rewarded with the announcement that her brother is dead. Perhaps it is necessary for the Duke to use Isabella's indignation in the accusation of Angelo he is planning, but this lie is very cruel indeed. The Duke is cruel, if only with souls and not bodies, but his cruelty is administered in the name of justice. He has a good reason for torturing her in this way as part of his taming of her. He has first gotten her used to dealing calmly with a certain carnality, and now he elicits from her a purely natural reaction to her brother's death, tinged with some guilt about her own unwillingness to act on his behalf. Revenge is for now her only motive, and she becomes utterly attached to her holy mentor and the ruler he serves. Both will be replaced in her esteem by the Duke as duke.

VI Most of Act IV takes place in the dark prison, where the Duke, as religious man, prepares his final rendering of justice, which will take place in the light of day in the public place in Act V. In the prison the Duke is at his most deceitful and Italianate—he claims to have been sent on a mission by the Pope. He commands the Provost, using the authority of the Duke's signs; in a parallel to his mission from the Pope, he acts in the name of a higher power. He is loath to act directly because he himself would appear to be partly responsible for the abuses he is correcting, and he is arrogating to himself a form of justice akin to that of Angelo. A significant part of the play is devoted to the disproportion between reality and seeming in the exercise of rule and justice. The Duke needs not only to resurrect the force of law but also to mitigate the disproportion of which he has spoken. His problem as a ruler, like Prospero's, is connected with a modesty about assuming the false godlike proportions of rulers and a distaste for all the hypocrisy surrounding those in high positions. This reticence is heightened by all the scenes with Lucio, who calumniates the Duke to the Duke, not knowing who he is. The comic delight of these scenes is connected with justice, for the audience knows surely that Lucio will repent of his loose tongue as soon as he knows whose face is hidden by the friar's cowl. Unawares, Lucio tells the awful truth when he says, "*Cucullus non facit monachum*," a cowl does not make a monk (V.i.261). As Prospero adopted magic to right the situation, the Duke uses the priest's deceits to do the same thing.

His prison is an interesting place where the treatment of the inmates is extremely gentle. The only death recorded is due to natural causes. As already mentioned, Pompey is enlisted as deputy executioner for executions that never take place. He likes the job and remarks that executioners ask for pardon of their clients much more often than do the whores to whom he has been the deputy in the past. They were probably dealing out death just as liberally as do executioners. The prison makes Pompey feel right at home because it is now populated with all the lowlifes who used to frequent the whorehouse. Nothing very serious seems to be happening to them, and the only ones we actually see being consigned to the prison have been so only after repeated offenses. While there, the Duke saves Claudio, who has learned his lesson. He interviews the alleged murderer Barnardine, whose head he intended to send to Angelo in place of Claudio's. Barnardine refuses to die on that day because he is suffering from a hangover, and the Duke agrees that he is no more ready for death than for life. He first says that he will wait for Barnardine to be ready to die. Then the only clearly chance happening that occurs in the play is made known. A pirate who resembles Claudio much more than does Barnardine dies, and his head is dispatched to Angelo. In the end, Barnardine is pardoned by the Duke, probably because there is some doubt about whether he actually committed the murder of which he was accused. The tone of the prison is conveyed by the Provost, who says that Barnardine could easily have escaped but never had the energy to do so. This prison in no way confirms the harshness of the law that it is supposed to represent. The ghoulish sending of the head intended to deceive Angelo, and the lie, the same lie connected with the head, told to Isabella about her brother's death, seemings rather than realities, are the only harsh deeds that emanate from this prison.

| VII |

Act V is the great affirmation of the Duke's policies and the public presentation of his refurbished position as dispenser of justice. He comes almost as a Messiah to satisfy the longing for justice on the part of the injured and to dispense punishment to the wrongdoers. All that has gone before, and particularly the subterranean activities of the disguised Duke in the prison, are the necessary preparations for his return to rule. The law requires much that is extralegal or even frankly illegal in order to be both just and applied. Shakespeare combines a Machiavellian critique of the law and of those who use it and abuse it with a classical, that is Platonic, Aristotelian, or Ciceronian, love of justice. The Duke is neither the dupe of the law nor a despiser of it.

He is met at the gates of the city in the public place by Isabella. Demanding redress from the Duke on whom she counts and who has asked for complaints, she is summarily clapped in prison for calumniating his minister of justice. This was extremely unpleasant for her and must be added to the list of things the Duke makes her undergo. One begins to pity her, in spite of her earlier stiff-necked self-righteousness. This scene mirrors the usual course of justice in states where the wronged are not believed in the face of the wrong-doers who are in the positions of respectability. The perpetual complaint against the law, articulated so powerfully by Thrasymachus in Plato's *Republic*, is that it is used by the rich and powerful to legitimize their aggrandizements.[7] This undermines men's confidence or hopes in the law. The final scene of *Measure for Measure* comically represents the realization of the human dream of the all-knowing and the all-powerful ruler or god who comes onto the scene to lift up the downtrodden and humiliate the arrogant. But it begins as a typical case of the disproportion between power and justice.

Isabella lies to the Duke, telling him that she acceded to the demands of Angelo in order to save her brother. Thus, she makes a public, if untrue, confession to the loss of her virginity. She is most probably wearing a religious novice's costume when she does so. In another sense, of course, she is vindicating herself before the public because she is claiming to have been willing to sacrifice herself for her brother's life. Finally, she is forced by Mariana's prayers to get on her knees and beg for Angelo's pardon. She explains that Angelo's career of crime began because of his being attracted to her. If she hadn't made such a big deal of it and had not placed such a high value on her virginity, Angelo would never have been corrupted.

Shakespeare in this play obviously tends to blame the sexual desires of males for most of the problems, and to pardon and to exculpate the women, but he also investigates the subtle mechanisms involved in the sexual relations between civilized, indeed over-civilized, human beings. He walks a narrow line between a legitimate concern and respect for the modesty of women and a sacralization of their virginity. In the three cases of offending males he judges in this scene, the Duke acts in favor of offended women in spite of the fact that they were apparently all consenting. The only exception is to be found in the treatment of Isabella.

As soon as Friar Lodowick is brought on the scene, with conflicting testimony about his character and reliability, the kind of conflicting testimony one finds so often in the exercise of human justice, the climax has been reached. His hood is ripped off him by Lucio, who has been the chief calumniator of both the friar and the Duke, a kind of chorus representing the shifting and dangerous moods of public opinion, and all the principals become aware that they are in the presence of a man who knows of their secret thoughts and doings and who can dispense superlegal justice to them. But it is Angelo, the doer of the only deed intentionally designed to harm others, who is most disarmed when he recognizes that he must meet his judgment day. He counted on a kind of Gygean invisibility to protect him from the consequences of his crimes, although his conscience distressed him with the possibility that there might be a divine observer. Now he finds himself in the presence of a human observer:

> O my dread lord,
> I should be guiltier than my guiltiness
> To think I can be undiscernible,
> When I perceive your Grace, like power divine,
> Hath looked upon my passes. (V.i.364–368)

The Duke appears as God to him, and the deepest guilt would be to believe that he will be unseen in his crimes. Men like Angelo, and in this respect there are a lot of them, must above all believe they are being seen by a higher power in order to remain just. The Duke gives Angelo and Lucio and many others the impression that he will always be spying them out in the secret crevices of their minds. The Duke's justice is speedily accomplished, and in all four cases before him the decision is for marriage. The Duke's policy is pro-family, with particular emphasis (the cases of Angelo and Lucio) on males taking responsibility for the children they made women bear. The Duke, unlike our moral reformers, who concentrate on peripheral issues like abortion, homosexuality, or pornography, goes to the heart of the problem. He looks to making and maintaining marriages. It is not, however, entirely an accident that these marriages look something like punishments.

The resolution of Angelo's case is the most curious of them all. The punishment of death, which the Duke first assigns and which is wished for by Angelo himself, is tempered by the clemency of the Duke, moved by the pleas of the two women. Mariana believes for a few moments that she must marry and become a widow on the same day, exactly the same kind of paradox she suffered for a day or two when she was both maiden and consummated wife. The sufferings of all other characters in this play seem to be fair, but it remains a mystery why Mariana must go through this torment, except as a means to the end of correcting Angelo. The Duke does test her in this way and confirms her implausible love of Angelo. She is to receive all his property, thus allowing her to realize the dream of many a widow. This would restore her to the situation that existed prior to her brother's death at sea and the loss of her dowry with him. The

Duke provides her with the means to look for a better husband, but she will have none of it. Although the play's title is *Measure for Measure*, a version of the *lex talionis*, it might be, at least for Mariana, *All's Well That Ends Well*. The Duke presents a soft version of an eye for an eye: a threat of death for a threat of death, not a death for a death. However, Angelo did do a horrible thing, intending really to kill Claudio. Claudio was, of course, under sentence of death, undergoing the rigors of a law that was on the books. The punishment is indeed severe, but Angelo was appointed, at least for the benefit of the public, to apply such laws. His fault is breaking the promise he made to Isabella-Mariana, which is a business outside the law. His legal crime is using his power to force a woman to have intercourse with him. The Duke has used Angelo in both ways—to reinvigorate the law and to soften the moral severity of the judge. It is possible that the Duke believes Isabella's account of the reasons for Angelo's crimes and thinks there is better stuff in him that will come out after the fall.

The Duke's providence is the cause of Isabella's not being violated and Claudio's not being beheaded. He performs miracles. Isabella is impressed by his action but thinks he failed to save her brother. All he has offered is "the appeal to heaven," for the punishment of wrongdoers. At the very end, she recognizes that his providence deals with everything that is most dear to her. One of the most interesting aspects of the Duke's justice is that he leaves no one with the satisfactions of indignation, of getting back at offenders, or even of repenting for sins committed. Marriages, reunions with brothers, natural satisfactions, are what the Duke deals in. Escalus is praised and the provost rewarded. Lucio is compelled to marry a woman who has, according to Lucio's own admission, borne him a child that he has denied and whom he now calls a whore, so that he is to receive, as he says, a cuckold's horns in return for having made the Duke a duke (by pulling off the friar's cowl). Teaching men to accept responsibility for their children is part of this punishment of Lucio, but the primary reason is, as I have said, his disrespect for the Duke and his tales of the Duke's own sexual conduct. The two reasons are perhaps identical: respect for the Duke must be respect for the Duke's law in these essential matters.

Claudio is assigned the marriage that he claimed he wanted without any discussion of the dowry he was waiting for. Since we know that Mariana has no dowry, and Lucio's blushing bride surely had none, the Duke is removing from women the burden of providing money to husbands.

And now we come to the case of Isabella and the Duke. He proposes marriage, once prior to the miraculous coming to life of Claudio, and once after. We never hear' her response, but his authority is such that we cannot doubt that she agreed. The Duke moves from the state of single man to the state of marriage, and he makes the whole population follow him in the move. This is a play that speaks almost not at all of love. It is full of sex and empty of eros. The kinds of marriage here ascend from Lucio's disgust, to Angelo's resignation and relief, to Claudio's easygoing satisfaction, to the Duke's apparent love. Shakespeare plays Jane Austen in giving everybody the kind of marriage he or she deserves. The Duke thinks he deserves the best. He has chosen a very attractive girl and has educated her before our eyes. She ends up with admiration for his wisdom and power, and gratitude for his having saved both her and her brother. He begins his marriage holding very good cards. He will need them because this is a woman very much with her own mind. Most of all, the Duke has robbed the convent of a promising sister to provide his bed with a delicious wife.

This last fact is the one that best teaches us about the spirit of the Duke's great reform. This is a terrible play in its threats, and a very sweet one in its results. The Duke understands effective law to be a delicate mixture of fear-producing force, wisdom, and, above all, natural inclination, producing as much happiness for individuals as human society admits of. He does not believe that sexual desire can express itself without limits in a decent society. He thinks sexual satisfaction is a good thing and that it does not take too much, unless there has been a total emancipation, to calm sexual desire sufficiently in the name of marriage. In the Holy Roman Empire we see a friar turning into a married ruler, a reform not unrelated to the Protestant reform. Everything he does is for the sake of natural satisfactions, in the first place, his own. Unlike his Enlightenment successors, he does not think that natural inclination is simply sufficient for the constitution of an orderly society, but he agrees in large measure with their aims.

Sexual education, the Duke agrees with Rousseau, is an essential part of citizenship education. The Duke, however, does not embark on a great transformation of man in order to overcome his dividedness. He simply introduces fear into the sexual scheme of things. The sexual prying of authority is distasteful, but the Duke engages in it so that it will not have to be done again. And he underlines by this activity that the sexual character of men is an essential component in their relation to the polity.

10. *Troilus and Cressida*

I

Troilus and Cressida, perhaps the bleakest of all Shakespeare's plays, presents itself as a wildly witty travesty of antiquity's greatest heroes. Shakespeare's message seems to be that heroes are not heroes, because they are either fools or knaves, and that love is a sham and deception. The atmosphere is very different from that of *Antony and Cleopatra*, so different that many interpreters can render the change intelligible only by supposing disappointments in love undergone by the Bard. Such explanations appeal to modern readers, who, under the persisting influence of Romanticism, understand writers as chroniclers of their own personal histories or their moods, sublime reproductions of the way most of us approach things. The notion that a writer overcomes his particular experience or feeling in the name of a more comprehensive and less personal view of things is rejected and treated as antipoetic, although this suggestion is enunciated by Shakespeare himself and discussed even in this play. It is more a commentary on ourselves that we take the autobiographical explanation as truth, when it is little better than an assertion, and an implausible one at that. We should at least consider that Shakespeare looks at the ancient heroes and love under different aspects in different plays and that each of the aspects is part of a total vision. Why should a man generally understood to be of such divine gifts not be able to discipline his thoughts? He may very well have used his moods to understand the psychology of the passions, that is, to reveal the human situation, not merely his personal experiences. The play, which actually exists and which we can keep before our eyes, has to be understood prior to our speculating about the poet's motives, which we really cannot know apart from their product, the play. Otherwise the unknowable becomes the basis for interpreting the knowable. These reflections are induced by reading the play itself, for it is most baffling. The high good humor, the outrageous anachronisms, and the ridiculing of a tradition that Shakespeare seems elsewhere to admire so highly, puzzle us. *Troilus and Cressida* contains very great poetry, but its form and its rhetorical character, including long speeches that could hardly be understood from the stage, seem to argue a dramatic failure. It is one of those plays that seem impossible to categorize as either comedy or tragedy.

Certainly if *Antony and Cleopatra* instills nostalgia in us, this play is the corrective of that dangerous sentiment. Nostalgia undermines the present in the name of the past, a historical moment that can never be reproduced, and ends up in empty snobbism. Here Shakespeare debunks the past, but it is not true that nothing is left standing. Nothing is left standing in the eyes of those who regard glory and love as the two greatest and most interesting human motives. But if, to put it bluntly, this is a play about wisdom, a thing neither understood nor desired by most people, then many of the play's formal difficulties disappear. One character, Ulysses, emerges, if in an understated way, triumphant. Shakespeare suggests in *Troilus and Cressida* that wisdom, austere and externally unattractive, is the one thing permanently available to man that is noble and choiceworthy. The difficulty Shakespeare has in presenting this theme is the old Platonic one: the lively and intense passions are what the imitative arts can depict, whereas the wise man (e.g., Socrates) has no important role on the stage that mirrors life. This is the same problem, in another guise, that Shakespeare grapples with in *The Tempest*, that is, how a wise man can be made interesting amid the passions, despite the popular lack of understanding of wisdom and distaste for it. Glory and love, always attractive and interesting, are central to *Troilus and Cressida*, but their splendor is dimmed by the corrosive of reason, and they become in the plot means to the ends of Ulysses. Just as Ulysses in Homer's *Iliad* is hardly a favorite character, Ulysses is not much liked in *Troilus and Cressida* and is very underrated by its critics. Prospero, the magician, can hold center stage. Ulysses, the intriguer and debunker, appears peripheral to the play's central action. But for a few choice viewers or readers he represents the consolation of philosophy in a dark world.

The characters in the play are very preoccupied with posterity's judgment and recognize that their glory depends upon poets. Shake-

speare really gives it to them. The only person who comes out looking good in the popular eye is Troilus, and even he seems a bit silly.
This play is written by an extremist who pulls no punches. Shakespeare chooses to represent the Trojans as much superior to the
Greeks, a very different picture from that given by the evenhanded
Homer. This allows Shakespeare to treat the victorious heroic tradition in an irreverent way. The Trojan men generally live up to their
legends, idealists of honor, whereas the Greek heroes are painted in
a most repulsive light, but one that reflects something of what they
really were. The rulers are not wise, the heroes are not honorable,
and there are no lovers among them. The presence of Ulysses helps
to bring all of this out or makes it worse than it might ordinarily
appear to be, but it is all too evident even without him, and
Shakespeare's play would seem to correct a great historical error, the
burden of which misleads men of later ages. It is Achilles, the hero
of all heroes, who is most transformed, and Shakespeare thereby
makes much more central what Plato hinted at in the *Republic*.[1]

This play inserts erotic motives behind the actions of the various
heroes in a way that is not evident in Homer, but it follows and enhances the erotic motive alleged to have been at the root of the Trojan
War. The struggle for the possession of Helen's beauty was supposed
to explain or give sufficient reason for the great sufferings and heroic
deeds of this war. The love of the beautiful can be considered a noble
motive for great dedication and great sacrifices in a way that the quest
for money or land cannot be. The Greeks and the Trojans elevated war
by their ideals. *Troilus and Cressida* demotes the war by ridiculing its
motives. This is exactly what Herodotus does at the beginning of his
History.[2] He does so in order to put the Persian War in the place of the
Trojan War as a truly noble war. Shakespeare, however, presents no
such noble alternative and in that resembles Thucydides, who leaves
understanding as the only satisfaction arising from the contemplation
of the ugliness of political history. The opposition between Venus and
Mars is underlined and undermined at the same time.

One of the peculiarities of the play is its turning the Greek and
Trojan, especially the Trojan, warriors into knights who, in the great
tradition of chivalry, have great ladies for whom they fight and
whose combats are enclosed in high, ridiculous forms. In *Troilus and
Cressida*, this reaches its peak with the combat between Hector
and Ajax, where each falls over the other with terms of endearment
and the enunciation of shared principles of honor. Not the slightest
harm is done by either to the other. The background of this combat
is senseless slaughter of both Greeks and Trojans. Thus the high

principles, the gentlemanliness of the leading combatants, is ridiculed, and the ugliness of the war revealed. In reading this play, one cannot help being reminded of the First World War, in which so many died for slight or even nonexistent goals. During a large part of this war there were civil and formal relations between aristocratic French and German officers, beautifully captured in Jean Renoir's film *Grand Illusion*. The difference between Renoir and Shakespeare is that Renoir solemnly teaches us about the vanity of war whereas Shakespeare presents this picture with unfailing gaiety. Folly is a permanent feature of human existence. The playwright cannot change that and can at best offer us consolation in laughter and the insight laughter brings with it. Never does he sermonize. The spoof of Christian chivalry in the context of the Trojan War, inherited from Chaucer, permits Shakespeare also to raise the question of the motives of classical warriors.

We are introduced to the play in a scene where Troilus has chosen not to go to war today because he is love-moody. The war is treated as something one can participate in or not according to whether one feels like it that day. Erotic life is viewed from a double perspective, as a war between the sexes and as a much more pleasant way of spending one's time than fighting. This picks up on a theme mentioned, but not insisted on, in the *Iliad*, where Paris is spirited away from the battlefield by Aphrodite to the bed of Helen and is chided for his sport by the ever serious Hector. The opposition between the erotic life and the most serious activity of politics, war, is the central message of this first scene, but it is never forgotten that this war as a whole is fought for Helen, so that the toils of war are means to the end of peaceful enjoyment of beauty. This robs of its intrinsic nobility the heroic fighting of an Achilles, and if Helen is a whore, then its instrumental nobility also disappears, as does the dignity of love. This is what Ulysses' action in the play accomplishes. It will ultimately restore peace, but peace that is lived merely for the sake of life, without the glory of war or the grace of eros.

Most of the love talk in this play rings false, and at best reminds us of a Ginger Rogers–Fred Astaire romance. Pandarus, the go-between, has a superficial urbanity and is a big booster of sexual connections, as opposed to either marriages or grand loves à la Romeo and Juliet or Antony and Cleopatra, where no go-betweens are needed. He is a character reminiscent of Viennese light opera. All these associations to literary types who have nothing to do with Homer show something about the range of Shakespeare's understanding of kinds of relatedness among men and women. When I was young I saw Tyrone Guthrie's production of *Troilus and Cressida*, and all I remember about it is that he made the meeting between the Greek and Trojan heroes in Act IV into a cocktail party, and it played very well as such. Shakespeare shows us real love, acted out solo by Troilus; gallantry, described by Rousseau as a parody of love, a routine form of passion with the certainty of consummation, represented by Pandarus, Helen, and Paris; and simple looseness and whorishness, played by Cressida and Diomedes. Ulysses is the only one who has nothing to do with anything of this, although he is a shrewd observer of it.

After Troilus' earnest but sophomoric love talk in scene i, we get Cressida playing the perfect coquette, prior to her descent into wantonness, with Pandarus. Whatever our prejudices about the appropriate behavior for men and women, we see immediately that someone who talks like Cressida cannot be serious. She plays the game of not taking Troilus seriously, and comparing him unfavorably with the other Trojan heroes who pass across the stage and upon whom she comments to Pandarus. And she proves her ecumenism by asking how Troilus would compare with the Greek Achilles, thus giving us a harbinger of her later conduct. She is much too experienced with sexual acts and sexual organs to be thought to be in any way innocent, or to respect their deeper meaning and mysteriousness. With her, it all hangs out. The innocent Juliet desires with purity and awe; Cleopatra knows it all and is witness to the qualitative superiority of Antony in the act. When Pandarus asserts that Helen loves Troilus, Cressida responds, "Troilus will stand to the proof" (I.ii.131).* Exclusivity is not within Cressida's ken, and she accepts with urbanity Troilus' presumed bodily movements when attended to by Helen. When Pandarus describes Troilus as a man of good nature and liberal education, Cressida remarks that these are the qualities of "a minced man; and then to be baked with no date in the pie, for then the man's date is out" (I.ii.261–262). Date refers to Troilus' intimate parts. It is not that Cressida speaks frankly in a "pagan" style; it is that this is all common currency for her. Hers is a lustful statement of what we know as the sexual teachings of Masters and Johnson. When, at the end of scene ii, she has a soliloquy in which she professes her seriousness about Troilus, one recognizes that it is a very relative seriousness indeed. She explains her coyness as a means to ensure Troilus' seriousness. By experience or report,

---

* All parenthetical citations in this chapter are to Shakespeare's *Troilus and Cressida*, ed. Kenneth Palmer, Arden Edition (1982; rpt. London: Routledge, 1989).

she knows that men are likely to despise what they get easily. She wants to appear difficult in order to maintain the upper hand after as well as before. She understands ordinary sexual relations to be a mere alternation of mastery and slavery. The disguising of her desires is only the better to satisfy them. This is a parody of a serious woman's reflections on her vulnerability. For her it is only an exercise in sexual economics. How different she is from Juliet, who recognizes the risk in giving herself so frankly, but accepts it. The acquisition of Troilus is merely an act of vanity. If she were to lose him, she would suffer from wounded pride, but not very much, because there are others where he came from.

II   The shift from Troy to the Greek camp in Act I, scene iii, is brutal. The Greek side is utterly unerotic, although there is a certain amount of brutish sex of the kind well known in armies. Here one finds a public debate about what is going wrong in the war. There are two ridiculous speeches, formal orations full of the commonplaces of public moral discourse, one by the king of kings, the shepherd of the host, Agamemnon, the other by his supporter and wise counselor, the aged Nestor (I.iii.1–54). These speeches are meant to hearten the host, but they are platitudes worthy of a current State of the Union address and could not arouse anyone. To a certain extent, they are cover-ups for the incompetence of the leaders. The difficulty, as is well known from the *Iliad*, is that Achilles is quarreling with the generals and keeping to his tent. But this is not mentioned by the speakers, who respond to the low morale in the army by explaining that the war is taking so long and costing so many men because of its place in the providential scheme of things. According to Agamemnon, this is Jove's way of testing the Greeks and showing what they are. Both speakers base themselves on a Stoic public morality, which, in distinguishing between virtue and fortune, makes human worth depend on the former while it holds out against the blows of the latter. True happiness is virtue, and the virtuous man will be happy and most himself when fortune is most hostile and he holds out against it. Dumb luck can procure all kinds of good things, including victory, but only those who have earned these things are truly admirable. It is an affront to human nature to say that what most counts depends on mere accident and not on the qualities of men. Therefore the current adversity is a blessing in disguise that will ensure the glory of the Greeks. Both Agamemnon and Nestor cheat a bit, probably unconsciously, in asserting that virtue is everything and then insisting that virtue will be rewarded by victory. Virtue should be its own reward, but this can never be believed by the multitude. Agamemnon and Nestor are simply haranguing the crowd in the hope that its members will learn patience.

Neither Agamemnon nor Nestor suggests that fortune can be conquered. It must be endured. Virtuous conduct is absolute and cannot alter itself to circumstances. There is in this an element of the noble classical teaching about what men must learn to live with, as opposed to modern teachings, which insist that they must be chameleons in thrall to chance. But this argument can easily turn into an excuse for idleness or stupidity. Machiavelli calls for the conquest of fortune in order to combat such passivity, which cripples the statesman's prudence and action. Although Machiavelli's generalization that what men call fortune is only the result of lack of foresight is not simply correct, there is much to it, and Ulysses' speech and the action later founded upon it are a page out of Machiavelli's book (I.iii.54–137).[3] His explanation of the problem the Greeks face amounts to an indictment of Agamemnon's inattention or incompetence, although he does not insist on making this conclusion public. Ulysses' rhetorical problem is that he has to persuade imprudent or unwise rulers of the proper course to follow, and they need not obey him as he must obey them, since his prudence or wisdom has no status in the order of things. Ulysses begins by praising Agamemnon for the position he holds and Nestor for his age. Agamemnon is king of kings because he is king of kings. There is no good reason for it. He was simply born to the position and the position must be respected. Nestor is respected for his age, since in traditional societies at least, age, simply because it is age, has authority. Reverence for the ancestral gives power, and the younger and wiser Ulysses must flatter Nestor. It is a rare thing when wisdom can peep through these thickets into the light of day, and a consummate rhetorician like Ulysses must present its case. He succeeds by making Agamemnon and Nestor indignant that their positions are being called into question by Achilles. Ulysses' wise plans succeed because he makes them appeal to the unwise passions of his hierarchical superiors.

And it is just the overturning of this rank order of things that Ulysses blames for the current discontents. Men do not obey their superiors. Why not? Because those superiors are incompetent and do not know how to control their inferiors. Actually, this means that the superiors are only conventionally superior. Ulysses, who knows how to right the situation and, in spite of the handicaps of his position, succeeds in doing so, is the only natural ruler on the scene. But natural rulers are not real rulers.

Ulysses dresses up his proposals in cosmic clothing. There is an order in all things, beginning with the heavens themselves, of which the human orders are a part. When priority is not observed, the whole falls into chaos. The good for everything is connected with this order of ruling and being ruled. This is a statement of the Great Chain of Being, about which so much nonsense has been written and which is supposed to have provided men with moral security prior to the Enlightenment. It is another one of those organic explanations of political relations that tell us about the way things ought to be but that are in fact only ideologies. Ulysses ridicules this cosmology as it is applied to human things. It is not unlike the divine order of things relied on by Richard II, which exempts him from having to accept the responsibilities of ruling.[4] The beehive is a favorite analogy to the political order, and Ulysses uses it. But in beehives nobody has to tell the workers what they must do or who the ruler of the hive is. There are no bees sulking in their tents. One might say that the hive is the model for the way things ought to be, but this is made questionable by the fact that nature does not produce human communities in the way that it does beehives. Human communities are much more a product of force and fraud exercised by rulers. Ulysses intentionally leaves his audience in some confusion as to whether the cosmic order itself has good and bad elements that require a cosmic ruler to control them or whether that order is permanent with all the parts ultimately contributing to a common good. This confusion has something to do with events such as killer storms that are not liked by human beings and seem to indicate disorder in the nature of things. If there were such disorder, men's rebelliousness and despair would have some justification. But if such storms are part of the good of the whole, then that whole is not necessarily friendly to human wishes or aspirations.

This beautiful cosmic picture amounts only to an indictment of the actual rulers. Ulysses presents high moral grounds, and immediately turns to a low and dishonest conspiracy to institute the proper relations of ruling and being ruled. Ulysses' speeches must be interpreted in the light of his deeds, and vice versa, for what appear to be low deeds become noble ones when understood in the light of the public good. This is Machiavelli's teaching.

Ulysses makes it clear that appetite, potentially "an universal wolf" (I.iii.121), must be subjected to power rather than allowed to make power its tool. This subjection comes from human action, not natural inclination. After his pompous elucidation of their difficulty, which has nothing to do with the fortune blamed by Agamemnon and Nestor, Ulysses gets down to cases and blames the couple, Achilles and Patroclus, as the source of rottenness in the state. This play, as I have said, ridicules almost all Greek things, and one of those well-known Greek things was pederasty. In this play, everyone takes Achilles and Patroclus to be sexually involved. The word "lovers" would be something of an overstatement, although these days the word is almost always an overstatement. This kind of sexual relation has none of the chivalry that one finds in the other kinds of connection in the play. It is treated as an expression of pride and factiousness (not particularly of lustfulness). This relationship will ultimately be politically useful, when Patroclus' death draws Achilles back into battle. The ancient view that couples of male lovers could be the source of conspiracy to overthrow tyranny, as in the case of Harmodius and Aristogeiton,[5] is not utterly rejected, if in any sense Agamemnon can be considered a tyrant.

Ulysses takes a very curious tack in describing the seditious speech of Achilles and Patroclus. He says Patroclus calls his jests "imitation." Ulysses appears to think that to call such subversive stuff imitation is a slander of imitation. Patroclus means by imitation what Aristotle means in the *Poetics*.[6] Patroclus is an artist whose art is subversive. If one looks closely at what Ulysses tells us about these "imitations," they are perfect representations of what we actually see in Agamemnon and Nestor—Agamemnon a blowhard, Nestor a doddering old fool. Patroclus does in bed with Achilles what Shakespeare does on the stage:

> With him Patroclus
> Upon a lazy bed the livelong day
> Breaks scurril jests,
> And with ridiculous and awkward action,
> Which, slanderer, he imitation calls,
> He pageants us. (I.iii.146–151)

Shakespeare's understanding of imitation can help to enrich the stiff modern interpretations of that term. Here the imitator produces a painting of a natural understanding of the political scenery, a painting that is subversive of the official understanding. The imitator imitates nature, as opposed to convention, and that is not so simple and stupid an activity as is often thought. Ulysses pretends to want to suppress, as do all tyrants in such cases, the mockery by Achilles' boyfriend, who thus amuses his senior partner. However, Ulysses silently but powerfully promotes an appreciation of the Greek leaders similar to Patroclus'. There is no doubt that imitation can be dangerous as well as salutary for civic morals. Only the loose and liberated are capable of such imitative art. The imitations are liberating, except for the fact that the audience, in this case Achilles, also needs imitations that would not simply flatter it. The imitator is limited by the nature of his audience, and that is indeed a problem for art, a problem that only the greatest of poets can solve. All the advantages and disadvantages of imitation as discussed by Plato are discussed in this passage. Shakespeare does for us, concerning all of what is handed down to us from Greece, what Patroclus does for Achilles concerning Agamemnon and Nestor.

The trouble with Achilles, according to Ulysses, is that he is all brawn and no brains. The heroes "count wisdom as no member of the war" (I.iii.198). They esteem only the battering ram and not the one who built it or the reason that guided the builder. This thought confirms the difficulty of Ulysses' position, which we have already noted. Unfortunately, poetry itself tends to share this point of view. It celebrates the glorious deeds of the heroes and not what does or should lie behind them. Strength and rage are made to seem to be the summit of human virtue and to contain within them all the other qualities. This is the reason why Ulysses, the wisest of the Greeks, must appear to be a very secondary character in the *Iliad*, and not a very sympathetic one at that. To repeat, wisdom is not in itself attractive. But Shakespeare in *Troilus and Cressida* brutally corrects the poetic preference for the warrior.

III The Greek council is interrupted by the arrival of Aeneas, another of the great Trojan romantics. He is there to propose single combat between Hector and any of the Greeks who is willing to face him. It is a challenge for lovers who assert the superiority in beauty and chastity of their beloveds over those of their opponents. Aeneas appears to believe in this nonsense, whereas it is utterly alien to the Greeks. It is pride in women that leads knights to fight. Rousseau said that men no longer dueled because they no longer believed in the chastity of women or its importance.[7] Aeneas is a man of the old order. Of course, there is a political intention underlying this challenge, because the Trojans expect Achilles to take it up and thus, perhaps, in this relatively cheap way, to end the war.

Aeneas' words bring out everything that is most ridiculous in Agamemnon and Nestor. Agamemnon assures Aeneas that some of his soldiers are lovers and hence will respond to the challenge, but promises, if there are none, he will do it himself. He does not say with whom he is in love. Clytemnestra is not mentioned. Nestor goes Agamemnon one better and declares himself ready to confront Hector, asserting that his dead wife is more beautiful than Hector's grandmother. This is rendered all the more hilarious by Patroclus' imitation of Nestor with palsied hand trying to put on a suit of armor. Aeneas responds to this with "Now heavens forfend such scarcity of youth." To which Ulysses, showing his own brand of humor, appends the single word "Amen" (I.iii.301–302).

As Aeneas goes off with Agamemnon for ceremonial visits in the Greek camp, Ulysses uses the occasion to speak to Nestor, who will presumably speak to Agamemnon, about the scheme he has conceived, connected with this challenge, to correct the chaos caused by Achilles. Simply, it is to set up a crooked lottery for the choice of the Greek combatant. The result of this lottery, which will appear to be chance but is actually controlled by Ulysses, will be that Ajax will go rather than Achilles. The defeat of Ajax would not, with Achilles still in reserve, completely dishearten the Greeks. If Ajax wins, so much the better. But in any case, Achilles will be humiliated and brought back into the order of things by the loss of reputation. Ulysses' shrewd management of this scheme is the theme of the rest of the play.

IV

The meeting of the Greek notables is paralleled by a meeting of the Trojan notables (II.ii) that, in its way, is a real deliberation about the purposes and conduct of the war. It all turns on Helen. Old Priam has received a communication from Nestor saying that the war can be ended simply by the return of Helen and that there will be no further demands. Priam is clearly inclined to meet Nestor's demand because he grieves for the terrible losses incurred during this war and fears for the very existence of Troy. The debate is initiated by the noble and decent Hector, who argues in favor of peace. He knows that no one can doubt his courage as a warrior, so he can confidently, without fear of accusation as a coward, take the side of ending the war on grounds of compassion. He concludes his first speech by saying that reason is on his side, and the entire debate becomes a disputation about the status of reason. This is, to say the least, an unusually theoretical, even academic, dispute in a play, especially a Shakespearean play. Of course, Shakespeare is not a crudely didactic writer who uses the stage as a platform for the direct propagation of his views. The arguments are a part of the action and are incomprehensible except in relation to the characters of those who enunciate them. They are opinions suitable to the individuals and teach us something about their dominant passions, which ultimately win out against any argumentation.

Hector's primary antagonist in the debate is the idealistic Troilus. He is unhesitating and equates fear and reason. No reason can be put in the scale to counterbalance the worth and honor of his father, the king. Reason is nothing against such "infinite" proportions. When he is chided by his older brother Helenus for being empty of reason, Troilus launches into a passionate attack on reason, which he identifies, like many of our contemporary men and women, with the mere calculating arm of self-preservation, which sees in glory only vanity. He stands foursquare for the noble and the splendid and seems certain that they cannot defend themselves against reason, if reason is credited. Reason cannot prove that the sacrifice of life in defense of a woman's honor or for the common good is preferable to safety and comfort:

> if we talk of reason,
> Let's shut our gates and sleep: manhood and honour
> Should have hare hearts, would they but fat their thoughts
> With this cramm'd reason: reason and respect
> Make livers pale, and lustihood deject. (II.ii.46–50)

It is almost as though Troilus and Shakespeare had read Hobbes, who was to write the *Leviathan* fifty years later, not to say thousands of years later. Troilus' position has just one weakness: he must use reason in his attack on reason, and this fact heightens the vulnerability of the position he enunciates.

Hector argues, in keeping with Troilus' description of the use of reason, that Helen is not worth the cost of keeping her, which forces Troilus into the position of saying that a thing is worth whatever it is valued at, that value is only subjective, a thing of men's imagination or fancy. This permits Hector to respond that esteeming must be related to the nature of what is esteemed if it is not to be mere folly:

" 'Tis mad idolatry / To make the service greater than the god" (II.ii.57–58). This gives Troilus the occasion to make his strongest point. We do not turn back to the merchant the silk we purchased from him when it is soiled. A wife no longer attractive is not thrown away. We make commitments, and we are supposed to stick by them. Here Troilus is closest to common opinion, and what he says is a truism, the logical extension of which is sticking by the Trojan decision to kidnap Helen in the first place. However, it is only an argument from common opinion, and one can very well sympathize with the desire to exchange old silks or old wives for new ones. Otherwise, one would have to agree with Troilus that the value of things is determined simply by our act of valuing them, and morality would be reduced to keeping one's promises not because they have a good result but merely because they are one's promises. This is the morality of Cephalus in the *Republic*. Reason most certainly challenges and tends to undermine the convictions that underlie ordinary morality. Troilus is a very moral man, and one can make no headway in getting him to doubt the desirability of being so. This is why he trusts Cressida. Ulysses is going to fix that for him, and thus destroy Troilus' dangerous idealism. This play treats reasonableness as a bleak thing, while casting in its lot with it.

The sham of rational debate is rudely interrupted by Cassandra's cries and her prophecies of doom for the Trojans. The conclusion of the debate, which is that the Trojans should stick by their guns no matter what, is heightened by Cassandra's reminder that this conclusion will bring about the disaster of Troy. Troilus' immediate response to her intervention is that the justness of acts is not determined by this or that outcome. Justice is an absolute. He is seconded by Paris, who understandably wants to keep Helen and use Troy and the Trojans to enable him to do so, unlike Hector and Troilus, who are disinterested. Priam intervenes to point out Paris' evident self-interest and thus to discredit his argument. Then, in one of the strangest and most hilarious moments in this play, Hector turns to Aristotle's authority to support his position (II.ii.167). Some interpreters have said that Shakespeare probably did not know that Aristotle came hundreds of years after Homer; they provide a counterpoint almost as funny as this scene is in itself. This entire deliberation is utterly implausible. When did heroes of any kind sit around and discuss first principles, let alone use philosophic texts to support their positions? Heroes are incarnate first principles that need no discussion. The very reflection on the status of heroic action undermines such action. It is only in the light of such reflection that you can have a strumpety Helen presented as the face "that launched a thousand ships."

The ultimate cause of the comic oddness of this play is the tension between heroic naíveté and reason. The intermediary between the two poles is constituted by the sexual nature of women. Hector points out that Paris and Troilus would not have been permitted by Aristotle to engage in serious moral deliberation. They can use words very well, but the proper use of words is connected to moral character. The young are too much under the sway of the passions to weigh those passions. The two passions that most affect young people, according to Hector's Aristotle, are pleasure and revenge. Paris seems to be more motivated by pleasure and Troilus by revenge, although this is not to say that Troilus' high-minded expectation of pleasure from love does not play a role in his arguments. Revenge is a passion closely allied to love of justice and is aroused by infractions of justice. Without its activity in the soul, justice would go unarmed. Perhaps the connection between pleasure and revenge has to do with protection of one's wife. Ulysses, confirming this interpretation, describes Troilus to Agamemnon as being:

> Manly as Hector, but more dangerous;
> For Hector in his blaze of wrath subscribes
> To tender objects, but he in heat of action
> Is more vindicative than jealous love. (IV.v.104–107)

These descriptions reflect a Platonic or Aristotelian tripartite division of the soul into appetite, anger, and reason. Having taken this scholastic high ground, Hector is able to argue on the basis of nature, the grounds of natural right to property. Helen was Menelaus' property and is therefore owed to him. It is a law of nature. The Trojans are breaking the laws of nature, and here Hector makes a sophisticated distinction between the laws of nature and the laws of nations (the *ius naturae* and the *ius gentium*). He concludes, "Hector's opinion / Is this in way of truth" (II.ii.189–190).

But, in an absolutely astounding and unexpected peripety, Hector chooses another way than that of the truth. After piling up good reason on good reason, he says, "Yet ne'ertheless . . ." His resolution is to keep Helen for the sake of all of their dignities. Thus he seals the doom of all of them. One could not present a starker picture of the contrariety of reason and heroic action. He reaches a conclusion without any arguments that have led to it. Shakespeare paints the folly of heroic choice, choice not preceded by deliberation, as vigorously as possible. Troilus, overjoyed by Hector's flip-flop, explains it by Hector's love of glory. The charming, thrilling love of glory is the villain of this play, and it works, in different ways, in both Hector and Achilles. No explaining it, but the heroes are distinguished above all other men by choosing glory over life. To put it in Nietzschean terms, here the noble man's instinct carries the day over slavish reason. Tragedy is somehow premised on the superiority of that instinct, and this is why *Troilus and Cressida* is not a tragedy. It ridicules, more or less brutally, the effect of that passion on men individually and on politics generally. Shakespeare does this in many other places, in particular in his portrait of Hotspur, the noble opponent of the cold and calculating Hal. No wonder that Ulysses, the bearer of the bad news about glory, is not very attractive to audiences who have a preference for the heroic. Socrates knows this and tries, ridiculously, in Plato's *Apology of Socrates*, to identify himself with the hero Achilles, who is the opposite of what he himself stands for.[8] This prejudice against reason explains why Ulysses' primary role in *Troilus and Cressida* is so often misunderstood by critics. The choice, as it presents itself to the popular imagination, is between dull, ignoble reasonableness and enspiriting deeds performed for the sake of the beautiful, whether one understands the word "beautiful" with respect to women of fair form or to glory.

V | These characteristics of heroic men are displayed in a much harsher light in the Greek camp (II.iii). Thersites, the low expression of the grievances of the vulgar against the alleged persecutions of the nobles, is transformed in this play into a fool in the medieval tradition, a clown who amuses kings and courts and has a right to say all the things nobody else is permitted to say because he does so in an amusing way and is not supposed to be taken seriously. He plays a role akin to that of Patroclus as described by Ulysses and resembles Shakespeare himself in his use of comedy. Thersites is an extreme of foul-mouthed destructiveness. He describes himself as related to the devil's envy. He is as low a character as one can imagine, and mad envy of greatness is surely his motive. But for precisely this reason, he is able to seek out the weaknesses of the great to whom he is intimately connected and by whom he is persecuted. Mostly, his theme is the lack of self-knowledge of the heroes in a play very much devoted to the problem of self-knowledge. Vanity is the great deceiver in telling us that we are what we are not and making us dependent on public opinion. The exchanges between Thersites and Ajax and Achilles reveal their pathological vanity. Thersites tells them that they are more fools than he is, and he makes it clear that Ajax is stupid and Achilles not too bright. They are needed to beat down the Trojans and are given an opinion of themselves that identifies their dumb physical prowess with all the qualifications of the noble and the good. Thersites tells them they are merely instruments manipulated by Ulysses and Agamemnon, although they think they are ends in themselves. These observations made in such distasteful ways by Thersites are confirmed in deed on the stage as Ulysses builds up Ajax's ego at the expense of Achilles. Achilles has reached such a summit of sensitivity to his position that his palate can no longer tolerate any nourishment other than that intended for the gods. Ajax's rivalry, his lust to equal or outdo Achilles, makes him into the dupe of dupes. One sees him inflating like a balloon as Ulysses pumps him up vis-à-vis Achilles. The comedy is very broad indeed as Ajax claims that he cannot understand what vanity is at the same time as he is, before our eyes, becoming the very exemplar of that vice.

| VI | The leading passions of Troilus and Achilles come to a climax in Act III, scenes ii and iii. In scene ii, Troilus and Cressida get together, make their declarations, and go off to |

their consummation. Troilus' speeches are beautiful and trusting, Cressida's coquettish. Pandarus brokers the whole thing with prurient attentiveness. There is no talk of marriage. The couple meet furtively, but *à la française*, without shame, and a rather large public is aware of what Pandarus has arranged. This situation heightens one's sense of Troilus' naive attachment to love. He seems to be utterly unaware of the circumstances, which indicate erotic levity on the part of Cressida. Troy is not like the Vienna of *Measure for Measure*. Troilus' father has been a solidly married man, and so is his brother Hector. But the moment is sufficient to satisfy expectations of eternity. Cressida complains when Troilus is about to go in the morning that all men leave too soon, not a remark made by an innocent. The scene ends with each of the three parties affirming his or her fidelity and predicting with confidence how posterity will view them. Troilus says that his name will be synonymous with truth; all men will say, "As true as Troilus." Cressida, strengthening her affirmation of her truthfulness, actually qualifies it by predicting that if she were to be false (a possibility in his own case that Troilus never even considered), her name will be idiomatic in "as false as Cressid." Pandarus casts Cressida's suggestion in a more neutral form and says, "If ever you prove false one to another," but then he accepts that it would be Cressida who would do the betraying: "let all constant men be Troiluses, all false women Cressids, and all brokers—between Pandars" (III.ii.180–202). Pandarus turns this into a prayer to which all say amen. It is a prayer that history has fulfilled, largely due to Chaucer and Shakespeare. The formula leaves Troilus as the only true person. And this is what the play teaches us. The question remains whether such unfounded idealism is simply admirable.

VII   Act III, scene iii details Ulysses' corruption of Achilles. It is in some aspects one of the most shocking deeds in all of Shakespeare, for it leads directly to the murder of Hector by an Achilles who no longer has any concern for nobility. Only if this deed serves a greater good can there be any justification of it. Ulysses has, in the best tradition of rhetoric, prepared Achilles to hear him. He has done so by engineering Ajax's choice as the Greek representative in the knightly combat and by orchestrating the snub of Achilles by the Greek chieftains. Achilles is confused and distressed and seeks out Ulysses on his own. He needs Ulysses and wants clarification. He is now ready to be instructed, although he does not expect what he is going to get. Achilles finds Ulysses reading. What an extraordinary conceit, a Homeric hero reading! And he is from all evidence reading *Alcibiades I*. This encounter reminds one of the procedure of Socrates. In general, Socrates attracts the students to him by engaging their vanity. They look for a kind of support from him, and he takes them on a long ride into unknown terrain to which they are receptive because of their need. No self-satisfied man is open to Socratic seduction. The first thing he does is to destroy that self-satisfaction. Socrates uses vanity while ridiculing it and attempting to destroy it. He furthers the Delphic command, "Know thyself," and points out that vanity is the great enemy to self-knowledge and the substitute for it. These students need Socrates for this moment because he gives the impression that only he can help them regain their loss of self-assurance.

Ulysses says that the writer he is reading claims that a man cannot "boast to have that which he hath" (III.iii.98) except by mirror-like reflection in others that returns his virtues to himself. There is a critical ambiguity here in that *boast* usually has the negative implication of an attempt to mislead others, although it appears to mean here merely a claim. Moreover, the formula leaves it unclear whether the man who does not possess such a mirror actually has his virtues nevertheless and is only unconscious of them, or whether the virtues are actually dependent upon being reflected in this way. Achilles is ultimately persuaded that the distinction is an empty one and that the virtues exist only in the reputation for them.

Achilles shows himself to be aware of this literature by actually quoting the sense of Socrates' observation in *Alcibiades I*:

> nor doth the eye itself,
> That most pure spirit of sense, behold itself,
> Not going from itself; but eye to eye oppos'd
> Salutes each other with each other's form;
> For speculation turns not to itself
> Till it hath travell'd and is mirror'd there
> Where it may see itself. This is not strange at all.
> (III.iii.105–111)[9]

Achilles knows the *Alcibiades* passage but has never been perplexed by it. Ulysses makes understanding it interesting for Achilles while perverting it. He leads Achilles into believing that what counts most or even exclusively is the image projected back on himself by the mirror and not the reality that is projected into it. Achilles was, up to this point, not a very appealing fellow, but he did have a salutary belief that he deserved his reputation because of his virtues. Such a man always remains a bit unsure whether the reputation for virtue is what is most important for him or whether virtue is its own reward, with reputation simply being a superadded pleasure. Aristotle discusses this question with great delicacy in the *Nicomachean Ethics* in the passage where he presents the proud man who claims great honors and deserves them. Such a man must have a certain contempt for honors, both because they come from individuals who are not his equals and hence not valid underwriters of his claims, and because virtue ought to be for its own sake.[10] There is in this description a fissure in the proud man's character that is important for the one who wishes to understand but on which it is imprudent to put too much stress, for fear that that character will split apart. This is the problem with the morality of the public man. Ulysses does put such stress on this historic model of the proud man and leads Achilles down the Machiavellian path that reputation for virtue is virtue, and that any means, fair or foul, are appropriate to getting that reputation. The plausibility of this conviction is attested to by the fact that Achilles kills Hector in the most ignoble way and gets perhaps the most brilliant reputation of any man in history by means of Homer's celebration of his deed. Shakespeare helps to correct this poetic abuse, but his correction does not lead in the direction of restoring the love of the kind of virtue professed by men like Achilles.

Ulysses speaks the best poetry in the play in the service of persuading Achilles of this terrible conclusion:

> Time hath, my lord, a wallet at his back
> Wherein he puts alms for oblivion,
> A great-siz'd monster of ingratitudes.
> Those scraps are good deeds past, which are devour'd
> As fast as they are made, forgot as soon
> As done. (III.iii.145–150)

These are truths, ugly truths, but truths. They are founded on Machiavelli's observations about gratitude and the bad character of men at large. Machiavelli suggests that the only way to deal with ingratitude is to keep men absolutely dependent on you so that your benefactions will never be in the past.[11] Of course, the critique of gratitude could very well lead to an abandonment of concern with public opinion altogether. This lack of concern for esteem would mean, however, a turn to private life or perhaps even to solitude, a position that at first blush would seem to diminish the scope of man and carries with it its own problems. Ulysses would seem to have drawn a similar conclusion from his analysis of the problem of fame. But he also knows perfectly well that there is a kind of man who has such a hunger for fame that all the critiques in the world fail to convince him. Such a man is Achilles, and the critique has the effect only of severing virtue from glory and making glory the only end. This is, not too surprisingly, the ultimate though unintended effect of Socrates' efforts in *Alcibiades I*. Socrates is dealing in Alcibiades with another loose cannon. His comparison of the eye of another with the soul of another is intended to make Alcibiades care about Socrates' opinion. He is trying to persuade Alcibiades to seek self-knowledge in company with a philosopher. But he also knows that Alcibiades is another man with the political hunger who turns to the city for the confirmation of his self. Alcibiades remains attached to Socrates but, at best, only halfway. Socrates ruins him by releasing him from the constraints that unconsciousness of moral ambiguity would have exercised over him and by reducing the dignity in his own eyes of the public acclaim that he so avidly seeks. Alcibiades clearly imitated Achilles, as did all men of heroic ambition, from Alexander to Caesar to Napoleon, whereas the Homeric hero to whom Socrates was regularly likened was Ulysses/Odysseus. Shakespeare presents Ulysses and Achilles imitating Socrates and Alcibiades who imitated Ulysses and Achilles.

Ulysses' point is seconded, in as touching an expression of affection as one finds on the Greek side, by Patroclus, who uses the epithet "sweet" in addressing Achilles. He tells Achilles that he, Patroclus, considers himself responsible for Achilles' loss of reputation, his affection for Patroclus having effeminated him (III.iii.215–224).

At the end of Ulysses' instruction of Achilles, he says that it was known that Achilles was keeping apart from the war because he was carrying on an affair with a Trojan princess. Achilles' motives in this play are unclear. The quarrel with Agamemnon over Briseis is not mentioned in the play, and Achilles' sulking is earlier attributed by Ulysses to his unwillingness to respect the rank order of things. Here Ulysses attributes it to a kind of treasonable connection across the lines of war, one that suits the medieval chivalry anachronistically connected with the Trojan heroes in particular. Ulysses reveals that the Greek intelligence system has knowledge of Achilles' secret deeds. He does this to show that the state is everywhere and one cannot hope to avoid its gaze. This love affair plays only a tiny role in the plot, and the death of Patroclus extinguishes it completely. Ulysses' instruction makes Achilles into a monster of glory, acquired by the reputation for virtuous deeds, not by virtue. It also shows him that his glory will have to be won in the context of the power of the Greek community. Ulysses liberates Achilles from moral concern and lowers his godlike pretensions.

Achilles' immediate response is an arousal of lust, to kill Hector. This is Achilles' authentic passion.

> I have a woman's longing,
> An appetite that I am sick withal,
> To see great Hector in his weeds of peace. (III.iii.236–238)

	Act IV is devoted to bringing the two great couples—
VIII	Troilus and Cressida, and Achilles and Hector—together
	in the same action. They represent the two interesting

motives in this play, love and glory, and they both are debunked by
Ulysses. War, in its unerotic necessity, separates Troilus and Cressida. Her father, Calchas the soothsayer, has defected to the Greeks
and wants his daughter back with him. *Raison d'état* dictates an exchange of the girl for the hero Antenor. All the seamy sides of a
Parisian-style erotic intrigue are again played out. It so happens that
Troilus is, at the moment when Cressida must be exchanged, in a
compromising position at her place. These are all men of the world,
and they get Troilus out without a public scandal. It is always the
comedy of this play that Troilus is faithful and wildly romantic in
settings and with kinds of persons more appropriate to erotic farces.
Troilus' farewell exhortations to Cressida are truly enchanting,
whereas her responses are only coy (IV.iv.12–137). His potential
jealousy of her is of the noble kind: he fears the Greeks will be more
attractive than he is and immediately confronts the insolent
Diomedes, who is sent to take possession of Cressida, and who
taunts Troilus with threats of fooling around with his beloved.

In scene v both Cressida and Hector are seen among the Greeks.
The supposedly heartbroken Cressida is liked by all the Greek heroes, with a single exception, Ulysses. The Greeks are full of prurient
interest; she loves the whole thing and seasons it with ridicule of
Menelaus, who, according to Pierre Bayle, was "the most debonair
cuckold of antiquity."[12] This kissing feast is promoted by Ulysses.
He gets her to ask him to kiss her, and then refuses her request.

ULYSSES: I do desire it.

CRESSIDA: Why, beg two.

ULYSSES: Why then, for Venus' sake, give me a kiss
When Helen is a maid again, and his.

CRESSIDA: I am your debtor; claim it when 'tis due.

ULYSSES: Never's my day, and then a kiss of you. (IV.v.48–52)

Ulysses, avid to discredit the romantic motives, has orchestrated
this little scene, and then humiliates Cressida by his refusal. Ulysses,
just as he is the only one with a general awareness of the whole
situation and with plans to change it, is a perfect reader of souls and
their characters. His implicit and explicit opinions of Agamemnon,

Nestor, Achilles, Hector, and Troilus are always perfectly on the mark. When Cressida exits, Ulysses makes a moralistic speech for the benefit of everyone there about Cressida's evident and disgusting sluttishness.

Then arrives the always gentle and enthusiastic Hector. He engages in all the formulas of knightly politeness, in which he actually believes. Aeneas speaks to Achilles of Hector's politeness and tells him that Hector cannot harm the foolish Ajax because Ajax is half Trojan. Achilles, continuing his erotic language about death, says, "A maiden battle, then?" (IV.v.87). Only the entry of the sword into the body interests him. The blurring of natural and historical differences, so characteristic of this play, makes what should be a climactic fight to the death between the two chosen representatives of the warring sides into a ceremonial gesture between chivalrous knights bound by blood without intention of doing harm. The great fight lasts only a second, a bit like the last trial by combat in *Richard II*.[13] It turns into a pageant with the exchange of the most exquisite compliments. The Greeks are perfect hypocrites in all this; Hector is a monster of sincerity.

As Ulysses has just dispelled the shadows of romantic illusion surrounding Cressida, Achilles chills us with his brutality, rendered much more extreme by the atmosphere of chivalric gentility in war. He comes in and looks at Hector as a butcher looks at a cow. Without any adornment he wonders how he will slaughter Hector, where on his body he will make the perforation out of which his spirit will fly, how he will dismember him. This is a rhetoric to which a Hector is unprepared to respond.

IX   Act V is devoted to Cressida's infidelity to Troilus and to Hector's death. The first of these is the darkest of the dark scenes in *Troilus and Cressida*. Ulysses, fully aware of what is going on at Calchas' tent, takes Troilus to it and gives him "ocular proof" of Cressida's betrayal. Ulysses subjects him to a terrible torture. The dog of envy, Thersites, who has just called Patroclus Achilles' male whore, slinks along to add a filthy counterpoint and conclude the scene with "Lechery, lechery, still wars and lechery! Nothing else holds fashion" (V.ii.193–194). Nothing could show us more clearly Ulysses' intention to demystify the romantic ideals. The torture of jealousy here is as intense as that in *Othello*. The difference is that the jealousy corresponds to the real deeds of Cressida. We do not find ourselves rooting for the couple and hoping against hope that it will prove to be a misunderstanding. Here we recognize that Troilus is a fool, a noble fool, for believing in Cressida. He is truly alone while the whole meaning of his life is staked on his being with her.

Our sentiments are complex when we contemplate this scene. On the one hand, it is difficult not to pity Troilus and to wish that it would all work out for the best for him. But we are persuaded of Cressida's falseness and know that a man should not live in false trust. Something like this excuses Ulysses' cruelty in sticking Troilus' nose into the mess. He may not be doing it for Troilus' sake, but it is not an unmixed act of cruelty. Othello does not believe in his beloved enough. Troilus believes too much in his. Under his own eyes he sees his beloved give his sleeve to his rival, whereas Othello had to fill in the argument that bridged the gap between his giving Desdemona his handkerchief and its possession by his supposed rival. Each one's heart was attached to the piece of cloth and was ripped out by its misappropriation. Troilus is made to pay a very high price for his opinion that "What's aught but as 'tis valued?" (II.ii.53). The noble soul creates value. But here an overwhelming reality makes it impossible to maintain a love that is not confirmed by its object.

When Troilus has been witness of Diomedes with Cressida, Ulysses says, "All's done, my lord," and Troilus agrees that it is. And Ulysses asks, "Why stay we then?" Troilus is compelled to stay in order to meditate on the meaning of what he has seen with his two eyes. What we witness is an epic culmination of the play's deepest theme, the quarrel between desire and reason. Troilus has always discussed his love as though it were equal or superior to the love of the gods. Belief or faith is his profoundest longing, although for him it is faith in the imaginations that emanate from his eros. He says "credence" gives birth to a hope that is "so obstinately strong" that it "doth invert th'attest of eyes and ears." He concludes on the basis of this logic of the heart with the question, "Was Cressid here?" Ulysses dryly responds that he cannot conjure. Troilus insists he is not mad, but goes on to exhort disbelief of what he has just seen for the sake of "womanhood" (V.ii.114–132). As we have seen, Troilus argues on the premises of moral commonplaces that he cannot bear to call into question. Here the consequence he draws from Cressida's infidelity is the infidelity of all women, especially the infidelity of mothers. The whole family moral order, which depends on the belief in the chastity of women, is collapsing. Of course, Troilus' logic is mad, taking the particular as the same thing as the general. At best, he could say, "Some are, some aren't." But this is a profound reflection of the logic of the heart or love in that when we love, we stake everything on an individual or a particular. If this particular is not the perfection itself of virtue, there is no virtue, and love as we know it disappears. Troilus has already declared himself the enemy of reason and is aware of love's inner necessity. Ulysses coldly accepts the rational conclusions from Cressida's behavior, but refuses to extend its meaning to all women. But Ulysses is emphatically not a lover. There is a war between reason and love. Unequivocal and unqualified love wants to attach a meaning to particular attachment, which reason can never allow.

Troilus piles up questionable premise upon questionable premise and tries to draw a necessary conclusion.

> If beauty have a soul, this is not she;
> If souls guide vows, if vows be sanctimonies,
> If sanctimony be the gods' delight,
> If there be rule in unity itself,
> This is not she. O madness of discourse,
> That cause sets up with and against itself!
> Bifold authority! where reason can revolt
> Without perdition, and loss assume all reason
> Without revolt. This is, and is not, Cressid. (V.ii.137–145)

This is a true conclusion. All of us who are particulars are and are not, partaking of being and nothing at the same time. But love insists on the universality and eternity of its object, and to the extent that its object is another human being, love is therefore either an illusion or a disappointment. True logic leads to human isolation, as one sees in the case of Ulysses himself, who is detached from his rulers and has no visible object of aspiration and no connections of love or friendship. Troilus' rejection of reason is based on a kind of insane attachment to the principle of noncontradiction, which is the very foundation of reason, and to the principle of causality. No speech in Shakespeare states the intellectual premises of love with such clarity. It is truly mad reasoning, but it is reasoning. If men were to turn their gaze to objects that do not admit of contradiction, there would be no problem. The question is whether one can love such objects. Ulysses can contemplate this scene without any need for self-contradiction and accept it with equanimity; he stands for the intransigent application of real reason to all things. But he is hateful to lovers, that is, to most of Shakespeare's audience. I do not think that he wishes to hurt Troilus. There is evidence that he pities him. What Troilus learns causes him to become angry and furious. He cannot learn merely to contemplate, as does Ulysses. The destruction of his ideal makes it impossible for him to live halfway sensibly as he did before. His noble enthusiasm for Cressida, and thus for Helen, and thus for war, has been effectively removed. Ulysses certainly believes that this war is unreasonable and does what he can to end it. *Troilus and Cressida* is the only Shakespearean play where reason, understood philosophically, is the theme.

X   Next we see the honest and idealistic Trojans prepare for war, with Priam, Andromache, and Cassandra trying to keep their men at home while Hector is unshakable in his dedication to honor. Troilus supports him while chiding him for being too gentle, himself declaring for all-out war without fair play and without pity. His only concern now is vengeance, a particular vengeance that he never gets.

The high-mindedness of the Trojans is unrelieved, and off they go to battle, perfect gentlemen and knights. Hector encounters Achilles, who has boasted so shamelessly of his superiority to his prey, but who now gets winded and excuses himself from the fray, alleging that he is out of shape and will come back when he is in better form. Hector agrees to this because he lives by the book of chivalry, and how one wins is more important than winning. Shakespeare presents this in the style of exposé. "You know the story. Now I will give you the story behind the story." After a scene where Hector kills a Greek in beautiful armor under which he finds a "Most putrefied core" (V.viii.1), which is symbolic of what we learn about the Greeks in this play altogether, Hector disarms himself. Achilles appears and then tells his troop of Myrmidons to surround Hector. When they do, Achilles orders them to kill him. It is, as I have said, a murder, a dastardly deed by Achilles and the opposite of the kind of death wished for by Hector. Cressida and Achilles belong together in their trampling on the dignity of love and war. Achilles ties Hector to his horse and drags him around in ignominious triumph. Achilles is very much what Socrates says he is in the *Republic*.[14] He beats up on a corpse. But the successful deed of getting rid of Hector, so long as its nature is not known, guarantees Achilles eternal fame. He got a good poet. Troilus screams in despair at Hector's loss and says that the war is over. In fact, it endured much longer, but Shakespeare treats it as though it ended here.

Shakespeare's very rough treatment of the spirited, combative man is, as I have noted, not exclusive to this play. He ridicules Hector's dressing up of the harsh thing in itself with the formulas of chivalry, and he more than ridicules the butchery by Achilles. The poetic prejudice in favor of the spirited, heroic man is subjected to a powerful critique by Shakespeare, just as it is by Plato. Warlike men are necessary, and like most everyone else, I suppose, they have their specific illusions that will enable them to believe in what they are doing. But the world is distorted by illusions, and a wise man must see through them. As far as it is in his power, he tries to mitigate the effect of these illusions. With boyish playfulness Hotspur is really just looking for someone to kill. The much more rational Hal makes fun of Hotspur's dining on deaths. Hal is perfectly willing to kill someone when it is reasonable to do so, and as a matter of fact he kills one notable person, Hotspur. In so doing, he is able to appropriate all of Hotspur's reputation at one stroke. This is reason, or the reasonableness of the political man.[15]

This leads us to a look at Ulysses. He is, I argue, the hero of the play. As we have seen, he does not always appear to be so because he represents something that is not to the taste of the audiences of tragedy or comedy: reason. This play is not satisfying to our moral sense. Achilles is not punished for his evil deeds; neither is Cressida. The only thing that rights the balance is the reasonable and just scheme of Ulysses, who takes the poetry, and hence the dangerous poison of its idealism, out of this war. He accepts it as an ugly business that reflects much of human nature and wishes to return to simple, if not honorable, peace. He is a modest presence in the play; but from his first appearance, he is not only saying the sensible things but manipulating the outcome with his profound sense of the politically necessary and his capacity to know and motivate men's souls. Ulysses does not produce a splendid or even especially just solution, but it is effective so long as wisdom does not become megalomaniacal and believe it can assure just and noble solutions to human problems. Ulysses does not hold that there are just gods upholding a providential order. What is going to be done has to be done by men with all the limitations of men, sometimes masquerading under higher apparent authorities. Ulysses' political scheme conduces, by deeds of questionable justice, to the common good, if one does not treat the common good too grandly. His goal seems to be peace, simple peace, without any need for gilding it, where a man like Ulysses, as shown by his deeds in the *Odyssey*, can take the center of the stage.

What Shakespeare has done in *Troilus and Cressida* is to subject classical heroism to a microscopic analysis. He would seem to underwrite the Christian notion that the Greek virtues are but splendid vices. He does not merely parody love and war, but from a comic perspective shows that it is imaginations and slaughters on which they live. But Shakespeare, unlike the Christian detractors of antiquity, does not join in their criticism of the pride of reason. After the heroes have been put in an acid bath, they all dissolve except for the one man among the Homeric heroes who represents wisdom. In this sense the play is a vindication of the Greeks over the Trojans, and antiquity over modernity. The Greeks have one man who singly counterbalances their ugliness. He is Ulysses *cum* Socrates. As I have said, such a figure is not very suitable to the stage. In Prospero we see a wise man whose gaiety covers over a hardly bearable vision of life. In Ulysses we see the wise man dealing with real life, and it can be a most disheartening experience. The gods and the heroes are unmasked, and the glory that was Greece turns out not to be glory at all. This can appear to be a combination of Enlightenment-style debunking and Célinesque nihilism. But Ulysses really practices neither, for the bleak surroundings serve to set off the beauty and dignity that belong to wisdom alone and to a way of life devoted to truth without illusion. I cannot resist comparing Ulysses to Thucydides, who chronicles without hope the decay of his whole splendid world and gets an austere pleasure from it. It is a solitary life, separated from the common goals and aspirations, one that is too detached for most men to bear. Thucydides represents the theoretical life in its opposition to all the charms of practical life, and so does this isolated Ulysses, who is among the Greeks but not really of them. Shakespeare puts him next to Troilus, the honest and appealing lover, as they together contemplate the spectacle of human vice. Troilus is too involved to enjoy it or accept it. Ulysses is the opposite. There is no question that love and its promises of the unity of two human beings become strongly doubtful from the perspective of reason. What human beings can really share without potential opposition is only reason, and that is pretty thin stuff on which to nourish passionate men and women. Shakespeare's plays about lovers have a kind of irony that does not suit the Romantic temperament. Love is wonderful, but the reasonable observer cannot help seeing through it, at least a bit.

The play ends with a lighthearted address to the audience by

Pandarus. In *Troilus and Cressida* very low people, like Patroclus and Thersites, are compared to the poets, and so is Pandarus, who is the only singing poet in the play. He is the pander who makes the connection between poetic imitation and the audience. Somehow a cynical reflection on the bad reputation of poets and actors would seem to follow appropriately from having seen this play. "O traitors and bawds, how earnestly are you set awork, and how ill requited. Why should our endeavour be so loved and the performance so loathed?" (V.x.37–40). Pandarus deals in a tainted kind of love that pleases most people as perhaps does the obscene side of Shakespeare. Pandarus ends by announcing that he and his audience both groan from venereal complaints, bitter accompaniments of the trade of love. In two months he promises his will will be made:

> Till then I'll sweat and seek about for eases,
> And at that time bequeath you my diseases. (V.x.56–57)

These are the last words of the play.

11. *The Winter's Tale*

The Winter's Tale takes place in Sicily and Bohemia at an uncertain date, and its characters seem to partake in equal measure of the religion and life of old Greece and Rome and of Christianity. It begins with the celebration of a classical-style friendship between two kings, Leontes and Polixenes, who have known each other from childhood and have a perfect harmony in their reciprocal admiration of each other's virtues. This very short beginning conveys the joy of confidence and trust combined with the enthusiasm of friendship. Human association for these two men is natural and a peak of pleasure. They do not use or need each other, at least not in any narrow sense. They understand each other, share views, and simply want to be together, although their kingly responsibilities keep them separate most of the time.

This glimpse of perfect friendship in action is immediately disturbed by an inexplicable and unmotivated storm of jealousy that destroys the atmosphere of trust and the friendship. Jealousy means doubt about the sexual fidelity of one to whom a person is attached.[1] Leontes suddenly comes to believe that his friend and his wife have had illicit relations. Leontes is both friend and husband, but there has never before been any tension between the two kinds of attachment. His wife, Hermione, seems to be just like him and to have adopted his friend as her friend. The openness and lack of reserve characteristic of friendship are not usual between a married woman and a man not her husband. But their friendship is apparently part of the old friendship between her husband and his friend. The sudden explosion of angry jealousy brings to light a problem about a married woman's blameless friendship with a man. The suspicions aroused make it impossible to have that confidence required for men and women to be together without tincture of erotic involvement. Moreover their new condition of marriage also raises doubts about the possibility of friendship between married men.

The arousal of jealousy, which is so sudden and seems such a mystery, needs interpretation. Leontes' jealousy is unlike that experienced by Troilus, whose beloved is guilty, and is akin to that of Othello, whose beloved is not guilty. Leontes' case, however, is much more extreme than that of Othello, who must be seduced into his passion by a subtle devil. Leontes' whole vision of the world changes in an instant and without provocation. Shakespeare usually treats this kind of terrible passion as a mistake on the part of the man. *Cymbeline* gives us another such case. What is so unusual about Leontes in this play is the speed of his change from trust to certitude of disloyalty. As soon as this takes place, the old world of friendship disappears. There is reconciliation and a happy ending, but it does not restore the old world, and it gives a definite primacy to marriage over friendship. Shakespeare seems preoccupied with the distrust in men about the genuineness of women's attachment and what it leads to. Shakespeare is fully aware of the difficulty of real unity between human beings, even, or especially, in love matters. But it is indicative of his temper that he concentrates so much on the unfoundedness of such suspicion, and hence affirms the possibility of unconstrained connectedness.

This inexplicable transformation is almost miraculous since one cannot treat Leontes as a sickly, weak soul, prone to suspicions. In Shakespeare one can almost always get guidance as to the character of a man by the kind of friends he has and how they behave with him. Not only is Leontes' wife a most remarkable woman, with whom he seems to have had up to now a free and open relationship, unstained by doubts, but he has also evidently been faithful and irreproachable in friendship. There are no villains in Leontes' entourage. On the contrary, they are all honest and forthright persons who serve loyally because of the character of the man they serve and are used to speaking with him on a level of frank equality. He has no flatterers, which makes it all the more difficult for him to follow the logic of his jealousy, because no one supports him in it. I can clarify the problem of his jealousy only by what immediately precedes it

(I.ii.1–108).* Leontes has failed to persuade Polixenes to prolong his stay with them in Sicily. He turns the task of persuasion over to Hermione, who succeeds. After she has done so, she starts asking questions about what the two friends were like when they were young. Polixenes tells her of their perfect joy in each other's company, which was most characterized by innocence. Polixenes makes it clear that he means by innocence sexual innocence and refers, pagan though he is, to the doctrine of original sin. Prior to sexual development they could have answered to heaven, except for the guilt associated with that sin that all men inherit, the Fall. Hermione slyly picks up on this and suggests that he, and perhaps her husband too, have "tripp'd since" that time of innocence. Polixenes rather ambiguously replies that there have been temptations since "the stronger blood" was born in them. She playfully returns to the assault and says that Polixenes' wife and she will answer for any sins connected with them. She refers to their married sexual relations here as sins, but affirms that there will be no punishment for them if there were no other sins committed with others. The formulation of her statement ("that you slipp'd not/With any but with us") could be interpreted to mean that it would be all right for Polixenes to have had sexual relations with her, although this is clearly not her intention. But she is playing around with an erotic theme, the difficulty of taming men's desires. It is not certain that Leontes hears these remarks. He has evidently been walking at some distance in order to allow his wife to persuade Polixenes to stay. He enters the conversation again at the end of this colloquy. When Hermione tells him that Polixenes will stay, he responds that she has never spoken to better purpose. She then plays a coquettish game with him, asking, "Never?" She talks about the nature of women and how they may be ridden more effectively with soft kisses than with spurs. She insists that he repeat what she said at the end of his long and hard courtship, "I am yours for ever." She thus links her persuasion of Polixenes to her giving herself to Leontes. Her first good speech "earn'd a royal husband," the second, a friend. With that, she grasps Polixenes' hand.

And then it happens. Suddenly Leontes lives in a world of temptations and betrayals. Every deed and gesture has an explicit sexual meaning. Lust is everywhere, and it cannot be controlled by the rules

* All parenthetical citations in this chapter are to Shakespeare's *The Winter's Tale*, ed. J. H. P. Pafford, Arden Edition (1963; rpt. London: Routledge, 1988).

of morality. The doubts about sexual attraction, which are always legitimate because thought and the movements of the sexual organs are not simply subject to will, become certitudes, and the whole world must be corrected. The first thoughts are about the legitimacy of one's children, then the ridicule attracted by a cuckold, a ridicule earned by the prejudice that a real man must be attractive to his wife always and exclusive of all others. Then there are thoughts of revenge, dignified as claims of simple justice. There is the fear that the whole world gives witness to the adultery, but there is also the certainty that those who do not see what he sees must be guilty of blindness and faithlessness. Everything is in the belief of the king, and all the subjects must support the king's belief or be subjected to the most terrible punishments. What we see is sexual doubt turning gentle and legitimate kingship into a tyranny that resembles the demands of a jealous god, rather than those of natural human attachment. As is always the case with love suspected of betrayal, the principle of noncontradiction is called into question. The belief that something can come from nothing seems to be required. Othello suffers this delusion, as does Troilus. Nothing else can account for such transformations from virtue to sin. Reason no longer rules the world; tyranny is the only way to forestall chaos. There is no solid center, opposites "co-act," and saint and sinner emerge from the same source. These are the mad affections of the man whose life is founded upon the necessity of another person's being always attracted to him.

The jealousy of Leontes follows its course. He orders his minister Camillo to poison Polixenes. Camillo suffers the conflict of the man who owes loyalty to a tyrant and is commanded to do something immoral. He leaves Leontes to follow Polixenes. When Leontes' tyrannical passion is deprived of the satisfaction of killing Polixenes, it turns on Hermione, whom he imprisons, and then on the daughter born to Hermione in prison, whom he orders to be abandoned to the elements in a remote spot outside his kingdom. He stages an inquisition accusing Hermione not only of adultery, but of conspiracy with Polixenes and Camillo to overthrow him. She has only her own testimony to defend herself against unfeeling and unhearing tyranny. Her sole supporter is the fierce Paulina, who will be her apostle and avenging spirit. Suspicions and unknowable intentions are more important than any deeds. A premise that all human beings, and especially women, are hot and unreliable has been established. This awareness makes trust impossible for those who care. Trials and prisons are the only remedy. Sexual desire, like heresy, an unknowable disposition of the mind, becomes the central object of justice.

When, in the midst of Hermione's trial, Leontes' ambassadors interrupt the proceedings to announce that the Delphic oracle proclaims her chaste and everyone else innocent, he simply dismisses the news. He has a new source of certitude that replaces his belief in the Delphic god. Immediately he is punished by the announcement of the death of his young prince, Mamillius, the only one of whom he is sure. Hermione faints. The death of the innocent boy causes the extinction of the tyrant's jealousy as quickly as it came into being. But it is too late. Hermione also dies, and the baby daughter, abandoned at his command, is lost. Now the atmosphere of Sicily is guilt and repentance, and Paulina becomes the minister of a cult devoted to the dead queen and her son. Leontes' tears at their chapel will be his recreation and his exercise.

Antigonus, charged by Leontes to get rid of the baby, deposited her on the Bohemian coast, and was himself immediately eaten by a bear. But here in Bohemia in a rustic setting that defies time and the distinctions between ancients and moderns, Shakespeare prepares the healing of the Sicilian wounds with the salubrious aid of nature. The characters here are beyond or beneath the changes of regimes and religions, and the necessary customs of the courts that differentiate them. We have a shepherd and his clownish son and a singing thief who has the same name and habits as Odysseus' grandfather.[2] Here, innocence and the spirit of comedy provide the seedbed for an overcoming of the tragic darkness of both the Sicilian and the Bohemian courts.

II Act IV is devoted almost exclusively to this pastoral dream of reconciliation with nature, and here eroticism frolics untainted by its fearful doppelgänger, jealousy. Time, as a chorus, introduces Act IV in a play where the distinctiveness of various times in human history is treated so cavalierly by Shakespeare. This provides a helpful guide to Shakespeare's understanding of that terrible master to which our lives are subject.

> since it is in my power
> To o'erthrow law, and in one self-born hour
> To plant and o'erwhelm custom. Let me pass

The same I am, ere ancient'st order was,
Or what is now receiv'd. I witness to
The times that brought them in; so shall I do
To th' freshest things now reigning, and make stale
The glistering of this present, as my tale
Now seems to it. (IV.i.7–15)

This is exactly the opposite of the way our contemporaries would think of time, which seems to be a co-conspirator with our necessary subordination to our own time. Time, as it expresses itself here, permits the playwright to see the coming into being and passing away of laws and customs, and hence to liberate himself from and laugh at them. Those laws and customs are not consubstantial with time. The spirit of this play is not to take the present, in particular here the new order of things in Sicily, seriously or to be overwhelmed by becoming and decay, but to look for a permanent standard and satisfactions outside the ephemeral systems of belief. Plays are subject to the immediate tastes of the audience, but, as Shakespeare indicates, the true playwright can teach an audience to despise the current attractions. Shakespeare, in such works as *Troilus and Cressida*, *Cymbeline*, and *The Winter's Tale*, plays very fast and loose with what we would call history, although as we have seen in *Romeo and Juliet* and *Antony and Cleopatra*, he can also stay very close to the real spirit of a particular time and place. *The Winter's Tale* and *Cymbeline* are among Shakespeare's very last plays, and here he permits himself the wildest flights of his kind of historical imagination. The very last play, *The Tempest*, is altogether the opposite, in that it maintains the classical unities of time and place, perhaps more rigorously than any other Shakespearean play. But this exception would only confirm the late freedom of Shakespeare from constraints normally imposed on us by the age in which we live, because in *The Tempest* we have only a dream, literally a play, which is outside of any historical situation, although it is related to one, Renaissance Italy. All three of these plays allow Shakespeare to show forth his ripest wisdom, looking at the laws and regimes of nations and the coming into being and passing away of religions from a perspective beyond history. Time, for Shakespeare, contrary to our belief, is not the destroyer of nature as a standard, but nature's accomplice in revealing what is always as opposed to what is merely made by man. This discourse of Time about time is the introduction to the great celebration of nature.

| | Act IV, scene iv, is one of the longest in Shakespeare, al-
| III | most 850 lines. In it we find a pastoral romance complicated
| | by reflections on nature and convention. A prince loves a
shepherdess, and there are two plots to use the pair of lovers, Camillo's to get back to Sicily, and Autolycus' to better himself ("all the
world loves a lover," because lovers are so easy to use). The central
theme throughout is the innocent, passionate, and restorative love
between Florizel, the son of Polixenes, and the shepherdess Perdita,
the lost daughter of Leontes, now grown up. This affair belongs with
those of Romeo and Juliet and of Ferdinand and Miranda as an
example of simple, uncomplicated love at first sight without the
slightest admixture of vanity on either side, a mutual attraction of
beautiful youngsters lucky enough to have found each other before
less happy experiences have made them distinguish between body
and soul in erotic matters. With them there is an eternity in the
present, a forgetfulness of what time will do to them as well as to
nations and their laws. Romeo and Juliet in the setting of Renaissance Christian Verona almost necessarily end in tragedy. Ferdinand
and Miranda have an untroubled courtship and prospects for an
untroubled future under the guidance of Prospero. Their marriage
will result in the union of two realms, Milan and Naples. Florizel and
Perdita are helped by nature, by the former's intense self-control,
fortune, and a bit of wisdom contributed by Camillo. For them it all
works out, but their success is less realistic than Romeo and Juliet's
failure; the atmosphere of a fiction is maintained throughout. As in
The Tempest, all petty motives are banished by the intensity of the
love of the beautiful shared by the two partners.

The cloud on Florizel and Perdita's horizon is formed by the conflict between the conventional inequality of the two and the authority
of Florizel's father to enforce that inequality. The greatest loves are
founded on inclination that is free of the constraints of propriety and
duty. The beauties of the body obviously leap over all artificial fences.
The prejudice of fathers is that breeding determines the soul and cannot be properly judged by youngsters whose bodily passions lead
them. Of course the fathers, especially when kings, are really less interested in the satisfactions of their children's love than in the succession to their kingdoms. This is a point Rousseau makes,
unequivocally taking the side of the children, if they are properly educated.[3] Shakespeare, who is usually respectful of the conventions,
vigorously sides here with Florizel. But the father undeniably has a
point. Ordinarily a boy who meets a country lass and becomes infat-

uated requires some restraint in order to be sure that he has found a suitable mate. In one of those twists that allow Shakespeare to preserve the conventional moral order, the object of Florizel's passion is really a princess. The issue is not noble versus commoner, but how to recognize a princess. Florizel appears to have that instinct. Shakespeare, who knew himself to be a commoner and also knew himself superior to all the nobles and the kings, does not permit the awareness of his own situation to determine the orders possible for society. He admirably mixes nature and convention; in doing this he finds a place in the world for his uncommon commonness.

This mixing is discussed by Polixenes and Perdita in the scene where she distributes flowers (IV.iv.70–167). Polixenes and Camillo, disguised as very old men, receive what they call winter flowers and would prefer to have a little less explicit reminder of their mortality. Perdita says there are flowers that would be appropriate but they are nature's bastards (which is what her own father suspected her to be as Polixenes' child), and she will have none of them. She wants nothing of an art that "shares with great creating nature." For her, nature alone produces legitimate offspring; art produces bastards. Her view is the opposite of that of kings. She has a kind of religion of nature, untouched and unassisted by human doings. Her very person makes a great case for her faith. Polixenes, accepting her view that nature should be supreme, argues that though there are indeed arts that are not natural, they are guided by a hierarchy that nature itself makes. He stands for the naturalness of the higher powers of intellect that intervene in raw nature for the sake of preserving the "intention" of nature. Polixenes makes a point opposite to that made by Melville in *The Confidence Man*, where a character asserts his eyes were made not by nature but by an oculist in Philadelphia.[4] The oculist has an art of which there is no natural pattern, but it is on the basis of study of the natural perfection of the eyes that the oculist can correct this particular case of weakness of sight. Thus the eyes are enabled to fulfill their universal vocation, a vocation not made by the oculist. Such a study or art of natural perfection generally would be philosophy, which judges where the specialized arts fulfill nature and where they contravene it. This is the most delicate of arts and the one least easily recognizable in those who possess it. But it is a much truer relation to nature than the acceptance of whatever raw nature produces as deserving of reverence. Perdita is the unconscious innocent who will have to be guided in her social relations by persons wiser than herself. Shakespeare's own art, which is one of the profoundest themes of this play, is close to the ones propounded by Polixenes, and admits of the necessity of art for understanding and living in the nature so dear to Perdita.

Polixenes, against his will, is somewhat taken by this charming girl. His reflections on art by no means make him a philosopher. But he is a ruler, and rulers exercise a kind of prudence in the government of a state and its people that is akin to the universal governance of reason in the world, a point made by the gardeners in *Richard II*, who use their rational governance of their garden as a standard to criticize Richard's governance of the state.[5] Unfortunately, the kingly art is most usually perverted and does not look to human nature and its fulfillment in making its decisions. Only Plato's *Republic* attempts to bring together the art of the natural whole and the art of the city in making philosophers kings. Polixenes, under the influence of this girl, makes the following reflection:

> You see, sweet maid we marry
> A gentler scion to the wildest stock,
> And make conceive a bark of baser kind
> By bud of nobler race. (IV.iv.92–95)

Here he speaks as the kind of eugenicist recommended in *The Republic*, where the philosopher kings are really marriage experts, mixing the stocks or natures of men to produce healthy citizens. Polixenes does not appear to recognize that he is producing plausible grounds for the marriage of his son to a wild child. For a moment his natural vision overcomes his political one.

Shakespeare gives the sympathies of the audience entirely to rebellious Florizel, not to his kingly father, Polixenes. Florizel maintains the outward forms of respect, but he is absolutely intransigent in his disobedience. Love is his only guide, his polar star. Perhaps Shakespeare so unambiguously takes sides because this couple is a kind of announcement of a new order that will take the place of a gloomy and neurotic old one, where regrets and guilts reign. In *The Tempest* we are entirely on the side of Prospero when he brutalizes Ferdinand, but this is because we are persuaded Prospero is wise and will bring things to the best end. Polixenes, on the other hand, is overtaken by a sudden rage that threatens death. After the dance of the satyrs, Polixenes unmasks himself and there is a risk that the mayhem that took place in Sicily sixteen years before will be repeated here, strangely turning on the parentage of this same child. This is not the sexual jealousy of Leontes, but it is again a tyranny attempting to control natural inclination. Florizel immediately plans flight with his beloved, and in this he contrasts sharply with Romeo, who first despairs and then relies on the superartificial schemes of his priestly accomplice. Florizel then accepts sensible counsel from Camillo, and instead of giving himself to the fortunes of the sea heads to Sicily. While he himself is deceiving Florizel in order to prepare his return home, Camillo suggests that Florizel deceive Leontes. The advice turns out to be good, but that is partly due to chance; and the interestedness of Camillo is food for thought about the counselors to princes.

IV The center of this scene is given to Autolycus with his high spirits and thief's intentions. At scene's end he is an instrument of the recognition, an instrumentality in which he sees possible advancement. Contrary to instinct he helps Florizel but unluckily gets no credit for it. He appears in the scene first as a purveyor of all those trinkets for female adornment that are so repulsive to Perdita. Florizel concurs that none of these vanities will mean anything to his Perdita. But Autolycus nevertheless makes a great hit with the other girls and reveals a permanent aspect of the nature of most women. He also sells ballads and sings them with the girls. The ballads are obscene, and Perdita, who is like Juliet unabashedly sensual, assures her brother, the Clown, that she does not care to think of such things. But the ballads are great entertainments and give the news of the day. In Act V the miraculous doings at the court of Sicily are said to be the stuff out of which ballads are made, although surpassing the art of ballad makers (V.ii.23–25). To put it bluntly, Autolycus is one of those figures invented by Shakespeare to represent at least a part of himself. He is an utter rogue, with nothing but contempt for the law. He never lets thoughts of his fate in the afterlife poison his pleasures of the day. He steals the money of his spiritual inferiors but reflects,

> How blessed are we that are not simple men!
> Yet nature might have made me as these are;
> Therefore I will not disdain. (IV.iv.746–748)

The simple are not blessed, but they are human and deserve human kindness. A man like Autolycus cannot help taking advantage of them, but he recognizes that it is nature, not himself, who deserves the credit for his superiority. He does not, however, concur with those, in particular Rousseau and Kant, who made the same observation and drew the consequence that nature contributes no part to human worth or dignity. No writer of entertainments for the people can avoid the recognition that a large part of the audience is made up of the simple who love vulgar displays and will always have a taste for untruth.

Autolycus is a supramoral character for whom Shakespeare wickedly gives us some sympathy. He does little harm, only engaging in petty thefts of property, and provides us with a liberating laughter in harmony with the lovely, but perhaps only momentary, rediscovery of natural paradise. When he fails to get recognition and promotion at the court, he sweetly recognizes his kind could never belong there. This is Shakespeare's comment on the question, raised earlier, about the place of his own commonness in the hierarchy of the court and the nobility. He wins out over them because they become his characters. Autolycus engages in a charming bit of casuistry to prove that his loyalty to Florizel is not in contradiction to his profession, because not informing the king of his son's plans is to defy the authority of a king (IV.iv.832–843). Thus we get a certain kind of explanation of Shakespeare's knavery, which supports the true moral order. In this late play Shakespeare permits himself the pleasure of putting the poet on stage. He is ridiculous, beneath the level of the great deeds acted on the stage, and does not in any way further the plot. He has only a fugitive place in the world of action, but he casts a revealing light on the actions. As the First Gentleman says, when telling of the miraculous events that have taken place, "The dignity of this act was worth the audience of kings and princes; for by such was it acted" (V.ii.79–80). The line between performing an act and acting (in the theatrical sense) is blurred. The illusion of the theater is that the deeds it mimics are the most important thing. But Shakespeare may very well think that "the play's the thing," that his stories present the highest thing, the moment of understanding, telling the story for all posterity. Autolycus is lighthearted toward the things that men and women take most seriously but which are not so serious from the point of view of the poet or that of knowledge.

> **V**   In Act V, scene i, we first get a picture of the gloomy world of Sicily with its guilt-ridden king living only to blame himself and for the sake of repentance. This world is orchestrated by Paulina, the apostle of the martyred Hermione, who spends her time reminding him of the perfection he has lost and of the fact

that he *killed* her. She puts herself in charge of Leontes' private life and makes him promise that he will not marry without her permission, even though there are the most pressing political reasons for him to marry again. The contrast between the this-worldly, one may say classical period of Leontes' rule and this one could hardly be more complete. Paulina preaches indifference to the succession, a problem that is absolutely central in Shakespeare's view of monarchy, as we learn from the history plays. Paulina of course knows Hermione is alive; but at this stage we do not know it, and we see only the terrible setting of personal guilt and political negligence promoted by her. And we must remember that Paulina has kept this going for sixteen years (IV.i.6). Without the discovery of Perdita, who knows how long she would have persevered? Certainly Leontes deserves punishment, but in fact neither Hermione nor Perdita is dead. The only dead one is the little boy, Mamillius, and the one really shocking aspect of the play is that he is nearly forgotten. He is remembered only by Leontes, and does not seem to play a role in Paulina's plan, for he would have stood in the way of Perdita's succession to the throne. She is the disciple and promoter of a cult devoted almost exclusively to Hermione.

When the arrival and great beauty of Perdita are reported by a most unusual servant, Paulina invokes the sacred name, "O Hermione," and says that the servant is forgetting his own writing, which asserted that Hermione "was not to be equall'd" (V.i.95–101). In both *Cymbeline* and *The Winter's Tale*, plays where sudden jealousy perverts trusting love, persons on the stage are said to be writers who teach something. There is a scripture that accompanies jealousy. In *Cymbeline* Posthumus Leonatus (note the similarity of names), after the most vivid of all the expressions of jealous imaginations —

> Perchance he spoke not, but
> Like a full-acorn'd boar, a German one,
> Cried "O!" and mounted;—

says, "I'll write against them, / Detest them, curse them."[6] The writings are an important part of the education of the adherents to the faith. The writings about Hermione are not necessarily in contradiction with the writings of Posthumus Leonatus against women. A new kind of woman characterized above all by chastity or purity becomes the center of this religion.

Although we are irresistibly inclined to believe that Hermione is not guilty, one ought to remember that, unlike Desdemona and Imogen, Hermione is not proved on the stage to be free of a guilty relation with Polixenes, and that Polixenes, in scene iii, calls himself the cause of Leontes' sufferings (one way or another, out of this affair Polixenes' offspring will reign in Sicily). The issue for Paulina here is not the proof of Hermione's innocence but the establishment of her as beyond criticism, whether or not she bore a child by a great king who was not her husband. Mamillius resembled his father, and in this Hermione was like the mare named Justice, as told by Aristotle, whose foals always resembled the stallions who engendered them.[7] Perdita resembles Hermione. The role of the father is reduced. The scriptor-servant engages in an exchange with Paulina in response to her reproach, admitting that the faith is likely to be forgotten under the influence of the present unless there is someone there to remind him.

SERVANT: Pardon, madam:
The one I have almost forgot,—your pardon, —
The other, when she has obtain'd your eye,
Will have your tongue too. This is a creature,
Would she begin a sect, might quench the zeal
Of all professors else; make proselytes
Of who she but bid follow.

PAULINA: How! not women?

SERVANT: Women will love her, that she is a woman
More worth than any man; men, that she is
The rarest of all women. (V.i.103–112)

This kind of religious language and appropriate accompanying feeling dominate the whole of Act V. This new religion overcomes the jealousy of women toward other women because this chosen woman is proved to be superior to man, showing how women can use the combination of attraction and guilt to accomplish the destruction of the old male-dominated world.

Leontes' meeting with Florizel and Perdita provides a mixture of pleasure and remorse. He is pleased by these unabashed lovers and pleased thus by proxy to regain contact with his old friend Polixenes. But it also reminds him again of all that has happened. He says that he lost a couple, meaning presumably Perdita and Mamillius, who "might thus have stood" as does the "gracious couple" standing before him. Leontes gives evidence of a certain confusion since his "couple" would have been brother and sister and would not properly have been "thus." He wishes that their stay be a good one because Florizel has a "holy father," against whose sacred person he has committed a sin. He interprets his lack of issue as heaven's punishment for that sin (V.i.123–137, 167–177). He filters the natural consequences of his jealousy through the gods, who continue to punish him and provide cosmic guilt for him.

Polixenes will arrive soon, angry at his son for his defection, at Perdita, and at all those who may have conspired with them. His anger is also death-threatening. Florizel asserts that fortune can stand in the way of his marriage to Perdita, but that it cannot alter his love, which appears to be the one absolute beyond fortune. He gives Leontes the occasion to be the one who softens his father. He tells Leontes that to him his "father will grant precious things as trifles." Leontes, unable to stop himself, says that then he will beg Florizel's precious mistress for himself (V.i.223–225). The old king is erotically aroused by her. He does not know that she is his daughter. Shakespeare's erotic imagination, which we have seen to be so active in *Measure for Measure*, tests the relation between natural attraction and the sacred laws. He does this in a way that is not shocking to his audience, although perhaps it should be. There is a similar scene in *Cymbeline* when Guiderius and Arviragus, living as children of nature but heirs to the throne, are sexually attracted to a boy who is actually their sister.[8] That scene poses a special problem because if you clean it up on one side it becomes all the dirtier on the other. There is more plasticity in sexual desire than conventional propriety admits. This scene in *The Winter's Tale* is a gentle and ironic presentation of the perpetual Oedipus question. The ever watchful Paulina reminds Leontes, not that sexual desire is improper, but that the lost Hermione is so much more attractive, even though she is not to be enjoyed in this world. Leontes excuses himself by saying that he saw Hermione in Perdita. Of course many fathers could say such things of their daughters. In fatherly fashion Leontes agrees to help the young lovers if they are truly chaste.

The classic recognition scene is not presented on the stage but is told by onlookers. This happy ending is farcically implausible, but it does the job in alleviating situations of revenge and remorse. The two old friends are reconciled. There is a survivor of Leontes' wrath. She is given a worth for Polixenes in addition to her beauty that makes her an acceptable bride, and love is given its due. This love will be the grounds for a new beginning, although one that comprehends the historical facts that preceded it. The scene ends with Autolycus' last appearance in the company of the newly ennobled shepherd and his son, the Clown. This scene is slapstick, for these are absurd gentlemen, but it shows Autolycus' capacity to adjust to a world in which the simple, the shepherds and the clowns, inherit the earth. He flatters them with all his habitual irony, and they agree to protect him. Autolycus will make do in whatever dispensation happens to dominate (V.ii.124–175).

VI Act V, scene iii, the culmination of *The Winter's Tale*, is one of the strangest tales in all of literature. We learned in scene ii that there was a statue of Hermione in the keeping of Paulina made by the Italian master Julio Romano. This egregious anachronism has shocked centuries' worth of critics, but it points to the meaning of the play. The praise of the artist is extravagant and is another important reflection on the meaning of art and manifestation of Shakespeare's unusual self-consciousness about it. He, Julio Romano, is good enough to steal nature's customers from her, but there are two immediate qualifications to his superiority over nature. First, he is only nature's perfect ape. His superiority might consist in producing beauty that nature intends but never actually produces. Something like this is suggested by Paulina, who refers to Hermione, the subject of the statue in question.

> If, one by one, you wedded all the world,
> Or from the all that are took something good,
> To make a perfect woman, she you kill'd
> Would be unparallel'd. (V.i.13–16)

The second defect, however, is decisive: he does not himself have eternity, which, according at least to the Gentleman who says all this, is solely in the possession of nature and makes it the supreme authority of all. And he cannot put breath in his work. The statue is a long-lived reminder of unattainable perfection, and at the same time a great consolation for those who have lost and longed for Hermione. The entire company goes to see this statue, "in hope of answer." The pilgrimage to the statue is set in motion by Perdita's hearing the tale of her mother's death.

> she did, with an "Alas," I would fain say, bleed tears,
> for I am sure my heart wept blood. Who was most marble,
> there changed colour; some swooned, all sorrowed: if all the
> world could have seen't, the woe had been universal.
> (V.ii.87–91)

Here we see marble turn into flesh, which parallels the role of the statue. Natural limits are surpassed under the influence of love and sorrow. This kind of statue and the tearful worship of it were and are well known in the Roman Catholic church, where sinning men and women have felt consolation and even response from statues, in a worship that has brought down on that Church the reproach of idolatry. Such statues have long existed, but this one had to be done by a Renaissance artist.

Paulina is the great animator. She has kept Hermione in her house for sixteen years. Leontes says that he has never seen the statue of Hermione when he visited Paulina's gallery. Paulina is apparently an art lover and has her own gallery like those of Renaissance princes and prelates. Since Hermione's statue is the greatest thing that an artist has ever made, she kept it separate, and she calls that spot not a gallery but a chapel. Paulina milks Leontes' first sight of the statue for all the regrets and sorrows imaginable. But Leontes, presumably under the influence of having seen Perdita, notices that there are more wrinkles on the statue of Hermione than when he knew her. This is not too good a harbinger of the erotic attractiveness of the statue were it to come to life. But Polixenes enthusiastically chimes in that the wrinkles do not exceed the original by much. Leontes returns to his worshipful attitude; and Perdita, first insisting in a traditional Catholic excuse that she is not superstitious, kneels and implores the statue's blessing, beginning her address with the word "Lady." This is all quite clearly an artistic aping, not of nature, but of the cult of Mary. Paulina then prepares them for more "amazement," which, if they are not ready to receive, they should leave the chapel immediately. She is about to exercise "magic" and professes fear that she will be thought to be a witch, "assisted/By wicked powers." She announces that "It is requir'd/You do awake your faith." She is mistress of ceremonies to a miracle. Hermione comes to life and the whole scene ends in present satisfaction. However, the disposition toward Hermione and her suffering, so carefully nourished by Paulina, will remain (V.iii.44–155).

	Hermione was an unusually attractive, frank, intelligent,
VII	and open woman. But her experience of the vulnerability
	of relations on this earth, the suspicions and distrust of

men, and the tragic loss of her children, give her finally a delicacy and depth that are conveyed to us by the description of her statue and her one speech after her resurrection expressing her love of her daughter. There are two other great women in Shakespeare who are victims of male jealousy, Desdemona and Imogen, and who as a result of the suffering imposed upon them by it and in response to the ugly, sinful description of sexual desire, become something more than they were and something new in the world. Desdemona is the pure victim in the tragedy; the other two, in what are called the Romances, plays that defy the classic categories of the drama, are spared by Shakespeare and become the gentle civilizers of the men, who perpetually expiate a crime of distrust of their relatedness to their women, and are refined by the self-consciously guilty love of them. Hermione's tears are imitations of Mater Dolorosa's, and her smiles through her tears are reconciliations and redemptions.

Shakespeare seems to have thought that Christianity effected a deepening of women and a new sensitivity of men to them. The manliness of men was diminished by this series of experiences, but the femininity of women and their power over men were greatly enhanced. The great pre-Christian portraits of women, Coriolanus' mother, Volumnia, Brutus' wife, Portia, and Cleopatra, are in their own ways extremely impressive. But there is among them none so deeply human as Desdemona or Hermione, or even Juliet. The cult of women in the tradition of chivalry, which is ridiculed in *Troilus and Cressida*, does, when shorn of its mumbo jumbo and histrionic, superhuman character, give women an influence that permeates all of life, from the quest for glory to the attachment to children, an influence absent in the ancient world. The souls of women have become more interesting than they ever were, and Shakespeare is the poet of women at least as much as he is of men. He clearly represents much madness, and many wounds to the souls of men and women, brought about by the coming of Christianity to the world, but he also chronicles great gains made in this history. It is not clear that he believes that there was a transformation or progress in wisdom beyond the kind one finds in Ulysses. But the possibilities of the human soul revealed by the new dispensation are worthy of contemplation by the philosophers and of imitation by the poets. In this play, where Shakespeare frees himself from the constraints of time in order to show us the things to which it gave birth, he puts on the stage a classical simplicity, the arrival of the Old Testament's jealousy, Christianity's turn to otherworldly hopes, loves and guilts, and something new that is all his own.

Jealousy seems to be the critical change, bringing new doubts and new forms of scrutiny. Modern Italy, as opposed to the ancient Rome that it replaced, seems to play a critical role in the transmission of this passion. It is the diabolical Iago who makes Othello jealous just for the sake of doing so, and Iachimo who makes Posthumus Leonatus jealous for the sake of proving a point. In *Cymbeline*, the dramatic date of which is the closest in Shakespeare's plays to the birth of Jesus,[9] Posthumus Leonatus goes to Rome to meet what is obviously a modern Italian villain and returns to a Britain on the brink of being Romanized and, in the long run, Christianized. These two plays, *Cymbeline* and *The Winter's Tale*, are the poet's phenomenology of the spirit.

The something new I just mentioned is Shakespeare himself and gets its expression in the play in Julio Romano, the artist who supposedly re-creates Hermione, the new Hermione with her new position bestowed on her for her sufferings. Julio Romano was a Renaissance artist, and so is Shakespeare. Romano was also an Italian, and Shakespeare is indebted to Italy for many things, not only the Catholic Christianity that one finds there, but also the corrupt but liberating political teachings of Machiavelli along with his religious criticism, and the notion of a special vocation of art. The Renaissance meant, if it meant anything, the rebirth of classical antiquity under the aspect of beauty. It was a rebirth or new life of art, emancipated from its subordination to religion. The experience of all those great artists was the rediscovery of beauty, beauty of bodies, living, breathing, desiring bodies, not bodies seen under the aspect of original sin or diminished by unrepresentable expectations of another life and world. They cast off world-weariness and felt themselves again in the prime of mankind's youth. The beauty of bodies, certainly problematic but also seen as divinatory, again became at least the beginning point. These painters would, on the one hand, turn again to the discredited heroes of antiquity and their deeds in war and in love, but, on the other hand, still devote themselves to the stories of the Christians and especially to that of the Virgin Mother and her Child, painted and sculpted, however, in a way that recalled classical sensuality and love of the body. They effected a kind of reconciliation between divine aspirations and the senses. This was to usher in an era of delight and a rebirth of both politics and love.

12. *Conclusion*

Shakespeare seems to have said, following Correggio, "I, too, am a painter."[1] He was a kind of Veronese or Titian, painting the vastest tableaux, turning his great mind to those most important moments in the past where one could find the expression of the most interesting human possibilities and trying to learn from them what a fully human or happy life might be. Such knowledge is not available to the man who is a slave to his own time, and it becomes accessible only by study and reflection. There is no inevitable march of history, only possibilities, learned from history about eternal nature, the true source of creation, as Perdita tells us. The survey of the human spirit, which is what Shakespeare's plays taken together are, instructs us in the complex business of knowing what to honor and what to despise, what to love and what to hate. Shakespeare's moment was a great one because all options were open, and one could imagine a future that could be, if not free from the perpetual conflicts that threaten man's happiness, nevertheless the stage on which the richness and fullness of human potential could be acted out. Shakespeare may well have considered himself and the plays, which when all is said and done really are that self, to be the perfect expression of all that a human being can be without the distortions imposed on him by the beliefs of this or that place. Julio Romano is said to surpass nature, but nature incarnated in Hermione surpasses Julio Romano. The movement is from nature to art to nature. But Shakespeare surpasses that nature in giving us his play, which shows that movement. This is not merely paradox, for nature in the classical sense is perfection, and the most perfect human being, not a fancy or a transcendent abstraction, is the perfection of nature. Hence this artist, who puts into his plays all possible human powers and confronts all possible human temptations, can be said to be the perfection of nature. Hence the artist and nature become one.

The Winter's Tale is a survey of Shakespeare's own soul, as a soul can be presented on the stage. In this play winter is used as the simile of old age, and it is a play that is written, if not in Shakespeare's old age, in the light of his anticipations of death. As Prospero tells us at the end of *The Tempest* that his "every third thought will be of the grave," so Shakespeare here may be showing us another third of the thought of the old wise man, thought of love. Mamillius says that sad tales are best for winter (II.i.25), and this play is indeed tinged with melancholy, but it is also an affirmation of a possible beauty of life. This beauty is best acted out in the play by the story of Florizel and Perdita, but their story is more than matched by the vision of the play as a whole. This play is not the expression of an old man's regrets of a lost youth. It is rather the artist's affirmation—a less immediate and less passionate affirmation than that of two lovers who contemplate each other—of the beauty of his contemplation and imitation of nature, nature that is most itself not in mountains and streams but in the microcosm, man. This is a lovely activity that is beyond love, but the experience of lovers and of an artist such as Shakespeare are mirror images of each other. In its own modest way, and without the radical self-regarding of later artists, this play is about the artist and nature under the aspect of mortality.

It may be thought by some that in interpreting these plays I have concentrated too much on the religious question. It is up to the reader to make up his own mind about this after reading the plays and their continuous explicit and implicit reference to religions ancient and modern. *The Winter's Tale* itself provides the most intricate weaving of the Greek gods and Christian practices. The Delphic oracle actually governs the play, but Hermione is a saint. Here Shakespeare's imagination blends the two, but they are kept separate and accurate in those plays that respect verisimilitude and are less revelatory of the poet's own state of soul. Shakespeare wrote prior to the separation of church and state, which, in spite of its manifest advantages, tends to make us forget that all earlier social and political orders were always ultimately governed by the gods and the vision of the good life mandated by their peculiar character. Politics, naturally, according to Aristotle, deals with the comprehensive good for man, and the first claims we encounter about that comprehensive good are made by the religions and their gods, supported by the authority of the state. No serious man could avoid confronting the conflicting claims of conflicting gods. They were all around him, and they constrained him. There can be no doubt that Shakespeare knew about and was influenced by ancient republicanism, and that it influenced his understanding of the medieval Christian monarchy he depicted in *Richard II*. In his histories he reformulated what monarchy ought to be partly on the basis of the real advantages to be found in ancient republicanism. Shakespeare taught us about the different kinds of political community and the relationships of individuals to them. It is impossible to believe that he was not powerfully aware of the different kinds of gods who patronized the different kinds of lives, particularly when one comes to the questions of love and eroticism. The meaning of erotic agitations and longings depends in large measure on the status of the body, and that status is differently appraised in the world of the Olympian gods and that of the biblical one. Shakespeare is compelled in characters as diverse as Cleopatra and Hermione, Angelo and Falstaff, to think thoughts that reflect on the moral teachings of the religious alternatives.

Shakespeare's erotic sensibility and imagination were obviously very far ranging and full of sympathy for many of the ultimately incomplete and imperfect solutions to the problem of what to do with this great force that brings human beings together and separates them, from Falstaff's whoremongering to Hermione's absolute fidelity, with many stops between. Shakespeare was no less addicted to the charms of the erotic union of two people than are we, nor was he less aware of all that separates us from each other in such relations than are modern artists and thinkers. No one can make us love love as much as Shakespeare, and no one can make us despair of it as effectively as he does. The difference, as I suggested in the beginning of this meditation on some of his plays, between him and us is that he does not assume on the basis of some philosophy that either separateness or union is the fundamental natural given from which the opposite has to be derived. He remains faithful to the phenomena, and shows us erotic connections along with their fault lines. He surely shows us that there is some element in man that is connected with other human beings and that his erotic inclinations lead him to them. But he shows us powerful motives of individuation—not only the obvious, defective motives such as self-preservation and desire for money, but the incapacity of a single individual to contain all that is beautiful, and the isolating effects of reason, which is not shared by lovers but which points to another kind of human connectedness, the common perception of the truth. In Shakespeare man remains the ambiguous animal, whose pleasures and pains are much more determined by his choices than by the kinds of accidents that afflict other animals. Of one thing we can be certain: there is a natural perception of and longing for the beautiful that is simply irreducible and cannot be derived from lower motives, an awareness that does not necessarily give us much guidance about the kind of loves we ought to pursue, that does not simplify our lives, as some might hope, but rather complicates them. Of course this awareness can be submerged by doctrine and by reasonings as well as by unfavorable circumstances, but it is a perennial beginning point for serious engagement with the world, and we need the poets to provide us with the words for its expression. This may seem unscientific to the modern mind, a mere fiction made to elevate poetry, but the test of any assertion about the nature of eros or any other part of man is whether it can account for what one actually experiences and for what one imagines. In this critical respect Shakespeare wins hands down against Freud or his kind, and, it seems to me, outdoes Rousseau and the Romantic novelists.

Yes, it is Shakespeare's naturalness and love of nature, not an environmentalist's love but a humanist's love of nature, that are his most salient characteristics. He can show us everything and let us sympathize with much without fear of undermining a teaching or a morality. It is not as some might like to think that Shakespeare is high and contemporary writers low, for Shakespeare is never high-minded. It is that Shakespeare knows so well that man is a mixture of high and low and that what is often understood to be low holds the key to what is highest. Enobarbus tells us this in his description of Cleopatra, in whom the "vilest things become themselves" in such a way that even "the holy priests bless her when she is riggish."[2] Shakespeare sees the natural beauties that are sometimes present within conventions, but he also blesses nature when it breaks through convention's encrustations. He certainly teaches us to love decency and is a writer who can be recommended safely to children, but he is also capable of showing us that an Autolycus or a Falstaff sees things that the "higher" types do not. We are so used to flipping through our TV channels, turning from vulgar sex and violence to PBS, where we find that the higher things are now bloated excrescences without a reality beneath them. But the lower things are also distorted without their relation to these higher ones. The distinction between high and low culture is completely foreign to Shakespeare, whose plays are both. Our current experiences do not attach us to the low; they make us despair of high and low. When an Enobarbus, a lowly soldier, speaks of Cleopatra, we know that he has higher experiences unknown to our fatuous orators. In Shakespeare there is never any speech that is not related to a real experience, and this is what distinguishes him. He never speaks with the clinical sterility of our scientists, nor with the impoverished ugliness of our popular arts. For us he is something of a miracle, for he neither really shocks our morality nor seems to repress our instincts by his morality. It is all there. He provides us incentives to be good without abandoning ourselves.

The result of this latest reading of Shakespeare for me is the renewed conviction that there is nothing I think or feel, whether high or low, that he has not thought or felt, as well as expressed, better than I have. This is a personal affront because one likes to think that one possesses a uniqueness and special worth that no one else can grasp. This is also a collective affront to the prejudice that our age really knows important things especially in matters sexual that give it a special superiority over all other ages. Even our nihilists pride themselves on their incapacity to say that this age is superior, which they think makes them superior. The one thing they are incapable of conceiving is that there is someone decisively superior to them, whom they ought to go study rather than chastise for failing to support their moralities. To our current disrespectful critics, I would only say, echoing my own experience, "Try it, you'll like it." Undeniably of course there are things that have happened to us that Shakespeare could neither imagine nor foresee, and we need, although we have only a small supply of them, writers who can help us to see ourselves in these times. But for the things that are permanent in us, the existence of which is best proved by Shakespeare's effect on those who read him seriously in all ages and countries, one must return over and over again to his plays. Once the immediate charms of the present are overcome one realizes that our dignity or lack of it comes from the way we confront that which is always in man. In thumbing through the various commentaries on Shakespeare's plays, which are mostly written by mediocre persons, I became aware that they were elevated by their roles as intermediaries between Shakespeare and us. Without necessarily being able to explain it, their reverence for him gave them a vocation in life that contributed to the continuing vitality of his works. A community of the mind is constituted by this great artist and the traditional interpretation that agglomerates around him. This is the closest thing there really is to a "great chain of being." His great soul informs their smaller ones, and thus elevates them, giving them a better *raison d'être* than they would have had had they struck out on their own. Such a tradition leads us back not to some obscure personal "roots," but to Shakespeare. It in no way incapacitates later great artists such as Goethe, who can look out over the valleys of obscure interpreters and face the challenge of the peak, Shakespeare himself. These interpreters cover Shakespeare with much dust, but they do not bury him by neglect. We can always dust him off, as did such a great man as Lessing, much to the chagrin of the English nationalists. It is this tradition of interpretation, not "creative misunderstandings," not empty rebellions against the "agony of influence," but submissive interpretation and delight at the opportunity to associate with one's betters that constitutes civilization for us. Shakespeare animates worlds and armies of men. The abandonment of the great network of interpretation is the abandonment of what was most important for the Duke of Vienna and for Shakespeare: quest for self-knowledge.

Interlude on Two Strange Couples:

Hal and Falstaff, Montaigne and La Boétie

| I | As a farewell to Shakespeare, we will look at one of the most unusual and powerful connections in his universe. Prince Hal, the future Henry V and, according to Shakespeare, perhaps the greatest of all English kings, has an intense involvement with Falstaff, a very surprising sort of associate for a man who has such a high vocation. Hal becomes a ruler equipped with all the political virtues: he succeeds, at least in his own lifetime, in bringing an end to the plague of civil war, establishing his own monarchy solidly, and expanding England's territory and influence. He has none of the defects of the other kings Shakespeare treats. His rule provides a textbook for future rulers, which could find its place among Plutarch's *Lives of Illustrious Men* and also satisfy Machiavelli's stern rules for the guidance of a prince. He was the son of a serious and highly moral king, but he chose to spend his youth with a fat, old, lecherous thief. Shakespeare, in the two *Henry IV* plays, which are presumably dedicated to the serious business of reestablishing the authority of the kings in England, spends an extraordinary amount of time putting the frivolous and immoral adventures of Hal and Falstaff on the stage. This is very curious, and his reasons are not quite evident. The story is not simply that of a young man who fools around while waiting to assume the throne. Hal from early on is too calculating and cold a man simply to idle, and we can, I believe, assume that his involvement with Falstaff reveals a part of his taste, which is visible only prior to his becoming king, but remains a hidden aspect of his character when he does rule. In some sense one

might say that in *Henry IV, Parts I and II* one sees a kind of education of Hal, not entirely unlike the education of another world-historical rascal, the *Education of Cyrus* invented by Machiavelli's rival Xenophon.[1]

And this relationship is really *invented* by Shakespeare inasmuch as Falstaff is an almost total fabrication, an exception in the history plays, which are in general fairly faithful to the historical record. Somehow Shakespeare had to have this antic fellow, who is not part of history, present in history in order to make his point. He is an Enobarbus in spades. He is also not unlike Autolycus, another Shakespearean invention—a minion of the moon, i.e., a thief and a balladeer. Falstaff is willing to have sex with man, woman, or child (Part II, II.i.14–17),* is riddled with venereal diseases, always drunk, a colossal glutton, and moreover, a blasphemer, a superior rhetorician, a man of great wit, and an exemplar of a kind of rationalism. For all of his vices he is one of Shakespeare's most engaging characters. He tramples on all of the rules, divine and human, without becoming repulsive to us. Shakespeare works this wonder by keeping Falstaff's thefts within relatively benign limits and showing that in spite of his bombast, he does not do bodily harm to people. His two loose women, Mistress Quickly and Doll Tearsheet, quarrel with him but love him. He is not actively leading conspiracies, nor is he a traitor to his friends. In general he is the beloved king of the Boar's Head Tavern, a little realm all its own. What might be considered his one really ugly act, wounding the corpse of Hotspur in order to get the credit for defeating him, is, for those who do not revere corpses, only a wound to a corpse. Most of all, his salvation for himself and for the audience is that he is screamingly funny. And, although there is much slapstick in him, the humor does not stop at that but touches on the great themes traditional to comic liberation—the gods, the city, and the family. He is a criminal not only because his uncontrolled tastes lead him in that direction, but also because he is a critic of the conventions.

This is perhaps enough to explain the shrewd Hal's attraction to Falstaff. From his earliest youth Hal seems to have known that the official versions of what is good and evil, noble and base, are defective and can hamper political activity. He was one of those who know that success will bring with it a reputation for morality, or that

---

* All parenthetical citations in this section of the Interlude are to Shakespeare's *King Henry IV, Part I*, ed. A. R. Humphreys, Arden Edition (1960; rpt. London: Routledge, 1988) or *Part II*, ed. A. R. Humphreys, Arden Edition (1966; rpt. London: Routledge, 1988).

the benefactor of the people will be held to be the good man, whereas those who follow the rules are burdened in such a way that the possibility of their success is compromised. Hal knows that his reputation is sullied by his associations, but turns the stain to his advantage. He who appears to be a low fellow and proves to be a superior one will have a better reputation for that. The noble Hotspur, the exact opposite of Falstaff, whom both Falstaff and Hal despise, spends his short life doing the works of nobility, and all Hal has to do is kill him; this one deed and all of Hotspur's reputation will accrue to him (Part I, V.iv.70–72). He is a takeover specialist.

Hal may very well have thought that Falstaff, who had gone a long way on nature's road, would be able to teach him about what is to be found along it. It is not sufficient to say that he enjoys the Boar's Head merely because he finds there the low, sensual pleasures. For in doing so he also learns something, that those pleasures are real pleasures though unavailable and frowned upon at the court. Nor is it sufficient to say he is there to find out about the lower orders, as he does in playing around rather cruelly with the tapster, Francis (Part I, II.iv.1–109). This would require very little of his time and less of his participation in the low deeds of the place. It is Falstaff who interests Hal there. Falstaff is of the place but expresses it with a spirituality that transcends it. He is a reliable guide to the charms of vice. Hal, it appears, finds life at the Boar's Head very enjoyable, but not so enjoyable as ruling, which makes it easy for him to give it up when there is imperious need to do so. Hal knows that he cannot be number one until his father dies, and he does not waste away observing the pieties while waiting. He surely wants to be king, which means that the prospect of his father's death is not an unmixed sorrow. Hal stays within the limits that require him to wait for his father's death before becoming king, but he tests them in thought at the Boar's Head.

Falstaff is the only inhabitant of the Boar's Head who has self-knowledge, and that seems to be irresistibly charming, at least for a time, to Hal. Falstaff's comments like "A plague upon it when thieves cannot be true one to another" (Part I, II.ii.27–28) remind Hal that there is a question whether civil society's morality is very different from that of thieves, only enjoying a better press. Hal, as opposed to Hotspur, seems to have understood politics the way Falstaff does. His only other comment about his motives in this stage of his life is one that is much more revealing than his statements about his improved reputation:

And we understand him [the Dauphin] well,
How he comes o'er us with our wilder days,
Not measuring what use we made of them.[2]

The French are about to find out what he learned in his apparently misspent youth. One thing he surely knows is that the usual view that dissipation of body and of mind destroys a man's strength of character is false, at least for men like himself. His bodily lusts are easily tamed by his political passions and set up no conflict within him, partly because he has been purged of romantic expectations from sex, and his intellectual lusts, by no means becoming an end in themselves, further his capacity to see well.

The Hal-Falstaff couple is in a way a parody of Aristotelian friendship, the union of two souls that appreciate each other and are rather indifferent to money or vulgar sensual pleasures, just delighting in each other even though every man loves himself more than anyone else, each heightened in the mirror of the other's understanding. This is a parody, but the parody contains some elements of the real thing. We have in these two a powerful natural connection, although shot through with tensions that make it doubtful. Hal enjoys Falstaff and admires him in a certain supramoral way. That the friendship can be broken off so brutally proves that it is not a true friendship, which is the most durable of all attachments. Hal, whose side decency forces us to take against Falstaff, has the upper hand in the relationship and performs the hard deeds connected with terminating it. This shows something about politics and the essentially friendless character of the king, who has no equals and must subordinate the highest things to *raisons d'état*.

Falstaff, of course, profits from the association with the heir apparent, who has money and, especially, sufficient influence to protect him from the full rigor of the law. He jokes about much greater expectations for the future when Hal will be king. But Hal's utility is not enough to account for the kind of attachment Falstaff expresses. In part, Falstaff is not really very ambitious. He wants some money, to stay out of prison, and to be able to influence appointments. He is a man of the present without extensive plans for the future. His primary concern is to live beyond the law, while avoiding the consequences of living in a society where there is law. In order to do so he has had to become a careful observer and very quick-witted. But just as Hal's attachment to Falstaff cannot be exhausted by the obvious low motives, Falstaff's motives contain something in addition to the obvious benefits of palling around with a man who is to be king. Part of it seems to be the pleasure of seeing a soul and a character he can hope to make like his own. This is a thrill of complicity, the complicity of understandings, which has a charm all of its own, one not always appreciated by vulgar psychologists. He has a sort of erotic attraction to this promising youngster in whom he would like to see himself reproduced. He looks forward to Hal's being king because he expects Hal on the throne to have a spiritual kinship with him. It is not so much the boast "I know the king" as "the king is mine" that moves him.

Falstaff has a touch of nobility in him, and unlike the others in his crowd, he could have made a political career for himself, although he could not seriously aspire to become a king. His failure to do so could be understood as the usual tale of a promising man undone by unbridled passions. But it is equally plausible that he has turned to that life of his, which he so evidently enjoys, because he sees through or beyond the political careers of the nobles. His reflections on the vanity of honor as opposed to the reality of life give some indication of the kind of critique he has made of such aspirations (Part I, V.iii.30–61). And there are many such reflections about men's not being able to be true to themselves. His descriptions of the pleasures are enticing, for example, his W. C. Fields–like praise of drink in response to his encounter with Hal's puritanical brother John (Part II, IV.iii.84–123).

One can see the charm of Falstaff's and Hal's association in the way they relate to each other in the first scenes. The pleasure consists primarily in their dialectical skill, each trying to outwit the other. It is a combat of masters of self-justification and sophistical argumentation. "I deny your major, if you will deny the sheriff" (where mayor of the city and the major premise of the syllogism by which Hal proves him to be a coward are conflated and sheriff is understood to be the subordinate of the mayor) is a perfect example of the exchanges that prove the dignity of speeches for their own sakes for these two men (Part I, II.iv.489). Hal recognizes the truth of Falstaff's assertion that not only is he, Falstaff, the possessor of wit, in all of its senses, but he also communicates it to others. Hal, who is one of those to whom he communicates wit, loves it and is gifted at it. The two elaborate scenes where Hal conspires to embarrass Falstaff, the double robbery at Gadshill, and the serving man's disguise adopted to overhear what Falstaff says about him, really have as their purpose to see how Falstaff will respond to being caught in his lies. And Falstaff gladly obliges and is breathtaking in his agility. There is nothing to say in response to Falstaff's justification that to say bad things about Hal among bad people is appropriate for a friend in order to protect him from the love of the wicked (Part II, II.iv.315–321). Hal delights in seeing not Falstaff's embarrassment but his skill at avoiding it. Things like this are what constitute the core of their love for each other.

Hal and Falstaff are a pair for whom nothing is sacred, at least in speech. They insult each other without any of the elaborate formalisms that characterize the court. Their insults are the courtesies of this world and are more honest than those in use among the nobles. The content of their discourse is from the outset dedicated to legitimizing the thieves, as if, when Hal takes over the law, they will become the true men. This is interlarded with lighthearted blasphemies. Law and religion are the first targets of these free spirits. Perhaps the most shocking game for Hal to play is the one where he asks Falstaff to play his father and then, as Falstaff puts it, deposes him and himself plays his father, the king (Part I, II.iv.371–475). The most sacred constraints of all, those on which the family is based and which are identical to politics in a hereditary monarchy, are themes here for the most radical theoretical and practical questionings. The question of a son's loyalty and duty to his father is tested to its limits in the two *Henry IV* plays, and Hal neatly straddles the issue by behaving and thinking as freely as he wants and then persuading his father that he is a good and true son. Hal lives in the perspective of his father's death and cannot help but come close to the stark question posed, according to John Locke, by the son stymied by his father: "Father, when will you die?"[3] Hal must be the good son in order properly to succeed his father, but what he brings to his rule is something radically different from and opposed to what his father brought to his. Hal shucks off the family pieties and shows something of his political genius by appearing to adopt them in the end. Falstaff probably taught him how to think this way and is certainly the only person with whom he can act it out.

The impious relationship of Hal and Falstaff, and the pious relationship between Hal and his father, pretty much represent the essential tension between philosophy and obedience to the ancestral so central to the life of Socrates. Falstaff is indeed Henry IV's rival. Hal knows that, although Henry IV does not. Falstaff, playing king, catechizes, as would any good father, his adoptive son on his disorderly friends and life. But, as king, he praises Falstaff. He does this in the form of great classical epideictic rhetoric, an art of which he is a master and which he uses at will throughout the plays. Then Hal wishes to take over the role and the imagined throne. The real son of the father epitomizes the father's role by an extreme attack on Falstaff, whom he calls "that villainous abominable misleader of youth" (Part I, II.iv.455–456). This is the complaint of the fathers against Socrates. And this charge, corrupting the youth, is really what brought Socrates down. He is the rival of the fathers in the education of their children, a function that belongs to the fathers in all traditional social orders, orders that are changed by the success of Socrates.

Socrates' questionings of the sons inevitably leads sons to question their fathers. The Hal-Falstaff relationship is not entirely unlike the one between Socrates and Alcibiades. Alcibiades was the young man of great family and unlimited political ambition with whom Socrates spent a certain amount of time and who was certainly influenced by him, although in ways that are difficult to gauge. Alcibiades' political career had an unlimited character unlike that of any other Athenian statesman, or perhaps any statesman ever. He seemed to want to live without the constraints of any law or convention and actually did so, but was brought down by the forces of convention. In order to see Falstaff and Hal as similar to the Socrates-Alcibiades pair, one must look to Xenophon, who lets us see an Alcibiades who ridicules his guardian, Pericles, using Socratic arguments,[4] and a Socrates who appears coarser and more buffoonish than in Plato. Falstaff tries to prove to the Chief Justice that he is younger than the Chief Justice, an argument not unlike Socrates' attempt to prove that he is the more beautiful than Critobolus, and is roundly ridiculed for it.[5] The Chief Justice avers that he is "well acquainted with your manner of wrenching the true cause the false way" (Part II, II.i.107—109). This is the ordinary accusation against Socrates, that "he makes the worse argument appear the better."[6] And this is not merely an empty accusation. Both Socrates and Falstaff practice such an art, which gives them freedom from conventional reasonings. And these are not the only reminiscences of Socrates in these plays. The death of Falstaff is akin to Socrates', as described in *Phaedo*,[7] in that his body appears to have grown cold from the feet up. And there is practically a quote from *Gorgias* in *Henry IV, Part I*, IV.ii.79–80, where Falstaff in Hal's camp describes his disposition to battle: "To the latter end of a fray and the beginning of a feast fits a dull fighter and a keen guest."[8] This comes closer to the heart of the real Socrates. Falstaff is not really a coward, and Hal knows it. Poins tells Hal that he will not "Fight longer than he sees reason" (Part I, I.ii.179). Falstaff is not avid of the glory of the battlefield. Life for him is more important than glory. But he often speaks of death, and in ways that indicate he accepts its inevitability. He will not change his life, for example his sexual behavior, in order to preserve it. He wishes to live as long as possible enjoying the real pleasures of food, drink, sex, and wit. A certain stiff piety surrounds the way we look at Socrates that makes it difficult to see the roisterous gaiety in symposia that are part of a shared philosophic liberation. Surely Falstaff is not Socrates, but this is a kind of comic picture of the Socratic life, no more outrageous than Aristophanes' picture of Socrates. It is actually more tender, because Shakespeare, the poet, has more in common with the philosopher than did Aristophanes, who was a spokesman for poetry in the old war between philosophy and poetry. Shakespeare's plays, as we have seen in this survey, are suffused with a love of reason and what Socrates calls a kind of human wisdom.[9] He reproduces here both the exhilaration of philosophical observation of human life and the kinds of relationships among human beings it can form.

Hal himself is as ambiguous as Alcibiades. He seems to have an irrepressible involvement with Falstaff but is unwilling to draw the conclusion from it, that politics is only a game. Alcibiades seems to have been liberated in the same way and to think that philosophy is in some way the highest, but he is unable to give up politics and so he practices a kind of unconventional politics. Hal does not mind Falstaff's walking through the battlefields ridiculing what goes on there. Falstaff even makes a comedy out of Hal's great moment, his defeat of Hotspur. By faking his own death, he gets a funeral oration out of Hal, as did Hotspur, showing up Hal's oratory, which ennobles the fallen who are no longer dangerous. Falstaff fools Hal by resurrecting himself. Hal seems to accept all of this easily and with amazing equanimity; he pursues his wars without the hot indignation that almost always accompanies warriors. He has certainly seen Falstaff's exposés of justice as it is really practiced in the cities of men, as in Falstaff's dealings with Justice Shallow. Hal as king acts with an efficaciousness unencumbered by morality but knows how to borrow the colors of morality. His simple abandonment of his old friend Falstaff, in order to improve his reputation for justice, follows from a teaching he could have learned from Falstaff. He uses the Chief Justice, whom he himself has struck in disrespect, to punish Falstaff. He therefore endorses the rigorous application of the law, which he does not really respect himself. Hal becomes a real Machiavellian king, which means (contrary to the conventional understanding of how a successful student of Machiavelli will appear) that he is reputed to be just, even while fighting unjust but successful wars. Above all, like the Machiavellian king, he appears to be very religious and manipulates the prejudice in favor of religion by using the prelates. But he is also Machiavellian in the sense that he gives up all the sub- or suprapolitical pleasures that he experienced with Falstaff. He proves the usefulness of Falstaff, but his political ambition allows him to suppress the charms of Falstaff. What is interesting and sinister about Hal is the degree to which politics consumes him even though he is the beneficiary of a powerful critique of it. Shakespeare always maintains for himself such joys as are beyond the unerotic necessities of politics. The depiction of Falstaff is his way of inserting such a reminiscence into the grim realities of English politics, as are Autolycus and Pandarus in other contexts, who are supplemented by truly philosophic presences like Ulysses and Prospero.

The relationship between Falstaff and Hal has something in common with the relation of pederasty described by Pausanias in the *Symposium*,[10] where an older man loves a beautiful and promising boy, and trades an education for intercourse. The attractiveness of the youth is given in exchange for the delightful discourses of the man. Hal may ultimately value Falstaff and the wisdom he imparts only for the political advantages gained from them. Hal and Falstaff can hardly be called friends, and certainly Hal is not a real friend, capable as he is of cutting Falstaff off even though Falstaff dies of his rejection. But there is also something Socratic in their relationship. Hal and Falstaff both have independent sex lives, but it is clear that they enjoy each other's company more than that of those with whom they sleep. They are soul mates, and without any touch of solemnity, they prove the possibility of a purely spiritual association, based upon mutual admiration of intellectual gifts, without necessary admixture of anything bodily, or of money, or of power. Those things are present, but they are not the core of the experience. It is, really, an erotic relationship, the attraction based on the potential for shared insight.

Shakespeare's portrayal of this relationship is precisely the opposite of the current attempt to understand human connectedness by what is called male bonding. As human beings we seem separated; it is only as brutes that we can believe in connection. That is a legacy of Konrad Lorenz's studies of animals where he discovered mechanisms of bonding that have bodily need as their ground. We are apparently unable to believe in anything that does not have a biological base. This is all part of the rebellion against reason. Shakespeare shows us an inspiring connection founded on what is available only to man and is highest in man, our reason. The wonderful recognition of a soul that interests us is treated as an experience as powerful as that of two beautiful young people first seeing each other and falling in love. This is a possibility of human connectedness that cannot be called sublimation or anything else derivative from the bodily sexual desires, although it may sometimes have a connection with them. This form of connectedness, shown at the extreme outer horizons Shakespeare presents to his audience, assures us that there is a certain natural community of men not included in the war of all against all or in the artificial community established to end that war and to protect individuals as individuals. For some moments, at least, there can be a community of men based upon common insights into the truth. This is a community not riven by the opposition of bodies and provides a kind of justification of nonillusionary adherence to eroticism. The souls need the conversation with each other and delight in the resulting common and thereby enhanced awareness of the way things are. Selfishness and selflessness become for a moment the same. Hal, of course, is an unsatisfying lover because he is too political to love for long.

Hal and Falstaff represent a raunchy comic view of friendship, while Michel de Montaigne in his essay "Of Friendship" describes his version of the delight of two souls with each other in the most exalted terms. But it must not be forgotten that the two phenomena are akin, and both bear witness to a passionate, exclusive attachment that stems entirely from a supraphysical involvement of two consciousnesses. In both accounts there is no element of preachiness or concentration on the higher things. Friendship does not here depend upon effort; it is described exactly in the way that the encounter between Romeo and Juliet is described, as an irresistible attraction. Montaigne tells of his first meeting with his friend Etienne de La Boétie at a great feast where there were many others but the two men were captivated by each other, drawing off into the exclusionary circle of their friendship, indifferent to all others. It was sudden and total. They became utterly indifferent to the throng that surrounded them there and in life thereafter. Montaigne does not try to describe what they said to each other or anything else about the substance of their relations. He tries only to describe from the outside the unbreakable and overpoweringly pleasant connection between the two of them.

Although this overwhelming experience seems akin to the love affairs that are so frequent and so attractive in the various literary genres, it does not lend itself to literary depiction. The experience of an attraction that leads to sexual intercourse is very easy to imitate on the stage and perennially appeals to the public. There is no need for the lovers actually to have sexual intercourse on the stage for everyone to imagine what is motivating them. But what it is that friends do in their intimacy is not so easily imagined, or, to put it otherwise, the core of the friendship is entirely intellectual, and most human beings do not have access to it and cannot imagine it. The bodily effect that leads to the spirituality of love belongs to everyone. Intellectual wonder as an end in itself, the basis of the kind of friendship praised by Montaigne, which he argues is higher than any other kind of human relationship, is almost unknown to mankind at large. Shakespeare can give a hint of it, but only reflected in the distorting mirrors of a carnival funhouse and as if it were part of an action of which it is not really a part. Even the essay form used by Montaigne cannot express the core of what he is talking about. He has to use externally admirable results of friendship, such as willingness to sacrifice one's property to a friend, in order to make it interesting and plausible to his readers. Such things, of course, are praiseworthy but they are not really appealing. When lovers make great sacrifices for their beloveds, the sacrifices are immediately understood as part of something very beautiful and exciting that almost everybody can imagine. The eros of souls for each other, experienced by two human beings who can share insights into the nature of man and of all other things, is much less palpable, and hence less believable, than the eros of bodies. This disbelief on the part of most men is strongly reinforced by pseudoscientific theories that tell us that this experience is founded on an illusion and is derived from the eros of bodies, bodies transformed by a semimiraculous faculty invented for the purpose, sublimation.

The rhetorical problem connected with explaining such friendship and making it attractive is thus very great: one has to give popularly accessible reasons for the sinister-appearing relation between two men to an audience that is not likely to grasp what it is that causes this relation. Such friends are suspect, for they seem to withdraw from the universal community of mankind in order to enjoy each other's company more perfectly and perhaps to be engaged in a conspiracy of one kind or another. This is the very problem of the Platonic dialogues, where Socrates seeks to make friends by way of conversation, which could not belong to any real literary form, especially not the stage. As Nietzsche, a great proponent of the drama, says, Plato is boring.[11] Actually, Socrates' conversations are not that boring if one follows them, but there is no dramatic way to imitate them. The only way to imitate thought is by thinking. Drama is concerned with actions; therefore thought can be present only as contributing to those actions, not for itself. This is also why there can be no real discipline called intellectual history. Deeds can be recorded by history without performing them; but thoughts are not essentially deeds and must be thought through and not recorded as if they were deeds. Actually, even the Platonic dialogues, boring as they may be for lovers of the theater, are not imitations of Socrates' thoughts, for Socrates is never shown speaking to an equal where the activity would be pure thought rather than pedagogy. He is not even shown talking to his best students, Plato or Xenophon. In Xenophon's works, Socrates actually does speak to Xenophon, but only in a comic context where he calls him a moron for his sexual incontinence.[12] The Platonic dialogues are, in fact, half dramas where Socrates talks to various kinds of people who have not yet thought, or are unable to think, or do not want to think. Such interlocutors are not likely to become his friends, though the discussions with them are full of interesting, sub-philosophical confrontations and seductions. This is what gives them whatever popular attraction they have. There are power struggles with characters like Thrasymachus and Callicles; there are amusing deceptions, like the one employed by Socrates to get rid of the father in the *Republic*, Cephalus, who would not have permitted the radical conversation that took place; there are ironic reassurances to men with a friendly disposition toward him who cannot understand why he does what he does, like Crito; and many other such little deeds. Deeds can be reproduced in speech, but thoughts cannot be reproduced in deeds, such as those in the drama. Plato leads us to the border of Socrates' encounters with those who could be true friends and share thoughts with him, but he never leads us into the promised land, which would really amount to a philosophic treatise to which only a tiny number of men would have access.

Montaigne does give an account of a meeting of two such equals but is forced simply to describe the facade of the edifice. He is talking about the engagement of two philosophers with each other, and he says that such a friendship is not likely to occur more than once in three hundred years. But make no mistake about it, in this circumspect account he is telling us about the most important part of himself, but only in such a way as to be plausible to a large audience. However rare the experience may be, if it is real, it shows the possibility of the natural unity between two human beings, which is what eros always desires but always somehow fails to achieve because of the naturalness of individuating selfishness. This possibility is capital for our understanding of human nature in that man's highest experience would cause us to reinterpret some of the lower experiences in its light. The conversation between two philosophic men would help us to see that the conversation between lesser men partakes at least a bit of this higher form. The banter of two buddies has a touch of the quest for mutual insight of two philosophers.

As Montaigne reminds us, Aristotle says that good lawgivers pay more attention to friendship than to justice because laws force men against their grain to an imperfect fulfillment of justice, whereas friends who really love each other as they love themselves perfectly fulfill justice without exhortation or punishment. But friends are something other than citizens. They are more dedicated to each other than to the polity, the goals of which they may not share. Montaigne insists that a man can have only one friend, that such seamless identity is possible only once, and that having two or more friends might well compel one to choose whether to serve the good of one or the other (141–142).* The pair of friends is a community of its own, which may or may not be in accord with the body of citizens as a whole. Friendship helps to explain what is wanted in politics but also leads to an awareness that politics cannot arrive at that desired end. Legislators want all citizens to have good will and friendly dispositions toward one another so that the law will not be obeyed only out of fear of punishment or calculation of profit, but they cannot want individual friendships that regard their connections as higher than the connections among citizens. In friendship, which is rare, the opposition between self and other is completely overcome, whereas in politics it can be, at best, partially overcome. The real interests of a large group of men can never be one in the way in which those of two friends of equal gifts and similar understanding can. For this reason, real friends, who are always off in a corner discussing privately with each other, are problematic for any community. "What are they talking about? What are they planning?" Their preference for each other

---

* All parenthetical citations in this section of the Interlude are to Montaigne, *The Complete Essays*, trans. Donald M. Frame (Stanford: Stanford University Press, 1976). Occasionally the translation has been modified.

is an affront to everyone else, and when they have high intelligence, distrust is increased. This is exacerbated by the fact that they probably could not be understood by the generality of mankind, which is another reason why they have to be so private in the first place.

This was Socrates' continuous problem as he carried on intimate conversation with young men and aroused the suspicion of the community and its leaders. He says publicly that he is always in public, but that assertion is gainsaid by Plato's and Xenophon's presentation of him as spending most of his time with well-born and well-to-do persons and carrying on critical discussions with certain individuals all alone. The crude suspicions were that he had sexual relations with his young companions against the stern interdiction of their fathers or that he was part of plots to overthrow the democratic regime, a charge made plausible by connections with Critias and Alcibiades, each in his own way a threat to democracy. Plato and Xenophon concentrated in their defense of Socrates on these vulgar charges, which are fairly easily rebutted, in order to avoid talking about what is truly shocking: having different thoughts about the highest things. What Socrates and his companions talked about and thought together, which is closer to the essence of friendship than is sex or politics, would seem on the surface to be more respectable than either of those two. But what Socrates talks about is surely subversive of the common faith of democracy as well as of any other actual regime. And the charge that he did not uphold the gods of the city and that he brought in new ones is closest to the mark of all. Socrates was not engaged in an active campaign to seduce the bodies of young men or to establish new regimes. What he did do was to make those who were attracted to him think differently, perhaps even about the authority of the religion that told them what to think. Ultimately, it is this withdrawal from the community of belief that is intolerable to the vulgar, and this is what philosophical friendship is all about.

These reflections can help us understand the relationship between Montaigne and La Boétie. They were both what we call Renaissance humanists, and this means, at the very least, that they admired classical antiquity, which was decisively different from Christian Europe in its beliefs and tastes. Intellectual historians tend to fudge this problem and to make us forget that, for those who really took them seriously, the books of Greek and Roman antiquity constituted a grave threat to their Christian faith. Intellectual historians do not like either/ors and do not share their subjects' desperate concern for the truth of things. In Montaigne's time, people were slaughtering one another mercilessly over questions of faith. Each of the orthodoxies demanded strict adherence to its version of a common faith and was equally severe with those suspected of being beyond any of the established camps. What did these two men together think about that situation? Montaigne was not just any private man who could isolate himself and think his own thoughts. He was to become famous throughout the whole Christian world and to be a mediator between Catholics and Protestants. He was a close associate of the Protestant king of Navarre, who was to become the Catholic king of France, Henri IV, who established peace between the warring factions. How one stood on these issues was a matter of life and death, and one's freedom of thought as well as one's influence in the delicate world of religious politics depended on finding prudent grounds that would conduce to the common good as well as protect oneself and one's thought from fanatic intolerance. Even Rousseau, two centuries later, when the vitality of these quarrels had lost much of its edge, suffered greatly as a result of his publishing about them. Montaigne, a more prudent and covert man in more difficult times, had to act and express himself with great reserve and subtlety. He only hints at how his dedicated reading of Plutarch, whose *Lives of Illustrious Men* he called his breviary (262), might affect his views of the quarrels of his own time and the manner in which he conveys them (115, 484, 761, 795).

Thus he tells us of the love at first sight between him and his new friend and adds enigmatically that they had heard of each other previously and had favorable dispositions toward each other. He told us earlier in the essay that he had already read La Boétie's treatise, given the title by him of *The Voluntary Servitude*, but called *Against One* by others. This treatise was a highly controversial discussion of the dominant religious issues and was used by the Protestant factions in France (against La Boétie's intentions, according to Montaigne, probably speaking ironically). He also tells us, in another passage in "Of Friendship," apparently connected with the first one about this treatise, that La Boétie had republican political preferences, quite an admission inasmuch as he lived under a monarchy, an admission that implicates Montaigne too because of his insistence on his oneness with La Boétie. He assures his readers that La Boétie's republicanism was innocuous because he was a religious observer of the laws of the country in which he was born. This defense is so problematic that I need not comment on it. And in the same context, Montaigne announces that he had intended to publish La Boétie's treatise as part of this essay but decided against it because it had been recently published, "with evil intent, by those who seek to disturb and change the state of our government" (144). He wants to protect his friend, he says, from ignorant prejudices, but he also means he wants to protect himself. Montaigne publishes in its place a series of insipid poems by La Boétie on love. The two men are engaged with theological and political questions of the greatest moment, but Montaigne diverts the readers' attention from them to the eroticism of the young man, which is apparently more publicly palatable. This eroticism is in one way beneath these great issues, but in another way it may point to something higher, the relationship between these two men. Montaigne, after reading La Boétie, was prepared to believe he had found a soul mate. He also makes it clear that what they thought together would be unpalatable to mankind at large, and particularly to the religious and political authorities. In telling us candidly about the power of their feelings for each other, he elaborately hides the contents of their shared thoughts. They were two young men, living in an age of passionate conformity and danger to independent thought. Montaigne subtly tells us that the mutual attraction was founded in the first place on their thought about religion and regimes. They discovered that they thought alike about the problems of their time; moreover they agreed about the importance of the literature of classical antiquity, which was ambiguously present in Christian modernity. What an explosion of joyful recognition this must have been! They could speak together without reserve, without fear of shocking each other, share each other's learning, and compare their thoughts. Certain kinds of persons would find such an encounter at least as attractive as the satisfaction of strong sexual desire. But they are, no matter what political deeds they may have intended, a subversive couple.

Montaigne tells us of this problem, as clearly as he tells us about anything, in the following passage:

> When Laelius, in the presence of the Roman consuls—who, after condemning Tiberius Gracchus, prosecuted all those who had been in his confidence—came to ask Caius Blossius, who was Gracchus' best friend, how much he would have been willing to do for him, he answered: "Everything." "What, everything?" pursued Laelius. "And what if he had commanded you to set fire to our temples?" "He would never have commanded me to do that," replied Blossius. "But what if he had?" Laelius insisted. "I would have obeyed," he replied. If he was a such a perfect friend to Gracchus as the

histories say, he did not need to offend the consuls by this last bold confession, and he should not have abandoned the assurance he had of Gracchus' will. But nevertheless, those who charge that this answer is seditious do not fully understand this mystery, and fail to assume first what is true, that he had Gracchus' will up his sleeve, both by power over him and by knowledge of him. They were friends more than citizens, friends more than friends or enemies of their country or friends of ambition and disturbance. Having committed themselves absolutely to each other, they held absolutely the reins of each other's inclination. Therefore, supposing this team to have been guided by virtue and governed by reason—and it could not have been driven otherwise—Blossius' answer was as it should have been. If their actions went astray, they were by my measure neither friends to each other, nor friends to themselves. (139–140)

The accusers inevitably think that such friends will burn temples, and Montaigne tells us that the response was imprudent, not untrue. He asserts that this "team" was necessarily "guided by virtue and governed by reason." This assertion reflects Montaigne's view that real friendship requires the presence of virtue and is a community of reason. But there is a quibble here because there seem to be two kinds of virtue, that of friends and that of citizens. By conflating the two, he can give apparent proof that this is a deed the two men would never have done. Montaigne continues his discussion of this question, attempting to reassure the world about friends, saying that he could answer such a questioner that he would never kill his own daughter. Two things are evident from this: he changes temples to daughter, and these two may have different statuses for him; and he makes it clear that he would never participate in a sacrifice of Isaac. God is not a friend, partly because he cannot be known.

Philosophy is what this friendship is about. The two help each other along on the path to truth. Friendship requires two souls and a reality to the understanding of which those souls are dedicated. They are solicited by the attempt to transform opinion into knowledge. It is nature, or being, or reality, prior to the souls, that provides the stuff that cements them together. That there is some kind of truth, about which they reason and about which they can agree or disagree, concerning which they can refute each other, is essential to the possibility of sharing. When two persons prove the Pythagorean theorem together, they are for that moment undeniably one, seeing and thinking the same things. They are really the same that moment in a way that persons are not in any other kind of relationship. Knowers can be friends in a way that creators cannot be, because knowers can be united in a common vision, but creators cannot be, each having his own unique vision. The experience of such common vision is relatively frequent in the natural sciences, and we all know something about it. The problem with the natural sciences is that they are only partial, that they do not engage the totality of a human being. Only if philosophy is possible is there the possibility of such total communication, because philosophy treats both of the whole of things and of those who try to know them. Montaigne—who was called by a great contemporary the French Thales[13]—and La Boétie obviously did not discuss only the movements of the heavenly bodies, but also things perhaps more gripping to them, like whether there is a heaven and a hell, what life will be the happiest for them (Montaigne began as a public man and finally chose to retreat into private life), and whether friendship is the highest kind of human association. This is a private association that, though it concerns itself with the most public or most common things, is necessarily private because the public opinions about these things are really dogmas and must be tested by those who insist on knowledge rather than opinions about them. Montaigne is famous for his skepticism, his *que sais-je?*, what do I know? This means that he recognized that he did not know what most people think they do know, and in itself bears witness to comprehensive reflection about the opinions of men, opinions sacralized in laws and modes of worship. This is the discussion the two friends shared with each other.

This is a possible, if rare, relationship. It requires two persons who experience the urgency of the need to know, who have the intellectual gifts for knowing, who are not overpowered by other passions of body or soul, and for whom knowing is more important and more pleasant than anything else. Obviously such a combination of gifts and tastes is rare. But filling this prescription is capital if one is to discover the possibility, the only possibility, of at least momentary perfect human union, where two men are like the two eyes focused on the same thing. This, as Montaigne tells us, is the only *ens per se*. He tells us, quite wittily, that in other relations he has no concern about the totality of virtue in his partners: he doesn't care about his doctor's or lawyer's religion, or his footman's chastity. These things have little to do with the performance of their functions, and that is what is important in these partial connections. At a dinner, he prefers a clever man to a wise one; in bed, he prefers beauty to goodness; in the society of discourse, he prefers competence, even if it is not connected with gentlemanliness. But in the total relation of friendship, all the qualities and virtues must belong to each of the members, not for their own sakes, but for the possibility of friendship. A man who is frightened of his shadow or who is always drunk does not have the time to be a friend. One cannot imagine a serious discussion of theology without wit. In a friend, he is concerned with all of these things, with the possible exception of the beauty he wants in bed. A certain perfection of virtue is part of friendship, but that perfection follows almost automatically from the common goal shared in friendship. Montaigne treats, as does Socrates, the moral virtues as merely the conditions for the exercise of the intellectual virtues.

Each of the two men loses himself, is no longer himself, in a common identity. Great patriots also lose themselves in the common identity, but this requires what Rousseau calls denaturing.[14] The appeal of what Montaigne talks about consists in its naturalness, in its being the result of primary inclinations. "One soul in two bodies." The services rendered between the two parties are no more praiseworthy than the services one renders to oneself. There is simply an expansion of individual consciousness to a common consciousness of the pair. Therefore, there is a perfect communism of property, overcoming the deepest source of separation among men. This means that friendship implicitly denies the sacredness of private property and is supportive of the old dream of communism, first articulated by Socrates and continued by Marx and his followers up to our own day. The concern with property is the concern with individual self-preservation, and when it is institutionalized, it means that men are separated forever. The longing for communism is perfectly understandable and reasonable. It is the precondition of a real community of persons. Something like such communism was always implicit in the relationship between husband and wife, in the era before prenuptial agreements, and gave that relationship a certain privileged status. But Montaigne shows us why it is a political absurdity: only two such friends are capable of it. This does not cause Montaigne to abandon the longing for communism or community; it causes him to have less hope for politics and to be unwilling to subordinate friendship to it. The complete involvement of a pair of friends with each other, a relationship that obviously has more dignity than the complete involvement of an individual with himself, is unjust from the point of view of the extreme demands of the political or social order. Montaigne, both in his political action and in his writings, attempted to restrain those demands, which are fueled by idealism, in order to protect the real possibility of friendship and the private life altogether.

This is the proper moment to look at the difference between Rousseau and Kant on the one hand, and Montaigne on the other, concerning the source of morality and the basis of human association. Rousseau begins from the naturally selfish and isolated individual, and, with his invention of the general will (the categorical imperative in Kant), constructs a path from the individual to the community. The trick is in the word "general." The individual continues to think about his needs and desires as he always did, but simply generalizes them to apply to all men. What could not apply to all men, the moral individual rejects. Another way to put it is that a man who wills should consider himself a legislator for all mankind. Any act of will that cannot conform to this role of universal legislator is illegitimate. There is no specific content to this morality. Its content comes from the ordinary wishes of ordinary human beings. What makes it moral is only the generalization. "I wish to lie in order to make money. All men may lie in order to make money. This is impossible. Therefore, I do not wish to lie." The moral man does not reflect on the character of the desire, but only on its generalizability. The possibility of a man's doing this is in Rousseau's teaching the essence of morality. It was elaborated in response to the liberal view of men's radical isolation from one another and their primary concern for their preservation and the corresponding assertion that all association is merely a calculating extension of one's concern for one's preservation. Rousseau and Kant responded that nature is too low to provide moral guidance, and that association thus derived is degrading. The act of generalization is not natural, it does not follow from anything given by nature. It attests to human freedom from the bonds of nature. The individual dedicated to the general will is moralized by that dedication and is morally reliable because he acts not from his natural impulse or individual will but from his general will. One moves from radical isolation to radical socialization. The man who wills generally not only is a member of a community but in a sense even is that community. But in between these two poles, there is almost no unity or community between individuals. Rousseau does indeed introduce romantic relationships as a kind of link between the two conditions. But, precisely for this reason, the love relation is undermined by both the natural lusts on the one hand and the demands of impersonal community on the other. From the point of view of morality, the charming connectedness of individuals and their aspirations to human completeness have no status. Love and friendship resist generalization, and community is a triumph over such relationships and their natural causes.

What Montaigne shows us is a natural connection, meaning a real concern for another that is not based on the overcoming of natural desire, but is itself a natural desire. That such a relationship is rare and almost unbelievable does not change the fact that it comes from nature and restores a natural basis for morality. It is the experience of oneness with another, and not abstract generalization, that ties Montaigne to La Boétie. If this is a real experience, it refutes the view of nature that underlies Hobbes, Locke, Rousseau, Kant, Freud, and most modern thinkers unto our own day. The relation between the particular and general will is a relation with oneself, whereas friendship is emphatically a relation with another. I have often in this book spoken of nature, and this is the crucial question about it: is nature the selfish atomization of individuals, or does it contain a unifying, and hence moralizing, impulse? The intermediary love relationship in Rousseau, as we have seen, is constructed out of *amour-propre*, out of a sublime self-regarding. Montaigne passionately asserts that wonder at the soul of another is natural and constitutes a natural community between those who admire each other. This overcomes the opposition between pleasure and morality that so strongly characterizes some Kantians. For them, if there is a reward for deeds performed for another, then the deeds are not moral. For such Kantians, and there are many of them among us, proof that one acts morally consists in saying, "I didn't enjoy doing it." Montaigne proudly asserts that his relationship is the highest form of association and proves it by saying, "I enjoyed it." Shakespeare and Montaigne present us in detail relationships formed from the natural inclination to society existing in men that is asserted by Aristotle and denied by Hobbes. This is the fundamental difference among our authors.

Montaigne tries to prove that friendship is the only perfect society by examining the other powerful claims to such perfection. All others, he says, have some end beyond this society or association itself, and are more or less subtle versions of the business association. Friendship as the end in itself becomes preeminently choiceworthy because nothing can threaten it, there can be no conflict of interest in the partners. It is like happiness, which can never be supplemented because it contains all good things. Nobody really says, "I am happy, but I would like to have a little more money or be better looking." This is an admission that one is not fully happy. In a sense, Montaigne argues that friendship is happiness, and is therefore desired for its own sake and with no need for anything beyond it. In order to prove his point, he investigates the other kinds of relationships, divided by the ancients into natural, social, hospitable, and sexual. He actually discusses only the natural, meaning blood, ties and the sexual ones. He engages in an activity that is contrary to our taste, determining a rank order or a hierarchy of these associations. This means that he recognizes that there can be conflicts among them, that one must choose, and that some people are going to be hurt by such choices. He faces up to the fact that our desire for the harmony of all good things is unfounded.

Montaigne begins with fathers and brothers, with the family, the original sovereign claimant to our loyalty. And he treats the family with Socratic levity. He speaks of the traditional family, not the democratic family we know, which he would treat as a halfway house, fulfilling neither the demands of family nor those of friendship, a tentative association doomed to disintegration. He says that the feeling of children for their parents is respect and not friendship. There is a kind of intimacy among friends that is utterly inappropriate between parents and children. The order of the family is founded on the instruction and precepts given by parents to their children. Fathers and mothers are authorities and not the objects of familiar intercourse. Parents and children are not equals, while friends must be. Education in the family is a one-way street, while in friendship it must be, and is, reciprocal. The family assumes the superior wisdom of the parents and does not admit of children's reproving their parents. He thinks of Aristophanes' depiction of a son, who was a student of Socrates, beating his father because of the father's ignorance and stupidity.[15] This illustrates the conventional character of the parents' claim to wisdom and the subordination of children to their parents. Montaigne does not think this can be changed, but the family would obviously be repressive of a wise child like Montaigne. He would seek a friend. He brings the witness found in the customs of some nations where children kill their fathers or fathers kill their children, "in order to avoid the impediments that they can sometimes become to one another." With a typically gently stated, but brutally thought, touch, Montaigne accepts the reasonableness of these horrid practices, founding himself on the maxim "Naturally, each depends on the ruin of the other" (136). Montaigne refers to the kind of things that we have seen in the relationship between Hal and his father, as opposed to his relationship with Falstaff. Both freedom and property for a son depended, in the traditional family, on the death of the father. And behind these facts lies the inevitable fact that the son's coming to manhood is connected with the decline and death of the father, and all the psychological baggage that the relationship must bear on that account. He completes this criticism of the blood tie by citing the bald statements of two philosophers. Aristippus, when he was asked about the affection he had for the children who came out of him, began spitting and said, "this too came out of me." Another philosopher, whom Plutarch wanted to reconcile with his brother, responded, "I don't esteem him any the more for having come out of the same hole as I did" (136). Such are the unsentimental reflections about fathers and the family by a man who had a remarkable father to whom he was a good son, in any usual sense of the word. Montaigne is a most unusual combination of harsh clarity and propriety of conduct.

Above all, the family's claim to provide the most compelling and important relationships for a man or a woman is what is most unacceptable about it. The coincidence between the qualities of a father or son or brother and those of a friend is extremely unlikely. The friend may very well be at the other end of the earth, sharing neither the laws, nor the religion, nor the customs that prevail in one's own country or family. The joy of friendship is to be found in choice and free will, whereas the friendships proposed by the family are founded on law and natural obligation. The family's imperious demands distort the quest for a good friend, and Montaigne expresses a delighted liberation from the constraints imposed by the family on his thoughts and his deeds.

From the constricted and constrained relationship of the family, Montaigne turns to the vivid one to be found in the erotic attraction to women. Of this he gives a much more favorable account. This surely comes from within us and is experienced as an act of freedom. Montaigne admits his interest in and experience of this kind of connection. He does not deny that the feeling in the erotic connection is more gripping and intense than in the friendly one. In the family, it was duty that stood in the way of friendship; here it is intense pleasure that compels us. This means, obviously, for Montaigne, that erotic relationships have an appeal superior to family ones. He confesses that there were moments of conflict in both himself and La Boétie when erotic attractions competed with their friendship, but they had no doubt about what is primary. Friendship keeps "its course in proud and lofty flight, . . . disdainfully watching the other making its way far, far beneath it" (137). This is very noble and proves that the two men are able "to put their priorities in order." But who would want to be the woman involved in any of these attractions? Montaigne's profound experience of both alternatives leads him unqualifiedly to prefer friendship over erotic love. Erotic love takes hold of us, as he says, by only one corner of ourselves. That corner may drag all the rest with it, but it really does not imply the general or total fitting together that one finds in friendship. Eroticism is impermanent, changing, full of highs and lows, whereas friendship is continuous and level. When one comes off the erotic high, which one must always do, one returns to the friendship with joy. And, most important of all, eroticism is more involved in the quest of its object than in its enjoyment. The real force of erotic desire is to be found in uncertainty. The doubt about the agreement of wills is the interesting thing, and while that doubt continues, eroticism is a totally gripping experience. Montaigne helps us to make the important distinction between eros and sex, a thing that often escapes us. As soon as there is mutual consent, which is, on the surface, what one sought for, the thing begins to lose interest. Sexual intercourse, habitually engaged in, becomes something like eating. In an erotic pursuit, there is a certain illusion about what one really wants. In friendship, the real pleasures begin after the acquisition, and the association of conversation engages men more totally than the association of sexual intercourse.

Now we come to marriage, one of the most privileged relationships in modernity, and about it Montaigne is savage. One has to remember that he was a solidly and dutifully married man, although he would certainly not say happily married man because happiness is not a category inherent in marriage. His great objection to it is that only the entry into this business, as he calls it, is free. There is no exit. Christians could not divorce. Freedom seems to be Montaigne's touchstone for what is most truly desirable and most truly human. The lack of freedom is central to his criticism of the family relations and, in another way, of the erotic ones. He apparently means by freedom something other than the two alternatives one finds in Hobbes, Rousseau, and Kant. The first of these is simply the capacity to do without impediment whatever brute impulse suggests to a man in the state of nature. The second is the freedom from imperious natural necessity demonstrated in the capacity to will generally or universally. When a man acts according to a general principle or maxim, he can be certain that he is not simply a brute guided by natural law, but a human being guided by the law he sets for himself. This latter is impressive and yields a satisfaction of self-esteem, but it is not very attractive, nor does it yield great pleasures other than those of a good conscience. Montaigne, on the other hand, means by freedom the capacity to choose the good and beautiful, unimpeded by the necessary, the conventional, or one's own. This is a sweet freedom. It implies that the noble or moral relations are natural, that there is a natural longing for union with a soul of another and for action in common with him. One does not anticipate that a friendship will break up any more than a marriage could in his time. But the very fact of the legal and religious constraint in marriage diminishes the daily reaffirmation of the will, which constitutes a large part of the pleasure of friendship.

Montaigne tells us that his wife cannot be his friend. This is not only because of the constrained character of the relationship itself. It is also because marriage is not an end in itself. The relationship exists for the care of the household and the production and education of children. These things go beyond, and even take primacy over, the simple being together that is friendship. The family is a unit conceived for the sake of the preservation of the species, and everything in it partakes of the original necessity. It is a man's citizen-duty to marry, but it is not his fulfillment. All these responsibilities of the family get in the way of the essential enjoyment of friendship. The sensible choice of a wife and the qualities in her or in the couple are determined in relation to the demands of family. Therefore, some of the things Montaigne says in his criticism of the family also apply immediately to marriage and all the relationships formed by it.

Moreover, he insists that the great virtues and charms of the friend are not likely to be found in the wife. Here the criticism he made about the sexual relation applies directly. He further believes that women rarely if ever have the philosophic gifts that are the essence of friendship. He does admit that if the virtues of the wife and the friend could be combined, and the original sexual attraction could maintain itself, this would be the perfect and complete relationship that one could not find elsewhere. But he appears really to regard this as an impossibility and to admit that the tension between the higher and lower loves he spoke of in his discussion of erotic relations is a permanent feature of our lives. We are forced to choose and to put things in order.

This indication provides for us the stark contrast between the classical articulation of the problem of marriage and that of the Romantics, as well as the practice of our own day. We have noted that there is almost no discussion of friendship as an end in itself in Rousseau and the Romantic literature, and almost no depiction of friends of the kind Montaigne talks about, whereas classical writings are full of such depictions, from Achilles and Patroclus on. Montaigne's view would clearly be that the common belief that one's wife should be one's best friend would, as we have remarked in our discussion of Jane Austen, corrupt both friendship and marriage. It would arouse unfulfillable expectations of what men and women would get from marriage, and it would set up arrangements that would make it impossible, and even immoral, to have a friend. It comes down to the choice of whom one would prefer to spend one's time with, and this choice must be made if one is to have friends. For Montaigne, it is clear that his wife has to accept that he prefers being with his friend to being with her, which would be almost impossible in our times. Actually, Montaigne married only after the death of La Boétie, but he makes no pretense that his marriage in any way replaces what he lost. In order for there to be friendship, there needs to be a rare leisure, and in addition, the institution of marriage has to have a limited status unlike our imperial version of marriage and the family. Montaigne would think that modern marriage demands the union of things that are almost impossible to unite, and therefore would fall of its own weight, except in the rarest of instances, where the gifts of husband and wife are high and equal. It is simply intolerable for us to say that our friend is preferred to our spouse, both from the point of view of pleasure and that of virtue. This can be seen in the practice of our time in the United States, where there is little time for friends and there are practically no facilities for the activity of friendship. Friends tend to be friends of the family, which means they are not friends in any sense intended by Montaigne. In countries like France and England, there are still reminiscences of the separateness of friends from marriage and the family. There are clubs and cafés where people meet who know each other very well but have hardly met the wife or children of their friends. These are two distinct kinds of relationship and, unfortunately, they are in conflict unless there is a natural rank order in which one takes precedence over the other.

Instead of the attachment of complementarity between man and woman proposed by Rousseau, Montaigne offers the natural attraction of "like to like." This analysis extends the brutal clarity of Montaigne in his attempt to put in order, without sentimentality, the various claims on us of our relationships. He makes his final statement about marriage in the essay that follows the one on friendship. It is a kind of dedicatory letter to a great lady on his publication of La Boétie's love poems. He apologizes for not having dedicated all of them to her, but he asserts that these are the ones full of a "fair and noble ardour." The others were written for his wife while he was pursuing the marriage and already express a *je ne sais quoi* of marital coldness (145).

Finally, he discusses what he calls "that Greek alternative (or licentiousness)," which is "justly abhorred by our morals" (138), that is, Christian morals. In spite of this, he goes on to discuss it dispassionately. His description of the practice of pederasty is drawn almost exclusively from Pausanias' speech in Plato's *Symposium*, which we will discuss later, and I will not try to make a résumé of Montaigne's résumé of that speech. He sees all kinds of difficulty in the erotic attraction of an older man for a young boy. He does not give biblical reasons for condemning this attraction, nor does he treat it as against nature. The essence of his objection to it is that the great disparity of ages means that it necessarily is an attraction of bodies rather than souls. Socrates addressed Alcibiades only when he was older and the real pederasts had deserted him, and this implies Socrates' agreement with Montaigne's criticism of the practice. But Montaigne does admit that the ideal implicit in the arguments of the Greeks for pederasty is friendship and that it is at least possible in some rare cases for this kind of attraction to culminate later in friendship. His condemnation is therefore only partial. He concludes with, "In short, all that can be said in favor of the Academy is that this was a love ending in friendship; which corresponds pretty well to the Stoic definition of love: 'Love is the attempt to form a friendship inspired by beauty.'[Cicero]" (139). Montaigne is far from prescribing Greek love, but it is the only one of the relations he discusses that is not contrary to friendship, and it links, however imperfectly, the eroticism licit in relations between men and women with friendship.

After this survey of the other human attachments, Montaigne can return to his friend La Boétie with a flight of poetry:

> For the rest, what we ordinarily call friends are nothing but acquaintanceships and familiarities formed by some chance or convenience, by means of which our souls are bound to each other. In the friendship I speak of, our souls mingle and blend with each other so completely that they efface the seam that joined them, and cannot find it again. If you press me to tell why I loved him, I feel that this cannot be expressed, except by answering: Because it was he, because it was I. (139)

The forces of attraction between the two were such as to defy rational explanation. But this does not mean that their relationship was not centrally founded on their sharing of reason. What Aristotle calls "the demonic" aspect of nature takes over and brings them together.[16] For Rousseau, attractions are sentiment or passion overcoming calculating and individuating reason, whereas for Montaigne, reason itself is a kind of passion that can cause irresistible attraction between souls. He and his somewhat older friend were lost in each other, and, to reiterate what I have already said, overcame the distinction between self and other, or I and thou. Here the we precedes the I and the thou, rather than being derived from it. Montaigne claims that he never recovered from the loss of his friend and that for the rest of his life he was only half a man. The friend had made him whole or completed him. Alone, a man is not sufficient for happiness, but a friend makes him whole. This must be contrasted with the view of another writer whom Montaigne knew very well, Saint Augustine. In his *Confessions*, he tells of the death of his friend and how inconsolable he was. But after the almost mortal wound had healed, he determined that he was glad his friend had died. This was because the friendship had fostered an illusory self-sufficiency of the couple constituted by the two friends, whereas man can never truly be self-sufficient except in giving himself to God. The friendship was noxious because it was impious. Man's love must be for God alone.[17] Both Montaigne and Augustine admit that man by himself is incomplete or imperfect with respect to happiness, and each teaches that man must search for that being which completes him. But Montaigne reasserts, against Augustine, the self-sufficiency of the purely human couple. This is altogether appropriate for a humanist.

PART THREE

The Ladder of Love

| I | I began this book with Rousseau, the most erotic of modern philosophers; I end it with Socrates, the most erotic of philosophers, period. Of the many beautiful Socratic dialogues, |

perhaps the most beautiful is Plato's *Symposium*, which was an inspiration for lovers throughout the ages, especially in those two fertile moments of return to classical antiquity that so marked our past, the Renaissance and Romanticism. Socrates says that he is an expert in the science of erotics (177d),* which must mean that he knows something that very many people think is important. But Socrates is also the prince of the skeptics, the man who said, "All I know is that I know nothing."[1]** This contradiction is usually resolved by taking Socrates' assertions about erotics to be an example of the famous Socratic irony, a kind of joke. This is a solution, but not a very satisfactory one, since it only fits our own sense of what a man like Socrates could take seriously, instead of being based on anything Socrates himself actually says. It is at least as possible that what he says about knowledge of ignorance is ironic. He insists most on his ignorance in the most public of contexts, his trial for impiety and corrupting the youth. By contrast, he speaks about his knowledge of erotics in much more intimate situations, understandably, because a man who claims he can teach erotics to young men would seem to be

---

* All parenthetical citations in Part III are to the Stephanus numbers used in most editions of Plato's *Symposium*.

** All translations from the Greek are the author's own.

vulnerable to the charge of corrupting the youth. But, in the absence of proof, as a preliminary working hypothesis, one might equate the two apparently contrary assertions. Socrates' statement that he only knows he knows nothing could be interpreted to mean that philosophy is impossible and that it is not worth going on. But Socrates interprets it in the opposite direction: knowledge of ignorance means that one's life must be dedicated to finding out the things that it is most important for man to know. If Eros,* put most generally, is longing, then the philosopher who pursues the knowledge he does not have could be considered erotic. He longs for knowledge. If the need to know is what is most characteristically human, then such philosophical Eros would be the privileged form of Eros. Moreover, it is generally agreed that Eros is connected with pleasure, a very powerful pleasure, and this would account for the philosopher's continuing in his uncompleted quest, which might appear to be very bleak without such accompanying pleasure.

Of course, all of this amounts to nothing more than an abstraction, the improbable assertion that thinking is erotic, unless there is some real connection between the activity of thinking and the phenomena everyone recognizes as erotic. This paradoxical philosophical eroticism does not accord very well with our usual image of philosophers, such as Aristotle, Thomas Aquinas, or Kant, especially at this moment when reason is in such low repute. More important, it does not accord with the depiction of Socrates by Aristophanes in the *Clouds*, which Socrates refers to in the *Apology* as the first accusation against him.[2] That play, which shows an atheist Socrates, accuses him not for his atheism, but for his lack of Eros and his lack of poetry. It is a poet's accusation. Aristophanes' comedy is hilarious, showing us a Socrates in a basket who is unable to distinguish between Sparta and Athens and does not know about the laws forbidding incest, who is literally above the world of concern to us. This is the consequence of the study of nature, a study that dissolves that world. Aristophanes suggests that poetry, independent of reason or philosophy, is the source of a more adequate grasp of man and his situation in the world. Aristophanes depicts himself as a man powerfully dedicated to his sexual attractions. The view that the lives of the poets are erotically interesting and that the lives of natural scientists are not is perennial. And, perhaps vulgarly, we identify that

---

* Eros is capitalized throughout Part III as in Greek, so as always to leave open the possibility of its divinity, rather than trying to distinguish instances of its divine from those of its human character.

eroticism with a certain human superiority. Nietzsche, another poetic philosopher, says in an aphorism: First-rate scientist, second-
rate man; second-rate artist, first-rate man.[3] And the situation
depicted by Aristophanes, where philosophy and science are practiced by unerotic, unpoetic atomists, is not unlike the one faced by
Rousseau, who undertook to reintroduce eroticism in the context of
Enlightenment materialism. Plato's Socrates performs the role that
Rousseau himself played in response to this condition. Not only is
Socrates the most erotic of philosophers, his spokesman, Plato, is the
most poetic of the philosophers. Plato's depiction of Socrates establishes on a new basis the link between Eros and poetry. The introduction of an erotic philosopher bridges the chasm between Eros and
philosophy that Aristophanes seems to argue is unbridgeable. Plato
gives us a Socrates who knows everything that is going on and
everyone who is a part of it, a gossip and a lover, who even tells us—
a unique admission among philosophers—of an erection he had
when he glanced down into a boy's cloak.[4] This Socrates, who is also
a married man with children, would seem to have the morals of a
bohemian. The problem with such a Socrates is to figure out how
such perverse or promiscuous details have anything to do with the
responsibility for knowing the first causes of all things. It is this that
Plato undertakes to do in the *Symposium*, the ascent from the most
common experiences toward the peaks, beginning with the real
bodily sexual attractions of individuals for one another.

He does this by making the characters in his dialogue—which in
this case is not really quite a dialogue but a series of elaborate rhetorical speeches—talk about their sexual desires. Socrates' famed dialectic consists only in compelling persons to articulate their opinions
concerning the things they care about most and to think these opinions through. Here, instead, the characters give speeches praising
the brute acts they perform, thus satisfying the distinctively human
need to explain oneself, to justify oneself, to think about why what
one does is good. In human beings alone every act is accompanied by
an opinion about the meaning or the goodness of that act. This is
what happens, implicitly and explicitly, in the *Symposium* with a
variety of lovers. In each case they believe their passion is good and
beautiful, and they are induced to praise it in speech. Like all others
in the Platonic dialogues, they give an account, a *logos*, of what is
dear to them. Their enjoyment of their acts has a lot to do with how
appealing or persuasive an account they can give of them—their
justification for performing them and taking them seriously within
the scheme of things. In the *Symposium*, since the subject is such an

appealing one and so dear to the hearts of the men who were there, the expressions are especially stirring and interesting. Of course, in stating these opinions, they are making their confessions and, unawares, showing whether they are serious or frivolous persons. It is impossible in reading the *Symposium* not to judge men's quality by their erotic practices and the way they celebrate them. There is a dialectic established among these rhetorical speeches because they contradict one another, and one must try to resolve the contradictions in order to get any kind of a coherent account of the phenomenon.

I have discovered in recent years that the feast to which the *Symposium* invites us is less appealing to students than it once was. They do not like to have to justify their sexual tastes or practices. Whenever they are asked to make a judgment about the quality of Phaedrus' or Eryximachus' statements, they are inclined to say, "Men and women have a right to do whatever they want in the privacy of their own bedrooms, provided, of course, one's partner or partners consent." This is probably true, but it is not sufficient. It bespeaks an unwillingness to think about one's experience and its relationship to the whole of life and the moral order. Today's students hesitate to articulate their reasons for loving—they must certainly have such reasons somewhere within them—for fear that they may come up with negative judgments about someone else's tastes or practices. This would be illiberal and might lead to persecution. Liberal society guarantees the right to privacy, even when nobody wants to keep anything private. A *de facto* equality among all preferences and practices is declared in order to avoid criticism and comparison. "You let me do what I want, and I'll let you do what you want."

After all, to this way of thinking, these are only preferences, not, as Plato thought, divinations into the nature of things. Preferences are value judgments, and value judgments cannot be reasoned about let alone judged. Judgment, which was one of the most cherished of the intellectual virtues, has become a vice, which we recognize when we call someone judgmental. This change may or may not contribute to a more tolerant society, but it surely provides a ready excuse for scanting that most valuable kind of judgment, the judgment of oneself. Even the old motive for making an argument about sexual tastes, provided by the laws forbidding many of them, has disappeared. And people no longer have a compelling need to search in literary and historical sources for "role models" in erotic activity. We've got it all, and need neither justification nor encouragement. All this tends to reduce sexual acts to their bodily and brutish expression and to repress a natural need to celebrate them in speech, while encouraging thoughtlessness about things that are of capital importance. Such thoughtlessness may seem to make things easy, but it robs us of more than half of our pleasure. Nothing so dear to one's heart as love, with its far-ranging influence on all one's tastes, can be experienced without opinions about its high significance. To abandon the attempt to articulate those opinions is to decapitate the experiences. The most splendid speech we know concerns love as it was once talked about by the poets. The *Symposium* can help us to regain the habit of saying, "This is what I do, and this is why it is so great!"

The need both to celebrate and to justify is fully satisfied in the *Symposium*, where seven persons praise the god Eros, each according to his fashion and his understanding of the god. There is no Greek word for sex, that late-nineteenth-century invention of sterile and timid imitations of science. The speech about the attractions of bodies is always in terms of either the god Eros or the goddess Aphrodite. This sense of the sacred and mysterious character of such attractions informs the discussion of them. This does not mean that any one of this group of friends believes that there actually are such tutelary divinities of desire, but their understanding of it is clearly affected by its allegedly divine origins.

These men represent what is most characteristic and appealing in the Athenian society that has been celebrated for so long. Still, there are aspects of that society which are peculiarly distasteful to us today, and one has to consider the degree to which it depended on these aspects. Simply, there are slaves and no women present. Each person who reads this dialogue must evaluate for himself in what sense his pleasure is diminished by these two facts and ask whether what is appealing in it is corrupted by them. One can only say that men and women of taste and intellect have, in ages that do not share the Greek prejudices, still loved the *Symposium* and still learned from it.

Among the participants, there is an atmosphere of perfect equality and a kind of democratic trust in one another. Their speech is both frank and exquisite. There is no aristocratic formalism and no democratic vulgarity. They speak openly about Eros, both taking it seriously and laughing about it. They know one another well and can ridicule one another delicately without offense. These men together celebrate a great occasion by making speeches. They are clearly having fun, without any opposition between edifying talk and enjoying oneself. There is nothing of the atmosphere where somebody clinks on his glass at the table and says, "Let's talk about serious things."

This is an utterly civilized entertainment of men who can drink and make love but who also can both rhyme and reason. There are no constraints of tradition or moralism. It is an association of friends, the substance of whose relations is speech. It would be very difficult to find another historical situation so favorable to this playful but philosophic friendship.

It must also be noted that although several of these men were married, their speeches mostly, although not exclusively, deal with love relations between men. This fact must neither be underestimated nor overestimated. In part, our judgment about the significance of this fact depends on how we regard heterosexual and homosexual relations: Are they essentially the same, as they were for readers like Rousseau or Shelley (who translated the dialogue into English)? Or does each have its own goal and arouse its own feelings, so that a choice must be made between the two or, at least, they must be regarded as supplementing each other rather than being equivalent? There is no doubt that Plato begins from the conventional Greek practice of pederasty, which does not mean that he accepted it, but only that he was required to begin from the prejudices of the participants even though he may very well transcend them. Plato clearly does not believe that homosexual inclinations, at least for some persons, are simply inborn and therefore not subject to choice, habituation, or education. He knew perfectly well that they flourished in some regimes, or, as we would call them, societies, and therefore were somehow connected with the fundamental legislation or way of life of such regimes.

At the very least, the choice of homosexual Eros has something to do with the freedom, perhaps shocking freedom, of the discussion, powered by erotic reflection and imagination. Homosexuality, as one recognizes as one reads the dialogue, was not utterly acceptable or legal. So this conversation immediately moves beyond the *nomos*, the law or the convention, which is always a morally questionable thing to do, but also stimulates the spirit of inquiry. This is a very private discussion, one the participants could not carry on in public. The homosexual bent of the conversation means that the law which governs marriage, and all that is connected with it, such as natural procreation and the family, are absent. This is Eros pure, ranging free, without benefit of law or teleology. It is for its own sake, not for the city or the family. The consequences, to overstate a bit, for anything other than the two individuals involved are forgotten.

To clarify the significance of this emphasis on homosexuality, it would be well to compare this with the other noble teaching about Eros flourishing at the same time, that found in the Bible. Not long after the *Symposium* was written, the contact of Jewish boys with Greeks and Greek practices caused a crisis in Judaism, echoes of which can still be heard. The Greeks' naked exercises, including those at the Olympic Games, scandalized the Jews when they encountered them, but they also attracted many of their young. Naked exercises obviously could contribute to an actualization of potential erotic attractions among males. But the gymnasia were not all that was objectionable about the Greeks. They were regarded as secondary emanations from their principal cause, Greek philosophy, which was quickly identified with Epicureanism, interpreted as the unbridled pursuit of pleasure. Among serious Jews, the very name Epicurus, in a Hebrew or Yiddish form, is still an ugly epithet.

This is not to say that Greekness meant pederasty, and Judaism meant condemnation of it. "There is an ancient law concerning sexual pleasures, not only of humans but of beasts, a law laid down even in nature, which this practice seems to have corrupted . . . , [in] cities that zealously practice gymnastics . . . the pleasure is given according to nature, it seems, when the female unites with the nature of males for procreation. Males coming together with males, and females with females, seems against nature; and the daring of those who first did it seems to have arisen from a lack of self-restraint with regard to pleasure." This is Plato's *Laws*.[5] "I am distressed for thee, my brother Jonathan; very pleasant hast thou been unto me; wonderful was thy love to me, passing the love of women." This is David lamenting his friend Jonathan, whose soul "was knit with the soul of David, and Jonathan loved him as his own soul."[6] So the Greek thinkers knew the problematic character of homosexual connections, and the Bible recognized their possible nobility. The difference seems to have to do with the status of the law. The Jewish law forthrightly condemned homosexuality and prescribed death to those who practiced it. Plato, who condemns it in the *Laws*, which implies that it is at odds with any system of laws, uses nature as his authority or standard. But nature, as even a careful look at the cited passage will show, is a much more ambiguous standard than the law. Nature must be studied and reasoned about, whereas a law requires only obedience. According to the Jewish law, there is nothing beyond the law, other than God who gave it, whereas, if not for all the Greeks, at least for the Greek philosophers, nature is beyond the law. For them, nature does not give laws, but it must be looked to in making the laws, and therefore is a perpetual source of dispute about the justice of laws. It is even doubtful whether any law can simply be underwritten by nature.

In less abstract form, this difference is expressed in the fact that the relationship between David and Jonathan is the only example in the Hebrew Bible of what one would call an admirable friendship.* It is a source of outrage to Jonathan's father, Saul, that his son prefers his friend to his father, which he indeed does. For Saul, the primacy of the family relations is so great that the threat to them posed by this friendship can only appear a perversion and a crime. In ancient Hebrew, there is no distinct word for friend; it is the same as that for neighbor or a fellow. By contrast, Plato and other Greek writers are full of tales of friends. And I would go so far as to say that the Greeks invented friendship, friendship as it is described by Montaigne, the free choice of total association without consideration of family or other legal ties. Friendship involves the possibility of conflict between itself and family, each bidding for the higher place. Of course,

---

* The only rival, but a serious one, to the depiction of David and Jonathan's friendship is the account of Ruth's love for Naomi. Indeed, Ruth's speech to Naomi expressing that love rivals in beauty David's lament for Jonathan (Ruth 1:16–17, see also 2 Samuel 15:21). While Ruth's love is admirable, its precise character and relationship to friendship is somewhat ambiguous. On the one hand, the origins of Ruth and Naomi's ties are familial, inasmuch as Ruth is the widowed daughter-in-law of Naomi. Moreover, Ruth eventually fulfills a most sacred familial duty (Ruth 3:9–13, 4:1–10; 12–17. Deuteronomy 25:5–10). Through her marriage to Boaz, a relative of her dead husband, Ruth produces a child who is considered the heir of both her dead husband and Naomi. On the other hand, their familial ties are, of course, not relationships of blood. Moreover and more striking, Ruth's affections transcend not only familial differences but the wider ones of ethnicity, inasmuch as Ruth was a Moabite.

However one is to understand the status of Ruth's love, the account of it still has an important bearing upon the story of David and Jonathan, since Ruth is David's great-grandmother. This is one expression of and serves to point one to the remarkable fact that in the Bible almost every depiction of what is or might be a friendship, good or bad, proves to have a connection with David or his family. (See Genesis 38:1–30, 2 Samuel 13:3–5, 15:32–37, 16:16–19, 17:5–15.) David, his ancestors and heirs, are remarkably and distinctively free in their attitude toward family, tribe, and even nation. (Consider Ruth in the light of Deuteronomy 23:3.)

The only potential exception of any weight is the depiction of Job and his friends. However, given the ambiguous status of this book and its teaching, it does not seem to affect the singularity of the story of David and Jonathan. Nor, for obvious reasons, does the possibility that God and Moses were friends (Exodus 33:11) affect the uniqueness of David and Jonathan except to underline it.

By way of conclusion, one may note that as far as the Law itself is concerned, its only reference to friendship occurs in a pejorative and penal context (Deuteronomy 13:6) and reads as follows: "If your brother, the son of your mother or your son or daughter, or your wife or *your friend who is like your own soul* entice you secretly, saying let us go and serve other gods . . ." (emphasis added).

the claims of the family were well known to the Greeks, and there were various and powerful expressions of anger at this new kind of relationship, which seems to have been connected somehow with that other new discovery of the Greeks, philosophy. To the extent that friendship expressed a longing for natural freedom, it is easy to see an erotic element in it.

It goes without saying that there is in the Bible no god Eros, but love surely has its place in the Bible. Abraham's enduring attachment to Sarah, and Jacob's willingness to undergo great and lengthy hardships in order to possess Rachel, belong in the chapter of memorable love affairs. David too had irrepressible longings for rare women and broke moral and religious law to have them. He was also a wonderful poet. This most ambiguous of the biblical heroes was both a great sinner and a great repenter, a style not much to the Greek taste. David, this great king, shows that none of the human virtues or temptations were absent from the Jewish world. But the Jewish law and the morals prescribed by it were almost totally directed to the family, though it would not be true to say that Judaism was simply a law made to protect and reinforce the family. For the family and all of its members were transformed by God's revelation and redirected toward the love of God, "With all thy heart, with all thy soul, and with all thy might."[7] The family is the instrument of this dedication. The covenant itself, and the circumcision to which it obliged men, were a sign of the directing of the procreative powers toward the increase of the Jewish people promised by God. But this dedication lives in and through families rather than individuals. God is the Father. What encourages and protects the family, along with the rules for worship of God, is the center of His law. Eroticism is totally confounded with the procreative function, and only that which contributes to it is celebrated and made beautiful.

This, of course, is found everywhere in Greece too, but there a struggle occurs, and a real opposition arises, one that is respectable and in certain ways wins out. The tragedies of Aeschylus and Sophocles treat of such issues, with the Oedipus story being the most evident one. The biblical incest laws are particularly sacred, and read out in the synagogues on the holiest of days, Yom Kippur. The Bible does not produce a hero, like Oedipus, who broke those laws. The extreme form of Greek impiety about such questions is found in Plato's *Republic*, where marriages, although called sacred, are nothing more than one-night stands arranged by eugenicists to ensure high-quality reproduction among the citizens, and very far-ranging incest was permitted, because everyone is at least a brother or sister to everyone else. Socrates is coolly indifferent to the sacred prohibitions, and the *Republic* really destroys the family. The unqualified authority of the ancestral is abolished in this city. Fathers and mothers hardly exist, and they can be ruled by their wise children. The older kind of family relationship is represented in many places in the dialogues. Cephalus, at the beginning of the *Republic*, treats friendship as a folding into the family of an outsider like Socrates.[8] But Cephalus is quickly dismissed in order to establish the new city, no longer founded on the family or on him. Aristophanes' *Clouds* accuses Socrates of antifamily activities, and the fathers in Athens were vigorous enough to impose the death penalty on him. Nonetheless, the Greek city itself required a certain subordination of the family.

The primacy of the family as the foremost or even exclusive erotic expression is connected in the Bible with an almost total absence of politics. Again by contrast, to make another overbold statement, it was the Greeks who invented politics. In an etymological sense, politics concerns those who live in a *polis*, a city, and not those who live in the country. Moreover, politics seems to require the availability of a republican alternative to monarchy. Elsewhere, one form of despotism or another was all there was. Even the establishment of a king in Israel was a subject of debate and only reluctantly accepted by God. The people of Israel was constituted by tribes, extensions of families, while the Greek cities were founded on a suppression of the tribes and of the claims of the fathers to rule. The rulers were no longer chosen because they were in any way blood relatives. This set up a permanent tension in the cities between the family and the political order, resulting in various compromises, since each needs the other. The political actors are not essentially family men, and their activities do not concern the same things as do those of fathers. The invention of politics is a liberation from the family order, although it may result in almost as total a subjection to the political order. The *Republic* is an impossibly radical scheme to suppress the family in the name of the city and thus to overcome the tension created by the dualism. The Bible is an attempt to solve this problem in the other direction, that of the family.

The actual Greek cities were dominated by associations of males, partly because war, defensive or offensive, was their most important function. This was the occasion for another kind of love than that promoted by the family. In the *Republic*, heterosexual relations are necessary for the perpetuation of the city, but eroticism is possible in all directions without the family and without "gender-specific" roles for men and women. Rousseau called this "civil promiscuity," and the more moderate Aristotle expressed shock at a city where fathers could have love affairs with their own sons.[9] Politics, pederasty, and friendship cluster together around the Greeks and have some connection with one another.

The family and the eroticism devoted to it are arguably more natural than what is found in the cities. The family certainly came first and cleaves closely to the evidently natural procreative function of men and women. But the Greek philosophers argued that the family is only imperfectly natural because it, more than perhaps anything else in human life, requires myths, conventions, and prohibitions to hold it together, all of which stand in the way of the full development of man's powers, particularly the intellectual ones. Cool consideration of the reasonableness of the incest prohibitions, for example, is something that belongs to philosophers and not to fathers. Even today, Montesquieu's nonchalance in such considerations can be deeply offensive to students, and not only students.[10] The psychological distortions resulting from family life remain the great subject of psychoanalysis. This pale afterglow of Greek philosophy still exacerbates parents' fear because psychologists may teach their children to blame them. Parents and families distort a child's eroticism by directing it toward the kind of spouses and offspring that are suitable to their projects. The family in principle prefers age to wisdom, and surrounds itself with all kinds of sacred terrors. Both intellectual and political freedom seem to depend upon some kind of a break with it. Pericles, who knew a lot about politics, at the end of his Funeral Oration told women, who in his view represented the family, to go home and keep quiet. The subjection of the family to the ends of both the city and the intellect is a primary task of classical political philosophy.

If one is aware of this problem, which the greatest thinkers treated but did not make too explicit, it leads one into the most secret recesses of their most important works, such as Plato's *Republic* and *Laws* and Aristotle's *Politics*. The family is necessary, but some distance from it in deed and thought must be acquired by anyone who desires to be a fully developed human being. This does not mean that the city does not develop constraints on freedom, sometimes as great as those of the family, which the truly free individual must also overcome. This movement is recapitulated in the *Republic*, with its noble lie, myths, and bizarre sexual regulations, where first the family is annihilated in the name of the city, and then the philosophers, who are to be its rulers, do not want to turn away from their contemplations to descend to the city's cavelike darkness. It is mostly around the family that the sacred things aggregate. The Greeks were the first to engage in religious criticism or even to become thoughtful atheists. There were impious and blasphemous persons everywhere and always, but only a very few Greeks would envision a world without gods. Herodotus makes up a story about an Egyptian who left his city, which was under attack. As he disappeared from view, its defenders on the walls yelled at him, "You will lose your gods and your children." He responded, pointing to his genitals, "I can make more." He either disregarded the gods or thought that they somehow came from the same organs as do children. Herodotus gives in a capsule something of what those marginal Greeks, who are the only ones we now really remember, were thinking about.[11]

Thus we are the heirs of two great teachings about the place of Eros or love in the life of man, the one passed down to us by the Bible, the other by the Greek philosophers, poets, and historians of the fifth and fourth centuries B.C. The former rests on the ultimate ground of God and His Revelation; the latter rests on nature and its rational study by philosophers. The Jews were characterized by a steadfast loyalty to and love of God; the obedience to His law is the sum and substance of that love. The Greek philosopher is a skeptical investigator of nature, which does not speak in a clear voice and does not give laws for the conduct of human beings; he is less a doer than a speculator. Piety is the highest virtue for the one, whereas an investigation of the divine, which for many seems an impiety, is the most human activity for the other. Membership in the family is what defines the biblical man and woman; the Greek was defined, on the one hand, by membership in a *polis*, or, on the other hand, by his philosophic individualism (a much less neat definition, deriving from the lack of the authoritative guidance provided by the Bible). The Jew's primary association and attachment is to mother, father, sister, brother, and, the only outsider, husband or wife. The wife left her family to follow the family of her husband and thus was incorporated into it. For the Greek, the attachment of all attachments was to the friend. For the Jew, the only laudable and beautiful human erotic expression is found in the relation between husband and wife. For the Greek, the erotic ties were more diffuse and, as one sees in the *Symposium*, concentrated less on fidelity than on the quest for the beautiful, wherever it may be found. Marriage and the family were of necessity important for the Greeks and, as a rule of thumb for most men and women, subject to severe law, but the character of the family was altered for the sake of the other kinds of concerns brought to light by politics and philosophy. For the Greek thinkers, the family was no more sacred than was private property, although they admitted the need for both. But this was more in the spirit of a compromise than something desirable in itself, as the *Republic*'s abolition of both indicates.

As heirs to these great contrary sources, we find ourselves always carrying on a certain balancing act between two visions of the good life, with primacy of one or the other to be found in different degrees in different times and places. The direct clash between the two has produced some of the greatest crises of our history. Such a clash occurred in Islam from the ninth century to the fourteenth century, until Greekness was rejected within Islam, though by then it had flowed into Judaism and Christianity. The sovereign works of men like Farabi, Maimonides, and Thomas Aquinas are the literary remains of these crises and the attempts to settle them. The Renaissance was another such striking instance of the quarrel. Our two heritages have endowed our instincts with mixed signals about Eros. Shakespeare gives us evidence of this in so many ways, epitomized in the contrasts between Cleopatra and Hermione, between the Roman Portia and Juliet. The Bible teaches us an intense but severely limited eroticism, one tainted by the Fall and the disobedience to God's command that brought it on. The Law condemns all Eros that does not contribute to the family's end and enhance it. In contrast, for the Greeks, who, for the sake of political and intellectual freedom, questioned the family and even the law, precisely those desires and yearnings that collide with the family and the law become the core of Eros, which in turn metamorphoses into the passion for free self-discovery.

Aristophanes, one of the two central actors in the *Symposium* and the greatest of all comic poets, expresses this Greek longing as well as anyone. His comedy itself is the literary form of such liberation, and the issue is to be found throughout his works. In his play the *Birds* he gives us two men who leave Athens in order to get away from the *nomos*, the law, and its meddling. They want to go up and live with and be as free as the birds. It turns out that they must, in order to get this freedom, not only leave the city but depose the old gods in the city and put the birds in their place. Their "original intent" in their outgoing is stated by each of them. One, the gentler and less ambitious of the two, wants to go to a place where a man will invite him to a wedding feast, saying that if he does not come now, in the host's prosperity, he should keep away when the host has hard times. This is the opposite of the spirit of private property: his fellow citizen commands him to take and backs this up with the threat of not taking in turn when he is needy. The second of the wanderers, the more daring and political of the two, explains his motives, also based on an expectation of finding a place where the laws are the contrary of what they are elsewhere, by saying:

> I long* for a place
> Where a father of a boy in the bloom of youth
> Will blame me for doing an injustice;
> "It's a fine thing that you did to my son, Stilbonides,
> Meeting him all bathed, leaving the gymnasium,
> You did not kiss him, speak to him, embrace him,
> Or grab his testicles."[12]

His hopes are far more radical than those of his friend, who merely longs for something like communism, whereas he wants to transform the nature of the fathers.

II

In the passage of the *Laws* I quoted previously, where the Athenian Stranger criticizes the practice of pederasty in Crete and Sparta, the Spartan responds, with nationalistic fervor, by attacking Athenian drunkenness. This gives the Athenian an opportunity to defend drinking, drinking together, as a mode of softening the rigid attachments to old laws that prevent rethinking them and reforming them. Alcohol is a great loosener of tongues, which are frequently tied by the law or the customs. He prescribes for his two elderly companions the practice of *symposia* if they are presided over by a moderate person so they do not get out of hand.[13] In the *Symposium* Plato combines the two practices: at a drinking party, the participants talk about pederasty. This might confirm Athenian suspicions that the aristocratic crowd with which Socrates associated consisted of disloyal Spartanophiles. The discussion is suggested by and presided over by the very moderate Eryximachus. The salubrious effects of drink in freeing men from convention portrayed here give us some idea of what the most secret conversations encouraged in the severe city of the *Laws* might be about. Drink is a necessary component of the freest association of men and helps them leap over the chasm separating *nomos* (convention) and *physis* (na-

---

* The verb *eraō*, related to eros.

ture). Something of our current problem is indicated by the fact that these men today would be considered guilty of "substance abuse." The evolution of the word "symposium" from this Greek association, with its drunken revelers telling one another what they care about most, to the symposiums of sober modern scholars, with their scientific detachment, is most instructive.

The titles of the great majority of Plato's works consist of the name of a person, like Phaedrus. Only the *Republic, Laws, Sophist,* and *Statesman* tell us what the subject matter is. The *Lovers* most probably refers to actors in the drama. The *Apology of Socrates* gives us both a name and the thing that is done. The *Symposium*, like the *Republic*, tells us about a kind of association. One might say, though, that this title is closest to that of the *Apology of Socrates;* and from the two dialogues we get very differing accounts about what Socrates characteristically does. The *Apology* insists on Socrates' knowledge of ignorance and contains not a word about Eros. The *Symposium* gives us a Socrates who in deed and speech is utterly preoccupied with the practice of the science of Eros. He is in the company of the young man whom he was preeminently accused of having corrupted, and the allegedly impious Socrates engages in the discussion of a god.

These revelers are, of course, not just anybodies. They include Aristophanes and Socrates, who need no introduction, as well as Agathon, the brightest light among the tragic poets who succeeded Sophocles and Euripides. And then there is the dramatic entry of the great Alcibiades. The others are worthy, if not world-historical, personages. This is what Athens could offer in its unrivaled moment, which still fascinates mankind.

It must be added that there is not among the participants a great appetite for drinking a lot on this particular evening. They were wildly drunk the night before in celebration of Agathon's victory in the tragic contest. God only knows what else they did. Socrates absented himself on that first night and comes only on this night when the members of the group are much diminished. The implication of this is that the wild party does not admit of serious speech. Socrates' behavior introduces a sobering reflection, indicating that the most unconstrained expressions of desire connected with food, drink, and sex must be disappointed if intellectual satisfaction is also to find its place. There is a tension that is reduced on this second night by having rhetorical speeches, not dialectic, from men who are a bit dull and made moderate by yesterday's indulgences.

One of the most striking aspects of the dialogue is the air of mystery surrounding what actually took place that night. The date when it took place is not known to those who have heard of it, and the accuracy of the reports about the contents of the speeches is compromised by the fact that it is repeated to the world third-hand, a distance from the original that is found in only one other dialogue, *Parmenides*.[14] The Platonic dialogues, with these two exceptions, are divided into acted and narrated dialogues. An acted dialogue is one where we see the participants as in a play. A narrated dialogue is one, such as the *Republic*, where someone tells of an encounter of Socrates with a person or group of persons. The *Symposium* is a subspecies of the narrated dialogue. The advantage of the acted dialogue is that one has the feeling of experiencing the thing as it actually happened. The advantage of the narrated dialogue is that, even if one is not sure of the narrator's accuracy, nevertheless he can tell us important things, like where Cephalus was sitting or that Thrasymachus blushed, that we would not learn from an acted dialogue. The *Symposium* does give us such distinctive descriptive elements, but the double narration—that is, an enthusiast of Socrates repeating what another enthusiast of Socrates told him, even though he claims he checked it out with Socrates himself—makes us somewhat doubtful. I would suggest that this covering by distance and time and narration has to do with the scandalous or dangerous implications of this meeting. Socrates, particularly in his relationship to Alcibiades, was, at the supposed date of this repetition, already becoming very well known and suspect. One can gather that the story is renowned, at least in certain circles in Athens, and that many persons are eager to hear it. And, as among Socrates' disciples in the *Clouds*, who say that his teachings are secret but blabber about them to anyone who comes to the Think Tank, the security arrangements here are porous. Whoever knows the story, repeats it. Socrates' lovers are also proselytizers.

The dates indicated by the speakers in the dialogue teach us something about what is going on in it. The date of the symposium itself is indicated to be around 416 B.C., at the last moment of Athenian splendor.[15] The victory of Agathon in the contest at the Lenaean Festival seemed to provide a continuation of the tradition of tragic poetry in the person of this attractive youth. And Athens itself was about to undertake the Sicilian expedition, the most splendid imperial exercise yet to be projected by the Athenians, under the instigation and leadership of Alcibiades. They prepared naval and ground forces of a size and beauty never yet seen, and were about to embark on a daring enterprise of conquest, completed only much later by the Romans. According to Thucydides, the Athenian people's distrust of Alcibiades was what caused the Sicilian expedition to fail.[16] The participants in this military expedition were, again according to Thucydides, infused with an Eros for Sicily, one of the few mentions of Eros by Thucydides, an Eros communicated by Alcibiades' rhetoric.[17] Just prior to the departure of the force, with its leadership divided between the radical Alcibiades and the conservative Nicias, a typical and self-destructive compromise made by the people, Alcibiades was accused of having mutilated the statues of the Hermae, religious statues scattered about Athens, and the profanation of the Mysteries, the most sacred and secret Athenian religious rite. The truth or falsehood of these charges is unknowable. But like Socrates, Alcibiades enjoyed a very bad reputation and his life was surrounded by rumors. He too seemed a threat to the democracy, although he was also at times its darling, as Socrates never was.

In short, the symposium seems to have taken place at just the moment when Alcibiades is supposed to have committed his impious deeds. As Alfred Dreyfus is purported to have said, where there's smoke, there's fire. Maybe Plato wishes to indicate that this private and fabled gathering, where the god Eros is unconventionally praised and a drunken Alcibiades enters to praise Socrates, was inflated by rumor into mutilation and profanation. The reserved Thucydides never mentions Socrates or any other intellectual or artistic figure, while both Xenophon and Plato lightheartedly make Socrates play a historical role through his relationship to Alcibiades, hinting that what was most radical and suspect in Alcibiades had something to do with Socrates. Do not forget that Aristophanes is a leading figure in this drama, and he was "the old accuser" of Socrates.

The retelling of what went on in the symposium took place around the year 404 B.C., a low point in Athenian history, when the Peloponnesian War was utterly lost and Athens stripped of its empire.[18] Agathon was in exile and Alcibiades was dead. And Socrates' increased renown was tending toward a storm that was to culminate in his execution five years later. This moment was the dividing line between the age that combined Athenian political greatness and the unparalleled flourishing of the arts, and that of the rise of the philosophers, who dominate the Athenian story from the fourth century on, beginning with Xenophon, Plato, and Aristotle. This dominance, as Nietzsche pointed out, is connected with Socrates' critique of the noble and artistic instincts. If philosophy did not destroy Athenian culture, it prospered in its demise. The accusation of philosophy's destructiveness was made on behalf of the political men and the poets. In this dialogue Socrates certainly engages with gentlemen, if not the ordinary citizens of the democracy, as well as one of the greatest statesmen of antiquity. This is the only place where we see him with the poets. This is an excellent vantage point for deciding what Socrates did and how he did it. Here we can examine the charges brought against Socrates by the Athenians and by Nietzsche, that proponent of a new renaissance, but one without Socrates.

In the small preface to the dialogue itself (172a–174a), which is directly acted out, one gets the impression that Socrates had some odd and fanatical groupies, not unlike those described in the *Clouds*. Apollodorus, the narrator, resembles the typical member of a cult or a sect. He spends most of his time listening to Socrates, as much as he is permitted to, and the rest of the time repeating to other men what Socrates said, while abusing them. He is far from the urbane men we see in the dialogue itself. He is a tormented fellow who hates himself because he is so far beneath Socrates, while being filled with contempt and anger at those who go on about their daily lives, especially concerned with the pursuit of money, without asking themselves whether what they do is good. He lacks only the placard with the message "The day of judgment is at hand." Such followers were not designed to win friends or influence people, although their capacity to retell Socrates' interesting speeches did have an effect in transmitting something of Socrates' teaching. This is a problem faced by all great teachers, the fanatic loyalists whose fanaticism is quite alien to the teacher's disposition. They develop an almost religious reverence for this man whose teaching they are so deeply impressed by but are not themselves in a position adequately to judge. The teacher himself may very well not want to discourage such people. They are the scholars who study him carefully and pass on what he has to say to others. But there is a danger that he will be misinterpreted or rigidified or codified by them in a way contrary to the spirit of his teaching. There is the further danger that the pupil's imprudence, partly connected with preening himself with this special learning, will attract undue and hostile attention to that teaching. Pupils can appear to be members of a crazy sect and permit onlookers to dismiss teacher as well as pupils. This risk may have to be accepted when one teaches, but it involves a real problem of responsibility or even self-protection. Among Rousseau's pupils is not only Goethe but also Robespierre. The former is a pupil Rousseau would have wanted, the latter one by whom he would have been horrified, but he could not have had one without the other, in addition to all the tiresome mediocrities who parroted him. What can be said of

Rousseau is true in spades for Nietzsche. So Socrates had not only Plato and Xenophon, but Apollodorus and Alcibiades. Plato, as we see here, is very much aware of the problem, and that awareness informs his artful mode of writing. But certain kinds of abuses, like Neoplatonism, were unavoidable. In Plato's case, at least, his teaching could never be used as the ideology for a tyranny.

The common source of the stories about the symposium was a man who is described as one of Socrates' chief lovers (*erastēs*, a derivative of Eros) at the time, Aristodemus. This use of the word "lover" provides us with a sharp contrast to the image of lover and beloved projected by the dialogue itself. Aristodemus is an ugly little man who, like Socrates, went barefoot and who was simply glad to be near Socrates. Socrates as beloved is a rather unusual notion inasmuch as he was older and himself also ugly. The heroic lovers and their beautiful young beloveds, as described in the dialogue, are very different from this odd couple, who it is not even clear have much of a relationship, and certainly not an erotic one in any common meaning of that word. There is a kind of lover of Socrates' speeches whose love is very different in spirit from the eroticism of the *Symposium*. There is obviously some connection between the two, but also a tension that makes us reflect on the problem of eroticism in ways not explicitly contained in the dialogue. There seems to be an independent eroticism around speeches that is not supported by the bodily Eros that all the participants in the dialogue seem to presuppose.

III Socrates encounters his lover, Aristodemus, on the way to the drinking party (174a–175a). It is an unusual Socrates, for he has just bathed and is wearing slippers. On this day Aristodemus resembles Socrates more than Socrates does, for Aristodemus is barefoot. Socrates says that he is on his way to Agathon's for the second night of the celebration, having missed the first night for fear of the mob, and has dolled himself up to be beautiful for his beautiful host. Socrates is ordinarily the virtuoso of the good and the useful, but tonight is dedicated more to the beautiful than the good. So we find an adorned Socrates, perhaps a less authentic one, as he approaches the question of Eros, which has much more to do with the beautiful than the good. What is the relation between these two things? Man responds to two different and powerful appeals in the good and the beautiful, and this dialogue investigates that dualism.

Aristodemus is next the victim of a trick of Socrates' that leads to his embarrassment. Socrates invites Aristodemus, who was not invited by Agathon, to Agathon's party. After a bit of byplay about whether the good go to the worse or the worse go to the good, a byplay on which Socrates' going to Agathon's is a commentary in itself, the two men start off.* As they walk together, Socrates stops and turns his mind on himself, contemplating silently. He tells Aristodemus to go on ahead, and that he will join him later. In this dialogue about the coupling of human beings, we begin with a Socrates who uncouples himself from his partner in order to think. This solitariness in what is properly Socrates' preferred activity is an important background to what is said in the dialogue. Alcibiades will pick up this theme and tell of Socrates' amazing powers of concentration. We get here at the outset a glimpse of Socrates in his most characteristic activity, one that cannot be shown in itself in the drama but can only be seen from the outside. Here he is alone, and those who see him can only wonder what is going on in his head; they have no access to what he is thinking about or how he is thinking about it. This in itself can cause envy and suspicion. He appears to be self-sufficient, a thing that puzzled Aristophanes, who tried to treat it as a mistake and a folly. In the rest of the dialogue, at the dinner party, we get the other Socrates, not found in Aristophanes, the perfectly urbane and sociable Socrates. He has paid attention to every individual and has made the subtlest psychological observations about each one, and his behavior is witty and graceful. Here we see Socrates combining what Pascal said could not be combined, *l'esprit de géométrie et l'esprit de finesse*, concern with the most universal principles and concern for the ultimate particulars, especially the different kinds of souls—brutishness and exquisite politeness. The ordinary view of Socrates as a pious sermonizer who ruins parties by stopping to ask people whether they care for their souls is hardly present in the dialogue, except for his imitator Apollodorus.

Aristodemus goes on by himself, wishing to hang around in front of Agathon's house until Socrates catches up, but he is met by a servant, who thrusts him into the dinner. The poor fellow is terribly humiliated by coming to a party where no one thought to invite him and without the cover of his friend, who was much desired by the

---

* In Greek, Agathon's name means "good," and is spelled the same as "good men's" in the proverb Socrates speaks of here: "Good men go of their own accord to good men's feasts."

others. Agathon proves his own urbanity by saying that he went around personally looking for Aristodemus but missed him; he however makes it clear who is really wanted by immediately asking, "Where is Socrates?"

Socrates does not appear until the dinner is well under way (175c). He is obviously a man who is respected and enjoyed by all, a prime catch for the host of a dinner party. The philosopher as good dinner companion is a kind of riddle. In being together, he is also separate. There is a certain truth to Aristophanes' picture of Socrates in his basket, monstrously unconcerned with what concerns most people. But there is another side of Socrates that has learned to live with people in a society and to learn from them. One can understand something of what his fabled irony means when it becomes evident that to cover the distance between the two sides of his life, Socrates must wear a mask. He makes himself somewhat like his companions. Moreover, he has learned to distinguish among them and simply to protect himself from those to whom he is not attracted, and to interest those to whom he is attracted. From this point of view, one can distinguish two kinds of dialogue, forced and erotic. A prime example of the former is the *Apology*, where, as it were, wearing handcuffs and accompanied by the police, he must defend himself on a capital charge before a largely hostile mob. Typical of the latter is the *Charmides*, where Socrates, back from his enforced stay with the army at the battle of Potidaea, with delight turns to the gymnasium where he can spend his time with the boys.[19] His interest in young men is a positive erotic impulse, a charm he freely chooses. There is nothing like this in Aristophanes' comedy about Socrates, and how it fits into Socrates' way of life is the theme of this dialogue in which he confronts Aristophanes.

Agathon, who clearly knows Socrates pretty well, in another example of his politeness, invites Socrates to sit next to him and somehow in contact with him. With a kind of self-protective counterirony, he says that from this contact he will be able to lay hold of the wise thing that Socrates has just thought out. Socrates parries by saying that he could only wish that wisdom were a bodily thing like water, which can by osmosis go from fuller to emptier. He obscenely parodies the erotic claim of pederasty to pass wisdom from the older man to the younger one. He wishes such osmosis were possible, he says, because he would be the gainer from his contact with Agathon. His own wisdom is dreamlike and contestable, whereas Agathon, although young, has proved his wisdom to the satisfaction of thirty thousand Athenian witnesses. The fair Agathon, although younger, is the full one who can fill the emptiness of the older Socrates. But would he want to? Agathon obviously is not attracted to the individual members of his audience, but he loves their collective admiration and worship. He is almost certainly not teachable, for, in order to be so, he would have to value Socrates' applause more highly than that of the people. Agathon plays at being erotic here, but he is too full of himself to feel a lack that only Socrates could fill. At the same time, he has a somewhat haunted sense that Socrates may be a better witness than all of the Greeks together, a sense he playfully tries to suppress. Socrates is not interested enough in him to go any further. Socrates' obscene contempt nettles the ever urbane Agathon, who accuses him of hubris, as if Agathon were a kind of god insulted by the impious Socrates. In one of so many references to Socrates' ultimate fate scattered throughout the dialogues, Agathon says that there will be a trial about Socrates' wisdom versus his own, with the god Dionysus the judge in place of the people.

After the dinner has concluded and the conventional libations and chants to the gods have been made, Pausanias says that they should consider how the members of the company should drink together, expressing the hope that it will not be really serious drinking because he has a hangover (176a–178a). Everyone agrees to this; and in the deliberation about it, Eryximachus makes a distinction between those who are good drinkers, like Agathon and Aristodemus, and those who can't hold their liquor well, like Phaedrus, and Eryximachus. Eryximachus exempts Socrates from the distinction because he is equally good at both drinking and not drinking, unaffected by drinking or abstinence. This distinction is represented in the dialogue by the fact that the first three speakers are poor drinkers and turn out to be less erotic, and that the two poets and the philosopher who follow are good drinkers and more erotic. Alcibiades, who turns up late and very drunk, fits in with the latter group. One of the things that provokes envy of Socrates is his indifference to things that affect other people most powerfully. In Aristophanes' depiction, he is a man of almost unbelievable continence, not to say insensibility. He is not hungry when others are starving,[20] and in Aristophanes' comic style, he does not notice that there are bedbugs in his mattress, which torture almost to death anyone else who happens to lie there.[21] Even Xenophon is irritated by this aspect of Socrates, and it raises questions of the extent to which Eros' love bites might affect him.[22]

Drinking cannot be their central activity of the evening, and one gathers that their erotic potency has been as much lamed as their potative capacity by the previous night's activity. They have a doctor in the house, Eryximachus, who says that he himself is always opposed to excess and that drunkenness is harsh on human beings. So he suggests that they amuse themselves by talking, with the evident implication that talking may be a sensible thing to do but is only second best. They are forced away from deeds toward speeches. Eryximachus suggests that they dedicate themselves to a rhetorical task that, he claims, has never before been undertaken, the praise of Eros. They are in a position of having to praise love rather than make it. He says that all the other gods have been praised by poets and rhetoricians, but never Eros. Phaedrus, who is interested in both speeches and Eros, as we learn from the dialogue bearing his name, has been complaining about this lack. Later on in his career, he was evidently adroit enough to get his older admirer Lysias to praise not love or the lover, but the nonlover, in the affairs of love.[23] All this would seem to imply that Eros is not a major deity, although his companion Aphrodite is. Eryximachus says that Sophists even praise salt, showing thereby an interest not in the thing but in the display of their rhetorical skill. All of this is evidently for Eryximachus merely trifling for an evening's amusement, not something to be taken very seriously. Socrates, though, eagerly votes for the proposal and says that the others, particularly Aristophanes, whose whole life work is about Dionysus and Aphrodite, would also vote for it. Any community requires a consensus based on the wills and opinions of diverse people looking toward a common good. Socrates here votes in favor of the formation of this community that will eagerly discuss Eros more readily than he does when, under some constraint, he votes to constitute the community necessary to discuss justice in the *Republic*.

So, Phaedrus begins with his praise.

IV Phaedrus is not a very appealing character, and it is strange that he is not only a major figure in the *Symposium* but also that his name is immortalized by the *Phaedrus*, the other great dialogue on love. He seems to be in the love business, someone who gets a lot of attention from older men—and likes it—but who himself is essentially unerotic. In the *Phaedrus* he is portrayed as being delighted by a speech presented to him by the great orator Lysias. This speech attempts to persuade a fair youth to accept the attention of a nonlover, because such a nonlover will in the long run serve the nonbeloved's interests better. Phaedrus is the audience in that dialogue for Socrates' praise of mad love, but almost certainly not the object of it. He must have been very good-looking, a frivolous young man who praises manliness but is an avid consumer of the wares of the Sophists and the rhetoricians, a culture buff. His speech emphatically insists on the distinction between lover and beloved, that unreciprocal attachment characteristic of pederasty, and he is just as emphatically the beloved who profits from the love of the lover. The beloved is the recipient of gifts, praise, and much more, as we shall see. Nice work if you can get it.

Phaedrus' speech (178a–180b) is a good student's imitation of conventional epideictic rhetoric. Of the three classical forms of rhetoric, in the *Symposium* we get a clear case of the epideictic, the rhetorician's display of his powers for the adorning of public occasions, the ancient Fourth of July oration; and in Pansania's speech we get the deliberative, the tool of the political man in attempting to influence public discussions about war and peace and the enactment of laws. The third kind, forensic rhetoric, used in courts for accusation and defense, seems missing here. It is possible that Alcibiades' speech in the *Symposium*, in which Socrates is playfully accused, is the missing forensic speech. A certain absence of the constraint of law seems to be the condition of having such a meeting, and the relative indifference to the law on the part of so many of the participants is what lent the meeting its public reputation of having been illegal. There is a letting go here that is probably dangerous.*

Phaedrus follows the rigid outlines characteristic of epideictic praises, which, as we have learned, can be lavished on anything. Only in the interstices of this rigid framework do Phaedrus' opinions and personal quirkiness peek out. He begins with a statement that Eros is a great and wondrous god for both men and gods. Then he goes directly to Eros' origins and asserts the god's greatness by reason of his antiquity. He accepts the prejudice that the good is the old, the opinion of traditional communities. He also reflects the opinion of the pre-Socratic philosophers that we learn most about what a thing is from examining its origins. In keeping with the point of view of the ancestral, Phaedrus takes the authority of the poets as proof of

---

* Socrates' most famous rhetorical endeavor, his *Apology*, was an example of forensic rhetoric. He also repeats in the *Menexenus* an epideictic speech by Aspasia, Pericles' mistress, in praise of Athens, a thing Socrates asserts is easy to do among Athenians. If he has any deliberative rhetoric, it is somehow to be found in the dialogues as a whole, where he influences people concerning the most important questions of their lives.

his assertions. He quotes Hesiod and mentions Acusilaus, who taught that Chaos came first, and then Earth and Eros. Perhaps Eros is what holds Earth together after Chaos has been overcome. Something similar is told by Parmenides the philosopher, who says that Genesis contrived Eros first of the gods. The eldest is necessarily the cause of the best.

Phaedrus asserts that the greatest of goods for a young man is to have a decent (or useful) lover, and for a lover to have a boy. The construction of the Greek sentence is such that it is difficult to decide whether Phaedrus says a decent boy or just a boy, a confusion not implausible in someone who speaks, as does Phaedrus, from the point of view of the beloved. His sole argument for this assertion is based on the shame felt by either lover or beloved when caught in doing ignoble deeds. Shame is an accompaniment of love of the noble. Men's object is to lead a life that is noble (or beautiful, the word is *kalon*, which means both, an ambiguity important for this dialogue). The greatest good is not the good life, but the noble life. The word for shameful is the same as the word for ugly. Men live nobly and do noble deeds out of fear of the bad opinion of privileged observers. Lovers are more concerned with the opinions of their beloveds, and vice versa, than with those even of their relatives. Eros produces shame, and shame is the best motivator for nobility, more powerful than family, honors, or money.

Such heroic concern for opinions is all very problematic, as is revealed in *Troilus and Cressida* and many other places. The opinion of others is obviously an important part of the heroic life, and Phaedrus, no hero, speaks only of the heroic, that is, the military, life. His innovation is to make Eros the crucial element in heroic ambition, which Homer certainly does not do. Phaedrus takes it for granted that the relationship between Achilles and Patroclus is a love affair.

The special vice that is avoided by lovers is cowardice. In Phaedrus' presentation, the emphasis is on the negative, the avoidance of vice, rather than any attraction or charm to be found in virtue. Vice draws us and can be counteracted by Eros. The avoidance of shameful deeds as a result of Eros is praised while the shame of erotic activity itself is not mentioned. Phaedrus never even alludes to the sexual act or any pleasure connected with it. This is understandable given his concentration on shame, for the most shameless things that men do are popularly connected with sexual desires and acts. Actually, he does not praise Eros, but the fruits of Eros, which can indeed be heroic but are not necessarily so. It is this glossing over by Phaedrus of the two-pronged character of Eros that provides the opening wedge for Pausanias' speech. Eros is not loved by this beloved, nor is virtue, but the one can be used to serve the other for the sake of good reputation in this life and the next. And it is this question of the next life that is the peculiar feature of Phaedrus' speech. To Phaedrus the most important effect of Eros is in war, the characteristic activity of the hero. The lover is ashamed to be seen by his beloved doing cowardly things and, above all, is willing to die to save his beloved. A pretty good deal for the beloved. (This theme is raised again by Alcibiades, who tells of Socrates saving his life.) If a not too courageous young man has a good lover, he will be protected from death and wounds by him. Phaedrus is a young Athenian who admires, as did many Athenian youths, the way of life and the virtues of the very military Spartans. But he is clearly not an eager warrior. What better for a man in this position than to have a lover who, because he passionately wants some dirty little thing from Phaedrus, will be his surest defender? To Phaedrus it seems a small thing to accede to the lover in exchange for such an insurance policy.

The rest of Phaedrus' speech is almost entirely devoted to deaths of lovers and beloveds for each others' sakes. The connection of Eros and death is one we have discussed earlier, and Phaedrus must be praised for his awareness of this weighty connection in love. But he does not state it very clearly nor as a necessary component of Eros. It is rather that Eros seems to provide some kind of motive for lovers to face death, a disposition that is otherwise obviously incomprehensible to him. This unerotic man sees in the erotic man a capacity to die for his beloved that is useful but beyond his ken. He is honestly in awe of this. But he understands it all as some strange frenzy that causes the lover to cease calculating, and in that, he sees the utility of Eros. He is, at least on some level, aware that this is not real virtue, but that Eros makes such a man equal to the one with "the best nature." There is such a thing as a good nature, which is higher than the virtue induced by Eros, but it is utterly alien to Phaedrus, and besides would not have the advantage of providing him with special attention. He says that an army composed of lovers and their beloveds would be an unbeatable fighting force that, although composed of the few, would conquer all human beings. He makes the distinction between men who are emphatically men (*andres*) and human beings (*anthrōpoi*), with a great preference for men. Real men are fighters, thus making the love of men for one another the highest kind of love for the cities that need defense and desire conquest. This is a manly speech, and the Greek word *andreia* or courage means manliness. Such a band of lovers was later founded at Thebes and contributed to its greatest victories in the first third of the fourth century.[24] This is the improvement on Sparta of which Phaedrus would have heartily approved. The erotic motive is easier to find than the pure love of virtue for its own sake.

Phaedrus' choice of examples to illustrate his argument is curious. Surprisingly, the first case that comes to his mind is that of a woman who performs the manliest of deeds, which poses a problem for Phaedrus' emphasis on *andres*. She is Alcestis, who was willing to die for her husband. She was rewarded for this by being sent back to the earth from Hades by the gods. The second case concerns the cowardly Orpheus, a poet, not a warrior, who tried to trick the gods and to get back his beloved Eurydice from Hades without himself dying. Phaedrus has nothing but contempt for a man who does not want to die for his beloved. In this case, the beloved is a woman and he interprets Orpheus' death to have been contrived by the gods as a punishment for his unwillingness "to dare to die for the sake of Eros." This death was the most humiliating one possible, appropriate to a mere lyre player, death at the hands of women. Dying seems for Phaedrus to be the only proper culmination and the only proof of Eros.

The third and final case is the most complicated and interesting one, that of Achilles, who has been in the background throughout this speech. Achilles is a man who did indeed die for his friend and in that sense fits the argument. But he is, according to Phaedrus, younger than his friend Patroclus. He insists, who knows on what authority, that Achilles was still beardless, that he was the beloved. Therefore, he is like Phaedrus, and Phaedrus makes a great effort to prove that Achilles was indeed the beloved. Aeschylus babbles when he asserts the contrary. Phaedrus makes himself a Homeric character on the basis of his training in the erotic attractions of men. His whole speech presupposes the superiority of Achilles as the model for those who wish to live well, but he succeeds in bringing that model down to his own level. But the problem is that Achilles' action, as Phaedrus himself admits, is a miracle, that is, an event without a natural cause. The lover has the god in him and is motivated thereby to the sacrifices he makes. Achilles, the more beautiful of the two, performs the more beautiful deed. Achilles chose to remain and die rather than go home and live comfortably till old age. Phaedrus explains this choice not, as Homer appears to, as a result of Achilles' general love of glory, but as somehow connected with Eros. He claims, moreover, that Achilles was as a reward sent to the Isles of the Blessed. In this he follows Pindar rather than Homer's *Odyssey*, where we see Achilles very unhappy about being in Hades. Phaedrus says that the gods honored Achilles more than they did Alcestis because he was a beloved and she a lover.

At this point, Phaedrus becomès a bit incoherent. The gods, he says, honor this virtue, which is connected with Eros, but they wonder more, are more delighted, and give more benefits when the beloved is attached (the word comes from *agapē*, which evolved gradually into the word for Christian love) to the lover than when the lover is attached to the beloved. And then comes the strange sentence: "for the lover is more divine than the beloved. He has a god in him." He insists that the gods honor more the one who does not have a god within him than the one who does. The implication is that the gods themselves are lovers and are grateful to those who respect lovers. This would imply, if Phaedrus knew how to think about it, that there is something higher than the gods, in this case, a return of affection to the gods, which the gods themselves worship. The gods are in a position to reward such return of affection most handsomely. Unfortunately, this appears most strikingly after death.

Phaedrus gives himself the *beau rôle*, while being unable in this praise of Eros to give an erotic explanation or, in fact, any explanation of the deeds of the beloved. The wonderful relationships he describes may be good for him and good for the city, but they are of questionable good for the lover unless one talks about things Phaedrus doesn't choose to talk about, and the unity of the couple is inexplicable except for the rewards the lovers and the gods may provide for the beloveds. There is here a hint of the strange relations between gods and men.

Phaedrus sums up by saying, "Eros is the eldest, the most honorable, and the most sovereign of gods with respect to the acquisition of virtue and happiness for human beings both living and dead." We have seen that Eros provides a kind of substitute for virtue and that the happiness provided by it consists of very limited kinds of satisfactions and may be fullest for the dead as opposed to the living. Phaedrus is a flawed exponent of Eros, because he profits from it without experiencing it. If he had been more attracted by the men who courted him, he would have spent more time doing than talking. He does not have the god within. He is a rather ordinary man who lives on heights provided for him by the poetic heritage. He makes an effort to justify himself and his own tastes in the context of the largest public good and the most beautiful heroic exemplars of courage. His speech is a good example of how people begin to think about their erotic tastes. We can imagine how, if this were a real dialogue, Socrates would put him to the test and refute him. The very fact that his imagination is allowed to take wing without fear of Socratic surgery causes him to speak more frankly about his self-consciousness. The speeches that follow will act as a corrective to his skewed vision. His is not a bad version of the Spartan military practice of love among males, a practice that probably cannot defend itself. His speech is almost forgotten later, but it, along with Pausanias' speech, represents the practical reality that is later forgotten in idealizations. In this way the *Symposium* is a bit like the *Republic*, where Thrasymachus describes the real practices of cities, which are forgotten as Socrates appeals to Glaucon's love of perfect justice by tempting him with an idealized city.

| V | Pausanias presents the lover's case, and his speech is an example of deliberative rhetoric (180c–185c). He is the person in the dialogue most concerned with the law (*nomos*) at the expense of nature (*physis*). We see that what he is trying to do is propose a new Athenian law concerning pederasty, which we learn is not quite so legal and acceptable in Athens as others would like to make us think. Actually, it appears that it is illegal, although at least partially tolerated. It needs a kind of justification, and Pausanias, who turns out to be a rather timid fellow, wants the protection of *nomos* for his practice. The problem seems to be getting to the boys whose fathers don't like these men buzzing around their sons. He never quite says this explicitly, but tries to put the best possible face on this pursuit, explaining how eroticism in general gets a bad name and how pederasty in particular can get out of hand. By a set of elaborate distinctions, he shows what good eroticism and salubrious pederasty can lead to and asks for laws that forbid the bad kind and approve his own kind.

Pausanias begins with the more comprehensive treatment of Eros that we began to feel the need for during Phaedrus' speech. He implicitly addresses the obvious question, "If Eros is such a wonderful god, why is it there are so many rapes, seductions, promises not kept, and so much general disorder to be found among his votaries?" Pausanias' theological response, admitting the accusations, is that there are actually two different gods with the same name. People understandably confuse them. He does not mention that in addition to the similarity of name, there is a similarity in the act desired by those who have these two gods within them. These two Eroses produce very different kinds of relationships, in keeping with their different genealogies. The first Eros he calls demotic, that is, belonging to the people or the mob, hence vulgar. Eros always accompanies Aphrodite, and there are two Aphrodites in the mythology. The vulgar or Pandemian Eros belongs to the Aphrodite who is the daughter of Zeus and Dione. The Uranian Eros is companion to the Aphrodite who was the daughter of Uranus without a mother. Uranus is, of course, heaven, one of the old cosmic deities who do not resemble human beings. And the Uranian, inhabited by the purer and higher Eros, is a special kind of human being, not just one of nature's mistakes.*

Pausanias interrupts his narrative to offer a bold thesis: no act is in itself beautiful (noble) or ugly (base). It depends upon the beauty or ugliness (not the goodness or badness) of the way in which the act is performed. He gives as examples what he and his companions are doing at this party—drinking, singing, and discussing. One could imagine other acts that would have made the thesis less convincing. One could also ask why Pausanias speaks of noble and base rather than good and bad. Perhaps Eros makes us think about the beautiful rather than the good and this disposition misleads us in deliberating about what acts we should indulge in and how they should be performed. We might get some guidance from Pausanias' examples in our attempt to understand why he needs to make the distinction; here they are drinking (*pinein*), whereas he must be thinking that in another kind of meeting, between two individuals, the deed done would be the erotic one (*binein*). The sexual act generally looks like a very brutish thing, not usually celebrated by poets and painters. Pausanias, for whom the bottom line is clearly this kind of satisfaction, has to defend it by declaring its neutrality in itself, and then making a case for the beauty of the way he does it. He doesn't really have the courage of his convictions or his attractions, and wants to make a publicly acceptable case for them. This is why he clings so closely to *nomos* in his presentation. He needs the support of public opinion, and we shall see why. He is a far cry from Hermes, who, when all the other gods stand around jeering at Ares and Aphrodite,

---

* Pausanias' speech, as a statement that unambiguously favors pederasty, remained popular in some circles up until the twentieth century. We have seen that Montaigne knew it very well and found it helpful in his exposition of friendship. French and British homosexuals had the habit of referring to themselves as Uranians. Classical texts were of interest at least insofar as they helped to explain and name a phenomenon about which the thoughts of the time had little good to say.

who have been ensnared in Hephaestus' golden net as they make love, says that he would not mind being laughed at as the price to be paid for being next to the goddess.[25]

Pausanias wants to make a popular and/or aesthetic case for the beauty of his own kind of sexual act. And, as we shall see, Pausanias is open to the charge of praising Eros not in itself but only for its consequences. His speech, like Phaedrus', is not really a praise of Eros, although in his way, Pausanias—unlike Phaedrus—has some experience of it. The Pandemian Eros is not choosy and is therefore indifferent to considerations of the noble and base. His votaries take it where they can get it; they love women as well as boys, they love bodies more than souls, and they seek the most foolish objects, looking only toward doing the thing. Pausanias makes the distinction Phaedrus fails to make, between body and soul. This distinction is the philosophical equivalent of the distinction between the two Aphrodites and their Eroses. Pausanias does not once use the words "courage" or "manliness" and, as we would expect, concentrates on the soul and the intellectual virtues. He is very Athenian in his taste, as Phaedrus was very Spartan. Pausanias is a soft gentleman; just as he does not mention courage, he does not mention war. His Eros, the Uranian one, is exclusively directed to males because they are the more robust by nature and have more mind or intelligence. His justification for pederasty is that it is an intellectual and educational enterprise, whereas Phaedrus justified it for its contribution to military virtue. Pausanias is going to get himself into one little problem, however: if souls are the concern, what is so important about this bodily desire and its satisfaction? He does not ever really solve this problem, and as a result his speech turns into an elaborate rationalization.

Pausanias is very high-minded, praising the sharing of minds and permanent connections. His defense of his kind of pederasty leaves all the other pederasts in the lurch. In support of his argument, Pausanias is forced to make another distinction, one that again fits his tastes and is more respectable: the Uranian, unlike the Pandemian, Eros leads to boys who already are beginning to grow their first beards. This might seem to be because they are more emphatically masculine, whereas young boys have much in common with girls and can more easily be the object of the taste for consuming charming flesh in all its forms. Pausanias, however, connects this first beard with the coming to being of mind or intelligence. He obviously still wants a good-looking boy, but the association will have much to do with the use of intelligence. Such a lover is looking for a permanent attachment, a being-together that lasts a whole life, and a sharing together, a sort of communism. This is the kind of relationship Pausanias apparently has with Agathon, who is pretty far over the hill from the point of view of Pandemian pederasty. The other kinds of men deceive foolish boys and mock them by running away to others as soon as they have enjoyed them. The Uranian lover is not promiscuous and likes what abides. The question is whether what abides is ever contained within a single human being.

Indeed, Pausanias waxes indignant at the other kind of pederast and says there oughtta be a law. At first blush one would think this law is to protect boys from the depredations of lovers. But no. It is to protect lovers. It is a shame to waste all that time and effort on an object so unformed that one cannot know whether he will be vicious or virtuous in soul and body. This boy might grow up to be either ungrateful or ugly, so it is very unwise of lovers to give in to the temptations presented by younger boys. Pausanias wants a law that will enforce some kind of reciprocity from the boy, the absence of which he deplores. His speech actually goes in two directions, one establishing the legitimacy of pederasty in the city, the other toward making the beloved care for the lover, a problem not adequately dealt with, from his point of view, by Phaedrus' speech. This law would have the effect of making Pausanias' kind of pederasty legal, although it seems to have as its intention to make Pandemian pederasty illegal. This will satisfy the moral indignation of the city and turn it away from the absolute condemnation of pederasty to which the city would likely incline. Pandemian pederasts bring disrepute, but the reason for outlawing them is to direct men's attention toward more lasting and spiritual attachments. How could one fail to admire such a noble and productive relationship as the one described by Pausanias? The very fact that it is evidently less erotic in the common sense of the word than the pursuit of younger boys helps to turn public attention away from the questionable character of the bodily deed. Now he says not that a deed done beautifully or nobly, but that one done lawfully and in an orderly way, could not justly be blamed. Law and order take the place of beauty. But much of the passion disappears with this substitution.

Pausanias reinforces his case with a disquisition on the *nomoi* of other cities. He begins by mixing up the two meanings of *nomos*, a law on the books, the infraction of which brings with it definite civil punishments, and a custom, with its less definite consequences for those who do not follow it. He distinguishes between two kinds of cities that have simple customs concerning pederasty. There are parts of Greece like Elis and Boeotia where it is respectable simply to gratify a lover without further ado. The reason for this is that the inhabitants have no gift for speech and therefore the lovers among them cannot persuade the youths. The implication is that pederasty is a necessity, and if the arts of speech are absent men will simply go ahead. In Athens, the links between pederasty and the mind are, according to Pausanias, first revealed. Athens is superior because in order to encourage the development of rhetoric, poetry, and philosophy, they make it a prerequisite to possessing a boy that one persuade him. Here we learn that pederasty is not according to the law or custom of Athens. But Pausanias is trying to explain that the lawgiver did not really mean to prohibit such relationships, but only wanted them to be of a certain kind. The Athenian prohibition is really only a ruse to get lovers to think and to cultivate the arts.

The other kind of city is to be found in Ionia, where they hold that pederasty is base. This custom is only a *nomos*, in the negative sense, where it is contrasted with nature, a *nomos* resulting from the fact that such cities live under the tyranny of the barbarians. The barbarians, because they are tyrants or live in tyrannical regimes, hold philosophy and love of bodily exercise (*philogymnastia*) to be shameful. This is the first mention of philosophy in the *Symposium*, and it is linked here with the cultivation of the body. Pausanias thinks that pederasty brings together philosophy and *philogymnastia*. "Gymnasium" and *philogymnastia* have as their root word *gymnos*, which means naked. Men exercising together naked was a Greek invention that profoundly shocked the barbarians or non-Greeks. The barbarians considered clothing a triumph over the life of the savages, an indication of the proper shame that turns primitive promiscuity into self-controlled channeling of sexual desire. The Greeks returned to the primitive nakedness because they did not need shame in order to be virtuous, or so they understood it, though naked exercises could lead to erotic attractions and activity.[26] It was in the gymnasia that the older men met the younger ones and they exercised and talked together. At various places in the dialogues, we see Socrates making his contacts there. Pausanias adds to the naked male exercises and their erotic accompaniment the philosophy that emerges from the associations in the gymnasia. These two things he takes to belong essentially to republican government. They are hated by tyrants because the strong friendship and community they form lead to great thoughts and an unwillingness to accept tyranny. We have here, again, a connection between body and soul that is not perfectly coherent, but the two do seem to go together in Greece.

One must not assume that Pausanias has a very well developed or technical notion of what philosophy is. It is in part just this capacity for lovers to talk to their beloveds with all the passion of their souls. The barbaric interdiction on pederasty he attributes to the tyrants' desire to protect their aggrandizements and to the cowardice of those they rule. This is the closest Pausanias comes to referring to courage, and this cowardice concerns the willingness to give up pederasty at the tyrant's command. In order to give respectability to his claim about the public utility of such friendships, he uses the old Athenian story, dear to the democratic faction, about how Harmodius and Aristogeiton, beloved and lover, destroyed the Pisistratid tyranny.[27] He sees a lustiness of body and mind that culminates in erotic friendships as essentially Greek and the foundation of republicanism. This is the linchpin of his persuasion of the Athenians to alter their custom, the limitations of which he indicates so tortuously in order to avoid direct confrontation.

He regards Athens as somewhere between simply accepting pederasty and simply condemning it. The presence of philosophy in Athens is what makes its custom about this topic so subtle. He attempts to further his analysis by examining the paradoxes in actual Athenian behavior. He speaks first of those things that seem to favor pederasty. If one looks at his list, one sees that they all concern encouragement of the lover. To be open about one's attraction is applauded in Athens. Victory in one's pursuit is counted beautiful and defeat shameful. The lover is encouraged in behavior that would win him reproach and shame if it were for any other object, like money or position. He can beg, make promises, sleep on his beloved's doorstep, and, in general, be nothing better than a slave. In sum, Pausanias tells us that all the world loves a lover, and shameless pursuit of a beloved as opposed to other kinds of objects is admired by the majority of men. There is something about Eros that is recognized to be superior.

But this unleashing of the lover imposes on the beloved all the responsibility for protecting himself against unworthy lovers who desire only his body. A lover is not to be held responsible by the gods for his oaths, since the oath under the influence of Aphrodite, an expression almost equivalent to our use of the word "sex," is no oath. This strange assertion fits our notions that the erotic connection can be insured only by Eros itself. When Eros disappears, the contract is no longer binding. This is a real observation, but it creates a problem for Pausanias that he never escapes: the boy to whom promises are made better watch out. Since the lover is older and more

experienced, he possesses wiles for seduction that it would be difficult for anyone to see through, let alone a youth. How would such
an undeveloped person be able to judge the honesty and the wisdom
of this man who subtly flatters him?

And here Pausanias starts presenting the other side of the paradox, which concerns the beloved, and immediately the fathers enter
the scene. In short, they are worried about child molesters, and
Pausanias, while compelled to agree that such persons are quite
unsavory and that public opinion is right in its indignation, wants to
make a case that some molestations can turn out well for the mo-
lested child. The fathers give their sons tutors who are supposed to
protect them from the depredations of men in the grip of erotic
attraction. These tutors watch the boys all the time, and, in addition,
their comrades chide the boys at any sign of such contacts. On the
boys' side of the question, everything seems to be negative about
pederasty in the Athenian *nomos*, and a rejection of the practice for
the sake of the young would appear fully justified by Pausanias' own
description of the lover. But Pausanias, in his supersubtle deliberative reasoning, interprets the rejection as only tentative, as only a
means of sifting out the vulgar Pandemian erotic man from the Uranian. There is nothing in the practices Pausanias describes that le-
gitimates this assertion, but it is what he wishes to impose on the
public.

The courtship of man and boy exists for the sake of finding a lover
who is not attached only to the prime of youth and will stay with the
boy when the boy's bloom has faded. Pausanias, however, as is his
wont, drifts from the testing of the lover, which at first seems to be
the most important thing, to the testing of the boy. He wants an
insurance policy, for he is aware that the erotic motives are not
shared by the boy. The boy knows that the lover is interested in him,
but he cannot know whether that interest will last or whether he will
keep his promises. The lover fears that it will only be the goods
extrinsic to himself that attract the boy, the gifts he gives him or the
future political advantages he might provide him. Pausanias invents
a third motive for the boy that would provide a more enduring
attachment to the lover himself. The boy must love virtue, especially
wisdom, and hope to improve in virtue by being together with the
lover. The prohibition against boys satisfying their lovers is, according to Pausanias, an attempt to do away with the most common,
interested motives of attachment, while encouraging the love of virtue, which can be furthered by a relationship with a man who can
teach the boy.

This seems a very neat solution. But if one thinks about it for a second, one sees the character of the exchange: the boy wants wisdom and the man wants sex. The youngster is the one who has the high motive, and the interests that tie the two together are utterly disparate. It is not the lover's love of wisdom that motivates him powerfully, but his attraction to the boy's body. He may just happen to have some wisdom, which is what appeals to the boy, if the boy just happens to love wisdom. Pausanias understandably concentrates on what the boy must be, and tells us nothing of where he got his own wisdom. This trick enables the lover to rectify the humiliating position of a man enslaved to a child, for the high-minded child reveres the virtue of his lover. The boy will be willing to undergo those perhaps unpleasant little moments when his lover insists on slaking thirsts that are not reciprocated. A kind of contact is really made between the incomplete youngster who needs to know a lot about life and the man who already knows something about it. Why should the man want to give that knowledge to the boy? A purely extrinsic cause is invoked, erotic attraction.

To put it shamelessly, but as Pausanias really intends it, the boy is a prostitute. Some prostitutes do it for money, some to get ahead, and others do it for wisdom. Wisdom is admittedly higher, but it is also cheaper. Sharing one's wisdom makes one no poorer. In a reciprocal relationship, each wants sexual satisfaction, and there need be no further questions. But in the relation of pederasty, the beloved must calculate in order to choose a course to which his passions will not lead him. Now we can understand fully Pausanias' assertion that nothing is good or bad in itself, but it all depends on how it is done. Prostitution is neither good nor bad in itself, but if the prostitute accepts wisdom as his pay, he is a splendid fellow. This shocking conclusion is what Pausanias cannot say publicly and can probably only half say to himself. Plato brings it out for us.

The kind of relationship favored by Pausanias is not so unusual nor is it entirely contemptible. In our speech about love, we have the habit, distantly derived from Romanticism, of admiring and perhaps even accepting only reciprocity. Movies about prostitutes mostly end up showing that the prostitute is really in love with the man who pays her. But, in fact, many perfectly decent relations are formed around interests that are not strictly reciprocal, quite apart from the careers made on the casting couch, or the fortunes acquired by poor persons who consort with the rich. Ava Gardner said that she learned an enormous amount from Artie Shaw. One need only think of Sartre's many girlfriends, who can hardly be interpreted as having been overwhelmingly attracted by his beautiful face or his well-proportioned body. It is not entirely certain that the benefits they may have gained from their association with him were of lesser value than the ones they got from the young men they also slept with. They could justify their attachments as Hal did his with Falstaff, by saying they learned a lot from him. This is exactly the justification Pausanias provides for the beloved when reproached for his mercenary lovemaking. It may somehow work, but this is hardly a praise of Eros, except as a kind of pimp. Again, as in Phaedrus' case, the dirty deed is justified as a means to a high end—here, wisdom—rather than praised as an end in itself.

The difficulty is described by Pausanias in a way that reminds us of the problem of the *Republic*. There, good politics is said to be impossible unless there is a fortuitous coincidence between philosophers and the people. The philosophers must be willing to rule, and the people must be able to recognize the philosopher—a thing not easy for the unwise to do inasmuch as there are so many fakers—and wish to be ruled by him. In fact, philosophers do not care to rule the people, and the people neither know who the wise are nor do they care to be ruled by them. The two elements of the equation are not drawn together by any natural inclination and their coincidence would be only a matter of the most improbable chance. Pausanias uses exactly the same language here as does Socrates there (184e3).[28] There must be a man who wants to improve the virtue of a boy, and there must be a boy who recognizes the virtue of the man and wants to get some of it for himself. This too is highly improbable, but not so improbable as in the *Republic*, where there is no Eros toward the people as a whole. Pausanias fails completely in his attempt to give a rational account of the erotic relationship between teacher and student. But there is still something real here, the image of which one finds in Socrates' relationship to his companions. And this will be at least partially addressed by Socrates himself. The teacher-pupil relationship is as mysterious as the lover-beloved relationship. Pausanias in his soft way has the merit of an awareness of a connection between the two kinds of relationship, and it would be in a more essential connection between the two that pederasty might get its justification. For him, however, wisdom is in no way erotic, and therefore the relationship between lover and beloved is the same as that between body and soul, the lover resembling the body and, paradoxically, the beloved resembling the soul.

Pausanias is aware of the dilemma for the boy in the practice about which he cares so much, and has to conclude his presentation with an exhortation to him. The boy, unlike the people, is attracted to wisdom and to the virtues in general, but like the people, he does not know exactly what they are. More likely than not, he will be disappointed in the expectations he had when he gave himself. Not to worry, says Pausanias. If your intentions were the right ones, you prove your good nature. Pausanias is forced into a Kantian argument: intentions are more important than good results. This is an extremely unsatisfactory conclusion inasmuch as the whole purpose of the relationship was to become better as a result of it. If this result is so rare, perhaps the youngster should try a different road to wisdom. Perhaps Pausanias sophistically might argue that having worked through such an unsatisfactory relationship would teach the boy a great deal. But this would not be any kind of tribute to lovers. Pausanias simply fails in his attempt to prove that the bodily sexual connection between man and boy is a salutary practice. Without the erotic motive, the lover would not be interested in the beloved.

Montaigne, in his criticism of Greek love in his essay on friendship, says most of the things we have observed in reading Pausanias. He asks why an ugly boy should not be more spiritually interesting than a very beautiful one—the case of the ugly boy, perhaps a Socrates, is in no way dealt with by this kind of love. The erotic attraction is sharp but ephemeral, and it is a one-way street. The exchange of body for soul is somehow disproportionate. The one thing that can be said for it, according to Montaigne, is that it can in the long run culminate in friendship, which is not in itself erotic. But this is really something and should give rise to further thought, inasmuch as the origin of friendship was in Greece. This is why Montaigne does not entirely share the horror at the Greek practice that was common in his time.

Pausanias' speech gives us a full account of the *nomos* that made pederasty in part respectable for the Greeks. One can say that this presentation is sufficient for a rejection of it inasmuch as no adequate reasons are presented for its being a good thing. This is not an account of homosexuality in general, in all its various forms. Plato does not speak of homosexuals, that is, persons who have reciprocal attractions to each other. If the boys were homosexuals in this sense, they would be attracted to one another and have no interest in what can only appear to them to be old men. It is difficult to know what Plato may have thought about reciprocal homosexuality. Since, in general, he supports family morals, he may very well have discouraged homosexuality as contrary to what is needed for the preservation of the species and the city. But it is also true that he is a critic of the family for the sake of both the city and philosophic individualism. Therefore, he may have been indifferent to homosexuality to the extent it did not get in the way of these other ends. Homosexual erotic activity as such is no more theoretically interesting than heterosexual erotic activity. Pederasty is specifically interesting because it has a certain connection with philosophy, and for Socrates, philosophy is the highest way of life. Rousseau, who follows the *Symposium* in trying to idealize erotic relations and connect them intrinsically with man's highest activity, does not think the philosophic life is highest and is therefore utterly contemptuous of pederasty. The Bible, with its concentration on the family and the love of God, condemns it absolutely. Plato finds some divination of philosophic connectedness, as opposed to family connectedness, in this Greek practice and uses it as a stepping-stone to a certain kind of liberation that was not available in other *nomoi*. Put more simply, Socrates' involvement with Plato was obviously much more important to him than his involvement with Xanthippe. This is what needs explanation.

Socrates was perfectly aware of the doubtful character of vulgar pederasty or the sexual relationship between boy and man. In Xenophon's *Symposium*, Socrates says, "The boy does not share with the man, as does the woman, in the excitement of the sexual act, but is a sober spectator of his lover's drunkenness in the sexual act. On this ground, it is not at all surprising if contempt for the lover is born in him."[29] This is really quite a repulsive picture. And that *Symposium* ends with a pair of young actors, a boy and a girl, who play Dionysus and Ariadne and who become visibly erotically attracted to each other and begin to make love. The spectators are delighted and recognize that this is really Eros. It does not do full justice to how erotic feelings seem for a moment to lead beyond themselves. But, in a simple sense, Socrates is aware that this is the exemplary phenomenon, Romeo and Juliet, Ferdinand and Miranda.

VI Next in the order of the speakers is Aristophanes, but he has a violent case of the hiccups and is unable to speak (185c–185e). Hiccups make a man ridiculous, and this suits the comic poet. It is a harmless disorder, which makes claims to dignity appear absurd. Man prides himself on his rational speech, but if every few seconds he makes a funny little noise that interrupts his discourse, everyone will laugh at him. This does not bother Aristophanes, since he is the maker of laughter, which also stops men from speaking. The comic vulnerability of man is his stock-in-trade. His hiccups are a kind of commentary on the serious speech that preceded the one he was supposed to make now. This suits the poet who presented a man who has cramps and is unable to leave the toilet while his wife slips out to take over the city.[30] Aristophanes is forced to ask the doctor, Eryximachus, to come to his aid, by either curing him or speaking in his place. In this dialogue about Eros, this is the only example enacted of one man's having a real need of another and associating himself with another. Eryximachus agrees both to cure Aristophanes, ultimately with another ridiculous bodily affection, the sneeze, and to speak in his place. This comic accident causes Aristophanes to be moved from the third position to the fourth. There are seven speakers, and thus Aristophanes becomes the central one, as we shall see, quite fittingly.

It is proper that Eryximachus be the next speaker (185e–188e) because he explicitly continues Pausanias' analysis of the two kinds of love, good and bad, whereas this distinction will disappear forever in the dialogue with Aristophanes. It is only a mode of temporizing with conventional morality, and trying to make the wildness of Eros conform to it. Eryximachus, it turns out, is an utterly unerotic man. And this apparently is the natural accompaniment of the fact that he is a specialist. A specialist cuts off an aspect of the whole of things man faces, orders it and becomes competent at dealing with it. The doctor or the engineer appeals to us on the basis of what might be called the charm of competence. Specialists represent an important and dignified human temptation, one in which the quest for knowledge is fulfilled as in no other domain. They can make claims to rational demonstration that those who want to face the whole cannot rival. They are good at reasoning except about the whole and their own place in it. This abstraction of a part from the whole provides intelligibility, but at the sacrifice of the erotic aspiration for completeness and self-discovery. The specialist lacks or suppresses such longing. Specialization is an attempt to make things utterly transparent and susceptible to rational analysis. Geometry is perhaps a perfect example of specialization, moving from clear first principles to necessary conclusions without any admixture of fortune or chance. Its practitioners have a sense of perfect insight and total control. But they have a tendency to resist reflection on the relationship of this abstract science to the world in which men actually live. Socrates admits that the practitioners of arts (*technai*) do actually know something, whereas poets and statesmen, who deal in one way or another with the whole, are like him in knowing nothing.[31] Socrates says he prefers his own condition of openness to the whole to an almost perfect clarity about a part bought at the expense of forgetting the whole. This is the Platonic way of approaching the problem of technology, so much discussed today, which transforms the world without being able to give an account of the goodness of what it is doing. This is connected with the old war between philosophy, understood as natural science, and poetry. Great natural scientists have it all over poets in technical precision, but great poets seem to be closer to the kind of wisdom we need to live well. Platonic philosophy, as represented by the poetic dialogue, is an attempt to combine these two charms.

Eryximachus' specialty, medicine, is of very special concern to men at large because it promises avoidance of death. It suits the two previous speeches in which Eros is really understood to be a bodily motion, but one that can have important nonbodily effects. Moreover, Eryximachus' specialty, like most specialties, is imperialistic. Although doctors are aware that they practice an art that is just one of many useful arts for man, they are often tempted to tell people how to live, as if the good life could be reduced to the healthy life. We need no further elaboration of this tendency of doctors. Health sometimes seems practically our only public concern today, and doctors, along with their biologist associates, dominate the nightly news, with its eager audience of millions who drink in the latest about the risks they run and the possibilities of immortality that are offered. The place of health in the scheme of things is a subject about which the doctors are utterly incompetent, but if their patients are already persuaded of its primacy, there is no problem. We see the specialist's imperialism all over the place, among economists, who interpret man totally in terms of the market, or anthropologists, who interpret everything totally in terms of culture, each peddling a competence that can interpret the whole from a perspectival nook that even the most superficial analysis would show is far too narrow.

And Eryximachus does indeed treat Eros as a medical question. It is all a matter of medical manipulation of desires in such a way that they contribute to, or do not harm, health. Eryximachus is a very moderate man, not in the grand Aristotelian style of moderation, but in the manner of your personal physician. His speech is somewhat incoherent, partly because doctors as such are not erotic, partly because of the problem posed by specialization itself in a domain that transcends the limits of any specialty. Eryximachus is compelled to connect Eros with the principles of the cosmos itself. What brings people together has to be understood in the same way as what brings and holds together the order of things.

Eryximachus is like so many specialists who seem all-wise when working within the confines of their skill, but who when tempted to talk about the world and life in general tend to utter confused banalities of which they are very proud. Not only are they without reflection on the larger world and without tools for investigating it, their tendency is to be deformed by the partial character of the principles used in their discipline. The doctor, for example, is excessively materialistic and thinks of everything in terms of bodies. Eryximachus is a pupil of what is called pre-Socratic philosophy and its characteristic atomism or materialism, not entirely dissimilar to that of the pre-Socratic Socrates depicted in the *Clouds*. The permanence of any kind of visible order in nature is a real problem for such atomism. The connectedness of the atoms in enduring shapes or forms is very difficult to explain. But the lack of a foundation for the phenomena of our world does not disturb atomists, who tend to despise the visible order as something ephemeral and from which one could not take one's bearings. This is, of course, not tolerable to lovers, who see something real and natural in their beloveds. The atoms themselves have no Eros in them in the way in which the bud of a flower, which could be interpreted as longing to be a flower, does. But there is no such "teleology" in a nature constituted by atoms, which are always fully actual. The pre-Socratics had a variety of means of approaching this problem of the order of the visible whole, none quite intellectually or emotionally satisfying. Socrates speaks of his own problems with atomism as a philosophy of nature and how he was forced to abandon it.[32]

Eryximachus reminds us a bit of Empedocles, who said that order is the result of two principles that work in nature, love and hate, synonymous with attraction and repulsion. Unfortunately, in this scheme hate is as important as love in providing the tensions required for the various kinds of holding together. If there were only love, then everything would be attracted into a single indistinguishable mass. Eryximachus quietly substitutes the distinction between the Uranian Eros and the Pandemian Eros for the distinction between love and hate, but it comes down to the same thing. From the outset, Eryximachus, unawares, admits that love is only half of it, and that hate, enmity, strife is coequal with love. What he actually does is to give himself and his art the principal role in bringing together things that are not really attracted to one another. The unerotic doctor plays the role of Eros, but he tries to make opposites that are not attracted to one another cohere. These are forced weddings, not ones based on mutual inclinations. He speaks as a dietitian who knows that there are desires for foods that make us sick and desires for foods that make us well, and who tries to wed the desires to the foods that will make us well. His speech contains no mention of natural attraction to the beautiful. Technique takes the place of love. He shares the point of view of the modern sexologist. Eryximachus faces the peculiar problem of the scientist who is a materialist.

Simple materialism would seem to imply chaos, whereas science would imply that there is some kind of transcendent order that pushes the atoms around. Eryximachus is an utter failure in giving cosmic support to Eros, and to the extent he believes in his science, there is no Eros possible. His comedy is best represented in his definition of medicine as a science of the eroticisms of the body with respect to fillings and emptyings. This is about as sexy a description of Eros as is that to be found in the contemporary science of sex. Nothing could be more repugnant to real erotic sensibility.

Eryximachus' confusion is revealed by his establishing two different kinds of dualism: the one, Uranian versus vulgar Eros, the other between the opposites that are constitutive of things like cold and hot, bitter and sweet, dry and moist. These latter opposites must be copresent for bodies to subsist, and one element of each pair is not higher or lower than the other element. Whether art or nature holds bodies together, the copresence of opposites is required. Male and female are such a pair of opposites, like dry and moist, and would be necessary components of the cosmic order founded on opposites. The science of bodies leads inevitably to the primacy of heterosexuality. This, of course, has the practical effect of undermining his case for pederasty, though Eryximachus is, of course, completely unaware of this.

He pauses to take exception to the philosopher Heraclitus, who tried to live with the copresence of opposites not subordinated to some higher principle. This is very close to what we could call nihilism and would seem to be the consequence of a pure materialism. Eryximachus seems to fear that there is really only chaos. He says that the tension between the opposites is overcome by the harmony itself. He imagines a pure science in control of the atoms, akin to the harmony among disparate sounds made by the musician, a perfectly ordered area that the science simply observes and codifies. Heraclitus would say that the musician is merely an ephemeral human being who produces a momentary, not natural, order.

As performed by men, contrary to its scientific purity, music depends on all kinds of human vagaries. But Eryximachus says that in a science like music there is no double Eros. The double Eros comes into being when dealing with men and their education. There the matter becomes recalcitrant, one part of it amenable to order, the other part disorderly. Unawares, he is making the distinction between soul and body, with soul superordinated in relation to body. This is exactly the contrary of what he wanted to do. The bodies are the enemies. His whole problem or confusion is to be found here. When he comes back to earth from his cosmic flights, he tells us that keeping bodies away from unhealthy foods that give them pleasure is a large part of his profession. This is the only place he mentions pleasure, a thing that would seem to be a fundamental part of Eros although it has hardly been mentioned by the first three speakers, who always want to justify Eros by something popularly thought to be more respectable than pleasure. Pleasure is a good thing, very much desired. Eryximachus clearly likes pleasure, but it must be controlled by his science of orderly bodies, for pleasure is wild and frequently destructive. Eryximachus knows only of bodily pleasures. He never mentions the intellectual pleasures connected with the sciences of which he speaks. Perhaps he has no real pleasure in them, or he has no basis for explaining such pleasures inasmuch as he is unable to articulate anything about the existence or power of soul. He is attracted by the lower, but acts in terms of the higher. Pleasure is a part only of the Pandemian Eros, so the doctor compromises with it, trying to subordinate it to the orderliness that is his stock-in-trade. The Pandemian Eros is really his Eros. What takes the place of the Uranian Eros? Health. He is the scientific bourgeois with "a little pleasure by day and a little pleasure by night, but always with an eye toward health."[33] This is hardly a ringing endorsement of the sublimity of Eros.

By a kind of unconscious necessity, Eryximachus is led back to reflections about the cosmic order as a whole. His previous argument implied that man has some special status that distinguishes him from the rest of nature, although his medicine wants to reduce man back to the nonhuman science of bodies. He now speaks of the disorderliness of nature, which he ascribes to the Pandemian Eros. He mentions storms, plagues, famines, and all such things that seem to happen by nature. Why are these not just parts of the relations between the opposites that constitute nature? Nature seems to get along just fine with such apparent disorderliness. From what point of view does one condemn these eruptions? It is obvious that these strictures against nature arise out of their inconvenience for men. Such things kill men who want to stay alive. The doctor is there as the servant of men's unreasonable hope of living forever and not as nature's servant or mere student. This scientist, like so many others, is not so much a knower as a conqueror of nature. Conquest of nature means making nature serve men's interests or wishes. The doctor represents man's self-preservative instinct, which is essentially unerotic and inimical to wild, death-defying Eros.

Eryximachus can do a lot to preserve men, but he must recognize both that death is inevitable and that all kinds of things, like lightning, are beyond his power to predict or to help men escape. His competence has limits, and beyond those limits he has to understand the hostile and uncontrollable as belonging to the domain of the gods. So his very attempt to control and master results in an excessive piety. The rational, scientific Eryximachus must turn to the gods and a pseudoscience that deals with the relations between men and gods, divining. There are false scientists who claim they can know the gods and help to improve men's relations with them. This is illusory, but if men wish to avoid such an illusion, they have to recognize that their individual existences are of little concern to nature. Instead they accept the doctor's rationalism to the extent it serves, but when it does not, they put themselves in the hands of other men who claim to have a science of the gods. Eryximachus' discussion of the shameless god Eros culminates in a submissive posture toward the old and more powerful gods. Eros for him means nothing more, so far as medicine is concerned, than the body's attraction toward food that will make it healthy. For nature at large, it means an improbable and implausible attraction to gods who can do us good or harm according to their whims. This does not do justice to the real experience of Eros nor to the kinds of Eros that seem to culminate in friendship. Both the actual practice of pederasty and the science of nature, which here attempts to provide pederasty with foundations, end in bankruptcy, debasing what are thought to be higher relationships and producing an incoherent philosophy of nature. Eryximachus can find no Eros in nature, only accidental concatenations produced as much by repulsion as by attraction, or arts that unerotically take the place of the absent god. Eryximachus knows only bodies but requires something like soul, which contains the pure principles that both govern nature and make it intelligible. But there is no place for soul in his cosmology, and therefore no place for the Uranian Eros.

Pausanias is the only one whose speech tended in the direction of the soul, but he was winded long before he got there. His supporter and continuer, Eryximachus, does not help him at all. A collection of various *technai* of the parts of the whole does not add up to the whole. His curious speech makes us aware of the art of the whole, philosophy. Perhaps Eros and soul will get their due when we confront it. We now need a new beginning, and this is what Aristophanes gives us. There will be another trio of speeches that respond to these difficulties and take the discussion to a much higher level, although one will hardly be able to say at the end that these problems are all solved.

VII

Aristophanes was struggling with his hiccups while Eryximachus was orating. This must already have been making some of the company laugh. All bodily noises have the effect of contradicting the pretensions of earnest speech. They assert the counterclaims of the low body, and Aristophanes' spirituality consists in a profound understanding of the meaning of belches, sneezes, farts, and so on, in relation to the *logoi*, which emptily tell us the way things ought to be. This is the genius of slapstick. Aristophanes wonders whether the order Eryximachus preaches is not contradicted by the sneezes he prescribes. One must listen to Eryximachus' speech while adding Aristophanes' sneezes in order to understand it and to see how Aristophanes' comedy undermines the respectable and reputable for the sake of the truth.

Eryximachus, presiding over this symposium, warns Aristophanes that he will be guarding against Aristophanes' saying anything laughable or absurd (189a–c). This is the polite way of saying that Aristophanes must not subvert the law. Eryximachus warns Aristophanes that he must be prepared to give an account of what he says. "Give an account" means both a defense in a trial and a justification in philosophical argument. Behind his jokes there must be, according to the ruler of the symposium, a serious and defensible line of reasoning. Perhaps, the ruler says, he might let Aristophanes off. This shows the fine line Aristophanes always walks. His mode of liberating men from a society's seriousness is to make them laugh. But authorities don't like to be laughed at. Of course, Aristophanes can always say, "I was only joking." Surely it is safer to operate with laughter than with solemnly rebellious speeches. It is the safer of two unsafe ways. The only safe way is to keep quiet, but for some reason, such men as Aristophanes and Socrates cannot keep quiet, although they are not, strictly speaking, revolutionaries. Aristophanes' comedy about Socrates is most hilarious, showing Socrates' utter ignorance about the consequences of speaking openly. Socrates tells any chance comer that Zeus does not exist. That is the truth, but he is blissfully ignorant of what is going to happen to him as a result of going around saying such things openly and seriously. When the giant, the *dēmos*, finally gets wind of Socrates, he will be crushed like an ant. The difference between the Socrates of the *Clouds* and the Socrates of the dialogues is that Socrates has, between the two, become witty, and this is a tribute to Aristophanes.

Comedy, as I have already said, is much more intimately related to Eros than is tragedy. Men and women tend to be serious in their erotic encounters, but it is easy to ridicule them. More important, those engaged in erotic affairs tend to laugh at conventions. Laughter cuts both ways, in dethroning erotic seriousness and in subverting the public opinion that disapproves of it. Taking Eros seriously is, at least from Aristophanes' point of view, connected with his opinion that man is primarily a comic being.

The comic speech of Aristophanes in the *Symposium* (189c–193d) is a masterpiece that shows as clearly as anything the level of Plato's literary genius. He puts into the mouth of the greatest of all comic poets a speech that is at least worthy of Aristophanes and perhaps, in the brilliance of its invention, surpasses anything Aristophanes could have done. This is the Aristophanes who conceived the *Clouds*, the *Birds, The Assembly of Women*, and so many other mad inventions. That the philosopher should be compelled to do such a thing teaches us something about the nature of ancient philosophy that we are all too likely to neglect. In ordinary histories of philosophy Aristophanes plays no role, whereas in Plato's presentation he is central. Plato is persuaded that the philosopher must meet this great poet on his own ground and try to surpass him. This shows that philosophy must be comprehensive, that it must contain all the charms within it, and that poetry is perhaps the most powerful of charms. The poets up to Socrates' own day had told men much more about man than had the philosophers. Plato's undertaking is a handsome admission of the truth in Aristophanes' characterization of Socrates as at one time a pre-Socratic philosopher, who could speak about the atoms and the other natural forces but could not give an account of man. It is also a kind of revenge in proving that Socrates, or his student Plato, could outdo Aristophanes. One must not forget that Aristophanes was said by Socrates to be his first accuser and to have made an important contribution to the actions that led to his execution. The strange relations among these very great men, who were at the source of what was perhaps the most extraordinary flowering of the human mind, demand reflection on our part.

The playfully serious confrontation of Aristophanes and Socrates shows friendly rivalry, and the result of this confrontation cannot merely be an abstract argument. It requires a comparison of the two men and the total views as well as the style expressed in their speeches. Socrates clearly despised most of the Sophists, but he did not despise Aristophanes. The writing of the *Clouds* can be interpreted not as an act of petty enmity but as a kind of warning to Socrates as well as a thoughtful criticism of what was then his teaching. They disagree about some very fundamental things, a disagreement that the comparison between the literary form of the comedy and that of the dialogue would help to elucidate, but they agree about the important questions, and Plato, in his invention, pays a tribute to Aristophanes' genius.

Moreover, Plato makes Aristophanes the expositor of the truest and most satisfying account of Eros that we find in the *Symposium*. There has probably never been a speech or poem about love that so captures what men and women actually feel when they embrace each other. Both the myth and the reasons that underlie it give a beautiful justification for taking love seriously, and this speech has the advantage of being much more comprehensive than the others in dealing with all species of love. To say, "I feel so powerfully attracted and believe I want to hold on forever because this is my lost other half," gives word to what we actually feel and seems to be sufficient. It does not go beyond our experience to some higher principle, which has the effect of diluting our connection to another human being, nor does it take us down beneath our experience to certain animal impulses or physical processes of which our feelings are only an illusory superstructure. Once one knows Aristophanes' speech, it is very difficult to forget it when one most needs it. It is the speech for an experience that is speechless.

Aristophanes' is the first speech in the *Symposium* that gives an erotic account of Eros. He, unlike his predecessors, describes embraces and orgasms. They are what Eros is about and are splendid as ends in themselves. The other speakers were afraid to say any such thing. He is all erotic and shows why men, with their squirmings and their grunts and their sweating and all the rest, are doing the best possible thing, the thing that most expresses their nature.

Eros is, according to Aristophanes' account, a very great god who provides man with the greatest of goods. But in the body of the speech, Aristophanes abandons all attempts to give a cosmic account of Eros. It is only human. Eros is not a god but a kind of consolation provided to men by Zeus. It is a very great good, but it is only a cure for a wound. In his telling, men were originally circular and resembled the cosmic deities, the sun, the moon, and the rest of the planets and the stars. They could revolve at great speed like them. They were children of the sun and the moon, and their three sexes were imitations of their parents' sexes. The sun was male, the moon female, and any combination of the two was both male and female. Thus, there were all male human beings, all female, and androgynes. The last, he says, was a perfectly respectable status in those ancient times, whereas androgyny has now become ridiculous because it is neither fish nor fowl after the separation of the two parts that constituted each of these circular men. Androgyny might appear to be a recapturing of that old unity, but in this later age no one has a natural right to it.

These circular men were ugly and ridiculous. They had two sets of sexual organs on the outside of the circle, which they hardly needed because they sowed their seed on the ground like crickets. But they were very proud beings, apparently full of a sense of their self-sufficiency, and so they rebelled against the gods. Aristophanes does not explain exactly why they rebelled, but they are apparently like those couples of men Pausanias described who rebelled against tyrants. And the tyrants here were not their parents, the cosmic deities, who apparently did not care or were powerless to help, but the Olympian gods. They were the great tyrants who give *nomoi*, before which these free-spirited circular men refused to bow. They apparently wanted only to revolve in freedom like their parents. When Zeus and the other Olympian gods recognized the threat posed by this rebellion, they had to debate what to do. In a bit of Aristophanean theology, the gods decided that they could not destroy men utterly because they would lose the honors and the sacred rites they were getting from men. The gods are not, as they are ordinarily thought to be, beneficent. These gods are really tyrants who rule for their own good, and who need what men give them. Unlike the cosmic gods, Olympian gods demand worship. Socrates found it much less difficult to believe in the cosmic deities than in these Olympian ones. In the *Apology* he does not even attempt to prove that he believes in the Olympian gods, but he does say that he has never denied that the sun and moon are gods. Unlike the Olympian gods, one sees the cosmic gods. Although one cannot count on them to come to the aid of individuals, they also do not make many demands on men. Socrates does not precisely wish to imitate them, but he would seem to prefer to live in their dispensation. Aristophanes suggests that that is impossible. He admires these old circular men with their freedom, pride, and self-sufficiency, and would like to join in a union with some other man in order to reconstitute his first nature, but he indicates that we must remain as we are and make do with our subjection to Zeus and all the others.

Zeus determined that he would weaken men by cutting them in half and put the fear of a further cut into them if they again became insolent. Apollo was ordered to cut them in half, and, lo and behold, men again resembled the gods, but this time the Olympian gods. This cut was all that was necessary to transform them. What a brilliant conceit! Human beings are always imitations of gods. In the first case, the circles, they imitate the cosmic gods; in the second case, they imitate the Olympian gods. The Olympian gods are beautiful and somehow make possible what we think of as the specifically human. These gods move around without necessity, they eat and they drink and they have sex, although they do not have Eros. They are partially models for men and partially objects of fear and disgust for them. It is at this point that man becomes separated from the cosmos and has a nature peculiar to him. He now fears the gods, must seriously worship them, and live within a world determined by *nomoi* that are not natural.

The cutting, the wound to human nature, inflicted by the Olympian gods gave birth immediately to what is most distinctively human: longing, longing for wholeness. Thus, what is perhaps the most important strand of philosophy and literature came into being. Man is essentially an incomplete being, and full awareness of this incompleteness is essential to his humanity and ground for the specifically human quest for completeness or wholeness. Man must resist spurious contentment because it conceals his fundamental condition. For both Aristophanes and Socrates, Eros, in its overwhelming and immoderate demands, is the clearest and most powerful inclination toward lost wholeness. Aristophanes clearly makes the distinction between what might be called sex and Eros. Itching, scratching, rubbing, and so forth can describe sex but the feeling that the other is part of oneself and that one wants to be together always is not contained in these merely bodily affects.

But the longing for the lost other half is not identical with Eros. It was simply the result of separating a whole into two parts, a condition akin to such experiences as losing a limb. In such cases we are no longer wholly ourselves, and we lament. We love the part of ourselves that is missing. We love our own. Of course in Aristophanes' tale it is half of us, and we can no longer be what we once were in the enjoyment of our old nature. So the first consequence of Zeus's act was that the two halves were moved to embrace each other as if they were still a whole. But this made it impossible for men to do anything else, and they starved to death. Zeus took pity on them, a pity suitable to Zeus's selfishness, because men were dying and he was losing worshipers. He moved the sexual organs that had been on the outside, that is the back, to the front. Apollo had already turned men's heads from what used to be the outside toward the inside, in order that, looking down at themselves, they would be reminded of what they had suffered. The mere sexual pleasure, which seems to have been like any other bodily function before, now becomes a mode of satisfaction and fulfillment as men and women hopelessly embrace one another. Their encounters produce intense pleasures, and their orgasms release them momentarily from the terrible pain of their loss. Sexual satisfaction is a momentary self-forgetting connected with the permanent remembering that afflicts men.

But man's condition soon worsened. In the beginning, their real other half was right there, and they could hold on to each other. But soon some of the halves died while others lived on, and in succeeding generations, the offspring of mixed couples reproduced together without necessarily being the true other half. Eventually there are no true other halves. The result is that men continue the quest, but it is hopeless. This justifies both fidelity and promiscuity. Those who are faithful to each other reproduce something of the original indivisibility imitated in bodily union. But they are not really the two halves of a whole. Those who go around continually trying new partners are free of the delusion that they have found the other half, but they are searching for what they cannot find. In both cases, the sexual satisfaction provided by Zeus makes this incurable wound at least tolerable. What is real is man's permanent separation from his truest nature, along with an unremitting longing somehow to correct the separation. Man now has a second nature, and that second nature is the result of a divine punishment that destroyed his first nature. It is unclear whether man would prefer to have that first nature without Eros or to have suffered his wound and have the pleasure of Eros. It is unclear even whether Aristophanes has thought this through, although his poet's art clearly belongs to this second stage of humanity. I might suggest that what Aristophanes means by the cut is man's necessary subjection to the *nomoi* of the family and the city, which wounds his bodily and intellectual freedom. His eroticism, untamed, is that longing for nature as opposed to what the *nomoi* demand. Man must compromise with Zeus and the other gods of his kind, and the one who is best equipped to deal with the reality of Zeus and the longing for the old gods is the comic poet.

Aristophanes' tale also accounts for the variety of sexual tastes without having to condemn some and approve of others according to some higher standard. Heterosexuals as well as homosexuals, male and female, are all doing what is natural and what is appropriate to their peculiar situations. Aristophanes' speech can appeal to members of all the major sexual lobbies. He expresses a certain preference for the all-male couples because of their manliness or courage, and hence their interest in politics. He denies what is said to be the shamelessness of boys in such couples, instead attributing their eagerness for erotic relations with men to frank acceptance of their all-maleness and delight in what is similar to them. He explains that adulterers, both male and female, stem from the original androgyne root. Forced by the law to get married, they take heterosexual relations very seriously, find it difficult to remain faithful to their false other halves, and want to get on with their search for the true ones. The basically homosexual males and females do not take marriage very seriously; and if they enter into it dutifully, they do not have much motive for adultery, at least in the usual meaning of that term. For heterosexual men and women, marriage is a conventional resting place; but for homosexuals, marriage is forever. It is among homosexual women that Aristophanes finds prostitutes, for they do not love men and are able to take money for what they are not serious about.

The seriousness or the engagement of the total person in the attraction to others is what makes Eros so important and so admirable. Practices that are simply loose belong to the sexual arena that is alien to their practitioners, while what is truly their own elicits great seriousness. This is crucial to Aristophanes' erotic teaching. The touchstone is the recognition of neediness and surrendering oneself to its possible cure. Aristophanes' favoring of seriousness is not moralistic, not a repetition of the reassuring litany that everything is all right so long as you care about your partner. Such seriousness comes from an inner necessity dictating the union between human beings, which is the most important thing in life. Unfortunately, such a partner is permanently unavailable to man. When Aristophanes imagines Hephaestus, the craftsman of the gods, coming to ask why a couple is so serious about their mutual embraces, they cannot say. The soul of each is incapable of saying what it wants, but it divines what it is in a riddling way. Hephaestus brings the reason to light by offering to weld the two together so they cannot be separated and will live and die together. Aristophanes sees that the essence of the soul is its divinatory power, which in spite of itself sees in connectedness something more than would immediately meet the eye, which sees only the brutish bodily connection. The serious erotic connection is a reminiscence of nature as it truly is, an access to nature nowhere else to be found, which, therefore, gives Eros its privileged status. But it is questionable whether such a couple would unreservedly want to be welded together, especially since they must not only live but die together. One of the defects of Aristophanes' presentation is a certain downplaying or even forgetting of death and its meaning for erotic attachments. These couples, holding on to each other, wanting to be in this position forever, delude themselves because they better than anyone are aware of the truth about nature. They are both sad and ridiculous. This Aristophanes most beautifully depicts.

He concludes his discourse with a praise of the god Eros along with an exhortation to piety. Somehow Eros, as understood by Aristophanes, is a gift of the Olympian gods for the enjoyment of men who live obediently under their rule. Eros is not in itself part of the natural order, but a compensation for the loss of the natural order. It is not what led to the rebellion against the Olympian gods. Eros, as an intense human satisfaction, is always threatened by Zeus. Eros is in one way daring, but in another timid. Aristophanes recognizes that the truly human world is one that has a strong element of *nomos* as opposed to nature. He tries to have it both ways, to love nature and to respect the *nomoi*. His comedy ridicules nature from the point of view of *nomos*, and *nomos* from the point of view of nature. The question is whether this leaves him any ground to stand on, although he can flatter himself that he has without risk seen through the conventions. The beauty that is to be found in man and his loves is not to be found in original nature, but depends on the combination of the old nature, which is unalloyed nature, and the new nature of man, which is alloyed by the power of the Olympian gods. This opens the way for a much more radical version of Aristophanes' total eroticism. Socrates, getting his revenge on Aristophanes, would say that Aristophanes lacks the courage to rebel against the gods himself and to find Eros in nature. Aristophanes legitimately noted the unerotic character of natural philosophy and tried to constitute a truly

human world separate from nature. Socrates will undertake to reform the understanding of nature and to find Eros within it. He will
therefore be more rebellious against the Olympian gods and their
nomos. Aristophanes has failed to give their due to the impiousness
and shamelessness he speaks of concerning the young males looking
for lovers. Socrates hints that Aristophanes' timidity or conventionality is connected with his art. The comic poet is dependent on the
approval of the citizens of the whole city, who are very much under
the sway of the Olympian gods. Aristophanes will not be put to
death by those gods or their worshipers, while Socrates will. Aristophanes has taken the safer course, but perhaps he might envy
Socrates' greater self-sufficiency and his willingness to follow Eros
wherever it leads.

Still, the great attractiveness of Aristophanes' tale is that it appeals to the love of ourselves, or, to use the ancient formula, our love
of our own. Such love seems to require no explanation; it is simply
immediately ours and to be respected as such. Family attachments
are instinctive in this way. But even more clearly, we say that our
arms, our legs, our hands, and our feet are simply ours. We have a
right to them; an immediate sense of justice tells us that no one can
take them from us. We need not explain why we do everything to
hold on to them. But Socrates later agrees with Diotima when she
says that we are willing to cut off our limbs for the sake of the good
(205e–206a). There is another kind of love, love of the good, which
is frequently and in many, many ways in conflict with love of one's
own. The social order is wracked with tensions resulting from these
two very human kinds of love. I think no healthy person can fail to
want Aristophanes' account somehow and in some way to be true.
Our loves are our most intimate form of ownness. Nobody really
wants to say that there must be some other justification for his connection with his beloved, for that leads to criticism and a certain
irresistible movement away from this beloved to some principle that
he or she may represent. Aristophanes' loves are pointed toward
each other horizontally, with no upwardness or transcendence implied in them. Socrates' loves, as we shall see, are vertical, pointing
upward and beyond. Aristophanes allows us to take our beloveds
with the utmost seriousness, and this is what we seem to want in
love. But, for those who have really plumbed the depth of the erotic
experience, there is a haunting awareness that one wants something
beyond, something that can poison our embraces. Aristophanes responds to this divination by saying that we really just want our
beloved. But he also admits that the soul divines and longs for the

old nature. This is not really satisfying, especially since Aristophanes gives in to the apparent impossibility of recovering the old nature. Socrates' entering wedge against Aristophanes is made here, at the point where our consciousnesses tell us that our loves are enchanting, but . . . This does not mean that Socrates' own account of love will be entirely or at every point more satisfactory than Aristophanes', for the love of our own and the love of our loves is one of the most powerful motives we meet in our lives. Aristophanes' discourse is a permanent text that satisfies us in our experience of love. This is more than can be said of Socrates' speech.

	Agathon, the representative of tragedy in this impressive
VIII	circle of men, is a distinct decline from the level set by
	Aristophanes. It is an interesting question why we should

be given the peaks of comedy and philosophy in this dialogue, but only a sadly diminished representative of tragedy. Perhaps that is all that was available in the decline of the tragic muse from Sophocles to Euripides and now to Agathon. It is a commonplace to say that in Euripides the tragic conflict and the tragic passions are much less extreme than they were in Aeschylus and Sophocles, and that Euripides was some kind of rationalist. Aristophanes even identifies Euripides with Socrates and connects them with the decline of Athenian greatness. Nietzsche says that Socrates killed the noble and the tragic. Although Aristophanes also attacked Socrates, they end up having much in common, and Socrates is much closer to being a comic than a tragic figure. Perhaps if Aeschylus or Sophocles had been there (of course, both were dead at the time of the action of the dialogue; but if Plato had needed them, he would have found a way), they would not have been so sympathetic to Eros, which seems not to have been so much a part of their poetry. If one were limited to a single adjective to characterize Agathon, it would have to be "soft," and he presents a praise of a soft Eros, in stark contrast to both Aristophanes and Socrates. His language is more rhetorical than poetic, and thus his arguments are faintly ridiculous. Altogether, he represents, in himself and for his audience, a distinct weakening of the fabled Athenian taste.

Agathon is, everyone agrees, a handsome, youngish man, gracious and cultivated. He seems to stake a tacit claim to being the most beautiful male present in a discussion about love of males, although

Phaedrus might like to contest the title with him and gives signs of a bit of envy. But it is Agathon's night. However, Agathon has already broken the thirty barrier and is way beyond the beardlessness that Pausanias, Agathon's lover, informs us was the classic taste of pederasts; Agathon is also years past the down on the chin Pausanias prefers. Still, Agathon remains something of a boy, always the beloved, never the lover. The permanent relationship between Pausanias and Agathon, untouched by the aspect of the argument about Eros that might encourage promiscuity, is a kind of denial of the power of time, an expression of the desire for permanence and even eternity. Agathon is unmanly and, hence, according to the prejudices of the time, ridiculous, both because of his effeminacy and because he resembles an older woman who tries to remain young by means of cosmetics. As Phaedrus was intransigently male, Agathon presents, at the very least, a certain androgyny that Aristophanes says is a thing now reproached (189d–e). In one sense this makes him an imperfect male, but he points to a mixture of male and female that may be more fully human, although his version of this mixture is clearly unsatisfactory. He praises Eros from the perspective of the beloved, as does Phaedrus. Pausanias and Socrates praise Eros from the point of view of the lover. Eryximachus and Aristophanes do not insist on the distinction. Agathon, in keeping with his making Eros similar to himself, extends his praise of the permanently beautiful by not mentioning death, just as his lover also fails to mention it.

Prior to Agathon's speech, Socrates engages in a kind of halfway dialectic (194a–194d), and does so a bit more extensively prior to his own speech. Agathon is the only person in the dialogue with whom Socrates, at least for a moment, uses his own characteristic form of speech, as opposed to the rhetoric of which this dialogue is composed. Agathon may very well be an imperfect copy of the young men to whom Socrates is attracted and whose lives he changes. We are reminded that Socrates is not really in his element here and that we should try to imagine what would have emerged from a more characteristic dialogue. This is another element of the covertness of the *Symposium*, in which Socrates' opinions are refracted through a somewhat alien element.

Socrates' little discussion with Agathon begins when the latter says that he is disturbed by the great expectations of his audience. Socrates responds by implying that Agathon is a hypocrite because Socrates has just seen him being so fearless before the Athenian public. This picks up Socrates' gentle mockery of Agathon at the beginning of the *Symposium*. Agathon, Socrates emphasizes, is a man of the great public: it is what he must please and the source of his self-esteem. The lover cannot love the people. But the beloved can enjoy the admiration of the people. Agathon, of course, recognizes the difference between the quality of judgment by the coarse multitude and by Socrates. Socrates insists on it, his difference, with the effect of undermining Agathon's self-satisfaction. One can try to ignore the contempt of a Socrates, but one never quite succeeds. Many or even most gifted young people look in the first place for brilliant success with the highest authorities of the general public. At the same time, they know that the politically powerful are not necessarily the best. But what good would it do Agathon to write only for Socrates? Socrates is merciless in pursuing this self-contradiction that belongs to all political men and all poets, and from which only Socrates himself is free. Again, Socrates can appear, and probably is, irrelevant to politicians and to poets, but there is a mysterious power in him that makes it difficult to forget him. He puts a little worm of dissatisfaction in the previously self-satisfied. Of course, in his heart of hearts, although he may be ashamed of it, Agathon would prefer being a god to being wise. To be the beautiful beloved winning the applause, love, and even worship of the whole city is probably what he secretly wants.

But Agathon, flustered, responds, out of shame, that Socrates should not think he is so full of the theater (and for Plato, the theater is an image for the city)[34] that he does not prefer the few wise to the many fools. However, if he were to carry this reflection to its conclusion, he would be forced to give up the theater. Somewhere in himself he has to recognize that, rather than being self-sufficient, he is dependent on the opinions of the theatergoers. Socrates denies that he has any such opinions about Agathon's respect for the few wise, but says that he and the others were also in the audience and therefore could not be wise. This bad argument leads in two directions: that the power of the many is such that Agathon can afford to and even must ignore the few wise; that every audience is mixed, containing many foolish and a few wise, and that the skilled poet or rhetorician must learn to talk to both at the same time. But if, Socrates continues, Agathon were actually to find a group of wise men, he would indeed be ashamed if he thought himself to be doing something shameful. Agathon agrees; and Socrates, having established that Agathon would feel ashamed before the wise, goes on to ask whether Agathon would be ashamed doing something shameful before the unwise many. The argument would seem to force Agathon to respond that he would not be ashamed in this case. But he cannot quite admit publicly that the central activity of his life is shameless, a hypocritical effort to please the incompetent. But if he does not make this admission, it means that he respects the opinion of the many, which he has just denied. Socrates himself never appears to be ashamed before anyone, which gives him great freedom. Shame in the face of public opinion limits a man's outer and inner freedom. This limitation is what Socrates accuses the poets of, because the public really counts for them. Socrates suggests that Agathon is ashamed when thinking of the wise as he addresses the public. He will never say anything the public will deeply disapprove of or be extremely shocked by. He is somewhere in between, recognizing the wise but appealing to the unwise. The implication of all of this is, of course, that there will always be an opposition between the opinion of the wise and that of the unwise. However, the popular Agathon has the advantage over Socrates that he can indeed appeal to the powerful many, who will condemn Socrates. But even this advantage is colored by the fact we learn of in the beginning of the dialogue, that Agathon has been exiled. The people are fickle. At all events, Socrates hints that Agathon's understanding of Eros will be conventional: he will be ashamed before the people to treat what is most shameless. Making love and carrying on philosophical discourse are both private acts.

But we never learn how Agathon would have dealt with Socrates' question because Phaedrus interrupts, noting that Socrates will give up the business they are all about if only he can find someone with whom to carry on dialectic, especially if he is beautiful. Phaedrus orders Agathon not to respond to Socrates, but to proceed with his speech. Socrates' peculiar form of seduction is forbidden, and we go on with the more popular forms.

Agathon's speech (194e–197e) is pretty silly, although it is another considerable literary achievement on Plato's part, a pastiche of rhetorical styles, particularly that of Gorgias. Its softness and its pyrotechnical use of language are part of that decay of taste that we have already noted. It appeals to an overrefined literary public in love with words, apart from the great questions that used to be the concern of the tragic poets.

However, Agathon, describing Eros pretty much as himself, makes a further contribution to the movement of the dialogue. He says that Eros is beautiful, and thus raises the question of beauty, which has been strangely absent in the earlier speeches. The *kalon* was mentioned by both Phaedrus and Pausanias, but in a sense tending toward the meaning "noble." Both Phaedrus and Pausanias said little about beautiful bodies, or did so in a denigrating way, for obvious reasons. They were looking to something "higher." Eryximachus talked about order, particularly as an aspect of health, where beauty is subordinate. Aristophanes is specifically indifferent to beauty, for one's own is chosen not because it is beautiful but because it is one's own. One may have an ugly nose, but one still loves it in the sense that one does not want to lose it. But everyone knows that love is beautiful and concerned with beauty. Agathon insists on this and explains why everyone should want his person and his speeches. But he fails to tell us why he wants to have others want him. This is the flaw in his speech on which Socrates will pounce. But he has made Eros for the beautiful the theme, as opposed to Eros for one's own, which was Aristophanes' theme. Aristophanes' comedy seems to accompany the ugly; tragedy seems to accompany the beautiful. Although Agathon is not a very tragic fellow, he reminds us that there is a cloud on the horizon within which the love of the beautiful takes place, a cloud hardly mentioned but that casts a dark shadow on such love.

In its way, Agathon's speech is a *tour de force*. He does something very rare, painting a god in words. He somewhat foolishly sets himself up as a rival to Homer, foolishly because the comparison is so unfavorable to himself. Homer gave descriptions of gods only in similes, whereas Agathon gives a full, direct description. Moreover, in addition to describing a god, he describes beauty itself, not just beautiful things. These two undertakings separately and together make for a stupendous task. I doubt whether many of us will really be satisfied with the execution, as many are with Aristophanes' execution, but the ambition is impressive. And Agathon makes us concentrate on what motivates us so powerfully. He says that the others have talked about what we get from the god but not told us what the god is really like. He is certainly right about this. Phaedrus and Pausanias, whatever they really believe about Eros, are concerned only with giving him a high place because of the wonderful results that come from taking eroticism seriously. They really think only about the erotic arousal they feel in themselves and what it leads to, without considering the sense in which this wonderful feeling might be considered a god. Eryximachus, in his cosmic description, breaks with his predecessors and thinks little of erotic experience, praising Eros' contribution to the visible order. And although at the beginning and end of his speech Aristophanes says Eros is a god, in its vital center Eros is in no way godlike but a delightful compensation given to men by the gods for their great loss. Agathon's speech is the only one where Eros is certainly a god, and it is, hence, the most religious of all the speeches. It is a celebration of the overwhelming power and attractiveness of beauty, beauty in all its possible forms.

He asserts that what was lacking in the previous speeches was an account of the character of the god, of "what sort of" thing he is. This, according to Socrates' usual mode of inquiry, is a secondary question. The primary question is not "what sort of thing" but simply "what."[35] To use Aristotle's categories, Agathon is concerned with the quality of Eros, not with his being. Socrates would characteristically say, "I am not concerned in the first place with whether a thing is beautiful or useful or praiseworthy; I need in the first place to know what it is. You provide me with the adjectives but tell me nothing about the noun itself." Socrates does not do this here because he knows what Eros is supposed to be, a god. The next question would be, "What is a god?" This one is too hot to handle so openly. Socrates, although he is not explicit, really raises this objection to Agathon throughout his own speech and gives his own answer to the implicit question, the most difficult and dangerous question of all philosophy. Agathon, the rhetorician-poet, has the vice of the rhetoricians in concentrating on the adjectives and not on the noun, piling up all the wonderful adjectives and attaching them to he-knows-not-what. He begins with attributing to Eros the highest of all goods for man, the end of all action, happiness. The god has achieved what all men wish to achieve. One cannot help wondering whether he gives happiness to men or whether he is admirable to men only because he is happy and they are not. Here the god represents human perfection or perfection simply. The element of longing in love, on which Aristophanes concentrates so poignantly, is absent. Men may love love, but love does not love. Agathon's Eros is in its way unerotic too and tells us almost nothing about the desires that Aristophanes explains so well.

Happiness is divided into two parts, beauty and goodness, the god being most beautiful and best. Agathon gives no explanation of why being beautiful contributes to happiness. Looking at or having sexual relations with someone who is beautiful undeniably contributes to being happy. But does anyone really enjoy being beautiful for its own sake? Narcissus did, but most of us are motivated by the beauty of another and would prefer to possess a beautiful other than to be beautiful ourselves. Agathon might very well say that being beautiful brings him many admirers, but that is an explanation of the value of beauty as a means rather than as an end or an intrinsic component of happiness. Everyone wants health for its own sake without thinking of what others may think of it. Health is not splendid, but it is good. This poet has a preference for the splendid over the good, and so do we all in a way. The old saw about happiness, "healthy, wealthy, and wise," leaves out the beautiful. It is a sober, peasant's view of happiness, but judiciously applied, it makes us question beauty.

Agathon proves Eros' beauty by his youth. In a direct confrontation with the first three speakers and in harmony with Aristophanes, he denies that Eros is the oldest of the gods. Agathon, the innovating poet, prefers the new to the old. He rejects the prejudice of antiquity and the love of the ancestral. If Eros is the greatest god or at least an important step forward, he is a reproach to the origins, and the true character of the origins has much to do with the character of our respect for gods and for nature. Agathon brings up the things that those who are more reverent about the past did not mention, for example the ugly wars among the gods. Necessity held sway before Eros came into being. Necessity is ugly, and Eros is beautiful because he is free. Eros, however, may be a dream merchant, because he is very swift in fleeing from old age, which also moves more quickly than we would like. Old age, which is real, for men at least, is escaped, not faced down, by Eros. Eros is not only young and swift, but also tender. He will, like Homer's Atē, not walk on the ground because it is too hard, but outdoes her by walking only on souls, and the soft ones at that. Atē walked on the heads of men, presumably on the bushy heads of heroes. But Agathon, presumably looking at Socrates' bald head, which is the head in itself, says that heads are too hard. He prefers the soft parts of the soul, as do all the imitative arts, according to Socrates, therefore neglecting the mixture of the hard and the soft that is required for a full human being.[36] Eros has a pliant form or shape. In this he is like Aristophanes' *Clouds*, who can easily imitate all shapes. Agathon gives here an explanation for the variety of beautiful forms we see in the world and is the first to raise the question of form or use the word for Form or Idea, but his forms are insubstantial or inessential. The god also is the cause of beautiful colors, as in flowers, and of their beautiful smells as well. This god, as described by Agathon, appeals to the delight of three of the five senses, softness for touch, pliancy and beauty of form for sight, and perfumed odors for smell. These are always the exemplars of pure pleasures, pleasures unmixed with pains, which do not stem from necessity but are choiceworthy for their own sakes. This makes a very good case for love. He does not mention either taste or hearing. The absence of taste is easily explicable because it is low and so closely allied with the neediness of eating. Of course he could have described Eros as sweet, but both Agathon and the god keep their distances and one isn't encouraged to lick them. Nor does he refer to the erotic act itself, unlike either Aristophanes or Socrates. Love does not make love. The explanation of the absence of hearing is more interesting and more complicated. Hearing is that sense to which Agathon's poetry appeals. Perhaps Agathon wishes to set himself on a higher level than the god.

Next Agathon turns to the goodness of Eros, which he interprets in a traditional way. Eros is good because he possesses the four virtues. Agathon gives no account of these virtues' contribution to happiness, and the proofs of Eros' possession of these virtues are in general sophistic. People in the grip of Eros do what they do willingly, and therefore there is no violence or injustice in Eros. In the fashion of Rousseau, erotic contracts are better observed and more heartfelt than business ones. Moderation results from the immoderation of Eros: Eros controls or diverts all other desires or pleasures. Socrates uses something like this argument in the *Republic*, where he proves the philosophers are moderate because they are immoderately in love with wisdom.[37] Similarly, Eros is courageous because the strongest men and gods can be subjected to love. The description of the first three virtues is amusing and contains some interesting reflections on the virtues. But none of this has anything to do with the true possession of the virtues in the soul. Eros is treated as a pleasant substitute for virtue, essentially as Phaedrus used it with specific reference to courage.

Agathon's presentation of wisdom, the fourth and the highest of the virtues, is most revealing although no less sophistic. It is also most incoherent because it contains elements that are very important to Agathon himself, which his position and character make it impossible for him to think through consistently. He means by wisdom particularly the kind of knowledge connected with the specialized arts (*technai*), above all his own art, poetry. Philosophy does not appear, whereas divining does, paired with medicine as in Eryximachus' speech. Eryximachus is mentioned by Agathon, and one remembers that although Agathon mentions medicine, Eryximachus did not return the favor by pointing out poetry (he does mention music, but only as the abstract mathematical science). Of course everybody would agree that medicine is important, whereas poetry seems less necessary. Medicine is good, and poetry is beautiful. This is Agathon's point. He says that the world of the old gods was dominated by necessity, and that is the one praised by Eryximachus, whereas Eros came later and brought poetry, the adornment of the world, in his wake.

Wisdom for Agathon is making, not contemplation. He does not make clear whether Eros and his arts deal only with the separate parts of knowledge and the world or whether they constitute some kind of art of the whole. But it would appear that Agathon, like his Eros, does not long for wholeness. Agathon does not discuss the being of the beautiful. Eros is described by him both as productive for the sake of the beautiful and as being the beautiful itself, the very Idea of the beautiful. Eros seems to imitate Agathon's own duality of aspiration to be both beautiful himself and productive of beauty. But that doesn't make much sense. Why should the beautiful love the beautiful? Agathon actually proves what was clear from Eryximachus' descriptions of the arts—they are not erotic but rather competent. Love, as is evident, produces all the animals. And the various arts produce things like prophecies, medical cures, weavings, and poems. Their essence is in these productions, which are separable from them. Nothing of the experience of seeing the beautiful in nature, especially in the beautiful bodies to which one is attracted, appears in this account. Eros provides a cosmic cosmetics that makes life and the world more attractive. It might even be interpreted as the artistic cover-up of harsh necessity. Agathon's account of Eros concentrates on the beauty of Eros and in no way tells us how that beauty becomes a part of the world. He clearly represents an argument for the superiority of poetry, of making over thinking. Eros and the art of poetry are treated as overwhelmingly beautiful, but neither is attracted by a beauty that exists outside of them. The trivialness of Agathon's praise is Plato's way of showing where this absolutization of poetry leads.

Agathon concludes with a kind of faked enthusiasm, as though he were possessed by Eros or the Muse, telling his audience that all the wonderful harmonious things dominate because of Eros. When one reads and thinks about it, it appears hopelessly callow. This is because one cannot really believe that all the harsh things have been overcome by the soft and gentle ones. The conquest exists only in words that are separated from facts. Hearing this, however, to our regret, appeals enormously to audiences, and Agathon's speech is greeted with thunderous applause. Agathon has turned the group into the audience at the theater, who like to be flattered and who like virtuoso displays. Even in Athens, the public can have very bad taste.

IX

Socrates picks up on Agathon's discussion of the few and the many, the knowers and the ignorant (198a–199b). He insults not only Agathon, but everyone there without their being quite aware of it. He implies that Agathon has indeed given an example of shamelessness before the mob, and that he, Socrates, is about to shame Agathon before the wise, that is, Socrates himself alone. He says that Agathon's praise of Eros is exactly what will appeal to those who do not know Eros, as opposed to those who know him. This means everyone else there except Socrates. Nothing could better illustrate Socrates' hubris. Earlier he spoke generally about possible knowers before whom Agathon might be ashamed, explicitly exempting himself from that group and implying that the fact that he went to see Agathon's play was a sign of his ignorance. Now he tells Agathon that he is the only true audience to whom Agathon must direct himself. Of course Agathon cannot oblige him. Socrates will now make his own poem about Eros, which may read well but which will never really please the audience in the theater.

Socrates finds himself in an uncomfortable situation. He is confronted by a noisy public that is not eager to hear him. He speaks of this at his trial, where the public was clearly unruly. How do you get people who are charmed by Agathon to listen to Socrates, who bores and shocks them? He always says that he is the only one who counts, the only one who knows, the only true witness, and is always greeted by jeers and insults. Here now he gives an example of how he goes about making himself heard. He begins by insulting Agathon and his speech. Then, like a wrestler, he gets Agathon, now with the permission of Phaedrus, to give him a wrestling hold, throws him and pins him. This is single combat, and at this Socrates is the unsurpassed master. Anybody who puts himself in the position of wrestling with Socrates always loses and goes away either angry, claiming that Socrates has cheated, or entranced by his unrivaled skill and strength. His problem is getting people's attention and finding an adversary who makes the mistake of letting Socrates get his first hold on him. Aristophanes says that Socrates can never have public rhetorical success, and the end of the whole Socrates story seems to prove him right. The poet can speak to the audience as a whole, but must flatter it in order to keep its attention. Socrates can force individuals to listen to him and to agree with him even when they passionately do not wish to do so. Each of the two alternatives has its distinct advantages in terms of influencing and controlling men. If Socrates' technique worked for whole audiences, he would be the superior. But it does not.

There are in Plato many imitations of the public arena in which Socrates gets control of a whole public, but they are always very special cases. The differences between the true public arena and the imitated one show the problem of Socratic speech, its essentially private character (on which Alcibiades is going to insist), as opposed to a public rhetoric that can influence the city and its laws. In the *Republic*, the *Gorgias*, and the *Protagoras*, Socrates arrives at an assembly where a rhetorician or a Sophist is holding forth to the great admiration and approval of the public. Socrates appears to be a nobody, and his talents are completely eclipsed by these great public figures. But by asking some naive question, he engages these important persons in a discussion that ends up humiliating them and turning the attention of the audience toward himself, not because it is attracted by Socrates, but because he is the conqueror of someone whose talents are respected and envied. In the *Republic*, his victory over Thrasymachus impresses the little public, puts Socrates at center stage, and finally allows him to attract the one young man who interests him, Glaucon, with whom he then can proceed to a more intimate form of conversation. That he succeeded somehow with Glaucon is indicated by the fact that at the beginning of the dialogue, Glaucon is the one who Apollodorus says questioned him about what was said at the famous symposium. To the extent that Socrates has learned a public rhetoric, it has as its purpose to attract individuals on whom he can act with his wonderful speeches in private. The political man is interested in individuals as part of the public; Socrates is interested in the public only to the extent that it includes individuals he can separate from it. This is why it makes sense to call the political man's speeches unerotic and the philosopher's erotic. You can only make love to individuals. Socrates' eroticism indicates that his primary activity is always private.[38] The Greek word for being together, *synousia*, has a wonderful ambiguity in that it can mean both a conversation and the act of coitus. The *Symposium*, a drinking together, discusses and provides a setting for *synousia*, a being together. Socrates' desire to be together with individuals is why Eros is the proper theme for such a gathering.

These mini-assemblies where Socrates is able to take over have a precondition never possible in a real public assembly, that is, one central actor, whom for one reason or another Socrates is able to get to. Not only does Thrasymachus want to persuade mobs of men, but he is vain enough also to want to show that his art is superior to Socrates'. Gorgias is an extremely polite man, and also vain, so he both greets Socrates and wants to make a case to him for the greatness of his talents. Such figures are halfway characters, spokesmen for the public but with pretensions to intellectual distinction. They are the suckers who are at least partially open to Socrates. Agathon plays this role here. After having made his guests into a rowdy public, an imitation of that theater where he triumphed the day before, and where Socrates would have been unnoticed and unheard, he is willing to talk to Socrates, who rudely knocks him down and prepares for his own rhetorical triumph. One can say that what one gets here is a confrontation of Gorgian versus Socratic rhetoric, or rhetoric versus dialectic. If one prefers the latter formulation, however, one must understand that dialectic is not only the method of truth but also the method of seduction.

Socrates' first tactic after Agathon's triumph is to threaten not to speak. This certainly catches everybody's attention. Socrates' irony is so transparent here that it can hardly even be called irony. It is closer to open contempt and sarcasm. It consists in saying exactly the opposite of what he believes, but in such a way that everybody knows it is the opposite of what he believes. His politeness is an insult, and we see a robust Socrates who strong-arms his competitor. Although Aristophanes' Socrates has no rhetoric and no irony, Socrates resembles, at this moment, the Socrates of the stage in his coarseness. He says that Agathon is just too good for him. Socrates, in all modesty, says that he only knows the truth and that he thought that Agathon would be a servant of the truth as well. But Agathon, a Gorgian Gorgon who turns his rivals into stone, simply took the biggest and most beautiful qualities he could think of and said they belonged to the thing he praised, Eros. Socrates, on the other hand, who had thought himself an expert about erotic things, would have begun from the facts about Eros and then adorned them with the best words he could find that were applicable. This, of course, could not rival Agathon, who had every beautiful qualification at his disposition. This would seem to make him the opposite of Agathon, but it is not quite the case. He too intended to adorn Eros to make him appear in the most flattering light. He implies that his rhetoric may very well try to see only the good or beautiful things about Eros, although they must somehow be connected with his true nature. He apparently contrasts rhetoric with dialectic in asserting that the former is concerned only with persuasion and the latter only with truth. But he overstates. Rhetoric has persuasion as its primary goal, and truth is secondary. Socrates' speech has truth as its primary goal and persuasion as its secondary goal. But such persuasion constrained by truth may very well be less persuasive than that of rhetoric. Perhaps rhetoric and dialectic need each other, inasmuch as teaching is ineffectual if it is not persuasive. The very speech that Socrates makes here is a piece of rhetoric intended to get his audience to listen to him and to overcome its predisposition in favor of Agathon. Socrates' most shameless statement here is that he knows the truth about Eros. This is a very daring assertion from a man who says that all he knows is that he knows nothing. It is much easier for a man who knows the truth about something to avoid the perils of rhetoric. Rhetoric's distance from the truth has a certain justification if it talks about those things about which we do not know the truth, but about which we almost necessarily have opinions. The most important instance of this might very well be the theme of this dialogue: a god or the gods. Socrates' claim to know the truth in this context is very bold indeed.

Socrates precedes his speech by a little dialogue with Agathon (199c–201c), and then turns his speech itself into a dialogue with Diotima, as we shall see. Whenever Socrates must give some kind of a rhetorical speech, he does something to bring it around toward dialectic in order to remind his hearers of his true power. Even in the *Apology*, which is the most constrained of Socratic speeches and necessitates a long, uninterrupted discourse, he is able to cross-examine his chief accuser, Meletus, which gives his audience a sample of the way he really talks and, at the same time, proves to them that, if he could talk to each member of the jury separately, he would succeed in defending himself and overpowering them.[39] This, by the way, does not necessarily make him very attractive to his audience; it certainly does not flatter them to show that Socrates is so superior to them. Dialogue, the intimate speech of two individuals, is Socrates' real mode, and he is always irresistibly attracted to it. Like a lover he always needs a response.

Socrates begins with making what should be a very simple point. He wants to get Agathon to admit that Eros is a relative term, that is, that love is not just love, but love of something, unlike the good or the beautiful, which stand by themselves. But the examples he uses make this point more difficult to understand and actually indicate that he is also thinking about something else beneath the surface that Agathon never quite gets. He says that when he asks whether Eros is love of someone or something rather than love of no one or nothing, he does not mean the love of a mother or a father, for that would be ridiculous. But this allusion is practically incomprehensible. Who would ever make this interpretation of Socrates' neutral question? Does love of a mother or of a father mean the love that parents have for their children, or does it mean the love that children might have for their parents? Socrates is going to continue by separating mother and father from Eros and simply using them as examples of relative terms: the words "mother" and "father" are meaningless without son or daughter. Quite obvious. But it is hard to resist the temptation to think that Socrates, by this momentary confusion, reminds us of a very delicate erotic problem, incest. By contrast, Agathon's unlimited praise of Eros is oblivious to certain limitations of Eros. Agathon, like all the others, to a greater or lesser degree, is conventional and keeps Eros within the bounds of the conventional. Socrates will think more shamelessly. He will speak about gods and about Eros, and the Oedipus story reminds us that the Eros between parents and children is naturally possible and forbidden by the gods. This willingness to entertain forbidden thoughts is a large part of what links Eros to philosophy. Socrates expands his point beyond what is necessary to make it clear by speaking of brothers and sisters too, incest between whom is a problem he faces more directly in the *Republic*.[40] Socrates continues with his only apparently superficial questions, immediately after mentioning love of mother or father, and then brothers and sisters, by asking whether Eros desires something, and whether it desires that thing to which it is related. Agathon need not have answered affirmatively, inasmuch as parents and children and sisters and brothers do not necessarily or properly desire each other. He simply says what he knows, but did not make much of in his speech, that Eros is desire and that one desires only what one lacks. He knows that Eros is a wonderful thing, but he also knows that lacking is not a wonderful thing, so he had just decided not to face the problem. Socrates is beginning to insist that Eros is a sign of our incompleteness, a condition we do not really desire. Agathon, unable to gainsay the fact, says that it is likely that Eros does not have what he desires. Socrates does not permit him to leave it at that and invokes the ugly word "necessity."

Then this pair, who are showing how two minds become one, go on to the examination of a further problem: people say that they desire something they already possess. For example, healthy persons say they want to be healthy. But this means that they are aware that health can depart, that they without lacking health lack eternity. The good underlying all the goods men desire is eternity. Persons who possess good things want to possess them always, and this, if we think it through, is impossible for mortal beings. Eros is the impossible desire for eternity, but that impossibility suggests something very ugly.

It is easy enough to say what it is that Eros desires, the beautiful. The immediate conclusion, of course, is that Eros cannot be beautiful.* This is fairly straightforward, but again, the examples Socrates gives push us somewhat beyond the explicit questions. He says that the gods contrived the things they did, the things they made, out of love of the beautiful. This means that all of these acting or making gods must lack beauty, just as Eros does. This is an important theological point, not emphasized by Socrates here, but absolutely essential to his thought. In order for the gods to act in the cosmos or in relation to human beings, they too must be needy or have a lack; otherwise they would remain whole and quiet. Socrates waits for Diotima to cross the T's and dot the I's even about Eros, and leaves it to the listeners to draw the consequences for all the gods. If the gods are beautiful and are always, they need nothing. If they desire the beautiful, if they are erotic, they are radically imperfect. For men, the gods must be both beautiful and useful to them, but they cannot be both. If the gods are lovers of the beautiful, then the beautiful cannot be a god, and we have to think about what the beautiful is in order to understand its co-relative, Eros. In this dialogue as a whole we learn a great deal about Eros, but not nearly enough about the beautiful.

This superficial, although useful, conversation with Agathon points to the depths but passes over them and continues with the gentle Agathon's acquiescing to Socrates' argument that Eros cannot be beautiful. He admits that he did not know what he was talking about. Socrates responds by saying that Agathon nevertheless spoke beautifully. This is not merely an insult, pointing out the disproportion between truth and the beauty of Agathon's speech, but an acknowledgment that such beautiful speeches may be a much desired consolation for men who lack what is beautiful always. Socrates' love of truth is an intransigent rejection of the temptation to forget death.

The last admission Socrates demands from Agathon is that Eros must lack not only beautiful but good things since good things are beautiful. This is false. Agathon admits it either because he finds himself incapable of disputing with Socrates or because his whole inclination is to make everything beautiful in accordance with the demands of his art. There are many things, like Locke's good bowel movement, that are good but which no sane person would call beautiful. The good is clear and reasonable: healthy, wealthy, and wise.

---

* A possibility not mentioned by Socrates but allowed by the argument is that Eros may be beautiful but not beautiful always.

It is precisely Socrates' attempt to reduce the noble or beautiful to the good that Nietzsche takes such strong exception to and uses to prove Socrates' ignoble character. The noble or beautiful, Nietzsche insists, is irreducible, and those who are motivated by it cannot give reasons for the love of it without destroying it.[41] One might be inclined to say in Agathon's defense that although not all good things are beautiful, all beautiful things are good. But this is also not true. Achilles' beautiful death for his friend is, at least on Achilles' testimony, not good. The beauty of tragedy does not persuade us that we want these beauties for ourselves in the same way we want the good things. Aristotle, in his incomplete treatise *Poetics*, tells us that comedy concerns the harmless ugly.[42] He may very well have meant to say that comedy's opposite, tragedy, is the harmful beautiful. Beneath these heights, it is easy to make an argument why something is good; it is not so easy to explain why something is beautiful; most difficult of all would be to explain why the beautiful is good. As I have suggested, this dialogue about Eros may very well teach us about something that is quite ugly.

Agathon concludes by saying that he cannot contradict Socrates, to which Socrates responds that it is not Socrates he cannot contradict, but the truth. This is a simple example of what Socrates means by the truth—the avoidance of self-contradiction. Here the contradiction in Agathon is that he wanted an Eros who is both beautiful and a lover of the beautiful. This is impossible.

Socrates, in this little dialogue and in what follows, insists on the lover's love of the beautiful. The overwhelming attraction we feel toward beautiful objects is central to eroticism, and it follows that eroticism is a painful and needy business and that the beautiful is a perfection outside of the lover. This insistence that the imperfect loves a perfection that does not love is, as I have noted before, in stark contrast to the Romantic ideal of love, which tries to sweeten the one-way character of Eros with the bourgeois myth of reciprocity. This Socratic teaching means from the outset that, in spite of the passion, pleasure, and excitement of Eros, it is something of a hopeless business. Cervantes gives the classic literary statement of this in Marcella's story in *Don Quixote*.[43] The Don encounters several despairing lovers who complain about the beautiful but cruel Marcella. They tell terrible stories of what she has done to them and others who are now dead due to her cruelties. On the basis of this, the Don and we are indignant about this terrible woman. Finally, we get a chance to see this monster whose appearance confirms the accounts of her ravishing beauty, which cannot help arousing powerful longing. She makes an apology or defense of her conduct, which is essentially that the sufferings of her suitors are not her fault. She did not pursue them or try to seduce them. She did not make herself beautiful; that is a fact of nature. They love her because she is beautiful; she is indifferent to them because they possess no beauty she lacks. That nature did not make them beautiful, and hence attractive, does not impose upon her a responsibility to be attracted to them in return. Case closed. The men have no justification for blaming her, and our indignation is misplaced, probably an attempt to make her give us what we want, a mere act of force masquerading as justice. The suitors should be content with contemplating her, except the erotic desire insists on possession, without which it makes life seem unlivable. Aristophanes satisfies that longing. By contrast, Marcella's speech is perfect Socrates, Plato, and Aristotle in their erotic, cosmological, and theological teachings. It is in the sharpest contrast with the teachings of Christian love.

	Socrates professes to have learned about Eros from a discus-
X	sion with a Mantinean woman named Diotima (201d–212c).

It is rare that Socrates professes to have learned from a woman, and it is especially noteworthy in this dialogue, where the interlocutors are all males and there is a preference, although not exclusive, for relations between males. The only similar occurrence in Plato is in the *Menexenus*, where Socrates repeats a speech he claims he learned from Aspasia, an unusually close friend of Pericles.[44] It too is a speech of praise, of Athens. The name "Diotima" means honored by Zeus, and the mention of the city Mantinea, in the grammatical form it appears in here, is identical with the word for the science of divining. She is clearly a made-up person. Socrates explains his conversion from Agathon's teaching about Eros to the one he now holds by his encounter with Diotima. This is one of several passages in Plato where Socrates describes how he stopped being a pre-Socratic philosopher, as he was presented by Aristophanes, and became the Socrates we know. In the *Apology*, the most famous of these passages, he tells of the Delphic Oracle, which he took to be a command to test other people's claim to wisdom.[45] In the *Phaedo*, the day of his death, in a discussion of the immortality of the soul, he tells directly of his dissatisfaction with earlier philosophy and his discovery that philosophy must study and speak of the good and mind, which necessitated something like examining opinions about the good. This he called his "second sailing."[46] Here, in the presence of Aristophanes, who thought him to be unerotic, he describes this conversion as a discovery of the truth about Eros. These different aspects of his conversion to what is specifically Socratic have to be compared in order to discover the whole truth about it. The *Apology* tells of his knowledge of ignorance. This dialogue tells of his knowledge of erotics. We must recognize that there is something in common between these two apparently opposite formulations. In a preliminary way, one might say that Eros itself is awareness or knowledge of a lack and therefore is linked to the knowledge of ignorance, which is obviously a kind of lack. Eroticism gives a more inward expression of what is so unsatisfactorily explained in the *Apology*, the turning of the lack into a quest. Socrates' assertion that prior to meeting Diotima he held pretty much the same position about Eros that Agathon did probably means that he was unerotic, as is the self-satisfied Agathon, a self-satisfaction mirrored in the atomism of the philosophers and the competence of their natural science.

It is amusing to see Socrates as a student sitting at the feet of his schoolmarm, who is severe in correcting his mistakes. After she has shown him the same thing Socrates has just shown Agathon, that Eros is neither beautiful nor good, Socrates asks her whether Eros then is ugly and bad. She rejoins by asking whether Socrates believes that whatever is not beautiful must be ugly. He says that is exactly what he thinks, and she says that there is a middle between the two. She does not tell us precisely, or even at all, what the middle between beautiful and ugly is, but says that there is a middle between wisdom and ignorance, which is right opinion. But she tells us very little about right opinion and how one determines it is right if one does not have knowledge. All that this incomplete and imperfect argument points to is that human beings hold opinions that, if examined, frequently turn out to be divinations of the truth about things. The ignorant person must either have no opinion whatsoever or have opinions that he thinks are knowledge or be unaware of the distinction between knowledge and opinion. This distinction defines what came to be known as Socratic doubt, the certain knowledge that one does not know. Of course, the fact that there may be a middle between wisdom and ignorance does not constitute a proof that there is a middle between beauty and ugliness. But using this example of knowledge and ignorance to illustrate her point about beauty and ugliness, she imperceptibly makes wisdom the theme in her discussion of Eros. Very quickly, the love of wisdom, philosophy, becomes her subject matter, and she makes this connection, which most men would never even think of, appear to be perfectly natural.

Diotima shows that, if one accepts that all gods possess good and beautiful things, Eros is not a god. At least to this point, Socrates is too conventional or too pious to doubt the perfection of gods. A god must be both beautiful and wise. Nietzsche's daring hypothesis that gods philosophize[47] would mean that the gods are still trying to find out what the good is, although they make the cosmos, which is supposed to embody the good. But Socrates at first refuses any such hypothesis. This is the only place in all the writings about Socrates where he discusses a god directly. Eros is not much of a god and has nothing of the status or awesomeness of Zeus. But it is still significant to see how Socrates, with the help of Diotima, goes about examining a god. In this one instance where he actually does it, the conclusion is that the god is not a god. When Diotima informs Socrates that he does not believe that Eros is a god, which he thought he did, he asks—beginning a series of rather impolite and peremptory questions to Diotima, a little in the style of Aristophanes' Socrates—whether Eros is a mortal. He, therefore, gives an indication of what he thinks is the most salient characteristic of a god, immortality. Diotima, following the pattern she has established with her discussion of the middle between wisdom and ignorance and beauty and ugliness, announces that Eros is neither mortal nor immortal. This is plausible only to someone who has been so carried away by Diotima's reasoning as to believe that there is a middle between all opposites. But what in the world is between living forever and dying? This seems to have mystified Socrates, who appears to have lost clarity about what is most important for him.

Socrates now asks the question "What is Eros?" that neither he nor Agathon raised, perhaps because they were constrained to believe that Eros is a god. Diotima now gives the important answer. He is a *daimōn*. *Daimōnes* are beings who are neither humans nor gods. They are expressive of the strangeness of this world that makes it seem, at least, to be divine. And here Diotima uses the word that is so inseparably connected with Socrates, *daimonion*. She uses the word as a synonym for *daimōn*. In what is perhaps the most famous passage in the *Apology* or even all of Plato, Socrates says that he has a *daimonion* who comes to him and tells him not to do certain kinds of things, for example, go into politics or beg for his life.[48] Here we are going to get a description of what a *daimonion* is and of a particular *daimōn*, Eros. Socrates has a *daimonion*, and Eros is a *daimōn*. Are they the same? There is a meeting here of philosophy, Eros, and theological criticism that, taken together, may sum up the problem of Socrates. The suspicions of religious innovation that surrounded Socrates had something to do with this *daimonion* of his. He was accused of bringing new gods into the city, and although a *daimonion*, as we learn here, is not a god, it is related to the gods. There was some theological incorrectness about Socrates, and here we are going to learn more about it than we ever will elsewhere. The fact that the account is a myth or a tale must not turn us away from taking it with the utmost seriousness. This is going to be a much more open description of Socrates' strangeness than one is likely to find elsewhere. Diotima, in response to Socrates' question "What power do *daimōnes* possess?" responds that they are the intermediaries between gods and human beings in all their various relations. If we apply this to Socrates, as we must, it appears that Socrates' strangeness among men consists in divinatory powers, his uncanny ability to look into each man's soul and to place it in the order of things. He prophesies and he tells tales of the life after death. Whatever these things may mean, they give Socrates a daimonic aspect. Socrates seems to be not quite a man but some kind of link between the whole order of things and men as they live here on earth.

This becomes clearer in Diotima's response to Socrates' next question about Eros, "Who are his father and his mother?" Diotima explains that his mother was Poverty (*penia*). This casts some light on Socrates' enigmatic assertion in the *Apology* that he lives in thousandfold poverty. Penia decided that she would seduce Poros (resource) at a party thrown for the birth of Aphrodite. She did this because, being Poverty, she needed resources for her child. She lay beside Poros in Zeus's garden when he was drunk and became pregnant with Eros. Eros is hence half Resource and half Poverty. It is to be noted that the word *poros*, with the privative prefix "a," means not only the same thing as *penia* but also the difficulty or perplexity that is provided by a contradiction in an argument. An *aporia* arises at the point in an argument when the interlocutor contradicts himself and must look for a solution but does not know quite how to do so. He is literally without resource. This is the critical moment in dialectic. It is identical to what Maimonides calls perplexity and indicates that philosophy is "the guide of the perplexed," particularly those who are caught up in the opposition between revelation and reason. This is indicated here in Diotima's own use of *aporia*. Eros falls into *aporia* but somehow will, due to his connection with Poros, always find some means. This is practically a definition of Socratic skepticism. We have some awarenesses that, if not definitive and complete, keep us from being utterly ignorant and without guidance. Diotima depicts Eros in the following way:

> first, he is always poor, and far from being soft and beautiful as the many suppose, is hard and dry and shoeless and homeless, lying on the ground without bedding in the open air, sleeping in doorways and on highways, having his mother's nature, always cohabiting with want. But, like his father, he plots for the beautiful and the good things, is manly, impetuous, and highstrung, a clever hunter, always weaving some stratagem, a desirer of and resourceful concerning prudence, philosophizing throughout his whole life, a clever juggler, purveyor of drugs, and sophist. His nature is such that he is neither immortal nor mortal, but at one time on the same day he flourishes and lives, when he has plentiful resources, and at another time, he dies, but he comes back to life again because of his father's nature. He is always getting resources but they are always flowing out. So Eros is neither without resource [the verbal form of *aporia*] nor is he ever rich; he is in the middle between wisdom and ignorance. (203c–e)

If ever there was a perfect description of Socrates, this is it, the man of the great hunt. It comes from the mouth of a diviner and is expressed in her style, but this is perhaps the perspective in which Socrates appears most clearly.

So Eros, the powerful attraction to the beautiful, is the same as Socrates, the man most powerfully attracted to wisdom. This is the identity Diotima wants to establish and explain. In an act of supreme hubris, Socrates uses Diotima to praise himself in the guise of Eros. The only bit of modesty he displays consists in his denying he is a god. But, for reasons that may soon become evident, he probably does not wish to be one. A god would have to be wise and therefore would not pursue wisdom. A man who is fully ignorant would not pursue wisdom, because he would not know that he needs it. He is self-satisfied and that is very ugly. Neither gods nor ignoramuses philosophize, and Socrates says that philosophy is the best, the most pleasant, and the most beautiful way of life.

Socrates has asked what Eros is, what his power is, what were his origins (still a pre-Socratic, believing that origins are essences), and now he asks what use Eros is to human beings. Socrates, although he is involved with the sublime things, is ever clear, simple, and utilitarian. This turns out to be a difficult question. Love is love of beautiful things, and the lover of beautiful things wishes that they be his. The possessiveness of love is underlined here. Love is not just contemplation of a beautiful object, but requires the active pursuit of it so as to possess it. Diotima says that this answer, that love is love of the possession of beautiful things, longs for another question. She indicates that speech itself contains a kind of Eros, a desire that pushes it toward completeness. The kind of speech they are carrying on here, the longing for clarity in the earnest student, is akin to the kind of motion initiated by Eros. The further question is, what will the man who gets the beautiful things have? Characteristically and revealingly, Socrates cannot answer. In order to clarify the question and to make an answer easier, Diotima changes the question to "What does the lover of good things love?" What she does here is, obviously, apparently only for the sake of example, change the object from the beautiful to the good. But in doing this she insists on the distinction between the beautiful and the good and raises all kinds of questions about the relation of the two and their differences, which men are apparently eager to forget.

In Greek moral philosophy, morality is divided into two parts, the noble or beautiful (*kalon*) and the good (*agathon*). A gentleman is called a *kaloskagathos*, a noble and good man. Full humanity is not attained just by being good or possessing good things. There is a certain irreducible splendor without which man would not be quite man, and a utilitarian morality, which does not give any status to such splendor, seems to diminish man. We shall see, in a few moments, Alcibiades, who is not distinctly a good man but is certainly a splendid one. The gloriousness of an Achilles is part of the moral phenomenon, though Hobbes and all those who followed him tried to suppress it and treat it as superficial and a mere expression of vanity. The noble and the good are both evidently requisite for a description of what we mean by morality, but they are also at tension with each other. Aristotle, in his general discussion of virtue at the beginning of the *Ethics*, says that men act for the sake of the highest good, happiness, and that the virtues are concerned with particular goods that contribute to happiness.[49] This is quite straightforward and makes the theoretical problem, at least of morality, quite simple. But when Aristotle gets around to discussing the virtues individually, such as courage, which leads to accepting wounds and death on the battlefield, he says that men act virtuously not for the sake of the good but for the sake of the noble.[50] Death in battle would probably never be chosen if the standard of the good were applied to it. It is difficult to believe that such a death is evidently good and will contribute to happiness, especially if there is no life after death, but it is an indisputably noble or beautiful deed. Aristotle is caught, as are we all, in a bind: we determine what we should or should not do according to the standard supplied by good and bad. Happiness is the end of life, and what contributes to happiness is good. The dignity of moral deeds seems to be in doing them for their own sakes and not for their consequences. But morality seems to lead to both happiness and an indifference to happiness.

Aristotle implies that there may perhaps be an ultimate unity in these two motives, but that there may also be a profound incoherence in morality. Kant resolves this difficulty by saying that happiness can never be the goal of the moral man because that would rob moral deeds of their specific dignity and freedom. Aristotle would do nothing so inhumane, and he both praises moral deeds and says they lead to happiness.[51] The intransigent Socrates always pursues the good, the good for himself—whatever that may be. Socrates is very easily able to answer Diotima's question about what the man who possesses the good has. It is happiness. He has a real difficulty with the beautiful, and this is what comes out here. What has one got when one has the beautiful? But love is the love of the beautiful, and that is why Socrates the lover is so problematic. Socrates is by nature or in the first place a lover not of the beautiful but rather of the good. We might express the issue here as the conflict between the aesthetic life and the utilitarian one. Socrates, at least at the outset, is intransigently utilitarian.

If men acquire good things, according to Diotima and Socrates, they are happy and this is a point beyond which no one has to go because happiness is the comprehensive good and self-sufficient. All men love all good things. In this sense—which does not distinguish Eros from desire—because all men are needy, all men should be called lovers. But they are not. Only a special category is called lovers. Again Diotima offers an example that is apparently chosen only for the sake of illustration, but that takes us very much further. She says that all the products of all the arts are poetic, that is, they are the results of *poiēsis*, which means "making" in Greek. The word "poet" should apply to the carpenter as well as to the maker of epics and tragedies. But it does not. The latter get the name "poet," while the others get the name "craftsman" or some such thing. She doesn't explain why these special few are called poets, but we can see that it has something to do with the beautiful. This is linked to and is perhaps identical with why only some are called lovers. Diotima alerts us to the mysterious fact that poetry is privileged because it caters to the longing for the beautiful. Without this signal from her we would not understand what follows, and the essential role of poetry in man's concern for the *kalon*. She continues her analysis without determining the specific character of those whom we call lovers, just as she has not determined the specific character of those we call poets, and says that all men are lovers, whether they are moneymakers, *philogymnastai*, or philosophers. Those who pursue these things are lovers, although they do not get the name. The three examples she offers refer to the classic distinction among three kinds of goods, external goods, goods of the body, and goods of the soul. These are all goods, and we know them to be goods. These are not value judgments. The problem, of course, is their rank order or hierarchy. In this purely rational analysis, the specificity of the lover as well as of the beautiful disappears. It is a debunking analysis, on the basis of which sexual union would just be one more good, like eating. This is the way Aristotle treats it explicitly in the *Ethics*. Both eating and sex belong to the sense of touch, the lowest of the senses, and produce a pleasure, one that leads lovers of food to desire necks as long as cranes, and lovers of sex, presumably, to desire similar extensions of the organs of their pleasure. There is nothing splendid or transcendent here, and it is this characteristically Socratic style of analysis, which Diotima is parodying, that provoked both Aristophanes and Nietzsche. It is so unpoetic and unerotic. But this is not the last word.

Diotima takes time out to criticize Aristophanes on the basis of her argument on behalf of the good. She says that men do not love their other half; they love the good. She mentions what I mentioned earlier, that men are willing to have parts of themselves amputated for the sake of the good. One's own things, she insists, are cherished only because they are good. Men love only the good. With this, Socrates heartily agrees.

But this cannot be, and is not, the whole story. Men, in fact, do love their own things, and because they are their own things, especially their countries, their families, and themselves. This is the first and perhaps the natural way, before men ever learned of the good. When they do learn of it, they sophistically identify the good with their own in order to remain at peace. If they really wanted to pursue the good simply, they would have to give up their cities, their homes, those whom by habit they call friends, and even perhaps themselves. This is what Socrates actually does. He lives in Athens but is not really of it, he is married and has children but pays little attention to them. Socrates' life illustrates the sharpness of these conflicts and makes him appear monstrous to the decent people who love their own. Most later philosophers, until the nineteenth century, did not marry, so the conflict between one's own and the good was not so evident.[52] The problem that Socrates poses for all of his interlocutors is that he urges them to break with their own in favor of the good. Hardly any are willing to go the whole way, and this willingness to go the whole way defines the potential philosophers, such as Plato himself. Erotic men seem to have some of this willingness too, but only if their Eros does not collapse into a defense of their own. Polemarchus, in the *Republic*, a decent man who loves his own things but accepts Socrates' view that they must be judged by the good, goes a long way in breaking with his own things, but becomes perplexed when Socrates tells him that he must share his wife with his friends for the sake of the good.[53]

Actually, what is defined in this bit of the dialogue is the essential split in man, which presents him with a harsh choice. All men have mothers and fathers, wives and children, and countries, and a large part of their lives is spent in concern for them. Their lives are apparently unified as long as a Socrates does not solicit another real part of their nature, their love of the good. They also want real friends, as Montaigne defines them, and good cities and just laws. Man's divided loyalties lead to intolerable conflict and much mythmaking. This is why men really do not love the truth nearly as much as they say they do. We all recognize that there is such a split in each of us, but it is not characteristic of political and moral philosophy in our time to insist on it. However, this mode of analysis of the human problem is, I am willing to assert, a distinctive advantage of ancient philosophy and one to which we can and should return.

Almost all tragic conflict concerns this split, but Socrates is completely indifferent to it. He is a strange duck. He seems to be able to resolve the conflict completely in favor of the good and appears, but only appears, to regard the love of one's own as completely nugatory. He has no difficulty in giving up his own, except himself simply, although the two interlocutors in this dialogue, Aristodemus and Apollodorus, seem to have given up even themselves, a kind of parody of Socratism. Socrates actually has to admit that one's own has a certain status because one wants the good things to be one's own—their existence alone is not sufficient. But he does represent to the highest possible degree the intransigent subordination of one's own to the good. Yet the noble deeds are almost always performed for the sake of one's own. This tension, which may very well ultimately have to do with the particularity and vulnerability of a man's body, which does not permit him to follow all the inclinations of his soul, helps define man as that being who loves both his own and the good. He is both a passionate and a rational being. The difficulty is best shown to us by the fact that none of us would want to give up either Aristophanes' or Socrates' account of love.

Diotima plows on and summarizes by saying that men love the good, that they love the good to be theirs, and finally, that they love the good to be theirs always. Eros is the Eros of the good that is to belong to oneself always. And it is this little word "always" that leads us to the heart of the matter. Men want a good dinner or a treatment for their ills. These are good things and perfectly amenable to rational analysis. But the pursuit of the good leads ineluctably to the wish to be always, and the desire for the state of contentment, happiness, or exaltation to exist forever is unreasonable because all human things are perishable and die. Eros, the beautiful, and poetry form a cluster around what is the greatest, but impossible, good. This is the fatal problem that Diotima either obfuscates or is unaware of.

On the basis of Diotima's exchange with Socrates one is almost forced to draw the conclusion that the beautiful is eternity, the always for man. The experience of longing for eternity, as when one holds one's beautiful beloved in one's arms, is constitutive of Eros as opposed to sex. This would obviously not be anything like a complete definition of beauty but, as frequently occurs in the Platonic dialogues, one crafted for the sake of making a particular point. Man is a poor, weak being. His greatest terror is his utter extinction. All the wonderful, rational goods are desired for the sake of being always, which is impossible and hence irrational. The beautiful is that which underlies and acts as goal for the pursuit of the good. Man's very imperfection makes satisfaction with mere humanism truly impossible. Human life is too ugly for anyone who thinks about it to rest content with it. This is the cause of the being of the gods, who underwrite the cosmic significance of human life. The old formula *timor deum fecit*, fear made god, has to be supplemented by *amor deum fecit*, love made god. This complicates a simplistic, antitheological theology. Eros may not be a god, but he animates the poets to create gods for the consolation and uplifting of mankind. This longing, impossible of fulfillment, culminates in the Olympian gods, always young, always beautiful. It is both necessary for man's spirituality and his most dangerous illusion. Diotima both encourages and demystifies this illusion in her mystifying speech. She feeds the aspiration that favors the beautiful and forces some, at least, to ask how they can live with the facts.

She tells Socrates that sexual desire is really pregnancy. She breaks down the distinction between male and female in asserting that both have a fetus within them to which they long to give birth and look for a partner with whom to bring it to the light of day. Without attempting to understand this completely, one can say that she points to a side of man's neediness that is often forgotten or misinterpreted. The picture of natural man given us by Hobbes or Locke, one confirmed by the practice of the market system, is that man barely holds on to life, needing food, shelter, clothing, and so many other things. His experience is beggarly; he takes, and does not give. It is possible to interpret sex in man in this way, but that means that it is only sex, and Eros is dead. This is what is generally thought today. But if one shifts the focus and looks at eroticism itself, it cannot be taken really to be like hunger; it gives rather than takes. Its oppressive character comes from fullness and the need to release the tension constituted by that overflowing presence. Hence, poverty is compensated by the productive search for eternity for which man seems made. Diotima's method of argument undertakes to attach all the wide variety of erotic phenomena to the most obvious one, reproduction. She describes the attraction to the beautiful, that which promises eternity, and the repulsion from the ugly, which is, in its most direct expression, the skeleton, by allusions to the movement of the phallus when it is in its most intense longing and about to overflow, and in its recoil in the presence of the ugly. Diotima and Socrates cannot regard the erection in the same way one regards the palpitations of the hungry stomach. Diotima is phallocentric here. This is a shortened version of Socrates' description of the wing that takes us from becoming to being in the *Phaedrus*, an utterly remarkable taking seriously of things that dignified philosophy usually considers beneath itself.[54]

The kind of immortality hoped for by acts of reproduction preached by Diotima is based on an implicit rejection of the fondest hope, that our individual souls will be saved. At the very outset, aware or unaware, the erotic persons have to give up any expectation that their own consciousness, which they treasure so much, will live on beyond them. On the day of his death as recounted in the *Phaedo*, a somewhat slacker Socrates, perhaps suitably so, given the occasion, tries not entirely successfully to persuade his grieving friends that his soul will survive always. This hope contains no element of Eros in it. In the face of immediate death Socrates, in his speech at least, is not erotic. This may be partly due to the very radical separation between body and soul required for that dialogue, in which immortality requires the soul's being without taint of the body's mortality. The fondest illusion of lovers, however, requires not only the significance of the bodily satisfactions but the permanence of those beautiful bodies that encase the souls. In all reflection on human beings, whether one is talking about the sciences, or politics, or literature, or Eros, some kind of distinction between two elements in man is necessary, whether it is expressed as body and soul, or more timidly and less persuasively, as mind and body, self and other, observer and observed. The mode of being of man, who contains these two elements, is of course extremely ambiguous. From the perspective of Eros, the separability of body and soul is at best questionable, and Diotima is by no means clear on the subject. Its first appearances are certainly in the body, and that is never forgotten. There is a similar aspiration in the soul, unless one tries to regard it as a calculator that exists for the sake of providing satisfactions for the desires of the body, if there are any such things. Rousseau and Freud try to treat the Eros of the soul as displacement from the Eros of the body. Plato does not resolve that question, and Diotima tries to explain the two harmoniously. This way of looking at body and soul is opposed to that found in the *Phaedo* or in Christianity, where the body is understood to be in complete contradiction to the soul and the source of evil, a thing to be fought and overcome. I would argue that Diotima's poetic description is more faithful to the phenomena in reminding us of the obvious interconnection of the two, although she somewhat underplays the impossibility of the perfect unity between them always hoped for by all of us. Certainly the desires of the body, at least in human beings, are never just desires of the body, but are informed by spirituality, and the soul's longing for knowledge is determined by man's particularity and mortality.

Diotima begins her presentation of the three kinds of immortality to which Eros can aspire with reproduction. Each individual man is in constant flux, as indicated by the growth of his hair and fingernails, as well as his forgetting and remembering. He is held together by a strange identity, but one that disappears with death. In the first kind of immortality, the continuity of that identity can be found in offspring. Why one should be concerned with a continuity of which one will not be conscious is not explained and is perhaps inexplicable. Nature attracts us to it, but perhaps for her own purposes alone. Moreover, this form of eternity presupposes the eternity of the visible universe with its species. Aristotle argues for this position, but it is not at all clear that Plato does. There is a very great difference between a long time and eternity, and eternity is what Eros insists upon. Whatever the satisfaction that comes from engendering may be, Diotima says that we delight in our immortality, as seen in our children. We love them because they are embodiments of the beautiful good, immortality, and because they are our own. They are our own immortality. This is undoubtedly a true observation of what men and women experience in the contemplation of their children. And to the extent this particular illusion of immortality becomes attenuated, the power of family attachments is also attenuated. It is very hard in our times, with the easy liberation from family ties and the movement of people from their ancestral homes, to see in children a succession that will endure for as long as the imagination can see. Today, one's children are with difficulty conceived of as one's own and as the continuers of something that began long before us and will continue long after us. This throws us back much more on our isolated selves.

But Diotima's account of the splendid imagination of the ancestral family is itself fraught with difficulties. In the first place, it is not nature that produces the family, but the law. Promiscuous encounters do not produce children, certainly not the kind who are one's own and who promise immortality to the family name. It is only within the context of the law that a man can really imagine that the offspring from his loins can people the world, and thus take his sexual acts with such cosmic significance. The law that gives names to families and tries to ensure their integrity is a kind of unnatural force and endures only as long as does the regime of which it is a part. The oldest existing families of which I have heard go back only to the Roman Empire, a mere two thousand years. The only slightly more common ones go back only eight or nine hundred years. And how many questionable individuals may have inserted themselves into these allegedly unbroken lines? Children are a great blessing and joy, but one must forget an awful lot in order to see eternity in them.

The sexual attractions of men and women in this first stage are justified only in terms of offspring. The love of the two individuals who make the children has no independent status, as it did in Aristophanes, where the children are treated as accidents. Diotima's way gives its full due to the natural cycle of reproduction, whereas Aristophanes' way gives full due to the immediate and powerful attractions. Diotima's nature, at least implicitly, puts more weight on the visible species and gives preference to the kind of motion to be found in the growth of plants and animals as opposed to that to be found in changes of place. In other words, she is not an atomist and is closer to being a biologist, one who views the atoms as controlled by the species or the Forms of things, the heterogeneity of kinds as superior to the homogeneity of atoms. Therefore, Diotima understands human beings much more as parts of nature and its purposiveness than do Eryximachus and Aristophanes. Diotima reflects a change in ontology or the understanding of nature, which is historically linked with Socrates' turning around from the blinding attempt to see the atoms to viewing the reflections of the various kinds of things. The atoms as such are never seen but are reasoned to as the substrate of the things that we see. The Forms or the Ideas in their etymological sense point toward the primacy of the eyes and what they see. There is a connection between natural philosophy understood in this way and the speculative or contemplative pleasure of the lover, who in the first place enjoys looking at the beauty of the beloved. None of the other speakers have concentrated so much on that purely speculative joy, although it was prefigured in Agathon's description of beauty. He himself was more interested in being looked at than in looking. Aristophanes concentrated on copulating with the beloved, on touching or feeling him or her.

After procreation, the ongoing continuation of the species, immortality in mortality like Eros himself, Diotima starts her upward climb. This is where the delicate question of rank order or hierarchy of sexual desires, a question repugnant to many contemporaries, is addressed. This is the category of those pregnant in soul, longing to beget prudence and the rest of virtue in the souls of others. The longing for fame or the love of glory that motivates men in this second stage is naturally preferable not because of its social utility, as it would be for Freud, but because it fulfills those subject to these kinds of pregnancy much more than does the mere act of sexual intercourse. At the same time, there begins to appear a certain separation of the erotic longing from the erotic act. The category of persons who practice this second kind of Eros is very broad, including poets, inventors, statesmen, lawgivers, and founders. But they are all described by Diotima as lovers who undertake to educate beautiful human beings and seem to resemble the pederasts, who, for obvious reasons, are not considered in the category of those whose longing for immortality is satisfied by producing babies. A lawgiver surely has to subordinate the interests of his family to those of the city, and although not everybody would agree with this ordering of priorities, it is readily comprehensible. For the lawgiver this is no great sacrifice, for his passion urges him to prefer his public acts over his private ones. Such persons tend not to be good husbands and fathers; they have no time for it.

The desire for immortality lifts men out of their exclusive concern for their mere selves, but it is not clear that the longing for immortal fame is an affect of eroticism. If it were, then the statesmen and the lawgivers would be erotic men. Elsewhere, however, the love of fame is treated by Plato as part of *thymos* or spiritedness, a great opponent of Eros. This is particularly so in the *Republic*.[55] It would seem that Diotima stretches things somewhat in order to give a totally erotic account of all man's powerful longings. Diotima tries to square the longings of these very public persons, founders and poets, with her thesis that all men and women are pregnant by pointing out that they produce something, a city or a poem, that makes the souls of those under their influence better and more beautiful. Moderation and justice are very attractive, and when one can say, "I put this into people," they are even more attractive. The contemplation of one's spiritual children can be held to be a higher thing than the contemplation of the children of one's body. This is the kind of satisfaction that Socrates offers to the young Glaucon in the *Republic*, a satisfaction coming from the founding of a city that educates men and women. Yet it is still difficult to see how the bodily Eros is also contained in this love of the generation of beautiful souls.

Perhaps this difficulty can be explained when one sees what Diotima says about the eroticism of those who undertake to educate beautiful human beings, and that it is strictly applicable to Socrates himself. It is well to point out that all three levels of Diotima's description fit the mature Socrates, who was a father, an educator, and a philosopher. The teacher is attracted to beautiful youths and wishes to form them in such a way that he can be proud of his influence on them. The change or transformation he wishes to engender in them, willy-nilly, leads from the body to a concern with their souls. An athletic trainer can improve the looks of a young person's body, but a serious man is interested primarily in what the young person does with his body. Here the connection between body and soul with respect to Eros is maintained, and what we really get is an aspect of the Socratic criticism of the lawgivers and poets. Theirs is an imperfect Eros. Their ambition is to influence whole peoples, and they have to deal with them in mass and without special concern for certain individuals. This ambition is in conflict with and attenuates Eros, which is concerned with individuals. Socrates wants a great reputation for improving the youth, as opposed to corrupting them, but his ambition must be limited by the power of his real attraction, beginning with their bodies but ending with their souls. Only the man practiced in the first powerful attractions that begin with the body will be capable of this transition. One can imagine that such a teacher will meet ugly youths whose spirituality is so distinguished that the body is forgotten. The strong attachment to a beautiful soul accompanied by an ugly body is more fulfilling than the attachment to a beautiful body accompanied by an ugly soul. The virtues preferred by the lawgivers are moderation and justice, the virtues that contribute most to political order and stability. Diotima does not say which virtues this educator loves, but I think one can rest assured that he is more concerned with courage and wisdom, the virtues that may characterize the lawgivers themselves but are not the ones that they propagate. This teacher, as opposed to the lawgiver, can actually propagate himself, and not just a distorted image of himself. In this way teaching is more erotic than lawgiving or poetry.

The picture Diotima gives us is of a wise and prudent man erotically attracted to a boy and carrying on conversations with him as a kind of intellectual seduction bringing forth from the boy responses and responsiveness that please the man. It is really very difficult to imagine a serious man perpetually involved with a dumb blonde with whom he can never hope to have any reciprocity of conversation. There is obviously a tension between the attraction to the body and the attraction to the soul, and it is difficult, in the case of a teacher and a student, to believe that it is possible to alternate between sex and conversation. Still, the whole relationship is suffused with a kind of intensity and doubt more characteristic of love than of friendship. A friend is an equal, and a beginning student is not an equal, but it is the very potential, the imperfection, that the teacher can actualize or perfect that constitutes the peculiar charm of this kind of relationship. The sexual act that produces children is more unified and more intense, from the point of view of the body. But there is an extraordinary power in this combination of body and soul, and it promises a continuity and unity between the two parties that is not a necessary consequence of the union of two persons for the production of children. This helps us to understand the post-Aristophanean Socrates, who spends so much time with young people from whom he could not expect to learn much new about the problems of philosophy. The spectacle of fresh and beautiful souls cannot help pleasing him. This later Socrates has discovered the soul, which is part of things as much as is matter. He has discovered or at least learned to take seriously Eros and its attraction to beautiful things, particularly beautiful human beings. It is a very high vocation, but one that begins with what is thought to be a low one, the desire to possess bodies. There is a golden thread that leads a man of

Socrates' talents from one to the other. It is not because he is sexually attracted that he wishes to teach, he is sexually attracted because he needs to teach. His delight in this one person can give him the hope that what he teaches, philosophy, will live on to all eternity in the midst of the changes of political orders.

In this passage on the love of glory, Diotima responds to both Phaedrus and Pausanias. To Phaedrus, she explains that the great deeds of Alcestis and Achilles, which he praised, were attempts to win immortal fame, not the kind of immortality Phaedrus described, that came to them in another world after their death. And she instructs Pausanias in the ways in which a man *can be* erotically disposed toward a youth's instruction as well as toward his body. The connection need not be "I'll show you how to work your computer if you'll let me have sex with you." The man can really find something beautiful, or potentially beautiful, in the soul of his beloved, which Pausanias is unable to articulate, something that both heightens the bodily attraction and contradicts it. Phaedrus and Pausanias gave praises of Eros that were defective and little better than ideologies justifying what they wanted to get from Eros. But those ideologies divined something about the nature of human attachments that was true and sublime. They were not just rationalizing, as we would say, in order to satisfy themselves, but rather pointed beyond themselves. They only had to be thought through more than Phaedrus or Pausanias wanted to or were capable of. Instead of stripping away their rationalizations in order to get at what is understood to be the real desire, Socrates would encourage them to see more in what they wish than they are yet aware of, while criticizing them gently and pushing them along the path as far as they can go. Erotic rhetoric is not merely rhetoric. Socrates makes use of such people while trying to help them. Men and women should engage in erotic apologetics, for it makes them better than they are. But as Diotima suggests, only the rarest of human beings can become initiates in the science of erotics.

One must remember that this second stage, too, really disappoints the longing for immortality, because even though poems, inventions, laws, cities, teachings, and the fame they bring with them are likely to last a much longer time than families do, they are almost certain to be extinguished with time.

This is what Diotima, in an insulting way, tells Socrates himself. She is ready to believe that he has understood the first two stages, but doubts that he will be able to understand the culmination to which they lead, and indeed, this last segment contains the most mysterious and mystical pronouncements of her teaching, and access to them is certainly beyond me. What she is trying to do is clear: she is undertaking to describe the philosophical experience as it would appear to a man who has become completely wise. This, of course, is impossible because no man is or has ever been completely wise. It is a description of the rewards in store for the one who undertakes the philosophical life, which are parallel to the rewards promised to the person who undertakes the Christian life. Of course, this description is much less admissible by a philosopher, who is by definition a doubter, than by a Christian, who is by definition a believer. But it helps to explain the partial experiences of a philosopher by an image of what they might mean if they were completed. This is why Socrates calls her a Sophist.

The splendid vision she presents is intended to make one believe that the philosophic is the most erotic life. Socrates always teaches that the philosophic life is the most necessary one and the best one. In the *Republic*, he tries to show that the philosophic life is the most just life, and elsewhere, that the philosophic life is also the most pious life and the most scientific life. He tries to present philosophy as the true fulfillment of all the other lives that men esteem and pursue. Here, Diotima simply says that if Eros is Eros of the beautiful, then what philosophers see is the most beautiful and hence the most erotic. But one has to give up an awful lot of what one originally understood to be desirable about Eros, just as one had to with justice or piety. The philosophic life may contain all the other ways of life, but in a way that is completely alien to those who lead them. It is justice without the city, piety without the gods, and Eros without copulation or reciprocity.

As soon as Diotima starts discussing philosophy, she is less insistent on her thesis that Eros is pregnancy. There is no product resulting from philosophic contemplation as there are from the link between male and female and the love of glory of lawgivers, poets, inventors, and teachers. She describes the movement from sexual attraction to a beautiful body, which remains for her the beginning, to philosophy as a recognition that this beautiful body is not beauty entire or in itself. One beautiful body, even one in which a man has engendered beautiful speeches, leads him to recognize that there are other and somewhat different beautiful bodies to which he is necessarily attracted if he is a true lover of beauty. Diotima is explicit that a man must love at least two bodies, and there seems no reason not to love at least a few more. The erotic problem as seen by the man who faces it consists in the almost inevitable attraction to many bodies in a lifetime and the temptation to consummate these attractions, accompanied by an awareness that there is also something wonderful and laudable about sticking together with a partner. The absolutization of the first alternative is incarnated in the person of Don Juan, and the second, in Saint-Preux or Werther. Each of the two seems somehow imperfect, and, according to Diotima, this is because men love the beautiful simply and wish to cleave to it always, whereas the flesh-and-blood individuals with whom one can actually copulate are only imperfect representations of the beautiful. Human, legal fidelity is only an imitation of true fidelity, and, to a certain extent, stands in the way of achieving it. The fidelity of two lovers represents something that ought to be but cannot be in this kind of relationship. Yet the simply loose and promiscuous man, although he does illuminate a problem, also looks for beauty where it cannot be found. The absolute Romantic preference for the permanent couple illustrates the difference between the classical taste and the Romantic one. The Romantics want to fix something that, according to the classics, cannot be fixed while remaining open to the truth. This aspect of Diotima's teaching is really very harsh. The movement of Eros leads away from the charm of the two people who embrace and want to be together always, the charm so marvelously captured by Aristophanes. It may seem wonderful to get a good argument in favor of promiscuity, but if one thinks it through, Diotima also destroys the pleasures of promiscuity. Promiscuity is only a means to the end of recognizing that what one is looking for is not to be found here and that the man who sticks to his looseness will soon become simply corrupt and never learn the lesson. In this respect, the permanent couples are clearly preferable.

This issue can be very well illustrated by the choice between remaining loyal to one's own country, or culture, as it would be styled today, and the freedom of cosmopolitanism. There are persons who make this choice in one direction or another very easily or instinctively and do not see the charms of the alternative, but each is incomplete. We all know how wonderful roots and traditional community are, the belonging and the unquestioned connectedness with other human beings that come from them. Those who are faithful to this kind of connection see the other kind of men as rootless cosmopolitans: selfish, because they are not dedicated to their community, and superficial, because they have not grown from the earth of a fatherland and been nourished by its history. The others recognize the injustices and stupidities that belong to their own particular culture while seeing in other ones all kinds of splendid opportunities they are denied at home. But is it possible at one's will to become part of other cultures, which will also, in their turn, reveal their specific injustices and stupidities? There is always something faintly ridiculous about persons who choose another country and try to become members of it. They seem to be merely imitating and never really a part. But if they do not try to cleave to an alien culture and make it their own, where are they to go in a world where there are only countries and cultures? They tend to become trivial tourists in both body and soul.

This could appear to be a tragic conflict between one's own and the good, between contented ignorance and unhappy knowledge, and this is the way it is most often represented today. This is how Nietzsche saw the problem when he tells us that men need horizons within which to live, but that all horizons are poetic creations of cultures, and when one knows that fact, one can no longer live within them.[56] But the status of such horizons, of course, is precisely where Plato and Nietzsche are at odds. Plato tries to make his view plausible in the person of Socrates, who remains in his native city, yet belongs nowhere and does not believe in any of the things the members of his community believe in but is hardly an unhappy or tragic figure. Socrates is the one whom Nietzsche most savagely attacked. Nietzsche believes that a man has to be seeking a new horizon, a new place in which to be rooted, whereas Socrates insists that the deepest source of inspiration is in nature or somehow in the cosmos and that a man can become fully human only by separation from the horizon within which he chanced to be born. Or, in other words, Socrates insists that there is an absolute horizon: he likens cities or cultures to caves, but philosophers can climb out of them into the light of the sun. Nietzsche says there are only caves and no sun. This is why Socrates says that the most important phenomenon in the soul is Eros, an overwhelming attraction toward the sun, which nourishes and expands the soul. Nourishment comes to a human being not through roots attached to the soil but through the eyes, which gaze on the permanent order of things. The highest virtue for Plato is love of knowledge, whereas for Nietzsche it is intellectual honesty, the resolve to look the ugly facts in the face. This is why Nietzsche cannot make Eros the center of his psychology, but is compelled to fall back on the will to power, which makes order rather than contemplating it. When Rousseau speaks of "a few great cosmopolitan souls," he refers to the Socratic phenomenon, in contrast to the trifling and justly despised cosmopolitanism that one ordinarily sees. An American who falls in love with the art of Italy may decide to go and live there and try to become a Renaissance Italian, or he can use that experience, as did Shakespeare, to open himself out onto beauties of which he was previously unaware and that ultimately belong to no nation. The ridiculous snobbism of a Bernard Berenson is indicative of what is wrong with the first alternative, whereas Shakespeare's person and his plays show what is splendid about the second. It is not so clear that Nietzsche is as right as most scholars today believe.

The harsh thing about Diotima's teaching is that one must leave behind so much of what constitutes the charm of life for us. Socrates tells us in the *Republic* that the philosopher is the only truly just man, but his justice is practiced all alone without a community that one could actually live in, which offers such satisfaction to most men.[57] Here must he love without the warm body and the adoring eyes of another.

The philosopher's movement up the ladder of love is an ascent toward the things that are always, as opposed to those that come into being and pass away. To see and perhaps to become one with what is always is the philosopher's way of reaching immortality. Diotima exhorts to philosophy by presenting its attainable goal as the completion of wisdom, which is a full grasp of beauty and immortality. That there are things which are always, whatever they may be, is almost certain. In the observation of men's bodies, that which is most permanent is their form or shape, while the flesh, blood, and bones are constantly in a flux of replacement. And after the death of these bodies, there are other bodies of like form which have been produced by the body that is now dead and can no longer reproduce. The visible forms of things are the most permanent things we know, and Diotima tells us that the truest, the most unchanging things are these forms, of which we get a reflection in bodies. Diotima outlines the Socratic teaching about the Ideas or Forms but in a way that both is very partial and avoids the manifest difficulties connected with that teaching. Philosophy is learning to become attached to these Forms, which are more real than the bodies that first attracted us. She reproduces Socratic dialectic, arguing that one moves from individuals, who are some kind of unity of body and soul, to the ways of life, the practices and laws, that govern men, and from there to the various branches of knowledge. The practices and the laws exist primarily in speech, and interest in them is the next thing after attraction to individuals because they form and rule individuals in communities. For example, Socrates will speak to Athenians about their laws, and will ineluctably be drawn toward a quest for justice, the standard against which laws or practices are measured. The Idea or Form of justice follows from the laws of men and from paying attention to what men say about them. Justice is not something one sees with the naked eye in nature, but is in the first place to be found in the opinions of men. And the inadequacy, or the habitually contradictory character, of opinions leads in turn to reflection on knowledge, as opposed to opinion, and the various kinds of knowledge. Ideas or Forms are essentially the kinds into which things are divided that constitute the heterogeneity of nature itself. These kinds, each of which has a specific kind of knowledge connected with it, articulate the whole and provide the objects of intellectual activity.

Diotima presents the movement from the first inclinations toward bodies as a smooth transition from the particular to the general, from the changing to the permanent, from the visible to the intelligible. Therefore, the contemplation of the whole is simply a perfection of the original erotic attraction to a single person and provides all the satisfaction one expected from that person. This is why she claims that the highest Idea, the Idea of Ideas, is beauty. Elsewhere, Socrates has said that the Idea of Ideas is the Idea of the good, which is much more in keeping with his clear and debunking rationalism.[58] This difference illuminates the inadequacy of Diotima's presentation and its "optimism." She teaches that the final experience will be as erotically satisfying as the first or even more so. Moreover, she implies that philosophy can overcome itself and turn into wisdom. In her account, there is no longer doubt or need to return to the particulars and the shadows from which the philosopher began in his quest for wisdom. Here is a reassuring account of things without the terrible and ugly doubts of the philosopher. She praises the philosophical life, as Agathon praised Eros, rather than describing it as it is. She tries to establish the dignity of the philosophical life, what must be if it is to be justified as the highest way of life. But she does what she criticized Socrates for doing; she forgets that Eros in its very nature is incompleteness and hence not beautiful. At best, philosophy can be only a divination of such an end as she describes, but full of tantalizing doubts that call it into question.

Philosophy and Eros resemble each other in their ugliness, in their alternation between death and immortality. Eros, as Diotima describes him, resembles Socrates, and Socrates is the philosopher *par excellence*. And this leads us to what is most unsatisfying in this hard climb up the ladder of love. The satisfaction that is promised at the end and for which the climb was undertaken in the first place is immortality. It is true that the objects of the philosopher's contemplation are immortal, but Diotima wishes to make us forget that the philosopher is not. She says that the philosopher is immortal if any human being is. That is a very big if. It is precisely the philosopher who will be most aware of and resistant to the self-forgetting induced by the beautiful. He knows that he will die, and his very contact with the things that are always provides the measure of the difference between them and him.

With such awareness, how can he go on? There will obviously be a certain splendor and magnanimity in his soul, aware as he is of the inspiring character of the whole and his special capacity to distinguish what is illusion and what is true. But he will have to come to terms with death and live always with the consciousness that in order to live well here in this short life, he must crush all hopes that will cloud his vision. He will enjoy the pleasures that are real and not those founded on the false anticipations of immortality that motivate all other men. At this point, Socrates becomes like the Epicurean Lucretius, for whom the hopes and terrors coming from the gods are done away with by philosophy, only to be replaced by the certainty of extinction. How the philosopher can live contemplating this terrible necessity is almost impossible for nonphilosophers to understand. And this, of course, is the great advantage of Diotima's description of philosophy, an attempt to reproduce the grandeur and the pleasure of philosophy for those who not only are not philosophers but do not even believe in the possibility of a life exclusively devoted to knowing. And she appears to reflect what it is that keeps the philosopher going even though he is fully aware of his situation, that is, the great pleasure that accompanies thinking for such men. He is really the child of Resource and Poverty, almost dying but brought back to life by the bit of immortality in him. Eros is both man's great deluder and his liberator, depending on how he is used.

What will the life of the real philosopher be like? He will constantly be looking for the causes of all things and asking "What is . . . ?" the questions such as "What is man?" "What is justice?" "What is beautiful?" and "What is a god?" But he, unlike the men described by Diotima, will not be able or want to live always on the heights. He will constantly have to return to those real, embodied persons with their opinions to whom he was first attracted and from whom he learned the problems. They are his only access to the Ideas, and as long as he does not see the Ideas completely, he has to interpret the Ideas in the light of the world that they must explain. The philosopher still has a body, and the Eros of the soul, no matter how powerful it is, does not do away with the body and its demands. Diotima makes it seem that everything that was implied in the first erotic attraction is fulfilled in philosophy. But a philosopher will still experience sexual attractions to bodies. He is not a saint who prides himself on the mortification of his flesh. He will do what pleases him, so long as it does not destroy the rank order of his pleasures. He will drink and have sex to such an extent as will permit or even encourage him to think. The youth to whom he was first attracted now becomes ambiguous: he is both an object of immediate erotic satisfaction and a stepping-stone to philosophy, and those two functions are not identical. Socrates did get married and have children, although the results were not entirely happy with either his wife or his children. And he hung around with some very attractive young men, although it is not clear he ever had sexual relations with them. If he did, he could not take them all that seriously. And there is, perhaps most important of all, that lonely speculator who cuts himself off from all others in order to speculate. These three layers of his real life reflect the architecture necessary to the fullness of a complex being such as man. Nothing fits together simply, and much must be overcome in order to put things in the proper order. He is most likely to cleave to the intellectual pleasures, which are more unmixed than the bodily ones, more enduring, and more self-sufficient. At the end, those persons to whom he is attracted disappear in the pursuit of that will-o'-the-wisp beyond them that one seeks even and especially in the moment of embrace. One would have to put Aristophanes and Socrates, or at least their arguments, together in order to get some clarity about what the whole man demands.

Diotima's teaching is both a failure and a success in trying to give a fully erotic account of human psychology. The primitive longings of Eros are denied their fulfillment, but Eros properly understood is that which most divines the human situation, mortality longing for immortality. She makes it clear that the Eros of the soul can never be understood as a mere borrowing from the Eros of the body. Therefore, she is able to give the soul, as well as the body, its due. But at the end of his praise of Eros, Socrates is able to say only that Eros is the best co-worker with man and to praise his power and his courage. Eros is the key to that mixture of daring and moderation that is essential for the good life. Above all, it provides the energy for flying out beyond *nomos*.

XI   Socrates is duly praised by everyone except, that is, for Aristophanes, who attempts to speak about the references to his own speech. We never get to hear his response, and we should try to figure out what he might have said. Unfortunately, he is interrupted but in such an enchanting way that we are disposed to forget him (212c–214b). Alcibiades, reputed to be the most beautiful and most talented man of his time, arrives roaring drunk and disguised as Dionysus himself. As we have already noted, this is the eve of his most daring undertaking, which might have led to empire beyond the previous dreams of the Athenians. Alcibiades is also at that moment when his recklessness leads him to the impieties which are to bring him down. He has godlike allures but shares the vulnerability of human beings. He is very erotic indeed, but more in the fashion of a beloved, as are the gods. He is no potential tyrant, although he wants to rule alone. He wants the people to love him purely and spontaneously, and they often did so, but never reliably. He was capable of making politics erotic. He made the citizens long erotically for Sicily. He wanted all good things to go together. He is a kind of peak of ambition and longing. His Sicilian scheme was the first step in a plan for world conquest that was later to be accomplished by Alexander the Great.[59] Even when he was an isolated exile without a political base he managed to become the arbiter of the affairs of Greece, first from Sparta, then among the Persians. This was an unparalleled achievement, his soul triumphing over the Greek body. He had an almost Socratic madness about the power of the soul. Like the philosopher he longed for the whole, but his whole was the real whole of this earth.

Alcibiades, as I noted, was the prime public example used by Socrates' accusers to prove that he was a corrupter of the youth. The other potential tyrant who actually became one and was linked to Socrates was Critias, but it is perfectly clear that he was never really close to Socrates and that Socrates was in no way attracted to him. Plato and Xenophon, who chronicled Socrates' life for us, tried to exculpate Socrates from the crude charges as much as possible, but if one looks closely, they always tell us the truth. Xenophon repeats a conversation that Alcibiades had with his uncle Pericles about so important a theme as the law, in which Alcibiades humiliates the great statesman and shows that Pericles does not know what law is. Pericles gives up the conversation saying this was the sort of thing he talked about when he was young, to which Alcibiades responds that he wishes he had known Pericles when he was at his best. Xenophon denies that Alcibiades was influenced by Socrates, yet he reports this conversation that is perfectly Socratic and a model of the kind of investigation that Socrates himself was continually performing. Nothing similar occurs with Critias. Actually, Socrates insults him, and Critias bears a great grudge against him.[60] Alcibiades, then, is exemplary of those young men who actually fell under Socrates' influence and in turn influenced Athenian public life. It is worth our while to reflect on this teacher-student erotic involvement and whether it was damaging to the polity. Socrates was surely attracted by this young man's soul, which in its way was prodigious. Certainly there is an extrapolitical immoderation in Alcibiades to which Socrates probably contributed. Socrates' criticism of *nomos* and the high place he gave to Eros fit the personality of Alcibiades as we know it, and Socrates' possible irresponsibility in encouraging such a gifted and dangerous man is worth questioning. Alcibiades himself admits that Socrates failed in his education of him (215e–216c), but should not such a diviner of souls, as was Socrates, have understood that this was inevitable? A failure with a high-risk person is almost as culpable as deliberate corruption. The Alcibiadean vision of politics seems like a political version of Diotima's vision of the Ideas and the beautiful. Maybe Socrates thought that Alcibiades was, all in all, a good thing for Athens. Or, perhaps he simply did not care. It would, however, be a great mistake, a mistake brought about by the brilliance of politics in the eyes of most men, to think that Alcibiades was Socrates' favorite student. His favorite student, without a doubt, was Plato, who, in Nietzsche's phrase, was the fairest growth of antiquity.[61] Alcibiades was attracted to philosophy only for a moment and obviously could not find vital sustenance from drinking at its source. Plato began from an attraction to the political life, one of those gifted young Athenians who believed that democracy was an outrage and an injustice to their vaulting natures, but lost all attraction to that life and left it forever without a moment of regret. Nietzsche says that Plato was the one whom Socrates corrupted by destroying his creativity and along with it his noble instincts.[62] We have to move from the relationship with the spectacular Alcibiades to an image of the relationship between Socrates and Plato, which neither Plato nor Xenophon grant us. We can speculate that Plato, if he had stuck to politics, would have been as talented as Alcibiades. We can judge Socrates, the master of erotics, by comparing the failure of his teaching with Alcibiades and its success with Plato. We can learn about the political man from Thucydides and we can know what Plato was from the dialogues. Here we get Alcibiades, Socrates' lover, praising

Socrates, and the Platonic dialogues as a whole are Plato's praise of Socrates. Few men have ever had such supreme testimonials from worthy lovers.

Alcibiades revitalizes the drinking party and forces his reluctant companions to drink. He comes on as a ruler and unilaterally takes over the presidency of the symposium, although he quite freely shares it with Eryximachus, whom he calls most moderate, when the latter insists. Eryximachus orders him to praise love, which is the convention of their little polity. When Alcibiades notices Socrates, he feigns shock, the shock of a rejected lover pained at unexpectedly meeting his beloved, particularly at seeing him in action with another. Socrates responds with the charge that he is being sexually harassed by Alcibiades and needs the protection of the others. All this is of course ludicrous. One only need imagine the looks of the two men. This is urbane comedy, but it reflects a profound and complicated relationship. The fair Alcibiades is the disappointed one, and Socrates means more to him than he means to Socrates.

At first, Alcibiades docilely accepts Eryximachus' command to praise Eros, but then he thinks better of it, saying that Socrates never permits him to praise anyone, god or man, other than Socrates himself and will strike him if he does so (214c–214e). This may appear to us to be a gross calumny, but on reflection, it is not so clear that Socrates, even though he does not care for popular acclaim, does not wish to be recognized as the best by the best. His conversations always end up with a recognition, willing or unwilling, by his interlocutor, that he is the superior. Wherever he goes, as one sees in this dialogue itself, he becomes the center of all attention and emerges the victor in the competition for attention. He affirms himself and appears to need confirmation. This seems to be a corollary of his imperfect wisdom.

So Alcibiades changes the subject and asks for permission to praise Socrates. But it comes down to the same thing, for Socrates is Eros. He resembles the description of Eros, he is the peak of Alcibiades' erotic longing, and he illustrates the gifts Eros gives. In a strange peripety, this ugly, imperfect being, whether it is Eros or Socrates, turns out to be the beloved and the possessor of the greatest beauties. The most imperfect turns out to be the most perfect. The explanation of this paradox will reveal the deepest strand of the *Symposium*. What a strange thing it is to watch the most desirable man of his time plausibly describing Socrates as the most desirable of all men.

The praise of Socrates is presented as an accusation of Socrates before the tribunal composed of the citizens of the polity. This is another, and a deeper, version of the charges made against Socrates by someone who knew him more intimately than did the Athenian *dēmos*. Alcibiades presents himself as an injured party Socrates wronged. But Alcibiades, in his charming and surpassing candor, admits that the wrong done him is essential to the admirable virtue of Socrates. He is an unrequited lover who complains about his beloved. Any such complaint, if deposed by an honest man, ends up being a praise of the qualities of the one who is loved. In his praise of Socrates, Alcibiades signals Socrates' courage, his moderation, and his wisdom, but never attributes justice to him. The city's complaint against Socrates was that he does injustice, and that comes down to saying that he did not love the *dēmos*, much as Alcibiades complains he did not love him.

Alcibiades' speech (214e–222b) has the function of trying to prove that Socrates is the most beautiful and attractive of men, and this is very difficult to do because he was admittedly an unusually ugly man. The genius of what Alcibiades does is equivalent to proving that philosophy itself, from the outside, in certain ways a very ugly activity, is the best and most beautiful way of life. What is so wonderful about what Alcibiades does is that he gives an account of his falling under Socrates' spell that is the opposite of a sermon given by a dry academic type. Nobody could be more full-blooded than Alcibiades, nor more capable of preserving the perspective of normal, healthy human beings, as opposed to that of converts, devotees, and fanatics. Moreover, he has an amazing candor, one might even say shamelessness, in his discourse, a candor that his speeches in Thucydides confirm. He speaks of his own habitual lack of shame, a godlike attribute, but it is never the decadent self-exhibition of the debauched man. He is a man with a capacious soul who wants to open it out to the world without the ordinary hypocrisy or the need to adjust it to public opinion. He wants to be loved, but for exactly what he is. He is perhaps the prime candidate of his time for comparison to one of the Homeric gods or heroes, as he compares Brasidas to Achilles and Pericles to Nestor or Antenor (221c–d). He is an utterly convincing witness, his drunkenness appearing only to confirm the veracity of his testimony.

In trying to make the attractiveness of Socrates plausible, Alcibiades begins powerfully by comparing him to Silenus or the satyr Marsyas. Socrates has no Homeric exemplar, so Alcibiades has to turn to mythological figures outside Homer to characterize him. The satyrs are obscene sylvan beings, connected with the flute and its erotic effects, which are banished from the *Republic* by Socrates.[63] The forest is alive with such erotic sensibilities, and these naked, ugly figures, frequently depicted with erect phalluses, run through it, inciting people to full expressiveness of their feelings. They are low but compelling. Socrates himself is frequently depicted to look something like them, with a pot belly and a coarsely sensual snub nose. They are not beings to whom one would be attracted, but ones who themselves desire without limit. They attest to a certain demonic character in nature itself. Beginning from this description, Alcibiades moves forward to a richer characterization of their appeal. He speaks of statues of Silenus that can be pulled open and contain images of gods. If one opens up this Silenus, there are gods within him. And shifting from what one can see within to the effect of Socrates, he speaks of the ecstatic states induced by the music of the flute. The science of flute playing was passed down from Marsyas and produced thrilling experiences akin to and connected with religious rites. There are great beauties to see for those to whom Socrates is willing to show his insides, and his speeches, unadorned by meter or the accompaniment of the flute, cause men to be possessed, as in the extreme and dangerous possessions one saw in the frenzied Corybantic dancers. Other kinds of rhetoric were cold exercises, but Socrates' speeches incited such responses, even when repeated by poor speakers—just as is in this dialogue narrated by Apollodorus. The speech, the *logos*, of Socrates is a life-giving and animating force. These experiences with Socrates made Alcibiades think it intolerable to go on living as he had been and not give himself over to Socrates completely. Alcibiades' rhetoric here does not try to say what those speeches actually were, but it succeeds in making his point by describing their effect on him.

It is one of the most difficult things in the world to make philosophy as a way of life plausible to anyone who has not seen a philosopher, as Herder indicated in his eulogy of Kant.[64] Philosophy, according to Plato, is not a doctrine but a way of life, one that rivals the ways of life of prophets or saints, and poets or artists, and statesmen or generals. Yet philosophy in itself has none of the splendor of any of those other types or kinds of lives. Those types are present almost anywhere where there is some kind of civilization, but philosophy appeared only in Greece and has persisted only in those to whom it was transmitted by the Greeks, beginning with the powerful and amazingly open Romans. Nations could do without philosophers but probably not without those who teach them about the gods, tell them their myths, and govern and protect them. Philosophy is both less necessary and less prepossessing, as the figure of Socrates himself makes evident, but he argues that philosophy is the one thing most needful. The other peak ways of life are public, useful for the people as a whole, and admired by the people. Philosophy neither needs the people so much nor is the object of their immediate respect. But philosophy must be accepted and respected in the city to reach fulfillment. In itself, again as represented in Socrates as we see him, it is essentially an activity carried on with individuals. This makes it closer to love than any of the others. The Platonic dialogues are a presentation less of Socrates' doctrines than of his activity and a kind of literary substitute for seeing and hearing him with one's own eyes and ears. Plato made Socrates a compelling and almost living figure for millennia. Such testimonies as that given by Alcibiades contribute to the living image of Socrates as the sorcerer. The golden speeches of Socrates can be found all over Plato's dialogues, but one sees them particularly powerfully in the *Symposium*, with its invention of Diotima and her perplexing and enticing teaching. Something similar is to be found in the great speech about divine madness in the *Phaedrus*.[65] For other types of tastes, the *Republic*'s founding of a city that features a community of women and children and philosopher-kings is equally spectacular.

But it is not simply his capacity to make beautiful and profound speeches that makes Socrates attractive. It is that they are tailored to evoke and elaborate the deepest longing of the persons to whom they are addressed. Socrates, the master psychologist and witch doctor of souls, knows the governing passion of everyone he meets, sometimes without his interlocutors' even knowing beforehand what that passion is. He satisfies it and then perplexes it. All whom he wishes to attract feel that he is the only one who has ever understood them, and then he makes them think that only he can help them in their perplexity. He is the author of their personal tragedy and the ecstatic state into which it puts them, and then he turns it into a comedy. They want him with them always, and they are soon forced really to observe him and find that he contains virtues that they have never really thought about but would now wish to possess. The contemplation of his virtues becomes a kind of religion.

All of this comes out in Alcibiades' tribute. It is not simply an exaggeration when he describes the state of possession in the same terms that Socrates, in the *Ion*, uses to describe the ecstasy of divine possession induced by the poets (215a–216a).[66] This dancing satyr with his flute forced Alcibiades to dance too. I believe there is no exaggeration in this account of Socrates' effect on Alcibiades. He had the same effect on Alcibiades that the Sirens had on Odysseus and all other men who heard them. Socrates ruined Alcibiades' life, because in Socrates Alcibiades saw a dazzling brilliance that caused him to want to be with him always. But Alcibiades was from top to bottom a political man who delighted in the admiration of the people to whom he wanted to give benefactions and play the god. Socrates created a division in this heretofore unified and self-satisfied man. Alcibiades must have been an infuriating object of love for all other men and women, because although he must have slept with a fair number of them, nobody could really get to him. Socrates got to him and was the only one probably who ever did. He needed Socrates' approval of what he did, but Socrates would not give it to him. Before Socrates, for the first and only time in his life, he experienced shame. He was as shameless as a god, but he knew that Socrates saw through him and that Socrates' judgment of his worth was valid. All this echoes the bit of foreplay to Agathon's speech about whom one ought to be ashamed before. Socrates is the model of what we call the inner-directed man, a man who marches only to the beat of his own drummer. Philosophy is the source of his independence, and Socrates would say that all others, including the poets, prophets, and lawgivers, depend in some measure on the opinions of the men of their own time. Alcibiades, although he is very confident of his capacity to seduce the public, could not help being awestruck by Socrates' self-sufficiency. Socrates saw what he saw and said what he said without thinking of anything other than the truth. He did not need money; he apparently hardly needed food; he did not need to have sexual intercourse with anyone; he was not afraid of anything; and, above all, he was utterly indifferent to applause or what people thought about him. He was as insensitive to all of this as is a bum, but Socrates was no bum. He was pure sincerity, authenticity, or what have you. And he was the only one like this Alcibiades ever met.

So, in his forthright way, Alcibiades decided he was going to have erotic relations with Socrates. One could hardly be more candid or graphic than is Alcibiades about his attempted seduction of Socrates. He enacts the boy described by Pausanias who gives in to the lover for the sake of getting his wisdom. He describes the stages of the affair in detail. Socrates appeared, like most other men whom Alcibiades encounters, to have an erotic interest in him. Alcibiades' interest was piqued by the fact that Socrates never declared himself. This in itself made Socrates more interesting: he is not your routine lover. So Alcibiades arranged it in such a way, for he was still a very young man at the time, that his tutor was absent in order that

Socrates have a chance to make his move. But Socrates did not, and with the self-deception of a man who considers himself attractive, Alcibiades thought that Socrates must be shy. Alcibiades was now engaged in a real seduction, and, without yet realizing it, he was a captive. Then he proposed wrestling, an interesting reflection on Greek athleticism. It is quite a picture, Socrates and Alcibiades wrestling naked together. We know what they looked like and we know the age disparity between the two of them. But Socrates seemed to feel no attraction, and in the state he was in, it would have been impossible to hide it if it were there.

Finally this beloved, who was, unawares, metamorphosing into a lover, invited his prey to dinner with the servants absent. Socrates dined and left. Alcibiades continued to attribute his behavior to shyness, confidently interpreting Socrates' implicit no really to mean yes. He invited him a second time, resolved on making his own move. But before he tells his audience what happened then, he stops to explain that his extraordinary revelation would be possible for him only in his drunken state and with an audience of persons who have undergone experiences similar to his own. He invokes justice. It would be unjust not to describe what from Alcibiades' point of view might be Socrates' greatest deed, his refusal of Alcibiades' advances. All of these individuals present have experienced philosophical *madness*, and Alcibiades attributes it to the adder's bite of Socrates' speeches when they infect a young soul with a good nature. He is a man about to make, in public, an enormous erotic confession. We are finally at the heart of the matter, the secret of passionate union. What is the secret? Nothing happened. He does say quite frankly that he was available, which is not totally respectable, as Pausanias taught us. Alcibiades makes the same argument Pausanias did, that prudent persons will not be shocked by a young man's acceding to the blandishments of a good lover. This is the argument he made to Socrates when he finally decided to confront him directly. This argument was both a self-defense and an exhortation to Socrates not to hold back out of some conventional motive of propriety.

And then Socrates responded in his infuriating ironic mode. Instead of jumping into bed, he said that they should deliberate. Alcibiades must see an overwhelming beauty in Socrates, eclipsing his own ephemeral bodily beauty; and if that is the case, it would be a bad deal for Socrates, a little like Glaucus' exchanging his golden armor for the bronze armor of Diomedes, which Homer himself says was foolish. This is a response to the problem we discovered in Pausanias' argument. For Pausanias, the higher urge is in the boy, and the low desire is in the man. The man is gripped by the need to satisfy his bodily Eros, and the boy sees the means of manipulating that Eros in order to learn. Socrates' disposition restores the proper superiority of man to boy and hence the superiority of wisdom to sex. Of course it seems to presuppose that Socrates, however hard that may be to believe, was really completely absorbed in intellectual beauty to the exclusion of the attraction to bodily beauty. Here Diotima comes to our aid in explaining the relation between lover and beloved in this kind of affair. Socrates' overflowing richness needed a receptive partner; he was really charmed by Alcibiades' interesting soul and wanted to sow his seed in it, but that would have been undermined by the boy's understanding of the lover's bodily desires. Lover and beloved in the highest sense are the teacher and student. Although a certain bodily attraction might occur, it is not the essence of the relationship and may even undermine it. The rank order of the value of things is reestablished in this Socratic moderation. Souls and what they contain are more beautiful than bodies. Man and boy both put the same higher value on wisdom or, as Alcibiades says, on being as good as possible. In this relationship the continuing superiority of the man over the boy is assured. Socrates might very well prefer the company of an extremely talented youngster to that of a fully developed man precisely because Socrates is pregnant. The erotic young Glaucon in the *Republic* makes Socrates give birth to his fetuses, which are the same as the three waves of paradox that make the *Republic* so extraordinary.*

Socrates has a real love of wisdom; it is his only profound passion, and this distinguishes him utterly from Pausanias, a cultivated trifler. But in the eyes of a young boy, they look the same, and Alcibiades assumed that the same motives of action were present in both. Socrates addressed directly the question raised by Pausanias about the boy who makes a mistake. Pausanias answered by saying that the boy's intention is what counts: he ought just to go ahead, and he won't be blamed for it. Socrates said that this is precisely the problem for the boy, and he must investigate the true qualities of his lover's soul. This means that he must philosophize, that intentions will not do. So they had to put off their erotic gratification until Alcibiades was in a position to know rather than merely to opine. But philosophy is an endless business, so they would probably never be able to get together. In fact, their relationship in philosophy would take the place of that more obvious kind of gratification; that is, they

---

* The Greek word *kyma* can mean either wave or fetus.

would become friends. But as Socrates well knew, Alcibiades was too attracted by politics ever to become his friend, even if he happened to have the intellectual gifts requisite for friendship.

This is what Socrates teaches Alcibiades. The desperate involvement with Socrates is caused by Socrates' unattainableness. Alcibiades recognizes that however gifted he may be, Socrates is not really interested in him. Unlike Sophists, Socrates cannot be bought; and what Alcibiades thinks is his trump card, his beautiful body, does not work. He is in a desperate condition. He wishes Socrates to be dead and at the same time knows that he prizes him too much to be without him. He is angry, but Alcibiades' great soul recognizes that he has no right to be. He tells what he calls the judges that he has been the victim of insult, hubris. He candidly tells the world that his passions make him think he has a right to the sole possession of Socrates, but his reason informs him that he does not. Everything is up to Socrates. He can have Alcibiades if he wants him. It is difficult to determine whether it is Alcibiades' Eros that is insulted or whether it is his *amour-propre*, whether Socrates has become necessary because he does not esteem Alcibiades as Alcibiades wants to be esteemed. It is probably a combination of the two, for Alcibiades really does love what Socrates says. He has natural good taste, which is proved by his recognition of Socrates' superiority. But he wants Socrates not only to be good but to be his own, his possession, and that he can never attain. Perhaps he would never have been attracted to Socrates if Socrates had not piqued his vanity in telling him that he did not know enough to rule.[67] The connection is an extremely complicated one.

Hubris is the central accusation against Socrates, the one Alcibiades brings before the jury in this strange mixture of praise and accusation. Hubris is a complex notion, including not only the kinds of insults in speech or bodily assault committed by insolent persons. It is also the flaw of tragic heroes who are too confident of themselves and, in the eyes of the gods, impious. This is a strange accusation from Alcibiades, who would normally have been considered the most hubristic Greek of his time. But it is almost certainly true. Alcibiades thinks of himself as a kind of god, and Socrates treats him with contempt. Socrates, he discovers, possesses more truly the qualities attributed to heroes than do those who are believed to be heroes. They think that they are self-sufficient and are brought down by the anger of the gods. Socrates cannot be brought down by the gods. He has no hostages to fortune, in a quest for either glory, conquest, country, or love. He is brought down by the city, but in a way that does not move him. He expected it, and he does not care. For him, his death is not a tragedy, although it may be for those men and boys who cannot do without him. Socrates' self-sufficiency is an insult to all those who are more or less dependent on something changeable. Alcibiades complains that Socrates does not really love anyone, even though he seems to promise to do so. This produces anger and admiration. Socrates is enviable and envied, once you pay any attention to him.

The charge of hubris is connected with Socrates' infuriating irony. Irony is always a sign of superiority, of speaking down to someone. Socrates is always ironic in the dialogues because he never speaks to an equal. With Alcibiades, Socrates speaks with apparent earnestness about having sex with him, but he is actually treating him as a child and is indifferent to having sex with him. Alcibiades is intelligent enough to know that Socrates speaks ironically to him (218d–e). Other interlocutors take Socrates' speech to be simply frank, and the comedy can be seen only by the onlookers. The prevailing Socratic irony is a continuing insult to everyone and wounds all pretensions to equality. It is particularly clear and poignant in erotic relations. Socrates may not be indifferent to Alcibiades' bodily beauty, but he cannot enter into the extremes of erotic rapture because there are other concerns, also in their own way erotic, that hold his attention.

Socrates gave Alcibiades a good lesson. Socrates, if attracted to Alcibiades, might very well have accepted his invitation to sleep with him. Such a deed would not have had for him great cosmic significance or been an unjust or sinful thing in the usual sense. But this wonderful lesson would have been lost. If he were vain, Socrates could exult in his triumph over Alcibiades. But this is surely not it. He teaches Alcibiades a three-quarter truth, that the soul is the only thing that counts. This has the effect of demystifying the extreme hopes engendered by normal bodily desire and helps to make clear the somewhat incoherent character of a human being—half god, half beast. The true Socratic teaching is that man is not a natural unity, but that there is no separability of the soul or that the body contains some of the wisdom that is necessary to the soul. There can be no great expectation of perfect satisfaction, as Montaigne tells us when he speaks of the disjunction between his friendship and his erotic adventures. Whether or not Socrates ever had sexual relations with young men, sex would never have been so important to him as to get in the way of a good lesson. One cannot believe that there was no element of the body in his interest in Alcibiades, but what the body demanded was different from what the soul demanded. It would be simply false to say that the soul's satisfaction provided also for that of the body. This is what Montaigne illustrates so marvelously. Socrates may have had an ordinary erotic life, with real romances; but his larger awareness forbade him the exciting illusions of the love of a couple. This is grim wisdom, but Socrates seems to have enjoyed life about as much as anyone could.

Did Socrates corrupt Alcibiades? He corrupted his best pupils in the way Nietzsche said, by turning them to philosophy; but in the more ordinary sense, it is legitimate to ask if Alcibiades was made a worse statesman by Socrates. His uncle Pericles, the greatest states-man of his time, had philosophic friends, such as Anaxagoras.[68] But they did not seem to try to convert him to philosophy and their teachings had nothing of the mad dance of the soul in them. He served his city much more loyally than did Alcibiades. Both Pericles' more naturally gifted predecessor, Themistocles, and his more gifted successor, Alcibiades, ended up advising the traditional enemy of Athens, the Great King of the Persians. Did Socrates' criticism liber-ate Alcibiades from the loyalty to the city, making him capable of arguing, when he joined the Spartans against Athens, that he loved his city and therefore was a traitor to it in order to possess it? The proof that he loves it is that he wants to use the Spartan armies to bring him back from his exile.[69] There is something Socratic in this apparently perverse argument. Socrates elicits from Alcibiades that he would like to rule over all men, that he would like to surpass the Great King.[70] Was he conscious of the extent of his desires before-hand? Such universal ambition may be a good beginning point for philosophy because the philosopher, in his way, has similarly uni-versal ambitions. The only thing that is required is to turn extreme political ambition around, to change its objects, to teach that only the philosopher can be possessor of the whole, by thinking about it. Did Socrates make a mistake, recognizing Alcibiades' talents but failing to recognize that he could not turn them around? Alcibiades is as a man, if not a statesman, much greater than Hal, who was able to get just what he needed from his Socrates, Falstaff, without tainting the prudence of his political goals, which he cared for more than any-thing. Who was more corrupted by Socrates, Plato, whom he with-drew from politics, or Alcibiades, whose political activities were probably informed by what he learned from Socrates? Politics, ac-cording to the ancient teaching, is perverted by philosophy and vice versa. Alcibiades may very well be such a hybrid. One can only speculate about Socrates' failure with Alcibiades, but he certainly did not, and did not care to, concern himself exclusively with Alcibiades any more than Aristotle took his pupil, Alexander the Great, all that seriously. Socrates was most certainly a kind of threat to the city's political life, and that threat was a result of his peculiar kind of Eros.

Alcibiades concludes his speech with a praise of Socrates' virtue, imitating the scholastic rhetorical style, recounting his virtues and the deeds that prove them. But this is not like Phaedrus' speech. It has an immediacy and an originality that cannot fail to impress. Alcibiades, as a military man, speaks entirely of what Socrates showed as a soldier on the two campaigns in which he did his citizen duty by taking part. Much of it has to do with Socrates' fabled endurance, which is different from, although akin to, moderation. It is almost an insensibility to cold and heat, hunger and drink. Alcibiades does not mention sex, but he has already given us a sufficient example of that. Something like this resistance is required by every philosopher so as to devote himself to thinking. It really remains ambiguous whether Socrates' indifference to bodily pain is just part of his nature or a result of his practice of philosophy. It does not, however, cripple his capacity to understand most of the passions; but it certainly aids his self-sufficiency, which enables him to taunt the Athenian people with the fact that when they were starving, he was doing just fine.[71] As an aspect of Socrates' endurance, Alcibiades tells of Socrates' marching over the ice barefoot in a terrible winter. He also tells of Socrates' standing without sleep for twenty-four hours thinking about something. It is a feat of endurance, but it is also a tribute to his philosophic intensity. This lonely contemplation, Socrates' soul engaging in dialogues with itself, proves that for all his involvement with human beings, he is essentially a solitary who can derive satisfaction from himself. This is Alcibiades' complaint, as well as that of many others whom he cites. A prophet, in order to be a prophet, must finally utter his prophecies, and a general must conquer his enemies, but Socrates does something that does not have to be spoken to anybody or shown forth in any other way. Nobody can know what he is thinking, and philosophy does not require him to reveal it.

Socrates' courage is illustrated by two deeds, one on each of the two campaigns in which he took part. In Athens' victory at Potidaea, Socrates saved Alcibiades' life, thus fulfilling the fondest hope entertained by Phaedrus, that his lover protect him from danger. But Socrates was not in love with Alcibiades, nor did he get the same kind of satisfaction Phaedrus' lover would get from him. Socrates acted *comme il faut*. He was nearby, and he did not calculate about the danger he would incur in saving the life of his partial friend.

He defends Alcibiades because the deed was forced on him; and he knows that many accidents occur in life, which if one tried to escape, one would live in constant, demeaning fear. The second deed Alcibiades cites was the orderliness of Socrates' retreat from the great Athenian battle at Delium. He marched in an orderly way, a way most calculated to keep one's wits about one and to discourage the enemy from attacking one. This actually seems to be much more an example of Socrates' self-control than of his courage. He was striving to escape and doing so in the most efficacious manner possible. Alcibiades underwrites Aristophanes' description of Socrates in the *Clouds*. Socrates walked on the retreat exactly as he did in Athens, "swaggering with his eyes protruding and casting glances in all directions" (221b).[72] Socrates' military exploits are limited to the protection of a friend and an orderly retreat. Each in its way was most impressive, but in neither of the two cases Alcibiades mentions is Socrates seen fighting or harming the enemy. His is not the real courage of the soldier or the heroic risk taker. Nothing here is proof of civic virtue.

Alcibiades concludes with two observations. The first is the already mentioned one that Socrates has no Homeric model to whom he can be compared (although Socrates is elsewhere compared to many-wiled Odysseus). Alcibiades again returns to the satyrs as the only possible model and highlights Plato's literary problem in making a hero out of Socrates. Then he goes on to point out that Socrates' speeches have a coarseness and ludicrousness appropriate to a hubristic satyr. He talks, for example, of pack asses—low things that gentlemen and high-minded people would never think about. Most people would be unimpressed or even put off by such things. In the *Apology*, when Socrates tries to prove that he believes in the gods because he speaks about *daimonia*, which are related to *daimōnes*, who are the offspring of gods and men, he adduces the example of mules, the offspring of horses and asses. Anyone, he says, who talks about mules must believe in horses and asses. Not only is the analogy defective, if one thinks it through, but mules cannot reproduce, which would imply that the heroes could not have produced the offspring who founded the Greek cities. This is connected with dizzying reflections on gods and their relation to men.[73] Socrates, like Aristophanes' dung beetle, can fly so high only because he goes so low.[74] The unprepossessing speech of real philosophers, which seems so unpoetic on the outside, is the literature that most deeply entrances.

Alcibiades ends his speech by appealing to his fellow sufferers like Charmides and Euthydemus, whose names were given to Platonic dialogues as was Alcibiades'. They are the witnesses against Socrates who were lacking at Socrates' trial. They know Socrates' injustice. Justice, the one cardinal virtue Alcibiades passed over in his list of Socratic virtues, is the virtue concerned with others. Socrates seems to be intent only on the virtues that perfect and benefit himself. But Socrates' perfection may very well be the greatest benefaction that he can give to others. There are two kinds of benefactors, those who deliberately provide us something that we want, and those who, although indifferent to us, by their example elevate us and make us more sublime. They represent the higher motives.

It is this reflection that teaches us what Alcibiades means, although he may not know it himself. Socrates' own speech showed us the incompleteness and imperfection of Socrates, an ugly spectacle that represents one aspect of philosophy and the philosopher. Alcibiades supplements Socrates' speech and turns him into the object of love. Man's longing for the completeness that he is aware he lacks ordinarily culminates in a rejection of man in favor of the gods. His own questioning forces Socrates to deny himself this satisfaction. But in that denial Socrates makes himself into the most perfect of the beings. He is the only being who knows both universal and particular, immortal and mortal, and he contains some of both in himself. The man who lives in full consciousness of this incompleteness, pursuing wisdom but unable to actualize it, in one perspective looks ugly, but in another perspective can appear to be that complementary being men seek for without ever really discovering. He is free of the vulnerabilities and boasting that make human lives appear to be so unattractive. The most complete of men is the one who truly knows that he is incomplete and can live in light of that fact. Socrates replaces the gods for aspiring human beings. They once took the wrong path, which ended up on Olympus, and Socrates brings them back down to Athens. This is the true humanism, if there can be one. Alcibiades teaches us, *mutatis mutandis*, to worship Socrates. Socrates is Eros and the fulfillment of Eros, and this is what he teaches to those in whom he lodges his shafts.

When Alcibiades has completed his speech, he and Socrates and Agathon carry on some urbane banter about a competition for the favor of Agathon (222c–223a). These very manly men seem to make an impossible combination of their manliness with erotic gallantry. This was present in the beginning of the dialogue; but in the light of what has transpired during it, these relationships take on a profound seriousness. The mixture of flirting and philosophy seems to make sense at last. They begin to engage in another round of praises with the theme now changed to praising one's neighbor. But there can be no praise equal to that appropriately given to Socrates. Happily they are interrupted by the intrusion of a mob of very loud and very drunken revelers who overwhelm the delicate atmosphere that has prevailed.

Everybody must now drink heavily. The weaker drinkers, each in his turn, slip away. The faithful Aristodemus himself falls off into a drunken sleep, but awakens to find Agathon, Socrates, and Aristophanes having a discussion, with only Socrates fresh and in full possession of his powers (223b–d). Socrates is forcing the two poets to agree that it would be possible for a man to be both tragedian and comedian, which each resists because Agathon regards tears as highest and Aristophanes regards laughter as highest, and they are opposites. For them there is no mean between the two that is as high as the two extremes. Socrates says that philosophy is such a mean and that a mixture of laughter and tears is the way to define man. Practically, Socrates is telling them that their two arts must be combined in order to depict him. This is the formula for the Platonic dialogues and perhaps for Shakespeare's plays. The other two nod away, and one is never sure whether Socrates could not persuade them. It is with this doubt that the dialogue ends.

XII

At the end it looks like Socrates is not a lover and is really all alone. Alcibiades does love Socrates, as do, each in his own way, Apollodorus, Aristodemus, and Plato. These are enduring attachments, quite passionate, and in no sense based upon illusions about the qualities of the man they love. They have seen him in all kinds of situations over a long period of time, and he meets all challenges that the loving or even the envious eye would set. Actually, the longer they know him, the more impressed they are as they find new virtues and beauties in him. Familiarity breeds worship in the exceptional souls who can recognize him for what he is. His example is a constant inspiration.

One might ask whether what Alcibiades and the others feel is really love, erotic love. It is, of course, very distant from the kind of sentiments Romeo and Juliet experience with regard to each other. It is not that simple eroticism one finds between young male and young female, nor is it that complete and reciprocal bodily union of which Aristophanes speaks. But these persons all want to possess Socrates and to be alone with him and to share his intimacy. That conventional and very questionable Greek love of men for boys conditions what these men felt for Socrates. In the prime of their youth they met someone who seemed to be an erotic aggressor and was also slightly repulsive to them, but whose speech excited them and gave them a fulfillment that was charged by their erotic longing, the great sense of excitement of youth along with its awareness of incompleteness. A youth with a good nature is an exciting thing to observe, pure potentiality longing for wonderful actuality, and at the same time touching in his aspect of vulnerability and self-doubt. When such a person meets a Socrates, it is not like a young man meeting a Nestor or a Mentor who can give him advice while he goes about his quest for love. It is as though he discovered love and the kind of exaltation love promises. Nietzsche in his *Schopenhauer as Educator* describes what his first encounter with philosophy was like for him, and it is worthy of Alcibiades' description of his encounter with Socrates.[75] And Nietzsche experienced it from books alone. The beautiful overflow from a generous nature that addresses the essential perplexities is at least akin to eroticism. No young person who has had such an encounter can find it easy to take his ordinary human love affairs all that seriously anymore. The intensity of the longing for bodily satisfaction is diminished by the enthusiasm for his primary love. Nonetheless he cannot quite relegate his bodily love and its objects to the tedious round of bodily needs and satisfactions, nor can he really, in a very coherent or serious way, try to get that bodily satisfaction from his teacher-beloved. Each person will have to work it out more or less satisfactorily between these two poles. This unsatisfactory but exciting search for complete satisfaction is a result of the complexity of human nature. The Eros of the body always tends toward and wishes to incorporate spiritual longings, and the Eros of the soul gets its power and its broad aspiration or vision from that of the body. The two are in tension but are hopelessly intertwined. The low and the high are hence reciprocal. And the urge to couple is as revealing as the love of truth in man.

Still there is the problem of Socrates, who ends up alone. Nobody serious ever promised eroticism really works out in its primary desire to be together always with someone who wishes to be together with you always. Erotic phenomena are too protean for such a neat solution, one that can be effected only by law and habit and by a certain renunciation of the real power of Eros. If Eros is something one can get over, with age or self-control, as I suspect many men and women hope, it can be done only by a closing of the full openness of the soul to its most distinctive longings. When I was criticized by a professor of philosophy at Oxford for spicing up my Plato with erotic allusions, I could, even without seeing his name attached to the review, have known that he was a specialist, someone utterly without experience of the longing for wholeness that is the essence of philosophy. As Socrates knows only too well, we are all selfish; we wish to be happy ourselves. This does not bode too well for the enduring and authentic permanent relationship. To the extent that Socrates was needy, he was obviously very much involved with others. But, finally, there was not much he needed or could get from other human beings. This does not mean he was a Narcissus or falsely attributed to himself the kind of self-sufficiency displayed by the gods. With full acceptance of his defectiveness, he was distant because now his quest could proceed by pure thought. But his arrival at this position came by way of full involvement with other bodies and souls. His selfishness is a sublime selfishness, the activity of a soul that has incorporated inclinations that raise it up far above the things that put human beings in ugly conflict. Neither food nor money nor position is at all motivating for him, and sexual desire has moved toward the most comprehensive erotic sympathies. The very being of such a soul is beneficent for his disappointed lovers. Socrates is alone but in a different way from the ways in which Rousseau and Nietzsche were alone. Natural human isolation, from which man began, is where Rousseau ends up: self-sufficient in the recovery of the pleasant sense of his own existence without the movements of *amour-propre* that involve human beings in relationships. That sentiment is distinctly his own and does not in any way even imply the existence of other human beings. Socrates' isolation is the culmination of his understanding of other souls and his own, and it therefore rests on a community of human beings, the community of knowers who have a true common ground on which their interests are the same and not in conflict. Nietzsche's solitude is a terrible situation that requires the utmost resolution to face, founded on the revelation that there is no cosmos but only chaos. Human beings are only others, with their own individual selves and with no possible authentic common ground. The soul of Socrates is solicited by an order of things of which the soul is a part and which stands above his own soul and that of others. The difference between Nietzsche and Socrates comes down to the possibility of that most ultimate form of community, mutual understanding. Socrates is persuaded that speech reflects being and that there is, beyond all misunderstandings, a possible understanding that is beyond language and for the grasp of which language is only a tool. For Nietzsche language can be nothing more than the oracular expression of absolutely individual selves and hence can never reach beyond mere perspectives to true universality, which would be understanding. At best one can have creative misunderstandings. Socrates talks of his good friends, Nietzsche of his best enemies.[76] Friendship is that relation constituted by *logos* and is logocentric. The Eros of Socrates and his fellow men joins in the common aspiration toward contemplation of the permanent order. Socrates' skepticism, which is identical to his Eros, *is* the authentic human posture and provides the grounds for contact with other human beings. Socrates' solitariness is no more characteristic of him than is the gentler image of beauty he has when he engages with an Alcibiades. Unfortunately, although we love both the particular and the universal, both what comes into being and passes away and what is always, these opposites meet only momentarily in the individuals to whom we are attracted. Our Eros sees both poles of opposition, but in their necessary separability we must choose which we prefer, or else hope, like Antony and Cleopatra, that we can, body and soul, ascend to heaven with our beloveds and maintain that unity between the particular and the universal. Socrates moves ineluctably from the particular to the general and loves the latter more, although he is a particular man who must die.

The whole question of Eros comes down to the question of psychology.

Psychology means the science of the soul. Socrates considered himself to be a psychologist; and he was what we would call a phenomenologist. Without presupposition or without constant sidelong glances to grounds or foundations, he looks at what goes on within himself and what he can gather about what goes on in others by the most acute examination of their opinions. The beginning point of his investigation is the consciousness that he has an inside, that he has opinions about things, and that that opinion-making faculty is a beginning point, not a thing that must be traced back to deeper sources. Marx or Freud will point out to us sources that determine opinion, but Socrates explains that not all opinions are determined by the kind of things Marx and Freud talk about, and that what they allege are at best preconditions rather than explanations of opinions. A rich old Greek man like Cephalus in the *Republic* will state conventional opinions about justice, but his various opinions about justice contradict one another and force him, or those who listen to him, to look for noncontradictory opinions about justice, opinions that are not conventional. Within his opinions there is a motor that sets him in dialectical motion. He is clearly informed by a divination of justice. It is this strange longing for the truth contained in almost whatever we say (and man is the being who has something to say about everything he does) that teaches Socrates that the soul is characterized most of all by longing, by the need for coherence and consistency. Thus it is man's speeches that are the core of his psychology. Longing in its most active form is Eros, and Eros is the backbone of the soul. The simplest sexual acts and even the slightest movements of his sexual organs are things about which man has opinions. As soon as he can be induced to speak or articulate those opinions to himself or another, he is beyond the bodily deed. Modern understanding of sex neglects or denies the importance of the opinions; and that is what is distorting about it, a rejection of the phenomenon for the sake of some theory. Man's divination of perfect love or perfect justice is most of all what proves he has a soul. For a number of reasons, some connected with democratic leveling and easygoingness, there is today an almost religious commitment to a denial of the soul's existence. Inasmuch as we cannot avoid thinking about what is in us, practically everyone gets the habit of quickly turning from what he really thinks and feels to one of the current categories that are intended to explain it: our selves, our consciousness, all half-baked substitutes for the soul. We lose the habit of taking ourselves seriously and examining the movements of our souls with delicacy and with that combination of affirmation and doubt that is the hallmark of the hunter of the rare psychological truths. A psychology that hopes to do any justice to the phenomena must begin by understanding the highest and most interesting human types. On the basis of such an understanding, one can easily understand lower and less interesting types simply by slicing off the peaks from the higher ones. But you cannot do it the other way around. You cannot get the causes and motives for the higher types from observing the lower ones, and any attempt to do so will be ludicrously distorting. Plato tries to show in the *Symposium* that philosophy is the most complete and most revealing form of Eros. On that basis he is capable of working down to the activities and hopes of persons who will never be philosophers or perhaps even know that there is such a thing as philosophy. But if one says that the fundamental erotic activity is the gross coupling of two individuals, you can explain the philosophic vision only as some kind of miraculous covering up of what one really wanted, rather than a cosmic solicitation. Try honestly to see whether one can say anything interesting or revealing about Socrates, Shakespeare, or Nietzsche in the psychoanalytic mode, and then you will see why we still need Plato. You may ask, what have Shakespeare, Caesar, and Socrates to do with me? But there is something of them, however small, in us; and we should not for the sake of simplistic explainers lose what may be most important in us.

The ingrained and stubborn unwillingness to think about the soul or admit its existence has much to do with the religious criticism of the seventeenth and eighteenth centuries. The study of the soul had become such a part of Catholic Christianity that its destruction in the name of something like consciousness seemed a necessity. But the Christian teaching was about a specific version of the soul characterized by separability from the body and immortality, great miracles that defied common sense and reason. Despite the doctrines apparently propagated by the *Phaedo*, the Socratic teaching makes no such presuppositions and investigates rather than preaches about the soul. I would nevertheless be inclined to think that a sensitive priest could give a better account of what is going on in a man than could a psychoanalyst. Since the soul was irreducible for a Christian and so much counted on its state, the most excruciating and tormented examination of the soul as it is, on its surface, led to a great delicacy of observation, the motives for which are lacking to the modern scientist. When Socrates appeared on the scene, there was likewise no place for soul in the natural philosophy he confronted. He was persuaded that something was lacking, and he made the soul the theme for philosophy. He said in prison on the day of his death that the pre-Socratics could explain that he was sitting in prison because of his bones, his flesh, and his blood. But Socrates counters by saying that his bones, flesh, and blood would be running down the road to Megara if he did not think it was good to remain in prison.[77] This pretty much describes the difference between a modern scientific psychology and Socratic psychology. The difference between Socratic and Christian psychology can be measured by the different status of Eros in the two.

Nietzsche was profoundly aware of what had been lost in human self-understanding by the suppression of the soul. He confronted the problem of psychology and said, echoing Socrates, that he was a psychologist.[78] He was rejected as such, by academic philosophy, academic philosophy that does not want to address the riddle of the Sphinx, the question "What is man?" but wants to get on with its work that is performed by men. Nietzsche wanted to destroy all scientific and metaphysical doctrines that would turn us away from a free examination of what we are and from taking ourselves seriously. He wanted to know the knower in order to evaluate what is said to be knowledge, and that is the most difficult of all philosophical undertakings. His is a model of the gifts and the dedication necessary for seeing what goes on within and developing adequate hypotheses about what it all means. He came to the conclusion that man is will to power, which is not, in the centrality of aspiration that it underlines, entirely without kinship with Eros. But Nietzsche could not call it Eros because he could not bring himself to believe that there is anything naturally beautiful. What we most of all need to do, for the sake of our souls, is to compare these two teachings, of Socrates and Nietzsche, and the psychological riches contained in them. Nietzsche's student Heidegger said that man is "being toward death," while Socrates says that he is being toward eternity. Socrates says the same thing when he says that man, or at least the best man, is Eros. This hypothesis can be tested by looking around you and seeing whether specialists or voluptuaries can even attempt to compete with a truly erotic man who despises the limits of the specialties and the pretensions of the self-satisfied.

When, after an absence of over twenty years, I recently gave a lecture at Cornell University, a group of students unfurled a sheet that they hung from the balcony with the following message, "Great Sex is better than Great Books." Sure, but you can't have one without the other.

EPILOGUE

Love is neediness, longing, awareness of incompleteness. It is a passion of the soul that palpably and visibly engages the body and points to the union, however uneasy, of the two. Love is a self-forgetting that makes man self-aware, an unreason that is the condition of his reasoning about himself. The pain it produces is linked to the most ecstatic of pleasures, and it provides the primary experiences of beauty and of life's sweetness. It contains powerful elements of illusion, it may be thought to be entirely illusion, but its effects are not illusory. Love can produce the most prodigious deeds in the most immediate way, without guidance by principle or command of duty. The lover knows the value of beauty and also knows that he cannot live well, or perhaps at all, alone. He knows that he is not self-sufficient. The lover is the clearest expression of man's natural imperfection and his quest for perfection.

The friend is similar to the lover in his recognition of his incompleteness and his need for exclusive attachment to another human being in order to attain fulfillment. Friendship too is imperious in its demands, but the experience of friendship is gentler, soberer, without frenzy. It, unlike love, is necessarily reciprocal. You can love without being loved in return, but you cannot be the friend of one who is not your friend. The correlate of lover is beloved; the correlate of friend is friend. Love is firmly seated in the body, and some of its feelings, if not its essence, are experienced by almost everyone. Friendship, which seems for a variety of reasons to be easier, is actually rarer. Its pleasures are wholly spiritual, and the self-overcomings required for it are not powered by bodily passions. The looks of the friend are almost a matter of indifference, whereas the looks of the beloved are a great part of love. Much of love consists in looking at the beloved, whereas most of friendship consists in conversations between the friends. Its satisfactions include the admiration of each for the other and the self-esteem confirmed by the admiration of such another. In any attempt to rank the relative importance of the two in a serious life, the different kind and degree of the body's involvement in friendship and in love can be counted as an advantage by each. Love engages the whole of us. Friendship is beyond mere bodily need and can be thought to be more distinctively human.

Whatever their selective rank, and it has to be thought through at some time by every serious human being, both love and friendship are splendid things, peaks of humanity, plausible candidates for election as the highest end of life. The capacity for love or friendship always indicates a superior and generous nature, and when we see them in life or art, they always engage our sympathies. They are witness to an expansive being that can in the pursuit of his own happiness encompass the happiness of another. In such a person the perennial tension between the pleasant and the noble seems to disappear. The lover or friend does what he most passionately wants to do and in doing so benefits the friend or the beloved.

For this reason love and friendship not only attract everyone but they flatter us by making us think well of ourselves. They seem to be the freest of activities, founded solely on choice, offering no advantage other than themselves. They require neither law nor theory to appear choiceworthy. Although they can favor reason, they are not calculating. An immediate and profound awareness of desirability is where they begin. Hunger and mere sexual desire are similar in directing us to immediate apparent goods; but they remain purely animal and constitute no morality in relation to their objects, while love and friendship are unthinkable without the will to benefit their objects. Love and friendship are distinctively human and inseparable from man's spirituality. They point to some kind of native need and capacity for community. Hunger and sex, even when they involve using other human beings, do not induce concern for them. Thus to be a friend or a lover, one must have somehow transcended the neediest of needinesses, the most self-regarding passions. The wonder is that this is done effortlessly in the case of the lover and the friend. It follows from the nature of the thing.

For this reason friendship and love are beyond justice. To be what they are, no contracts are required and no divisions of mine and thine. The good of the other is willed; and if there is inequality of benefits, it is because the parties want to give more, not because they want to take more. One cannot imagine taking someone to court and seeking an injunction compelling him to be one's friend or lover. Political justice is merely an attempt to approximate in larger groups by the use of rewards and punishments the kind of association friends and lovers have without the need of either. When stated thus, love and friendship may seem hopelessly idealistic. But friendship and love are that way; they mean unity. A moment's reflection will prove that if there is a need for reward and punishment between the two members of a couple, they are not friends or lovers, they are associates. Both love and friendship necessarily carry with them notions of virtue without which neither is possible. They require a trust that seems to be mad daring to those who cannot believe in the reality of such notions. Trust of this kind would indeed be mad in business or international relations, where there is no true common good. But without well-founded trust, there is no real love or friendship, only imitations of them; once such trust is shaken, love and friendship degenerate into tyrannical jealousy or lose all their intensity and reality. If one cannot believe in such virtue and trust, then love and friendship have to be explained as composite effects of simpler, lower causes. Such reductionism is, I fear, the direction taken by modern interpretation, which is constitutionally unable to believe in the independent existence of higher phenomena, looking instead for biological, economic, neurotic, or power-seeking sources of human connectedness and depriving the phenomena of their richness and charm.

But the *ideas* of love and friendship remain in popular discourse. When we say, "she's only interested in his money," or "he has made useful friends for his career," or make any other similar observation, we have in mind more perfect relations that act as the standard for recognizing the less perfect ones. The low is known to be what it is only in light of the awareness of the high. That awareness is native to man and is the ground of his being able to see the human world, to judge the motives of men, and to guide himself sensibly and sensitively through life. Persons dominated by low motives doubt the existence of high ones but pay their tribute to them in their envy of friends and lovers. Somehow they know that delight at the sight of and in the company of another admirable human being, delight that eclipses other pleasures and makes even duties seem trivial, exists. They are regretfully too busy to open themselves to it.

It must be remembered that in spite of the favorable disposition most of us have toward both friends and lovers, they nevertheless are problematic. Love and friendship are strange combinations of freedom and necessity. They involve freedom from all the ordinary commands of duty and loyalties to country and family. They are not given by birth or by any accident of race, religion, or nationality, and realize the ideal of cosmopolitanism. Many great love stories are about persons who come from enemy nations, and almost all involve some kind of conflict with convention and conventional authority. True love always seems to be a discovery of nature, of natural beauties and natural virtues. And friendship is even more so, in that it does not even point back to the claims of civil society in the production of children, and it contains nothing resembling the legal covenant of marriage. It is strictly on its own. It really knows no country and no family and frequently is the object of profound suspicion on the part of both. Socrates, it must be remembered, was tried and executed on the basis of the accusations of fathers who thought he corrupted their sons in making them his friends. As they loved Socrates more, it was thought, they loved their fathers less. Friendship as end in itself does not fit in the established order of things, for it is a law unto itself, one that is not easily deducible from the civil or divine law. Passionate love is also antinomian, but family and polity try to tame it, because it is necessary to them. It is an unreliable partner, however. Love can lead to children, whom the family and polity spurn if produced without their blessing, but it does not have to, and so many of the great love stories are about persons who do not want children or who even abandon them for the sake of their love. And, of course, many children are not the fruit of what one would exactly call love. Reproduction and love constitute an uneasy pair in their shared organs.

The necessity in love and friendship is that of nature. Once entered in this world, we are free of all other constraints, but the power of the beloved or the friend over our whole being does not itself admit of free choice in the usual use of the term, and there seems to be no act of the will involved. We simply walk into a magnetic field and are drawn by it. We are not the movers, we are moved. We may be lucky and attract the one to whom we are attracted; but he or she is affected as are we, not moved by our will. The objects of our attraction are not figments of our imagination, however much imagination may embellish them. They are real human beings whom we need and whose union with us will make us complete and whole, and heal the wounds that their separation from us seems to have inflicted on us. These are experiences of the soul, dangerous and thrilling, next to which almost all others pale.

Love and friendship do not emerge out of petty passions, but they lead to a self-sufficiency that is not easily tolerated. The fabric of all societies is woven out of needs of individuals, which tie them to it. Real couples, of lovers or friends, are constituted by special kinds of needs, and their being together tends to separate them from the rest of the community. Lovers and friends inevitably appear disloyal to rulers and families and are accused of self-indulgence by them. Selfish individuals are less suspect, and so shrewd an observer as Thomas Hobbes thought they could more easily be integrated into and controlled by societies than those who are in the grips of higher passions and are concerned with something more than their own preservation and comfort. If there is moderation in love and friendship, it is not of the sort encouraged by the vulgar considerations for safety.

Love and friendship are rendered even more problematic by the doubt whether the passionate lover and the dedicated friend are roles that can be played by the same person. Love and friendship each make a demand of loyalty and exclusivity that is likely to bring them into conflict. Then, which do we choose? Each can make a claim that it is higher. The man or woman in love may have a friend, but it is very hard for the lover to be a friend to that friend. Why shouldn't lovers be friends? Maybe, but it is a lot harder than is ordinarily believed, for reasons that should have become clear in the course of this book. At all events, love and friendship make total demands that do not easily admit of division. There is no doctrinaire resolution to this problem, and only life can teach a full human being, one capable of both love and friendship, how he will resolve it. But understanding love and friendship in their manifold experiences is the key to self-knowledge.

NOTES

When referring to classic works, generally accepted systems of reference are used (e.g., Stephanus numbers for Plato, Bekker numbers for Aristotle, or standard book, chapter, or section numbers), rather than page numbers in any particular current edition. This should facilitate reference for readers using any of a wide variety of available editions. All translations are the author's unless otherwise indicated.

INTRODUCTION: THE FALL OF EROS

1. Jean-Paul Sartre, *No Exit*, in *No Exit and Three Other Plays*, trans. Stuart Gilbert (New York: Vintage, 1949), p. 47.

2. Alfred C. Kinsey, Wardell B. Pomeroy, and Clyde E. Martin, *Sexual Behavior in the Human Male* (Philadelphia: W. B. Saunders Co., 1948).

3. Aristotle, *Politics*, 1278b21–25.

4. Thomas Hobbes, *Leviathan*, Part I, Chapter 13.

5. Herbert Marcuse, *Eros and Civilization* (1955; rpt. Boston: The Beacon Press, 1966).

6. See Sigmund Freud, *Leonardo da Vinci and a Memory of His Childhood*, in *The Standard Edition of the Complete Psychological Works of Sigmund Freud* (hereinafter referred to as *S.E.*), trans. James Strachey (1957; rpt. London: The Hogarth Press, 1968), Vol. XI, pp. 63–137.

7. Freud, *Dostoyevsky and Parricide*, in *S.E.*, Vol. XXI, p. 177.

8. Jean-Jacques Rousseau, *Discourse on the Origin and Foundations of Inequality*, in Roger Masters, ed., *The First and Second Discourses* (hereinafter referred to as *Second Discourse*) (New York: St. Martin's Press, 1964), pp. 91–92.

9. Xenophon, *Memorabilia*, Book I, Chapter vi, Section 14.

10. Denis de Rougemont, *Love in the Western World* (1940), trans. Montgomery Belgion (1956; rpt. Princeton: Princeton University Press, 1983).

PART I: ROUSSEAU AND THE ROMANTIC PROJECT

CHAPTER 1. ROUSSEAU

Unless otherwise indicated, all works in this chapter are by **Jean-Jacques Rousseau.**

1. Edmund Burke, *A Letter to a Member of the National Assembly,* in *The Writings and Speeches of Edmund Burke,* ed. L. G. Mitchell (Oxford: Oxford University Press, 1989), Vol. VIII, pp. 316–17.

2. Ibid., p. 313ff.

3. Thomas Mann, "Goethe's Career as a Man of Letters," in *Freud, Goethe, Wagner* (New York: Alfred A. Knopf, 1937), p. 97.

4. *The Confessions of Jean-Jacques Rousseau* (hereinafter referred to as *Confessions*), trans. J. M. Cohen (New York: Penguin, 1953), Book III, pp. 108–9, 90–91; Book V, p. 189; Book I, pp. 25–28, 36; Book VI, pp. 240–41; Book VII, pp. 297–302; Book V, p. 194; Book VII, pp. 320–22; Book II, pp. 71–72.

5. *Confessions,* Book I, p. 36; *Les Confessions de J. J. Rousseau,* in *Oeuvres complète* (hereinafter referred to as *O.C.*), eds. Bernard Gagnebin and Marcel Raymond, 4 vols. (Paris: Gallimard, 1959–1969, Bibliothèque de la Pléiade), Vol. I, p. 1247, note (a) to p. 27; *Confessions,* Book V, p. 189.

6. Aristotle, *Nicomachean Ethics,* 1118a24–b8.

7. John Locke, *Some Thoughts Concerning Education,* §215.

8. Ibid., §§23–28.

9. Diogenes Laertius, *Lives of Eminent Philosophers,* Book VI, Section 69.

10. *Confessions,* Book III, pp. 108–9; Book IV, p. 166.

11. Aristotle, *Nicomachean Ethics,* 1152b16–18, 1153a20–24.

12. Sartre, *No Exit,* p. 47.

13. *Considerations on the Government of Poland,* Chapter II; *On the Social Contract* (hereinafter referred to as *Social Contract*), Book II, Chapter 7.

14. See Allan Bloom, *Giants and Dwarfs: Essays 1960–1990* (New York: Simon and Schuster, 1990), pp. 211–13.

15. *Second Discourse,* p. 117ff.

16. Ibid., pp. 221–22, note (o).

17. See Choderlos de Laclos, *Cecilia ou les mémoires d'une heritière* in *Oeuvres complètes,* ed. Laurent Versini (Paris: Gallimard, Bibliothèque de la Pléiade, 1979), p. 469; *Lettres de la prison de Picpus,* à madame de laclos, 2 juin 1794, ibid., p. 825; note also *Les Liaisons dangereuses,* trans. P. W. K. Stone (New York: Penguin, 1961), pp. 15, 79.

18. Plato, *Republic,* 518b–c; *Theaetetus,* 148b5–151d6.

19. *Second Discourse,* pp. 148–50.

20. G. A. Harrison *et al., Human Biology* (New York: Oxford University Press, 1964), pp. 318–20.

21. Kant, "Speculative Beginning of Human History," in *Perpetual Peace and Other Essays,* trans. Ted Humphrey (Indianapolis: Hackett Publishing Company, 1983), pp. 54–56.

22. John Aubrey, *Aubrey's Brief Lives,* ed. Oliver Lawson Dick (London: Secker and Warburg, 1949), pp. xcv–xcvi.

23. Goethe, *Faust,* lines 12110–11; Nietzsche, *Beyond Good and Evil,* aphorism 236.

24. Nietzsche, *Beyond Good and Evil*, aphorism 168.

25. *Social Contract*, Book IV, Chapter 8.

26. *Second Discourse*, pp. 128–34; cf. Marc F. Plattner, *Rousseau's State of Nature: An Interpretation of the Discourse on Inequality* (De Kalb, Illinois: Northern Illinois University Press, 1979), pp. 82–87.

27. Alexis de Tocqueville, *Democracy in America*, Vol. II, Book 3, Chapter 1.

28. *Reveries of the Solitary Walker* (hereinafter referred to as *Reveries*), trans. Charles E. Butterworth (New York: Harper & Row, 1979), cf. Third Walk and Fourth Walk; *Quatre lettres à M. le Président de Malesherbes*, in *O.C.*, Vol. I, pp. 1140–42.

29. Karl Barth, *Protestant Thought: From Rousseau to Ritschl*, trans. Brian Cozens (1959; rpt. Salem, New Hampshire: Ayer Co., 1987), Chapter II, pp. 61, 62.

30. Kant, *Critique of Judgment*, §42.

31. Arthur M. Melzer, *The Natural Goodness of Man: On the System of Rousseau's Thought* (Chicago: University of Chicago Press, 1990), p. 280.

32. Cf. *Confessions*, Book II, pp. 65–74; Book III, pp. 92–95; Book III, pp. 117–18.

33. Ibid., Book I, pp. 25–28.

34. *Reveries*, Seventh Walk; *Lettres sur la botanique*, in *O.C.*, Vol. IV, pp. 1151–95.

35. *Second Discourse*, p. 144.

36. Ibid., pp. 91–92, 104–5, 183–86, note (c).

37. Kant, *Critique of Pure Reason*, trans. Norman Kemp Smith (1929; rpt. New York: St. Martin's Press, 1965), pp. 635–44; *Critique of Practical Reason*, trans. Lewis White Beck (New York and London: Macmillan, 1989), pp. 3–14, 137–39, 166.

38. Cf. Richard Velkley, *Freedom and the End of Reason: On the Moral Foundation of Kant's Critical Philosophy* (Chicago: University of Chicago Press, 1989).

39. *Second Discourse*, pp. 160–61.

40. *Reveries*, Fourth Walk, p. 43.

41. Barth, *Protestant Thought*, pp. 97–117.

42. Kant, "Speculative Beginning of Human History," p. 54.

43. Aristotle, *Politics*, 1253a9–18.

44. *Confessions*, Book III, pp. 108–9.

45. Pascal, *Pensées*, trans. A. J. Krailsheimer (1966; rpt. New York: Penguin, 1985), pp. 210–12.

46. Aristotle, *Politics*, 1252a35–b9.

47. Voltaire, *Philosophical Letters*, trans. Ernest Dilworth (Indianapolis: Bobbs-Merrill, 1961), pp. 41–45.

48. Plato, *Republic*, 405a–b, 406d–e, 409e–410a.

49. Tocqueville, *Democracy in America*, Vol. II, Book 3, Chapter 12.

50. Aristotle, *Politics*, 1253a2–3, 1253a19–25; but contrast *Nicomachean Ethics*, 1162a17–19.

51. Cf. *Julie, ou La Nouvelle Héloïse*, in *O.C.*, Vol. II, p. 693.

52. Herodotus, *The History*, Book I, Chapters 7–14.

53. Kant, "Speculative Beginning of Human History," p. 54; see also Velkley, *Freedom and the End of Reason*, pp. 152–63.

54. *Social Contract*, Book I, Chapter 1.

55. Shakespeare, *Julius Caesar*, ed. T. S. Dorsch, Arden Edition (1955; rpt. London: Routledge, 1988), IV.iii.142–94.

56. Plato, *Republic*, 389e–390a.

57. *Emile et Sophie, ou les solitaires*, in *O.C.*, Vol. IV, pp. 881–924.

58. *Letter to M. d'Alembert on the Theatre*, ed. and trans. Allan Bloom, in *Politics and the Arts* (New York: Cornell University Press, 1989).

59. See Robert Darnton, "Readers Respond to Rousseau: The Fabrication of Romantic Sensitivity," in *The Great Cat Massacre and Other Episodes in French Cultural History* (New York: Basic Books, 1984).

60. *La Nouvelle Héloïse*, in *O.C.*, Vol. II, p. 153.

61. Stendhal, *On Love*, Book II, Chapter 59.

62. *La Nouvelle Héloïse*, in *O.C.*, Vol. II, p. 490.

CHAPTER 2. STENDHAL, *THE RED AND THE BLACK*

1. Stendhal, *On Love*, "Second Attempt at a Preface."

2. Stendhal, *The Charterhouse of Parma*, trans. Margaret R. B. Shaw (1958; rpt. New York: Penguin, 1983), Chapter 6, p. 130; Chapter 24, p. 427.

3. Rousseau, *Confessions*, Book VII, p. 272.

4. Stendhal, *On Love*, Book II, Chapter 59.

5. Hippolyte Taine, *Nouveaux Essais de critique et d'histoire* (Paris: Hachette, 1909), p. 225.

6. Rousseau, *Emile*, pp. 135–37.

7. Rousseau, *Emile*, pp. 215, 245, 337; *Constitutional Project for Corsica*, in *Political Writings*, trans. Frederick Watkins (Edinburgh: Thomas Nelson and Sons, 1953), pp. 325–26.

8. Goethe, *Faust*, line 328.

9. Nietzsche, *Beyond Good and Evil*, aphorisms 39, 254; *Ecce Homo*, "Why I am so Clever," Section 3; *The Gay Science*, aphorism 95.

10. Nietzsche, *Thus Spoke Zarathustra*, Part I, "Of War and Warriors."

11. Machiavelli, *The Prince*, Chapter XXV.

12. Aristotle, *Nicomachean Ethics*, 1119b29–30, 1120a30–33, 1120b15–20, 1121b16–17.

13. Rousseau, *Confessions*, II, pp. 65–74.

14. Hippolyte Taine, *Nouveaux Essais de critique et d'histoire*, pp. 241–42.

15. Goethe, *Elective Affinities*, Part I, Chapter 2; Part II, Chapter 8.

16. Rousseau, *Letter to M. d'Alembert*, Chapter VII, esp. pp. 67–73.

17. Nietzsche, *Thus Spoke Zarathustra*, Part I, "On Little Old and Young Women."

CHAPTER 3. AUSTEN, *PRIDE AND PREJUDICE*

1. Leo Strauss, *On Tyranny*, eds. Victor Gourevitch and Michael S. Roth (New York: The Free Press, 1991), p. 185.

2. Xenophon, *Oeconomicus*, Chapter VII.

3. Aristotle, *Nicomachean Ethics*, 1124b18–20, 1124b30–31.

4. Rousseau, *Letter to M. d'Alembert*, Chapter IV; cf. Bloom, *Politics and the Arts*, pp. xv–xvi.

5. Xenophon, *Anabasis*, Book V, Chapter viii, Section 26.

6. Aristotle, *Nicomachean Ethics*, 1156b7–24.

7. Ibid., 1152b16–18, 1153a20–23.

CHAPTER 4. FLAUBERT, *MADAME BOVARY*

1. Montesquieu, *The Spirit of the Laws*, Part I, Book IV, Chapter 4.

2. Nietzsche, *Thus Spoke Zarathustra*, "Zarathustra's Prologue," Section 5.

CHAPTER 5. TOLSTOY, *ANNA KARENINA*

1. Rousseau, *Social Contract*, Book II, Chapter 8; *Considerations on the Government of Poland*, Chapter III.

2. Rousseau, *Social Contract*, Book II, Chapter 7.

3. Nietzsche, *Thus Spoke Zarathustra*, Zarathustra's Prologue, Section 5.

4. Rousseau, *Emile*, pp. 240–43.

5. Ibid., p. 441.

6. Tolstoy, *Anna Karenina*, trans. Constance Garnett (New York: Random House, The Modern Library, n.d.), Part I, Chapter I, p. 3.

7. Rousseau, *Letter to M. d'Alembert*, Chapter VI, p. 65.

CHAPTER 6. CONCLUSION

1. Céline, *Journey to the End of Night*, trans. Ralph Manheim (New York: New Directions, 1983), p. 424.

2. Ibid., p. 431.

3. Leo Strauss, *Spinoza's Critique of Religion*, trans. Elsa M. Sinclair (New York: Schocken, 1965), p. 11.

4. Sartre, *No Exit*, p. 47.

5. Nietzsche, *Beyond Good and Evil*, aphorism 218; see also aphorism 254.

PART II: SHAKESPEARE AND NATURE

1. Unless otherwise indicated, all works cited in this part are by **William Shakespeare.**

CHAPTER 7. *ROMEO AND JULIET*

1. Machiavelli, *The Prince*, Chapter XVII.

2. Homer, *Odyssey*, Book XI, lines 489–91.

3. Plato, *Republic*, 604e; *The Republic of Plato*, trans. with notes and interpretive essay by Allan Bloom (New York: Basic Books, 1968), pp. 430–32; *Letter to M. d'Alembert*, Chapters II and V.

4. Aristotle, *Metaphysics*, 982b11–19.

5. *The Tempest*, ed. Frank Kermode, Arden Edition (1954; rpt. London: Routledge, 1988), V.i.310–11.

6. Eric Partridge, *Shakespeare's Bawdy* (London: Routledge, 1947), p. 379.

7. Aristotle, *Politics*, 1327b40–1328a1.

8. Alexis de Tocqueville, *The Old Régime and the Revolution*, Part III, Chapter 5.

9. Leo Strauss, "The Problem of Socrates: Five Lectures," in *The Rebirth of Classical Political Rationalism: An Introduction to the Thought of Leo Strauss*, ed. Thomas L. Pangle (Chicago and London: University of Chicago Press, 1989), p. 107.

10. Rousseau, *Emile*, p. 324; *Social Contract*, Book IV, Chapter 7, Rousseau's second note; Goethe, *Wilhelm Meister's Apprenticeship*, Book V, Chapter 16; letter to Schiller, 14 March 1798.

CHAPTER 8. *ANTONY AND CLEOPATRA*

1. Plato, *Phaedrus*, 253d–254a.

2. Homer, *Iliad*, Book III, lines 31–56; Book VI, lines 281–334; Book XIII, lines 765–75.

3. Plutarch, *Comparison of Demetrius and Antony*, Chapter III.

4. Hobbes, *Leviathan*, Part I, Chapter 10.

5. Lessing, *Laocoön*, Chapters XX–XXII.

6. *King Richard II*, ed. Peter Ure, Arden Edition (1956; rpt. London: Routledge, 1988), V.iv, V.vi.30–52.

7. Plutarch, *Life of Antony*, Chapters LXVII and XXXVI; Plato, *Phaedrus*, 253e–254a.

8. Gibbon, *The Decline and Fall of the Roman Empire* (New York: Random House, The Modern Library, n.d.), Chapter II, p. 52.

9. Winston Churchill, *Marlborough: His Life and Times* (New York: Charles Scribner's Sons, 1933), Vol. I, p. 40.

CHAPTER 9. *MEASURE FOR MEASURE*

1. Montesquieu, *The Spirit of the Laws*, Part 4, Book 24, Chapter 25; Part 3, Book 14, Chapter 11.

2. Machiavelli, *The Prince*, Chapter VII.

3. *King Henry IV, Part II*, ed. A. R. Humphreys, Arden Edition (1966; rpt. London: Routledge, 1988), V.v.69–95.

4. Nietzsche, *Beyond Good and Evil*, aphorism 168.

5. Lessing, *Laocoön*, Chapter I.

6. Allan Bloom (with Harry V. Jaffa), *Shakespeare's Politics* (Chicago and London: University of Chicago Press, Midway reprint, 1986), pp. 101–103.

7. Plato, *Republic*, 338c–339a.

CHAPTER 10. *TROILUS AND CRESSIDA*

1. Plato, *Republic*, 388a–391c.

2. Herodotus, *The History*, Book I, Chapters 3–5.

3. Machiavelli, *The Prince*, Chapter XXV.

4. *King Richard II*, III.ii.1–62.

5. Thucydides, *The Peloponnesian War*, Book I, Chapter 20; Book VI, Chapters 53–59.

6. Aristotle, *Poetics*, 1448a–1449a.

7. Rousseau, *Letter to M. d'Alembert*, Chapter VII, p. 71, note.

8. Plato, *Apology of Socrates*, 28b–d.

9. Plato, *Alcibiades I*, 132c–133e.

10. Aristotle, *Nicomachean Ethics*, 1123b27–1124a20.

11. Machiavelli, *The Prince*, Chapter IX.

12. Pierre Bayle, "Hélène," remark G, *Dictionnaire historique et critique*, 4th edition (Leiden: Samuel Luchtmans, 1730), Vol. II, p. 703.

13. *King Richard II*, I.iii.

14. Plato, *Republic*, 388a–391c.

15. *King Henry IV, Part I*, ed. A. R. Humphreys, Arden Edition (1960; rpt. London: Routledge, 1988), V.iv.70–72.

CHAPTER 11. *THE WINTER'S TALE*

1. Cf. Bloom, *Shakespeare's Politics*, pp. 36–38, 51–54.

2. Homer, *Odyssey*, Book XXIV, lines 234–35.

3. Rousseau, *Emile*, p. 400.

4. Melville, *The Confidence Man*, Chapter 21.

5. *King Richard II*, III.iv.24–91.

6. *Cymbeline*, ed. J. M. Nosworthy, Arden Edition (1955; rpt. London: Routledge, 1988), II.iv.167–69, 184–85.

7. Aristotle, *Politics*, 1262a21–24.

8. *Cymbeline*, III.vii.41–68.

9. Cymbeline became king in 33 B.C. and reigned for thirty-five years.

CHAPTER 12. CONCLUSION

1. Words attributed to the Italian painter Correggio on seeing Raphael's *St. Cecilia*; cf. Montesquieu, *Spirit of the Laws*, Preface.

2. *Antony and Cleopatra*, II.ii.238–40.

INTERLUDE ON TWO STRANGE COUPLES: HAL AND FALSTAFF, MONTAIGNE AND LA BOÉTIE

1. See Machiavelli, *The Prince*, Chapters XIV and XVII; *The Discourses*, Book II, Chapter 13; Book III, Chapters 20, 22, 29.

2. Shakespeare, *King Henry V*, ed. J. H. Walter, Arden Edition (1954; rpt. London: Routledge, 1990), I.ii.265–67.

3. Locke, *Some Thoughts Concerning Education*, §40.

4. Xenophon, *Memorabilia*, Book I, Chapter ii, Sections 40–48.

5. Xenophon, *Symposium*, Book V, Sections 1–10.

6. Plato, *Apology of Socrates*, 19b–c, 23d.

7. Plato, *Phaedo*, 118.

8. Plato, *Gorgias*, 447a.

9. Plato, *Apology of Socrates*, 20d.

10. Plato, *Symposium*, 181c–185a.

11. Nietzsche, *Twilight of the Idols*, "What I Owe to the Ancients," Number 2.

12. Xenophon, *Memorabilia*, Book I, Chapter iii, Sections 8–13.

13. Justus Lipsius in a letter to Montaigne, 23 May 1583.

14. Rousseau, *Emile*, p. 40; *Considerations on the Government of Poland*, Chapter II; *Social Contract*, Book II, Chapter 7.

15. Aristophanes, *Clouds*, lines 1321ff.

16. Aristotle, *On Prophecy in Sleep*, 463b14–15.

17. Augustine, *Confessions*, Book IV, Chapters 4–9; see also *City of God*, Book XIX, Chapters 8–9.

PART III: THE LADDER OF LOVE

Unless otherwise indicated, all works cited in this part are by **Plato**.

1. *Apology of Socrates*, 21d.

2. Ibid., 18a–d.

3. Nietzsche, *Beyond Good and Evil*, aphorism 137.

4. *Charmides*, 155d.

5. *Laws*, 636b–c.

6. 2 Samuel 1:26; 1 Samuel 18:1.

7. Deuteronomy 6:5, 13:3.

8. *Republic*, 328c–d.

9. Rousseau, *Emile*, p. 363; Aristotle, *Politics*, 1262a32–40.

10. Montesquieu, *The Spirit of the Laws*, Part 5, Book 26, Chapter 14.

11. Herodotus, *The History*, Book II, Chapter 30.

12. Aristophanes, *Birds*, lines 128–43.

13. *Laws*, 635e–674c.

14. *Parmenides*, 126b8–127b1.

15. Athenaeus, *Deipnosophists*, Book V, 217a is our source for the date of Agathon's victory at the Lenaea, and hence of the symposium.

16. Thucydides, *The Peloponnesian War*, Book II, Chapter 65; Book VI, Chapters 15, 91–93; Book VII, Chapter 2.

17. Ibid., Book VI, Chapter 24.

18. Apollodorus the narrator still spends time with Socrates (172c), so the retelling must be before 399 B.C., when Socrates was put to death. The retelling is some years after Agathon's departure from Athens (172c), which is believed to have been around 408 B.C. (See R. G. Bury's edition of *The Symposium of Plato* [Cambridge, England: W. Heffer and Sons, 1973], p. lxvi.)

19. *Charmides*, 153a–d.

20. Xenophon, *Apology of Socrates*, Section 18.

21. Aristophanes, *Clouds*, lines 633–34, 694–745.

22. Xenophon, *Memorabilia*, Book I, Chapter iii, Sections 8–15.

23. *Phaedrus*, 230e–234c.

24. Athenaeus, *Deipnosophists*, Book XIII, 561f, 602a; Plutarch, *Life of Pelopidas*, Chapters XVIII–XIX.

25. Homer, *Odyssey*, Book VIII, lines 296–342.

26. See *Republic*, 452c, 457a, 458d.

27. See Thucydides, *The Peloponnesian War*, Book I, Chapter 20; Book VI, Chapters 53–59.

28. *Republic*, 473d2–3.

29. Xenophon, *Symposium*, Chapter viii, Sections 21–22.

30. Aristophanes, *The Assembly of Women*, lines 311–73.

31. *Apology of Socrates*, 21b–22e.

32. *Phaedo*, 96aff.

33. Nietzsche, *Thus Spoke Zarathustra*, Zarathustra's Prologue, Section 5.

34. For example, *Laws*, 817a–d.

35. For example, *Gorgias*, 448d–449a.

36. *Republic*, 410a–412a; *Statesman*, 306–11.

37. *Republic*, 490a8–c6.

38. See Nietzsche's connection between Socrates' agonistic dialectical wrestling and his erotics in *Twilight of the Idols*, "The Problem of Socrates," Number 8.

39. *Apology of Socrates*, 24c–28a.

40. *Republic*, 461d–e, 463c.

41. Nietzsche, *Beyond Good and Evil*, aphorism 191; *Twilight of the Idols*, "The Problem of Socrates," Number 5; *The Birth of Tragedy*, Sections 12–15.

42. Aristotle, *Poetics*, 1449a32–37.

43. Cervantes, *Don Quixote*, Volume 1, Book 2, Chapters 4–5.

44. *Menexenus*, 235e and 249d; see also Xenophon, *Memorabilia*, Book III, Chapter xi.

45. *Apology of Socrates*, 20e–23c.

46. *Phaedo*, 96–99.

47. Nietzsche, *Beyond Good and Evil*, aphorism 295.

48. *Apology of Socrates*, 31c–32a.

49. Aristotle, *Nicomachean Ethics*, 1095a14–21, 1097a15–b21, 1098a7–19.

50. Ibid., 1115a30–32, 1115b11–14, 1115b21–25, 1117b7–17.

51. Ibid., 1098b30–1099a8, 1101b10–27.

52. Compare Nietzsche, *Genealogy of Morals*, Essay III, Section 7.

53. *Republic*, 335d–336a, 449a–450a.

54. *Phaedrus*, 246c–e, 251a–252c, 255b–d.

55. *Republic*, 548c.

56. Nietzsche, *The Use and Abuse of History*, Sections 1–5.

57. *Republic*, 486b, 496d, 517b–d, 591–592, 619b–d, 620c.

58. Ibid., 505a, 508e, 517c.

59. Thucydides, *The Peloponnesian War*, Book VI, Chapters 18, 90.

60. Xenophon, *Memorabilia*, Book I, Chapter ii, Sections 12–18, 40–46, 29–38.

61. Nietzsche, *Beyond Good and Evil*, Preface.

62. Ibid., Preface; aphorism 190.

63. *Republic*, 399d.

64. Herder, "Briefe zur Beförderung der Humanität" (Letters for the Advancement of Humanity), in *Sämmtliche Werke*, ed. Bernard Suphan (Berlin: Weidmann, 1877–1913), Vol. XVIII, pp. 324–25.

65. *Phaedrus*, 243e–257b.

66. *Ion*, 535e–536d.

67. *Alcibiades I*, 106cff.

68. Plutarch, *Life of Pericles*, Chapters IV, VIII, XVI.

69. Thucydides, *The Peloponnesian War*, Book VI, Chapter 92.

70. *Alcibiades I*, 105a–106c, 119b–124b.

71. Xenophon, *Apology of Socrates*, Section 18.

72. Aristophanes, *Clouds*, line 362.

73. *Apology of Socrates*, 27b–28a.

74. Aristophanes, *Peace*, lines 1–179.

75. Nietzsche, *Schopenhauer as Educator*, Section 2.

76. Nietzsche, *Thus Spoke Zarathustra*, Part I, "Of the Friend."

77. *Phaedo*, 98b–99a.

78. For example, *Beyond Good and Evil*, aphorisms 12, 23, 45; *Twilight of the Idols*, Foreword; and letter to Carl Fuchs of 29 July 1888, in *Selected Letters of Friedrich Nietzsche*, ed. and trans. Christopher Middleton (Chicago: University of Chicago Press, 1969), p. 305.

INDEX

Achilles:
  Agamemnon and, 200
  anger of, 135, 200, 349, 371
  death of, 283, 337, 457–58, 500,
    517
  Emile compared with, 134, 135
  Odysseus compared with, 169
  Patroclus and, 355–56, 357, 361, 366,
    368, 374, 426, 457
Acusilaus, 455
Address on Religion (Schleiermacher),
  72*n*
adolescents, sex education for, 13, 19,
  24–27, 54–62
adultery, 16, 110
  heterosexuality and, 482
  love vs. motherhood in, 178–79, 237,
    238, 239–41, 244–45, 249
  modern conception of, 240–44
  in Romantic novels, 90, 119, 209
  in Rousseau's *Confessions*, 41
  stoic response to, 138–39
  as term, 179–80
Aeschylus, 274, 439, 457, 485
Against One (La Boétie), 415–16
Alcestis, 457, 458, 517
Alcibiades I (Plato), 363–66
Alexander the Great, 525, 537
All's Well That Ends Well (Shakespeare),
  344
Anaxagoras, 536
androgyny, 479–82, 486, 511
anger:
  of Achilles, 135, 200, 349, 371
  as male prerogative, 116
  as tragic passion, 135

Anna Karenina (Tolstoy), 231–58
  adultery in, 233, 237, 238–49
  amour de soi in, 246–47
  amour-propre in, 235, 237, 244, 246
  Anna Karenina in, 233, 235–36, 237,
    238–49, 250–51, 252, 254, 255, 258
  aristocracy in, 234, 239
  atheism in, 253–54
  Betsy Tverskoy in, 241
  bourgeois society in, 233, 247–48
  conscience in, 255–56
  Constantin Levin in, 233, 235–36,
    237, 238, 246, 250–58, 260
  convention in, 239, 243–44, 248
  depression in, 251, 253, 254
  Dolly in, 236–37, 246
  Emile compared with, 244, 246, 251,
    252
  eroticism in, 236–38, 242, 245, 246
  family in, 233, 238–41, 250, 252, 257,
    258
  guilt in, 239, 240, 249
  happiness in, 246–47, 249, 250, 260
  intellectualism portrayed in, 252, 253,
    254, 256–57
  jealousy in, 246–48
  Karenin in, 233, 240, 241, 245, 246, 248
  Kitty in, 233, 237, 244, 246, 251–53,
    256, 257
  love in, 238, 241–42, 243, 248
  Madame Bovary compared with, 238,
    239, 249
  marriage in, 233, 236, 237, 240–41,
    252, 253, 254, 258
  morality in, 241, 244, 249, 254,
    255–58

Anna Karenina (cont.)
  mortality in, 237–38
  motherhood in, 237, 238, 239–41,
    244–45, 249, 252
  Oblonsky in, 236–38, 251
  parallelism in, 235–36, 254, 258
  paranoia in, 247–48
  Platon in, 255
  pregnancy in, 236–37
  Red and the Black compared with, 238,
    239, 241, 244, 246, 248
  reform as theme in, 233, 240–41, 251,
    256
  religion in, 253–57
  Rousseau's influence on, 157, 233–35,
    236, 238, 241, 242, 244, 246, 251,
    252, 255, 256
  Russia as represented in, 233–34, 250
  seduction in, 239, 242, 245
  self-consciousness in, 240, 244–45,
    251
  sensuality in, 236–38, 251
  Seryozha in, 239–40
  sex as treated in, 236–37, 242–44,
    246, 257–58
  suicide in, 245, 248, 249, 253, 254,
    255
  tragedy in, 235, 239, 240, 254
  Vronsky in, 233, 236, 239, 240, 244,
    245–48, 252
  War and Peace compared with, 231,
    235, 236, 249–50, 252, 255
Antony and Cleopatra (Shakespeare),
    297–325
  amour-propre in, 305
  Antony and Cleopatra's passion in,
    299, 301, 302, 303, 304–7, 319–25,
    351, 543
  Antony in, 299–300, 301–4, 308, 309,
    310, 314–23
  Antony vs. Octavius in, 299, 301,
    303–4, 310–12
  art vs. nature in, 308–10
  Battle of Actium in, 299, 306, 314–15,
    317, 321
  beauty in, 300, 307–9, 396
  Caesar mentioned in, 305, 306, 311,
    314, 315, 318
  Charmian in, 303, 306
  Christianity in, 298, 299, 300, 301,
    303, 318, 319
  Cleopatra in, 133, 175, 300, 304–10,
    314, 315, 318, 319–25, 351, 396,
    397
  decadence in, 300, 324
  desire vs. duty in, 299, 301, 303–4,
    306, 310, 315–17
  end of antiquity in, 301–2
  Enobarbus in, 287, 300, 303, 307, 308,
    309, 312, 314, 315–18, 319, 321,
    324, 396, 402

  Eros the servant in, 322
  eroticism in, 300–303, 304, 306–9, 323
  fortune in, 312, 314, 322–23
  friends in, 302
  Fulvia in, 304, 305
  Henry IV compared with, 402
  Hercules in, 303, 322
  heroism in, 298, 304, 313, 317
  historical background of, 297–302,
    313, 318–19, 380
  immoderation in, 302, 316–17
  infidelity in, 304–5
  Iras in, 323, 324
  Julius Caesar compared with, 299, 318,
    319
  justice in, 313, 319
  language of, 300, 306–9
  love in, 298, 301, 302, 303, 305, 306,
    310
  lover vs. warrior in, 301, 303–4, 313,
    314–17
  loyalty in, 313, 316, 317–18
  Machiavellianism in, 310–11, 312,
    313, 314
  marriage in, 304, 305, 306, 312
  monarchy vs. republic in, 299, 310,
    311, 312, 314, 320
  morality in, 304, 312–13
  Octavia in, 306, 312, 319
  Octavius in, 299, 302, 303–4, 306,
    310, 314, 315, 318–19, 320–21, 322–
    323, 324–25
  Plutarch as source for, 298–99, 302,
    310, 315
  Pompey in, 304, 311–13, 314
  prolepsis in, 307–8
  reason in, 315–17
  Roman political order in, 298–99, 301,
    302–4, 305, 310–19, 322–23
  Romeo and Juliet compared with, 274,
    287, 298, 300, 305, 307
  sex as treated in, 302, 304, 307, 316
  soldiers in, 302, 315
  suicide in, 319–25
  Tempest compared with, 301, 307
  triumvirate in, 311–14
  Troilus and Cressida compared with,
    347, 348, 351
  Ventidius in, 313–14
  vice vs. virtue in, 302, 306, 318
  witnesses in, 317–18
Aphrodite, 435, 453, 460–61, 464, 504
Apollo, 480
Apology of Socrates (Plato), 361, 432, 445,
    451, 454, 479, 494, 497, 501, 502,
    503, 538
Aquinas, Thomas, 432, 443
Archimedes, 61
Ares, 460–61
Aristippus, 423
Aristogeiton, 355, 464

Aristophanes, 274, 289, 443, 476–77
  Socrates ridiculed by, 408, 422, 432,
    440, 446, 447, 448, 450, 451, 472,
    477–78, 496, 503, 508, 538
Aristotle:
  Alexander the Great as pupil of, 537
  on barbarism, 100
  Christianity and, 298
  as classical authority, 359, 360
  on comedy, 500
  on communication, 87
  desire as concept of, 44
  on eros, 120, 432, 501
  on family, 441
  on friendship, 68, 147, 196, 205, 207,
    286, 404, 413, 421
  imitation defined by, 355
  on irony, 199
  on marriage, 199–200, 195, 206, 207
  metaphysics of, 75
  moderation as concept of, 302, 471
  on nature, 387, 428
  on pleasantness of life, 336
  on politics, 19, 256, 394–95
  Republic as viewed by, 441
  sex discussed by, 45, 47–48, 508
  on soul, 70
  taste discussed by, 94
  on virtue, 364, 506–7
  on wonder, 284
art:
  for art's sake, 229
  beauty in, 263
  creativity in, 22–23, 32, 47–48, 259,
    264
  morality and, 257
  nature and, 43, 308–10, 382–83,
    393–94
  pleasure from, 142
  science vs., 263–64
  society and, 159–60, 226, 227–28
  subversive, 167, 226
Aspasia, 454, 501
Assembly of Women, The (Aristophanes),
  477
atheism:
  in Greek philosophy, 442
  morality and, 154
  rational, 155, 156, 233
  standards for judgment lacked by, 74
Athens:
  democracy in, 314, 526
  dēmos of, 477, 528
  pederasty as illegal in, 459, 463, 464
  Sicilian expedition of, 446–47, 525
  vs. Sparta, 94, 444, 456, 457, 459, 461
Aubrey, John, 57–58
Augustine, Saint, 428
Austen, Jane, 191–208
  on adultery, 191, 195
  bon sens of, 191

classical influence on, 193–96, 195,
    201, 205, 207
  conventionality of, 191, 194, 202, 207
  emotional rage represented by,
    191–92
  Flaubert compared with, 227
  on friendship, 196, 203, 205–8, 426
  irony of, 193–94
  on love, 195–96, 238, 244
  on marriage, 191, 195–96, 252, 345, 426
  moderation of, 193, 315
  parental authority depicted by, 195–
    196, 202–3
  as Romantic, 195–96
  Romantic hero as represented by,
    191, 197
  romantic interaction portrayed by,
    157–58, 194
  Rousseau's influence on, 33, 157–58,
    195, 196, 206, 207
  Shakespeare compared with, 345
  Stendhal compared with, 157–58,
    192, 193, 194, 195, 205
  Tolstoy compared with, 251, 252
  virtues and vices represented by, 33,
    192, 193–94, 195, 196–97, 228
  Xenophon compared with, 193–94,
    195, 205
  see also Pride and Prejudice
authenticity, 260–61, 290
authority:
  obedience to, 90–91, 134–36, 140,
    150, 151, 240
  parental, 117, 119, 120, 121, 422

Bacon, Francis, 40, 301
Balzac, Honoré de, 168, 192
Barnave, Antoine-Pierre-Joseph-Marie,
  174, 175
Barth, Karl, 72*n*, 85
Bayle, Pierre, 367
beautiful, beauty:
  education as love of, 15, 26
  eros as longing for, 21, 40, 41, 54, 91,
    113, 130, 164, 241–42, 258, 263,
    277, 279–80, 281, 282, 396, 499, 511,
    518–19
  as eternity, 510
  good vs., 94, 449–50, 490–91, 492–93,
    499–500, 506–8
  ideal of, 121–22
  natural, 75, 78–79, 80, 493, 550
  physical, 516, 517, 518–19, 524, 533
  in poetry, 507–8
  Renaissance conception of, 392
  Romantic dedication to, 40
  spiritual, 515–16, 517, 523, 533, 541–
    543, 544
Bellow, Saul, 209, 291
Berenson, Bernard, 521
Beyond Good and Evil (Nietzsche),

Bible:
　authority of, 161, 298
　David and Jonathan in, 138, 437–38
　eros in, 437–39, 442
　family in, 440, 442, 469
　friendship in, 437–39
　God as represented in, 75, 135
　homosexuality in, 436–37, 469
　love in, 439
　Naomi and Ruth in, 438*n*
　reading of, 142
　Rousseau's views on, 63, 73, 85, 88
　sexual teachings of, 64
　Symposium compared with, 436–39,
　　442
Birds, The (Aristophanes), 443–44, 477
birth control, 106, 107, 237
Blake, William, 63, 85
Boccaccio, Giovanni, 63
body:
　natural teleology of, 138
　"rights" over, 64
　soul vs., 34, 81, 84, 174–75, 236–38,
　　239, 247, 461, 463, 474, 511–12, 516
Boethius, 189
books, 25, 30–33, 63
Borgia, Cesare, 330
bourgeois society, 34, 47, 49, 59, 62, 85,
　　100, 142, 152, 159–61, 162, 167,
　　192–93, 209, 210, 214, 217–18, 226,
　　259
Brief Lives (Aubrey), 57–58
Buber, Martin, 261
Burke, Edmund, 39–40, 41, 49, 143
Burroughs, William, 142

Callicles, 412
capitalism, 44*n*, 106
Catholic Church, Catholicism:
　Enlightenment vs., 76–77, 214–15
　idolatry in, 390, 392
　Protestantism vs., 77–78, 171, 415
　Rousseau's views on, 76–78
　vaccination opposed by, 107
Cato the Younger, 317, 320
Céline, Louis-Ferdinand, 259–60
Cervantes Saavedra, Miguel de, 141,
　　500–501
Charmides (Plato), 451, 539
Charterhouse of Parma, The (Stendhal),
　　162, 169, 178, 186
Chaucer, Geoffrey, 63, 350, 363
children:
　continuity of identity through, 512–14
　education of, 56, 58, 59–61, 62, 140,
　　153
　eroticism of, 441
　in family, 422–23, 425, 441, 550
　innocence of, 55
　legitimacy of, 106, 149, 328, 333, 343,
　　344, 513

naming of, 217
as natural savages, 68
nurturing of, 99, 102
parental attachment to, 103, 106–7,
　　249, 497–98, 512–13
as sacred, 241
sexual abuse of, 17, 27
vaccination of, 107
women as devoted to, 103, 110, 154,
　　237, 238, 239–41, 244–45, 249
China, People's Republic of, 28–29
Christianity:
　body vs. soul in, 512
　conscience as concept in, 82, 158,
　　262, 315
　decrepitude of, 212, 218
　divorce in, 424
　eros and, 63–65, 84, 332
　guilt in, 315
　love in, 35, 274, 458, 501
　monogamy in, 18
　original sin as concept in, 34, 62, 73,
　　84, 124, 140, 280
　psychology in, 544, 545
　questions of faith in, 414–15
　reason in, 315
　rewards of, 518
　"splendid vices" of ancients in, 298,
　　373
　suicide as sin in, 319
　see also Catholic Church, Catholicism;
　　Protestantism
Churchill, Winston, 319
Cicero, Marcus Tullius, 427
civilization:
　Athenian vs. Spartan, 94, 444, 456,
　　457, 459, 461
　culture vs., 234, 519–21
　love vs. motherhood in, 178
　nature vs., 96
　passions distorted by, 42
　sexuality and, 21–22
Clarissa (Richardson), 141
Clouds, The (Aristophanes), 432, 440,
　　446, 448, 477, 478, 491, 538
communism, 29, 419, 444
Communist Manifesto (Marx and Engels),
　　100
Confessions (Rousseau):
　fame of, 71
　masochism in, 76
　masturbation in, 93
　Red and the Black and, 161
　religious education in, 171
　self-examination in, 42–43
　Tolstoy influenced by, 236
Confessions (Saint Augustine), 428
Confidence Man, The (Melville), 382
Correggio, 393
cosmopolitanism, 232, 519–21
courage, 44, 162, 165

courtship, 124–33
  dating vs., 124
  imagination and, 124–25, 129
  modes of, 26
  quarrels in, 130, 132
  religion and, 129–30
Critias, 414, 525, 526
Critique of Judgment (Kant), 96n
Crito, 412
culture:
  civilization vs., 234, 519–21
  generalization of private sphere in,
    73
  nature vs. society in, 127
  unification of man in, 72–73
  "westernization" of, 117
Cymbeline (Shakespeare), 376, 380, 386,
    388, 392
Cynicism, 47

Dante Alighieri, 271
death:
  acceptance of, 282
  eros and, 456–57
  fear of, 134, 136, 336–37
  of God, 15, 166, 172
  love and, 136, 137, 238, 279, 281–82,
    322, 323–24
  philosophical speculation on, 282,
    337–38, 339
  by suicide, 319–20
Death of Ivan Ilyich, The (Tolstoy), 254,
    255
debauchery, 89–90, 92, 113
de Beauvoir, Simone, 99
deconstructionism, 24, 28, 30
Defoe, Daniel, 63, 125, 141
democracy:
  artistic development and, 94
  Athenian, 314, 526
  compassion as basis of, 71
  family and, 119, 145
  friendship and, 414
  isolation in, 100–102
  leveling process in, 15, 28, 98, 101,
    123, 217–18, 265, 544
  liberalism and, 232
  monarchy vs., 440
  platitudes of, 20, 104
  self-protection in, 15, 25–26
de Orco, Remirro, 330
Depardieu, Gérard, 123
Derrida, Jacques, 20, 32
Descartes, René, 79, 107, 183, 270,
    301
desire:
  amour-propre and, 102
  compassion and, 73
  duty vs., 49, 56, 90–91, 118–19, 121,
    131–33, 134, 150, 155, 178, 205, 218,
    249, 276

  expressions of, 42–43
  frustration of, 148, 154
  heresy compared with, 378–79
  hierarchy of, 514
  illusory powers of, 47, 121–22, 137–
    138
  legal restraints on, 56, 130
  lust vs., 26, 43, 84, 130, 206
  marriage vs., 126–27, 195
  meaning of, 86–87, 90
  of middle-aged men, 96–97
  morality vs., 65, 134–36
  objects of, 20, 51, 91–92, 121–22, 135
  as pregnancy, 511, 512, 514, 515,
    518
  restraints on, 64–65
  satisfaction of, 43–44, 61
  scientific examination of, 18, 19–20
  for self-preservation, 56, 58, 67, 69,
    160, 168
  self-respect vs., 130, 133–34, 137, 139,
    164, 181
  virtue and, 104, 105, 109, 112–13,
    133, 134, 136–37, 279
  waning of, 138, 140
  will vs., 120–21, 378
  see also sublimation
Dickens, Charles, 31, 163
Diogenes Laertius, 47
Diogenes the Cynic, 47
Dionysus, 453, 525
Discourse on Method, The (Descartes),
    107
*Discourse on the Origin and Foundations of
    Inequality, The* (Rousseau), 29, 60,
    67, 99, 126–27, 142
Discourse on the Sciences and Arts (Rous-
    seau), 48
divorce, 117–18, 240–41
  prevalence of, 125, 424
Donizetti, Gaetano, 223
Don Quixote (Cervantes), 141, 500–501
Dostoyevsky, Fyodor, 231
  emotional range of, 192
  love as theme of, 29
  psychoanalytic theory on, 23, 29
  Tolstoy compared with, 231, 250,
    254–55
drama:
  actions vs. deeds in, 412
  aristocratic nature of, 142
  Greek, 141, 167, 485
  see also tragedy
Dreyfus, Alfred, 447
duty:
  desire vs., 49, 56, 90–91, 118–19, 121,
    131–33, 134, 150, 155, 178, 205, 218,
    249, 276
  rights vs., 117
  self-interest vs., 68, 71, 80–82
  standards of, 191, 205

economics, 45, 54, 87–88
education, 96*n*
    of adolescents, 54–62, 65–66
    of children, 56, 58, 59–61, 62, 140,
        153
    compassion in, 66–71, 127
    democratic, 104
    development of, 57–59
    egalitarianism in, 28–29
    enlightenment as goal of, 73–74
    imagination and, 65–67, 86
    liberal tradition in, 46–47
    literary, 25, 30–33
    motivations for, 59–62
    pedantic, 126
    public opinion and, 66, 74–75, 77, 78,
        92, 127, 133
    religious, 63, 73, 171, 177, 211–12
    for self-preservation, 56, 58, 67, 69
    sentimental, 15, 24–26, 30, 65–66, 67,
        71, 73, 119, 129, 132–33, 165
    sex, 13, 19, 24–27, 54–62
    teacher-student relationship in, 27,
        134–36, 140, 143–44, 467, 516, 526,
        533
    utilitarian, 94
Education of Cyrus (Xenophon), 402
Einstein, Albert, 41
Elective Affinities (Goethe), 180–81
Emile: or On Education (Rousseau), 44–
    140
    adultery in, 133, 138–39
    amour de soi in, 51–52
    amour passion in, 92
    amour-propre in, 50, 51–53, 54, 60, 69,
        76, 86, 96, 102, 104, 105, 125–26,
        130–31, 137, 196
    anger discussed in, 135–36
    art as subject in, 94–95
    as *Bildungsroman*, 97
    books discussed in, 63, 70, 85, 125
    compassion discussed in, 66–71, 73
    conscience discussed in, 82, 114–15
    contract in, 88, 90–91, 134–36
    courtship in, 124–33
    education in, 53, 54–62, 64, 108–13,
        123, 126, 127, 129, 140, 142, 144,
        165, 173
    Emile as carpenter in, 131–32
    Emile compared with Sophie in, 114,
        117, 125–26, 129–30
    Emile in, 60, 63, 69–70, 74–75, 83,
        86–87, 90–92, 104, 109
    Emile's separation from Sophie in,
        133–40
    feminine ideal in, 91–92, 97–123, 139
    first encounter described in, 125–26,
        128
    food as subject in, 50–51, 52, 70, 92
    friendship in, 147
    gender relations in, 98–108

    locales of, 89, 94–97
    marriage as subject of, 86–87, 117–21,
        195, 244
    motivation in, 59–62
    nature vs. society in, 49–50
    Nouvelle Héloïse compared with, 144,
        145
    Paris as locale for, 94–97
    Pride and Prejudice compared with,
        196
    puberty in, 54–62
    "real" Sophie in, 121–22, 124, 125
    Red and Black compared with, 165–66,
        173
    religion as subject in, 62–64, 73
    as Romantic novel, 97, 99, 126
    in Rousseauan canon, 140
    Rousseau's personal development
        described in, 75–77, 80, 83, 86, 87,
        96–97, 115
    sex as treated in, 44–48, 74, 86–93
    Sophie in, 91, 97, 108–23, 252
    Sophie's "death" in, 133, 135
    Sophie's name in, 126
    stoicism in, 133, 138–39
    sweets used in, 57, 60–61
    taste discussed in, 94–97
    Tolstoy influenced by, 236
    virtue discussed in, 112–14, 115,
        116–17
    see also "Profession of Faith of the
        Savoyard Vicar, The"
Emile and Sophie (Rousseau), 138–39
Empedocles, 472
Encyclopedists, 172, 233
Enlightenment:
    Catholicism opposed by, 76–77,
        214–15
    cosmopolitanism of, 232
    heroism and, 236
    materialism of, 433
    optimism of, 183–84
    progress as doctrine of, 214, 220, 221,
        235
    rationality of, 88–89, 169, 269
    religion and, 74, 75, 76–77, 85–86,
        155, 171, 214–15, 225–26
    scientific tradition of, 16, 42, 107,
        214, 220, 269
    society and, 63, 234, 345
envy, 68, 69, 92
Epictetus, 139
Epicureanism, 437
eros:
    agape vs., 33, 63, 274, 458
    arousal and, 20, 24, 42, 43, 93
    author's approach to, 30–35
    as contractual relationship, 15, 28,
        261, 273, 492
    corruption of, 63–65, 84, 332
    death and, 456–57

decline of, 13–35
Freudian, 13, 20, 21, 264, 512, 514
God and, 256
as Greek word, 13, 21
human connectedness in, 14–15, 28,
    30, 100, 101, 186, 207, 219, 261–62,
    265, 395–96, 409, 410
justice and, 25, 413, 548–49
law and, 514–15, 516
as longing for beautiful, 21, 40, 41,
    54, 91, 113, 130, 164, 241–42, 258,
    263, 277, 279–80, 281, 282, 396, 499,
    511, 518–19
nature and, 21, 28, 29, 80, 84, 89,
    474–75, 482, 483–84, 489
necessity vs., 491, 492–93
Nietzschean, 63, 332, 433
origins of, 454–55, 491, 504–5
physical preferences in, 15, 115
Platonic, 35, 84, 89, 128, 301, 501,
    542, 545
poetry and, 23, 24, 433
qualities of, 490–93
Rousseauan, 54, 63–65, 80, 84, 89, 91,
    100, 101, 113, 115, 130, 262, 492,
    512
sensuality of, 491–92
sex vs., 15, 17, 24, 109, 264, 424, 480–
    481, 508, 510, 511, 541, 544
spiritedness vs., 513
transcendent pleasures of, 26, 35
wholeness and, 478–85, 489–90, 493,
    498–99, 501, 506, 508–10
see also desire; love
Ethics (Aristotle), 196, 298, 506, 508
Euripedes, 445, 485
Euthydemus (Plato), 539
Existentialism, 99

family:
    ancestral, 513
    children in, 422–23, 425, 441, 550
    collapse of, 15, 106, 107–8
    as conventional vs. natural structure,
        99, 100–101, 105, 119
    democracy vs., 119, 145
    friendship vs., 422–23, 438–39
    Greek conception of, 440–43
    homosexuality vs., 468–69
    legal basis of, 513
    parental authority as basis of, 422
    Platonic eros vs., 35
    politics vs., 101, 440–42, 514
    property and, 442–43
    romantic love vs., 34, 86, 239, 243–
        244, 249, 257–58, 550
    sacredness of, 441–43
    society vs., 119, 120
    as sublimating structure, 49, 139–40
    in U.S., 111, 264–65
    will of, 123

women as central to, 107–8, 114, 240,
    369
see also children; fathers; mothers;
    parents
Farabi, al-, 443
fathers, fatherhood, 102, 103, 106–7,
    138, 153, 497–98, 512–13
Faust (Goethe), 167
feminism, 26–28, 98–100
Fénelon, François de Salignac de La
    Mothe-, 121, 125, 126
Flaubert, Gustave, 209–29
    aestheticism of, 210, 215–16, 218,
        226–29
    as anti-Romantic, 209–10, 228
    Austen compared with, 227
    as novelist, 210
    Rousseau's influence on, 33, 157
    Tolstoy compared with, 227
    see also *Madame Bovary*
Fontenelle, Bernard Le Bovier de, 95n–
    96n
Franklin, Benjamin, 215
freedom:
    compassion vs., 66
    conscience and, 81–82
    as illusion, 252
    intellectual, 443
    moral, 118
    natural, 46, 132
    suicide and, 320
free will, 423, 424–25
French Revolution, 162, 170, 171, 212,
    228, 235, 250
Freud, Sigmund:
    creativity examined by, 22–23, 32, 264
    eros as concept of, 13, 20, 21, 264,
        512, 514
    influence of, 158, 231
    Kinsey compared with, 21, 22, 24, 62
    Marx and, 21, 54, 158, 543
    moralism of, 21–22
    objectivity of, 41–42
    Rousseau vs., 41–42, 43, 61–62, 158
    sexual theories of, 20–24, 29–30, 41–
        42, 43, 61–62, 151, 264
    Shakespeare vs., 396
friendship:
    admirable, 438
    Aristotle vs. Rousseau on, 68, 147–48
    Biblical view of, 438–39
    "bonding" vs., 409
    citizenship vs., 416–17, 425
    common identity in, 419–20
    community vs., 411–12, 413–14
        420–21
    completeness of, 428
    as conspiracy, 411–12, 413–1
    democracy vs., 414
    equality in, 516
    expectations in, 418–19

friendship (*cont.*)
  experiences shared in, 33
  family vs., 422–23, 438–39
  free will as basis of, 423, 424–25
  general will and, 420–21
  as happiness, 421–22
  intellectual basis of, 411, 414, 416,
    417–18
  as irresistible attraction, 410–11, 426,
    427–28
  love vs., 281, 410–11, 423–24, 547–51
  marriage and, 196, 203, 205–8, 375–
    376, 424–27
  morality based on, 418–20
  pederasty and, 427, 468, 533–34
  of philosophers, 412, 417–18, 425,
    438–39
  political, 413, 414, 416–17, 419–20
  puberty and, 147
  public opinion and, 413–14, 416, 418
  rarity of, 411, 413, 418
  reason in, 409–10, 417–18, 427–28
  reciprocity in, 34
  religion and, 414–15, 416
  Romantic conception of, 147–48
  speech in, 147, 410, 411–12, 436, 543,
    548
  spiritedness and, 286
  unerotic nature of, 196, 411, 413, 414,
    416, 423–24, 427
  as union of souls, 404, 410, 411
  virtue in, 281, 417, 418–19

Gardner, Ava, 466
gender as cultural vs. natural phenom-
    enon, 28
general will, 420–21
"Genius" (Rousseau), 72n
geometry, 58, 61, 470
Gibbon, Edward, 318
gluttony, 45, 61, 116
God:
  belief in, 84, 130, 155–56
  covenant of, 64, 439
  death of, 15, 166, 172
  eros and, 256
  existence of, 79
  fear of, 510
  as first cause of motion, 79
  goodness of, 154
  guidance from, 74
  laws of, 49, 64, 437, 439
  love of, 137, 428, 442, 469, 510
  man as imperfect, 81, 155
    corrupted by, 63
    e and, 75; 155, 256
    passion and, 62, 72
    y of, 75, 156
    wable, 417
    ann Wolfgang von:
    rks of, 97, 271

  on love, 180–81
  love life of, 41
  on morality, 167
  on obscenity, 289
  as Romantic, 62
  Rousseau and, 80, 90, 448
  Shakespeare and, 398
good, goodness:
  beautiful vs., 94, 449–50, 490–91,
    492–93, 499–500, 506–8
  common vs. individual, 81–82, 261
  comprehensive, 394–95
  love of, 484, 508–10
  morality vs., 136–37
  natural, 165, 168, 255–56
  virtue vs., 136–37
Gorgias (Plato), 407, 495–96
Gracchus, Tiberius, 416–17
Grand Illusion, 350
Guthrie, Tyrone, 351

Hamlet (Shakespeare), 270
happiness:
  affirmation of, 260
  as commandment, 136
  eternal, 82–83
  friendship as, 421–22
  love as, 90
  morality vs., 118–19, 139
  natural equilibrium as basis of, 43–44
  nobility and, 284
  opinions and, 54
  virtue as, 44, 153, 154, 352
Harmodius, 355, 464
Hedda Gabler (Ibsen), 145
Hegel, Georg Wilhelm Friedrich, 23, 40,
    50, 262
Heidegger, Martin, 546
Henri IV, King of France, 415
Henry IV, Parts I and II (Shakespeare),
    401–10
  Antony and Cleopatra compared with,
    402
  blasphemy in, 402, 406
  Boar's Head Inn as locale of, 332, 403
  Chief Justice in, 332, 407, 408
  Falstaff as Socratic figure in, 406–8,
    536
  Falstaff in, 287, 289, 332, 395, 401–10,
    422, 536
  father-son relationship in, 406–7,
    422–23
  Francis the tapster in, 403
  friendship in, 401–10, 422–23, 467
  Hal (Henry V) in, 332, 401–10
  Henry IV in, 406–7
  historical background for, 402
  Hotspur in, 361, 372, 402, 403, 408
  language of, 402, 405–6
  law in, 404, 407, 408
  Machiavellianism in, 402, 408–9

monarchy in, 401, 404, 406–7
obscenity in, 287, 289
Poins in, 407
political morality in, 402–3, 404, 406,
    408–9, 410
reputation in, 402–4
Romeo and Juliet compared with, 287
sex as treated in, 402, 404, 408, 409
vice in, 402–3
Winter's Tale compared with, 402, 409
wit in, 402, 405–6
Hephaestus, 460–61, 482–83
Heraclitus, 473
Herder, Johann Gottfried von, 529
Hermes, 460–61
Herodotus, 123, 349, 442
heroes, heroines:
    compassion for, 70, 92
    monetary indifference of, 129
    Napoleon as model for, 70, 228, 232–33
    reason and, 360–61
    Romantic, 144, 156, 161–63, 177–78,
        191, 193, 197, 210, 278
    Shakespeare's criticism of, 167, 228,
        347–50
Hesiod, 455
historicism, 21, 29, 107, 108, 228, 234,
    297, 320*n*
Hobbes, Thomas:
    amour-propre in philosophy of, 261
    antiquity and, 306
    on death, 134
    egalitarianism of, 100
    on freedom, 424
    on human nature, 60, 67, 70–71, 261–
        262, 421, 511, 551
    Machiavelli's influence on, 301
    rationalism of, 67, 74
    self-preservation as doctrine of, 136,
        358
    virtue described by, 201
    "war of all against all" as concept of,
        20–21, 48, 53, 101, 127–28, 410
Homer, 125, 134, 142, 283, 298, 307,
    489, 491
    see also Iliad; Odyssey
homosexuality:
    as crime, 16
    family morals and, 343, 468–69
    female, 482
    heterosexuality vs., 436, 473, 482
    marriage and, 482
    Plato's views on, 436–37, 468–69
    prevalence of, 17
    see also pederasty
Hugo, Victor, 31
human nature:
    denaturing of, 419
    evil in, 52
    idleness in, 59
    incoherence of, 535
    inequality in, 54, 60, 69, 228
    nature vs., 384–85
    otherness and, 261–62, 264, 265
    permanence of, 107
    pessimism about, 260–61
    reason and, 19, 68
    repression of, 336
    rights of, 132–33
    selfishness in, 48–49, 51–53, 68, 73,
        127–28
    see also man
Hume, David, 83*n*

Ibsen, Henrik, 145
Iliad (Homer), 135, 169, 283, 307, 336
    Troilus and Cressida compared with,
        348, 349, 350, 352, 356, 365
    see also Achilles
imagination:
    compassion and, 66–71
    education and, 65–67, 86
    erotic dreams vs., 23
    hope and, 137–38
    ideal woman created in, 91–92, 113,
        137
    independence of, 66–67
    literary, 31
    obscenity and, 290–91
    poetic, 23, 138
    reality vs., 151
    reason vs., 263
    Romantic, 24–25, 169, 176, 177
    sadomasochism and, 187
    sentiment vs., 65–66
    sex and, 45, 48, 50, 51, 57–59, 64, 94
    sublime and, 156
    superstition vs., 73–74
incest, 35, 41, 432, 439, 441, 498
individuality:
    in anarchy, 314
    liberal, 14, 100, 262
    morality and, 420
    natural law vs., 42
    property and, 63
    reproduction and, 101–2
    Rousseauan, 48, 51
    society vs., 14, 48–49, 67–70, 87, 100–
        102, 201, 234, 395, 413, 419, 420–
        421, 551
innocence, 62, 90–91, 131, 145, 150
intercourse, sexual:
    as culmination of commitment, 124,
        129, 411
    desire for, 43, 129, 140
    differences between women and men
        in, 102
    as greatest pleasure, 45
    as habitual practice, 425
    physical details of, 175–76, 460, 492
    see also orgasms; sex
Ion (Plato), 530

jealousy:
  erotic nature of, 123, 549
  as form of *amour-propre*, 130–31
  rationalism and, 153
  self-esteem and, 176, 186–87
Jesuits, 170, 172
Johnson, Virginia E., 290n, 351
Journey to the End of Night (Céline),
    259–60
Joyce, James, 259
Judaism:
  Hellenism vs., 437, 440, 442, 443
  laws of, 437–38, 439
  monogamy in, 18
Julie; ou La Nouvelle Héloïse (Rousseau),
    see Nouvelle Héloïse, La
Julius Caesar (Shakespeare), 299, 318, 319
justice:
  anger and, 135
  compassion vs., 69, 71, 78
  conscience and, 80–82
  eros and, 25, 413, 548–49
  law and, 516, 521–22
  of men vs. women, 116
  perfect, 139
  social, 69, 81, 231

Kant, Immanuel:
  on civilization, 72–73
  on freedom, 424
  on happiness, 139, 507
  on human nature, 420–21
  Hume's influence on, 83n
  metaphysics of, 79
  morality of, 468
  on nature, 384–85
  as philosopher, 432, 529
  postulates of, 83n
  Rousseau's influence on, 14, 40, 50,
    55–56, 72–73, 83n, 86, 96, 126–27,
    255, 264, 420–21
  sublime as conceived by, 14, 61, 75
  taste analyzed by, 97
King Lear (Shakespeare), 270
Kinsey, Alfred Charles:
  Freud compared with, 21, 24, 62
  political agenda of, 16–17
  sexual practices researched by, 15–20
Kinsey Report, 15–20
Kojève, Alexandre, 264

La Boétie, Etienne de, 410–28
Laclos, Choderlos de, 53, 104–5, 144,
    212, 260
Laelius, 416
law:
  divine, 49, 64, 437, 439
  eros and, 514–15, 516
  justice and, 516, 521–22
  natural, 360, 424–25, 437–38
  rhetoric of, 454

Laws (Plato), 437, 444, 445
Lessing, Gotthold Ephraim, 270, 307,
    336, 398
Leviathan (Hobbes), 261, 358
Liaisons Dangereuses, Les (Laclos), 53,
    104–5, 144, 212, 260
liberalism:
  censorship and, 226–27
  in education, 46–47
  equality and, 160
  individuality in, 14, 100, 262
  laisser-aller attitude in, 28
  modern, 47, 232
  rationalism of, 67
  reforms in, 235
  toleration in, 25–26, 28, 171
  utilitarianism of, 184
libertinism, 63, 87
Lincoln, Abraham, 27
literature:
  alienation and, 85
  classical, 95n–96n, 116, 298, 416
  criticism of, 31–33, 158, 159, 180, 275,
    308–10, 397–98
  didactic, 142–43
  drama vs. novel in, 141–42, 147
  love as concept in, 25, 29–35
  nihilistic, 142
  philosophy and, 157–59
  reading of, 25, 30–33
  taste in, 157
  see also novels, Romantic
Locke, John, 46, 60, 74, 97, 100, 234,
    301, 406, 499, 511
Lorenz, Konrad, 409
Louis Philippe, King of France, 170,
    220
love:
  abstraction vs., 22, 23, 28, 30
  capacity for, 57, 102
  consolation of, 189–90
  "crystallization" in, 125–26
  death and, 136, 137, 238, 279, 281–82,
    322, 323–24
  deception and, 110
  de-eroticization of, 15, 27–28
  experiences shared in, 33
  fanaticism vs., 277
  feminist critique of, 26–28
  fidelity in, 65, 105, 138, 139, 481, 519
  at first sight, 273, 381
  fortune and, 125, 134, 139
  friendship vs., 281, 410–11, 423–24,
    547–51
  gallantry in, 39, 95, 109, 351
  general will and, 420–21
  of God, 137, 428, 442, 469, 510
  guilt and, 149–50, 151
  of head vs. heart, 174
  history of, 35
  ideal, 57, 91–92, 121–22, 149, 162

as illusion, 91, 112–13, 124, 150, 175–176, 196, 241–42
intimacy in, 19, 176–77
isolation in, 280–81
literary conception of, 25, 29–35
merit and beauty as components of, 54
modern conception of, 13–35
motherhood vs., 178–79, 237, 238, 239–41, 244–45, 249
natural foundation for, 209, 246, 276
of order, 152, 155
Platonic, 91, 239, 242, 274, 275
possessiveness of, 506
as power struggle, 26, 27–28, 30
propriety and, 276–77, 281
reciprocity in, 34, 43, 51, 113, 131, 138, 176–77, 179, 201
redemptive power of, 162, 166
relationships and, 238, 262–63
as religion, 279
romantic, 34, 86, 195–96, 239, 243–44, 249, 257–58, 550
Romanticism and, 34, 241–42, 259–65, 466, 500
in Romantic novels, 25, 34, 259
self-justification of, 278
sexual basis of, 19, 43, 57
of single partner, 54, 56, 71
social forms for, 110–11
speech about, 13–14, 25–26, 29, 87–90, 95–96, 289–91, 466, 506, 517
Stoic definition of, 427
sublimity of, 264–65
as supreme happiness, 90
types of, 42–43
unrequited, 138
wholeness in, 56, 108, 476–85
Lucia di Lammermoor (Donizetti), 223
Lucretius, 47, 91, 337–38, 523
Lycurgus, 49

Macbeth (Shakespeare), 238, 275–76
Machiavelli, Niccolò:
   political vision of, 51, 63, 168, 277, 285, 300–301, 310, 312, 314, 392
   priests criticized by, 293, 329–30
   Shakespeare influenced by, 277, 313, 341, 392
Madame Bovary (Flaubert), 209–29
   Abbé Bournisien in, 214–15, 218, 225–26
   adultery in, 209, 216–24
   amorality of, 218, 226–28
   amour-propre in, 219
   ancien régime in, 213–14
   Anna Karenina compared with, 238, 239, 249
   anticlericalism in, 214–15, 220
   blind beggar in, 225, 226
   bohemianism in, 219, 226

boredom in, 210–11
bourgeois society in, 209, 210, 214, 217–18
Canivet in, 229
Charles Bovary in, 210, 212–13, 216, 222, 224, 229, 321
children in, 217–18
comedy in, 215, 216
criminal trial on, 226–28
education in, 211–12
Emma Bovary in, 209–214, 216–26, 238, 239, 249, 259
Enlightenment lampooned in, 214–216, 220, 225–26, 229
eroticism in, 209, 210, 216
Hippolyte in, 222
Homais in, 214–16, 217, 218, 219–220, 222, 224, 225–26, 229
journalism attacked in, 214, 220, 226
language of, 210, 216, 219–22
Larivière in, 228–29
Léon Dupuis in, 216–18, 223–24
Lheureux in, 224
love in, 209–10, 223–24, 259
Marquis d'Andervilliers's ball in, 212–14
marriage in, 210, 217, 218, 227
materialism in, 216, 218
medicine in, 222, 229
Pride and Prejudice compared with, 219
Red and the Black compared with, 190, 210, 219, 220
religion in, 211–12, 214–15, 218, 224–226, 227
Rodolphe in, 218–23, 224
Romanticism criticized in, 209–10, 216–17, 220–21, 226
Rousseau's influence on, 157, 211, 212, 215
seduction in, 221–23
self-deception in, 213–14, 216
sex as treated in, 218–23
suicide in, 214, 224–26
virtue in, 211–12, 227, 229
Yonville county fair in, 219–22
Maimonides, 443, 504
man:
   as "botched creation," 63
   civilized, 42–43, 46, 49–50, 51–54, 75, 90–91, 93, 94, 102, 127, 134
   divided nature of, 43, 56, 62–63, 81, 90–91, 94, 114, 126–27, 134, 137, 264, 279, 345, 478–85, 509–10
   economic, 46, 100, 101
   Fall of, 62, 90–91, 150, 261, 332,
   high vs. low in, 275
   as imperfect God, 81, 155
   natural, 29, 42, 43, 46, 49–50, 62, 73–74, 78, 80, 100, 118, 134, 136, 137, 177, 253

man (*cont.*)
   as political animal, 120
   socialist, 93
   see also human nature
Mandragola, The (Machiavelli), 300
Mann, Thomas, 41
Marcuse, Herbert, 13, 21
marriage, marriages:
   arranged, 117, 119
   choice in, 117–23, 195, 203–4, 206–8
   classical vs. Romantic views on, 425–26
   cohabitation before, 124–25
   as communal arrangement, 419
   communication in, 123
   consent in, 119, 120
   as contract, 28, 90, 117, 150
   conventions of, 178
   desire vs., 126–27, 195
   equality in, 200
   friendship and, 196, 203, 205–8, 424–27
   homosexuality and, 482
   irrevocable nature of, 117–18
   legal basis of, 240–41, 243
   loneliness overcome by, 97
   monogamous, 16, 18
   morality of, 118
   physical attraction in, 119, 120–21, 123
   respectability of, 179
   romantic love and, 34, 195–96
   in Romantic novels, 118–19, 425–26
   sacredness of, 117, 140, 150, 242
   social status and, 119, 120, 123, 205
   wealth and, 119, 120, 123, 128–29, 205
Marsyas, 528, 529
Marx, Groucho, 31
Marx, Karl:
   class struggle described by, 171–72, 262
   economic critique of, 27, 44*n*, 54
   Freud and, 21, 54, 158, 543
   influence of, 158
   Rousseau vs., 54, 100, 158, 162
   on rural life, 235
   Socrates vs., 419
Marxism, 93, 217, 235
masochism, 17, 41, 76, 186–88
Masters, William H., 290*n*, 351
masturbation, 16, 17, 41
   education and, 58
   Rousseau's views on, 47, 65, 93, 143
Measure for Measure (Shakespeare), 327–45
   Angelo and Isabella in, 331–34, 337, 2
   o in, 330, 331–34, 335, 337, 339, 342–44, 345
   ine in, 341
   in, 331–38, 342, 344

Claudio and Isabella in, 334–38, 339–40
Claudio in, 330, 332, 333, 334–38, 339–40, 341, 344, 345
comedy in, 327, 328, 336–37, 340
death in, 335–38
dowries in, 331, 334, 343–44
Duke and Isabella in, 338–45
Duke Vincentio in, 327–30, 331, 333, 334, 335–336, 337, 339, 340, 341–45, 398
Escalus in, 328, 331, 344
family in, 328, 332, 343
Friar Thomas in, 327–28
guilt in, 332, 339–40
imagination in, 332, 337
Isabella in, 331–45
Juliet in, 331, 333, 334, 335
justice in, 340, 341–44
law in, 327, 328, 329, 331, 334–35, 341, 344, 345
Lucio in, 331, 333–34, 340, 342, 343, 344
Machiavellianism in, 329–30, 341
Mariana in, 331, 338–39, 342, 343–44
marriage in, 328, 329, 330, 331, 333, 334–35, 339, 343–45
mercy in, 334, 342
Mistress Overdone in, 328, 339
morality in, 330–31, 332, 333, 334, 335–38
political intrigue in, 329–30, 331, 340
Pompey in, 328, 331, 340
prison in, 340–41
promiscuity in, 329, 335
prostitution in, 328, 333, 335, 340–41
Provost in, 333, 340, 341
punishment in, 331, 335–38, 342–44
Puritanism in, 332, 333
religion in, 327, 329–30, 332, 335, 338
Romeo and Juliet compared with, 327, 335
sex as treated in, 327–29, 331–38, 339, 342, 345
sinfulness in, 331–32, 334, 335
Stoicism in, 335–36
Tempest compared with, 327, 340
Troilus and Cressida compared with, 362
venereal disease in, 328–29
Vienna as locale of, 328–29, 333, 335, 362
Winter's Tale compared with, 388
Melville, Herman, 382
Melzer, Arthur, 75
Mémorial de Sainte-Hélène (Napoleon), 161
men:
   character of, 52–53, 103–4, 108, 112–113, 117, 391
   double standard and, 105

as fathers, 102, 103, 106–7, 138, 153
fidelity of, 105, 106, 132
as gentlemen, 26, 94, 146–47, 506
as husbands, 123, 132
intelligence of, 109–10
self-esteem of, 117
sexuality of, 26, 114
Menexenus (Plato), 454, 501
moderation, 44, 279, 283, 302, 471, 492
Molière, 201, 270
Momigliano, Arnaldo, 269, 300
money:
  equality destroyed by, 132
  power of, 160, 166, 173
  sex vs., 144
Montaigne, Michel de, 410–28
  on freedom, 424–25
  on friendship, 196, 410–28, 438, 468,
    509, 535, 536
  as humanist, 414–15, 428
  marriage of, 425–27
  on pederasty, 427, 460*n*, 468
  Platonic philosophy and, 35
  que sais-je? formulation of, 418
  religious views of, 414–15, 416
  Rousseau vs., 420–21
  sex life of, 40, 63
  Thales compared with, 418
  see also "On Friendship"
Montesquieu, Charles-Louis de Secon-
    dat, Baron de La Brède et de, 98,
    211, 329*n*, 441
morality:
  amoral quest for, 65, 229
  bourgeois, 29, 167–69, 175, 257
  compassion and, 66–71, 92, 168
  conscience and, 80–82
  conventional, 17, 18, 84, 167–69, 191,
    194
  deeds and, 421
  desire vs., 65, 134–36
  friendship as basis of, 418–20
  goodness vs., 136–37
  in Greek philosophy, 506–7
  happiness vs., 118–19, 139
  immortality and, 82–84
  internalization of, 130
  mercenary, 135
  nonjudgmental, 26
  obligations of, 80–82, 227
  pleasure vs., 421
  relativism in, 26, 43, 92, 123
  self-interest vs., 134, 168
  self-legislated, 90, 91, 138, 160
  utilitarian, 506, 507
Moses, 49, 438*n*
mothers, motherhood, 102–3, 109, 178–
    179, 180, 190, 237, 238, 239–41,
    244–45, 249, 497–98, 512–13
Mozart, Wolfgang Amadeus, 22–23
music, 473–74, 528–29

Napoleon I, Emperor of France, 31,
    192, 236
  as hero, 70, 228, 232–33
Narcissus, 490
nature:
  as abstraction, 309
  art and, 43, 308–10, 382–83, 393–94
  beauty of, 75, 78–79, 80, 493, 550
  conquest of, 235, 475
  convention vs., 18, 99, 100–101, 105,
    119, 120–21, 146, 166–67, 203, 276,
    444–45
  demonic aspect of, 428, 529
  environment vs., 396
  eros and, 21, 28, 29, 80, 84, 89, 474–
    475, 482, 483–84, 489
  estrangement from, 64, 85, 93
  form vs. matter in, 188
  as "full of gods," 88
  God and, 75, 155, 256
  human nature vs., 384–85
  laws of, 360, 424–25, 437–38
  order in, 79–80, 83, 152, 155, 474–75,
    483
  society vs., 20–21, 43–44, 48–50, 56,
    127, 146, 264, 421
  sublime in, 75, 79
  symbols in, 88
  teleology of, 472
Neoplatonism, 449
Newton, Isaac, 41
Nicias, 447
Nicomachean Ethics (Aristotle), 364
Nietzsche, Friedrich:
  Bildung ridiculed by, 21
  on bourgeois society, 221
  contempt and, 218
  cultural horizons as concept of, 520,
    521
  death of God asserted by, 166, 172
  decline of West announced by, 162
  on distrust, 247–48
  eros as concept of, 63, 332, 433
  followers of, 449
  on friendship, 543
  gods portrayed as philosophers by,
    503
  on good vs. evil, 228
  on morality, 168
  as philosopher, 541, 546
  Plato vs., 412, 520, 526
  psychological insight of, 545–46
  Rousseau vs., 50, 62, 157, 260
  on sex, 287
  on Socrates, 447, 448, 485, 500, 508,
    520, 526, 536
  solitude of, 542–43
  on Stendhal, 179–80, 262, 263
  Superman of, 93
  "will to power" as concept of, 188
    262, 520, 546

nihilism, 142, 228, 254, 260, 373, 397, 473
No Exit (Sartre), 14
Nouvelle Héloïse, La (Rousseau), 140–56
  Abelard and Héloïse as model for, 143
  atheism in, 154, 155, 156, 180
  Burke's critique of, 40, 49, 143
  Claire in, 145, 146, 149, 154
  corruption by, 144–45, 167
  M. de Wolmar in, 145, 150, 152–56, 253
  didacticism of, 142–43, 152
  duel in, 146–47, 150
  Edouard Bomston in, 146–48, 151
  education in, 56, 143–44, 152, 153, 242, 250
  Emile compared with, 144, 145
  as epistolary romance, 116, 143, 146, 149
  friendship in, 147–48, 153
  guilt in, 149–50
  irony in, 143, 151
  Julie d'Etange in, 116, 117, 143, 145, 148–56, 228, 233, 236, 238, 239, 242, 253
  law in, 144, 149
  locale of, 143, 154
  marriage in, 145, 148, 152, 153, 180
  ménages à trois in, 152–53
  parental authority in, 117, 144, 145, 146, 148–49, 150, 153
  Red and the Black compared with, 159, 163–67, 180
  religion in, 150–51, 154–56
  reputation of, 140–41
  as Romantic novel, 147, 156
  Saint-Preux in, 143–45, 146, 148–56, 159, 242, 519
  sex as treated in, 143, 144, 145–46, 148, 154
  suicide in, 148, 156
  teacher-student relationship in, 143–144, 152
  tragedy in, 146, 147, 156
  virtue in, 145, 147, 150, 152, 153, 154
novels, Romantic:
  adultery in, 90, 119, 209
  autobiography in, 347
  chance meetings in, 125, 201–2
  convention vs. nature in, 119
  corruption by, 144–45, 167
  democratic nature of, 142
  desire as theme in, 18
  domination as theme in, 188
  as educational novels, 97
  literary criticism of, 31–33
  love as theme in, 25, 34, 259
  marriage as theme in, 118–19, 425–26
  modern novels vs., 259–60
  phenomenology of, 263

  psychological insight of, 262–64
  reading public for, 157
  Rousseau's influence on, 140–43, 157–59
  virtue as subject of, 147
  see also specific novels

obscenity, 65, 285–91, 296, 300, 307, 374
Odyssey (Homer), 25, 134, 169, 373, 457–58
Oeconomicus (Xenophon), 195
"On Friendship" (Montaigne), 410–28
  community vs. friendship in, 411–12, 413–14, 420–21
  essay form of, 411
  family vs. friendship in, 422–23
  happiness defined as friendship in, 421–22, 428
  La Boétie's treatise discussed in, 415–16
  love vs. friendship in, 410–11, 423–24
  marriage vs. friendship in, 196, 424–27
  pederasty discussed in, 427
On Love (Stendhal), 159
On the Nature of Things (Lucretius), 47
orgasms:
  in animals, 55
  peak age for, 18
  perfect, 46
  simultaneous, 290n
Orpheus, 457
Othello (Shakespeare), 270
  Desdemona in, 386–87, 391
  Iago in, 392
  jealousy in, 246, 376, 378, 386, 391, 392
  Othello in, 376, 378, 392
  Troilus and Cressida compared with, 368–69
  Winter's Tale compared with, 376, 378, 386–87, 391, 392

parents:
  authority of, 117, 119, 120, 121, 422
  children loved by, 103, 106–7, 249, 497–98, 512–13
  obedience to, 150, 151
  see also fathers; mothers
Parmenides, 455
Parmenides (Plato), 446
Partridge, Eric, 286
Pascal, Blaise:
  on boredom, 210–11
  l'esprit de géométrie of, 94
  religious analysis by, 184, 210–11
  Stendhal's admiration for, 172
Paul, Saint, 303
Paul and Virginia (Saint-Pierre), 40, 211
pederasty, 35, 409, 436, 441, 451–69, 486, 532–34, 541

as erotic activity, 35, 459–60, 461,
  462, 463, 464, 465, 467
illegality of, 459, 462–63, 464
Montaigne's views on, 427, 460*n*,
  468
philosophy and, 461, 463–68, 469,
  514
promiscuity and, 461–62, 463, 464
as prostitution, 466–67
reciprocity in, 462, 463–68, 469
as unnatural, 473, 475
Peloponnesian War, 446–47, 525, 536,
  537–38
Pericles, 407, 441, 525–26, 536
Persian Letters (Montesquieu), 98
Persian War, 314, 349
pessimism, 228, 260–61
Peter the Great, Czar of Russia, 233,
  234
Petrarch, Francesco, 271
Phaedo (Plato):
  body vs. soul in, 512
  immortality in, 545
  philosophy in, 501–2
  Socrates' death described in, 407,
    511–12
Phaedrus (Plato):
  divine madness in, 530
  erotic rhetoric of, 28, 87, 95, 301, 314,
    316, 511
  immoderation discussed in, 316
  Lysias in, 453–54
  Phaedrus in, 453–54
phenomenology, 30, 543
Philosophical Letters (Voltaire), 107
philosophy:
  atomistic, 262, 472, 473, 502, 513–14
  barbarian disapproval of, 463
  consolation of, 189, 348
  death as subject of, 282, 337–38, 339
  as erotic activity, 316, 432–33, 509,
    518, 522–24, 541–43, 544
  and friendship, 412, 417–18, 425,
    438–39
  Greek, 35, 67, 68, 94, 437, 439, 441–
    442, 447–48, 506–7, 529
  as "guide of the perplexed," 504
  literary influence of, 157–59
  materialist, 64, 264–65, 433
  modern, 35, 64, 67, 68, 75, 94, 262,
    471
  pederasty and, 461, 463–68, 469, 514
  poetry vs., 74, 113, 471, 485, 487
  politics vs., 256, 487, 525, 526, 531,
    534, 536–37
  pre-Socratic, 472, 477, 501–2, 505, 545
  tolerance in, 85–86
  virtue and vice in, 44
  see also individual philosophers
Pindar, 457–58
pity, 67, 82, 92, 128

Plato:
  dialogues of, 284, 412, 477, 526–27,
    530, 540
  eros as conceived by, 35, 84, 49, 128,
    301, 501, 542, 545
  on good vs. evil, 255
  on homosexuality, 436–37, 468–69
  on knowledge, 91
  literature attacked by, 167
  Nietzsche vs., 412, 520, 526
  as philosopher, 447
  on politics, 256, 257
  on reciprocity, 34
  Rousseau vs., 35, 105
  Socrates as described by, 194, 361,
    407, 412, 414, 433, 477, 525, 526–
    527, 536, 538, 540
  soul and, 70
  on theater, 487
  transcendent Ideas of, 80, 137
  on wisdom, 284, 348
  see also individual works
pleasure:
  aesthetic, 142
  control of, 44
  intellectual, 425, 523–24
  as measurement of taste, 96
  morality vs., 421
  transcendent, 26, 35
Plutarch, 228, 401, 423
  Montaigne and, 415
  Rousseau and, 70, 82, 85, 142, 164,
    232, 250
  as source for *Antony and Cleopatra*,
    298–99, 301, 310, 315
Poetics (Aristotle), 355, 500
poetry:
  beauty in, 507–8
  epic, 142
  eros and, 23, 24, 433
  imagination in, 23, 138
  muse of, 263
  philosophy vs., 74, 113, 471, 485, 487
  religion and, 158
  Romantic, 138
politics:
  abstractions in, 30
  beehive analogy for, 354
  community as goal of, 14–15
  family vs., 101, 440–41, 514
  friendship in, 413, 414, 416–17,
    419–20
  as Greek invention, 440
  human need for, 19, 21
  legal basis of, 139
  philosophy vs., 256, 487, 525, 526,
    531, 534, 536–37
  power as basis of, 27
  selfishness in, 49
  unerotic nature of, 409, 525
Politics (Aristotle), 441

pornography, 27, 175, 343
pregnancy, 56, 102, 103, 105, 106,
    236–37
  desire as, 511, 512, 514, 515, 518
Pride and Prejudice (Austen), 191–208
  amour-propre in, 196–97, 198, 207
  Mr. Bennet in, 197, 198, 199, 202–3,
    204
  Mrs. Bennet in, 202–3, 204
  Mr. Bingley in, 192, 193, 198–99, 201,
    204
  Charlotte Bennet in, 204
  Mr. Collins in, 192, 193, 197, 198,
    200, 204
  country gentry in, 192–93
  education in, 199, 200, 201, 203
  Elizabeth Bennet in, 193, 196–206
  Fitzwilliam Darcy in, 192, 193, 195,
    196–206
  Emile compared with, 196
  Mr. Gardiner in, 192
  humor in, 193, 194
  irony in, 193–94, 199, 202, 204
  Jane Bennet in, 193, 198–99, 203, 204
  Lady Catherine de Bourgh in, 192,
    198, 199, 204
  Lydia Bennet in, 192, 199, 202, 204,
    205
  Madame Bovary compared with, 219
  marriage in, 198–99, 200, 201, 203–8
  Mary Bennet in, 197
  matchmaking in, 192, 194
  misunderstandings in, 197–98
  morality in, 199, 202–3, 204
  opinions in, 196–97, 198, 199
  prejudice in, 196, 199, 200
  pride in, 196–97, 199, 200
  Red and the Black compared with, 192,
    193, 194, 195, 197
  as Romantic novel, 201–2
  Rousseau and, 157, 196, 206, 207
  self-deception in, 193, 197, 200, 205
  sex as treated in, 206–7
  social order in, 191–93
  vanity in, 197, 198
  virtue in, 191, 199, 200–201, 202, 204,
    205
  Mr. Wickham in, 192, 198, 199, 201,
    202, 204, 205
  wit in, 202, 203
priests:
  attacks on, 214–15, 220
  celibacy of, 77, 242
  Machiavelli's criticism of, 293, 329–30
  power of, 74
  "Profession of Faith of the Savoyard
    Vicar, The" (Rousseau), 71–86
    amour-propre in, 76, 77, 80, 83
    Catholicism in, 76–78
    science in, 80–82, 115
    ___ of, 71–72

happiness as theme in, 78
  Kant influenced by, 72–73, 83n
  locale of, 78–79, 89
  morality in, 80–85
  natural religion in, 75, 78, 79–80, 83
  Savoyard Vicar in, 77–78, 84, 284
  sensitive rationalism in, 74–75
  sexuality in, 77, 84, 89, 97, 108
  as theological treatise, 72–76, 84–86,
    129–30, 152, 215, 255
promiscuity:
  "civic," 440–41
  as erotic phenomenon, 35, 246, 273,
    519
  legitimacy of, 16, 125
  mortality and, 486
  origins of, 481
  pederasty and, 461–62, 463, 464
property:
  family and, 442–43
  individuality and, 63
  natural right to, 360
  self-preservation and, 160, 419
prostitution, 41, 93, 143, 147, 242, 247,
    252, 466–67, 482
Protagoras (Plato), 495
Protestantism:
  Catholicism vs., 77–78, 171, 415
  liberalism and, 171
  religious reform by, 345
  sexual desire and, 84
Proust, Marcel, 259
psychology:
  biography in, 22–23
  ironical attitude as result of, 22
  motivation in, 22–23
  relationships examined in, 14, 151
  science of, 20–24, 29–30, 41–42, 43,
    61–62, 151, 263–64
  as "science of soul," 543–46
  Socratic, 263, 543–46
  see also Freud, Sigmund
puberty:
  beauty as perceived in, 79
  crisis of, 54–55
  double nature of, 55–56, 64, 65
  education and, 54–62, 65–66
  friendship and, 147

Racine, Jean, 270
rape, 26, 27, 102
reality:
  acceptance of, 133
  appearance vs., 276
  ideals vs., 283
  imagination vs., 151
  individual consciousness as basis of, 67
reason:
  as calculation, 315
  classical views on, 315–16
  fanaticism vs., 85–86, 89

friendship and, 409–10, 417–18, 427–28
heroic action vs., 360–61
human nature and, 19, 68
imagination vs., 263
isolation as result of, 395
passion vs., 48, 315–17, 361, 369–70, 428
pride of, 255
sentiment vs., 66, 67, 73
sexual arousal and, 42
Red and the Black, The (Stendhal), 157–90
   Abbé Pirard in, 166–67, 172, 174
   adultery in, 19–20, 159, 174–90
   ambition in, 163, 173, 177, 183, 188
   amour-propre in, 164, 168, 174, 176, 177, 179, 181–82, 183, 188, 189
   ancien régime in, 170, 172, 183
   Anna Karenina compared with, 238, 239, 241, 244, 246, 248
   aristocracy in, 160, 170–71, 172–73, 177, 181, 184–85
   boredom in, 183–84, 188
   bourgeois society in, 159–61, 162, 167, 170–71, 184
   Charterhouse of Parma compared with, 162, 169, 178, 186
   comedy in, 181–83, 194
   compassion in, 165, 166, 168
   Conte Altamira in, 185
   convention vs. nature in, 166–67
   Curé Chélan in, 166–67, 172, 174
   Mme. de Rênal in, 163, 164, 166–67, 174–83, 185, 188–90, 210, 238, 239, 244, 248, 315–16
   M. de Rênal in, 164, 170–71, 178, 179, 181
   duel in, 179, 182–83
   education in, 161, 163–64, 165, 170, 171, 173, 177
   Elisa in, 179
   Emile compared with, 165–66, 173
   female submissiveness in, 174, 177–178, 180
   heroism in, 160, 161–63, 166, 173, 177–78, 182
   honor in, 174, 179, 182–83
   hypocrisy in, 161, 165
   imprisonment in, 189–90
   jealousy in, 176, 186–87
   Julien Sorel in, 19–20, 32, 160–69, 174–90, 192, 194, 197, 315–16
   love in, 162, 164, 166, 167, 174–90
   Madame Bovary compared with, 190, 210, 219, 220
   Marquis de La Mole in, 172–73, 174, 182, 188, 220
   Mathilde de La Mole in, 32, 166–67, 168, 172, 174–77, 179, 183–90
   morality in, 167–69

   motherhood in, 178–79, 180, 190
   Napoleon's influence in, 161–63, 173, 181, 182, 250
   Nouvelle Héloïse compared with, 159, 163–67, 180
   novels in, 167, 177, 184, 185
   passion in, 177, 178, 315–16
   Pride and Prejudice compared with, 192, 193, 194, 195, 197
   pride in, 160, 161, 181–83
   psychology in, 163, 165, 179–80
   religion in, 161, 163, 165–66, 170, 171–72, 180, 181, 189, 190
   romantic illusion in, 175–76
   Rousseau's influence on, 157, 159–67
   sadomasochism in, 186–88
   seduction in, 164, 166, 174–90
   seminary in, 171, 181, 185
   sex as treated in, 19–20, 174–76
   shooting in, 163, 188–90
   sincerity in, 165, 168, 173
   social hierarchy in, 171–73, 183, 220
   vanity in, 160, 173, 182–83
   vengeance in, 164, 181
relationships:
   commitments in, 14, 53, 118, 124, 136, 151
   contractual basis of, 27–28
   love and, 238, 262–63
   mutual misunderstanding in, 185–86
   as pseudoscientific term, 14
   rank order in, 422, 426
   reform of, 26–27
   truth of, 176–77, 185–86
religion:
   abstractions in, 30
   education and, 63, 73, 171, 177, 211–12
   Enlightenment and, 74, 75, 76–77, 85–86, 155, 171, 214–15, 225–26
   fanaticism in, 85–86, 111–12, 156, 172, 256, 332, 333
   friendship and, 414–15, 416
   natural, 46, 75, 78, 79–80, 83, 155, 256, 382
   piety in, 189, 211, 442
   rationalizations for, 151
   religiosity vs., 74, 254
   revealed, 75, 85
   science vs., 253–54
   spiritual examination in, 544, 545
   see also Christianity; Judaism
Remembrance of Things Past (Proust), 259
Renaissance, 298, 390, 392, 431, 443, 521
Renoir, Jean, 350
reproduction, 43, 54–55, 64, 101, 103, 106, 107, 237, 252, 439, 511, 516, 550
Republic (Plato):
   anger discussed in, 135, 349, 371

Republic (cont.)
  Cephalus in, 359, 412, 440, 446,
    543–44
  Christianity vs., 298
  "civic promiscuity" in, 440–41
  Glaucon in, 130, 459, 495, 515, 533
  human nature in, 261
  incest in, 498
  laws in, 342
  marriage in, 439–40
  morality in, 130, 359
  music criticized in, 528–29
  philosopher-king in, 383, 530
  as Platonic dialogue, 412, 446
  Polemarchus in, 509
  political order in, 440, 467
  rhetoric of, 495
  sexual differences in, 98, 105, 440
  Socrates in, 440, 530, 533
  Symposium compared with, 301, 445,
    446, 459, 467, 492, 498, 515, 521
  Thrasymachus in, 342, 412, 446, 459,
    495
  title of, 445
  wisdom in, 492
Reveries of a Solitary Walker (Rousseau),
    96, 140, 236
rhetoric:
  aporia in, 504–5
  art of, 87–89
  deliberative, 454, 459
  dialectic vs., 496–97
  economic, 87–88
  epideictic, 406, 454
  erotic, 517
  forensic, 454
  as persuasion, 87–88, 496–97
  public, 25, 494–95
  scholastic, 537
  Socratic, 494–96
Richard II (Shakespeare), 368, 383, 395
Richardson, Samuel, 141
Robespierre, Maximilien de, 235, 448
Robinson Crusoe (Defoe), 63, 125, 141
Romanticism:
  boredom in, 183–84, 193, 221
  Christianity vs., 212
  classical influence on, 431, 519
  distinctions between male and female
    in, 108
  friendship in, 147–48
  heroes of, 144, 161–63, 191, 197, 210,
    278
  heroines of, 156, 177–78, 193, 210
  imagination in, 24–25, 169, 176, 177
  legacy of, 259–65
  love in, 34, 241–42, 259–65, 466, 500
  nature in, 89
  passion vs. reason in, 315–16
  post-Napoleonic pathos in, 161–62
  risk accepted by, 238

  Rousseau's influence on, 34, 39–40,
    43, 62, 93, 148, 151, 262, 289
  sexual revolution in, 39–40
  Shakespeare and, 269–70, 273, 274,
    278, 300, 307, 347, 373, 396
  sublime in, 260
  wholeness sought by, 43, 56
  see also novels, Romantic
Romeo and Juliet (Shakespeare), 273–
    296
  Antony and Cleopatra compared with,
    274, 287, 298, 300, 305, 307
  banishment in, 282, 286, 293, 294
  beauty in, 277, 279–80, 281, 282
  Benvolio in, 279, 291
  Capulet in, 291–92
  Capulets in, 276–78, 280–81, 286,
    287–88, 291–92, 293, 294, 296
  conspiracy in, 278, 292–93, 295, 296
  convention in, 276, 296
  death in, 279, 280, 281–82, 286, 292–
    295, 296
  denouement of, 276, 282, 293
  eroticism in, 280, 287, 289, 291, 300
  family in, 276–77, 282
  Friar John in, 295
  Friar Lawrence in, 277–78, 280, 281,
    282, 283, 285, 286, 292–95
  friends in, 278, 279, 280, 286–87
  good intentions in, 287–95
  guilt vs. innocence in, 282, 291
  Henry IV compared with, 287
  historical background of, 280
  Juliet in, 276, 280–82, 292–95, 305,
    307, 351, 384, 391
  Lady Capulet in, 288
  language of, 275, 285–91, 293–94,
    296, 300, 307
  love in, 273, 274–83, 289, 293, 298
  Macbeth compared with, 275–76
  Machiavellianism in, 277, 293, 296
  marriage in, 293, 294
  Measure for Measure compared with,
    327, 335
  Mercutio in, 279, 283, 285–87, 288,
    290n, 291, 294, 296, 300, 307
  moderation in, 279, 283
  Montagues in, 276–78, 280–81, 287–
    288, 291, 292, 294, 296
  Nurse in, 286, 288, 293
  obscenity in, 285–91, 296, 300, 307
  parental authority in, 276, 277
  Paris in, 288, 295
  philosophy in, 282–83
  political order in, 277–78, 292–93,
    295, 296
  popularity of, 273, 275
  Prince of Verona in, 277, 292, 293
  Queen Mab speech in, 286–87, 296
  relationships in, 14, 281
  religion in, 279, 292, 293–94, 295, 296

Romeo and Juliet's passion in, 14, 175–77, 278, 281, 292–95, 381, 410, 540
Romeo in, 275–76, 278–81, 282, 286, 290n, 292, 293–95, 384
Rosaline in, 278–79, 286, 291
sex as treated in, 278, 280
sinfulness in, 280, 291
suicide in, 275–76, 280, 293, 295
Tempest compared with, 283–85, 291, 296
as tragedy, 274, 276, 282, 285
Troilus and Cressida compared with, 274, 351
Tybalt in, 277, 280, 281, 286, 291, 292, 294
virtue in, 279, 280
West Side Story and, 273
Winter's Tale compared with, 381, 384, 391
wisdom in, 279, 283
Roosevelt, Franklin D., 27
Rossini, Gioacchino, 250
Rousseau, Jean-Jacques, 39–156
aesthetics of, 94–95
on *amour-propre*, 50, 51–53, 76, 125–126, 130–31, 421
on Bible, 63, 73, 85, 88
books "hated" by, 63, 85
Burke's criticism of, 39–40, 41
Calvinism of, 64, 109
on complementarity of men and women, 98–108, 110, 123, 205, 426
conservatism of, 139–40
on cosmopolitanism, 520
didacticism of, 142–43
on education, 53, 54–62, 64, 108–13, 143–44
eros as concept of, 54, 63–65, 80, 84, 89, 91, 100, 101, 113, 115, 130, 262, 492, 512
exile of, 62, 72
on freedom, 424
on friendship, 147
Freud vs., 41–42, 43, 61–62, 158
gallantry attacked by, 39, 351
on human nature, 14, 42–43, 49–54, 73–74, 90–91, 419, 420–21
intellectual legacy of, 50, 54, 55–56, 72–73, 83n, 126–27, 448–49
Kant's critique of, 55–56, 86
literary influence of, 33, 40, 41, 47, 140–43, 157–59
on love, 34, 39–40, 264, 381, 421
on marriage, 46, 86–87, 117–21, 145
as naturalist, 55, 384–85
as novelist, 93, 140–43, 257
on obscenity, 289
as philosopher, 33–34, 66–67, 93
Plato vs., 35, 105

Plutarch cited by, 70, 82, 85, 142
political influence of, 234–35
private life as subject of, 63
psychological analysis by, 41–42, 52, 61–62
religious views of, 62–64, 72–76, 84–86, 109, 129–30, 211, 415
on *Republic*, 440–41
Romantic project of, 34, 39–40, 43, 62, 93, 148, 151, 262, 289
self-knowledge sought by, 41–43
sentimentality of, 255
sex life of, 40–41
on sexual desire, 41, 47–48, 345
Shakespeare vs., 269, 280, 300, 396
sincerity as concept of, 260
social contract of, 48, 67, 71, 90, 118, 119, 131
Socrates vs., 41, 431
on soul, 70–71
sublimation as concept of, 61–62, 71–72, 96, 166, 260
sublime as concept of, 61–62, 71, 72, 260
virtue as concept of, 201
on wisdom, 284
see also individual works

Sade, Marquis de, 187, 188
sadism, 17, 41, 186–88
Saint-Pierre, Bernardin de, 40, 211
Salammbô (Flaubert), 228
Sartre, Jean-Paul, 14, 49, 260, 466–67
Schleiermacher, Friedrich Ernst Daniel, 72n
Schopenhauer as Educator (Nietzsche), 541
science:
art vs., 263–64
behavioral, 22
demystification by, 88, 107
in Enlightenment, 16, 42, 107, 214, 220, 269
knowledge from, 270, 470–72
materialism of, 15, 24, 28, 253–54, 259, 472, 473
natural, 21, 58, 66, 259, 442, 471
objectivity of, 15–16, 290
observation in, 263
psychological, 20–24, 29–30, 41–42, 43, 61–62, 151, 263–64
reductionism of, 15, 19, 34, 80, 353–354, 259, 260
religion vs., 253–54
of sexuality, 15–20, 40, 41–42, 290, 435, 544
as unerotic activity, 433
Scott, Walter, 212, 228
seduction, 20
as evidence of desirability, 52
force vs., 188

sex:
  in animals, 19, 55
  as behavior, 18–19, 22, 24
  as "brutish experience," 20–21, 435
  consent in, 26, 434
  energy of, 45–46
  eros vs., 15, 17, 24, 109, 264, 424,
    480–81, 508, 510, 511, 514, 544
  fantasies in, 23, 45, 48, 124–25
  feminist critique of, 26–28, 98–100
  Freud's analysis of, 20–24, 29–30, 41–
    42, 43, 61–62, 151, 264
  frustration in, 148, 154, 264
  gratification in, 19–20
  guilt about, 16, 28
  hunger compared with, 24, 45, 47,
    50–51, 511, 548
  imagination and, 45, 48, 50, 51, 57–
    59, 64, 94
  meaning of, 86–90
  neuroses of, 23, 47, 125
  objectivization of, 290
  preferences in, 15–20, 434–35
  private nature of, 63
  as pseudoscientific term, 13
  punishment in, 17, 41, 76, 186–88
  scientific investigation of, 15–20, 40,
    41–42, 290, 435, 544
  as self-forgetting, 481, 547
  as sinful, 34, 62–63, 64
  thinking and, 47–48, 176, 207
  see also intercourse, sexual; reproduc-
    tion
Shakespeare, William, 269–410
  Austen compared with, 345
  characterization by, 287, 319–20, 385
  classical heritage of, 228
  comedies of, 274–75, 289, 540
  commentaries on, 397–98
  cowards as portrayed by, 319–20
  didacticism absent from, 142, 269,
    358
  eroticism of, 274, 388, 395–96, 443
  Freud vs., 396
  gender reversals used by, 108, 273–74
  heroism criticized by, 167, 228,
    347–50
  high and low culture in works of,
    396–98
  historical imagination of, 297–302,
    380
  history plays of, 274, 287, 386, 395
  as humanist, 396, 521
  humanity as portrayed by, 269, 270,
    393, 395–96, 421
  influence of, 270–71, 397–98
  irony of, 373
  love as theme of, 29–30, 34–35, 270,
    273, 395
  Machiavelli's influence on, 277, 285,
    301, 313

  morality of, 167, 396–97
  nature represented by, 34–35, 166,
    269–71, 393–94, 396
  obscenity and, 285–91, 296, 300, 307,
    374
  personal experiences of, 347–48
  popularity of, 270–71
  on reason, 315–17, 409–10
  religion and, 394–95
  as Renaissance artist, 392, 393–94
  Romanticism and, 269–70, 273, 274,
    278, 300, 307, 347, 373, 396
  Rousseau vs., 269, 280, 300, 396
  sex as treated by, 63, 175
  tragedies of, 274–75, 289, 540
  on truth, 269
  women as portrayed by, 273–74, 307,
    391–92
  see also individual works
sexes:
  complementarity of, 98–108, 110, 123,
    205, 426, 479–85
  differences between, 98–108, 174,
    206–7, 511
  origin of, 480–82
Shaw, Artie, 466
Shelley, Percy Bysshe, 436
Silenus, 528, 529
sincerity, 191, 194, 260
Social Contract, The (Rousseau), 71, 131,
    139, 140, 142, 234
socialism, 44n, 93, 170
society:
  artists vs., 159–60, 226, 227–28
  Enlightenment and, 63, 234, 345
  family vs., 119, 120
  individuality vs., 14, 48–49, 67–70,
    87, 100–102, 201, 234, 395, 413,
    419, 420–21, 551
  inequality in, 69–70, 92–93
  justice in, 69, 81
  nature vs., 20–21, 43–44, 48–50, 56,
    127, 146, 264, 421
  patriarchal, 55, 145
  quality of life in, 107
  repression in, 20–22, 65
  solitariness in, 14, 34, 93, 120, 127–
    128, 176–77, 207, 420–21
Socrates:
  Achilles compared with, 361
  Alcibiades and, 365–66, 407, 408, 414,
    427, 446, 449, 525–41
  Aristophanes' parody of, 408, 422,
    432, 440, 446, 447, 448, 450, 451,
    472, 477–78
  attractiveness of, 528–40
  character of, 449, 450
  continence of, 445, 452, 531, 537
  courage of, 534, 537–38
  Cynicism derived from, 47
  daimonion of, 32, 503–4, 538

death of, 189, 320–21, 407, 447, 477–
478, 511–12, 534–35, 539, 550
Delphic oracle consulted by, 32, 501
dialectical skills of, 459, 488, 494–96,
497, 521
Diotima as teacher of, 284, 497, 499,
501–24, 526, 530, 533
eroticism of, 58, 144, 323, 431–33,
445, 452, 484–85, 492, 495, 502,
505, 516–18, 527, 540–46
Falstaff compared with, 406–8, 536
followers of, 448–49, 509
friendships of, 32, 412, 414
Homeric models and, 528, 538
hubris of, 494, 505, 534–35
ignorance professed by, 431, 432,
497, 502
as intellectual "midwife," 27, 53, 242,
363
irony of, 168, 193–94, 431, 451, 496,
532
literature important to, 32–33
lovers of, 446, 448–49, 463, 467, 468,
484, 507, 524, 526–27, 532–41, 542
marriage of, 433, 469, 524
maturity of, 515, 516–17
Meletus as accuser of, 497
military service of, 451, 456, 534,
537–38
morality of, 433
Nietzsche's views on, 447, 448, 485,
500, 508, 536
on pederasty, 469
as philosopher, 432, 447–48, 450, 452,
472, 477, 501–2, 505, 509, 515–17,
521–22, 524, 528–40, 542–43
philosophy defined by, 60, 282, 316,
530
Plato's account of, 194, 361, 407, 412,
414, 433, 477, 525, 526–27, 536,
538, 540
as pre-Socratic, 472, 477, 501–2, 505
private discourse of, 494–96, 497
psychological insight of, 263, 543–46
religious views of, 414, 432, 477, 479,
480, 503–4
Rousseau vs., 41, 431
as satyr, 528–29, 538
"second sailing" of, 502
seduction by, 496, 532–40
self-sufficiency of, 534–35, 537,
542–43
sex life of, 40, 469, 531, 535, 536
skepticism of, 504–5, 543
speeches of, 529, 532
on *technai*, 470–71
ugliness of, 449, 527, 528, 539
Ulysses compared with, 363–66, 373
urbaneness of, 449, 450, 451
vanity manipulated by, 495–96
on virtue, 44, 419

as wise man, 348, 452, 505, 531, 533,
539
wit of, 477
Xantippe and, 469
Xenophon's account of, 32–33, 168,
194, 407, 412, 414, 452, 525, 526
youth "corrupted" by, 407, 414, 431–
432, 448, 515, 525, 526, 527–28, 530,
550
Sophist (Plato), 445
Sophists, 495, 518
Sophocles, 274, 286, 439, 445, 485
soul:
beauty of, 515–16, 517, 523, 533, 541–
543, 544
body vs., 34, 81, 84, 174–75, 236–38,
239, 247, 461, 463, 474, 511–12, 516
construction of, 133, 137, 182
divinatory power of, 483, 484–85
"hydraulics" of, 65, 69
immortality of, 82–83, 511–15, 545
ladder of, 86, 138, 514, 515, 517–18,
521, 522–23
rank order of, 66, 70–71, 207–8
strength of, 136–37
tripartite division of, 70, 360
Sparta vs. Athens, 94, 444, 456, 457,
459, 461
speech:
in friendship, 147, 410, 411–12, 436,
543, 548
about love, 13–14, 25–26, 29, 87–90,
95–96, 289–91, 466, 506, 517
scientific, 18, 20
see also rhetoric
Spinoza, Baruch, 40, 301
Statesman (Plato), 445
Stendhal, 19–20, 32, 157–90
Austen compared with, 157–58, 192,
193, 194, 195, 205
cynicism of, 159
egalitarianism criticized by, 159–60
fantasy life of, 169
on justice, 160–61
on love, 125–26, 239
on morality, 31, 257
Nietzsche's views on, 179–80, 262, 263
opera as interest of, 160, 173
psychological insight of, 163, 165,
179–80, 262, 263
realism of, 162–63
romantic interaction portrayed by,
157–58
Rousseau's influence on, 33, 157–58,
159–67
sentimentality of, 165
on sexual frustration, 148–49
Tolstoy compared with, 249, 250, 257
see also Red and the Black, The
Stoicism, 133, 138–39, 322, 335–36, 352,
427

Strauss, Leo, 193, 289
sublimation, 20–24, 61–62, 71, 72, 104, 114, 119, 120, 133, 137, 166, 219, 260, 410
sublime:
  God as source of, 75, 156
  illusion of, 113
  imagination and, 156
  love and, 264–65
  in nature, 75, 79
superstition, 73–74, 390
Swift, Jonathan, 55
Symposium (Plato), 431–546
  Agathon and Socrates in, 451–52, 486–88, 497–500, 539, 540
  Agathon in, 274, 449, 450, 451, 452, 485–86
  agathon in, 506
  Agathon's speech in, 445, 446, 447, 488–93, 496, 522
  Alcibiades and Socrates in, 427, 446, 449, 456, 526–40, 541, 543
  Alcibiades' entrance in, 445, 525–27
  Alcibiades in, 447, 506
  Alcibiades' speech in, 454, 526–40
  amour-propre in, 534, 542
  andreia in, 456
  andres vs. *anthrōpoi* in, 456–57
  androgyny in, 479–80, 486
  Apollodorus in, 450, 495, 509, 529, 540
  aporia in, 504–5
  Aristodemus in, 449–51, 452, 509, 540
  Aristophanes and Socrates in, 477–478, 480, 484–85, 524, 525, 540
  Aristophanes in, 469–70
  Aristophanes' speech in, 108, 443, 447, 476–85, 486, 489–90, 491, 492, 501, 508–10, 513, 514, 519
  Athens as locale for, 444, 445, 446–448, 459, 463, 464, 525, 536
  beautiful as subject in, 442, 460, 461, 483, 488–89, 499, 500–501, 505, 507–8, 510, 515, 518, 522, 526
  beautiful vs. good in, 449–50, 466, 468, 470, 471, 490–91, 492–93, 496, 497, 499–500, 502, 503, 506–8, 510
  Bible compared with, 436–39, 442
  body vs. soul in, 461, 463, 474, 475–476, 509–10, 511–12, 516, 535–36, 541, 543
  comedy in, 476–78, 485, 540
  cosmic order in, 471–72, 474–75, 479–480, 489, 493, 510
  courage in, 455, 464, 492, 506–7, 516, 534
  daimōnes in, 503–4
  death in, 456, 457–58, 471, 475, 483, 499, 506–7, 521, 523
  desire in, 498–99, 500–501
  dialectic vs. rhetoric in, 496–97

  drinking in, 444–45, 452–53, 525, 528, 532, 540
  dualism in, 472–74
  eros defined in, 35, 431–33, 435, 449, 451–52, 459–61, 478, 492, 503–46
  Eros the god in, 432, 435, 436, 442, 447, 449, 453, 454–55, 456, 458, 467, 469, 478, 489–90, 491, 498, 503
  Eryximachus in, 452, 453, 527
  Eryximachus' speech in, 434, 444, 470–76, 486, 489, 492, 514
  fame discussed in, 514, 515, 517
  friendship in, 435–36, 468, 533–34
  glory discussed in, 514, 517, 518
  happiness in, 490–91, 506, 507, 510, 542
  health in, 471, 474, 489, 491, 492, 498
  historical background of, 445–48
  hubris in, 452, 494
  human nature in, 478–85
  immortality in, 498, 503, 511–15, 523–24
  justice in, 515, 516, 518, 520, 521–22, 528, 532, 544
  kalon in, 455, 488, 506, 508
  logos in, 433, 476, 529
  love of one's own vs. love of the good in, 35, 484–85, 489, 508–10, 519–21
  lovers discussed in, 453–54, 459, 461–462, 464–68, 486, 533
  materialism in, 472, 473
  medicine in, 470–72, 492
  military service in, 456–57
  moderation discussed in, 492, 515, 516
  morality in, 470, 506–7
  as narrated dialogue, 446
  nature in, 474–75, 483–84, 513–14
  necessity in, 491, 492–93, 498
  nobility in, 455, 488–89, 500, 506
  nomos in, 436, 443, 444–45, 459, 460, 462, 463, 465, 468, 479, 482, 483, 524, 526
  oaths in, 464–65
  Olympian gods in, 460–61, 479–80, 483, 484, 499, 510
  Pandemian vs. Uranian Eros in, 459–460, 461, 462, 465, 472–74, 475
  parental love in, 497–98
  Pausanias in, 452, 486, 488–89
  Pausanias' speech in, 409, 427, 459–469, 470, 475–76, 479, 517, 531, 532–33
  pederasty discussed in, 409, 427, 436, 451–69, 473, 475, 486, 514, 531, 532–34, 537
  penia in, 504–5, 523
  Phaedrus in, 452, 453–54, 486, 488, 494

Phaedrus' speech in, 434, 454–59,
    488–89, 517, 537
philogymnastia in, 463, 508
philosophy in, 461, 463–68, 469, 476,
    477, 490, 501–3, 504, 505, 508, 509,
    518, 521, 540
physis in, 444–45, 459
as Platonic dialogue, 431, 433, 445–
    446, 449, 451, 478, 497, 501, 502,
    526–27, 529, 540
Platonic Ideas in, 491, 493, 514, 521,
    522, 523–24, 526
poetry in, 471, 485, 487, 492–93, 494,
    507–8, 510, 515, 516, 517
poros in, 504–5, 523
preface to, 448
public opinion in, 460–61, 486–88,
    493–96, 502, 522, 531, 543–44
reading of, 434, 436
religion in, 477, 479–80, 490, 498
Republic compared with, 301, 445,
    446, 459, 467, 492, 498, 515, 521
rhetorical speeches of, 433–36, 445,
    446, 454, 459, 467, 476, 486, 488,
    490, 494, 496–97, 537
Rousseau's admiration of, 63, 95, 469
sensuality in, 491–92
sex as treated in, 455, 460, 464, 492
shame discussed in, 455, 463, 464,
    487–88, 494, 528, 531
Socrates' speech in, 494–525, 539
Spartan culture discussed in, 444,
    456, 457, 459, 461
symposium in, 444–45, 449–51, 495,
    527
synousia in, 495
technai in, 470–71, 476, 492
theater in, 487, 493, 494, 496
title of, 445
tragedy in, 485, 486–88, 489, 540
trust in, 435–36
truth in, 496, 497, 499, 500, 502
types of love presented in, 433–35
tyranny in, 463, 464, 479
vanity in, 534, 535
virtue in, 456–57, 458, 461, 463, 465,
    466, 467, 468, 492, 506–7, 514, 516,
    528, 530, 537, 538
wisdom in, 465–68, 487–88, 492, 494,
    502–3, 505, 516, 518, 522, 531, 533,
    539
Xenophon's *Symposium* compared
    with, 469
see also Socrates
Symposium (Xenophon), 469

Tacitus, 172
Taine, Hippolyte, 163
taste:
    as compilation of ordinary qualities,
    115

critical, 31, 157
development of, 24–25, 94–97
justification of, 434–35
sexual relations and, 95–96
Tchaikovsky, Peter, 250
Tempest, The (Shakespeare):
    Antony and Cleopatra compared with,
    301, 307
    classical unities maintained in, 380
    Ferdinand and Miranda in, 283–85,
    291, 296, 307, 381, 383
    Measure for Measure compared with,
    327, 340
    political order in, 283, 284–85, 296,
    301
    Prospero in, 283, 284–85, 296, 301,
    327, 340, 348, 373, 381, 383, 394,
    409
    Romeo and Juliet compared with, 283–
    285, 291, 296
    Troilus and Cressida compared with,
    348, 373
    utopia of, 297
    Winter's Tale compared with, 380,
    381, 383
    wisdom in, 284, 394
Thales, 418
Themistocles, 536
Thucydides, 349, 373, 446–47, 526, 528
Thus Spake Zarathustra (Nietzsche), 172
Tocqueville, Alexis de, 71, 94, 111,
    162
Tolstoy, Leo, 231–58
    as aristocrat, 232
    Austen compared with, 251, 252
    author's rereading of, 231–33
    characterization by, 232, 236, 238,
    250, 252
    didacticism of, 232–33, 249–50
    Dostoyevsky compared with, 231,
    250, 254–55
    on Enlightenment, 232, 233–35, 250
    Flaubert compared with, 227
    on love and friendship, 232
    modernity of, 231
    nationalism of, 232, 234
    Plato's influence on, 256, 257
    political views of, 232, 235
    psychological insight of, 231, 232
    rationalists as depicted by, 254
    as Romantic novelist, 233, 249, 250,
    254–55, 257–58
    Rousseau's influence on, 33, 70,
    232, 233–35, 236, 241, 250, 25■
    252, 255, 256
    sentimentality of, 233, 255
    Stendhal compared with, 24■
    257
    see also Anna Karenina; Wa■
tragedy:
    Greek, 141, 274, 485, 48■

tragedy (*cont.*)
  passion vs. reason in, 48, 361
  Shakespearean, 274–75, 289, 540
Troilus and Cressida (Shakespeare),
    347–74
  Achilles in, 349, 350, 351, 353, 357,
    361, 362, 363–66, 368, 371, 372
  Aeneas in, 356–57, 368
  Agamemnon in, 352–53, 355, 356,
    357, 360, 366
  Ajax in, 349, 357, 362
  Antony and Cleopatra compared with,
    347, 348, 351
  autobiographical element in, 347–48
  beauty in, 349, 350
  Calchas in, 367, 368
  Cassandra in, 359, 371
  chastity in, 356–57, 369–70
  chivalry in, 349–50, 355, 366, 368,
    371, 372
  combat in, 349–50, 356–57, 365, 366,
    368, 371–72
  comedy in, 350, 357, 361–62, 373
  conspiracy in, 353, 357, 363–66,
    372–73
  coquetry in, 351–52, 362, 367–68
  cosmology in, 354–55
  Cressida in, 351–52, 359, 362–63, 367–
    371, 372
  Diomedes in, 351, 367, 369
  duty in, 358–60
  eroticism in, 349, 350, 367, 369
  fortune in, 352, 353
  glory in, 348–49, 356, 361, 363–66,
    367, 371, 373
  Greeks in, 349, 352–57, 361, 368
  Hector in, 349, 356, 357–61, 362, 366,
    368, 371–72
  Helen in, 349, 350, 351, 357–61, 371
  Helenus in, 358
  heroism criticized in, 347–50, 356,
    359–61, 363–66, 371–72, 373
  historical transformation in, 349, 380
  idealism in, 358–59, 363, 372
  Iliad compared with, 348, 349, 350,
    352, 356, 365
  imitation as subject in, 355–56, 357,
    374
  infidelity in, 362–63, 367–71
  jealousy in, 367, 368–69, 376, 378
  justice in, 359, 360, 372
  language of, 348, 351, 352, 353, 354,
    358, 363, 374
  ⋯ in, 347, 348, 350–52, 362–63, 367,
    ⋯70, 371, 373
  ⋯avellianism in, 353–55, 365
  ⋯*for Measure* compared with,

  ⋯in, 364–65, 366
    352–53, 355, 356, 357
  ⋯pared with, 368–69

  Pandarus in, 350, 351, 362, 363, 373–
    374, 409
  Paris in, 351, 359, 360
  Patroclus in, 355–56, 357, 361, 366,
    368, 374
  peace in, 350, 372–73
  Platonism and, 348, 349, 356, 360,
    361, 363–66, 371, 372, 373
  political order in, 353–56, 365–66
  power analyzed in, 354–55
  Priam in, 357, 359, 371
  public opinion in, 359, 362, 365, 455
  reason as subject of, 358, 360–61,
    369–71, 372–73
  reflection as subject of, 359–61
  Romeo and Juliet compared with, 274,
    351
  self-knowledge in, 361–62, 363, 372
  sex as treated in, 351–52, 360, 362
  Tempest compared with, 348, 373
  Thersites in, 361–62, 368, 374
  as travesty, 347, 355, 361
  Troilus in, 349, 350–51, 358–59, 360,
    361, 362–63, 367, 368–72, 373, 376,
    378
  Trojans in, 349, 357–61, 366
  Trojan War as subject of, 349, 352,
    366, 367, 371, 372, 373
  tyranny in, 355, 356
  Ulysses in, 348, 349, 350, 353–56,
    357, 360, 361, 362, 363–66, 367–74,
    391, 409
  vanity in, 352, 362, 363–66
  virtue in, 352–53, 356, 364–65, 370,
    373
  Winter's Tale compared with, 376,
    378, 391
  wisdom portrayed in, 348, 356, 361,
    372–73, 391
truth:
  belief vs., 166
  common insights into, 410
  love of, 42, 263
  of relationships, 176–77, 185–86
  self-contradiction and, 500

Ulysses (Joyce), 259
utilitarianism, 57, 94, 185, 201, 241, 505,
  506, 507

vanity, 59, 60, 71, 104, 160, 173, 197,
  261, 506
venereal disease, 56, 242, 329n, 374
Virgin, cult of, 105, 390, 391, 392
virginity, 18, 92, 124, 178, 210, 238
virtue, 53, 201, 274
  chastity vs., 113–14, 115, 116–17
  corruption of, 63, 331, 332
  desire and, 104, 105, 109, 112–13,
    133, 134, 136–37, 279
  in friendship, 281, 417, 418–19

goodness vs., 136–37
as happiness, 44, 153, 154, 352
intellectual vs. moral, 419
vice opposed to, 33, 44, 62, 63, 164, 227
wisdom as, 279, 283
Voltaire, 107, 142, 172, 185, 201, 215
Voluntary Servitude, The (La Boétie), 415–16

War and Peace (Tolstoy):
amour-propre in, 233
Anna Karenina compared with, 231, 235, 236, 249–50, 252, 255
aristocracy in, 234
heroism in, 70, 232–33
Kuragin in, 236, 252
Kutuzov in, 250
Napoleon in, 232, 236, 250
Natasha in, 252
Pierre Bezuhov in, 70, 232–33, 254
Platon in, 255
Prince Andrei in, 70, 232–33
Sonya in, 237
Weber, Max, 161, 130
Wilhelm Meister (Goethe), 97
will, 19, 80, 130
commitment vs., 118
construction of, 114
desire vs., 120–21, 378
eroticization of, 186–87
familial, 123
free, 423, 424–25
general, 420–21
internalization of, 138
to power, 27, 30, 188, 262, 520, 546
triumph of, 183
Winter's Tale, The (Shakespeare), 375–92
adultery in, 375, 378–79, 386–87
aesthetics in, 382–83, 389–90, 392, 393–94
Antigonus in, 379
Autolycus, 381, 384–85, 388–89, 402, 409
Bohemia in, 375, 379
Camillo in, 378, 381, 382, 384
Christianity in, 375, 390, 391, 392, 394
Clown in, 384, 388–89
convention in, 381–82
custom in, 379–80
Cymbeline compared with, 376, 380, 386, 388, 392
Delphic oracle in, 379, 394
eroticism in, 379, 388, 390
Florizel in, 381–84, 385, 387–88, 394
friendship in, 375–76, 377
guilt in, 376, 377, 378, 385–86, 388
Henry IV compared with, 402, 409
Hermione in, 375–79, 385–87, 388, 389–92, 393, 394, 495

jealousy in, 375–79, 383, 386, 388, 391–92
Julio Romano and, 389, 390, 392, 393
legitimacy of children in, 378, 382
Leontes in, 375–79, 383, 384, 385–90, 390
love in, 381, 382–84, 388
loyalty in, 378, 385
Mamillius in, 379, 386, 387, 394
marriage in, 375–76, 377, 383, 386, 388
Measure for Measure compared with, 388
monarchy in, 383, 386
nature in, 379, 381, 382, 384–85, 389, 393
Othello compared with, 376, 378, 386–387, 391, 392
as pastoral, 379, 381
paternal authority in, 381–83
Paulina in, 378, 379, 385–86, 387, 388, 389
Perdita in, 379, 381–84, 386, 387–88, 389, 393, 394
Polixenes in, 375–76, 378, 381–83, 387, 388
religious cult in, 379, 385–86, 387, 391, 394
Romeo and Juliet compared with, 381, 384, 391
sex as treated in, 377–79, 388
Sicily in, 375, 380, 384, 385
statue of Hermione in, 389–91, 392, 393
Tempest compared with, 380, 381, 383
Time as chorus in, 379–80
Troilus and Cressida compared with, 376, 378, 391
tyranny in, 378–79, 383, 386
wisdom:
consent vs., 119
dramatic representation of, 284, 348
love of, 126, 130, 254, 465–68, 492, 502–3, 533
self-sufficiency of, 131, 156, 283
as virtue, 279, 283
women:
attractiveness of, 109, 115, 116
barren, 237
chastity of, 27, 95, 113–14, 115, 116–117, 128, 131, 149, 174–75, 206, 211, 244, 342, 356–57, 369–70
children central to, 103, 110, 154, 237, 238, 239–41, 244–45, 249
chivalry as cult of, 391
in classical literature, 116
conscience of, 112, 114–15
dependency of, 108, 110–11, 194
dissimulation by, 104
dowry of, 120

women (*cont.*)
  duties of, 117, 119
  education of, 108–13, 123
  equality of, 99
  families centered around, 107–8, 114,
    240, 369
  feminine nature of, 97–108, 116
  fidelity of, 105
  household duties of, 109, 116, 206
  ideal for, 91–92, 97–123, 137
  imagination of, 121–22
  intelligence of, 109–10, 116
  in labor force, 106, 107–8
  as ladies, 26–27
  manipulation by, 110
  men's character influenced by, 52–53,
    103–4, 108, 112–13, 117, 391
  modesty of, 102–3, 128, 206, 280,
    342
  natural talents of, 115–16, 117
  opinions important to, 110, 112, 128

  philosophy and, 425
  religious beliefs of, 111–12, 115, 116,
    155, 180
  reputation of, 128, 146
  sexuality of, 20, 26, 97–108, 114–17,
    123
  as slaves, 100, 123
  in society, 117, 146, 150, 211–12
  submissive, 174, 177–78, 180
  vulnerability of, 352
  as wives, 109, 116, 122–23, 132

Xenophon, 402, 447
  Austen compared with, 193–94, 195,
    205
  on friendship, 32
  Socrates as described by, 32–33, 168,
    194, 407, 412, 414, 452, 525, 526

Zeus, 477, 479, 481, 482, 503
Zola, Emile, 145, 163

ABOUT THE AUTHOR

Until his death in October 1992, Allan Bloom was co-director of the University of Chicago's John M. Olin Center for Inquiry into the Theory and Practice of Democracy and the John U. Nef Distinguished Service Professor in the Committee on Social Thought and in the College. He also taught at Yale, Cornell, the University of Toronto, Tel Aviv University, and the University of Paris. His books include *The Closing of the American Mind*, *Giants and Dwarfs*, *Shakespeare's Politics* (with Harry V. Jaffa), and translations of Plato's *Republic* and Rousseau's *Emile*.